Management

third edition

About the Authors

Louis E. Boone (B.S., M.S., Ph.D.) holds the Ernest G. Cleverdon Chair of Business and Management at the University of South Alabama. He formerly chaired the Division of Management and Marketing at the University of Tulsa and has taught management in Greece and the United Kingdom.

Professor Boone has authored or coauthored a number of books, including the widely acclaimed *The Great Writings in Management and Organizational Behavior* (Donald D. Bowen, coauthor). His research interests include the areas of management information systems and executive behavior, and he has published articles in such journals as *Business Horizons, Journal of Business Strategy, MSU Business Topics, Business,* and the *Journal of Business of the University of Chicago.*

Professor Boone is a member of the Academy of Management and of the editorial review boards of the *Journal of Experiential Learning and Simulation* and the *Southern Business Review.*

David L. Kurtz (B.A., M.B.A., Ph.D.) holds the Thomas F. Gleed Chair of Business and Finance in the Albers School of Business, Seattle University. He was formerly a professor and department head at Eastern Michigan University. During 1974, Professor Kurtz was the Ian Potter Foundation Visiting Fellow at the Caulfield Institute of Technology (Melbourne, Australia). He also previously taught at the University of Arkansas and Davis and Elkins College.

Professor Kurtz is the author or coauthor of numerous books, and more than forty articles, monographs, cases, book reviews, invited papers, and computer simulations. Professor Kurtz's textbooks, including *Contemporary Business,* coauthored with Louis E. Boone, are widely used in collegiate schools of business. Professors Kurtz and Boone are now engaged in an extensive research project concerning chief executive officers.

A member of numerous professional associations, Professor Kurtz has also served in editorial capacities with five academic journals in business administration. Professor Kurtz has been involved in consulting and training activities in business and has been the president of a small corporation.

Management

third edition
Originally called Principles of Management

Louis E. Boone
Ernest G. Cleverdon Chair of Business and Management
University of South Alabama

David L. Kurtz
Thomas F. Gleed Chair of Business and Finance
Seattle University

Random House Business Division, New York

To Pat and Diane

Third Edition
9876543
Copyright © 1981, 1984, 1987 by Random House, Inc.

Library of Congress Cataloging-in-Publication Data

Boone, Louis E.
  Management.

   Rev. ed. of: Principles of management. 2nd ed. c1984.
   Includes bibliographies and indexes.
   1. Management. I. Kurtz, David L. II. Boone, Louis E. Principles of
      management. III. Title.
HD31.B619 1987   658   86-27957
ISBN 0-394-36305-1

Manufactured in the United States of America
Cover photo by Paul Silverman

Photo Credits (at end of book) appear on pages: C-1 and C-2

Preface

During the six years since the publication of the first edition, *Management* has become one of the most frequently used texts for introductory management courses in the nation's colleges and universities. Its thorough treatment of the managerial functions is combined with separate treatment of such important management subjects as international management, operations management, management information systems, ethics, management of nonprofit organizations, and careers in management. Perhaps an even more important determinant of the success of the previous editions is its extensive use of hundreds of real-world examples to emphasize the **application** of fundamental management concepts discussed in the text. A recent review of the ten leading introductory management texts ranked *Management* highest in the use of examples.*

In preparing the new Third Edition, both authors relied heavily on reviewer feedback with the intention of producing a significantly strengthened text. Reviewer suggestions focused on five areas: (1) the need for increased emphasis on organizing, organizational structure, and organization design; (2) the need to integrate microcomputers into the introductory management course; (3) the need to better integrate more detailed examples in the chapter materials through the use of recurring theme boxes; (4) the need to strengthen the treatment of environmental forces affecting management; and (5) the need to add new cases of varying lengths to provide maximum instructor flexibility.

The new Third Edition of *Management* addresses each of these issues.

A COMPLETELY REWRITTEN SECTION ON ORGANIZING

No part of *Management* received more extensive work than this section. The result is a major strengthening—both in breadth and depth of coverage. A new chapter on organizational design and job design complements the introductory chapter analyzing the fundamental organizing concept. The section ends with a separate chapter devoted to the management of organizational development and change, resulting in a vastly improved treatment of this critical management function.

* Allen C. Bluedorn, "Resources for the Introductory Management Course," *Academy of Management Review,* Vol. 11, No. 3 (July 1986), p. 687.

INTEGRATING MICROCOMPUTERS IN *MANAGEMENT*, THIRD EDITION

A growing number of colleges and universities are seeking ways for students to use microcomputers in solving analytical problems in the basic management course. The new edition of *Management* includes computer-assisted instruction for analyzing and solving three cases, of which one is from the text and two are new supplementary cases. This exciting new component, PC-CASE, was prepared by Professors Daniel Baugher and Andrew Varanelli of Pace University. These computerized cases are intended to allow the student to interact with a computer system when trying to make critical business decisions. Topics covered include: (1) the use of the business matrix as a planning tool; (2) the use of situational leadership theory and motivation as a method for employee selection; and (3) the use of cost-volume-profit analysis in a manufacturing environment. In addition, Random House has developed several other software programs to accompany this text, including self-assessment software and a self-testing microcomputer study guide.

STOP ACTION CASES

An exciting feature of the new edition of *Management* is the inclusion of **Stop Action Cases** in each chapter. These real-life cases emphasize the application of management concepts presented in each chapter. Every chapter begins with a description of a firm experiencing a management problem involving concepts discussed in the chapter. Students are given background information, a statement of the problem, and the assignment to use materials in the chapter to assist the firm's decision makers in solving the problem. In **Solving the Stop Action Case** at the end of the chapter, the students learn how the firm's decision makers resolved their problem. Examples of **Stop Action Cases** include:

- Microsoft Corp.
- Stouffer Foods Corp.
- Gerber Products Company
- Hardee's Racing Team
- Jaguar Cars, Ltd.
- Monsanto
- BMW of North America
- Burger King
- Hershey Chocolate Co.
- the Kansas City Royals

THEME BOXES LINKED TO IMPORTANT CHAPTER CONCEPTS

Unlike the frequently interruptive boxed illustrations in many management texts, *Management* uses specific theme boxes to identify each extended example. For example, one recurring theme is entitled **Management Successes.** Students are introduced to a succesful organization whose efficiency is linked directly to the correct application of management concepts described in the chapter. Specific examples include the following:

- Payless Cashways Inc.
- Mylan Laboratories
- The Great Pyramid
- Live Aid Benefit Concert for Ethiopia Famine Relief
- Olivetti
- *TV Guide*

The counterpart of the success theme is a second feature entitled **Management Failures.** These case examples are also designed to emphasize chapter concepts by introducing an organization whose failure resulted from the incorrect application of management concepts. Specific examples include:

- RCA SelectaVision
- People Express: Airline's Ills Point Out Weaknesses of Unorthodox Style
- Atari
- The Firestone 500 Automobile Tire
- Parker Pen Company
- The Workaholic Boss
- Schlitz Is No Longer No. 1
- Ideal Basic Industries

A third theme, **Computers in Management,** describes the specific implementation of computer systems in modern organizations and their impact on performance, morale, and/or productivity. Specific examples of **Computers in Management** boxes include the following:

- Managing the New York Mets by Computer
- Programs that Make Managers Face the Facts
- Counseling by Computer
- Monitoring Performance at Savin Business Machines
- The World's Most Computerized Organization

The fourth theme box is titled **Management: The Lighter Side.** Humorous examples are included to demonstrate the correct and incorrect application of management concepts discussed in the chapter. Examples of specific boxes in this category include:

- The World's Worst Forecasts
- What Happens When Japanese Managers Meet U.S. Production Workers?
- "What They Really Meant Was . . ."
- Cultural Mistakes in International Management

A final theme, designed to introduce management students to well-known books frequently read by practicing managers, is titled **The Manager's Bookshelf.** In addition to reviewing the major contributions of the book, each theme box relates the book to concepts discussed in the chapter. Specific examples include:

- Peters and Waterman, *In Search of Excellence*; Peters and Austin, *A Passion for Excellence*
- Sloan, *My Years with General Motors*
- Porter, *Competitive Strategy*
- Townsend, *Further Up the Organization*
- Levering, Moskowitz, and Katz, *The 100 Best Companies To Work for in America*

ADDITIONAL CASES OF VARYING LENGTHS ▬▬▬

Through the inclusion of cases of varying lengths throughout the text, instructors who prefer to make extensive use of cases in their courses are provided with greatly increased flexibility. In addition to beginning each chapter with a **Stop Action Case,** each chapter in *Management,* Third Edition, ends with a relatively short case entitled **Managerial Incident.** Each incident involves an actual firm or individual dealing with a managerial problem related to concepts discussed in the chapter. Specific examples include:

- Winnebago Industries
- Guidelines for Change at Volvo
- Munsingwear
- Walt Disney Productions
- The Female Boss
- Legal Services Corporation

Longer, more comprehensive cases are included at the end of each Part of the text. There is also one major, comprehensive case, Xerox Corporation, included in the complementary student supplement that accompanies the text.

INCREASED EMPHASIS ON THE MANAGEMENT ENVIRONMENT ▬▬▬

Chapter 2 has been expanded and is devoted exclusively to the evolution of management thought. Environmental factors, previously discussed as part of a longer chapter, are now the exclusive subject of Chapter 3. In addition, the management environment is discussed in detail in the chapters on organizing. These revisions represent a major strengthening of the new edition.

PROBLEMS AND SKILL REINFORCEMENT EXERCISES IN EACH CHAPTER ▬▬▬

The beginning of each chapter contains a **Management Fact or Fiction** quiz that requires students to respond to statements about concepts contained in the chapter. The correct responses are shown at the end of the chapter.

PHOTO ESSAYS EMPHASIZE IMPORTANT MANAGEMENT CONCEPTS ▬▬▬

A total of seven four-color photo-essays are included to emphasize important concepts discussed in the text. These essays focus upon the following subjects: (1) Entrepreneurship and Intrapreneurship, (2) Milestones in the

Development of Management Thought, (3) Microcomputers in Management, (4) Technology and Production, (5) Leadership and Corporate Culture, (6) International Business and Management, and (7) Social Responsibility.

MANAGEMENT CAREER SUPPLEMENT

Although many textbooks ignore the subject of management careers, the subject is of considerable interest throughout the student's collegiate career. Even in textbooks that include a separate chapter or appendix on management careers and career planning, many professors skip them, arguing either that class time is inadequate to cover all topics or that such a topic is a four-year subject for the student, not one that can be treated totally in the introductory management course. However, other professors desire coverage of this topic as an integrated chapter within the text.

Our solution in *Management,* Third Edition, is to provide all students with a separate supplement entitled *Organizational and Entrepreneurial Career Options with Comprehensive Case*. This special supplement—bound together with the regular text—provides the student with detailed information on such topics as the job search process, employment trends, strategies for career advancement, obstacles to achieving managerial career objectives, the entrepreneurship career option, and intrapreneurship.

Provision of a separate supplement at no additional cost permits the student to retain these materials throughout a college career as a part of his or her management materials. The instructor is offered considerable flexibility. Instructors have the option of assigning this supplement as additional text material to be discussed in class and covered on course examinations. Teaching and testing materials on the supplement are included in the *Instructor's Resource Manual*. Alternately, the instructor can encourage students to read the supplement and to retain it for future reference in advanced management courses.

Specific features of previous editions are regularly cited by users as important to their classroom instruction. These features have been retained in the Third Edition.

THOROUGH TREATMENT OF ESSENTIAL MANAGERIAL FUNCTIONS

Certainly one of the most noticeable features in this new edition of *Management* is the major strengthening of the discussion of universal management functions. Part Two, a four-chapter section titled "Planning and Decision Making," is markedly improved with a significant strengthening of the introductory chapters on planning fundamentals and strategic planning. Part Three, which considers organizing and staffing, has been improved with the addition of a second chapter on organizational design and job design. Part Five is a tighter component of the entire text, with a completely rewritten chapter on controlling and a thorough updating of the management information systems and production/operations control and productivity chapters.

SEPARATE CHAPTER COVERAGE OF IMPORTANT MANAGEMENT SUBJECTS

While many textbooks neglect emerging areas of management by merely making occasional passing references or lacking coverage altogether, the areas of international and comparative management, operations management, management information systems, and management ethics are simply too important to ignore. Each of these subjects is treated in detail in separate chapters.

EXPLAINING MANAGEMENT IN BOTH PROFIT AND NONPROFIT SETTINGS

Management is a universal concept. *Management,* Third Edition, employs cases, examples, and applications from nonprofit as well as business settings to reflect the growing importance of effectively managing nonprofit organizations in today's society—a subject often neglected in other texts.

PROVIDING ACCEPTED, ORTHODOX COVERAGE

The study of organization and management is characterized by a number of different "approaches," each focusing on specific aspects of management thought. But most professors tend to follow a certain sequence in their basic management classes. *Management* provides a mainstream treatment of organization and management, matching the subject coverage of most introductory courses. Instructors do not have to spend hours adjusting their course plans to the text.

STRESSING PEDAGOGICAL SOUNDNESS

The emphasis on student learning in *Management* is evident on the first page of each chapter. Specific learning objectives open each chapter; whereas, management terms close each chapter. Vocabulary-building is further stressed by the inclusion of definitions in the margins and by a comprehensive glossary at the end of the book. Each chapter ends with a summary, a set of review questions, problems and experiential exercises, and a **Managerial Incident** which describes actual applications of the chapter subjects in a profit or nonprofit organization.

EMPHASIZING READER INTEREST

Instructors who used the previous editions of *Management* reported that students actually enjoyed reading and studying the text! Unlike some other texts that either lack substance or use technical jargon to report research study after research study, *Management* incorporates research findings in a clear manner and focuses on real managers facing real situations and decisions. Hundreds of examples from the real world breathe life into a text that is both comprehensive and rigorous. The cases and examples are designed to illustrate the application of fundamental management concepts discussed in the text. *Management* avoids sexist language and portrays women in realistic roles.

DOCUMENTING RESEARCH FINDINGS IN THE TEXT

The management discipline is populated with many writers, researchers, and philosophers who are continuing to contribute to its understanding. Much of their work is carefully documented in this text.

A COMPLETE INSTRUCTIONAL SUPPORT PACKAGE

Management is a complete teaching/learning package for the introductory management course. In addition to the text, the instructional support—already the most comprehensive ever assembled for this course—has been revised and expanded for the Third Edition. It consists of the following supplementary teaching aids.

INSTRUCTOR'S RESOURCE MANUAL

These instructional materials consist of the following elements for each chapter in the text:
- Changes from the Second Edition
- Annotated Learning Objectives
- Management Terms
- Stop Action Case
- Lecture Outline
- Transparency Notes
- Answers to Review Questions

- Problems and Experiential Exercises
- Teaching Notes for Managerial Incident
- Guest Speaker Suggestions
- Term Paper Suggestions
- Profile
- *Great Writings in Management and Organizational Behavior* Reading Assignment
- Film Guide

Instructor's Notes for Study Guide also appears in this Manual.

TEST BANK AND TESTING SERVICES

A completely revised Test Bank comprised of approximately 1,600 questions was prepared for this edition. A computerized version of the printed test bank is also available for IBM® PC/PC-XT and Apple® IIe/IIc microcomputers. This special testmaker program enables the instructor to view, edit, and scramble questions to create exams. Instructors may also order customized tests by calling the Random House Customized Test Service; tests prepared in this way can be mailed to the instructors within 72 hours. The Test Bank was prepared by Professors Daniel Baugher and Andrew Varanelli of Pace University.

STUDY GUIDE

The all new Study Guide was especially developed by Professors Daniel Baugher and Andrew Varanelli of Pace University to complete this edition of *Management.* Included for each text chapter is a set of learning objectives, Key Term Exercises, Chapter Reviews and Self-Tests. The Self-Tests were designed with a programmed learning emphasis and consist of two levels of questions. Level 1 questions test for basic factual knowledge while Level 2 questions test the student's conceptual understanding.

The Study Guide also includes ten original experiential exercises. These exercises, which relate to a range of topics in management, have each been classroom-tested. Detailed Instructor's Notes for the exercises have also been provided in the Instructor's Manual.

The Study Guide is available in two formats—the standard print version and a special edition, which will be shrink-wrapped with the new PC-CASE computer software (see full description provided earlier).

GREAT WRITINGS IN MANAGEMENT AND ORGANIZATIONAL BEHAVIOR, SECOND EDITION

This highly regarded and widely adopted book is an important collection of the classic writings in management and organizational behavior. Use of the materials in the introductory management class is facilitated by including a photograph and biographical sketch of each management writer, a detailed outline of each selection, and a programmed learning review at the end of each selection. The author of each selection or a guest expert updates each article to 1987 by preparing special retrospective commentaries which are included at the end of each selection.

A separate *Instructor's Manual* has been prepared to accompany *Great Writings*. It contains a summary of each selection as well as true-false, multiple-choice, and discussion questions for use in student testing. *Great Writings* was prepared by Professor Louis E. Boone of the University of South Alabama and Professor Donald D. Bowen of the University of Tulsa.

MANAGEMENT SIMULATION

DECIDE, a computer simulation, is available for use with *Management*, Third Edition. This management game was prepared by Professor Thomas F. Pray of Rochester Institute of Technology and Professor Daniel R. Strang of SUNY College at Genesco.

FULL-COLOR OVERHEAD TRANSPARENCIES

This innovative component includes a set of 101 original, color acetates. Without duplicating the presentation of material in the text, each transparency is a striking graphic illustration of a concept discussed in *Management*.

ACKNOWLEDGMENTS

Management would not have been possible without the concerted efforts of a number of dedicated professionals. Our energetic editor, Susan Badger, and the fine staff at Random House were responsible for assembling a team of reviewers whose suggestions, criticisms, and advice markedly assisted in the book's development.

The authors are grateful for the suggestions made by the following academicians who reviewed the current or previous editions of the text: **Mildred E. Buzenberg,** Kansas State University; **Franklin Cantwell,** Texas Wesleyan College; **Wayne Cioffari,** Mercy College; **James Conley,** Eastern Michigan University; **Jagdish Danak,** Eastern Michigan University; **Thomas W. Faranda,** University of Minnesota; **William C. Feldbaumer,** Trenton State College; **C. Patrick Fleenor,** Seattle University; **Giovanni B. Giglioni,** Mississippi State University; **Marjorie M. Gilmore,** Community College of Denver-Auraria; **Douglas Gordon,** Arapahoe Community College; **J. Kenneth Graham,** Rochester Institute of Technology; **Michael F. Heil,** Miami University; **C. N. Hetzner,** University of Rhode Island; **Robert W. Higgins,** Middlesex County College; **John W. Lloyd,** Monroe Community College; **Vincent P. Luchsinger,** University of Baltimore; **Earl F. Lundgren,** University of Missouri; **Joe Manno,** Montgomery College; **Daniel W. McAllister, University of Nevada-Las Vegas; George R. McDonald, University of North Alabama; James McElroy, Iowa State University; Israel B. Markowitz, Metropolitan State College; Ina Midkiff-Kennedy, Amarillo College; James G. Pesak, Clarion University; E. Leroy Plumlee, Western Washington University; David L. Short, Lansing Community College; Susan Smith, Central Michigan University; Harriet B. Stephenson, Seattle University; Jeffrey C. Susbauer, Cleveland State University; Glen L. Tischer, Bergen Community College; H. Ralph Todd, Jr., American River College; Jay Todes, Northlake College; Jerry L. Wall, Western Illinois University; Irving Weschler, Borough of Manhattan Community College; and Bert W. Weesner, Lansing Community College.

We would also like to thank the following academics who contributed to our marketing research: Abshire, Roger, University of Southern Mississippi—Natchez; Adkins, Robert T., Southwest Baptist University; Ash, Robert, Santa Ana College; Armstrong, Ken, Olivet Nazarene College; Ashbaugh, Donald L., University of Kentucky; Babcock, Daniel L., University of Missouri—Rolla; Bartrem, Richard L., Briar Cliff College; Beckerink, K. W., SUNY at Alfred; Bentley, Gerald H., Niagara University; Bernthal, Wilmar F., University of Colorado; Bluedorn, Allen, University of Missouri; Bornfriend, Arnold, Worcester State College; Brady, Teresa, Holy Family College; Burgess, John F., Concordia College; Cadden, David T., Quinnipiac College; Cabral, Albert C., Nazareth College; Carey, Alan D., Bloomsburg University; Carvey, Davis, Pacific Lutheran University; Cavanagh S.J., Gerald F., University of Detroit; Champion, John M., University of Florida; Couch, Peter D., Illinois State University; Craven, Thomas, York College of Pennsylvania; Cupo, Anthony, County College of Morris; Curry, Tom, Shelby State Community College; Dahlstrom, Thomas A., Eastern College; Davis, Thomas S., Clarion University; Drumm, Robert H., University of Texas—San Antonio; Duckworth, Linda, Northeast Mississippi Jr. College; Edwin, Edward M., York College; Emmett, Dennis, West Virginia College of Graduate Studies; Forbes, Ben, John Carroll University; Forbus, Frank, Liberty University; Freedman, Sara M., University of Houston; Frost, Charles H., Tampa College; Fuller, Olene, San Jacinto College North; Fudala, Patricia, Cleary College; Gent, Michael J., Canisius College; Guidicessi, Rick, Des Moines Area Community College; Gordon, Gary, SUNY at Oswego; Grandfield, Raymond, Delaware State College; Greenlee, Tim, Piedmont Technical College; Gum, Anthony, West Virginia Wesleyan College; Guzell, Stan, Youngstown State University; Hartley, Lorraine, Ft. Lauderdale College; Headley, Dean, Kansas Newman College; Herden, Richard P., University of Louisville; Hochner, Arthur, Temple University; Hopkins, David, University of Denver; Hulcher, Wendell E., Florida Southern College; Imrik, Andrew, University of Albuquerque; Joshi, Gopal, Central Missouri State University; Kennedy, Jim, Navarro College; Kizzier, Donna, Kearney State College; Kozmetsky, George, The University of Texas at Austin; Kramer,

Robert J., Business International Corporation; Lamberton, Lowell, Central Oregon Community College; Leitner, Lewis, Stockton State College; Lentz, Christine, Rider College; Lussier, Robert, Springfield College; Mack, John E., Salem State College; Mackenzie, Kenneth, University of Kansas; Manno, Joseph R., Montgomery College; Marcellis, Sister Anita, College of St. Elizabeth; Mason, Irving, Herkimer County Community College; Matheny, John E., Wytheville Community College; Matsey, Michael, Ancilla College; Matukonis, Mike, SUNY at Oneonta; McDonough, Jack, Menlo College; McKendall, Marie, Grand Valley State College; Menzin, B., Queensborough College; Mills, Ed, Kendall College; Morse, John J., Florida International University, at Miami Campus; Mulholland, Joanna D., Philadelphia College of Textiles and Science; Natiello, Thomas A., University of Miami; Necessary, J. R., Ball State University; Peper, Merle, Southwestern Louisiana University; Polchow, Raymond, Muskingum Area Technical College; Reilly, Bernard J., Widener University; Richardson, Peter, Southwest Missouri State University; Roswell, Robert, Jackson Community College; Shipper, Frank, Arizona State University; Slagle, Michelle, George Washington University; Spencer, Jerry W., College of Charleston; Spohn, Robert, Northwestern Connecticut Community College; Sullivan, Jack, Oklahoma State; Templeton, Bob, Piedmont Technical College; Tews, Michael, Texas State Technical Institute; Thibodeaux, Mary S., North Texas State University; Todd, H. Ralph, American River College; Van Fleet, David, Texas A&M; Vecchio, Bob, University of Notre Dame; Vijayaraghavan, V., Kent State University; Waterston, Tom Lee, Dallas Baptist University; Wells, Pat, Oregon State University; Whitehill, Arthur M., University of Hawaii at Manoa; Whitehurst, J. Robert, Miami University; Wood, Carol, Lourdes College; Yost, Edward, Ohio University.

We especially thank our capable secretaries and research assistants Colleen Keleher, Jeanne Lowe, and Linda Troup for their invaluable assistance in securing needed data and in typing the manuscript. Finally, we acknowledge and thank the following contributors of original material: Edgar T. Busch, Western Kentucky University; K. Tim Hostiuck; Thomas F. J. Pipal; and Phillip K. Sherwood, Oral Roberts University.

January 1987

LOUIS E. BOONE
Mobile, Alabama

DAVID L. KURTZ
Seattle, Washington

Contents

PART TWO   PLANNING AND DECISION MAKING   79

CHAPTER **6**
MANAGERIAL DECISION MAKING   150

CHAPTER **7**
QUANTITATIVE TECHNIQUES IN PLANNING AND DECISION MAKING   189

PART
THREE   ORGANIZING AND STAFFING   245

CHAPTER **8**
FUNDAMENTALS OF ORGANIZING   246

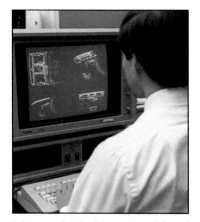

PART
FOUR   LEADING AND MOTIVATING   393

PART ONE INTRODUCTION

1 THE NATURE OF MANAGEMENT

LEARNING OBJECTIVES

After studying this chapter you should be able to

1. Identify the functions of management and how they are applied in practice.

2. Demonstrate that management concepts have universal application to both profit-oriented and nonprofit organizations.

3. Describe the managerial hierarchy.

4. Draw a capsule profile of top management.

5. Identify the basic skills needed to be a manager.

6. Explain the roles managers are expected to play.

7. Discuss whether management is an art or a science.

STOP ACTION CASE

Microsoft Corp.

Microsoft Corp.'s Bill Gates is the embodiment of the burgeoning personal computer business. His thick-lensed glasses, his youthful appearance (he started Microsoft when he was only twenty), his tendency to throw objects across the room when he is upset mark Gates as one of America's latest breed of entrepreneurs. Since dropping out of Harvard in 1975 to form Microsoft, Gates has turned his software company into one of the major forces in the lucrative personal computer market. But not all of Gates's success can be attributed to his superior programing capabilities—he has also had to learn something about managing a company.

Back in 1975, Gates, then a Harvard sophomore, teamed up with a friend and wrote a version of the Basic programming language for one of the first microcomputers on the market, the Altair. The program sold well enough to convince Gates that his future lay in the software industry. In 1980, Gates's Microsoft landed a contract with a computer giant, IBM. Microsoft was to provide IBM's new PC home computer with an operating system (the program that allows a computer to work applications software). IBM sold a half a million PCs, and Gates's operating system, the Microsoft Disk Operating System (MS-DOS), became the industry standard. By 1984, Microsoft had made over $100 million from MS-DOS alone. Today, Microsoft provides the operating systems for 45 percent of the business computers made in America.

Gates knew that his deal with IBM relieved him of the entrepreneur's usual problem in cracking a marketplace. But Gates had higher ambitions. He wanted to dominate the highly profitable applications software field. Gates had always run Microsoft like a small business; now he needed professional management.

Use the materials in Chapter 1 to develop a management plan that will position Microsoft for significant growth in the applications software market.

M anagement is a difficult term to define. It has a variety of applications and interpretations, all correct within a given set of parameters. Sometimes it is used to describe the activities of executives and administrators of an organization, as when one talks of labor-management negotiations. In other cases, it suggests the professional career path aspired to by most business administration students. And in still others it refers to a system for getting things done.

This textbook follows a systems-type definition. *Management* is the use of people and other resources to accomplish objectives. This definition is applicable to all organizational structures, both profit-oriented and not-for-profit. The process of management is as important to the effective functioning of a hospital or fire department as it is to Procter & Gamble.

Management involves the creation of an environment in which people can most effectively use other resources to reach stated goals. It involves the implementation of four important functions—planning, organizing, leading, and controlling. Management is a fundamental part of the operation of all organizations.

Part One of *Management* consists of three chapters. This opening chapter discusses the general nature of management. Chapter 2 will explore the evolution of management thought, and Chapter 3 will look at the environment within which management decisions are made.

Management is the use of people and other resources to accomplish objectives.

MANAGEMENT FACT OR FICTION

	FACT	FICTION			FACT	FICTION
1. Management is as important to the Omaha Fire Department as it is to General Foods.	☐	☐	4. Resource contributors are sometimes more influential than customers in the case of nonprofit organizations.		☐	☐
2. Frederick W. Taylor is usually credited with identifying the basic functions of the managerial process.	☐	☐	5. Most chief executive officers are now in their forties.		☐	☐
3. The functions of management are performed at all levels in the managerial hierarchy.	☐	☐	6. Management is generally considered to be an art rather than a science.		☐	☐

The materials in this chapter will assist you in separating management fact from fiction. Your answers can be checked on page 21.

THE FUNCTIONS OF MANAGEMENT

The managerial process consists of four functions that must be performed by every manager: planning, organizing, leading, and controlling. Henry Fayol, the distinguished French management theorist and practitioner, is usually credited with identifying these four basic functions of the managerial process. Fayol's contributions to the study of management are discussed in detail in Chapter 2. Figure 1–1 is a model of the managerial process based on these four functions. It is important to note that these functional activities must be performed within a general environment for management. The various components of the managerial environment are discussed in Chapter 3.

PLANNING

Planning is the process of setting objectives for the future and developing courses of action to accomplish them.

Planning can be defined as the process by which managers set objectives, assess the future, and develop courses of action to accomplish these objectives. All managers are involved in planning activities. In fact, all of the functions of planning, organizing, leading, and controlling are performed

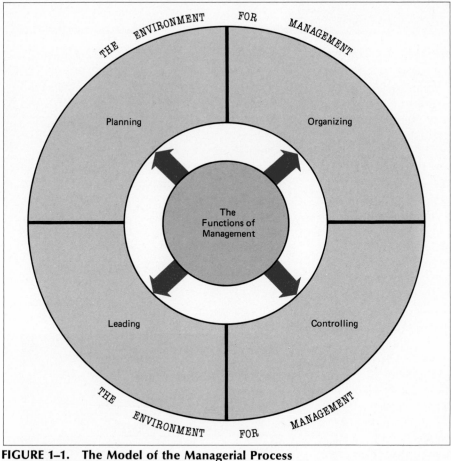

FIGURE 1–1.   The Model of the Managerial Process

by all levels of management—from a first-line supervisor to the company president. Let us look at the way one executive is involved in planning.

Dr. Henry Harper, Jr., has always been a keen observer of market opportunities. His observations have led to development of effective business plans. When Harper was a high school junior, he noted that Little League players would bypass a nearby ice-cream vendor to walk a mile to a snow-cone seller. So Harper decided to buy 300 pounds of crushed ice, syrup, a motor scooter, and go into the snow-cone business. He made $3,000 in just half a season.

As the young entrepreneur planned for next summer, he knew he wanted to expand. So he used the $3,000 he had earned to buy two pickup trucks. Harper then hired his father and brother to help him in his business venture.

After getting a medical degree, Harper worked in emergency rooms in Iowa and Texas. Again, he saw a business opportunity and began planning

COMPUTERS IN MANAGEMENT

Managing the New York Mets by Computer

New York Mets manager Davey Johnson gnawed on a wad of chewing tobacco, contemplating what radio announcer Bob Murphy aptly described as "one of those war-of-nerve situations that a manager gets paid to manage for." One out in the bottom of the seventh on this late-June afternoon, and the Mets had already blown an early 6–1 lead to the Phillies before rallying to tie against Philadelphia reliever Bill Campbell. Now they had the go-ahead run at second, and the crowd at Shea Stadium was screaming for more. With first base open and first place at stake, all eyes turned to the home dugout to see who Johnson would send out to hit for his pitcher.

"It'll be interesting to watch Davey's move here," noted Murphy from his press-box perch, thinking aloud as any knowledgeable fan might. "He's got [right-handed slugger] George Foster and [left-handed pinch-hitting wizard] Rusty Staub both in reserve, but Rusty hasn't had much success against Campbell, even though he's one of the better pinch-hitters in the league. Foster's the obvious home-run threat, but the Phillies could always walk him to pitch to Staub. You can almost hear the wheels turning in both dugouts." Or the faint hum of computers.

Down on the Phillies' bench, manager Paul Owens was shuffling through lineup cards and considering a variety of possibilities: If Foster came in and was pitched to, it meant the potential winning run was at the plate—with a game-breaker in the batter's box; Staub was the better clutch hitter, but at .067 lifetime against Campbell, he was no historical favorite to do heavy damage. Either guy could be walked to get to the other, setting up the double play. And Owens had Jim Kern, another short reliever, warming up in the bullpen. Johnson, on the other hand, was squinting at

how to take advantage of it. Harper noted that emergency rooms properly took immediate care of the 5 percent of their patients who were serious emergencies. The others had to wait.

Harper's planning led to the first MedStop in Dallas. Today, his Medical Networks, Inc., has franchised thirty-four medical clinics. With an eight-figure net worth, Harper continued to plan and set objectives such as $90-million revenue in 1986, up from $15 million two years earlier. Harper

the mound and pondering the inadequacy of certain statistics. Roughly sixty feet down the stadium tunnel, or about the distance from the pitcher's mound to home plate, sat his IBM P C/XT microcomputer, Johnson's so-called sixth coach, which he consults before each game.

One for fifteen, yeah, he thought, trying to visualize his printout on Staub vs. Campbell, *but how many of those balls were hit hard? Where did they go, infield or outfield, right side or left side? Were there men on base? How many outs? Late innings or early innings? Night games or day games? Home or away? Was Staub playing hurt? Would Owens risk walking Foster? Would Campbell have to pitch Staub too carefully? Is Rusty loose? Is he due today?* Having no terminal to consult for an immediate answer, Johnson scratched his head and motioned for the right-hander.

Foster took four wide ones and trotted down to first. As the crowd buzzed with anticipation, the portly forty-year-old Staub tossed aside his batting donut and settled into a semicrouch at the plate. Campbell glared in for the sign. "I regarded it," Johnson would later say of this second-guesser's smorgasbord, "as your classic 'unfavorable chance deviation.' " Staub regarded Campbell's first pitch as a meat-high fastball, and roped it to right for the game-winning RBI.

Hardball hunch meets personnel pool meets disk drive, produces line drive: "The media has a lot of fun with this computer thing," sighed Staub, child of another baseball era, in the warm Shea twilight of next day's batting practice, "but I think you can make too much of statistics. There's no substitute for baseball sense. Dave's no slave to the computer. Sometimes, I swear, I have no idea *what* he's doing."

What Johnson is doing is taking a small but highly visible business with only one tangible product to sell—the performance of its people—and managing it, using that most tangible of new business tools, the computer. Once the very symbol of baseball ineptness, the Mets have assumed an aura of slick proficiency by becoming the latest professional sports franchise to experiment with the computer as a major strategic weapon. Johnson's challenge: to integrate what the computer can tell him with what he already knows about the business of winning baseball games. Against a backdrop of pennant pandemonium, this is management at a technological crossroads.

Source: Joseph P. Kahn, "Get Your Program Here," *Inc.,* September 1984, pp. 60-61. Reprinted by permission. Copyright © 1984 by Inc. Publishing Company, 38 Commercial Wharf, Boston, MA 02110. Photo courtesy New York Mets.

explained his success this way: "I saw a hole in the market"—something he has been doing since high school.[1]

ORGANIZING

The second function of management is *organizing,* the process of arranging people and physical resources to carry out plans and accomplish organi-

> **Organizing** is the process of arranging people and physical resources to carry out plans and accomplish objectives.

zational objectives. Organizing is a continuing process in any enterprise. The effectiveness of a firm's organizational structure is a key ingredient in its eventual success or failure.

Consider the organizing activities of the management of Fluor Corporation, an international engineering, construction, and natural resources management company with annual sales of more than $4 billion. The largest engineering and construction group of its kind among publicly held companies, Fluor has the ability to manage both small and very large, complex projects on a worldwide scale.

A $5-billion Saudi Arabian gas conservation facility, designed to convert wellhead gases burned off as wastes into fuel, is only one of the mega-projects Fluor Corporation has worked on since its inception in 1912.

J. Robert Fluor, chairman and chief executive officer (CEO) of Fluor Corporation from 1968 until his death in 1984, recognized that the rapid growth of the company and the vast scope and location of its projects made a major organizational change essential. Realizing that organizational size, advanced technology, and the far-flung nature of big construction projects made the horizontal structure of the company inefficient, Bob Fluor reorganized his personnel by projects. Each job is assigned its own set of designers, procurement specialists, engineers, and so forth.

▼ FLUOR CORPORATION

Current chairman and CEO David S. Tappan, Jr., has continued to implement and expand on Fluor's original goal for a more decentralized management structure. New and smaller divisions, located in key areas throughout the world, have been established to meet the needs of the ever-changing marketplace Fluor Corporation serves.[2]

LEADING

Leadership is a critical activity in all organizations. For example, the win–loss records of athletic teams often depend on the leadership skills of the coaches and key players. The same is true of business organizations. *Leading* can be defined as the act of motivating or causing people to perform certain tasks intended to achieve specified objectives. It is the art of making things happen. Sandra Kurtzig is an excellent illustration of someone who knows how to make things happen.

Leading is the act of motivating or causing people to perform certain tasks intended to achieve specific objectives. It is the art of making things happen.

Before her recent resignation as CEO, Sandra K. Kurtzig made ASK Computer Systems, Inc., the company she founded, a great success story even for Silicon Valley. ASK, with its 460 employees, now regularly posts annual sales increases of 70 percent.

But Kurtzig started on a much smaller scale. After getting degrees in chemistry, math, and aeronautical engineering, she went to work for General Electric. But she later quit to write software programs at home and to raise a family. Kurtzig's initial product was software that allowed weekly newspapers to account for carrier activity. Today, ASK concentrates on software designed to improve a manufacturer's productivity.

Kurtzig's business grew and she began to hire young graduates. At one time, the staff even slept in sleeping bags at Hewlett-Packard so they could use a computer at night. Kurtzig, who is ASK's chairman though she limits her role to active board member, is well known in Silicon Valley for her leadership style. She describes her approach to managing people as providing "enough rope to see if they can do the job."

ASK is a friendly place to work largely because of Kurtzig's leadership. She puts it this way: "To work here, you must adapt to the ASK environment. You must be able to drink at the company's Friday beer blast." It is clear that Sandra Kurtzig's leadership style provides the basis for effective management at ASK Computer Systems, Inc.[3]

CONTROLLING

Controlling is the fourth function of management. *Controlling* can be defined as the process by which managers determine whether organizational objectives are being achieved and whether actual operations are consistent with plans. Controlling is what makes Browning-Ferris Industries so successful in its field.

Controlling is the process by which managers determine whether organizational objectives are achieved and whether actual operations are consistent with plans.

Harry J. Phillips, Sr., probably knows as much about trash collection as anyone. Phillips is chairman of Browning-Ferris Industries, a $1.1-billion trash hauler that serves 425,000 commercial/industrial customers and 3.3 million residences. Browning-Ferris handles anything from garbage to chemical wastes Its customers are worldwide. For example, Browning-Ferris is now hauling trash in Saudi Arabia, Malaysia, Australia, United Kingdom, and Kuwait. The company is also involved in negotiations to build waste-to-energy plants in New Jersey, Texas, Massachusetts, and Connecticut.

Browning-Ferris is a very profitable firm with an operating margin in excess of 35 percent. Much of its success should be credited to Harry Phillips's efforts to control costs. Phillips explains:

> Your costs in this business are associated with time. If it costs $9.42 per hour to operate a garbage truck, and if you have enough market share to make a stop every seven minutes instead of fifteen, then your cost per stop drops from $10.50 to $4.90.

As a result, Browning-Ferris drivers are paid according to the number of stops they make, rather than by the hour. Phillips also closely monitors parts and fuel costs. Engines and gear ratios are selected according to the terrain and type of driving that characterize each market. Sales personnel are expected to sign up to 80 to 100 new clients annually. Drivers are given extensive safety training in order to control insurance costs, which average 3 percent of revenues. Harry Phillips clearly recognizes the importance of management control in the garbage business.[4]

THE MANAGER'S BOOKSHELF

In Search of Excellence, by Tom Peters and Robert Waterman

 Five years later, analysts are still trying to explain the huge success of *In Search of Excellence,* Tom Peters and Robert Waterman's look at American business techniques. *In Search of Excellence* (Harper & Row) was a dispassionate look at forty-three well-managed American companies. The authors' "America's-still-got-it" message was admittedly one that Americans wanted to hear. But 5 million copies were sold in fifteen languages, so it is obvious that the Peters and Waterman message had international applications.

The basic premise of *In Search of Excellence* was that excellently managed companies are characterized by certain attributes. These include:

1. A bias for action.

2. Closeness to the customer.

3. Employee productivity.

4. Adequate controls.

5. Concentration on the business with which management is familiar.

6. Lean organization with minimal bureaucracy.

7. Central corporate values that guide the organization.

8. Encouragement of entrepreneurship through autonomy.

In Search of Excellence has been called "the business book of the century" and has propelled its authors, particularly Peters, into the national spotlight. Peters, perhaps applying some of his own principles, has staked out his own search-of-excellence mini-industry: He lectures, leads seminars, and sells leather-bound Excellence calendar books.

Now he has written a sequel with Nancy Austin, a former Hewlett-Packard consultant. The new book, *A Passion for Excellence* (Random House, 1985), fine-tunes and somewhat expands the arguments advanced by *In Search of Excellence.* Peters and Austin have narrowed their list of components of business success to two: Take exceptional care of your customers and innovate constantly. Once again, the book is chock-full of American companies that have achieved success because of their distinctively American managerial approaches. *A Passion for Excellence* also includes nonprofit areas; the authors have added a look at managing in education, sports, city government, and the United States Air Force. Altogether, it is a reminder that the key to the resurrection of American business does not necessarily lie across the Pacific Ocean. Peters and Austin's message is that the Japanese could also learn a few things from us.

Sources: "A Passion for Excellence," excerpted by Tom Peters and Nancy Austin, *Fortune,* 13 May 1985, p. 20; and *In Search of Excellence.*

MANAGEMENT CONCEPTS HAVE UNIVERSAL APPLICATIONS ▰▰▰▰▰▰▰▰▰▰▰▰▰▰

Although the problems and organizational constraints vary widely between private enterprises and nonprofit organizations and between small firms and industrial giants, the functions performed by managers are nearly the same. All managers operate in organizations with specific objectives. They must plan, organize, lead, and control so that these organizational objectives are met. The functions of planning, organizing, leading, and controlling are similar regardless of geographical location or the ownership or type of organization that is involved. The universality of management practices in both the private and public sectors is a well-known concept.[5]

ADAPTING TO ENVIRONMENTAL CIRCUMSTANCES

Environmental circumstances change from one managerial situation to another. Government organizations, for example, require an executive to adjust to a different set of environmental parameters than would be common in business. Management styles have to adjust to the particular factors confronting the decision maker. This adaptive approach is referred to elsewhere in this text as *contingency management*.

George Shultz provides an excellent illustration of the transferability of management concepts to different problem-solving situations. Shultz has been a top manager in three different environments. He was dean of the University of Chicago's business school, Secretary of the Treasury, and then president of the Bechtel Group, a major construction company. But he gave up his $500,000-a-year-post at Bechtel to become Secretary of State, a job that pays about one-seventh as much.[6]

Consider the following remarks about the similarities and differences between management in the private and public sectors:

> One very important thing you have to learn in Washington is the difference between appearance and reality. At Bendix, it was the reality of the situation that in the end determined whether we succeeded or not. In the crudest sense, this meant the bottom line. You can dress up profits only for so long—if you're not successful, it's going to be clear. In government there is no bottom line, and that is why you can be successful if you appear to be successful—though, of course, appearance is not the only ingredient of success.
>
> W. Michael Blumenthal[7]
> *(Blumenthal now heads Burroughs Corp. He served as Secretary of the Treasury after being Bendix's board chairman.)*

Many of the similarities stem from size, and there are certain things unique to big organizations. They require a variety of competencies, along with

MANAGEMENT FAILURES

Lenin and Management Science

The Prekhanov Institute of the National Economy is a business school with an extensive program for educating practicing managers. The school is part of the Soviet Union's attempt to introduce modern management practices to its ineffective industrial sector.

Many of the courses at Prekhanov Institute would be familiar to business students in North America. The school offers classes in organizational design, management psychology, information processing, and decision making. Lectures are the usual teaching method, but cases and business games are also used.

Management science has always been popular with Soviet leaders. In fact, Lenin believed that Frederick Winslow Taylor's work would shortly allow Russia to surpass the Western nations in productivity. Systems theory, which tries to integrate the various aspects of the organization, is well received today. However, the students at Prekhanov Institute—

most of whom have technical or engineering backgrounds—seem most interested in management psychology.

The management education received by these executives, all members of middle or top management, is often in conflict with Marxist philosophy. For example, Marx believed that class motivates individual behavior. But today's Soviet business student is also taught about informal group behavior, and Soviet academics debate whether a theory of personal leadership is acceptable to a Communist state.

So far, the results of Soviet management education are mixed. While techniques are learned easily, it does not appear that management practice has changed significantly. Apparently, management science will not be the panacea that Lenin had hoped.

Source: Mark R. Bessinger, "Soviet Factory Directors Go to Business School," *Wall Street Journal,* 2 November 1981, p. 26.

intricate planning and budgeting. However, planning in a business is more analytical and thoughtful than in government. You are in a less reactive mode.

Donald Rumsfeld[8]

(Rumsfeld has held posts as G. D. Searle & Company's chief executive, a member of Congress, secretary of defense, and White House chief of staff.)

MANAGING A NONPROFIT ORGANIZATION

Nonprofit organizations provide an excellent illustration of the concept of the universality of management. Effectively managed nonprofit organizations accomplish their goals, while poorly managed ones do not. Good management is a key ingredient in the success of any organization—profit or nonprofit.

The not-for-profit sector of our society is exceedingly diverse. Nonprofit organizations include hospitals, government agencies, unions, art and cultural institutions, colleges and universities, and cooperatives, among others.[9]

Features of Nonprofit Organizations. The following features often characterize nonprofit organizations and constrain the managerial approaches and techniques that are employed:

1. Service is intangible and hard to measure. This difficulty is often compounded by the existence of multiple service objectives.

2. Customer influence may be weak. Often the enterprise has a local monopoly, and payments by customers may be a secondary source of funds.

3. Strong employee commitment to professions or to a cause may undermine their allegiance to the enterprise.

4. Resource contributors may intrude into internal management—notably fund contributors and government.

5. Restraints on the use of rewards and punishments result from 1, 3, and 4 above.

6. Charismatic leaders and/or the "mystique" of the enterprise may be important means of resolving conflict in objectives and overcoming restraints.[10]

Consider a few examples. The second characteristic in this list—"Customer influence may be weak"—might be illustrated by a public health agency. The customer, or patient, may pay only a minor portion of the cost of treatment. In fact, the nonprofit organization, the health agency, may be more attuned to satisfying the government officials who provide the bulk of the funding. Characteristic 6—"Charismatic leaders"—might be demonstrated by the immense importance of Ralph Nader to the consumerism movement. While consumerism may be considered a broad social movement consisting of numerous nonprofit organizations, Nader's key role is seldom questioned.

Management Problems Unique to Nonprofit Organizations. The characteristics of nonprofit organizations create obstacles to effective operation. Two primary problems in such operations are:

• Lack of direct-line responsibility.

Bottom line reflects company profitability on the income statement.

- Lack of a *bottom line,* industry jargon for a measurement of performance such as profitability.[11]

Nonprofits typically do not possess a direct line of responsibility similar to the owner/board of directors/management hierarchy that characterizes profit-oriented institutions. A nonprofit has no true owners (with the exception of government agencies, where the taxpayer might loosely be given this designation). Management levels are also often confused. In some not-for-profit enterprises there can be three separate hierarchies—administrative, professional (such as doctors or curators), and voluntary. All have an impact on the overall management of the organization.

Nonprofits also suffer from lack of a clearly identified bottom line. The output of the entity's activities goes to its customers, rather than providing benefits to the organization itself. A related issue concerns the nonprofit's lack of such work incentives as bonuses and stock option plans. Thus, a sense of personal satisfaction and accomplishment becomes more important as a motivator in the not-for-profit sector.

THE MANAGERIAL HIERARCHY

Management acts as a catalyst for getting things done within an organization. In some cases, these organizational objectives can be accomplished through a simple management–subordinate hierarchy. In many small businesses, the owner–manager is the only member of the management team. But as the organization becomes larger and more complex, a more sophisticated structure is required.

Figure 1–2 illustrates the three basic levels of management: (1) top management; (2) middle management; and (3) supervisory management. Many people describe this hierarchy as a pyramid since there are relatively fewer positions as one progresses to higher levels of management. Similar hierarchies exist in both profit and nonprofit organizations.

Top management is usually appointed, elected, or designated by the organization's governing board. The president of General Foods is selected by the firm's board of directors, representing the stockholders. The president of a college or university is appointed by the institution's board of trustees, regents, or governors. Top management is concerned with overall management policy and strategy, and ultimately it is responsible for all decisions made within the managerial hierarchy.

Middle management deals with the actual demonstration and operation of the organization's activities. As Figure 1–2 suggests, the head of the accounting function and an army captain are examples of middle management. These people possess considerable responsibility and authority in the performance of their assigned missions. But they look to top manage-

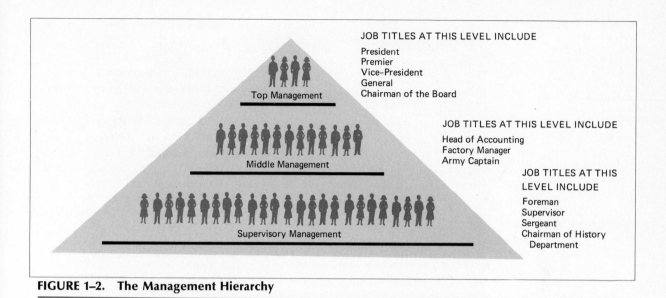

FIGURE 1–2.   The Management Hierarchy

ment for direction and guidance and are responsible to these higher ranking executives.

Supervisory management includes the managers who have ongoing, direct contact with subordinates. Typically, a supervisor is the leader for some type of work group, such as a college's history department or the paint shop in a factory. These managers are often involved in the actual tasks carried out by the unit. For instance, a district sales manager will often call on key accounts with his or her local representatives.

The management hierarchy provides an overall framework for the accomplishment of objectives. Chapters 8 and 9 describe the organizing function in detail, noting how management uses the hierarchical structure to reach its goals.

A PROFILE OF THE CHIEF EXECUTIVE

Heidrick and Struggles, a management consulting firm specializing in executive search, reports that managers are a hard-working occupational group (see Figure 1–3). Those at the top of the nation's largest corporations work long hours. Over 68 percent of the chief executive officers of industrial companies with earnings over $2 billion spend at least sixty hours a week at their jobs—but the rewards are also high for those who succeed. In a recent year, the typical chief executive officer earned $473,500 in salary and bonuses, and had stock options, a company car, club membership, and extra life insurance paid for by the company.[12]

&& By working faithfully eight hours a day, you may eventually get to be boss and work twelve hours a day. &&

Robert Frost

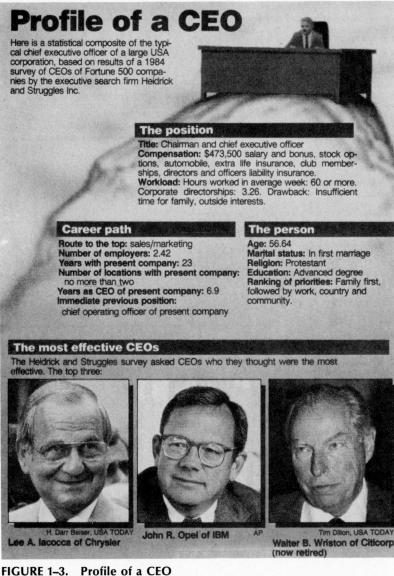

Profile of a CEO

Here is a statistical composite of the typical chief executive officer of a large USA corporation, based on results of a 1984 survey of CEOs of Fortune 500 companies by the executive search firm Heidrick and Struggles Inc.

The position

Title: Chairman and chief executive officer
Compensation: $473,500 salary and bonus, stock options, automobile, extra life insurance, club memberships, directors and officers liability insurance.
Workload: Hours worked in average week: 60 or more. Corporate directorships: 3.26. Drawback: Insufficient time for family, outside interests.

Career path

Route to the top: sales/marketing
Number of employers: 2.42
Years with present company: 23
Number of locations with present company: no more than two
Years as CEO of present company: 6.9
Immediate previous position: chief operating officer of present company

The person

Age: 56.64
Marital status: In first marriage
Religion: Protestant
Education: Advanced degree
Ranking of priorities: Family first, followed by work, country and community.

The most effective CEOs

The Heidrick and Struggles survey asked CEOs who they thought were the most effective. The top three:

H. Darr Beiser, USA TODAY
Lee A. Iacocca of Chrysler

John R. Opel of IBM   AP

Tim Dillon, USA TODAY
Walter B. Wriston of Citicorp (now retired)

FIGURE 1–3.   Profile of a CEO
Source: USA Today, 16 August 1985, p. B1. Data from Heidrick and Struggles, Inc. Copyright, 1985 USA TODAY. Reprinted by permission.

THE SKILLS AND ROLES OF MANAGEMENT

All managers must possess specific managerial skills if they are to adequately perform the management functions discussed earlier in the chapter. In addition, managers must adopt certain roles in order to accomplish the different objectives for which they are responsible.

Entrepreneurship and Intrapreneurship

Do you enjoy a challenge? Are you self-motivated? Energetic? Full of ideas? If so, you may be the entrepreneurial type. Entrepreneurs start and operate their own businesses, an exciting option for many new business people.

If the idea of working within a corporation and enjoying greater financial support and corporate clout appeals to you, but you also have all of the qualities of an entrepreneur, you are a potential "intrapreneur." Although an intrapreneur embraces the concepts of the entrepreneur, he or she works within the established structure of a large firm.

Entrepreneurs and intrapreneurs, with their creativity and their willingness to take risks, are essential for the growth of new business opportunities. Here are some examples of entrepreneurial and intrapreneurial successes.

Although Stephen Huse was successful in his previous job with a corporation, he decided to go into business for himself by establishing what has grown into the large pizza chain he still owns, Noble Roman's. Based in Indiana, Noble Roman's sales exceed $36,000,000 annually and it employs 4,000 people.

(Left) AT&T is another company that encourages employee creativity. Intrapreneurs, like this group shown, develop and market new products with cross-divisional authority.

(Below) Many new entrepreneurs are women. Mary Kay Ash of Mary Kay Cosmetics, pictured here checking products, is a nationally known success.

(Right) Given the freedom and authority to utilize information given to her by experts in sales, promotion, production, and technical development, Ann Fudge considers herself an intrapreneur in her job as Marketing Director for the Golden Valley Division of General Mills.

(Above) Bill Gates, in true entrepreneurial spirit, dropped out of Harvard in 1975 to form Microsoft, a computer software company which today provides the operating systems for almost half the computers made in this country. His achievements are discussed in

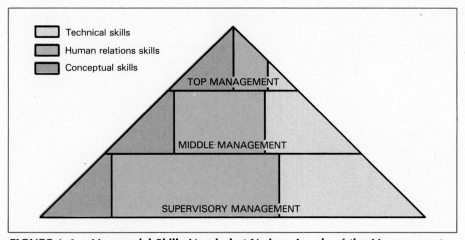

FIGURE 1–4.   Managerial Skills Needed at Various Levels of the Management Hierarchy
Source: Based on Robert L. Katz, "Skills of an Effective Administrator," *Harvard Business Review* (September–October 1974): 94–96.

THE SKILLS NEEDED FOR EFFECTIVE MANAGEMENT

What skills do managers need to possess? Robert L. Katz has suggested three specific skills that are required in all types of managerial situations.[13] Katz's managerial skills relate to technical, human relations, and conceptual factors in the manager's job. The importance of each of these skills at different levels of management is shown in Figure 1–4.

Technical skills refer to the ability to use various tools and methods to accomplish specific managerial aspects of a work task. A good illustration of the importance of technical skills is the factory supervisor who must be familiar with how machinery works in order to correct problems that may arise on the plant floor.

Human relations skills refer to the ability to lead and motivate people so as to accomplish certain objectives. Human relations skills are also important during interactions with supervisors and people outside the work unit such as vendors, customers, and the general public. Human relations skills are important at all levels in the organization.

Conceptual skills refer to the ability to understand and coordinate the full range of organizational objectives and activities. This ability to analyze the entire organization is particularly important to top management. It is a necessary ingredient in the development of a strategic plan for the organization.

MANAGERIAL ROLES

Henry Mintzberg's studies of executive behavior led him to conclude that managers are required to play a variety of roles.[14] These roles can be grouped into three main categories: interpersonal, informational, and

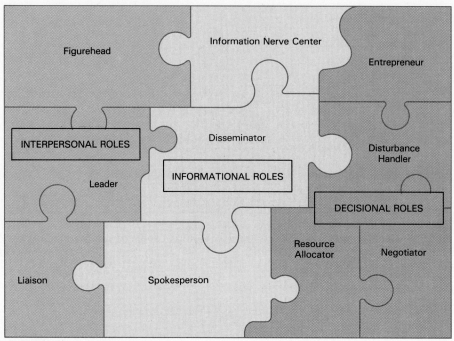

FIGURE 1–5.   Managerial Roles
Source: Based on Henry Mintzberg, "The Manager's Job: Folklore and Fact," *Harvard Business Review* (July–August 1975): 49–61; and "Managerial Work: Analysis from Observation," *Management Science* (October 1971): B97–B110.

decisional (see Figure 1–5). Mintzberg believed that all three roles were common to all levels of management.

Interpersonal roles result from the fact that managers are called upon to interact with numerous groups and individuals. The three interpersonal roles are figurehead, leader, and liaison. The *figurehead role* refers to ceremonial duties such as throwing out the first pitch for a Little League team the company sponsors. The *leadership role* refers to the manager's work in motivating subordinates to meet the unit's objectives. The *liaison role* comes from the manager's responsibility to interact with various groups both within and outside the organization.

Informational roles exist because managers are important conduits of information in the organization. In fact, managers spend a great deal of their time collecting and disseminating information. The three informational roles are information nerve center, disseminator, and spokesperson. The *nerve center role* means that the manager is the major information receiver within the work unit. The *disseminating role* refers to the task of informing subordinates of information that is important to them and necessary for their job performance. The *spokesperson role* is implemented when the manager communicates with parties outside the organization; a speech at the local Rotary Club would be an example.

MANAGEMENT SUCCESSES

Payless Cashways, Inc.

Payless Cashways, Inc.—a chain of hardware stores that is geared primarily toward the do-it-yourself homeowner—seems to know how to motivate its store managers. It gives them a great degree of independence, and it gives handsome incentives to managers who can translate their independence into profits.

Payless store managers determine their own inventory, set their own prices, and handle their own advertising. They devise their own business strategies, and they even select their own target net profit margins, which affect the size of their incentive reward. As a result, Payless store managers frequently earn annual salaries of more than $30,000, in addition to 3 percent of their store's pretax profits—and up to 25 percent more if their store achieves certain net margin targets.

Not only does this policy help the store managers, but it has appeared to work for Payless itself. In 1984 the firm made more than $1 billion, due largely to the dramatic addition of seventy-eight new stores—half the current total—in only five years. Its profits have since dropped a small amount, partly because of a decline in lumber prices, but Payless is still a strong contender in the $65-billion-a-year home-building supplies field.

Payless's strong performance can be explained by its handling of its store managers to a certain extent. But it is also attributable to the growing importance the chain is placing on retailing. "We're a building materials specialty retailer," comments Payless CEO David Stanley, "and the operative word is retailer. The others are just adjectives." This means that Payless stores are no longer merely lumberyards. Lumber is still a staple, but sophisticated hardware is an increasingly key component of the chain's merchandise, enabling Payless to reap higher margins.

Its new direction has led Payless to adopt a tighter grip on its store managers by using corporate merchandising programs. The managers still draw healthy incomes—a top performer may well earn $75,000 a year—but it will be interesting to observe how the new policy of centralized authority will affect a company that's succeeded by doing without it.

Source: Lisa Gross, "Do It Yourself," *Forbes,* 11 October 1982; and Daniel McConville, "Lumbering Giant," *Barron's,* 14 January 1985, p. 22.

Decisional roles refer to management's decision-making process. The four managerial roles in this category are entrepreneur, disturbance handler, resource allocator, and negotiator. A manager is playing an *entrepreneurial role* when he or she initiates projects to improve the department or work unit. When problems such as a missed delivery to a key customer arise, the manager must adopt a *disturbance handling role.* The decision on how to allocate the unit's money, time, materials, and other resources is referred to as the manager's *resource allocator role*. Finally, the *negotiator role* refers to situations where the manager must represent the unit's interests with others, such as suppliers, customers, and government.

MANAGEMENT: AN ART? A SCIENCE?

The question of whether management is an art or a science or both is a common one in the discipline's literature. A basic understanding of this issue is crucial to the discussion of management that follows.

Science is a systematic study that leads to a general body of knowledge about a subject. The discussion in Chapter 2 of the history of management clearly indicates that management has been the target of systematic study for centuries and that general principles or concepts have been derived from this effort. Most observers would classify management as a developing science. Society already knows a great deal about management science, but considerably more needs to be learned. By most recognized standards, then, management qualifies as a science.[15]

Management is also an art. In fact, one source has even defined management as the "art of making decisions with insufficient information."[16] The artistic process is generally seen as having three vital aspects: craft, vision, and communications.[17] The process of management qualifies as an art form in all three instances. Managers must have the tools (craft) to accomplish their tasks. They must possess vision in order to implement innovative strategies, and they must be able to communicate effectively in the work environment and elsewhere. Before he retired, AT&T's director of corporate planning, Henry B. Boettinger, put it this way: "To manage is to lead, and to lead others requires that one enlist the emotions of others to share a vision as their own. If that is not an art, then nothing is."

A balanced perspective suggests that management is both an art and a science. The management process follows the general scenario for the artistic process. But its craft or tool aspects are clearly based on a scientific body of knowledge that has been accumulated over time. It seems likely that the discipline of management will always maintain both scientific and artistic components.

> 66 Being good in business is the most fascinating kind of wit. 99
>
> Andy Warhol

SUMMARY

Management is a difficult term to define because it has a variety of applications and interpretations. In this text, we define it as the use of people and other resources to accomplish objectives. The managerial process consists of four functions: planning, organizing, leading, and controlling. Chapter 1 develops a model (Figure 1–1) illustrating how these functions are performed within a general environment for management.

Management concepts have universal application to all problem-solving situations. The concepts of effective management are as appropriate to the Red Cross, a church, or a public agency as they are to a major corporation. Nonprofit organizations have characteristics different from those of the profit-oriented sector, but the management concepts are similar.

There are three basic levels of management: (1) top management; (2) middle management; and (3) supervisory management. This hierarchy is often described as a pyramid since there are relatively fewer slots at each higher level. These levels of management are common to both profit-oriented and not-for-profit enterprises.

Chapter 1 also presented a capsule profile of top management, looking at the specific skills needed for management, as well as the different roles that managers have to play.

The management literature often discusses whether management is an art or a science. A balanced view of this argument reveals that management has both artistic and scientific components.

SOLVING THE STOP ACTION CASE

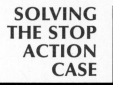

Microsoft Corp.

Bill Gates knew he had always operated Microsoft as a small business. Now it was time to assemble a team of experienced, professional managers. Gates himself made an interesting observation about the departure of fellow computer entrepreneur Steve Jobs from the company he founded, Apple Computer. "Steve wasn't getting things done. They needed to use a team approach. He needed to become part of a team."

After the first professional managers Gates hired failed to work out, he hired Jon Shirley, a Tandy Corp. manager with a reputation for toughness and efficiency. Shirley cut manufacturing costs by 20 percent, eliminated a massive backlog of unfilled orders, and restructured the Microsoft sales force. Although there is still some confusion over which parts of Microsoft Gates personally controls, Shirley has positioned Microsoft Corp. for future growth in the applications software market. If Gates continues to succeed, this still-young Harvard dropout may become one of the standouts of late twentieth-century American business.

Recently, Microsoft has gone public, and it is now worth $350 million.

Source: Stratford P. Sherman, "Microsoft's Drive to Dominate Software," *Fortune*, 23 January 1984, p. 82. Gates is quoted in Mike Gowrylow, "Microsoft Expects to Excel," *Journal-American,* 1 October 1985, p. D2.

FACT OR FICTION REVEALED

1. Fact 2. Fiction 3. Fact 4. Fact 5. Fiction 6. Fiction

MANAGEMENT TERMS

management	**organizing**	**controlling**
planning	**leading**	**bottom line**

REVIEW QUESTIONS

1. Define the following terms: (a) management (b) planning (c) organizing (d) leading (e) controlling (f) bottom line.

2. Why is management a difficult concept to define?

3. Explain the model of the managerial process presented in Figure 1–1.

4. Does management have universal application? Discuss.

5. How is the management of a nonprofit organization both similar to and different from the management of a profit-oriented organization?

6. Outline the basic levels of management.

7. Develop a capsule profile of top management.

8. Outline the specific skills required in management.

9. Identify and explain the roles that managers must play in their work environment.

10. Is management an art or a science?

PROBLEMS AND EXPERIENTIAL EXERCISES

1. "In terms of functional aspects, I didn't find all that much difference between heading a large corporation and the Federal Reserve Board. That surprises my friends in business. Coming here, I feel, was a very easy transition. Here, we deal in defining issues through objectives and priorities, mobilizing information, convincing ourselves, including whoever is chairman, of the correct decision and dealing with such outside constituencies as Congress, the banks and the public. A corporation is much the same. Their objectives have to be in terms of bringing a product to production or to market or acquiring a company or spinning off a company. And then you have to convince your organization to implement it because you can't just order them to do it. If they don't believe in it, they'll make it hard."[18]

G. William Miller

(Miller, now an international financial consultant, once headed the Federal Reserve Board. He later became Secretary of the Treasury. Miller was also formerly chief executive officer of Textron.)

Comment on the viewpoint expressed by Miller.

2. Consult three other texts in your library and develop a list of definitions of management. What do these definitions have in common? How are they different?

3. Select one of the following not-for-profit organizations and prepare a brief report on the management of the organization:
   a. your college or university
   b. the Girl Scouts or Boy Scouts
   c. a local hospital
   d. the local police department
   e. a public school system
   f. United Way

4. Request permission to observe the daily routine of a manager of a local firm. Record what he or she does during the day. How would you categorize the various tasks performed by the manager?

5. Write a brief essay on your conceptualization of management. File the essay away until the completion of the course you are now taking. Then make an analysis of whether, and how, your views have changed.

MANAGERIAL INCIDENT: Advice for Future Managers

Frank R. O'Keefe, Jr., president of the Armstrong Rubber Company, suggested a nine-step formula for "winning and succeeding in the business world" to the University of Massachusetts School of Management students:

1. **Bust your butt.** "Every successful person I know has 'busted his butt'—not frenzied activity and not working to exhaustion, but intensive, intelligent, directed activity."

2. **Show mental and physical energy.** "Energy—that's what all successful people seem to have; the energy to do what has to be done to satisfy your boss or your subordinates, and to inspire them with your sense of urgency and purpose."

3. **Become an active player instead of a spectator.** "You have to make things happen. If you do not, then things will happen to you and to your business. And you may not like what happens."

4. **Show enthusiasm for whatever you do.** "Enthusiasm is life. Boredom is death. You cannot become a leader if you are detached and cynical, uninvolved and cool."

5. **Know when to jump—when to make a vital career decision.** "You may like your job, your associates, and your location. But watch out! At some point, you have to decide that you are no longer on a training program, that you are no longer an understudy and that you are ready for another and bigger challenge. You are the one who decides it is time to jump—to take a new job, to take a risk or even to leave a company."

6. **Keep in touch with the realities of your business.** "Business is inhabited by people who see the world the way it is, and by others who see it the way they wish it to be. Winners tend to be realists; they go for the singles and doubles and get on base. The dreamers are always looking for home runs, and they often end up losers. One of your most valuable traits to an employer will be your ability to give him or her a faithful picture of that part of the universe assigned to you."

7. **Gain and maintain a reputation for credibility.** "Establish credibility. It's not just truth-telling. It's delivering as promised to your boss, to your customers, and ultimately to your shareholders."

8. **Show respect for people.** "You can be charging and you can be aggressive, but you have to show sensitivity to others. There will be many people in a company who are older than you or have less formal education, but they are often the core and the continuity of the company. You can learn from them. Respect them."

9. **Pick good bosses.** "A good boss is a person who lets you try something, who lets you stick out your neck and take a chance."

Questions and Problems

1. Do you agree or disagree with each of the nine ideas offered by O'Keefe? Why?

2. Relate these guidelines for "winning and succeeding in the business world" to the material presented in Chapter 1.

Source: Reprinted from Larry Walker, "Bust Your Butt," *Oregon Business*, May 1985, p. 9.

2 THE DEVELOPMENT OF MANAGEMENT THOUGHT

LEARNING OBJECTIVES

After studying this chapter you should be able to

1. Identify the early contributors to management theory.

2. Explain the two divisions of the classical school of management and identify the major contributors in each area.

3. List and discuss the major contributors in the behavioral school of management.

4. Distinguish among the quantitative school, systems theory, and contingency theory.

STOP ACTION CASE

Midvale Steel Co.

The young engineer was born in 1856 in Germantown, Pennsylvania. He received his early education in France and Germany and at Phillips Exeter Academy, but his poor eyesight compelled him to temporarily give up attending college. He went to work as an engineer at Midvale Steel Co. There he became fascinated with the differential piece-rate system devised by the company's superintendent.

The machine shop at Midvale seemed like a logical department in which to improve and extend the superintendent's work. At the time, jobs like grinding tools were shared by all workers. But the young engineer wondered if there was a more efficient way to accomplish the unit's tasks.

Use the materials in Chapter 2 to devise a system that would significantly improve employee efficiency at Midvale Steel Co.

Like most modern disciplines, contemporary management thought rests on a historical framework enriched by the many significant contributions of earlier theorists and practitioners. Many of these contributors are featured here in Chapter 2. Still others are discussed in the chapters that follow.

Management's historical framework has both theoretical and applied components. Important management contributions have come from both groups. The rich diversity of management's contributions was clearly illustrated by a plan to request that the U.S. Postal Service issue a series of commemorative stamps to honor people who made outstanding contributions to business and management practice and thought. Nominations were sought from the Business History Conference, the History Division of the Academy of Management, and a random sample of other Academy of Management members. Each group's candidates reflected its own biases. The Business History Division group favored entrepreneurs and practicing managers; the Academy's History Division was oriented toward academicians from the scientific management school; and the Academy of Management sample also favored academicians, but with less bias toward the scientific management school. The composite of these surveys is shown in Table 2–1. Frederick Taylor headed the list for each survey as well as the composite ranking.[1]

Management's rich historical background is explored in this chapter. Part One will then conclude with an environmental chapter that completes the missing links in Figure 1–1.

THE HISTORICAL CONTEXT

Most management students today think of management as a business- or industry-related discipline. But historically, people were more concerned with the management of other organizations such as the state, church, military, tribe, or household. The very earliest examples of management come from nonbusiness entities.[2] These management techniques were later adapted to commercial applications.

The list below identifies some of the most important ancient and medieval contributors to our knowledge of management techniques.[3]

MANAGEMENT FACT OR FICTION

	FACT	FICTION		FACT	FICTION
1. A survey indicated that Henry Ford is considered the most outstanding contributor to management thought.	☐	☐	5. Mary Parker Follett is usually associated with the quantitative school of management.	☐	☐
2. Charles Babbage produced the first computer prototype over 150 years ago.	☐	☐	6. Douglas McGregor first proposed the concepts of Type A and Type B management behavior.	☐	☐
3. Henry Fayol's major work was not published until he was seventy-five years old.	☐	☐	7. The quantitative school of management began with military, rather than business, situations.	☐	☐
4. Max Weber is considered the father of scientific management.	☐	☐			

The materials in this chapter will assist you in separating management fact from fiction. Your answers can be checked on page 47.

- The Sumerians were concerned with record keeping in 5000 B.C.
- By 4000 B.C., the Egyptians were aware of the importance of planning, organizing, and controlling.
- Staff advice existed in Egyptian management by 2000 B.C.
- Socrates discussed the universality of management in 400 B.C.
- Xenophon recognized management as a separate art in 400 B.C.
- Plato described specialization in 350 B.C.
- Alexander the Great used a staff organization extensively during his military campaigns from 336 to 323 B.C.
- Alfarabi listed the traits of a leader in A.D. 900.
- Ghazaei suggested the traits of a manager in A.D. 1100.

TABLE 2-1   OUTSTANDING CONTRIBUTORS TO MANAGEMENT THOUGHT AND PRACTICE: A COMPOSITE RATING

Rank	Contributor	Number of Votes	Points	Total Points	First-Place Votes
1	Taylor, Frederick W.	108	850	958	51
2	Barnard, Chester I.	81	516	597	9
3	Gilbreth, Frank	70	414	484	0
4	Mayo, Elton	61	368	429	3
5	Gilbreth, Lillian	61	348	409	2
6	Sloan, Alfred P., Jr.	55	313	368	3
7	Follett, Mary Parker	55	302	357	2
8	Ford, Henry	48	262	310	4
9	Maslow, Abraham	45	209	254	3
10	Gantt, Henry L.	40	211	251	2
11	Roethlisberger, Fritz	41	203	244	2
12	Wharton, Joseph	40	196	236	0
13	Lewin, Kurt	33	172	205	2
14	Edison, Thomas A.	27	171	198	6
15	Du Pont, Pierre	28	148	176	0
16	Carnegie, Andrew	32	143	175	2
17	Whitney, Eli	21	123	144	3
18	Rockefeller, John D.	23	114	137	1
19	Slater, Samuel	19	116	135	3
20	Watson, Thomas	18	102	120	2

Source: Daniel A. Wren and Robert D. Hay, "Management Historians and Business Historians: Differing Perceptions of Pioneer Contributors," *Academy of Management Journal* (September 1977): 476. Reprinted by permission.

The movement of manufacturing to a factory system (where products are produced in a centralized location) from a craft-like cottage system (where production was contracted to a family living/work unit) had a significant impact on management as well as on social history. This movement, which occurred in Europe (particularly the United Kingdom) in the mid-1700s, is usually called the *industrial revolution.*

Management had to be adapted from its public administration applications to use within the developing factory system.[4] The industrial revolution had launched an industrial era within which modern management concepts had to be developed.

Four major contributors can be identified in this early era of management thought: Robert Owen, Charles Babbage, Andrew Ure, and Charles Dupin. All were forerunners of later developments in management. Owen's concern for human welfare preceded the behaviorist school; Babbage was a pioneer in scientific management, operations research, and management science; and Ure and Dupin were early advocates of management education.[5]

Industrial revolution was the mid-eighteenth-century movement of English manufacturing to a factory system (where products are produced in a centralized location) from a cottage system (where production was contracted to family living/work units).

MANAGEMENT SUCCESSES

The Great Pyramid

It is easily the most massive building ever built on earth. Its height equals one and one-half football fields, while its square base covers more than thirteen acres. The most incredible fact about the Great Pyramid is that it was built more than 4,600 years ago by men who had neither machinery nor iron tools. The two million stone blocks that made up the planned resting place of the Pharaoh whom the Greeks called Cheops sometimes weighed more than fifty tons each. Some were moved from nearby quarries; others were transported by boat from southern quarries down the Nile. The stones, cut with copper chisels and saws, were so finely cut that the joints measured less than one-fiftieth of an inch in thickness.* The building's outer casing of white polished limestone was laid so smoothly that the Great Pyramid appeared to have been cut from a single stone. Not surprisingly, some observers have speculated that such a marvel of architectural perfection must have been constructed by extraterrestrial beings.

Construction of the Great Pyramid required immense organizational skills. Several thousand skilled workers were employed for more than twenty years on the project. Unskilled workers added their services when Nile floods made farming impossible. Numerous specialties were required: surveyors, quarry workers, toolmakers, overseers, priests, engineers, and scribes. Teams of peasants dragged the stones from the quarries or boats to the building site. Ramps were used to drag the stones to the next layer. Some men specialized in pouring milk under the sledges to lubricate the runners and move the stones upward. The rewards for service to the organization were wages paid in bread, onions, meat, salt, and beer. The pride of the workers is reflected in the graffiti found on many of the pyramid blocks. The names of the work gangs are proudly listed: Boat Gang, Enduring Gang, Sceptre Gang.** The results of this effort of organizing human and other resources—one of humanity's most spectacular achievements—are even more impressive when one remembers that the construction dates back to the very edges of prehistory.

Sources: *Peter Lemesurier, *The Great Pyramid* (New York: St. Martin's Press, 1977), pp. 3-5.
**Rafael Steinberg, *Man and the Organization* (New York: Time-Life Books, 1975), pp. 13-14.

ROBERT OWEN: HUMAN RESOURCES MANAGEMENT PIONEER

A successful factory owner at eighteen years of age, Robert Owen (1771–1858) became an early advocate of improved management of human resources. He attempted to better the situation of the pauper children employed at his Scottish factory (child labor was a common practice of the era). He proposed legislative reform that would limit the hours and usage of child labor. Owen's proposals were viewed as radical at the time.

Owen used what he called the *silent monitor* to encourage productivity. Blocks of wood were painted in four different colors, with each color signifying a different level of accomplishment. The blocks were then attached to each machine in the factory. Employees were graded daily, and the appropriate color was turned so that all could see.

Owen urged other manufacturers to adopt his concern over improving the human resources they employed. He claimed that returns from investments in human resources would far exceed those in machinery and equipment.

Later, Owen suggested the establishment of "villages of cooperation" based on communal sharing of the output of their inhabitants. In 1824, he set up the first such village in New Harmony, Indiana. Later, in 1834, Owen's socialist views were evident in his direction of the British trade union movement. While Owen's reforms failed, he has to be considered a forerunner of the behaviorist school because of his concern for human welfare.

CHARLES BABBAGE: INVENTOR AND MANAGEMENT SCIENTIST

Charles Babbage (1792–1871) was an early pioneer in areas that now are known as scientific management, operations research, and management science. In 1822, Babbage produced the first practical calculator, which he termed his *difference machine*. He also produced a rudimentary computer—termed the *analytical machine*—that included the various aspects of contemporary computer hardware. Babbage also developed gaming programs that were precedents of more modern quantitative methods.

Babbage published his views on management and manufacturing processes, including his belief that the division of labor was a necessary aspect of all developed economic systems. He also proposed observational procedures for studying manufacturing operations.

The inventor realized the importance of the human factor. He believed that management and employee interests were closely linked. Thus, Babbage advocated use of profit-sharing and employee suggestion plans—techniques that are still used.

THE MANAGER'S BOOKSHELF

My Years with General Motors, by Alfred P. Sloan, Jr.

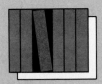 The 1980s have witnessed an explosion of interest in business books. Everyone seems to be searching for excellence, upping the organization, catching megatrends, or learning to manage by one-minute installments. It's hard to remember now, but there was a time when a book about business was its own worst enemy.

One of the first books to crack the best-seller list—and the very first "management book" to reach the number one spot—was Alfred Sloan's *My Years with General Motors* (Doubleday, 1964). Published over two decades ago, Sloan's account of his thirty-three-year reign over the world's largest manufacturing enterprise remained on the best-seller list for nearly six months.

Alfred Sloan was one of America's great corporate organizers. Men like Sloan, Walter Teagle of Standard Oil, and Theodore Vail, who created AT&T, gave the modern corporation its distinctive form. Industrial America had been carved up by the great "robber barons" of American economic history: the Carnegies, the Rockefellers, the McCormicks. But it was this second generation of American entrepreneurs, the corporate organizers, who set the stage for American dominance of the world economy.

General Motors started as a loose conglomerate; it was assembled from about twenty-five smaller firms, and it barely survived a couple of early financial crises. Sloan had been general manager of the Hyatt Roller Bearing Company, which was absorbed into the GM network in 1918. When GM founder William Durant stacked up a $20-million market speculation debt, he was bailed out by GM's investors but required to leave as part of the agreement. Sloan was then brought in as president.

More than any other person, Alfred Sloan was responsible for the shape the organization has taken and the strategies it has pursued. He

---

ANDREW URE AND CHARLES DUPIN: MANAGEMENT EDUCATION PIONEERS

Andrew Ure and Charles Dupin were early proponents of management education, Ure in the United Kingdom and Dupin in France. Ure, who taught in Glasgow, published a book outlining various principles and concepts of manufacturing. He was responsible for educating many of the managers of his day. Ure argued that the factory system produced numerous advantages for society, far offsetting the problems it presented.

Dupin was a French engineer. He was impressed with Ure's work, which he came to know when visiting the United Kingdom from 1816 to 1818. Shortly thereafter, Dupin's appointment to a professorship in Paris commenced a long career. Dupin's writing and curriculum, well known throughout France, may have influenced Henri Fayol's subsequent contribution to management thought.

is justifiably famous for his organizational system, which was copied by thousands of other would-be General Motors corporations.

Sloan's motto for his organizational set-up was "decentralization with coordinated control." Three elements went into this equation. First, an elaborate system of long-run financial controls was applied to every activity of the corporation. Everything was evaluated in terms of return on invested capital at the average volume of business and level of costs and prices that could reasonably be expected for that activity. Second, a system of short-run market forecasts, continuously revised in the light of actual sales, served as the basis for a very close scheduling of production, purchases, and inventories. Third, an executive bonus system gave the executive team a personal stake in the welfare of the company as a whole.

Before this system was instituted, divisions in GM were run like separate fiefdoms, often by the very managers whose companies had been absorbed into the General Motors network. Divisions sold their parts to other divisions (e.g., a battery division to a car division) with a predetermined percentage tacked on.

The executives at the top of the corporation had no idea which units were profitable and which were not. Divisions would often hoard cash to fund later investments.

Sloan changed all this by treating each division as a separate company, with the corporation on top acting as a holding company. He then measured the rate of performance on investment consistent with attainable volume. In other words, divisions were rated according to their performance, not just their profit figures.

Sloan was also a great leader, which probably accounts for the way he was able to bend to his will the various division heads, many of whom were older and more experienced than he. *My Years with General Motors* doesn't offer many leadership clues, and it doesn't have the kind of gossipy detail or personal vendetta we've come to expect from our managerial biographies. Nevertheless, it reveals the creation of an organizational system that became so pervasive that we take it for granted.

Note: Adapted from New York Review of Books, March 19, 1964, p. 12, "The Company He Keeps," by Daniel Bell.

CLASSICAL APPROACHES TO MANAGEMENT

Classical approaches to management thought include two separate schools: one on administrative theory and a second on scientific management concepts.[6] The two major components of this school of thought are best represented by the work of Henri Fayol and Frederick W. Taylor, respectively.

ADMINISTRATIVE THEORY

Henri Fayol and Max Weber are cited here as pioneers in administrative theory. Many others could be mentioned. For example, Fayol is usually credited with the development of the functional or management process school. But R. C. Davis of Ohio State University probably did more to popularize this school than anyone else in the United States.

HENRI FAYOL: DEVELOPER OF MANAGEMENT'S FIRST GENERAL THEORY

Fayol (1841–1925) was Europe's most distinguished management theorist and the first to develop a general theory of management.[7] Born of French parents in 1841 in Istanbul, Fayol was trained as an engineer at the Ecole de Mines in Saint-Etienne. At nineteen he joined a large mining company and during the next twenty-eight years he distinguished himself as a scientist and engineer. In 1888 he became the managing director of the company, which at that time was near financial ruin. Intrigued by the problems of management, Fayol reorganized the company and made it prosper.

Fayol insisted that the "administrative function" of an organization be viewed as distinct from all other functions. He quickly pointed out that this function was not the sole responsibility of the chief executive officer, but was part of the responsibilities of subordinate managers and supervisors. Fayol felt that the proportion of time the individual manager devoted to the administrative function was positively correlated with that individual's position in the firm; the higher the level of the position, the greater the administrative responsibility.

Fayol's Writings. Fayol spent a lifetime in industry, observing and applying management practices, and ultimately developed a philosophy and theory of management. They were expressed in his book *Administration generale et industrielle,* first published in 1916 when Fayol was seventy-five years old.

Fayol's work was published in France in the midst of World War I and was not translated and published in the United States for another thirteen years. As a result, it received very little attention in Europe until the 1920s. In the United States, management study focused on the scientific approach of Frederick Taylor to effective shop management, and Fayol's methodology for top management was almost unknown. Nearly two decades passed after the death of Fayol in 1925 before U.S. management theorists became familiar with his work.

The basis of Fayol's theory was that industrial undertakings consisted of six separate activities: (1) technical (production, manufacture, adaptation); (2) commercial (buying, selling, exchange); (3) financial (search for and optimal use of capital); (4) security (protection of property and persons); (5) accounting (stocktaking, balance sheets, costs, statistics); and (6) managerial (planning, organizing, command, coordination, control).

Fayol concentrated on the last of these activities, the managerial activities. He went on to create the first general theory of management with his identification of fourteen basic principles of management:

1. Division of work (specialization belongs to the natural order)

2. Authority and responsibility (responsibility is a corollary to authority)

3. Discipline (discipline is what leaders make it)

4. Unity of command (people cannot bear dual command)

5. Unity of direction (one head and one plan for a group of activities having the same objectives)

6. Subordination of individual interest to the general interest

7. Remuneration (fair, reasonable rewarding of effort)

8. Centralization (centralization belongs to the natural order)

9. Scalar chain (line of authority, gang-plank principle)

10. Order (a place for everyone and everyone in his place)

11. Equity (results from combination of kindliness and justice)

12. Stability of tenure of personnel (prosperous firms are stable)

13. Initiative (great source of strength for business)

14. Esprit de corps (union is strength)[8]

Fayol's Other Contributions to Management Thought. In addition to the development of a comprehensive management theory, Fayol is credited with enunciating the universality of management concept discussed in Chapter 1.

Since no formal training was available for the study of management in France at the time, Fayol spoke out strongly in behalf of developing formal education programs in management. All organizations, he insisted, from departments of government to small or large private firms, require effective management. Acting on these convictions, he founded the Center of Administrative Studies in France—the first institution of its kind.

MAX WEBER: FOCUSING ON AUTHORITY

Max Weber (1864–1920) was a German contemporary of Fayol who was concerned with the study of organizational sociology. As a result of his conceptual work in this area, Weber is considered part of the classical school of management. His wide-ranging contributions, however, make it difficult to limit him to any given discipline.[9]

Weber believed there were three types of authority: charismatic, based on the peculiar powers of the leader; traditional, based on loyalty to the individual; and rational-legal, based on a system of formal, explicit rules— typically a bureaucracy. *Bureaucracy* refers to a management approach based on a formal organizational structure with set rules and regulations. Unfortunately, the term is now held in low regard because of its association with inefficiency and incompetence in many organizations. Weber's concept of bureaucracy, however, still provides us with some basic organizational principles.

Bureaucracy refers to a management approach based on a formal organizational structure with set rules and regulations.

Weber's thoughts on organizational behavior were based on his analysis of capitalism as it exists in the modern Western world. Capitalism had existed in earlier eras, but the important point for Weber was that the modern form was characterized by a bureaucratic organizational structure. He believed that the combination of bureaucracy and the capitalistic framework created the current economic system.[10]

Bureaucracy required various specialists. Weber believed that the use of specialists in a bureaucracy provided advantages over other forms of organization. He also specified various requirements for an effective bureaucracy: technical training for its personnel; appointment on the basis of merit; set salaries and retirement benefits; guaranteed careers; divorce of people's private lives from their organizational positions; set hierarchy of jobs and offices; implementation of an adequate control system; rational rules and regulations within the organization; and certain obedience to a superior's command.[11]

Like Fayol, Weber's conceptual developments were not widely known to American management for several decades. It was not until years after his death that the importance of Weber's studies was widely recognized. His work is now considered an integral part of classical organizational and management theory.[12]

SCIENTIFIC MANAGEMENT

Scientific management is a school of management popularized during the early 1900s that is based on the application of the scientific method to the workplace and management activities.

Scientific management refers to a school of management thought that became popular in the early 1900s. It was based on the notion that the scientific method could be applied to the workplace and the related management activities. Among its major early contributors were Frederick W. Taylor, the Gilbreths, and Henry L. Gantt.

FREDERICK W. TAYLOR: FATHER OF SCIENTIFIC MANAGEMENT

Frederick W. Taylor (1856–1915), who is profiled in the stop action case for this chapter, is credited with the development of scientific management. An engineer and inventor, Taylor first began to experiment with new managerial concepts in 1878 while employed at Midvale Steel Co. He went on to work in a variety of capacities. He retired in 1901 to devote full time to the dissemination of scientific management techniques.[13]

The Development of Scientific Management. Taylor outlined four principles that constitute scientific management:

1. Develop a science for each element of a person's work, which replaces the old rule-of-thumb method.

2. Scientifically select and then train, teach, and develop the worker, whereas in the past he chose his own work and trained himself as best he could.

3. Heartily cooperate with the workers so as to insure all of the work being done in accordance with the principles of the science which has been developed.

4. There is an almost equal division of work and responsibilities between the management and the workers. The managers take over all work for which they are better fitted than the workers, while in the past almost all of the work and the greater part of the responsibility were thrown upon the workers.[14]

Taylor differentiated these principles from such mechanisms of management as time study, standardization of tools, time-saving devices, and so forth.[15] His comprehensive system of scientific management had five basic features:

1. Organizational and technical improvements such as better machine operations, cost accounting, purchasing, and stock and tool room control.

2. A planning department that was responsible for coordinating the overall operation and assigning jobs.

3. The use of functional foremen who were responsible for a single functional activity within the manufacturing process.

4. Time study to determine the rate at which a job should be done.

5. An incentive wage system.[16]

Scientific management became the accepted management philosophy in part because it provided a response to the labor unrest and problems that prevailed at the time. The incentive wage system advocated by Taylor was the dominant remedy for labor problems during the early 1900s. While Taylor's system was a far more comprehensive approach to management, its labor-oriented features facilitated its acceptance by management.[17]

Taylor's Views Reconsidered. Taylor's views were an important step in the evolutionary development of management thought. One management writer put it this way: "Considering that it has been over sixty-five years since Taylor's death and that a knowledge explosion has taken place during these years, Taylor's track record is remarkable. The point is not, as is often claimed, that he was 'right in the context of his time' but is now outdated, but that most of his insights are still valid today."[18]

THE GILBRETHS: TIME AND MOTION STUDY PROPONENTS

The Gilbreths—Frank B. (1868–1924) and Lillian M. (1878–1972)—were responsible for many contributions to management theory and are generally identified with the scientific management era. Frank Gilbreth is considered the father of motion study because of his early studies of bricklaying. *Motion study* refers to the determination of the best sequence and number of motions to accomplish a specified task. Gilbreth's modification of the bricklaying process increased hourly output from 120 to 350 bricks.[19] Lillian Gilbreth was active in much of the research concerning motion studies. Later, she became a widely recognized industrial psychologist, management consultant, and professor of industrial engineering.[20]

Working as a team, the Gilbreths pioneered the study of time-saving techniques for both the home and industry. Their rambling Montclair, New Jersey, house was a model of precision and efficiency. Assembly calls, family council budget meetings, and a system that awarded household jobs on a contractual basis to the lowest bidder were all part of the family routine for the Gilbreths and their twelve children, two of whom described the Gilbreth family in *Cheaper by the Dozen* (see Figure 2–1). Charts and follow-up systems determined the flow of work, and work centers and

Motion study refers to the determination of the best sequence and number of motions to accomplish a specified task.

FIGURE 2–1.   Frank and Lillian Gilbreth with Eleven of Their Dozen Children

work surfaces turned the house into a kind of well-oiled family factory. What could have been a chaotic child-rearing situation became a model of what Lillian Gilbreth could accomplish if she put her mind to it.[21]

During the course of their studies, the Gilbreths identified seventeen basic hand motions which they called *therbligs* (except for the transposition of the *t* and *h*, *therblig* is *Gilbreth* spelled backward). The Gilbreths were also responsible for such management tools and techniques as the process chart, the flow diagram, and a merit-rating system for employees.[22]

> **Therbligs** is the term coined by the Gilbreths to refer to the seventeen basic hand motions they identified in the course of their studies of motion.

HENRY LAURENCE GANTT: FATHER OF THE GANTT CHART

A teacher and an engineer, Henry Laurence Gantt (1861–1919) joined, in 1887, the steel company that employed Frederick W. Taylor. Gantt later followed Taylor to other employers and became one of his best-known disciples.[23] He was a prolific writer and successful consultant.

Gantt made several contributions of his own to the scientific management school. He exhibited a humanistic concern for his workers. Gantt dropped Taylor's piece-rate pay system for a "task work with a bonus system." In Gantt's plan, workers received a bonus for completing all of their daily tasks. He also awarded bonuses to supervisors who were successful in getting all of their subordinates to meet the output goal.

> 66 I know of no way of judging the future but by the past. 99
>
> Patrick Henry

Gantt later refined his management thoughts in three books and in numerous papers presented to professional organizations. His work in employee relations was crystallized in a presentation to the American Society of Mechanical Engineers in 1908 in which he proposed what was then a revolutionary policy. It was the responsibility of management, said Gantt, to train workers to become more skilled rather than to just drive them to increase their output. He also believed that it was management's role to help employees learn better, more efficient working habits. As a result of this paper, Taylor, who supported a much more mechanistic view of workers, severed his long-term personal and working relationship with Gantt. Although Gantt experienced a personal loss, time vindicated his views on human resources management. Years later, after World War I, Gantt's theories became generally accepted as a part of management thought.

During World War I, Gantt volunteered his management services to the government and developed an innovative method for comparing actual to planned work performance. As Figure 2–2 reveals, the Gantt Chart, as it came to be known, was a visual method of comparing production output with the time it took to complete a task. For the first time, managers could use a simple visual device to maintain production control. His charting procedures had ready application to industrial management and were the forerunners of today's PERT (program evaluation and review technique), discussed in Chapter 18.

EXPLANATION OF PROGRESS CHART

When the machines are running, it is necessary to know whether or not they are doing the work which is most needed and also at what rate they are doing it.

Our chart system for presenting these facts is based on the following principles, and is very effective:

1. The fact that all activities can be measured by the amount of time needed to perform them.

2. The space representing the time unit on the chart can be made to represent the amount of activity which should have been performed in that time.

Bearing these two principles in mind the whole system is readily intelligible and affords a means of charting all kinds of activities, the simplest as well as the most complex.

These charts force us to make a schedule: They show how the schedule is being lived up to, by showing at a glance a comparison between what has been done, and what should have been done.

Charts of this kind, if kept in sufficient detail, also indicate with great accuracy the probabilities of future performance, and enable a manager to anticipate his needs and make preparations therefor.

In a manufacturing establishment the schedule portions of the charts are taken from whatever promises have been made. Performance is charted at intervals against the schedule. If these charts are kept entered to date they will enable a manager to concentrate his efforts on those operations which are being delayed.

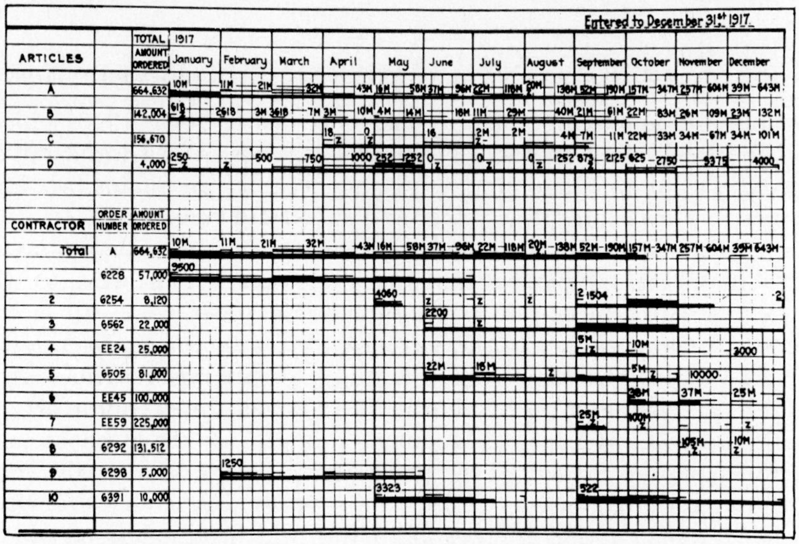

Entered to December 31st 1917.

KEY TO PROGRESS CHART

At the left of the chart is a list of articles to be procured. The amounts for which orders have been placed are shown in the column headed "Amount Ordered." The dates between which deliveries are to be made are shown by angles. The amount to be delivered each month is shown by a figure at the left side of the space assigned to that month. The figures at the right of each space indicate the total due at that date.

If the amount due in any month is all received, a light line is drawn clear across the space representing that month. If only half the amount due is received, this line only goes half way across. In general, the length of the light line indicates the amount delivered during that month.

The heavy line shows cumulatively the amount delivered up to the date of the last entry. It will be noted that, if this line is drawn to the scale of the periods through which it passes, the distance from the end of the line to the current date will represent the amount of time deliveries are behind or ahead of the schedule. It is thus seen that the short lines are the ones which require attention as they are farthest behind schedule.

A, B, C, and D are summaries.

A is a summary of the orders shown on the lower part of the chart.

FIGURE 2–2. A Typical Progress Chart Prepared by Henry Gantt

OTHER DISCIPLES OF SCIENTIFIC MANAGEMENT

Figure 2–3 summarizes the key thinkers in the development of classical management thought. F. W. Taylor had many disciples. Gantt, Carl E. Barth, Morris L. Cooke, H. K. Hathaway, Hollis Godfrey, Royal R. Kelly, C. Bertram Thompson, and the Gilbreths were some of the better known proponents of Taylor's scientific management concepts. These people played a major role, particularly after Taylor's retirement in 1901, acting primarily as consultants to firms interested in installing scientific management. In many cases, they had to make changes in Taylor's original system.[24] Taylor's disciples had a decided impact on management thought;

Administrative Theory

    Henri Fayol—General Theory of Management
    Max Weber—Authority

Scientific Management

    Frederick W. Taylor—Development of Scientific Management
    Frank B. and Lillian M. Gilbreth—Time and Motion Studies
    Henry L. Gantt—The Gantt Chart

FIGURE 2–3.   Key Thinkers: Classical Approaches to Management

---

in fact, one, Morris L. Cooke, has recently been credited with preparing a portion of Taylor's book, *The Principles of Scientific Management.*[25]

BEHAVIORAL APPROACHES TO MANAGEMENT

The *behavioral school* in management thought is nearly as diverse as the classical school. Essentially, behaviorists believe that those involved in the organization are the prime determinants of organizational and managerial effectiveness.

    Behaviorists moved away from supervisory procedures and industrial engineering techniques and focused their attention instead on the motivation of people. Members of this school see human behavior as a complex subject and as the most vital aspect of management. Selected major contributors are discussed in the section that follows. Others such as Levin, Homans, Whyte, and Festinger are discussed elsewhere in the text.

> **Behavioral school** is a managerial approach that emphasizes employee motivation as a primary determinant of organizational and managerial effectiveness.

MARY PARKER FOLLETT: FOCUSING ON GROUP INFLUENCE

For most of her early working life, Mary Parker Follett (1868–1933) devoted herself to serving the poor and underprivileged in Boston's Roxbury section.[26] After graduating summa cum laude from Radcliffe College in 1898, Follett organized evening centers in the hope of getting young people off the streets and finding them jobs. She soon became a national figure in the community center movement and was elected vice-president of the National Community Center Association.

    From this unlikely beginning as a social worker, Mary Parker Follett became a modern management pioneer who advised businesspeople on personnel problems and made important contributions to the field of human resources management. Even though she never set foot in a factory except as an observer or participated in the management of a company, Follett understood the critical role managers play in bringing about the kind of constructive change that enables businesses to function.

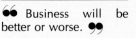
❝ Business will be better or worse. ❞

Calvin Coolidge

Attracted to the practical approach of business managers and their need to translate theories into changes that produced results, Follett applied what she had first observed in her community center activities to the management of business. She focused on the cross-fertilization of thinking that occurs when people operate in groups. She observed that the ideas that came out of group thinking could not be duplicated by any individual working alone and that all group participants undergo important changes in thinking simply because of their participation in the group. Follett believed that when group members take part in a discussion, they begin to think in a more compatible, harmonious way. Follett believed the role of the manager was to cultivate this group interaction so that it produced the optimal results.

Central to Follett's theory is the concept of integration—the harmonious blending of the differences of group members to produce a solution acceptable to all. This solution is usually short-lived, for new differences are always arising. However, Follett believed that new solutions are always contained within the differences themselves and that it is the function of the manager to preside over the process of integration. Managers who try to dominate the group for the purpose of bringing about a preconceived goal usually fail, for the process of talking and ironing out differences is ever-changing. Managers have little advance notice of the most appropriate solution when conflicts first appear. Follett advises them to use the goals of the evolving situation as a guide to their own behavior as long as they are willing to change these goals as new differences and new possible integrations arise.

Follett likened this process to planting an unfamiliar seed and cultivating it without knowing whether to expect a flower, or a fruit, a tree, or bush. Only after the results appear does the manager know what he or she has been working toward all along.

ELTON MAYO: APPLYING BEHAVIORAL APPROACHES TO MANAGEMENT

Elton Mayo (1880–1949) is most often associated with the famous Hawthorne studies described in Chapters 12 and 14.[27] These studies emphasized the impact of human motivation on productivity and output. When he began the first phase of his famous Hawthorne experiments, Mayo firmly believed that every social problem was "ultimately individual." At the Hawthorne Works of the Western Electric Co. in Chicago, where he and his assistants did their study, however, Mayo soon found that group rather than individual psychology was the key factor in the production performance of the workers.

Based on the premise that fatigue was the main factor affecting output, Mayo's study had three phases. The first phase was a day-by-day statistical evaluation of the output of five female telephone assemblers who were segregated in a controlled work environment. The analysis of their work performance was carefully related to changes in their working conditions

❝ Once you get into this great stream of history, you can't get out. **❞**

Richard M. Nixon

that were periodically introduced, as well as to the characteristics of their work environment (temperature and humidity, for example) and variations in their personal routines (for example, different meals, few or many hours of sleep). Mayo and his team were puzzled to find no correlations of any significance. Though the output of the women rose as coffee breaks were added and hours shortened, it did not decline when the group was once again required to work under the original control conditions. These findings revealed that the determining factors were the significance the experiment had for the workers and their desire to cooperate with the researchers and facilitate their work.

This discovery launched the second phase of the Hawthorne studies: interviews, somewhat psychoanalytic in nature, of thousands of workers to determine the meaning they ascribed to their work and personal relationships within the factory. Eventually, Mayo developed the revolutionary hypothesis that "the working group as a whole actually determined the output of individual workers by reference to a standard, predetermined but never clearly stated, that represented the group conception of a fair day's work." His research also indicated that "this standard was rarely, if ever, in accord with the standards of efficiency engineers."

The final phase of Mayo's investigation consisted of the observation of a group of workers and served to verify his hypothesis that the group, not the individual worker, plays the crucial role in setting standards for output. He further concluded that even economic needs and interests of the individual are subordinated to the group's standards. "Management," Mayo wrote in his *Social Problems of an Industrial Organization* (1945), "in any continuously successful plant, is not related to single workers but always to working groups. In every department that continues to operate, the workers have—whether aware of it or not—formed themselves into a group with appropriate customs, duties, routines, even rituals; and management succeeds (or fails) in proportion as it is accepted without reservation by the group as authority and leader."

The Hawthorne studies were a milestone in the development of the behavioral school (see Figure 2–4). They emphasized the impact of human

FIGURE 2–4. Elton Mayo and the Hawthorne Studies

Prejudgments	Findings
Job performance depends on the individual worker.	The group is the key factor in worker job performance.
Fatigue is the main factor affecting output.	Perceived meaning and importance of the work determine output.
Management sets production standards.	Workplace culture sets its own production standards.

motivation on productivity and output. Mayo's work pointed out the existence of a workplace culture that sets its own productivity standards, and it is considered a cornerstone in the evolution of management thought.

ABRAHAM H. MASLOW: FOCUSING ON HUMAN NEEDS

Abraham H. Maslow (1908–1970), a Brandeis University psychologist, suggested that a number of different human needs exist and that organizations relying solely on money as a motivator may be ignoring important needs. He felt that human needs could be arranged in the following hierarchy: (1) physical and physiological needs; (2) safety or security needs; (3) love or social needs; (4) ego or status needs; and (5) self-actualization, self-realization, or self-fulfillment.[28]

Maslow believed that people progressed from satisfying the most basic needs in the hierarchy to attempting to fulfill the next higher level needs. He saw this conceptualization as a general model that was subject to certain deficiencies and constraints, for example, the tendency of some people to fixate at a given level. Maslow's hierarchy of needs model, which is described in detail in Chapter 13, has played a key role in the acceptance of behavioral science in management.

DOUGLAS McGREGOR: CHALLENGING TRADITIONAL ASSUMPTIONS ABOUT EMPLOYEES

Douglas McGregor (1906–1964) spent most of his career at the Massachusetts Institute of Technology, with a six-year stint as president of Antioch College.[29] His primary contribution to management thought is the now famous dichotomy of the two alternative management views of subordinates. According to McGregor, Theory X managers believe their subordinates are uninspired workers who seek to avoid responsibility and work assignments. By contrast, Theory Y managers hold that all subordinates view work as rewarding if given the chance by their superiors.

McGregor thought that management's perception of subordinate behavior played a significant part in determining the type of leadership style that was employed. Theory X suggested supervision and evaluation as the key management functions. On the other hand, a Theory Y conceptualization implied that providing improved communications and greater employee participation in decisions would be the most desirable format for management. McGregor's theories are discussed in detail in Chapters 13 and 14.

CHRIS ARGYRIS: MATCHING HUMAN AND ORGANIZATIONAL DEVELOPMENT

Chris Argyris is a contemporary advocate of the behavioral school of management thought. The Yale University professor believes that people normally progress from a stage of immaturity and dependence to maturity and independence and that many modern organizations keep their employees in a dependent state, thus preventing the individual from achieving his or her fullest potential. Further, Argyris believes that several of the basic concepts and principles of modern management—such as specialization—inhibit the natural development of a "healthy" personality. He feels that the incongruence between the organization and personal development can be alleviated through such management actions as job enlargement. Under this approach, a person is given greater work-related responsibilities, such as an increase in the range of tasks to be performed or more opportunity to participate in the decision-making process.[30]

Model I and Model II.[31] According to Argyris, most organizations are guided by unilateral defensive strategies that pit one worker against another. These "Model I" organizations are predicated on four overriding values: define your purpose, then achieve it; do everything you can to win; restrain all negative emotions; and above all be rational. When these values are put into action, workers are motivated by the desire to manipulate others and to protect themselves from others. There is little opportunity for risk-taking or new learning.

Argyris believes that organizations can break out of this self-defeating model by adopting procedures that enable them to learn from their mistakes and keep up with the changing demands of society. These "Model II" organizations are governed by a very different set of values: give workers access to information so that they can make free and informed choices; allow them to design their own work settings, contribute original thoughts to a project, express feelings about it, and ultimately take responsibility for their contributions along with others involved; and set up a sophisticated system for monitoring the results of workers' decisions. Workers in a Model II environment, says Argyris, are less manipulative and more willing to learn and to take risks.

The cornerstone of Argyris's Model II organization is his theory of "double loop learning," the process in which one's underlying values and assumptions are changed in the face of complex problems. Double loop learning enables managers to break out of the cycle of ineffective behavior by asking the right questions, creating an effective problem-solving network, and effectively channeling the energy and commitment of workers to produce the solution.

Figure 2–5 gives an overview of the key thinkers in the behavioral management school.

MODERN APPROACHES TO MANAGEMENT

The classical and behavioral schools form the initial basis for the study of management. But other approaches are now playing significant roles in

> *Mary Parker Follett*—Group Influence
>
> *Elton Mayo*—Impact of Human Motivation on Productivity and Output
>
> *Abraham Maslow*—Human Needs: Hierarchy of Needs
>
> *Douglas McGregor*—Leadership Style: Theory X and Theory Y
>
> *Chris Argyris*—Human and Organizational Development: Model I and Model II

FIGURE 2–5.   Key Thinkers: Behavioral Management

the discipline. These include the quantitative school, systems theory, and contingency theory. These approaches to management are introduced in this section and then covered in greater depth in later chapters.

THE QUANTITATIVE SCHOOL

The quantitative school had its origins in military applications. One of the earliest examples occurred in 212 B.C. when Archimedes assisted the city of Syracuse with military strategy when the Romans attacked the city.[32] Quantitative research was employed by both the United Kingdom and the United States during World War I. And this approach became widely accepted during World War II when it was used to plot strategies for protecting troopships and the like. After the war, the benefits of using quantitative methodology in industry became readily apparent. Today, the quantitative school is an established part of management thought.

Two separate chapters are devoted to discussion of the quantitative school of management. Chapter 6 deals with the decision-making process itself, while Chapter 7 deals with the quantitative techniques for planning and problem solving.

SYSTEMS THEORY

Systems theory is another facet of management thought. It is sometimes linked to the quantitative school along with decision theory and management science. Systems thinking, viewpoints, and terminology have also been adapted from the military by many diverse organizations—both profit and nonprofit—and have come to assume a central role in the modern world. Words like *feedback, input,* and *synergy* have found their way into the language of many academic disciplines and are a part of the manager's vocabulary.

The basic notion of a system is simply that it is a set of interrelated parts. A person might be considered a system of organs, a molecule may be thought of as a system of atoms, and a group as a system of individuals.

Implicit in these concepts is a degree of totality or "wholeness" that makes the whole something different from, and more than, the individual units considered separately.[33]

The term *system* comes from the Greek word *systema*, which refers to an organized relationship among components. It denotes plan, order, arrangement, and method. The human body is a system made up of circulatory, skeletal, and nervous subsystems. Only when each of these subsystems is functioning properly is the total system effective. A firm's components might include such interrelated areas as production, marketing, and finance. Coordination of these subsystems allows the business to achieve its objectives.

A *system* may be defined as an organized group of parts, components, or subsystems linked together according to a plan to achieve specific objectives.[34] The system's components may be as simple as a single machine or a complex assemblage of both people and clusters of machines.

The opposite of systematic is chaotic. An orderly coordination of components is required if the system is to function efficiently. Just as the traffic manager must consider speed of alternative transportation modes in choosing the most efficient distribution system, so also must the manager consider all components in developing an optimum business system.

System is an organized group of parts, components, or subsystems linked together according to a plan in order to achieve specific objectives.

CONTINGENCY THEORY

Contingency theory is one of the more recent attempts to synthesize earlier management thought. The earliest studies with a contingency orientation can be dated in the immediate post-World War II era. Contingency theory—sometimes termed *situational management*—simply says that management actions and styles should be dependent upon the circumstances of the situation confronting the manager. Environmental factors such as public opinion might have impact on the decision-making process. So might employee and management attitudes. The appropriate decisions to make in a given situation or the proper management style may be determined only after these and other situational factors are carefully considered.

The historical evolution of contingency theory is described in Chapter 13. The development of contingency theory, like that of other schools, suggests the rich historical framework upon which the study of management is based.

Contingency theory, often called **situational management,** is a managerial approach that emphasizes adjusting managerial actions and styles to the specific circumstances of the situation confronting the organization.

SUMMARY

This chapter has looked at the development of management thought, describing the historical environment for management as well as major schools of management. The chapter began with a listing of outstanding contributions to management thought, and selected precedents to management theory. Attention then shifted to early industrial era contributors—Robert Owen, Charles Babbage, Andrew Ure, and Charles Dupin.

The classical school of management thought can be divided into administrative theory and scientific management. The major contributors to administrative theory were Henri Fayol and Max Weber. Fayol was Europe's most distinguished management theorist, and the developer of the field's first general theory. Weber discussed bureaucracy and types of authority. The scientific management school applied the general scientific method to solving managerial and work-related problems. Frederick W. Taylor is considered the "father of scientific management." Other major contributors to scientific management were the Gilbreths and Henry L. Gantt.

The behavioral school is based on the idea that people are the primary determinants of organiza-tional and managerial effectiveness. The importance of motivation in the work environment was the common thread that ran through the studies and theories of the behaviorists. Major contributors to this school of management thought were Mary Parker Follett, Elton Mayo, Abraham H. Maslow, Douglas McGregor, and Chris Argyris.

Systems theory, which was introduced in this chapter, looks at the organization as a set of inter-related parts. The quantitative and contingency theory schools, briefly discussed here, will be covered in detail elsewhere in the text.

SOLVING THE STOP ACTION CASE

Midvale Steel Co.

The young engineer in this stop action case was Frederick Winslow Taylor. He improved the efficiency of the machine shop at Midvale Steel Co. by specializing the work responsibilities of each individual. For example, he gave the job of grinding tools to one person, rather than sharing the task among the workers as had previously been the case.

Taylor was promoted to chief engineer. In this position, he was able to conduct scientific time and motion studies on a large scale. With the aim of standardizing all points along the production line, he analyzed each job, break-ing it down into as many basic movements as possible. Then he found the most skilled workers and, with a stopwatch, measured how much time they needed to complete each given task. That amount of time, expanded slightly to allow for unavoidable delays, initial slowness of new workers, and rest periods, became the standard for determining how much work each employee in the shop should produce in a specified time period.

Taylor's success in increasing production at Midvale was phenomenal; the shop output shot up to 300 percent of what it had been. Consistent with Taylor's philosophy that good work should be well rewarded, the pay of his workers moved up by 25 to 100 percent. Efficiency engineering—or *Taylorism,* as his techniques became known—quickly captured the imagination of man-agement everywhere.

Taylor left Midvale in 1890 to assume the position of general manager of the Manufacturing Investment Co.'s paper mills. Later, in 1893, he established his own consulting business, but in 1901 he gave up gainful employment to avoid what he believed to be the dehumanizing effect of too much money. During his retirement he continued his research and authored several books on his findings, among them *Principles of Scientific Management* (1911) and *Shop Management* (1903).

Before his death in 1915, Taylor had applied his creative mind not only to streamlining factory shop and yard production techniques but also to inventing and refining equipment to enhance his efficiency measures. Perhaps the most significant of his numerous inventions were the development of a cutting tool and, in collaboration with J. Mansel White, of a method for heat-treating chrome-tungsten tool steels that effectively doubled their efficiency. For this contribution to industry, he was awarded a gold medal at the Paris Exhibition and the Elliott Cresson medal of the Franklin Institute.

Sources: The National Cyclopedia of American Biography, Vol. 23. s.v. "Taylor, Frederick Winslow." Norman M. Pearson, "Public Administration: Fayolism as the Necessary Complement of Taylorism," *American Political Science Review* 39 (February 1945): 66-80. Paula Smith, "The Masterminds of Management," *Dun's Review* (July 1976): 17-19. Edwin A. Locke, "The Ideas of Frederick W. Taylor: An Evaluation," *Academy of Management Review* (January 1982): 14-24.

FACT OR FICTION REVEALED

1. Fiction   2. Fact   3. Fact   4. Fiction   5. Fiction   6. Fiction   7. Fact

MANAGEMENT TERMS

industrial revolution
bureaucracy
scientific management

motion study
therbligs
behavioral school

system
contingency theory

REVIEW QUESTIONS

1. Define the following terms: (a) industrial revolution, (b) bureaucracy, (c) scientific management, (d) motion study, (e) therbligs, (f) behavioral school, (g) contingency theory, (h) system.

2. Why do you think Frederick W. Taylor was rated so highly in the survey reported in Table 2–1?

3. List and identify the early contributors to the development of management thought.

4. Explain Henri Fayol's contributions to management.

5. What were the three types of authority according to Weber?

6. Describe the development of scientific management. Who were the main participants in its development?

7. Identify the major contributors to the behavioral school of management thought.

8. Describe the origins of the quantitative school.

9. Explain the systems approach to management thought.

10. Discuss the contingency theory concept.

PROBLEMS AND EXPERIENTIAL EXERCISES

1. Organize a classroom debate. The issue in the debate is "Who contributed the most to the development of management thought as we know it today—Henri Fayol or Frederick W. Taylor?" A team should be selected to argue each viewpoint with the rest of the class serving as judges.

2. Frank and Lillian Gilbreth's large family has been described in this chapter. Using many of the same techniques that proved successful in their home, the Gilbreths applied their motion studies to factory routines and to the design of model nurseries and kitchens. After Frank's death in 1924, Lillian continued their work. She took over control of Gilbreth, Inc., consulting engineers in management, where she concentrated on what she knew best: improving the efficiency of the American home. She conducted detailed analyses of how American homemakers could make kitchens more efficient. At a National Organization of Better Homes in America meeting, for example, she interrupted the work of 4,000 busy women to measure the distance from their elbows to the floor, obtaining figures she needed to calculate the optimum height for stoves and sinks.

Lillian Gilbreth's mission to streamline the operation of the home and factory could not have been accomplished without a keen sense of effective planning, organization, leadership, and control. Her commitment to creating a truly effective managerial system pervaded her entire life—surmounting even the grief she felt after her husband's death. Two days after Frank Gilbreth's funeral, Lillian boarded an ocean liner bound for Europe. There she took Frank's place at a convention, delivered his speeches, and attended committee meetings. She explained her ability to overcome her grief in this way: "I am only adhering to my husband's principles—the elimination of wasted motion."[35]

Suggest other possible uses of motion studies in daily living situations.

3. Prepare a paper on one of the people listed in Table 2–1 as a major contributor to the development of management thought. Choose someone not discussed in this chapter.

4. Select one of the end-of-part cases in *Management*. Then write a brief report on how each of the contributors to management thought described in this chapter would approach the case.

5. Prepare a report on a woman who has contributed to the development of management thought in the last twenty-five years.

MANAGERIAL INCIDENT: The Career of A. P. Sloan, Jr.

A single-minded devotion to business characterized the career of Alfred Pritchard Sloan, Jr., whose twenty-year career at the helm of General Motors transformed the auto firm into one of the industrial giants of the world. His prowess in corporate decision making led him and the companies he shepherded along a straight path to financial success. The principles he espoused called for a direct approach to management problems and decision making: "Get the facts. Recognize the equities of all concerned. Realize the necessity of doing a better job every day. Keep an open mind and work hard. The last and most important of all. There is no short cut."

Born in 1875, Sloan soon exhibited a talent for scientific disciplines. As a teenager, he passed the entrance examination for the Massachusetts Institute of Technology, but he was too young to gain admission. When he was finally permitted to enter that institution, he completed the four-year curriculum in three years, obtaining his B.S. in electrical engineering at the age of twenty.

Sloan's first job after college was at the Hyatt Roller Bearing Company as a drafter. Six years later he had advanced to the

Milestones in the Development of Management Thought

Because of the dynamic process of human communication, experience, and learning, the schools of management thought have not developed within neat, progressive time periods. In light of application and research, management theories are constantly being reexamined and are often revised. Despite this process of development and change, this time line will help to clarify this evolution by putting the major management thinkers and their ideas in a chronological perspective.

5000 B.C. *Sumerians* emphasize record keeping as a control technique.

4000 B.C. *Egyptians* recognize the planning, organizing, and controlling functions.

400 B.C. *Socrates* discusses the universality of management.

Xenophon recognizes management as a separate art.

350 B.C. *Plato* describes specialization.

336–323 B.C. *Alexander the Great* makes extensive use of a staff organization during his military campaigns.

900 A.D. *Alfarabi* lists the traits of an effective leader.

1750s *The Industrial Revolution* begins in the United Kingdom.

1822 *Charles Babbage* produces his "difference machine"—forerunner of today's computer.

1834 *Robert Owen,* human resources management pioneer, directs the British trade union movement.

1898 *Mary Parker Follett,* a pioneer who discovered the benefits of group thinking and group participation, graduates from Radcliffe College and begins a career in social work that will help to shape her management ideas.

1911 *Frederick W. Taylor* publishes Principles of Scientific Management.

1923 *Alfred P. Sloan* uses modern management techniques to build General Motors into an industrial giant.

colleagues begin their study of the Hawthorne Works of Western Electric (pictured), which will mark the birth of the human relations movement.

1928 *Ludwig von Bertalanffy* introduces systems theory.

1929 *Henri Fayol's* works are translated into English.

1938 *Chester I. Barnard* publishes his classic book on organizations.

1938–1945 *Allied Forces* use operations research techniques in the war effort.

1943 *Abraham Maslow* proposes his theory of a hierarchy of human needs.

1947 *Kurt Lewin* proposes a model of individual change.

1948 *Lester Coch* and *John R. P. French, Jr.,* conduct their classic study on resistance to change.

1950s *Emergence of the Human Relations School.*

Herbert A. Simon conducts his pioneering work on decision theory.

1951 *Kurt Lewin* emphasizes environmental factors as determinants of behavior.

1952 *IBM* introduces the first widely available electronic data processing system.

1953 *Keith Davis* describes the importance of the informal organization and coins the term "grapevine."

1954 *Peter Drucker* popularizes management by objectives (MBO) in his book The Practice of Management.

1957 *Chris Argyris* publishes Personality and Organization: The Conflict Between the System and the Individual.

1959 *Frederick Herzberg* publishes the two-factor theory of motivation.

1960 *Douglas McGregor* describes Theory X and Theory Y managers.

1956–1958 *PERT* and *CPM* are developed.

1961 *Rensis Likert* develops a leadership systems model using the contingency approach.

1964 *Robert Blake* and *Jane Mouton* develop Managerial Grid® of leadership styles.

1965 *Joan Woodward* publishes her findings about impact of technology on various methods of organizing.

1971 *Intel Corp.* introduces the "computer chip" microprocessor, leading to the development of personal computers and the rapid diffusion of information technology to managers at every level.

1973 *Victor Vroom* and *Philip Yetton* develop a normative model of decision making.

1974 *Robert J. House* and *Terence R. Mitchell* propose the path-goal theory of leadership.

1980s *Managers place increasing emphasis on **strategic planning** in competing with domestic and international firms.*

1981 *William G. Ouchi* describes how U.S. managers could adopt modifications of Japanese managerial practices in an approach that he labels Theory Z.

company presidency.

Curiously, the firm's major product at the time Sloan came to work there was billiard balls. But Sloan could foresee the tremendous expansion that was about to take place in the automobile industry and he began to redirect the company in the task of perfecting steel roller bearings to be marketed to the auto manufacturers. Sloan not only perfected the new product; he dedicated himself to the task of selling it. As Hyatt's chief traveling salesperson, he became intimately acquainted with all aspects of automobile production as well as all the important personalities in the industry. Under Sloan's leadership, Hyatt's profits soared.

Fearful that the great auto manufacturers might decide to produce their own steel roller bearings, Sloan negotiated the merger of his firm with United Motors, an organization established by General Motors in 1916. Two years later, the two firms merged, and Sloan became a vice-president and member of GM's executive committee. He assumed the GM presidency in 1923, and by 1936 he was the highest paid executive in the United States. The following year he was named chairman of GM's board of directors.

General Motors' prosperity under Sloan's guidance has been attributed to his management style, which underlined the importance of individual executives exercising their own initiative. Sloan emphasized this fact in his statement that "the organization of which I am now president would be impossible without the principle of individual initiative." To eliminate the possibility that a decentralized management philosophy might lead to divisions operating at cross-purposes, Sloan instituted a set of "standard procedures" and a committee system, both of which functioned to keep information circulating in an orderly fashion.

Alfred P. Sloan retired in 1956 after a sixty-year career in business. Business was his life—both his work and his hobby. He had no other significant interests. He died in 1966 at the age of ninety-one.

Questions and Problems

1. Why do you think Sloan ranked sixth on the list of "outstanding contributors to management thought" presented in Table 2–1? Discuss.

2. Explain the factors that went into making Sloan such a successful executive.

3. This chapter discusses several major contributors to the development of management thought. With which ones do you think Sloan would have identified? Why?

Source: "Businessmen in the News," *Fortune,* May 1956, p. 55; *Current Biography* (1940) s.v. "Sloan, Alfred Pritchard, Jr."; and *Current Biography Yearbook* (1966), Obituaries, s.v. "Sloan, Alfred Pritchard, Jr.," p. 471.

3 THE ENVIRONMENT FOR MANAGEMENT

LEARNING OBJECTIVES

After studying this chapter you should be able to

1. Differentiate between management's internal and external environment.

2. Discuss the importance of monitoring the managerial environment.

3. Discuss the concept of a corporate culture.

4. Identify the six dimensions of management's external environment.

5. Explain what is meant by reactive and proactive response modes to the managerial environment.

6. Explain the need for effective planning for an uncertain future.

7. Identify the attributes and style of successful management in the late 1980s.

STOP ACTION CASE

Monsanto Company

Monsanto is known as a company that makes tremendous efforts to alleviate potential problems with its new products. Technology risk reviews—using both employees and outside experts—are conducted to determine whether the new product creates a potential hazard of any kind.

But even this conservative and reasonable approach cannot spot all potential risks in the firm's external environment. Monsanto spent $100 million developing Cycle-Safe, a recyclable plastic beverage container designed to help eliminate the nation's litter problems. Cycle-Safe bottles—technically known as acrylonitrile-styrene-copolymer bottles—could be ground up and made again or could be washed and refilled. Monsanto went to great lengths to be sure this new product would be safe. Experts in both the government and the private sector were consulted. A scientific symposium was held in Boston. Federal Food and Drug Administration and Environmental Protection Agency personnel liked the test results profile. Management now had to decide whether or not to launch the new container given the environmental circumstances they faced.

Use the materials in Chapter 3 to determine whether Monsanto should launch their new recyclable plastic beverage container.

Monsanto

The essential managerial functions—planning, organizing, leading, and controlling—were identified in Chapter 1. Effective managers perform these functions in their pursuit of the goals that have been specified for their organizations. However, the performance of these functions is affected significantly by a number of environmental factors. Monsanto, for instance, was affected by its regulatory situation. The environment for management decision making is the subject of this chapter.

CATEGORIZING MANAGEMENT'S ENVIRONMENT

The environment for management can be classified into internal and external factors. The *internal environment* refers to factors within the firm itself. For example, tradition—the customary way of doing something— plays a major role in management decision making. Similarly, the image cultivated by a firm forms an internal expectation for management. The image of firms like Bloomingdale's and Neiman-Marcus as prestige retailers could affect a variety of management decisions. These could range from employee training decisions to merchandising practices. Similarly, McDonald's motto "quality, service, and cleanliness" is the cornerstone of much management decision making at the offices of the fast-food giant.

Internal environment refers to factors within the firm itself.

The *external environment* refers to factors outside the organization. This environmental category consists of the competitive, political-legal, economic, social and cultural, technological, and international dimensions. The external environment influences companies in various ways. Consider the failed attempts to limit textile imports. Higher tariffs or import quotas would benefit manufacturers employing U.S. workers. But what about importers and shippers in ports like Seattle? In this case, the effect would be negative, not positive.

External environment refers to factors outside the organization.

MANAGEMENT FACT OR FICTION

	FACT	FICTION		FACT	FICTION
1. There are no business heroes in a firm with a strong corporate culture.	☐	☐	4. Johnson & Johnson has adopted a proactive response mode.	☐	☐
2. Even a business luncheon can be considered a corporate ritual in some instances.	☐	☐	5. Sewell Avery is considered the first future-oriented manager.	☐	☐
3. The French sounding "Le Car" made Renault an instant hit in Quebec.	☐	☐			

The materials in this chapter will assist you in separating management fact from fiction. Your answers can be checked on page 67.

The environment for management is summarized in Figure 3–1. It shows that the functions of management are performed within the context of the organization's internal environment, and that the decision-making process is also influenced by a host of external factors.

THE IMPORTANCE OF MONITORING THE MANAGERIAL ENVIRONMENT

It is important to monitor both the internal and external environment. The internal environment effectively delineates the goals, strategies, and tactics of an organization's management. While corporate traditions and long-standing operating practices are difficult to change, it can be done. Successful change, however, often involves the removal of top executives or even the company's founder. The departure of Steven Jobs from Apple Computer is an example of how an internal environment might be changed.

Environmental Modifiers. P. N. Khandwalla has discussed how a firm's external environment can affect managerial strategies.[1] Khandwalla identifies five environmental modifiers: turbulence, hostility, diversity, technical complexity, and restrictiveness. These can be described as follows:

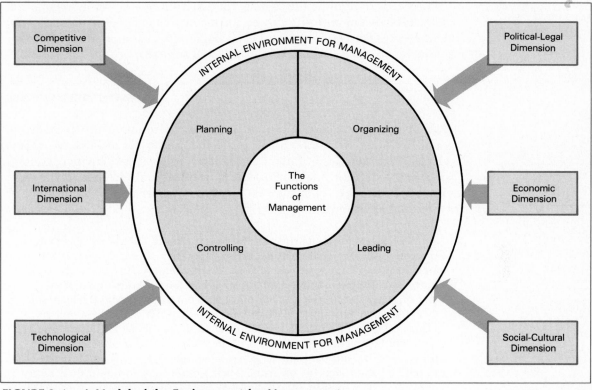

FIGURE 3–1.   A Model of the Environment for Management

- Many firms face an increasingly turbulent environment where changes occur quickly and frequently. The changing structure of the airline industry illustrates this attribute.

- A hostile environment is one that threatens the organization. Johnson & Johnson had to take prompt and decisive action to counter the hostile environment associated with the discovery of cyanide-laced Tylenol capsules in 1986.

- Diversity also characterizes the external environment. This is particularly true in the competitive environment of the late 1980s. Fast food is an example of an industry affected by this modifier.

- Technical complexity can be another attribute of the external environment. For instance, defense contractors face more complex technical questions than do most service industries.

- Organizations also face a variety of restrictions on the way they operate. The pharmaceutical industry faces a variety of environmental requirements during the conduct of its business.

The need to monitor the managerial environment is widely recognized today. Effective monitoring can be the factor that differentiates successful firms from unsuccessful firms. Let us begin our examination of the managerial environment with the internal environment.

THE INTERNAL ENVIRONMENT

Most firms foster a certain type of internal environment in which managerial decisions are made. Some pride themselves on innovation; others on a lean, spartan organization; and still others on a participative, consensus style of decision making. At NCR, the internal environment is very sales-oriented. The following tale has become part of NCR tradition, or its internal environment.

> S. C. Allyn, a retired chairman of the board, likes to tell a story about his company—the National Cash Register Corporation. It was August 1945, and Allyn was among the first allied civilians to enter Germany at the end of the war. He had gone to find out what had happened to an NCR factory built just before the war but promptly confiscated by the German military command and put to work on the war effort. He arrived via military plane and traveled through burned-out buildings, rubble, and utter desolation until he reached what was left of the factory. Picking his way through bricks, cement, and old timbers, Allyn came upon two NCR employees whom he hadn't seen for six years. Their clothes were torn and their faces grimy and blackened by smoke, but they were busy clearing out the rubble. As he came closer, one of the men looked up and said, "We knew you'd come!" Allyn joined them in their work and together the three men began cleaning out the debris and rebuilding the factory from the devastation of war. The company had even survived the ravages of a world war.
> A few days later, as the clearing continued, Allyn and his co-workers were startled as an American tank rumbled up to the site. A grinning GI was at its helm. "Hi," he said, "I'm NCR, Omaha. Did you guys make your quota this month?" Allyn and the GI embraced each other. The war may have devastated everything around them, but NCR's hard driving, sales-oriented culture was still intact.[2]

THE CONCEPT OF A CORPORATE CULTURE

The concept of a corporate culture was first suggested in Terrence E. Deal and Allan A. Kennedy's book of the same name. It has become the subject of numerous publications and speeches and is now an accepted concept in modern management.

Corporate culture refers to generally accepted behavior patterns within an organization that are adopted by each new generation of employees. A corporate culture deals with an organization's traditions and basic values.

Corporate culture refers to generally accepted behavior patterns within an organization that are adopted by each new generation of employees.

THE MANAGER'S BOOKSHELF

The New Competitors, by D. Quinn Mills

 This fad-free guide for managers (Wiley, 1985) presents tomorrow's executives as they appear today: managers in their thirties and forties who barely resemble their predecessors. The new-generation manager, Mills says, is better-educated, less conformist, and—the old-style managers will tell you—less impressed with hard work. In these respects, the new competitor is a cause-and-effect of the changes that are sweeping over management in the late 1980s. The old, rigid, authoritarian system of orders being passed down to subordinates is being replaced by a new baby-boom looseness which is changing the way organizations plan and make decisions.

The author begins with a profile of the typical old-style managers. In most cases, he says, such managers were introduced to large organizations when they served in the Armed Forces during World War II. This caused them to realize that survival, and perhaps even effectiveness, depended on strong leadership, a clear chain of command, decisiveness, and clear directions for the rank and file. In other words, they absorbed the value of a top down, hierarchical organization in which the top-level strategy was developed in secret.

Most GIs realized that the military wasn't exactly the paragon of organizational structure, Mills says. On the other hand, it seemed to have won the war, and that caused many returning vets to believe that a similar system might work well in peacetime industries.

That's not the impression many of the veterans of Korea and Vietnam took away from their stints in the services, however. Many of these vets came away disillusioned with the way the military conducted their particular war. Therefore, Mills says, these young managers looked elsewhere for their organizational models: to churches, political groups, clubs and associations, and to business.

Since these groups don't tend to rely so heavily on clear lines of authority or unambiguous direction, Mills says, today's rising managers "do not identify with carrying through a task given them by others." They seek, instead, environments where people are creative and cooperative, and where everybody carries a fair share of the work load. Most of all, they want to participate in decisions rather than simply follow orders.

The New Competitors offers a series of case studies that show competent and incompetent managers trying to deal with new-style issues—everything from planning compensation systems and leadership succession to employment security and participatory management. What these case studies provide is a good look at the new business climate and at the new business managers who are trying to work within it. Mills does not necessarily share the older executives' view that younger managers are short on ambition. The younger manager may be defining a new kind of ambition, Mills says; one that balances the desire to advance within the company with other equally important responsibilities. The new competitors may be just as competitive as the old; they just like to compete at many different things.

Many of these attributes are expressed in corporate slogans like Du Pont's "Better things for better living through chemistry."[3]

The Newhouse organization presents a good example of how a corporate culture can have an impact on organizational behavior. The late Samuel Irving Newhouse started what is now the nation's biggest privately held media enterprise. The Newhouse chain consists of newspapers like the New Orleans *Times-Picayune,* Newark's *Star-Ledger,* Cleveland's *Plain Dealer,* and the St. Louis *Globe-Democrat;* numerous cable television units; magazines like *Vogue, Glamour, Parade, Self,* and *House & Garden;* and Random House, the publisher of this text.

The size of the Newhouse empire is a remarkable accomplishment for a privately held company that does not have a headquarters office. The Newhouse company is a family-run operation. Nearly two dozen Newhouses work for the organization. The senior Newhouses maintain their offices at different publications. They each visit a set group of operations and report their findings to other family members through memos. The professional managers of each enterprise deal only with the Newhouse assigned to their particular operation.

The management framework of the Newhouse organization is characterized by a strong corporate culture. Samual Irving Newhouse, the founder, prepared an outline entitled "A Memo to the Children of S. I. Newhouse" that described how he built the company. The first newspaper was bought with funds borrowed from family members, whom he later hired. The message was clear that "the ties that matter are the ties to each other."[4]

THE ELEMENTS OF A CORPORATE CULTURE

Deal and Kennedy suggest that there are five basic elements of a corporate culture: business environment, values, heroes, rites and rituals, and the cultural network. While not all firms have a strong culture, those that do tend to exhibit each of these five determinants.[5]

1. *Business Environment.* Each firm faces a specific business setting that largely determines the type of organization that is needed to prosper in the marketplace. NCR faces a highly competitive environment; so, as noted earlier, a sales orientation is part of its corporate culture. (The next section of the text will discuss the competitive dimension of management's external environment.)

2. *Values.* Values shared by all employees constitute the basic character of the organization. Values are what drive the collaborative efforts of the organization's members. As indicated earlier, values are often specified in corporate goals or slogans. Caterpillar's "24-hour parts service anywhere in the world" is an example.

3. *Heroes*. Certain individuals are sometimes closely identified with a firm's corporate culture. For instance, the corporate culture of the revitalized Chrysler Corporation is closely linked with its hero, Lee Iacocca.

4. *Rites and Rituals*. Regular activities and events are also part of a corporate culture. Lore Harp, the founder and president of Vector, initiated a ritualized lunch called the "Friendship Lunch." A sign is posted weekly inviting nine people to sign up to go to lunch with either Harp or a vice-president.[6]

5. *The Cultural Network*. Corporate cultures are communicated through an informed network. Stories of earlier corporate ideals and heroes are transmitted throughout the organization and between successive generations of employees. (The workings of a firm's "grapevine" are discussed in detail in Chapter 14.)

THE EXTERNAL ENVIRONMENT

The manager must also deal with his or her external environment. Factors outside the organization can often play a major role in whether or not the firm or unit is successful. Figure 3–1 identified six dimensions of management's external environment: (1) competitive dimension; (2) political-legal dimension; (3) economic dimension; (4) social and cultural dimension; (5) technological dimension; and (6) international dimension.

COMPETITIVE DIMENSION

The *competitive environment* refers to the firm's relative situation in the marketplace. It includes such factors as how the firm rates in market share, technological innovation, financial strength, involvement in growth industries, and the development of its human resources. Our earlier discussion indicated that the competitive environment sometimes plays a major role in the development of a corporate culture, the basis of a firm's internal environment.

Competitive environment refers to the firm's relative situation in the marketplace.

A firm might be financially strong, have good personnel, and dominate its industry; yet if the company is positioned in a declining industry, management may have to take aggressive action to move it into new, expanding markets. Similarly, a firm in a growth industry may lack the financial strength to compete in the long run. Management might consider a merger with another enterprise in order to correct this deficiency.

One of the major lessons any manager must learn is that the competitive environment is not static; it is dynamic. To paraphrase the classical maxim of the TV weather forecaster: If you don't like the competitive environment that exists—just wait, it will change soon! The real question for

MANAGEMENT SUCCESSES

Olivetti: An Energy Boost from Pasta

Carlo De Benedetti is the chairman of Olivetti, a giant Italian corporation that manufactures data processing and office automation equipment. Olivetti is now a leader, but when De Benedetti took over in 1978, it was in desperate trouble—it owed more than $1 billion and was losing $6 million a month. De Benedetti turned Olivetti around by looking to the future—and keeping an eye on the competitive environment.

De Benedetti immediately saw that he would have to instill the need for foresight and planning into the firm. He increased spending on research and development, and he pulled the company out of the production of mechanical equipment such as typewriters. He also slashed his payroll by a third. Over each of the next two years, productivity jumped 22 percent.

But these were just beginnings. De Benedetti realized that Olivetti would have to go international if it were to survive in the electronics industry. Italy alone could not provide the large markets the firm would need to maintain the extensive investments in research and development or the demands for industrial automation. De Benedetti says, "In our business there is no future in becoming a second, third, or fourth ranked company. Either you win or die."

Previously, Olivetti had not met with success in its attempts to enter the highly profitable U.S. computer market. To make Olivetti a world leader, though, De Benedetti cultivated close ties with American firms. And, in December 1983, American Telephone & Telegraph bought a 24 percent share in the Italian firm for $260 million. De Benedetti then forged an alliance with Japan's Toshiba Corp. He intends to take advantage of these relationships to tackle IBM.

Early in 1985, De Benedetti acquired a large chunk of Industrie Buitoni Perugina, one of the top food producers in Italy, and, in May of that year, he bought 51 percent of SME, a food subsidiary of Italy's mammoth government-owned holding company, IRI. So De Benedetti is now in an odd combination of computers and food, but this is what he planned. The food industry is stable, but it generates a dependable cash flow. Electronics is just the opposite—hefty profits, but equally great risks. De Benedetti claims the pairing is ideal: one venture can finance the other. This strategy typifies De Benedetti's attempt to cope with his future competitive environment.

olivetti   ET 221

Source: Spencer Davidson, "A Mix of Microchips and Pasta," *Time,* 13 May 1985, p. 48.

management is whether or not the new setting will be more favorable than the previous one.

POLITICAL-LEGAL DIMENSION

Political and legal factors are another important aspect of the external environment. The general political climate can dictate the range of flexibility available to managers. In recent years, this range has been expanded considerably. The Carter administration introduced the concept of deregulation in certain industries and the Reagan administration has been generally pro-business.

The *legal environment* for management consists of federal, state, and local regulations, as well as those of foreign nations in which the business may operate. Some aspects of the legal environment have very broad goals, such as the preservation of the competitive environment. The Sherman and Clayton Acts, which ban efforts to restrict competition or monopolize a market, are examples. Other laws, like the Occupational Safety and Health Act, may deal with issues as specific as the storage height of fire extinguishers.

Effective managers must be cognizant of the political and legal factors that can impact a particular situation. This environmental dimension forms the parameters within which the managerial process must operate if it is to continue to receive public sanction.

ECONOMIC DIMENSION

Consider how the contemporary economic environment affects management. During prosperity, firms will expand their work forces and seek out new markets. Recessionary periods mean cutbacks in personnel, plant closings, and the like. Of course, not all firms are affected in the same fashion. While many manufacturing industries prospered in the mid-1980s, the agricultural sector lagged behind.

The economic dimension is one of the most dynamic aspects of the external environment. Even possible future events can have a profound influence on managerial decision making. Tax reform and the federal deficit illustrate this point. Most tax reform proposals offer lower rates in exchange for cutbacks elsewhere. Many of these offsets would have a disproportionate impact on business. Longer depreciation schedules and elimination of the investment tax credit could affect a variety of investment decisions on the part of managers. Similarly, if the federal deficit goes unchecked, it may mean higher interest rates and less access to capital markets for businesses. Again, economic uncertainty and constant change influence the external environment of the firm.

All management decisions must reflect the economic realities of the times. Some markets should be avoided because of minimal profit opportunities. A product refinement may price the item too high relative to its

66 The less government interferes with private pursuits, the better for general prosperity. 99

Martin Van Buren

Legal environment refers to federal, state, and local regulations, as well as those of foreign nations in which the business may operate.

66 A billion seconds ago it was 1951. A billion minutes ago Jesus was alive and walking in Galilee. A billion hours ago no one walked on two feet on earth. And a billion dollars ago was 10.3 hours in Washington, D.C. 99

Alexander B. Trowbridge
President, National Association of Manufacturers

MANAGEMENT FAILURES

Why Schlitz Went Flat

 Schlitz used to be one of the major brewers in the United States, but now the brand is owned by Stroh's. The reason lies largely with the regulatory environment.

In the late 1970s, Schlitz's lawyers feared that the Food and Drug Administration (FDA) was going to order that all beer ingredients be listed on the can. The attorneys advised that Schlitz remove from its beer any ingredients that could make consumers uneasy.

Schlitz's managers believed that one ingredient—an enzyme stabilizer, which gives beer a longer shelf life—might be a problem. They therefore replaced the enzyme stabilizer with a substance called Chill-garde; because Chill-garde could be filtered out of the final product, it would not have to be included on the label. But Schlitz did not realize that Chill-garde, when mixed with the beer's foam stabilizer, made the beverage look cloudy. There was no threat to anyone's health, but many customers just didn't like the look of the new Schlitz.

How did management resolve this situation? It kept using Chill-garde, and it removed the

foam stabilizer. What happened? The beer went flat. Eventually Schlitz got its old froth back, but, ironically, the FDA never actually called for the labeling that the lawyers had been worried about!

Source: Jacques Neher, "Lost at Sea," *Advertising Age,* 20 April 1981, p. 49. Copyright 1981 by Crain Communications, Inc.

competition. Resistance to higher wage demands may reflect management's inability to pass increased costs along to the consumer. The economic setting is clearly a key influence on the management process.

SOCIAL AND CULTURAL DIMENSION

The external environment includes a social and cultural dimension that is quite important to management. Decisions must be in general agreement with the social structure and culture that prevails in a particular situation. Many writers have pointed out the existence of regional differences in work attitudes. General Motors, for example, made its decision to locate the new Saturn plant in Tennessee partially on the basis of the strong work ethic of the local people who would be hired. Managerial philosophies also differ from region to region. The go-go tradition of Silicon Valley stands in marked contrast to the more staid business communities of other cities.

The marketplace confronted by managers also varies according to demographic factors. Florida has the highest percentage of aged citizens in the United States. Religious influences—another demographic factor—can also affect management decisions. Salt Lake City's Mormon influence, New York's Jewish influence, and St. Cloud, Minnesota's, Catholic influence suggest some of the variations that can exist.

Renault's experience in Canada provides a good example of the social and cultural dimension of management's external environment. Renault used the identical "Le Car" theme used in the United States to introduce the model to English-speaking Canada. But French-speaking Canadians would translate "Le Car" as the absolute number one car, which would not have been a credible advertising theme. So Renault's management used "Le Chameau," which stresses economy, as the theme for French Canada. The result was a ten times greater market penetration than Renault achieved in English-speaking Canada.[7]

TECHNOLOGICAL DIMENSION

The technological dimension of the external environment also has an important implication for management. The availability or state of technology for an industry may set parameters on management's decision making.

Technology may be defined as the science of applying information and knowledge to problem-solving situations. Much information becomes a part of human knowledge without being applied to the solution of problems. Technology refers to the process of putting knowledge to work for humanity. The technology of most industries of the late 1980s is relatively advanced, at least in developed nations. But much more can be done.

Technology is the science of applying information and knowledge to problem-solving situations.

It is difficult to anticipate the impact of technology. For instance, a 1930s government study of technology failed to foresee television, jets, organ transplants, laser beams, and the ballpoint pen.[8] Nevertheless, technology has provided significant breakthroughs in the past, and improved technology is seen as the answer to many of today's business and societal problems. Technological innovation may also be a way to improve America's productivity, a measure of the nation's output of goods and services. The U.S. annual manufacturing productivity gain between 1973 and 1983 was less than 2 percent. By comparison, Japan had a 7.3 percent annual gain.[9]

INTERNATIONAL DIMENSION

Managers in the late 1980s must increasingly compete on an international as well as a domestic basis. International and comparative management is the subject of Chapter 19 of the text. But for our present purposes, it is important to note that managerial practices differ from nation to nation. For instance, in some nations a business relationship takes much longer to develop than in the United States. In Japan, business entertainment is never done in the manager's home. Restaurants and hotels are considered the proper setting for such situations.

While managerial practices may vary, world marketplaces are often similar. As a result, there has been a gradual shift in management's approach to international markets. American firms traditionally used what is called a *multinational strategy,* by which products are designed and marketed for specific overseas markets. Ford Motor Co. is an example of a firm employing this strategy. Recently, U.S. companies have begun to adopt a *global strategy,* one that uses standardized manufacturing and marketing approaches to serve markets worldwide. Toyota produces models that are essentially the same except for the position of the steering column. Black & Decker, Revlon, and Sony are examples of other companies now using a global strategy.[10]

Multinational strategy is one by which products are designed and marketed for specific overseas markets.

Global strategy is one that adopts standardized manufacturing and marketing approaches to serve markets worldwide.

MANAGERIAL RESPONSES TO THE ENVIRONMENT

Environmental factors were traditionally considered a "given" for management. They were viewed as uncontrollable, so management's task was to become knowledgeable about such matters and to respond in the best possible manner when required to do so. In certain circumstances, management's environment can be changed. For example, Lee Iacocca was successful in changing the internal environment at Chrysler. Similarly, lobbying efforts by the nation's banks stopped a plan to subject interest earned on savings accounts to federal withholding.

REACTIVE AND PROACTIVE RESPONSE MODES

For years, business executives took a passive attitude toward the organizational environment that faced them. Since these factors were viewed as uncontrollable, the best approach was deemed to be a low profile to avoid increasing exposure to environmental threats. For instance, only recently would executives speak out on controversial public issues. Management for the most part would respond only if forced to do so. This approach might be called a reactive response mode. Figure 3–2 shows that environmental factors tended to act upon management with only limited interaction or response.

By contrast, the modern management approach might be called a proactive response mode to environmental threats. Figure 3–2 shows that management is acted upon, but that managers also attempt to influence their environmental setting. Johnson & Johnson's decision to discontinue the

66 I have learned a long time ago not to flinch when someone says they are going to hit you. 99

David M. Roderick
Chairman, USX Corp. (formerly U.S. Steel Corp.)

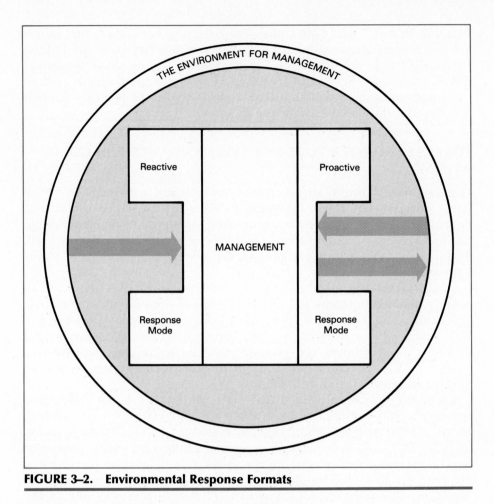

FIGURE 3–2.   Environmental Response Formats

use of all capsules in the wake of the 1986 Tylenol poisoning is an example of a firm adopting a proactive response mode.

A proactive response mode also assumes that the manager is involved in assessing his or her future environment. This topic is discussed in the section that follows.

THE MANAGEMENT ENVIRONMENT OF THE FUTURE

Managers are responsible for monitoring the organization's environment and forecasting future changes in its dimensions. But not all forecasts prove to be accurate assessments of future events. Many forecasts are substantially off-target and must be altered or discarded. Others prove true only in a different time frame than originally envisioned. Still others are lost in comparison with larger, more significant trends, or are at least partially offset by countertrends. Thirty years ago, a common prediction was that managers in the late 1980s would commute to and from work in their personal helicopters. In some cases, people will magnify current events and unjustifiably extrapolate them into the future.

FORECASTS OF OUR FUTURE ENVIRONMENT OFTEN GO ASTRAY

Generations of business administration students know the story of Sewell Avery's decision to protect Montgomery Ward from a post-World War II depression (that never came) by accumulating cash rather than expanding like its rival, Sears.[11] The two retailers were about the same size in 1946. Today, Sears is the nation's largest retailer, several times the size of Montgomery Ward.

Similar examples are abundant. Underwood—once the big name in office machines but now only part of Olivetti—passed up the electric typewriter. Curtiss-Wright—the equal of Douglas and Boeing combined in 1945—decided to put its money into an improved piston engine instead of jets.[12] When it finally did get into jets, Curtiss-Wright's management poured millions of dollars into ill-fated projects, such as trying to get the government order for an SST engine.[13]

Kemmons Wilson fulfilled novelist Sinclair Lewis's earlier belief that someone would become rich by offering a national chain of standardized hotels. A self-made millionaire builder, Wilson set off on a family vacation in 1951. The family's unpleasant experiences in several motels convinced him that standardized, quality motels would be well received by travelers. He built the first Holiday Inn on Sumner Avenue in his hometown of Memphis. The phenomenal growth of Holiday Inns is now one of the greatest success stories in United States management history. But even a successful manager like Kemmons Wilson can make a business mistake. Wilson admits that one of his worst errors was a decision not to invest in a contract of a young Memphis rock singer—Elvis Presley.[14]

A SHIFTING ENVIRONMENT MAKES EFFECTIVE PLANNING VITAL TO MANAGERS

An action by General Electric illustrates management's realization that assessments of a wide range of future events can have a significant influence on a firm's success. GE created a Business Environmental Studies group in 1967 to examine various changes in the political and social environment and to see how these possibilities could affect the company.[15]

General Electric's management clearly recognized the integral relationship between effective planning and future managerial decision making. Chapter 8 notes the importance of planning in the overall process of

MANAGEMENT: THE LIGHTER SIDE

The World's Worst Forecasts

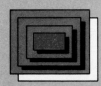

"Man won't fly for a thousand years."
>—Wilbur Wright to brother Orville after a disappointing flying experiment (1901)

"I think there is a world market for about five computers."
>—Thomas J. Watson, IBM (1958)

"Gaiety is the most outstanding feature of the Soviet Union."
>—Joseph Stalin (1935)

"X-rays are a hoax."
>—Lord Kelvin, engineer and physicist (c. 1900)

"Who the hell wants to hear actors talk?"
>—Harry M. Warner, Warner Bros. Pictures (c. 1927)

". . . by 1983 my program can bring about a balanced budget and begin to bring in surpluses so that we can have additional tax cuts beyond those we already suggested."
>—President Ronald Reagan (1981)

"Ruth made a big mistake when he gave up pitching."
>—Tris Speaker (1921)

"Sensible and responsible women do not want to vote."
>—President Grover Cleveland (1905)

"The Americans have need of the telephone, but we do not. We have plenty of messenger boys."
>—Sir William Preece, chief engineer of the British Post Office (1876)

"There is no likelihood man can ever tap the power of the atom."
>—Robert Millikan, Nobel Prize in Physics (1923)

". . . and I cannot conceive of anything more ridiculous, more absurd, and more affrontive to sober judgment than the cry that we are profiting by the acquisition of New Mexico and California. I hold that they are not worth a dollar."
>—U.S. Senator Daniel Webster (1848)

"Everything that can be invented has been invented."
>—Charles H. Duell, Director of U.S. Patent Office, urging President McKinley to abolish the office (1899)

"We have the happiest Africans in the world."
>—Ian Smith, Prime Minister of Rhodesia (1971)

"I cannot imagine any condition which could cause this ship to founder. I cannot conceive of any vital disaster happening to this vessel. Modern shipbuilding has gone beyond that."
>—E. J. Smith, Captain of the *Titanic* (1912)

Source: Wayne Coffey, *303 of the World's Worst Predictions* (New York: Tribeca Communications, 1983). Reprinted with permission.

managing any organization. The uncertainty of the future environment demonstrates why planning is so important to modern business.

Plans must be developed to cope with expected long-run trends. But even these are not enough. *Contingency plans* provide alternative scenarios for use in case of deviations from expected trends. Consider the possible contingencies that must be evaluated. Examples might include the adoption of new management styles and structural changes such as a significant increase in public ownership. While none of these are dominant factors in contemporary management, all must be considered in the future. Contingency planning is what allows some managers to succeed where others fail.

Contingency plans provide alternative scenarios for use in case of deviations from expected trends.

THE FUTURE-ORIENTED MANAGER

Future-oriented managers are managers who think ahead and take appropriate steps to stay ahead.

Future-oriented managers are those who think ahead and take appropriate steps to stay ahead. They keep up with events and changes in management philosophy, thought, and theory. They are well read and probably participate in continuing education programs both directly or indirectly related to their work. Future-oriented managers are also good listeners; they realize that much can be learned from even the most casual conversation. Above all, future-oriented managers attempt to broaden their experience, seeking out additional and varied responsibilities that will lead to further professional development.

Management style will also vary in the years ahead. A decade ago, George S. Odiorne developed a list of ten elements of a management style for a future manager. Obviously, these are broad generalizations subject to numerous exceptions. But the elements do form a conceptual basis for counseling today's managers. Odiorne's elements are:

1. *Less bureaucratic, more individualistic.* This is predicted to become the accepted operational method of the future.

2. *More systematic.* Wide adoption of the systems approach will be facilitated by the availability of mini- and microcomputers.

3. *Development-centered management.* Increased attention will be given to developing the organization's human resources.

4. *Situational management.* Directive and charismatic leadership will be replaced by contingency management.

5. *Management by commitment.* Effective managers will seek personal commitments from their employees and then hold them responsible for their performance.

6. *Achievement motivation.* A high achievement orientation in managers usually means that their organizations accomplish more.

7. *Group management processes.* Team building will be stressed from the

board of directors down. Task forces will be used in a more innovative fashion.

8. *Due process in personnel decisions.* Due process protection will become
   an integral part of most personnel procedures.

9. *Management by information.* Accurate, timely information will be the
   key to good management communications systems.

10. *Physical aspects of workplace.* Tomorrow's workplace will be altered
    by the desire to improve occupational health, safety, and security
    and employee motivation.[16]

Today's management student has an interesting opportunity to assess
history. Simply file this book away on an appropriate bookshelf and then
pull it out again, say, in twenty years.

SUMMARY

The environment for management can be divided
into the internal and external environment. The
internal environment is largely based on tradition
and customary methods of conducting business. A
firm's internal environment delineates management's goals, strategies, and tactics. In recent years,
the concept of a corporate culture has become popular. A corporate culture can be defined as a generally accepted behavior pattern within an organization that is adopted by each new generation of
employees. Its primary elements include: business
environment, values, heroes, rites and rituals, and
a cultural network.

The external environment for management consists of six dimensions: (1) competitive, (2) political-
legal, (3) economic, (4) social and cultural, (5) technological, and (6) international. These environmental factors are sometimes influenced by modifiers
such as turbulence, hostility, diversity, technical
complexity, and restrictiveness.

Environmental factors were traditionally considered uncontrollable by management. Managers only
reacted to an environment that was accepted as a

"given." But today, contemporary thinking holds
that managers can interact with, and influence, their
environment. This is referred to as a proactive response mode.

Some managers are able to forecast the future
business environment accurately. But such forecasts
are often inaccurate and may lead to substantial
managerial errors, such as when Sewell Avery re-
strained Montgomery Ward's growth after World
War II. A great deal can be learned by reviewing
earlier forecasts to see where they went wrong.

The uncertainties involved in assessing the environment make an effective planning function vital
to management. General Electric's Business Environmental Studies group illustrates this concern
about the impact of future political and social
trends.

Effective managers for the coming decade are
those who keep up to date, think ahead, and take
appropriate action to remain viable leaders. Chapter 3 concludes with some elements of a management style that is expected to predominate in the
late 1980s.

FACT OR FICTION REVEALED

1. Fiction   2. Fact   3. Fiction   4. Fact   5. Fiction

| SOLVING THE STOP ACTION CASE | Monsanto Company |

Given the favorable response to Cycle-Safe, Monsanto decided to launch the new soft drink container. But just a few years later (in 1977), the Food and Drug Administration issued an edict that banned Cycle-Safe—an action that cost 800 jobs. The FDA claimed that some acrylonitrile would leak into soft drinks, so it had to be classified as a food additive for which Monsanto did not have clearance.

Monsanto believed that the FDA's action was largely the result of the intense environmental concerns that permeated society at the time. In response to the FDA claim, Monsanto argued that the amount of acrylonitrile that got into the soft drinks would be negligible, and it would be nearly impossible to extract it. Monsanto initiated legal action.

In 1979, a judge ruled that the matter should not be dealt with judicially. Therefore, the FDA was left to handle the issue. Monsanto refiled Cycle-Safe with the FDA and the container material was finally approved for beverage packaging. The Cycle-Safe case shows the difficulty in predicting management's future environment.

Sources: John W. Hanley (interviewed by David W. Ewing and Millicent R. Kindle), "Monsanto's Early Warning System," *Harvard Business Review* (November–December 1981): 107-116; Kenneth Labich, "Monsanto's Brave New World," *Fortune,* 30 April 1984, p. 68; and "Acrylonitrile Bottles May Act as a Second Shot," *Chemical Week,* 6 April 1983, pp. 12-13; "Monsanto Presses Case on Cycle-Safe Bottle Delaying Provision Dispute," *Chemical Marketing Reporter,* 9 April 1984, pp. 7, 54; and correspondence from Paul Dalton of Monsanto, 5 December 1985.

MANAGEMENT TERMS

internal environment
external environment
corporate culture
competitive environment

legal environment
technology
multinational strategy

global strategy
contingency plans
future-oriented managers

REVIEW QUESTIONS

1. Define the following terms: (a) internal environment, (b) external environment, (c) corporate culture, (d) competitive environment, (e) legal environment, (f) technology, (g) multinational strategy, (h) global strategy, (i) contingency plans, (j) future-oriented manager.

2. What is meant by management's internal and external environment?

3. Discuss Khandwalla's work on the managerial environment.

4. What is meant by the term "corporate culture"?

5. Outline the basic elements of a corporate culture.

6. List and explain the various dimensions of management's external environment.

7. Discuss the shift that has occurred in terms of management's response to its internal and external environment.

8. Why is the future environment for managers difficult to predict?

9. Discuss the role of planning with respect to assessing the future environment for management.

10. Discuss Odiorne's views on the management style of a future executive.

PROBLEMS AND EXPERIENTIAL EXERCISES

1. Prepare a brief report on the corporate culture of a selected firm. Discuss the major conclusions you reach from your research.

2. Discuss the major threats and challenges facing management in each dimension of its external environment. This exercise might use teams to deal with each of the environmental dimensions.

3. Management expert George S. Odiorne has remarked: "Too often, managerial reactions are responding to the environment of the fading decade when the new one engulfs them. In part, this is because problems and solutions require lead time, and lead time appears to be collapsing on management."[17] Do you agree with Odiorne's comments? Explain.

4. Management consultants Arnold Brown and Edith Weiner identified some responses to changes that have occurred in the workplace. These are reprinted below.

   Do you agree with Brown and Weiner? Can you expand their list?

5. Albert Einstein once remarked: "I never think of the future. It comes soon enough."[18] Would Einstein's observation be an appropriate philosophy for a manager today? Comment.

Workplace Changes

Driving Forces	Flexible hours	Work at home	Support for networks	Stress management	Restructuring of jobs	New recruiting and promotional considerations	New compensation schemes	Professional contacts
Two-wage-earner households	✓	✓				✓	✓	
Broadened social and self-awareness	✓		✓	✓	✓	✓		✓
Explosive growth of service economy	✓	✓	✓	✓	✓		✓	✓
Economic, demographic, and technological challenges to middle-management positions				✓	✓	✓	✓	
Time of rapid change and an uncertain future			✓	✓	✓	✓	✓	✓

Source: Arnold Brown and Edith Weiner, *Supermanaging* (New York: McGraw-Hill Book Co., 1984), p. 101. Reprinted by permission.

MANAGERIAL INCIDENT: Walt Disney Productions

Walt Disney Productions zealously guards its reputation as the dominant movie maker for the family and the five-to-thirteen-year-old markets. Walt Disney was an innovator in this particular segment of the entertainment industry, and his firm continues to work on plans that he conceived (Disney died in 1966). Donn B. Tatum, a company director, commented on the traditions existing within the firm: "There was a time after Walt died that I wondered whether the Disney spirit could be transmitted to succeeding generations. But I have now seen it transmitted through four generations with no apparent diminution."

Disney has now set up Touchstone Films, a second motion picture label to deal with more contemporary themes. The move proved highly successful with the 1984 hit film *Splash*, and in 1985 with another comedy success, *Down and Out in Beverly Hills*. The new division's success continued in 1986 with the film *Ruthless People*.

While Touchstone was enjoying box-office success, Disney's original film studio was releasing popular films for children. Two 1986 successes aimed at the children's market were *Flight of the Navigator* and *The Great Mouse Detective*.

Questions and Problems

1. Relate this case to the material presented in this chapter.

2. Explain how Disney's tradition can be both an advantage and a disadvantage to the firm.

Source: Tatum quote from "Can Disney Still Grow on Its Founder's Dreams?" *Business Week,* 31 July 1978, p. 67. Updated by Erwin Okun of Walt Disney Productions, 23 August 1985.

CASES FOR PART ONE

CASE 1 The City of Sageview: The Management Process at Work in the Public Sector

At 3:30 the Sageview team is to hold its first meeting. The team consists of Dave Foster, director of the Municipal Assistance Center (MAC) at Western State University, and three Western State MBA students. The purpose of the team's meeting is to find ways to respond to Steve Morris, Sageview's city manager of six months. Morris has asked MAC to assist in improving employee productivity and satisfaction in the Sageview city organization.

Dave especially wants the Sageview team's efforts to be successful for two reasons. First, Steve Morris is an old and close friend. Second, Morris enjoys a high reputation for innovation and effectiveness among other city managers. Many city managers will thus watch with interest MAC's efforts in Sageview. If a low-cost, high-benefit program can be implemented in Sageview, many other cities should fund similar work with MAC.

A week ago, Dave visited Sageview and gathered preliminary information on Sageview and its problems. He sifted through it in preparation for the team's meeting.

DEMOGRAPHICS

Sageview is a prosperous western city with a population of approximately 100,000. Its economy is diversified among energy production and agribusiness. One manufacturer accounts for 10 percent of the employment. This manufacturer is expanding, and two medium-sized, high technology firms have located in the city in the past three years. Un-

employment is less than 4 percent. Housing is adequate but falling behind and becoming very expensive.

The city is politically homogeneous. Few political divisions have been exhibited in city elections in two decades. Like most western cities, Sageview is very conservative fiscally. Its property tax rate is low for a city of its size in the West. Sageview, however, is not without problems. New growth is demanding expansion of city services and the creation of new programs.

PREVIOUS CITY MANAGERS

During the thirteen years that preceded Steve Morris' arrival in Sageview, two city managers had served the city. Jim Lynch was the first of Morris' predecessors. Having managed several prominent western cities—one three times the size of Sageview—Lynch was well respected by other city managers.

Lynch told Dave several years ago that he had come to Sageview to retire. He wanted to make no major changes. Changes, Lynch felt, stirred up things, and he was tired of the hassle from public furor. Thus, his unwritten policy was that no major changes were to be proposed to him by his staff. This policy was well understood by the city staff and was in effect throughout Lynch's tenure in Sageview. When Lynch retired he was comforted by the knowledge that he had done a good job in Sageview. No major public protests had occurred while he was city manager.

(Continued on next page.)

Lynch was followed by Bill Jones. A civil engineer by training, Jones came to Sageview from a city half its size. He prided himself on keeping taxes down. His standing order was "no new programs, no new taxes."

The net result of these two management styles was the stifling of change. Fred Henderson, who served as the planning director under both managers, found this very frustrating. "For years I tried to get improvements in our zoning ordinance. The response was 'There's no money in the budget'; 'We're not going to get into that mess right now.' Now we're paying the price. Today, we have real problems with development."

The Sageview City Council usually preferred not to ask for new taxes, but now the council recognized that needed changes had been put off too long. City hall rumors circulated that the council "encouraged" Jones' early retirement. During the initial interview with the council, Steve Morris was told in no uncertain terms that changes had to be made. No specific demands were made except that his administration bring the city into the "last half of the twentieth century."

MORRIS' MANAGEMENT STYLE

Morris was thirty-eight years old and known to city management professionals as a "progressive, effective" city manager. Before coming to Sageview, he served four years each as city manager in two cities with populations of 30,000 to 50,000. Both these cities had been facing serious financial and development problems before Morris began his tenure. Both were in strong fiscal shape when he left, and Morris believed both were also progressing well on the development of new or better city services.

In each city, Morris felt that he had done a good job and had the support of the city council. Each time he changed jobs, it was to accept a position with a larger city that he felt would offer new professional challenges for him.

Steve Morris sees his management style as having three key components. First, he emphasizes providing opportunities for individuals to reach their full potential and grow in their jobs. "I believe in hiring good people and giving them freedom to try new ideas."

The team concept is the second major part of Morris' style. Upon reaching Sageview, he formed his assistants and division heads into a top management team (see Exhibit 1). He holds frequent team meetings where any major problems facing the city as a whole are thoroughly discussed. Division heads are encouraged to bring up problems from their specific areas to the team, and when appropriate, several divisions work together on a common problem.

The last component of Morris' style is the use of task forces to solve city problems. A task force may be headed by a division head, but its members are drawn from all levels and departments in the organization. Memos are sent to employees describing the problem and soliciting volunteers for a task force. Those employees selected for the task force are given time off from regular duties to work with the task force. Morris thinks that this broadens the scope of employees' jobs and lets the city avail itself of the talents and interests of many more individuals than a rigid structure allows.

Morris believes all three components of this management style have worked well for him. He believes that they have started to improve how Sageview employees view their jobs. He hopes Sageview employees see him as a city manager open to suggestions, concerned for the welfare of all employees, and equally concerned with the efficiency and quality of city services.

EXHIBIT 1   City of Sageview—The Top Management Team

Below is a short description of the people who make up Sageview's top management team and Steve Morris' perceptions of their views on recent changes.

HENRY WILLIAMSON—Chief of Police. Graduated from Sageview High School; joined the Sageview PD immediately after army service in World War II; became the chief in 1963. He is now 61 years old. Henry generally favors Morris' changes.

FRED HENDERSON—Planning Director. Master of Urban and Regional Planning; began working for the city in 1969; became director in 1973. Fred is very excited about the opportunities to expand the scope of his department's operations under Steve Morris.

RON BYERS—City Attorney. Started to work for the city in 1977 right out of law school; became city attorney in 1980; sees some of his authority as having been challenged because Steve has asked that he be kept informed of the legal office's activities. Ron likes to remember that formally he is appointed by the council, not the city manager.

BILL BRIGGS—Safety Officer. Master of Educational Administration; was hired by Steve Morris in August 1983 and is very favorable to the changes Steve has made.

DAVID WILKES—City Engineer (Acting Public Works Director). B.S. in Civil Engineering; started with the city in 1956; became city engineer in 1966. David feels that recent changes have produced too much work. A division director cannot worry about others' problems and adequately handle his own.

FRANK TUTTLE—Utility Director. B.S. in biology; started working for Sageview in 1967; became director in 1981. Frank shares many of Wilkes' views about recent organizational changes.

SAM SHILLING—Director of Community Services. M.A. in Parks and Recreation; started with Sageview in 1974; made director in 1980. He is very positive toward Morris' management style.

ALLEN FLEET—Fire Chief. Associate of Arts in Fire Technology; joined the Sageview FD in 1957; made chief in 1982; doesn't see any reason for everybody to know what other departments are doing; running the fire department is as much work as he needs.

BOB BILLINGWORTH—Finance Director. B.B.A. in Finance; came to Sageview as finance director in 1982, having been an assistant finance director in a smaller community. He is generally positive toward Morris' management style but is uncertain of the real impact of organizational changes.

DICK MARLIN—Traffic Director. M.S. in Civil Engineering; came to Sageview as traffic director in 1979. Dick is very concerned over how proposed organizational and pay scale changes will affect his department.

TOM HARRIS—Assistant City Manager. M.A. in Urban Studies; came to Sageview with Steve Morris, having worked with him in his previous city. Tom works closely with Steve, so closely that it is often hard to tell which one originated a particular idea or action.

TED FILLER—Administrative Assistant to the City Manager. Master of Public Administration; Sageview is his first job since graduating and he came to the position two months ago. Predictably, he is very supportive of Steve's and Tom's ideas.

(Continued on next page.)

SAGEVIEW'S ORGANIZATION

The City of Sageview employs approximately 860 employees. It is structured into forty-seven departments grouped into nine divisions (see Exhibit 2). The nine division heads, safety officer, assistant city manager, and city manager make up the top management team.

FIRE AND POLICE UNREST

Before Morris' arrival in Sageview, the police and firefighters had petitioned for formal collective bargaining rights. Under the city charter, a public referendum had to approve the granting of collective bargaining rights to any municipal employees wanting to unionize. Ten months before Morris' arrival, the vote was held, and Sageview citizens turned down the proposition.

More recently, the police petitioned for a referendum to grant police officers an immediate 25 percent pay raise. This petition was submitted after the police in another city won a similar referendum.

The Sageview Police Officers' Association (SPOA) conducted a well-organized publicity campaign modeled after that in the other city. TV ads showed police officers willing to lay down their lives for citizens and asked, "How much is law and order worth to you?"

Several council members openly opposed the SPOA campaign, and the city's only daily newspaper carried an editorial against the pay raise. In one of Morris' first actions, the city manager's office released to the press a wage and salary study showing that Sageview's police salaries were about average for other western cities.

The proposition lost at the polls. Morris, however, knew his problems with the police and firefighters were not over. Resentment had developed between police and fire officers and city management.

OTHER PROBLEMS

Police and fire disputes were not the only problems facing Steve Morris. The public works director was fired four months after Morris took office. He had been with the city for fifteen years and openly opposed changing his operations. For example, he refused to allow the Engineering Department to work on the Planning Department's new flood plan even though Morris had directed him to provide engineering assistance to Planning.

The firing had an unknown impact on the rest of the staff. Morris sensed that most employees understood why the firing occurred, but there was some evidence that a few "old-timers" were apprehensive about contradicting Morris' ideas. Morris didn't want the firing to build a wall between him and the staff.

Dave found that a wall was already developing. During a coffee break, Sageview's shop foreman responded to Dave's question on what he thought of his new city manager this way: "Well, I guess Mr. Morris is all right. Bill (the former manager) was a pretty good manager, too. He'd just drop by and chew the fat with you. I seldom see Mr. Morris."

The apprehension of many city employees toward Morris was also increased by a new wage classification program he instituted. Salaries and job classifications had not been analyzed in many years. Morris felt that a wage study was essential to insure that equal work received equal pay. Such a study, however, takes time; and while it was being conducted, employees voiced interest and concern over its possible effects on their jobs and salaries.

Morris told Dave, "I'm worried that my management style, personnel changes I've made, the police and fire agitation, and the other new things we're working on could have lowered the staff morale. This is especially likely given the previous administra-

(Continued on page 76.)

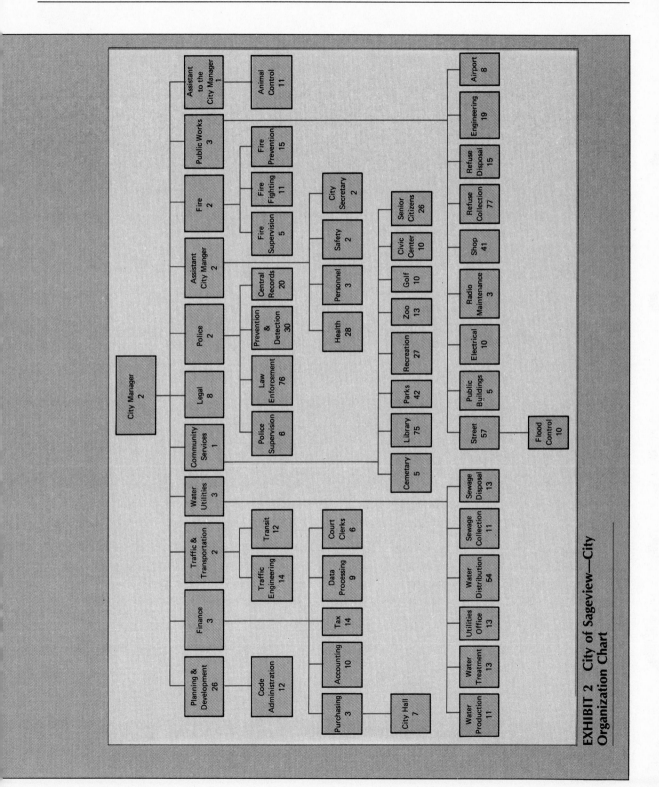

EXHIBIT 2 City of Sageview—City Organization Chart

tion's 'go slow' policies. Dave, I don't want to wait for some of our people to catch up before we start to make more improvements. But I don't want to lose their participation either."

With his thoughts collected, Dave walked into the conference room. The Sageview team meeting was about to start.

QUESTIONS

1. What should Foster say at the team meeting?

2. Evaluate the decision-making approach used by the City of Sageview.

3. How can Morris introduce the changes demanded by the city council within the city's existing managerial framework?

Source: This case was prepared by William R. Fannin, Assistant Professor of Management, University of Houston–Clear Lake; Don C. Moore, Vice-President, Lockwood, Andrews, & Newman, Inc.; Lisa C. Guinn, research associate, and Rebecca A. Baysinger, Candidate for the Ph.D. in the Department of Management, Texas A & M University. Adapted and reprinted by permission of the authors.

CASE 2   The Bhopal Chemical Disaster

The cloud of poison gas that oozed death and agony through a sleeping city in India has awakened the world to a danger hanging over mankind.

It's a nightmare come true—the 2,000 dead and 100,000 injured in the city of Bhopal—of what can happen anywhere that people live close to the powerful tools they try to use to master their environment.

Bhopal became a hell. Seventy funeral pyres, stacked 25 bodies high, all burning at once. Mass graves near overflowing. Babies gasping for breath in hospitals that reported a death a minute. Streets strewn with carcasses of animals. Swarms of flies. Skies with circling vultures.

The city of 900,000 people stank of death. The leaves on trees shriveled and yellowed. Ponds got scummy. Turnips and spinach grew scorched in the fields. Milk turned foul. Everywhere sounded the wails of grieving relatives, moans of survivors in pain and cries of hungry children.

BUSINESS TOLL

The legacy of this man-made horror—the worst chemical-industry disaster in history—portends financial misery, too, for corporations engaged in hazardous enterprises near population centers.

To U.S.-owned Union Carbide, damages from the leak of the pesticide methyl isocyanate from its Bhopal plant could be staggering. The company lost 832 million dollars in market value in one week on Wall Street. Legal experts say that damage claims could total hundreds of millions of dollars and even threaten the financial structure of the firm, which had total assets of 9 billion at the end of last year. Union Carbide officials said publicly that they do not expect the company to fail.

Yet the company certainly is facing formidable trouble. When Union Carbide's chairman, Warren Anderson, stepped off a plane in Bhopal after flying from his Connecticut headquarters to assess damage and offer aid, he was arrested along with the two top executives of the Indian subsidiary and charged with "negligence and corporate liability." Notes an Indian Supreme Court lawyer and former judge: "It is probably the first time in India that a senior multinational executive has been arrested on a negligence charge."

Anderson was freed on bail—only to face demands of India's Minister of Chemicals and Fertilizers that the firm pay U.S. compensation rates to victims.

That stand signals new and higher risks for foreign corporations doing business in undeveloped nations. Legal experts predict long trials over the comparative economic values of Indian and American lives, noting that per capita income in India is only $226 a year, vs. $11,680 in the U.S.

Though Union Carbide reportedly has up to 200 million dollars in insurance, analysts said that its coverage could be canceled if company officials were proved to have "recklessly or intentionally" caused the disaster.

SAFETY STANDARDS

Union Carbide insists that the Bhopal facility was built by Americans to the same safety standards as U.S. factories. However, the company also says that it had not installed a computerized safety system at Bhopal, despite having one at a sister plant in West Virginia. Meanwhile, Union Carbide ordered an immediate halt to its production of methylisocyanate gas worldwide.

KEY QUESTIONS

What caused 25 tons of the agricultural pesticide to spread over 25 square miles and, in the words of a missionary, make all of Bhopal "like a big gas chamber"?

Company officials blamed the leak on a malfunctioning valve in the underground tank used to mix the gas. Yet Indian authorities held six supervisors of the plant under house arrest, sealed the facility to prevent any tampering with evidence and put a 24-hour armed guard on a critically gassed employe thought to be the only eyewitness to the leak. One point investigators want to clear up is why—when so many died outside the plant—only one of the 120 workers inside was killed.

The *Washington Post* reported that two workers responsible for stemming the leak ran away rather than try to stop the high-pressure burst of toxic fumes.

The chemical is known to be many times more deadly than a poison gas of World War I—phosgene—which is one of its key ingredients. If inhaled, it causes rapid swelling of moist lung tissues, because of water accumulation. Victims drown in their own fluids.

Methyl isocyanate, used to make a fairly low-toxicity insecticide called Sevin, itself is highly volatile, which is why it boiled out of its tank in such a huge cloud.

The Bhopal incident creates a challenge to the government of Rajiv Gandhi. The disaster gives ammunition to opponents of Gandhi's plans to open India's economy to foreign technology.

The Soviet Union, which has strong relations with India, was quick with a propaganda attack, charging that the accident shows that U.S. corporations endanger the Third World in a callous search for profits.

The British relief agency Oxfam cites 375,000 cases of pesticide poisoning plus 10,000 deaths in developing countries in 1982 alone.

A major point of contention in India—and all around the globe—is the locating of such plants in areas of high population density. "Life for poor people like us," said a woman who escaped the gas, "is difficult enough

(Continued on next page.)

without rich people and their companies making it dangerous for us to live here."

In Bhopal, however, the closest residents were squatters who began putting up shanties and mud hovels on government-owned land surrounding the factory about eight years ago.

Many survivors of the gassing said they had no idea that lethal materials were manufactured next to their homes. Some said they never heard sirens that were supposed to blare in case of a leak. Others said they were never told what the sirens meant.

"IT IS TOO LATE"

Even while medical authorities argued the possibility of long-term contamination, many Indians returned to the shantytown. "We came back," said truckdriver Ram Narain, "because we've nowhere else to go." Bihari Vlal, coughing and wiping white fluid stream-

ing from his eyes, said, "Now they must take the Union Carbide plant away. But now it is too late."

To analysts of the chemical business, the incident stands as a 1-in-a-million chance that will alert the industry to its hazards. To the people of Bhopal, there is no understanding to be gained. They know it only as "The Devils' Night."

QUESTIONS

1. Do you think the Bhopal disaster will affect management's external environment? If so, what industries will be affected? How will they be affected?

2. How will this tragedy affect Union Carbide's internal environment? Discuss.

Source: Reprinted from "India's Tragedy—A Warning Heard Around the World," *U.S. News & World Report,* 17 December 1984, pp. 25-26.

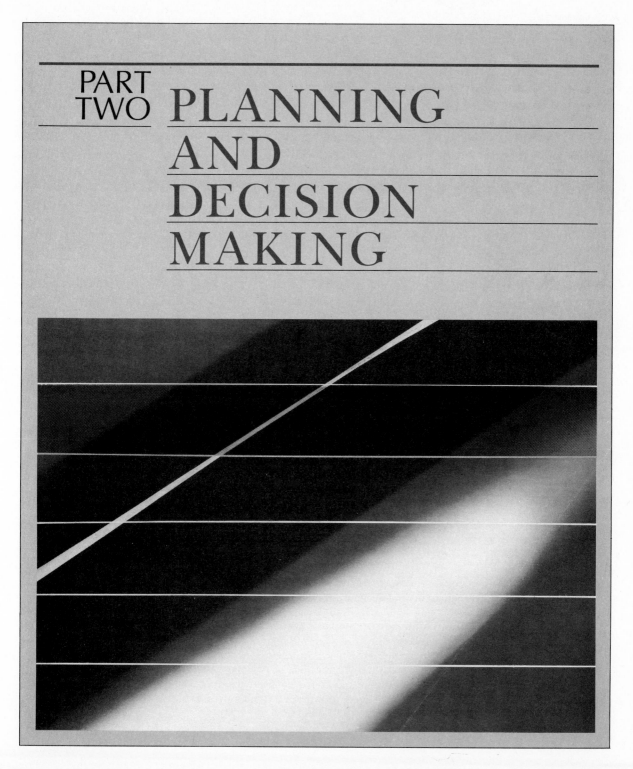

PART TWO

PLANNING AND DECISION MAKING

4 FUNDAMENTALS OF PLANNING

LEARNING OBJECTIVES

After studying this chapter you should be able to

1. Identify the steps in the planning process.

2. Explain the relationship between planning and decision making.

3. List the major benefits of planning.

4. Categorize plans on the bases of time, use, and scope (or breadth).

5. Identify the major categories of forecasting methods.

6. Identify the factors that determine how an organization will structure its planning activities.

7. Explain the relationship between time management and planning.

STOP ACTION CASE

Stouffer Foods Corp.

Meticulous planning and major inputs from present and potential customers have long been the underlying keys to the success of Stouffer Foods. The Solon, Ohio-based company, a subsidiary of the huge multinational Nestlé firm, has long been a widely recognized supplier of frozen foods. Recent changes in the marketplace, however, concerned the firm's top management. The huge growth in the number of two-wage-earner households had pushed up the sales of convenient frozen food products. Moreover, these shoppers were much more likely to purchase higher-priced, higher-quality frozen food dinners.

A second trend in food purchasing was the increased concern for diet, nutrition, and the caloric content of food. Stouffer's, which had entered the frozen food business in 1950 and whose frozen food sales had reached $165 million annually by the early 1980s, was determined to maintain sufficient flexibility to adjust its product offerings to match changes in food shopper tastes and preferences.

Stouffer's managers, unwilling to risk their current market position with an ill-conceived plan, took a cautious approach. Elena Coccari, consumer affairs manager for the firm, stated, "We've always stuck to the philosophy that Stouffer's looks good, tastes good, and offers value, and it took a lot of testing before we developed a product line that matched that philosophy. Stouffer's doesn't go for fads. Taste, texture, and appearance are important here, so we take a long, healthy look at things before going to the market with it."

Use the materials in Chapter 4 to recommend a course of action for Stouffer Foods managers.

Don Shula, head coach of the Miami Dolphins, tells his listeners that planning is the key to his organization's success and that many of his team's victories can be attributed to careful pregame planning. The director of the local United Fund organization echoes Shula's statements concerning the necessity of careful planning to achieve yearly goals. Most organizations—profit and nonprofit—develop plans and then work closely within the framework of these plans to accomplish objectives.

Managers engaged in the ongoing process of planning count on at least one constant in the fast-paced world of the late 1980s: *change.* U.S. exporters are affected by government policies restricting sales to Nicaragua. Cable television companies that previously enjoyed monopoly positions in their market areas make drastic modifications in their operations when city governments permit new competitors to offer similar services. Plans for a new production facility may have to be revised if the local zoning authority does not approve the zoning changes required for construction of the facility.

Although unexpected developments are not always negative, they can often devastate the ill prepared. Planning forces managers to anticipate change and to prepare to cope with it. Change can often result in new opportunities, new markets, a chance for growth—if plans have been made to capitalize upon such change.

The ability to develop effective plans and the need for planning are not limited to large organizations. Although larger organizations often have the added resources, specialized talent, and time to allow them to develop detailed plans, effective planning may be even more important to smaller organizations. In many cases, small organizations possess limited resources and cannot afford the luxury of trial and error or of failure.

The planning process and its resultant plans have become increasingly sophisticated as organizations recognize that no managerial function is

●● Plans are nothing; planning is everything. ●●

Dwight D. Eisenhower

MANAGEMENT FACT OR FICTION

	FACT	FICTION		FACT	FICTION
1. *Decision making* is a broader term than *planning*.	☐	☐	more time on the development of single-use plans than do managers at the supervisory level of the organization.	☐	☐
2. The commitment principle emphasizes the relationship between the acceptance of a plan by all members of its organization and the likelihood of its success.	☐	☐	6. Smaller firms are likely to use the expertise of staff planning groups more than larger organizations, which do not require such outside consultants.	☐	☐
3. Three basic types of standing plans are programs, projects, and budgets.	☐	☐	7. Managing time effectively requires the establishment of a system to handle two major sources of interruption: the telephone and staff planning meetings.	☐	☐
4. Contingency plans are the answers to "What if?" situations facing the organization.	☐	☐			
5. Top management spends relatively					

The materials in this chapter will assist you in separating management fact from fiction. Your answers can be checked on page 109.

more important than planning. Quantitative techniques and computers are frequently employed. Yet all plans use one crucial component: *human resources*. People engage in planning, develop plans, are part of them, and are directly affected by them. Their understanding, motivation, and productivity must be major factors in any planning activities.

WHAT IS PLANNING?

- "Should we open a new branch bank in Woodland Hills to capitalize on the city's growth in that direction?"

- "Will our concert audience be offended if we add a Pops series to the Philharmonic's offerings this season, or will this new series enable us to increase the number of season ticketholders?"

- "Suppose we commit $1.9 million to battery capacity research; what if the market for battery-driven autos grows by only a 3 percent rate between now and 1999?"

Questions such as these are frequently posed in small firms as well as in very large organizations. Managers must anticipate future environmental changes that may affect operations. These might consist of changes in the inflation rate, technological innovations by competitors, raw material shortages, or political disturbances in a country where the firm has production facilities. While these situations are beyond the control of managers, effective planning aids in reducing risk and preparing the firm to withstand the roller coaster ride of future uncertainty.

Planning can be defined as the process by which managers set objectives, assess the future, and develop courses of action designed to accomplish these objectives. As the definition states, planning actually includes determining appropriate objectives and the optimum timetable for achieving them. Effective planning often means the difference between success, mediocrity, and failure. It is a continuous function that directs the organization through a change-oriented environment in the pursuit of established objectives. It also specifies the actions needed to reach these objectives.

Planning is a process by which managers set objectives, assess the future, and develop courses of action to accomplish these objectives.

As Figure 4–1 indicates, organizations are recognizing the importance of the planning function by actively seeking people who exhibit skill in this vital area. The recruitment ads are typical of those found in the classified section of any major newspaper.

PLANS VERSUS PLANNING

As the formal definition states, planning involves the continual reevaluation, analysis, and adjustment of organizational activities toward defined and agreed-upon objectives. One writer stated that successful planning must be based on a searching look within, a broad look around, and a long look ahead.[1] The *look within* involves thorough reviews of organizational assets, including human resources, facilities and equipment, location, and patents and trademarks. The *broad look around* is relations oriented, focusing on such factors as the organization's relations with suppliers, lenders, customers, and the community. The *long look ahead* combines these factors with forecasts that relate the present to the future. The alternative to planning is random behavior.

Plans are natural outgrowths of the planning process. They are detailed expressions of actions necessary to accomplish stated organizational objectives. Once plans are formulated and implemented, they are periodically evaluated to determine their success in moving the organization in the direction of its stated goals.

Plans are detailed expressions of actions necessary to accomplish stated organizational objectives.

FIGURE 4–1.   Classified Advertisements for Qualified Planners
Source: Wall Street Journal, 10 December 1985. Reprinted by permission of the companies.

PLANNING VERSUS DECISION MAKING

Decision making is the process of identifying options and choosing those courses of action necessary to perform a given task.

Decision making occurs at all managerial levels. It involves identifying options and choosing those courses of action necessary to perform a given task. Decisions trigger actions designed to keep plans in motion. Decision making is closely related to planning, since all planning involves making decisions. However, not all decision making is planning. (Decision making will be discussed in detail in Chapter 6.)

Planning, as an area of decision making, involves three special characteristics:

- *Anticipatory decision making.* Managers must decide what to do and how to do it *before* action is required.

- *System of decisions.* Managers should recognize the interconnections between one decision or set of decisions and others. As a result, an entire network of decisions is present, and each impending decision should be considered not only in isolation but also in terms of how it will affect every related decision.

- *Creation of desired future states.* Managers engage in decision making concerning the objectives for their organization. This important decision vitally affects all other decisions and organizational activities by focusing decisions and activities on the attainment of agreed-upon objectives.[2]

THE IMPORTANCE OF PLANNING ▰▰▰▰▰▰▰▰

While planning does not automatically guarantee success in accomplishing organizational objectives, it is rare for an organization to succeed solely by luck or circumstance. Careful planning should result in the development of a blueprint describing the means to accomplish objectives. Such a blueprint will typically include checkpoints at which actual operations can be compared with expectations to determine whether specific activities are moving the organization toward its objectives. There are several reasons why planning is considered to be a vital function for every manager.

AFFECTING PERFORMANCE

A number of empirical studies provide evidence concerning the importance of planning in organizational success. An investigation of thirty-six firms in the machinery, drug, food, steel, oil, and chemical industries revealed that companies that engaged in formal planning consistently outperformed those firms that did not.[3] A follow-up study by David M. Herald showed that the performance superiority (measured by such factors as return on equity and invested capital, sales, and growth in earnings per share) of firms engaged in formal planning had increased since the original study.[4] Similar results were obtained by Wood and LaForge, Stagner, and Eastlack and McDonald.[5]

FOCUSING ATTENTION ON OBJECTIVES

Organizational objectives, discussed in detail in Chapter 5, are part of the planning process. They may be considered *ends* because they serve as the focal point for organizational decisions and activities.

Once organizational objectives are defined, the planning process involves developing methods for achieving them. Plans continually reinforce the importance of these objectives by focusing on them. Every decision is measured in terms of its contribution to the achievement of organizational objectives. Having plans that focus on these objectives helps to prevent overinvolvement of managers in less important decisions and activities.

The importance of establishing organizational objectives as guidelines for planning activities is illustrated by the success enjoyed by the Rolm Corp. during the past twelve years in competing with the communications giant AT&T as a supplier of telecommunications systems to corporations. Rolm's introduction in 1975 of a 400-line computerized branch exchange (CBX) with sophisticated switching gear proved highly successful in serving smaller organizations, but the major corporations required greater line capacity. Following careful analysis of such factors as cost, market potential, and competitive offerings, Rolm first introduced two larger versions, a 1,500-line system and a 4,000-line system. But achieving its objectives of serving the communications needs of the world's industrial giants would

❝ No amount of sophistication is going to allay the fact that all your knowledge is about the past and all your decisions are about the future. ❞

Ian E. Wilson

MANAGEMENT FAILURES

RCA SelectaVision

Technological advances during the past two decades have created numerous opportunities for business firms throughout the world. In the consumer electronics field, innovations made it possible for consumers to purchase machines that would allow them to play prerecorded entertainment and educational programs on their television receivers—at their convenience. Radio Corporation of America, long a pioneer in consumer electronics and entertainment, was actively involved. At least three alternatives were available: videocassette recorders capable of recording television programs for replay as well as playing prerecorded programs; laser-disc videodisc players capable of very high visual quality programs but incapable of recording new programs; and less expensive diamond stylus videodisc players whose quality was poorer than that of the

laser-disc models but considerably better than that of the videocassette recorders.

RCA planners recognized several possible "futures":

- Acceptance of the diamond stylus videodisc player would be poor because of its inability to record.

require even larger systems, and Rolm's planning activities shifted in this direction. In 1983, the firm announced the CBX II, a digital PBX that accommodates corporations requiring more than 10,000 voice and data lines. Since then, all thirty of the largest corporations in the United States have installed Rolm equipment. Clearly, Rolm Corp. has successfully met the objectives it set for itself.[6]

OFFSETTING UNCERTAINTIES AND ANTICIPATING PROBLEMS

A significant aspect of any planning process is the collection of information for use in forecasting the future. The three "alternative futures" considered by RCA in the Management Failures box illustrate the development of contingency plans based on possible future events. A *contingency plan* is an alternative plan to be put into effect if certain events occur. For instance, the strong negative reaction to New Coke forced managers at the world's largest soft-drink company to implement their contingency plan and re-

Contingency plan is an alternative plan to be put into effect if certain events occur.

- The lower price (initially $599 but later reduced to $299 less retailer discounts) of the videodisc player would more than compensate for the added features of the videocassettes. In addition, the higher price of the laser-disc player would force consumers to settle for the diamond stylus videodisc.

- Although the laser-disc player would be priced higher than its competitors, its greater capacity (the entire *Encyclopaedia Britannica* can be stored on a few discs) and quality picture would offset the higher price, especially to industrial users and government purchasers.

RCA chose the second scenario and introduced SelectaVision in 1982, following expenditures of over $200 million in development. Although expected sales for the first year were 200,000 units, the firm sold only 65,000—even after a last-minute $22 million advertising campaign for the Christmas season.

Actual sales continued to trail projections during 1983 as the strategic plan began to unravel. To a large extent, the culprit was technology. Retail prices for both videocassette players and prerecorded tapes plummeted as imports began to arrive in the United States from South Korea and Japan. A bare-bones videocassette recorder could be purchased for as little as $200. In addition, a huge retail video tape rental industry developed, offering thousands of tapes to the videocassette recorder owner. The price gap between RCA's videodisc player and the videocassette recorders disappeared.

Although RCA continues to market and manufacture videodiscs and to provide parts and service for its SelectaVision disc players, the firm admitted defeat in 1984 when it ended production of its videodisc player. The continuing losses and dim future prospects were tangible evidence of the failure of the firm's planners to recognize the "future" that actually occurred prior to launching the new venture.

introduce Coca-Cola in its original formula as Classic Coke. Seattle University's contingency plan for possible volcanic ash fallout that might result from an eruption of Washington's Mount St. Helens is shown in Figure 4–2.

Identifying alternative futures and developing contingency plans in case any of these alternatives occur produces at least three benefits: (1) it permits quick response to change; (2) it prevents panic in crisis situations; and (3) it makes managers more adaptable by encouraging them to appreciate just how variable the future can be.[7] Forecasting the occurrence of alternative futures is discussed in detail in Chapter 5.

PROVIDING GUIDELINES FOR DECISION MAKING

Since plans specify the actions necessary to accomplish organizational objectives, they serve as the bases for decisions about future activities. Eastman Kodak's plans for penetrating the Japanese market are an example.

Seattle University
FOUNDED 1891

SEATTLE UNIVERSITY

Interoffice Memorandum

TO: All Seattle University Faculty, Administrators, Staff

FROM: Office of the President

SUBJECT: Ash Fallout Plan

In the event that future inclement winds bring ash fallout from Mount
St. Helens to the Seattle area, the following procedures are to be
implemented as of this date by all university personnel to reduce or
preclude costly damage to our facilities:

    DUE TO THE ABRASIVE CONTENT OF THE ASH, WE ARE RECOMMENDING,
AS OF NOW, THAT ALL EQUIPMENT, i.e. TYPEWRITERS, CALCULATORS,
COPY MACHINES, AND ANY OTHER EQUIPMENT THAT IS OPERATED BY
AN ELECTRICAL MOTOR, BE COVERED AT THE END OF THE WORK DAY.
ALL WINDOWS SHOULD BE CLOSED AS WELL AS ALL DOORS (INCLUDING
INTERIOR DOORS) WHEN LEAVING THE BUILDING AT THE END OF THE
DAY. IN THE EVENT OF AN "ASH ALERT" DURING THE WORKING DAY,
IT WILL BE MANDATORY TO SHUT DOWN ALL ELECTRICAL EQUIPMENT.

FIGURE 4–2.   Seattle University's Volcanic Ash Fallout Plan
Source: Reprinted courtesy of Seattle University.

Although the familiar yellow boxes of Kodak film produce over $10 billion in world wide sales for Eastman Kodak Co., it is strictly a small player in the Japanese market, where Fuji Photo, one-third the size of Kodak, commands a whopping 70 percent share of the market as compared with only 15 percent for Kodak. Kodak's plans for increasing its Japanese market share include moving responsibility for Japanese sales from its regional division for Asia, Africa, and Australia to a new Japanese subsidiary. Kodak managers seek to boost their firm's visibility by sponsoring numerous events in Japan and listing the company on the Tokyo Stock Exchange. It has replaced most of its independent agents with its own marketing and sales staff. Finally, its plans also call for establishing a large number of joint ventures with Japanese firms to improve its visibility in Japan.[8]

FACILITATING CONTROL

Controlling is the continual analysis and measurement of actual operations against the established standards developed during the planning process.

Although the evaluation and control process is discussed in detail in Chapter 16, it is closely related to the planning process. *Controlling* involves the continual analysis and measurement of actual operations against the established standards developed during the planning process. Failure to provide follow-up control mechanisms is similar to enacting a new law without bothering to develop methods of enforcing it. Control is the safeguard that ensures plans are properly carried out. Well-developed plans can aid this process in two ways.

A major contribution of planning to control systems is the development of an early warning system to inform managers of possible plan deviations. Once the possible contingencies have been identified during the initial planning process, management may establish a schedule of review dates or warning signals to alert it to deviations. These review systems may take the form of monthly operating statements or even daily reports of deviations from specified production, sales, or even profit levels. Such deviations can then be investigated, and remedial action may be considered.

Failure to create an effective early warning system has proven costly for contact lens manufacturer Bausch & Lomb during the past decade. The firm had roughly 90 percent of the soft contact lens market in the 1970s, but success blinded management to the fact that extended-wear soft lenses were the wave of the future. By 1982, the firm's share of the contact lens market had dropped to 55 percent. CooperVision and Continuous Curve Contact Lenses (a Revlon subsidiary) now dominate the $50 million to $60 million extended-wear market.[9]

TYPES OF PLANS

Since organizations may be involved with thousands of plans of widely varying degrees of importance, a method of classifying plans must be developed. As Figure 4–3 indicates, plans can be classified along three dimensions: *time, use,* and *scope* (or *breadth*).

THE TIME DIMENSION IN PLANNING

Of all the ingredients in the planning process, time is the most critical, most elusive, and most often abused. The time available to conduct a major research and development effort, correct a safety hazard, react to a business downturn, or acquire another firm varies widely. Certain types of plans take years to complete. When the six-foot, four-inch political candidate Abraham Lincoln was asked how long he thought a man's legs should be, he replied, "Long enough to reach the ground." Planning should be considered in the same manner. Plans should reach far enough into the future to cover the subject under consideration.

Consider, for example, the planning horizon for Weyerhauser Corp., which reaches into the twenty-first century. Weyerhauser managers know that it takes ninety-nine years to grow Douglas firs in the Northwest. Only by planting seedlings today is it possible to guarantee pulp supplies in ninety-nine years.

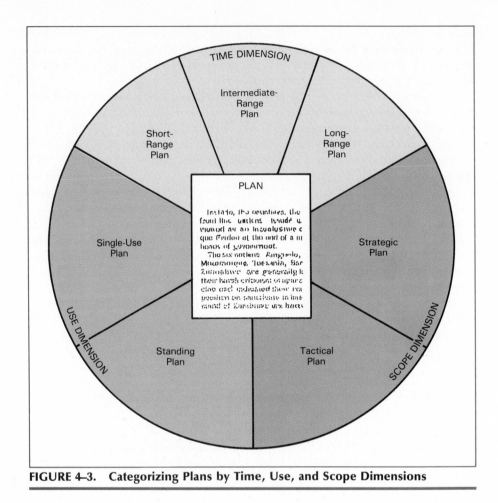

FIGURE 4–3.   Categorizing Plans by Time, Use, and Scope Dimensions

Short-Range, Intermediate-Range, and Long-Range Planning. The following time frames are typically used by managers in describing planning periods:

- Short range: one year or less

- Intermediate range: between one and five years

- Long range: five years or more

Figure 4–4 lists several examples of planning activities for each of the different planning periods.

The planning activities for each of the different time horizons may vary among organizations. General Motors Corp., for example, has invested more than ten years in research activities aimed at developing an improved capacity battery storage system for electric cars. A utility company such as

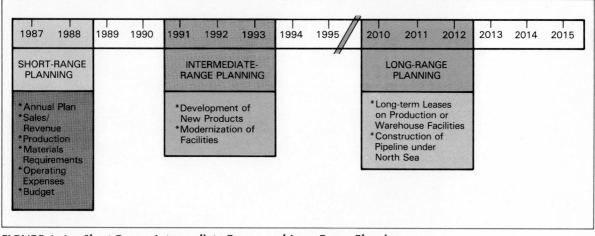

FIGURE 4–4.   Short-Range, Intermediate-Range, and Long-Range Planning

Consolidated Edison may view five years as a relatively short planning period in planning major expenditures for new generating facilities. On the other hand, a sportswear firm such as Ocean Pacific may view six months as a relatively long planning period.

The Commitment Principle. The period of time covered by organizational planning should be related to the commitments of the organization. The *commitment principle* states that an organization should plan for a period of time in the future sufficient to fulfill the commitments resulting from current decisions.[10]

For example, Toyota's decision to open an automobile assembly plant near Lexington, Kentucky, required long-range commitments in facilities, raw materials, and component parts, as well as commitments to the 2,000 American workers it employs. Long-range planning by Toyota managers reaches into the twenty-first century, as they attempt to capture an increased share of the nearly three million imported automobiles purchased annually in the United States. Sears, Roebuck and Co. commits itself for a period of six months when it distributes millions of semiannual catalogs to its mail-order customers.

The commitment principle is also in operation at Rolls-Royce Motors, the British firm renowned throughout the world for its luxury motor cars. Rolls-Royce models such as the Ghost, Phantom, Silver Shadow, and Corniche have long been regarded as the benchmark of automotive excellence. Of the 100,000 or so motor cars built by Rolls-Royce since 1905, more than half are still on the road. Consequently, when a new Rolls-Royce such as the Corniche convertible shown in Figure 4–5 is introduced, the firm's management recognizes that the odds of it still being in use and still

The **commitment principle** states that an organization should plan for a period of time in the future sufficient to fulfill commitments resulting from current decisions.

FIGURE 4–5.   The Rolls-Royce Corniche: An Eighty-Year Commitment
Source: Courtesy Rolls-Royce Motors, Inc.

requiring replacement parts in the year 2067 are at least 50 percent. The planning horizon for mechanical training and parts availability at Rolls extends over this period.

Planning must encompass a sufficiently long time frame to meet the commitments of current decisions. A long-range plan is built upon the foundations of short- and intermediate-range plans, all attainable within a specified time frame.

THE USE DIMENSION IN PLANNING

Plans may be divided into two major categories on the basis of their use: single-use plans and standing plans.

Single-Use Plans. *Single-use plans* are predetermined courses of action developed for relatively unique, nonrepetitive situations. The decision of a corporation such as American Airlines to move its home office from New York to Dallas required numerous one-time plans. The three basic types of single-use plans are programs, projects, and budgets.

Single-use plans are predetermined courses of action developed for relatively unique, nonrepetitive situations.

A *program* is a large-scale, single-use plan involving numerous interrelated activities. A program will typically specify the objectives, major steps necessary to achieve these objectives, individuals or departments responsible for each step, the order of the various steps, and resources to be used. Programs are often major undertakings, as was the joint British and French program to develop the Concorde supersonic airplane or the U.S. space program that landed astronauts on the moon. On a smaller scale, programs may be developed for reducing absenteeism and improving employee morale in an organization. Still other programs may be developed by a school superintendent to improve mathematics test scores of high school graduates.

A **program** is a large-scale, single-use plan involving numerous interrelated activities.

A *project* is a single-use plan that is a component of a program or is on a smaller scale than a program. The Concorde program was originally divided into numerous specific subprograms. The subprograms were then divided into specific projects. Each project was then assigned to a government contractor for completion. These projects resembled small-scale programs, since each contractor's assignment contained the same steps present in a program. Other examples of projects include the conversion of police vehicle engines from gasoline fuel to gasohol, the installation of new machinery in a manufacturing facility, or the enlargement of the seating capacity of the Orange Bowl.

A **project** is a single-use plan that is a component part of a program or is on a smaller scale than a program.

A *budget* is simply a financial plan listing in detail the resources or funds allocated to a particular program, project, product, or division. Budgets are discussed in detail in Chapter 16 as important devices for controlling organizational activities. In addition, they are important components of both programs and projects. However, budgets are also considered single-use plans because the process of developing budgets is clearly planning and because budgets take objectives into account in deciding in advance how to allocate resources among alternative activities. Many organizations use the budget as the basis for planning and coordinating other activities.

A **budget** is a financial plan listing in detail the resources or funds assigned to a particular program, project, product, or division.

Standing Plans. *Standing plans* are predetermined courses of action developed for repetitive situations. Such plans speed the decision-making process and allow managers to handle similar situations in a consistent manner. Standing plans are developed for situations as diverse as the Sears policy of promoting employees from within the organization whenever possible, a local supermarket's check-cashing policy requiring customers to complete an application and have a checking account at a local bank, or a rule prohibiting smoking in the company dining room.

Standing plans are predetermined courses of action developed for repetitive situations.

For example, several years ago managers at Scott Paper Co.'s Mobile, Alabama, manufacturing facility had become increasingly concerned with tardiness and absenteeism. The rate of absenteeism had risen to 7 percent by the early 1970s, and a plan was developed to deal with the problem. The plan, which called for a five-step system of oral and written warnings and suspensions, was incorporated into the firm's labor agreement. As a

MANAGEMENT SUCCESSES

Mylan Laboratories

The headquarters of Mylan Laboratories, Inc., tucked into the corner of a refurbished building in a neglected area of Pittsburgh, looks more like an insurance sales office than the home of a star in the exploding generic-drug industry. But in some ways, the location is fitting: Mylan's future wasn't always so bright. And its success, Chairman Roy McKnight argues, owes much to the troubles Mylan weathered a decade ago.

When McKnight took over in 1976, Mylan was fading fast: "We had no money, a severe negative net worth, and no credibility. We were in bankruptcy and just didn't admit it," he says. At the time, McKnight had no experience in pharmaceuticals, but after thirty years in electrical equipment sales he could recognize Mylan's symptoms: It had expanded too fast into too many products and was plagued by high production costs. McKnight took classic remedial action: He cut staff by a third, revamped the product line, and persuaded bankers to extend more credit. The crisis galvanized Mylan's management team, and by 1977, McKnight had pushed the com-

pany back into the black. It has been prospering ever since.

Open Window. Mylan is now universally regarded as the leader among generic drug makers, leaving McKnight, sixty-four, much more time to relax with a regular round of golf. The company "always beats the competition" in bringing new generic drugs to market, says Hemant K. Shah, an analyst with Mabon, Nugent & Co. Although Mylan paid no dividends until 1984, it is a darling of Wall Street. Its stock has split six times since 1979, while sales have more than doubled, to $53.6 million, and earnings have increased nearly seven times, to $12.5 million, for the year ended March 31. And the Street believes the best is yet to come: Mylan's stock sells at forty times earnings.

Mylan is reaping the rewards of the rush to contain health care costs. Generics, costing 30 percent to 70 percent less than branded drugs, claim 6 percent of the $17.9 billion prescription drug market, and their share is growing. Since September, five big brand-name drugs with total estimated yearly sales of $1.2 billion have lost their patent protec-

result, tardiness has lessened, absenteeism has dropped to 4.4 percent, and almost seventy employees have been dismissed in the past five years.

Standing plans may be categorized as policies, procedures, or rules on the basis of their scope. *Policies* are general guidelines for decision making. Many organizations provide parameters within which decisions must be made. Human resources policies may focus on hiring from within; purchasing department policies may prohibit gifts from suppliers; pricing policies may permit district sales managers to meet the lowest prices of competitors.[11]

Policies are general guidelines for decision making.

tion. "For the generic-drug industry, this is the best window of opportunity [ever]," says David F. Saks, an analyst with Morgan, Olmstead, Kennedy & Gardner, Inc.

A major share of the spoils has come to Mylan because it spends heavily on the clinical research needed to convince the Food & Drug Administration that its product is the same as a branded drug. "Our R&D expenditures have been 40 percent to 50 percent above anyone else's for the past four to five years and have grown at a higher rate," McKnight boasts. And Mylan has targeted high-margin drugs that treat chronic conditions, such as high blood pressure, while deemphasizing, say, antibiotics, which are typically used for two weeks. In April 1984, for example, Mylan introduced indomethacin, the first generic version of Merck & Co.'s Indocin, an antiarthritic drug with annual sales of $110 million. Within four days, Mylan had booked more than $4 million in orders, and in its last fiscal year it sold in excess of $10 million worth of the drug.

'On the Lookout.' Mylan has further separated itself from the pack by being the first generic manufacturer to introduce a patented drug. Last October, it brought out Maxzide, a diuretic, to compete with SmithKline Beckman's Dyazide, whose $250 million in annual sales make it the No. 3 patented prescription drug in the United States. Instead of copying Dyazide, Mylan spent more than $5 million to develop a version that is more easily absorbed and has to be taken just once a day. Dyazide often must be taken twice. "I'd be disappointed if [Maxzide] didn't reach $100 million in sales by 1987," says James J. Mauzey, vice-president of Lederle Laboratories Div., the large U.S. drug maker that distributes Maxzide for Mylan. With that number as a lure, there may be more patents in Mylan's future. "We're much more on the lookout than before, because we know we can do it now," McKnight says.

McKnight, who has amassed a fortune of $33.8 million from Mylan's stock, is still surprised by the company's revival. "I never dreamt it would turn out like this," he says. The same may be said for the twenty other millionaire employees that Mylan boasts, thanks to a stock-option plan that extends even to the company's switchboard operator. Despite his success, though, the amiable CEO is still known to answer the phone occasionally at headquarters and chat with callers when the receptionist is out to lunch.

Source: Matt Rothman, "A Classic Cure Put Mylan in the Pink." Reprinted from May 27, 1985, issue of *Business Week* by special permission, © 1985 by McGraw-Hill, Inc.

Procedures are guides to action that specify in detail the manner in which activities are to be performed. They tend to be narrower in scope than policies and are often intended to be used in implementing policies. Scott Paper Co.'s policies regarding tardiness are implemented by a set of written procedures.

Procedures are guides to action that specify in detail the manner in which activities are to be performed.

Rules are the simplest type of standing plans. They are statements of actions that must be taken or not taken in a given situation. Rules serve as guides to behavior. Most organizations use a great variety of rules. Certain rules may require employees to wear protective head coverings and safety shoes on construction sites. Other rules may prohibit food and

Rules are statements of actions that must be taken or not taken in a given situation.

drinks in a retail store. Although procedures may incorporate rules, rules do not incorporate procedures. Rules, unlike procedures, do not specify a time sequence. They permit no deviation from a stated course of action, and the manager's discretion is limited to deciding whether or not to apply a rule in a given situation.

The six types of single-use and standing plans—programs, projects, budgets, policies, procedures, and rules—are categorized on the basis of their usage in Figure 4–6.

THE SCOPE (OR BREADTH) DIMENSION IN PLANNING

The third method of categorizing plans is by scope or breadth. Some plans are very broad and long range, focusing on key organizational objectives. Other types of plans specify how the organization will mobilize to achieve these objectives. The two basic types are strategic plans and tactical plans.

Strategic Planning. *Strategic planning* is the process of determining the major objectives of an organization and then adopting the courses of action and allocating the resources necessary to achieve those objectives.[12] Such planning provides the organization with overall long-range direction and leads to the development of more specific plans, budgets, and policies. Strategic planning formed the basis of such fundamental management decisions as:

> **Strategic planning** is the process of determining the major objectives of an organization and then adopting the courses of action and allocating the resources necessary to achieve those objectives.

- Levi Strauss & Co.'s product line expansion from men's blue denim work pants to women's and children's clothing, fashion-oriented clothing, shoes, and automobile seatcovers.

FIGURE 4–6.   Classifying Plans on the Basis of Usage

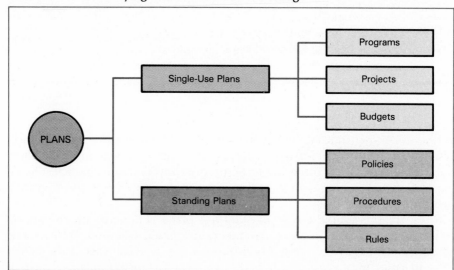

- Motorola's decision to abandon the consumer-goods market and concentrate on industrial products.

- General Electric's decision to acquire RCA.

Tactical Planning. Although strategic planning focuses on what the organization will be in the future, tactical planning emphasizes *how* this will be accomplished. *Tactical planning* refers to the implementation of activities and the allocation of resources necessary to achieve the organization's objectives. Many writers mistakenly consider tactical planning as short term and strategic planning as exclusively long term. In some instances, strategic planning is short term. The advertisement shown in Figure 4–7 describes the underlying rationale for ITT Corporation's short-term—but strategic—plan to redirect the focus of the firm away from food products through the sale of its Continental Baking subsidiary.

In most cases, however, strategic planning is associated with longer-term planning. Tactical planning, on the other hand, typically focuses on short-term implementation of activities and resource allocations.

Strategic planning is the critical ingredient in the long-term success of the organization. The importance of this topic is emphasized by the fact that an entire chapter (Chapter 5) is devoted to an analysis of strategic planning and the steps involved in developing strategic plans for the organization.

Tactical planning refers to the implementation of activities and the allocation of resources necessary to achieve the organization's objectives.

FIGURE 4–7.   Implementing the ITT Strategic Plan
Source: Reprinted by permission of ITT.

FORECASTING: CRITICAL PLANNING INGREDIENT

Forecasts are estimates or predictions of future events or outcomes for a specified time period. While most firms focus on forecasting such tangible future occurrences as sales or production, planners may also attempt to predict technological breakthroughs, economic changes, or variations in the legal or societal environments. Forecasts play critical roles in the planning process, and their accuracy is reflected in the accuracy of plans that are developed.

The forecasting process is a difficult undertaking for most organizations. One management writer has pointed out that there are only three certainties about the future:[13]

- The future will not be like the past.

- The future will not be what we think it's going to be.

- The rate of change will be faster than ever before.

Even though forecasts involve uncertainty, they are the foundation for all organizational production, financial, personnel, and marketing planning. They also provide the basis for the establishment of performance standards. Actual performance is then compared with these standards. Without such standards, comparisons would not be possible, since inadequate performance cannot be recognized without some definition of *adequate* performance.

Forecasts may be short run or long run. Long-run forecasts attempt to predict variables such as company sales for five, ten, or even twenty or more years in advance. They are quite general and typically are not used to predict the sales of specific products. Short-term forecasts attempt to predict sales, production, or other variables for one year or less, often by specific territories, product lines, or divisions. They are used to regulate production, materials purchases, and inventory. They also aid in planning cash requirements and establishing sales quotas.

Any forecast tries to include both facts and executive judgment. Most forecasting techniques attempt either to limit the areas in which judgment must be totally relied on or to improve the quality of judgment by reinforcing it with concrete data.[14]

FORECASTING METHODS

Forecasting methods may be divided into two broad categories: quantitative and qualitative (or subjective). *Quantitative forecasts* are based on statis-

Forecasts are estimates or predictions of future events or outcomes for a specific time period.

Quantitative forecasts are estimates or predictions of future events or outcomes that are based on statistical techniques and produce numerical forecasts.

tical techniques and produce numerical forecasts. They include such techniques as statistical trend extensions based on past data, statistical correlation, computer simulations (which are treated in detail in Chapter 7), econometrics, and mathematical programing.[15]

Qualitative forecasts may produce numerical forecasts, but they rely heavily on the subjective predictions of key executives; estimates by the field sales force; surveys of customer attitudes, opinions, and intentions; and the expectations of experts in the industry who might participate in attempts to predict future events.

Qualitative forecasts are subjective estimates or predictions of future events or outcomes based upon customer surveys, sales force estimates, key executives, and other industry experts.

Each method contains advantages in assessing an uncertain future. It is, therefore, not surprising that most organizations use a combination of methods in their attempts to produce more accurate predictions of future events.[16]

One type of qualitative forecast that has proven extremely useful in analyzing new products, planning research and development, allocating resources, and predicting scientific breakthroughs is *Delphi forecasting*. The Delphi method is based on two premises: (1) those who are most knowledgeable in a given field will make the best forecasts, and (2) the combined knowledge of several persons is better than that of one person. However, the method does not use a committee of experts but rather a panel of experts acting individually with provisions for anonymous interaction among all the experts.

Delphi forecasting is a method of forecasting in which a group of experts in a given field work individually until a consensus about the future is reached.

The method works as follows: Several experts in one field of interest are invited to participate. At first, they may be asked to list the major developments or areas of concern in their field of knowledge. From these initial inputs, a group of questions is formulated about when certain things are expected to happen (or when they will happen within a fifty-fifty chance). The experts answer the questions individually; then their answers are compiled and sent to all panel members. A second round of answers to the same questions is requested, and the panelists are urged to include statements that challenge or support predictions that fall outside the central range of answers. The process is repeated until answers stabilize. The consensus answer is indicated by the average answer of the panelists' predictions for each question. This technique has produced economic forecasts that compare favorably with those made by the most sophisticated mathematical models, and some efforts have been made to predict political and natural environmental changes.[17]

While managers are not expected to be experts in every forecasting technique, they should be thoroughly familiar with the strengths and weaknesses of each and sufficiently knowledgeable to determine situations in which one technique is superior to another. In most instances, the choice of forecasting method will depend on its purpose and the way in which it will be used. Table 4–1 shows appropriate techniques at each stage in a product's life cycle: product development; introductory stage; growth stage; and maturity stage.

TABLE 4–1   FORECASTING TECHNIQUES FOR EACH STAGE OF THE PRODUCT LIFE CYCLE

	Product Life Cycle Stage			
	Product Development	Introductory Stage	Growth Stage	Maturity Stage
	Delphi method	Consumer surveys	Tracking and warning systems	Time series analysis and projection
Forecasting Techniques	Historical analysis of comparable (substitute) products	Test market data	Market surveys	Market surveys

Source: Reprinted by permission of the *Harvard Business Review.* An exhibit from "How to Choose the Right Forecasting Technique" by John C. Chambers, Satinder K. Mullick, and Donald D. Smith (July–August 1971). Copyright © 1971 by the President and Fellows of Harvard College; all rights reserved.

ORGANIZING THE PLANNING FUNCTION

66 No plan can prevent a stupid person from doing the wrong thing in the wrong place at the wrong time—but a good plan should keep a concentration from forming. 99

Charles E. Wilson
Former president, General Motors Corporation

Planning is a major responsibility of every manager. As a result, managers at every level in the organizational hierarchy spend part of their workdays engaged in planning activities. Top management of most organizations spends greater proportions of its time engaged in planning than do middle- and supervisory-level managers, whose plans tend to be derivative. In addition, top management typically focuses its planning activities on the development of long-range strategic plans, while middle-level managers generally concentrate on planning for their divisions, and supervisory management focuses its planning activities on developing action programs to meet the goals of its divisions. Figure 4–8 shows how managers at various levels might allocate their planning activities in a typical organization.

While the figure provides an indication of the relative emphasis of different managerial levels on different types of planning, the categories are by no means exclusive. The firm's president and other members of top management are involved on a regular basis in developing short-range plans, tactical plans, and single-use plans. Similarly, department heads and other supervisors who comprise the supervisory level of management frequently develop standing plans for use in their work areas and make contributions to long-range, strategic plans.

STRUCTURING PLANNING ACTIVITIES

A number of factors affect the method used by an organization to structure its planning activities. These include the size of the organization, the

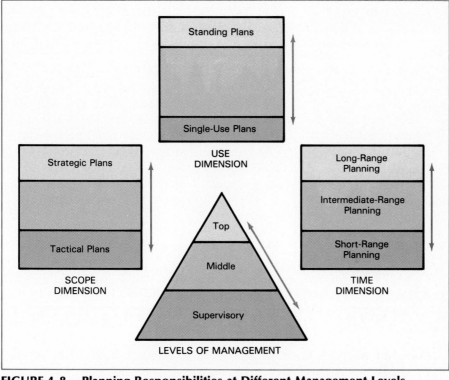

FIGURE 4–8.   Planning Responsibilities at Different Management Levels

degree of decentralization, the personality of top management, and the nature of the product.

Size of the Organization. The larger the organization, the greater the number of people and planning specialists available to plan. Smaller organizations may be forced to rely on one—or a few—managers to perform any significant planning activities. Larger organizations can afford to use planning specialists and may be in a better position to free their managers from the time required to engage in planning.

At Sonat, Inc., a Birmingham-based energy company, members of the planning staff provide expertise and perform a supporting role for each of the firm's operating units. Some firms even hire such trend-spotting firms as the Naisbitt Group, Weiner Edrich Brown, SRI International, and Perception International to assist them in their planning activities. Southwestern Bell used the Naisbitt Group's reports of the growing political and economic force of the elderly as the basis of its $100-billion decision to launch the Silver Pages, a directory of businesses catering to the elderly.[18]

COMPUTERS IN MANAGEMENT

Farming with a Computer

 If David Richardson, a hog and cattle farmer near the central Oklahoma community of Pocasset, survives today's agricultural crisis, his computer will get part of the credit.

To squeeze more out of his operations, Richardson uses a computer to calculate feed mix for his livestock, their gestation time, and when to sell their offspring for top dollar. His son Wynn, seventeen, has designed programs to write checks, keep books, and track inventories.

"Times have changed and I've got to change with them," says Richardson.

While less than 10 percent of the nation's farmers own computers, the current fiscal crunch is boosting business. Peggy Blunier, an Illinois farmer's wife, says that the only major purchase her family has made recently was a computer to monitor expenses and help them market grain. "In the 1960s and 70s, there was technology to produce more," she says. "Now, what makes the difference is how you manage."

On-Line Help. Farmers are using computers to measure a cow's milk output and to tell how much feed the animal needs. Some use the keyboard to plan how much and when to plant. Others keep an electronic eye on market prices and commodity-futures trading. Microsensor devices attached to tractors control seeding, fertilizing, and spraying of fields. One research project is testing a "talking tractor" that tells when to shift gears for fuel efficiency.

Bankers are delighted when farmers come in for loans armed with computerized spreadsheets instead of pulling a little notebook out of their back pocket. "Many farmers are running million-dollar businesses, but they're still doing arithmetic with pencils and tablets," says Henry Neal, vice-president of the production credit association in Sugar Land, Texas.

"Some of the ag high tech is pie-in-the-sky stuff," observes Lawrence Lippke of Texas A&M University. "But if the average farmer implemented even one aspect, he would see some benefit."

Source: Sarah Peterson, "One Way to Survive: Computerize," *U.S. News & World Report,* 20 May 1985, p. 75. Copyright © 1985 U.S. News & World Report. Reprinted by permission.

Degree of Decentralization. Planning in a multiproduct, decentralized organization is likely to be more diffused than in a centralized organization. Each division or production facility in a decentralized operation is likely to play a significant role in developing major plans. Although such plans may be coordinated by a planning authority located at the headquarters office, managers of decentralized organizations are likely to have more responsibility for planning than their counterparts in highly centralized operations. (The centralization–decentralization issue is discussed in detail in Chapter 9.)

The movement of planning "into the trenches" in a decentralized organization is illustrated by recent changes at one of the world's largest corporations:

> Only eight years ago, General Motors Corp. had no strategic planners in its divisions, let alone in a lowly car plant. But as Raymond K. Fears, the strategic planner for GM's Buick City complex in Flint, Michigan, amply demonstrates, times have changed. Fears, who turns thirty in mid-September, moved from GM's corporate strategic-planning group in 1983 to Buick City—the trio of sixty-year-old plants that GM aspires to turn into the world's most efficient auto factory. His assignment: "To get [operating managers], who are used to thinking in terms of nuts and bolts, to think in strategic terms." That, he concedes, "is a major educational job."
>
> Fears' transfer is part of GM Chairman Roger B. Smith's master plan to integrate strategic planning "into our daily lives." In Smith's book, that means "true integration with the operating organization."[19]

Personality of Top Management. Some top managers prefer to work with a specialized planning staff. Others desire participation from middle- and supervisory-level managers and require them to assume the major responsibility for planning.

At General Motors, staff planners have been converted to "facilitators" to help operating managers do the planning themselves. By contrast, Avery International, a Pasadena, California, manufacturer of labels, tape, and office products, has expanded its centralized planning operations from one vice-president to two. One focuses on such long-term strategic issues as competition, technology, and acquisitions. The second vice-president concentrates on operational issues. Both report directly to the firm's president.

Nature of the Product. Multiproduct companies may assign planning responsibilities to relatively low organizational levels. This may be particularly true in organizations such as department stores, where fashions and customer tastes change rapidly and where single products do not represent major portions of total sales. In the automobile industry, by contrast, planning and decision making take place at numerous levels within the organization. Such diverse subjects as design, marketing, and government regulations must be coordinated at the highest levels. Planning arrangements such as General Motors Corporation's "management by committee" approach result from this need to oversee and coordinate the inputs of numerous departments.[20]

THE USE OF STAFF PLANNING GROUPS

The growth in the size of organizations and the recognition of the importance of planning in achieving organizational objectives have led to the

Staff planning groups are specialized groups that assist managers by developing a planning system, guiding the development of corporate and divisional plans, and gathering and evaluating needed information.

development of specialized *staff planning groups* within the organization. Such groups assist the managers by developing a planning system, guiding the development of corporate and divisional plans, and gathering and evaluating needed information. These specialized groups combine many talents and can devote the time necessary to planning major, long-term activities. They can also provide an important service by coordinating the overall planning efforts of the organization, ensuring that the more specific plans at the middle- and supervisory-management levels are consistent with the broader plans developed by top management.

The advent of specialized staff planning groups is a relatively recent phenomenon. Du Pont has been in existence since 1802, but it did not establish a corporate planning staff until 1975. Although the danger always exists that some managers will accept the planning group's recommendation as a substitute for their own decisions, the use of such groups is widespread among large enterprises.[21]

TIME MANAGEMENT—ENSURING THAT MANAGERS HAVE TIME TO PLAN

❝ You may ask me for anything you like except time. ❞

Napoleon Bonaparte

An all-too-frequent barrier to effective planning is finding time to engage in planning activities. Lack of sufficient time to devote to planning is a common complaint of managers and a frequently expressed explanation for planning deficiencies. To ensure the best use of time, managers should evaluate their time use, establish priorities, and manage time effectively.

EVALUATING TIME USE

Busy managers have two alternatives in finding a way to save time: Do less or work faster. A considerable portion of most managers' daily activities could be performed by subordinates. Executives who assign tasks to subordinates may use a format such as that illustrated in Figure 4–9 to identify the amount of authority being granted to subordinates and the freedom of action granted to them.

The second method of saving time is to perform at a faster rate. Some research studies have shown that the average manager wastes two hours or more every day and that managers spend as much as 80 percent of their time on relatively unimportant matters that produce only 20 percent of the results.[22]

To improve the effectiveness of time on the job, managers should analyze how they are currently using their time. Such analysis might take the form of a logbook recording a manager's actions at fifteen- or thirty-minute intervals throughout the day. Analysis of the logbook data may prove quite revealing, especially the first time such data are collected.

The manager should then critically assess his or her use of time by asking such questions as:

- "Should I perform this task or assign it to a subordinate?"

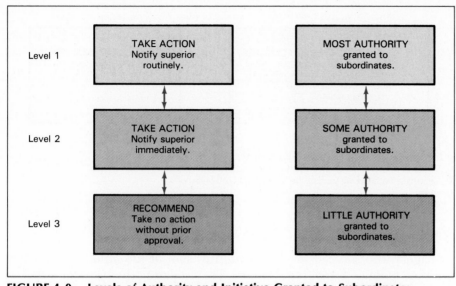

FIGURE 4–9.   Levels of Authority and Initiative Granted to Subordinates
Source: Adapted from Thomas V. Bonoma and Dennis P. Slevin, "In Pursuit of Time Management," *Managing* (# Two 79): 6. Reprinted with permission of the publisher, University of Pittsburgh Graduate School of Business.

- "Can I perform this task at a faster rate?"

- "How much of my time is wasted, and how can I reduce this waste?"

- "How can I reduce the amount of time I spend on the telephone?"

ESTABLISHING PRIORITIES

Analysis of actual time usage should be followed by the establishment of priorities. Many hard-working, enthusiastic managers are ineffective because of a lack of priorities to guide their use of time. Priorities can help prevent the following types of problems:

- The division executive who reads and deals with all of her own mail but doesn't get around to writing the working paper on the division's strategic direction.

- The production manager who spends half of every day fighting fires on the shop floor but doesn't have time to work with his staff on production planning and scheduling systems.

- The quality control director who wades through the detailed results of every quality trial but can't find the time to organize much-needed quality improvement projects.[23]

Figure 4–10 illustrates a typical approach to developing priorities.

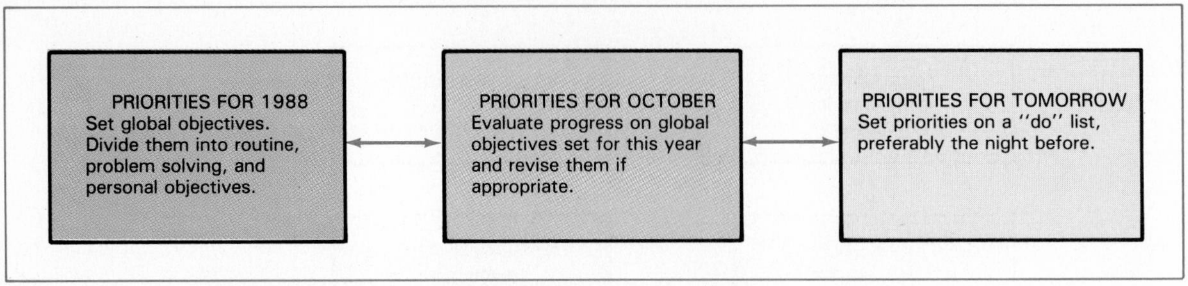

PRIORITIES FOR 1988	PRIORITIES FOR OCTOBER	PRIORITIES FOR TOMORROW
Set global objectives. Divide them into routine, problem solving, and personal objectives.	Evaluate progress on global objectives set for this year and revise them if appropriate.	Set priorities on a "do" list, preferably the night before.

FIGURE 4–10.   Establishing Priorities: Annually, Monthly, and Daily
Source: Adapted from Thomas V. Bonoma and Dennis P. Slevin, "In Pursuit of Time Management," *Managing* (# Two 79): 7. Reprinted with permission of the publisher, University of Pittsburgh Graduate School of Business.

MANAGING TIME EFFECTIVELY

Managers who succeed in solving the problem of too little time typically use time budgets for working hours. They set aside the necessary time to devote to major tasks and assign less important activities to subordinates. By separating the essential from the nonessential, they ensure that larger amounts of time are devoted to priority areas.

Two major sources of interruption are the telephone and paper flows.[24] Filtering systems should be established to protect the manager from most telephone calls while retaining access in case of emergencies. Most calls can be grouped together and returned in the late afternoon.

Time management specialists frequently recommend that a manager handle each piece of paper only once. Secretaries or assistants may be used to sort incoming mail and other paper flows into one of the three categories shown in Table 4–2. Such screening of paper flows and other interruptions should result in time savings and improved performance.

TABLE 4–2   SYSTEM FOR HANDLING PAPER FLOWS

Category	Required Action
1. Action: immediate	Read and take appropriate immediate action to dispense with the piece of paper.
2. Action: pending	If you can't take action immediately, you may place the paper in a pending file, but only after initiating action on the matter.
3. Read and distribute or discard	These are items read for information purposes. Distribute only those items that you are confident will benefit the individuals to whom you send them. (Be considerate of their time, also.) If the item is of no value, discard it.

Source: Thomas V. Bonoma and Dennis P. Slevin, "In Pursuit of Time Management," *Managing* # Two 79, p. 7. Reprinted with permission of the publisher, University of Pittsburgh Graduate School of Business.

SUMMARY

Planning is a critical function of management and a continuing responsibility of every manager. It consists of setting objectives, assessing the future, and developing courses of action designed to accomplish these objectives. Plans, the natural outgrowths of the planning process, should contain methods for controlling the implementation of the plan.

Planning is important for a number of reasons:

- Many research investigations report a positive relationship between formal planning and organizational performance.
- Plans focus attention on objectives.
- Plans help offset uncertainties and anticipate problems.
- Plans provide guidelines for decision making.
- Plans facilitate control by specifying concrete data for use in comparing actual and planned performance and by establishing early warning systems for possible plan deviations.

The numerous types of plans in any organization may be categorized on three bases: time, use, and scope (or breadth). Classifying plans on a *time* dimension involves three categories: short range (one year or less), intermediate range (between one and five years), and long range (five years or more). A classification scheme based on *use* divides plans into single-use and standing plans. Programs, projects, and budgets are all one-time, single-use plans. Standing plans are predetermined courses of action developed for repetitive situations; they include policies, procedures, and rules. The third classification method is based on *scope* (or *breadth*) and includes two types: strategic planning and tactical planning. Strategic planning focuses on what the organization will do in the future and involves determining major objectives and then adopting courses of action and allocating resources necessary to achieve these objectives. Tactical planning is much narrower in scope; its primary focus is on how the activities specified by strategic plans are to be accomplished.

Forecasts are estimates or predictions of future events or outcomes for a specified time period. Forecasting is vital in establishing a basis on which to develop plans. The forecasting period is typically tailored to the needs of the organization, and many firms develop both short- and long-term forecasts.

Forecasting methods can be divided into quantitative methods, which use statistical techniques to produce numerical forecasts, and qualitative methods, which rely more heavily on subjective predictions of executives, sales personnel, customers, and industry experts. Since forecasting typically involves the combination of facts and executive judgments, both methods play important roles in the final forecast. One type of qualitative forecasting that has proven extremely useful in analyzing new products, planning research and development, allocating resources, and predicting scientific breakthroughs is Delphi forecasting.

Although managers at every level in the organization engage in planning, top management tends to devote relatively more time to planning and is more likely to focus on the development of long-range strategic plans. Middle managers and supervisory managers tend to be involved in derivative plans for their divisions and in developing action programs to meet division goals. Planning activities in an organization are affected by the following factors:

- Size of the organization
- Degree of decentralization
- Personality of top management
- Nature of the product

Specialized planning groups or departments are frequently found in larger organizations. Although such groups are advisory in nature, they can assist the managers by developing planning systems, coordinating planning activities at the various levels of the organization, and gathering and evaluating needed information.

Effective planning requires a precious commodity: time. Managers must develop plans for using their valuable time if they are to have sufficient time to engage in planning. Time management results from a critical assessment of how the manager's time is being used and the establishment of a priority system for activities. In some cases, time management results in assigning activities that were previously performed by the managers to others in the organization and minimizing such interruptions as telephone calls and distracting, nonessential personal contacts. The result of a time management system should be the generation of sufficient time to engage in the vital process of planning.

Stouffer Foods Corp.

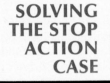

Stouffer's managers knew their starting point in developing a plan designed to move the corporation toward its objectives: consumer research. They began by interviewing current and prospective consumers to find out what dieters didn't like about diet meals.

Four objections repeatedly voiced were: The food doesn't look good; it doesn't taste good; it isn't filling; it's monotonous and drab. "They walked away from the table with a feeling that they had eaten an incomplete meal," [Stouffer representative Elena Coccari] said. So it was important to develop meals with ample portions but with less than 300 calories.

The 300-calorie hook was developed because the American Dietetic Association recommends 1,200 calories a day for women (1,600 calories for men), with 400–500 calories allotted for the main meal. Lean Cuisine, therefore, permits the consumer to enjoy a salad or other food item with his meal.

To keep the calorie count low, meats which were low in fat content had to be used. Only 21 percent of Lean Cuisine's calories come from fat, for example. Stouffer's grinds beef that is 90 percent lean for dishes calling for beef. . . .

Heavy use of vegetables was made, and extra herbs were used. Some dishes never made it out of the test kitchen. Consumer panels in Cleveland tried each dish before test marketing began in Cleveland, Cincinnati, and Columbus, Ohio; and Omaha, Denver, and Philadelphia.

Dieters dislike the word *diet* or *diet food,* and Stouffer's wanted to position the line for broader appeal anyway, so the name Lean Cuisine was chosen over four others. That kind of positioning led to the package design. To appeal to all consumers interested in eating light, a white package was chosen to distinguish the line from Stouffer's regular red boxes and to signal the light concept to shoppers.

"We target to women, but Lean Cuisine appeals to anyone interested in eating light," according to Jerry DeCroce, marketing vice president. "The target audience really is based on attitude, not demographics." Instead of selling a frozen meal per se, he said the company is selling a product that fits into the lifestyle of today's working women and smaller households. These people want quality, and they will pay a premium for convenience foods which deliver it.

Lean Cuisine was an immediate hit in test markets, Coccari said, and consumers from other markets soon were calling the company to inquire about the line. "Dieters have an amazing word of mouth network," she said. "A Chicago woman heard about Lean Cuisine while on a cruise ship, and she called us and wanted us to ship the product to her because she felt left out."

By the time the product was introduced nationally in 1982, Lean Cuisine was on its way to a classic product success. Sales were triple the anticipated amount and the firm's production managers had to scramble to meet demand. By 1983, Stouffer's share of the $500-million frozen entree market had soared from 33 percent to 46 percent. About half of its sales came from the Lean Cuisine line. Cautious, deliberate, step-by-step planning had paid off.

Source: Paragraphs 2–7 from Kevin Higgins, "Meticulous Planning Pays Dividends at Stouffer's," *Marketing News,* 28 October 1983, pp. 1, 20. Reprinted by permission.

FACT OR FICTION REVEALED

1. Fact   2. Fiction   3. Fiction   4. Fact   5. Fact   6. Fiction   7. Fiction

MANAGEMENT TERMS

planning	**program**	**strategic planning**
plans	**project**	**tactical planning**
decision making	**budget**	**forecasts**
contingency plan	**standing plans**	**quantitative forecasts**
controlling	**policies**	**qualitative forecasts**
commitment principle	**procedures**	**Delphi forecasting**
single-use plans	**rules**	**staff planning groups**

REVIEW QUESTIONS

1. Distinguish between:
   a. plans and planning
   b. planning and decision making
   c. plans and contingency plans

2. What are the chief benefits of planning?

3. Identify and explain the three methods for classifying plans.

4. Distinguish between short-range, intermediate-range, and long-range plans. Include an example of each type.

5. Categorize the following plans on the basis of use:
   a. rule
   b. program
   c. project
   d. procedure
   e. budget

6. Distinguish between strategic planning and tactical planning.

7. Identify the two categories of forecasting methods and give two examples of each.

8. Identify the factors that collectively determine how an organization will structure its planning activities.

9. Explain the contributions that can be made by staff planning groups. What are the potential dangers facing organizations that use these planning specialists?

10. Relate the concept of time management to planning.

PROBLEMS AND EXPERIENTIAL EXERCISES

1. "I keep six honest serving men
   They taught me all I knew:
   Their names are What and Why and When
   and How and Where and Who."[25]

   Rudyard Kipling

   Refer to the questions in Kipling's poem. Provide a one- or two-sentence answer to each question by relating the questions to the appropriate part of Chapter 4.

2. Confusion is possible concerning the meaning of the following terms:
   a. *plans* and *planning*
   b. *planning* and *decision making*

   Explain how to avoid confusion by contrasting each term. Include examples to emphasize the difference in the terms.

3. This chapter discussed several factors that affect the planning activities of an organization and the

approaches that might be used. Briefly explain each factor and provide an example from your own experiences of how these factors affect organizational planning.

4. Give an example of a strategic plan, tactical plan, policy, procedure, rule, program, project, and budget that might be appropriate for each of the following:

a. Atari Division of Warner Communications
b. The Boeing Company
c. Kinney Shoes retail outlet
d. Baltimore Museum of Art

5. Prepare a log book of your activities for a single day. Use your logbook analysis to explain how you could apply time management concepts to your activities.

MANAGERIAL INCIDENT: Piedmont Aviation, Inc.

By now everybody knows that People Express has been the fastest-growing airline since deregulation opened the skies to all-out competition. But which is second? Here are a few hints: It's based in Winston-Salem, N. C., sports a bluebird on the tail of its planes, and has a 63-year-old chief executive who collects antique cars and motorcycles as avidly as his passengers go after frequent-flier coupons.

Give up? It's Piedmont Aviation Inc. Since 1978, Piedmont has grown from a regional airline serving the mid-Atlantic to one that blankets the East and much of the Midwest. Revenues will hit around $1.4 billion this year, up sixfold from $204 million in 1978, while Piedmont's 1984 net margin was the third-highest among major airlines. Last year earnings were a record $58.2 million, and this year should be even better. Says Marc Klee, an analyst with National Aviation & Technology Corp., an aviation stock mutual fund: "Piedmont will show well-above-average growth for the next several years."

But it won't be easy. People Express Airlines Inc. has horned in on its turf. And rampant fare wars are already taking their toll on Piedmont's profits. Although net income was up 20%, to $50.7 million, for the first nine months of 1985, operating earnings dropped 12½%, to $87 million. The entire net gain comes from lower interest costs and a $25 million investment tax credit.

CAPTIVE CUSTOMERS. To counterattack, Piedmont is spreading its wings farther north and south. It recently bought Empire Airlines Inc., a small carrier in New York, and has launched an innovative commuter network in Florida, linking 12 cities there with small, cost-efficient jets.

Until now, Piedmont has prospered by keeping out of harm's way. Since deregulation, the big airlines have tried to muscle in on each other's largest markets. But Chief Executive William R. Howard, hired from Eastern seven years ago, knew Piedmont was too small to do that. Instead, Piedmont flies into large cities from dozens of small and medium-size cities ignored by the biggies. On over half of its nonstop routes, no other carrier flies comparable jet service.

Howard also skirted competition by building hubs in Baltimore, Dayton, and Charlotte, N. C. Since it is the dominant carrier at those airports, Piedmont keeps 95% of its passengers making connecting flights. The result: Piedmont has maintained strong margins and until recently, avoided the fare wars dragging other carriers into the red.

Howard's strategy worked so well, in fact, that other airlines are moving in on Piedmont's territory. In June, People Express set up shop across the terminal in Dayton and Charlotte—it now flies on 30% of Piedmont's routes. "We've been heavily impacted by People Express," Howard admits, adding that People caused much of the dent

in Piedmont's third-quarter operating earnings.

Piedmont faces an even tougher challenge from American Airlines Inc., the nation's most profitable major carrier. American plans to lure passengers from Piedmont's Charlotte and Baltimore hubs when it opens its new hub at Raleigh-Durham, N. C., in mid-1987. Piedmont, predicts Wesley G. Kaldahl, American's senior vice-president for airline planning, will be one of "the carriers to feel the slowdown in growth most."

But Piedmont has been busily expanding as well. It will spend an estimated $735 million to buy 35 Boeing 737-300s in the next

three years so that it can add flights throughout its route system. The first push is already starting. By January, Piedmont will operate 94 flights daily between 12 cities in Florida. Until the carrier expanded, business travelers there had to rely on slower commuter planes or flights at odd hours on major carriers. By providing timely early-morning and late-evening jet service, Howard claims, Piedmont turned a profit only two weeks after it opened its doors in Florida in October.

The flights have already nicked Piedmont's competitors. Eastern will begin jet service in mid-December between Key West and Miami, a new Piedmont route. "We have felt some pressure from Piedmont within the state," admits Paul C. Auger, an Eastern marketing vice-president. And Provincetown-Boston Airline Inc., Florida's biggest commuter, dropped about half of its Tampa-Jacksonville flights after Piedmont entered the market. PBA, however, has other problems: A fatal plane crash in December, 1984, forced the company into Chapter 11 bankruptcy reorganization.

Howard says the Florida routes will add $100 million to revenues in 1986. To make sure they generate profits, too, Piedmont is crisscrossing the state with 65-seat jets instead of conventional Boeing 727-200s. The smaller jets cost less to operate than the 150-seaters typically used on short-haul flights. Piedmont can make money filling only 40% of the seats on the little planes, for example, while its bigger jets don't break even until 46% of the seats are filled.

FEEDING TIME. Up north, Piedmont will pick up passengers through Empire, a commuter line based in Utica, N. Y. But more important, Howard wants to feed the new customers from the Northeast and Florida into Piedmont's existing routes. Empire doesn't share a single route with Piedmont. Howard is trying to hook its 1.2 million passengers a year into other Piedmont flights by linking them up at the Baltimore hub. If all goes well, Howard projects Piedmont will double in size, to roughly $2.5 billion in revenues, by yearend 1988.

But getting there won't be all smooth sailing. Both People Express and USAir Inc. fly on many of Empire's routes. USAir is also trying to build its business by funneling people from small cities in New York down to the rest of the East Coast. Because of the competition, Empire lost $1.4 million through the first nine months of 1985.

With its solid growth record, Piedmont has expanded without financial strain. Debt as a percentage of capital is down to 52% from 64% in 1983, although Piedmont will borrow another $100 million in 1986 for new planes. But some observers worry that it may be striking out in too many directions at once. Says analyst Klee: "The question now is whether they can manage the system they've built."

Howard, a cherubic-looking man who made his first solo flight at age 16 in a yellow Piper J3 Cub, has no doubt Piedmont will be ready for the coming battle for passengers. He is beefing up flights out of Raleigh-Durham and argues that his Charlotte and Baltimore routes will be out of American's range. Howard plans to open a fourth hub in late 1986. He hasn't chosen a site yet, but Piedmont has talked informally with officials in Wichita. And margins will be up in the fourth quarter: After its initial splash in Dayton and Charlotte, People raised fares and pulled back slightly on competing routes. Nonetheless, Howard may be forced to chart a different course for Piedmont.

His days of skirting the competition are ending—the competition is flying straight at him.

Questions and Problems

1. A number of benefits that result from planning are discussed in the chapter. List these benefits and indicate how Piedmont's actions can be related to each.

2. Explain how the decisions made by Piedmont's chief executive William R. How-

ard are likely to affect Piedmont's future performance. What potential dangers are present?

3. Make additional recommendations that Piedmont Aviation should consider in its attempts to maintain and improve its competitive position.

Source: Scott Scredon and Jane Sasseen, "Piedmont's Secret for Success Isn't a Secret Anymore." Reprinted from December 9, 1985, issue of *Business Week* by special permission, © 1985 by McGraw-Hill, Inc.

CHAPTER

5 STRATEGIC PLANNING AND ORGANIZATIONAL OBJECTIVES

LEARNING OBJECTIVES

After studying this chapter you should be able to

1. Distinguish between strategic planning and tactical planning.

2. Identify the steps in the strategic planning process.

3. Distinguish between *mission* and *objective* and identify the major contributions of objectives in improving organizational effectiveness.

4. List the steps involved in the management by objectives (MBO) process and identify the chief benefits of MBO as well as the common problems encountered in installing an MBO program.

5. Distinguish between corporate strategies, business strategies, and functional strategies.

6. Explain the role of the strategic business unit (SBU) concept in strategic planning.

7. List the names and characteristics of products and businesses in each cell of the SBU market growth/market share matrix.

BMW of North America

Even though BMW is scarcely one-third as large as its Munich neighbor, Mercedes-Benz, the two competitors have virtually identical market shares in the highly profitable U.S. market. During 1985, the two German car makers sold an estimated 87,000 models in the United States. BMW's per car profit in the United States is estimated at $2,900. Although one of BMW's 300-series cars sells for about $9,600 in Germany, the addition of EPA-mandated anti-pollution devices and other options that are included as standard equipment pushes the retail price of the car to approximately $19,500 in the United States.

The BMW, with its image of handling, engineering technology, and prestige, has long been a favorite of the Yuppie market. As one writer put it, "BMWs are so closely identified with under-forty, affluent, urban professionals that they can be 'worn' as a badge of success. BMW plays off that in a magazine headline, 'Winning isn't everything, but the trophies do have a certain appeal.'"

The growth in sales of both BMW and Mercedes-Benz to younger, more affluent U.S. buyers has been at the expense of domestic luxury cars. Over the past ten years, Cadillac's market share has declined by almost one-third as buyers turned to both European and Japanese models for quality, road performance, and perceived value. As a recent *Business Week* article pointed out, "That is precisely what Cadillac seems to lack. The car has not shaken its stodgy, 'grandpa's car' image among younger consumers, many of whom think imports are sportier and provide more value for the dollar." That helps account for the popularity of the Maxima and Cressida, which compete primarily against such American midsize models as the Buick Century and the Oldsmobile Cutlass. Notes the general manager of a Toyota dealership in Detroit: "We transfer a lot of Cadillac-type buyers into the Cressida because it's a little cheaper, and the quality of the car is much, much better."

But the Japanese car makers, who have produced almost two decades of nightmares for Detroit, are also anxious to secure a share of the U.S. luxury car market. Even though the Japanese strengths have traditionally been at the lower ends of the auto market with their emphasis on high-quality, competitively priced compacts and subcompacts, their most expensive cars—such as the Nissan Maxima and the Toyota Cressida—earn their manufacturers an average of almost $6,000 per sale.

The first wave of Japanese models aimed at the top-of-the-line market came ashore in 1986 in the form of the Honda Legend, an $18,000 executive luxury car, and Honda's sportier Integra. To avoid a clouded image for these cars and Honda's established U.S. dealers, a separate marketing unit called Acura was established and separate showrooms were opened. The Honda plan even stipulated that the Acura showrooms must be located at least ten miles from the nearest Honda showroom. Although the new models were intended to provide some competition to the Audi 5000 and the Mercedes-Benz 190 "baby Benz," the precise target was BMW's four-cylinder BMW 318i. While purists argued that the 11.6 seconds the new models took to accelerate from zero to sixty miles per hour was much too slow to match the BMW image, 50,273 of the cars were sold in the United States within two years following their late 1983 introduction.

But the Honda luxury cars were merely the first among many six-cylinder top-of-the-line Japanese imports. The Mazda 929 and new models from Nissan, Mitsubishi, and Toyota are expected to be available in the United States by 1989. BMW's managers, who are heavily dependent on the U.S. market, prepared to defend themselves against the Japanese attack.

Use the concepts discussed in this chapter to suggest strategic and tactical planning decisions to aid BMW managers in protecting their market.

Sources: Quotation in paragraph two from Jesse Snyder, "BMW Accelerates Plan to Defend Its Turf," *Advertising Age,* 25 November 1985, p. 53. Quotation in paragraph three from "Detroit Beware: Japan Is Ready to Sell Luxury," *Business Week,* 9 December 1985, p. 118. Estimates in paragraph one from "BMW's Plan to Avoid Being Flattened by Mercedes," *Business Week,* 9 December 1985, p. 53.

The critical subject of planning was introduced in the previous chapter. Plans were classified on three bases: time, use, and scope or breadth. The chapter also examined the subject of forecasting and discussed the use of both quantitative and qualitative techniques for developing estimates or predictions of future events or outcomes that serve as bases for the planning process. Finally, the importance of time management in ensuring that managers have sufficient time to engage in planning activities was discussed. This chapter continues the treatment of the planning function by focusing on two vital planning elements for every organization: strategic planning and the formulation of organizational objectives.

Strategic planning is the process of determining the major objectives of an organization and then adopting the courses of action and allocating the resources necessary to achieve those objectives.

In Chapter 4, *strategic planning* was defined as the process of determining the major objectives of an organization and then adopting the courses of action and allocating the resources necessary to achieve those objectives.[1] The word *strategy* is derived from the Greek word *strategos,* meaning "the art of the general." Strategic plans provide the organization with long-range direction. They focus on relatively uncontrollable environmental factors that affect the achievement of organizational objectives. Although strategic planning is generally associated with long-range planning, it is also involved in such short- and intermediate-range questions as whether to merge with another organization or whether to broaden activities from a domestic to an international market.[2]

The strategic planning process develops answers to three questions:

- Where are we now?

- Where do we want to be at a specified future date?

- How will we get there?

MANAGEMENT FACT OR FICTION

	FACT	FICTION
1. The term *mission* refers to a broader concept than does the term *objective*.	☐	☐
2. While more firms are likely to list social responsibility as a corporate objective today than in the past, more firms today also list growth and profitability as specific objectives.	☐	☐
3. If objectives are measurable, they are too specific.	☐	☐
4. One shortcoming of MBO programs is that since each member of the organization is responsible for selecting his or her individual objectives for the year, the		

	FACT	FICTION
chosen objectives may not mesh with overall organizational objectives.	☐	☐
5. The strategic-window concept is more applicable in the automobile and construction industries than in extractive industries and firms that provide services.	☐	☐
6. The four categories of strategic business units are cash cows, stars, kittens, and dogs.	☐	☐
7. As a pet, dogs are often called "man's best friend." As an SBU category, they are also a business firm's best friend.	☐	☐

The materials in this chapter will assist you in separating management fact from fiction. Your answers can be checked on page 148.

Answers to the first question are developed from data on current operations. Information concerning the organization's financial status, current market share, and relative strengths and weaknesses (human, financial, material) is utilized in an overall assessment of the firm's present position in relation to organizational objectives. This assessment is important in answering the second question and developing premises related to these objectives. Forecasts of market growth, economic conditions, political and legal changes, and technological developments—all discussed in Chapters 3 and 4—are invaluable in the development of strategic plans.

66 Business is like war in one respect. If its grand strategy is correct, any number of tactical errors can be made and yet the enterprise proves successful. **99**

Gen. Robert E. Wood
Former president, Sears, Roebuck & Co.

Answering the third question involves determining the activities necessary to achieve established goals. It requires the planner to identify resources necessary to implement the plan as well as establishing a monitoring system to review actual performance and inform management of possible adjustments that should be made in the plan.

The final steps in the strategic planning process involve choosing the most appropriate strategy to use in accomplishing organizational objectives and methods to implement and control the selected strategy. The chosen strategy becomes the basis of annual plans, budgets, and policies and procedures used throughout the organization. It serves as a grand design for guiding the firm's management in decisions and activities.

Implementation is the subject of Chapters 6 and 7 on decision making, as well as Chapters 8 through 15 on organizing, staffing, and leading. The final component, controlling, is treated in detail in Chapters 16 through 18.

In discussing the importance of strategic planning in the accomplishment of organizational objectives, it is equally important to understand what is *not* strategic planning. According to Peter Drucker:

- Strategic planning is *not* applying quantitative techniques to business decisions. It is analytical thinking and a commitment of resources to action.

- It is *not* forecasting. Drucker stresses that strategic planning is necessary *because* of the difficulty of forecasting beyond a relatively short time period with any degree of precision. Forecasts are regularly upset by entrepreneurs who develop innovations that, by definition, alter the course of economic, political, and social events.

- Strategic planning does *not* eliminate risk. It aids managers in weighing the risks they must take.[3]

STRATEGIC PLANNING VERSUS TACTICAL PLANNING

Tactical planning is a type of planning that focuses on short-term implementation of current and pending activities and the allocation of resources for those activities.

The outcome of strategic planning is to provide the organization with an overall context for the development of more specific plans, policies, forecasts, and budgets. While strategic planning focuses on what the organization will be doing in the long term, *tactical planning* places emphasis on how these activities will be accomplished in the short term. Tactical planning is concerned with current and pending activities, focusing on the effective allocation of resources to assure their implementation. While wars are guided by strategic planning, single battles may be won (or lost) due to tactical planning.

One writer, using the military analogy, contrasted strategy and tactics as follows:

Strategy may be defined simply as "doing the right thing." It deals with the allocation of resources to the battle. In his famous book, *On War,* Clausewitz says that strategy sets the point *where,* the time *when,* and the force *with which* the battle is fought. . . . Tactics is best defined as "doing things right." It deals with the deployment of resources. . . .[4]

Although strategic and tactical planning are different, both should be integrated into an overall system designed to accomplish organizational objectives. Strategic plans form the basis for the development of tactics. American Hospital Supply Co. managers incorporate both types of planning into an overall corporate plan. A five-year strategic plan is established, and tactical plans for the next twelve months are then developed. Because of rapid environmental changes, the assumptions of the five-year plan are reviewed annually, and the plan is reworked. By reviewing and adjusting plans annually, American Hospital Supply Co. decision makers can keep both strategic and tactical plans sufficiently flexible, permitting their adjustment to changing environmental factors while maintaining their focus on organizational objectives.[5]

Whenever possible, plans should contain built-in means of changing direction in response to unexpected environmental developments. Such flexibility is particularly valuable in long-range strategic planning, where unexpected future events may disrupt operations. The ability to shift direction is built into the strategic plans at Westinghouse Electric. The firm's strategic plans contain built-in "milestones," points at which adjustments can be made in response to changes in environmental factors. Publius Syrus noted the importance of flexibility 2,000 years ago: "It is a bad plan that admits of no modification."[6]

STEPS IN THE STRATEGIC PLANNING PROCESS ▬

Strategic planning involves both the development of organizational objectives and specifications for how they will be accomplished. Development of strategic plans forces managers to broaden their concerns from an exclusive focus on short-range matters to an examination of broad organizational issues. The six steps involved in the strategic planning process are identified in Figure 5–1.

DEFINING THE MISSION OF THE ORGANIZATION ▪

To determine the more specific objectives and goals, a firm must first assess its mission. "The *mission* of a business is the fundamental, unique purpose that sets it apart from other firms of its type and that identifies the scope of its operations in product and market terms. The mission is a general, enduring statement of company intent."[7] Each enterprise ex-

Mission is a general, enduring statement of company intent.

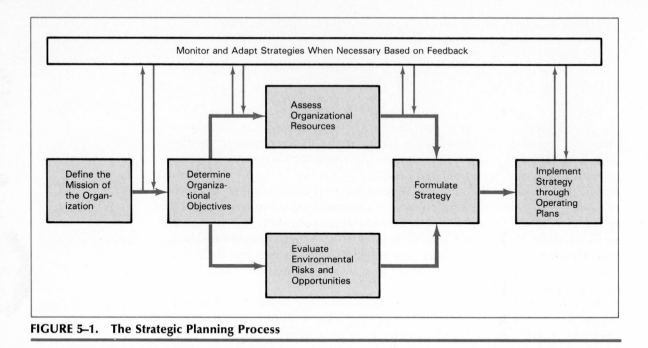

FIGURE 5–1.   The Strategic Planning Process

presses its mission in its own unique way, but the tendency is to express what the company is and why it exists. The following examples illustrate how firms define their business, their markets, and even how they will conduct their affairs.

> *McCormick & Company* will seek overall growth both from businesses in which it is now engaged, as well as new businesses. We define new businesses as products, services, customers, geography, or channels of distribution. However, these businesses will be relatable to and compatible with the areas or activity where we have strengths, are comfortable, and can perform well. Our "niche" will continue to be flavors, seasonings, and specialty food, and the company will continue to pursue these opportunities within the food industry. . . .[8]

> The mission of *Northwestern Mutual Life* is to deliver high-quality insurance and financial products to its policyowners through personalized, value-added service.[9]

> The purpose of *Simmonds Precision* is to conduct our business in such a way that we are considered an outstanding company by, among others, our employees, our parent company, our suppliers, and the communities in which we operate. We will provide our customers with a series of essential and distinct high-quality products and services, and in so doing, earn significant profits and a high return on invested capital. . . . We intend to make management in the '80s an increasingly participative process at all levels

throughout the company. . . . We will be a demanding organization which always strives for excellence, rather than efficient mediocrity. We place a high value on an environment inside the company which encourages individual development and promotes dignity and respect for each employee. We recognize and reward individual and group initiative and performance. We believe strongly in the free enterprise system, in defending that system, and in the purification process of the marketplace. We accept the social responsibilities of business. In our commitment to be an outstanding company, we reject the use of any unethical methods to achieve success. We are as dedicated to the quality of the process as we are to the result itself and to managing our business according to these principles.[10]

These written mission statements identify the uniqueness that has led to the creation of the organization and serve as reference points for future decisions. They represent the foundation for priorities, strategies, plans, and work assignments. Although the mission of a firm can be modified over time to reflect changing environmental conditions or different managerial philosophies, it always serves as a reference point for managerial thought and action at a specific point in time.

NEED FOR SPECIFIC DEFINITION OF THE FIRM'S BUSINESS

Mission statements should be sufficiently narrow to help the company determine its proper market niche. One of the easiest ways to fail is to attempt to satisfy everyone. Because of the different characteristics of customers and geographic areas, and varying product preferences, a firm attempting to satisfy a large group of diverse customers is forced to make compromise decisions in virtually every aspect of its pricing, product features, and service policies. Consequently, it finds itself failing to satisfy anyone completely. Other competitors are likely to move into the industry and develop plans that involve focusing on narrow market niches. And the original firm, in its attempt to retain a large, diverse market, frequently finds this market disappearing into smaller slices being served by other firms with narrower focuses.

In 1985, the British conglomerate Imperial Group sold its Howard Johnson hotel/restaurant subsidiary for less than 50 percent of the $630 million it had paid for the firm back in 1979. The buyer, Marriott, began the process of dismantling the company by converting the 418 company-owned HoJo restaurants to its own Big Boy franchise and selling off the motels and franchised restaurants to Prime Motor Inns. How did the well-known chain reach this end? In 1965, Howard Johnson's sales exceeded the combined sales of McDonald's, Burger King, and Kentucky Fried Chicken. But its demise can be blamed on competitors with narrower focuses. As a *Forbes* article described it:

When franchised operators began expanding the motor lodges to 200 rooms and more, the chemistry changed. Now came a second set of customers, business travelers. Business travelers didn't want a frank and a soda; and they didn't want to sit next to a noisy kid with a sticky face. The business types wanted a drink and a steak, and maybe a little action in the bar. The HoJo restaurant offered them little. . . . Down the street, competitors such as Marriott were starting from scratch, busily building motels and restaurants as packages tailored to carefully selected markets.

Meanwhile, HoJo couldn't counter what Ray Kroc, the dynamo behind McDonald's, was doing to the food market. "We fooled with fast food for a while," [company president and son of the company's founder] Johnson recalls, "but we put our HoJo Junctions in the wrong place, out on the highway, instead of in town. . . ."

But had Howard Johnson successfully concentrated solely on coffee shops, for instance, it might have been another Denny's, now the nation's largest coffee shop operator. Certainly, Denny's expanded rapidly. But it also evolved. While Denny's offers regionally flavored dinners and low cholesterol entrees, HoJo's standard fare seems unexceptional and its menu graphics strangely outdated. Says Denny's [chairman Vern] Curtis, "If you're not willing to adapt to a changing market, the world is going to pass you by. I don't see a lot of difference between the Howard Johnson's of today and that of ten to twelve years ago."[11]

DEVELOPING ORGANIZATIONAL OBJECTIVES

Objectives define standards for what the organization should accomplish and provide direction and motivation.

Once the firm's mission has been determined, it is translated into more concrete objectives. *Objectives* represent the desired outcome that management hopes to attain eventually. They are more specific than missions and often include a time schedule for completion. Objectives represent the specific means by which an organization's mission is achieved. Plans are developed to accomplish them. Policies, procedures, and performance standards all result from objectives. Control methods are based upon comparisons of performance with expectations.

In Chapter 1, management was defined as the use of people and other resources to accomplish organizational objectives. Determining objectives is a primary management responsibility. Objectives become guideposts in defining standards of what the organization should accomplish in such areas as customer service, profitability, and social responsibility. Without clearly stated objectives, no means exist to make these evaluations. As the Cheshire Cat told Alice in Lewis Carroll's *Alice in Wonderland,* "If you don't know where you are going, any road will get you there."

Objectives improve the effectiveness of an organization by producing three major benefits:

Objectives Provide Direction. Clearly defined objectives specify an end result for the organization. In the same way that the beacon of a lighthouse guides ship captains to safety, objectives direct the efforts of managers into certain channels in the pursuit of these objectives.

MANAGEMENT FAILURES

Parker Pen Company

 The failure was so great that the company even changed its name. The Parker pen, which celebrates its one hundredth birthday in 1988, had become the victim of dreadful planning that had seriously tarnished its image as a prestigious writing instrument. In 1985, top management at the Janesville, Wisconsin-based firm decided that its limited funds should be earmarked for its thriving temporary help subsidiary and that the company would be renamed Manpower, Inc. The pen business was sold to several of the firm's European managers, who continued to operate as Parker Pen Co.

Why had the Parker pen fallen on such hard times? Serious blunders among the firm's management during the 1970s led them to take on such low-priced competitors as Paper Mate and Bic in a vain attempt to compete profitably in the disposable pen marketplace on a price basis. The plan failed and, even worse, seriously tarnished the Parker image among status-conscious purchasers. The result was a virtual surrender of the prestige market in the United States to A. T. Cross Co. By 1985, United States sales had declined to only 20 percent of Parker's annual totals. As one book on product image points out, "It's bad enough when other companies take your position away; it's worse when you do it to yourself!"

But the image problems are largely limited to the United States, and the prestige associated with the Parker pen continues in 160 other countries. The new owners of the firm benefit from heavy discounts they received when they purchased Parker's manufacturing facilities in France, England, and Wisconsin. Even more lucrative is the efficiency of the plants, which benefit from approximately $30 million invested over the last four years for automation and modernization. The firm's new owners have no plans to tamper with the pen's quality image in its worldwide market.

Sources: Quotation in paragraph two is from Al Ries and Jack Trout, *Positioning: The Battle for Your Mind* (New York: McGraw-Hill, 1981), p. 120. The sale of the pen division is described in Subrata N. Chakravarty, "No Place for Sentiment," *Forbes,* 16 December 1985, pp. 136-138.

Objectives Serve as Standards. A temperature of 70° Fahrenheit reflects the homeowner's standard for a comfortable setting. In a similar manner, objectives serve as standards for the manager. Accomplishments can be measured against these standards and performances can be evaluated. Without clearly defined objectives to serve as standards, managers possess no tools for evaluating performance; no means of deciding whether work is satisfactory or unacceptable.

Objectives Serve as Motivators. In addition to serving as standards and providing direction, objectives perform a role in encouraging workers to put forth their best efforts to achieve the end goals.[12] Employees who understand the objective of profitability and their role in generating profits may be motivated to work harder or more efficiently under a bonus or other profit-sharing program. Mangement professor Edwin A. Locke argues that, so long as people view objectives as instrumental in achieving their own personal needs, they serve as powerful motivators.[13]

CHARACTERISTICS OF SOUNDLY CONCEIVED OBJECTIVES

Objectives are derived from the general organizational aims of profitability, market position, customer service, human resources development, growth, public attitudes, and aims related to the general public and the environment. Soundly conceived objectives possess a number of common characteristics.

Specificity. Objectives should be specific. Perhaps the most common weakness of organizational objectives is that they are stated in too general terms. While some flexibility is desirable, objectives that are too general become little more than platitudes. An organizational aim of growth must be reflected in specific objectives specifying what is meant by growth. Specific growth objectives could then specify adequate sales growth ("a 5 percent sales increase over last year"), market position ("attain a 15 percent share of the market by 1989"), and profitability ("a 10 percent increase in profits over last year"). Specific high-level objectives also simplify the process of setting objectives by lower levels in the organization.

Measurability. A second characteristic of soundly conceived objectives is that they have built-in performance indicators. An objective of increasing market share by 5 percent during the next fiscal year allows each manager to measure progress during the year and to compare performance with expectations. It also implies specific actions for all of those persons involved in activities affecting the accomplishment of the objective. In contrast, a general objective of increased market share is of little value since its meaning will differ with different people. Both a 1 percent increase and a 40 percent increase in market share would meet the general objective. The measurable objectives provide mutual understanding and a definite basis for comparing actual performance with expectations. Four examples of specific measurable objectives by well-known firms are listed in Figure 5–2.

Some objectives are more difficult to measure than others. How can a manager make such objectives as improved employee morale, good corporate citizenship, and provision of a safe workplace measurable? Although it is more difficult to translate these objectives into measurable terms than sales and profit objectives, it is certainly not impossible. Employee safety might be translated into an objective of reducing employee workdays lost as a result of accidents by 5 percent over the previous year. Employee morale may be reflected in terms of absenteeism or turnover,

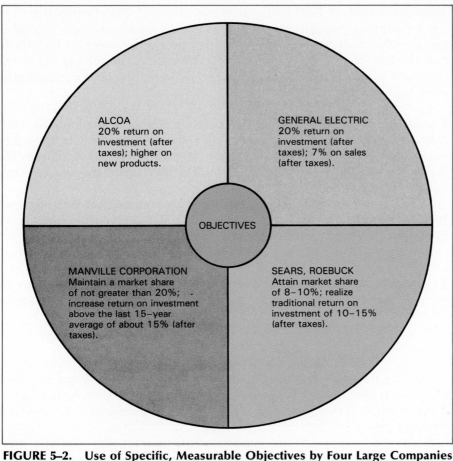

FIGURE 5–2.   Use of Specific, Measurable Objectives by Four Large Companies
Source: Data from Robert F. Lanzillotti, ''Pricing Objectives in Large Companies,'' *American Economic Review* (December 1958): 921–940.

and specific objectives may be developed to apply to these areas. Corporate citizenship may be reflected in the number of hours employees devote to civic roles, reduction of pollution by a stated amount, or the hiring of hard-core unemployed. Once measurements are determined, management can establish control procedures to determine whether performance is acceptable in each area.

Time-Specific. Objectives should also be time-specific. They should have time frames within which they will be accomplished. In addition to being measurable, objectives should indicate the period in which they are to be attained. Within the organization, objectives may be set on a daily, weekly, and annual basis.

Focus on Results. A fourth characteristic of sound objectives is that they focus on results, not activities. Activities are the means by which objectives are accomplished. Additional training for production workers may facilitate the accomplishment of the firm's objective of improving employee productivity by 5 percent within the year. However, the objective continues to be the productivity increase.

Challenging but Realistic. Objectives that are unrealistically high are ineffective as soon as employees realize they are unattainable. On the other hand, those objectives that call for the best efforts of all employees for their accomplishment provide a sense of achievement and are effective means for motivating people.

Management must ensure that objectives are communicated to all members of the organization. Each employee should understand how his or her individual work objectives relate to the overall organizational objectives. Objectives should not be so numerous or complex that they confuse rather than direct members of the organization. Management must also be prepared to periodically refine—or even replace—objectives with new ones. As the organization and the environment in which it operates change, objectives may require adjustments to reflect these changes.

TYPES OF OBJECTIVES

"What are the objectives of business?" Ask ten people this question and the most typical answer is "profits." The success stories of such firms as Twentieth Century-Fox and IBM are typically summarized in sales and profit figures.

But profits are not the only objective of an organization—even a business organization. Peter Drucker argues that profits are not even a major objective.

> There is only one valid definition of business purpose: to create a customer. . . . What the business thinks it produces is not of first importance— especially not to the future of the business and to its success. What the customer thinks he is buying, what he considers "value" is decisive—it determines what a business is, what it produces, and whether it will prosper.[14]

Henry Ford was even more adamant that profits are merely a means to an end. He had formed Ford Motor Company with a simple—but specific—objective in mind: to provide the American public with inexpensive transportation. According to Ford, "If one does this, one can hardly get away from profits."

Profits are obviously necessary for the survival of a business firm. But profitability may also be viewed as a measure of the firm's ability to serve its customers by providing desired goods and services. Customer service is of equal importance in the nonprofit organization.

MANAGEMENT SUCCESSES

Carlson Companies

 For the past fifty years, Curt Carlson has been setting goals for himself. Goal setting began in a small way in 1937 when he began selling soap for Procter & Gamble to grocery stores for eighty-five dollars a month. He noticed that some stores were generating considerable increases in sales by offering trading stamps and decided there was room for another trading stamp company that concentrated on the grocery field. His company, the Gold Bond Stamp Company, was started in Minneapolis with $50 in borrowed funds. Carlson recorded his goals for the company on a piece of paper and put it in his wallet.

Soon the company had grown to the point where Carlson could quit the job at P&G and expand beyond his native Minneapolis. Having reached his first goal, he replaced the paper in his wallet with another one. In 1952, Carlson signed up Super Valu, his first large grocery chain. Others followed in the next few years, and he soon earned his first million. By this time, he had replaced the paper-in-the-wallet technique with a giant wall chart in his company headquarters. But he continued his practice of replacing accomplished goals immediately with new ones.

When trading stamps began to lose favor in the mid-1960s, Carlson diversified by acquiring the Radisson Hotel in Minneapolis and building it into a twenty-five-unit "collection." Today, his privately owned Carlson Companies generates nearly $3 billion in annual sales in a diverse range of businesses that include hotels, catalog showrooms, restaurants, sales incentive and motivational programs, property

development, manufacturing, travel agencies, and construction.

Carlson Companies employs more than 45,000 people and ranks among the top 15 privately owned businesses in the United States. The firm's wall chart of goals, which lays out company goals by years, occupies a prominent location at headquarters and is updated on a regular basis. At the top of the chart is the current goal: "$4 billion by '87."

Sources: Current data provided by Thomas J. Polski, Public Relations Director of Carlson Companies. See also Maurice Barnfather, "Capital Formation," *Forbes*, 29 March 1982, pp. 94-95.

Short-range objectives are organizational aims to be accomplished within a period of one year or less.

Long-range objectives are organizational aims to be achieved within a time period longer than one year.

External objectives are organizational aims focusing upon service to customers and to society as a whole.

Internal objectives are organizational aims designed to satisfy groups within the organization.

Social objectives are organizational aims designed with the larger interests of society in mind.

Short-Range and Long-Range Objectives. Some of the firm's objectives may be labeled *short range,* since they refer to a time period of one year or less. Intermedics, Inc., has achieved rapid growth since it introduced the first small lithium-battery pacemaker in 1976, increasing the life of heart-regulating implants from two years to six or more. Its corporate objective for the current year is a sales increase of 30 to 40 percent over last year's sales. However, its long-term objective is to capture the number one position in the medical implants industry by surpassing the leader, Johnson & Johnson's Iolab, Inc., in sales. Since Intermedics' top management feels that achieving this aim will take more than a single year, this represents a *long-range* objective.[15]

External and Internal Objectives. Objectives may also be divided into external and internal aims. *External* objectives are service objectives. They include service to customers and to society as a whole. Every socially responsible organization operates in a manner designed to attain these external objectives. Failure to consider such responsibilities often results in adverse publicity, passage of restrictive legislation, establishment of consumer and environmental protection agencies, and impaired sales and profitability.

Internal objectives are those aims designed to satisfy groups within the organization. These objectives include such areas as sales, profitability, growth, and market standing. They affect such groups as managers, operative employees, and stockholders. Other internal objectives may be directed toward employees in such forms as safe working conditions, equitable wages, and attractive fringe benefits programs.

Even though objectives may be classified as internal and external, they are not totally independent. In a very real sense in the business world of the 1980s, organizations must recognize their responsibilities to both customers and to society as a whole if they are to accomplish their internal objectives.

Firms increasingly recognize a number of *social objectives.* These may include such areas as providing job opportunities for all qualified workers, paying fair wages, making factories and offices safe places to work, offering job training to handicapped workers and the hard-core unemployed, and being a good corporate citizen of the community. Figure 5–3 describes the objectives of a large public service company.

In an attempt to determine the actual objectives of business, Y. K. Shetty surveyed a group of managers of large American business organizations and asked them to indicate specific organizational objectives.[16] Figure 5–4 shows the results of this study and compares them with the results of a similar survey conducted twelve years earlier by George W. England.

Profitability and growth were the objectives most often mentioned by the respondents of both studies. However, the two studies differ greatly in the emphasis placed on the objectives of social responsibility, resource conservation, and multinational expansion. The listing of these objectives by the respondents in the more recent study is evidence of the impact of the environment upon the organization and its objectives. Such objectives were rare in the 1950s and 1960s, and many managers argued that the attainment of objectives related to efficiency, productivity, and profitability was prerequisite to accomplishing social and employee objectives.[17] While many managers continue to hold this viewpoint, the typical statement of organizational objectives in the late 1980s includes these social and employee aims as explicit objectives of the firm. In addition, the more consumer-oriented environment of the past decade and the increased international competition for resources and markets influenced one respondent in four to specify multinational expansion as an organizational objective in the recent survey.

HIERARCHY OF OBJECTIVES

Not only do most organizations have a number of objectives, but these objectives typically exist in a hierarchy. At the top are the overall objectives of the entire organization.[18] The broader aims of service, market share, sales, profitability, and return on investment are then broken down into objectives for each division, operating facility, department, work group, and individual employee. Once this is accomplished, each member of the organization can relate his or her contribution to the overall organizational objectives.

The number of levels in the hierarchy depends upon the size and complexity of the organization. Large, multiproduct firms generally have more levels of objectives than do smaller organizations. Figure 5–5 illustrates the hierarchy of objectives for a typical firm.

MANAGEMENT BY OBJECTIVES

What do General Motors, Du Pont, RCA, General Foods, 3M Company, Honeywell, the Air Force Logistics Command, Paul Revere Life Insurance, and the City of Tulsa Parks Department have in common? All of these organizations have successful management by objectives (MBO) programs in operation.

A growing number of managers recognize that, whenever possible, objectives should be set by the people responsible for accomplishing them. It is much easier to obtain commitment to objectives when those persons responsible for their accomplishment have played a role in developing them. Linking individual and organizational objectives is facilitated when individual employees are permitted to participate in establishing their own objectives for a specified time period and know in advance that their performance will be evaluated by comparing actual results with expected, agreed-to-in-advance performance. This is the promise of such programs.

Few management techniques have received more publicity in the past two decades than management by objectives. Although MBO has been

66 Fixing your objective is like identifying the North Star—you sight your compass on it and then use it as the means of getting back on the track when you tend to stray. 99
Marshall E. Dimock

Customer Service and Product Quality

To supply gas and electric service for the home, the community, commerce, agriculture, industry, and government
- at the lowest possible cost
- in the quantities customers demand
- with constantly improved quality
- with increasing beneficial uses of our service.

Profitability

To earn an adequate profit so that
- investors' risk and replacement and obsolescense of capital assets can be provided for
- earnings can be reinvested and new capital can be attracted and retained
- the company's total efforts and net effectiveness will be financially sound.

Employee Attitudes and Incentives

To attain skillful, safe performance, loyalty and teamwork of individual employees by
- establishing good wages, benefits, and working conditions
- maintaining security of employment
- preserving individual human values and human dignity
- assuring opportunity for self-improvement, advancement, and self-realization.

Managerial Performance and Development

To provide for a continuity of managerial leadership and company progress by
- stimulating continuous moral and technical self-development of managerial personnel
- soundly designing a dynamic organization structure
- clearly defining objectives, policies and standards of managerial performance
- assuring opportunity and authority to perform within the bounds of capacities, objectives, and job functions
- establishing incentives proportionate to responsibilities, risks, and results.

Physical and Financial Resources

To provide for the future financial and physical needs of the

FIGURE 5–3. Eight Objectives of the Arizona Public Service Company

employed by a few firms since the 1930s, it was first popularized by Peter Drucker, who described it this way:

> The objectives of the district manager's job should be clearly defined by the contribution he and his district sales force have to make to the sales department, the objectives of the project engineer's job by the contributions he, his engineers and draftsmen make to the engineering department. . . . This requires each manager to develop and set the objectives of his unit himself. Higher management must, of course, reserve the power to ap-

company by planning and providing for
- continuing sources of adequate fuel and power
- adequate office facilities, tools, and equipment
- capital supply requirements.

Productivity

To attain constantly improving productive performance of all employees through
- effective and balanced utilization of human and material resources
- development and adoption of new tools, equipment, and methods, and through refinements of proven methods of work
- feasible but challenging standards of performance for individual employ-

ees and each segment of the organization.

Innovation and Research

To engage in research and study in all fields and areas of work relating to business and the utility industry by
- contributing to, developing, and utilizing technological advances
- developing sensitivity to changing conditions—economic, technological, and scientific
- developing new, better, and more efficient methods of rendering service to customers
- keeping up with advances in knowledge and skills in all major areas of activity.

Public Responsibility

To recognize the company's public responsibility and earn public confidence by
- leading in efforts to bring about community and industrial growth, development, and betterment
- opposing efforts to destroy individual initiative and the private business system
- maintaining constructive and forthright relationships with governmental bodies
- contributing to the development and strength of the utility and allied industries, sharing our advances and benefiting from experience and ideas.

prove or disapprove his objectives. But their development is part of a manager's responsibility; indeed, it is his first responsibility.[19]

Management by objectives (MBO) often carries different labels: *managing for results, management by results, goals management,* and *management by commitments.* MBO may be defined as a process whereby the superior and subordinate managers of an organization identify objectives common to each, define areas of responsibility in terms of expected results, and use these measures as guides for operating the unit and assessing the contri-

Management by objectives (MBO) is a process whereby the superior and subordinate managers of an organization identify objectives common to each, define areas of responsibility, and use these measures as guides for operating the unit and assessing the contribution of each member of the organization.

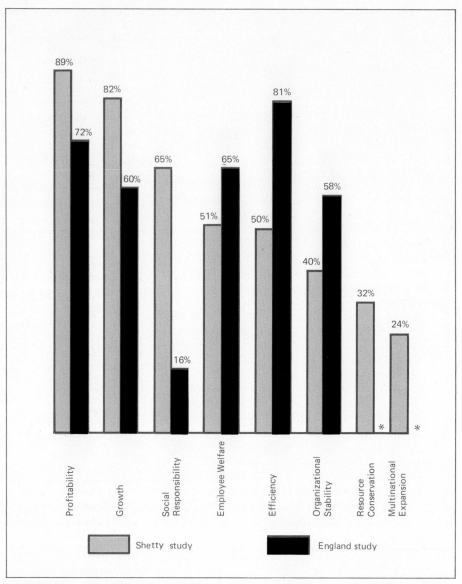

FIGURE 5–4.   The Objectives of Business: A Comparison of the England and Shetty Studies
Source: The Shetty data are adapted from Y. K. Shetty, "New Look at Corporate Goals," *California Management Review* 22, no. 2: 73. © 1979 by the Regents of the University of California. Adapted by permission of the Regents. The England data are from George W. England, "Organizational Goals and Expected Behavior of American Managers," *Academy of Management Journal* (June 1967): 108.

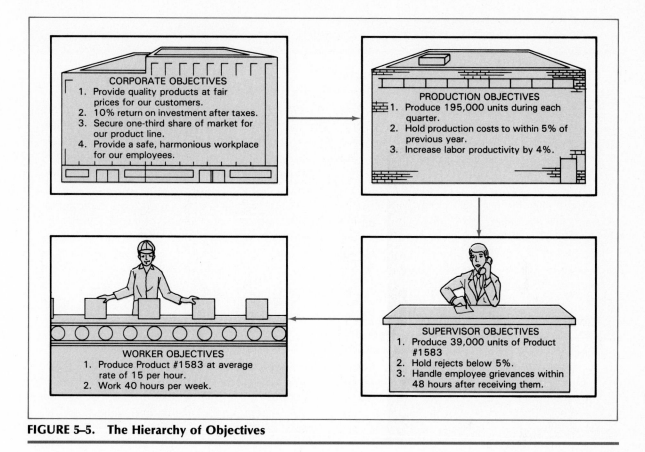

FIGURE 5–5.   The Hierarchy of Objectives

bution of each member of the organization.[20] MBO programs are designed to improve employees' motivation through their participation in setting their individual objectives and knowing in advance precisely how they will be evaluated.

MBO is a particularly flexible management technique that can be implemented for a single department or for the entire organization. It is generally agreed that an MBO program should begin with the chief executive officer setting specific organizational objectives in consultation with the board of directors. The process should then extend throughout the organization.

Although early applications of MBO were limited to business organizations, it has since spread to such diverse organizations as the Department of Defense, educational agencies, local government bodies, and charitable organizations. MBO has considerable merit in settings where performance measures are vague or lacking.[21]

THE MANAGER'S BOOKSHELF

Competitive Strategy, by Michael E. Porter

 Harvard Business School professor Michael Porter wrote his best-selling *Competitive Strategy* (The Free Press, 1980) not for the general reader and not for academics, but for the practitioners themselves, the many business managers "seeking to improve the performance of their businesses." Porter's book isn't chock-full of anecdotes, like so many business best-sellers these days, and it certainly doesn't offer any immediate cure-alls for a company looking for a successful plan to break into a new market. What *Competitive Strategy* does offer, however, is a framework and method for understanding how various companies can compete within their different environments.

During the 1970s, many American companies shifted their strategic emphasis from sales growth to dominance over their competitors. Porter's framework is designed to help managers planning to enter or exit markets to anticipate the competitive response to their decisions, to predict how the industry will continue to evolve, and to analyze the industry as a whole. He does this by applying economics to the science of managing.

Porter first describes competitive relationships that occur among the various aggregate actors: suppliers, buyers, potential entrants, substitutes, and industry competitors. Most analysts, Porter says, have ignored four of these actors in favor of the fifth: industry competitors. Porter suggests that all five are of equal importance. Within this first "ideas" section of the book, he includes chapters on market signals, competitive moves, strategy toward buyers and suppliers, structural analysis within industries, and industry evolution.

An astute planner not only finds suitable alternatives, Porter says, but also creates them. Toward this end, the author proposes three viable strategy options: overall cost leadership, differentiation, and focus. Differentiation and low cost leadership apply within industry-wide market targets. A focus strategy means specializing in a market segment, a portion of a product line, or a geographical region. The real danger, says Porter, is in failing to choose among these options, being (in the author's words) "stuck in the middle."

The second section of *Competitive Strategy* deals with the concept of industry life cycles (as opposed to individual product life cycles) and their associated effects. Each stage in an industry's life cycle, Porter says, has its own set of relationships, and one must begin by analyzing where in its life cycle an industry is. The last section of the book deals with those types of decisions that are only loosely linked to industry life cycles. These chapters examine vertical integration, capacity expansion, and entry into new businesses.

One of Porter's main points is that the relationship between market share and profitability differs widely. (Between 1963 and 1965, Porter says, the follower companies in 15 of 38 tested consumer industries were more profitable than the leaders.) Market planning, not market share, is the major determinant of profitability, and *Competitive Strategy* lays a comprehensive groundwork for understanding the theory and practice of market planning.

STEPS INVOLVED IN AN MBO PROGRAM

To be effective, an MBO program must involve clear communication of the overall organizational objectives to each organizational member. Each manager then has the opportunity to structure personal objectives and the work of his or her unit to these broader objectives. Most MBO programs follow this sequence:

1. Unit managers list objectives for their departments or work groups that mesh with the overall organizational objectives. Performance measures for subordinates are also established.

2. Individual members of the department or work group list their major performance objectives for the coming period with target dates for accomplishing them.

3. Unit manager and individual employee meet to discuss objectives and performance measures. The result of the meeting is agreement by both parties on specific objectives and how performance will be measured.

4. Unit manager and subordinate meet on a periodic basis to discuss intermediate progress and make revisions or update objectives as necessary.

5. At the end of the period, the subordinate prepares an "accomplishment report" which lists major accomplishments and comments on the variances between expected and actual performance.

6. Self-appraisal is discussed with unit manager. Reasons for objectives not being met are explored.

7. New set of objectives is established for the coming MBO period.

The result of Steps 1–3 should be a document similar to the one shown in Figure 5–6. While they represent challenges for the plant manager, they are achievable. Finally, they are consistent with overall organizational objectives. The relative priority (A = high; B = low priority) of each objective is indicated in column 2 and the expected completion date for each objective is given in column 3. Actual outcomes or results are noted in column 4.

Benefits of an MBO Program. The major benefit of any MBO program is the linking of objective setting with individual motivation. Since the individual employee participates in setting his or her own goals, there is a commitment to them. Workers know both the tasks to be accomplished and how they will be evaluated. Improved morale may also result from regular face-to-face communications between employees and their superiors.

MANAGERIAL JOB OBJECTIVES

Edward S. Thompson   7-2-87   PLANT MANAGER
Prepared by the manager   Date   Manager's job title

J.K. Hawkins   7-2-87   PRESIDENT
Reviewed by supervisor   Date   Supervisor's job title

Statement of Objectives	Priority Level	Completion Date	Outcomes or Results
1. To increase deliveries to 98% of all scheduled delivery dates.	A	6/30/88	
2. To reduce waste and spoilage to 3% of all raw materials used.	A	6/30/88	
3. To reduce lost time due to accidents to 100 days/year.	B	2/1/88	
4. To reduce operating cost to 10% below budget.	A	1/15/88	
5. To install a quality control radioisotope system at a cost of less than $53,000.	A	3/15/88	
6. To improve production scheduling and preventative maintenance so as to increase machine utilization time to 95% of capacity.	B	10/1/88	
7. To complete the UCLA Executive Program this year.	A	6/30/88	
8. To teach a production management course in university extension.	B	6/30/88	

FIGURE 5–6.   MBO Administrative Form
Source: Adapted from Anthony P. Raia, *Managing by Objectives* (Glenview, Ill.: Scott, Foresman, 1974), p. 60. Copyright © 1974 by Scott Foresman and Company. Used by permission.

Problems with MBO. Experience with MBO programs indicates that they can make significant contributions to the organization if used with judgment and a great deal of planning. However, one study of the top 500 manufacturing firms in the United States revealed that only 10 percent of the industrial giants were totally satisfied with their MBO programs.[22]

When MBO programs fail or do not measure up to management expectations, one or more of the following problem areas are likely to exist:

- Lack of support and involvement by top management

- Lack of commitment

- Objectives handed to subordinate rather than decided upon as the result of joint agreement

- Poor implementation methods

- Little coaching and assistance

- Overemphasis on appraisal

- Overemphasis on paperwork.[23]

MBO programs are doomed without the total support of top management. All too often, top management begins an MBO program as the "latest fad" and delegates its implementation to subordinates. In some instances, top management specifies organizational goals and leaves no flexibility for subordinates. In other cases, organizations rush into implementation of an MBO program without sufficient preparation or understanding. Hollman and Tansik quote one manager in a public sector organization who expresses the confusion that often results from a hurried, inadequately planned implementation:

> First we heard all about MBO. We took a three-day workshop and were told how to go about doing MBO in a city government. Then somebody in Personnel began pushing a Management by Results (MBR) seminar. Right now we don't know what we're *supposed* to be doing. I do know what we are doing though—just what we've always done. We'll react when their intentions are clear.[24]

Some MBO programs suffer from managers' unwillingness to devote time to the regular face-to-face meetings required in MBO programs. Still others fail as a result of a mechanical approach relying on volumes of paperwork for both superior and subordinate.[25]

MBO programs have a greater probability of success when they are implemented by top management in an orderly, unhurried fashion and all participants receive training prior to implementation. Other programs in similar organizations may be studied. Limited testing and debugging of the proposed program may prove extremely beneficial. The normal time for implementing a successful MBO program on an organization-wide basis may be three years or more.[26]

ASSESSING ORGANIZATIONAL RESOURCES ■■■■■■

The third step in the strategic planning process involves the assessment of the firm's strengths and weaknesses in comparison with those of other organizations. This assessment of organizational resources is used to iden-

Equifinality is the principle that organizational objectives can be achieved through more than one course of action.

tify appropriate strategies for accomplishing organizational missions and objectives. Specialists in systems theory use the term *equifinality* to describe an important principle of organizations—that organizations can achieve their objectives through several possible courses of action, not just one.[27] The principle of equifinality requires managers to remain flexible in choosing the appropriate means to achieve the firm's objectives. Rather than an endless search for the "one best way," the manager may choose from a variety of satisfactory alternatives. The manager must recognize, like Huckleberry Finn, that there are "more ways than one to skin a cat."

Selection of the most appropriate strategies for accomplishing the organization's mission and its more specific objectives should result from an evaluation of the firm's strengths and weaknesses in comparison with those of present and likely future competitors. Every aspect of the organization may serve as a source of competitive advantage—or disadvantage. IBM, frequently ranked among America's most admired corporations, summarizes its key strengths this way:

> A commitment to excellence and a commitment to customer service. The fundamental thing is that the people who work in the company make it a good company. That's really the secret: the people. It's our good fortune to have superior people who work hard and support each other. They have adapted to our set of basic beliefs—the standards we expect of one another—and follow those standards in dealing with one another and with people outside the company. I know it sounds corny, but it's true, and there's no point in trying to analyze it much more than that. Mr. Watson, Sr. [IBM founder Thomas J. Watson, Sr.] used to say, "You can take my factories, burn up my buildings, but give me my people and I'll build the business right back again." And he was right.[28]

Superior marketing is the primary competitive advantage possessed by Atlanta-based Lanier Business Products Co. All products are manufactured outside the United States and are sold through a strong network of sales representatives located in major cities throughout the nation. The major source of competitive advantage for Du Pont has long been its technological leadership resulting from extensive research and development efforts. Du Pont has created entirely new industries through such major new products as nylon, cellophane, Teflon, Kevlar, and Lucite.

By contrast, limited financial resources and limited production and marketing facilities may force a firm to concentrate on small segments of an industry rather than directly attacking industry leaders in every market segment. Rather than taking on automobile giants such as General Motors, Ford, Chrysler, Toyota, Nissan, and the other major competitors in the U.S. auto industry, the Yugoslavian-made Yugo is aimed at a segment of car buyers who seek the ultimate in economy from a subcompact car. Recognizing that they could not compete with foreign sporting goods manufacturers, Spalding Sporting Goods managers have chosen to forego manufacturing and, instead, to license their highly regarded brand to dozens of foreign producers.

Resource assessment should be accomplished in the following sequence:

- Develop a profile of the organization's principal resources and skills in three broad areas: financial; physical, organizational, and human; and technological.

- Determine the key success requirements of the product/market segments in which the organization competes or might compete.

- Compare the resource profile to the key success requirements to determine the major strengths on which an effective strategy can be based and the major weaknesses which must be overcome.

- Compare the organization's strengths and weaknesses with those of its major competitors to identify which of its resources and skills are sufficient to yield meaningful competitive advantages in the marketplace.[29]

EVALUATING ENVIRONMENTAL RISKS AND OPPORTUNITIES

The fourth step in the strategic planning process is the evaluation of risks and opportunities in the environment in which the firm operates. Environmental factors—both within the organization and from the general external environment—play major roles in determining the effectiveness of different strategies in achieving organizational objectives. Antiquated production facilities at many U.S. steel mills have rendered many companies unable to compete with more modern facilities in Japan and South Korea. Cooperative efforts between several Japanese firms seeking major international construction projects and Japanese banks that provide the necessary financing have made them formidable competitors against firms in nations whose antitrust laws discourage such cooperative efforts. Changing customer tastes that led to a rapid decline of the U.S. market for double-knit clothing turned Monsanto's plans to increase production capacity by adding new production facilities in North Carolina into disaster. A $500,000 investment by Hella North America in a Flora, Illinois, manufacturing facility to produce automobile diesel engine components was largely wasted when demand for autos with diesel engines plummeted in the mid-1980s.

By contrast, Teddy Ruxpin dolls, which utilize computer chip technology to produce toys that talk and move their eyes and mouths in synchronization with the words, have proven enormously successful. Domino's Pizza, Inc., managers have taken advantage of consumer demands for convenience. Acceptance of the concept of thirty-minute free deliveries of hot pizza has been so great that the firm has already opened over twenty-three hundred stores in the United States, Canada, and Australia.

In developing its strategic plan, the Allstate Insurance Group gives careful consideration to the current environment and the changes ex-

●● All men can see these tactics whereby I conquer, but what none can see is the strategy out of which victory is evolved. ●●

Sun Tsu
3000 B.C.

pected in the planning time frame. Critical to this appraisal are environmental factors that might affect current or anticipated businesses either positively or negatively. These include economic, demographic, social, technological, and regulatory trends, among others. Allstate planners feel that a thorough understanding of the industry and competitive environment is essential. They focus on both by addressing the following issues:

A. *Industry*
   1. What is the nature of the industry currently?
   2. How large is it? Is it growing?
   3. How is the industry structured currently?
   4. What are the segments and market targets?
   5. What are the prospects for profitability?
   6. How will all of these factors change during the plan period?

B. *Competitors*
   1. Who are the major competitors in terms of key measurements?
   2. What data can be provided which describes competitors' current positions, their revenues, profits, rankings, market shares?
   3. What are the competitors' strengths and weaknesses?
   4. Where do they appear to be headed strategically?
   5. What is their product/service assortment?
   6. How are competitors achieving growth?
   7. Who is likely to enter the business and why?[30]

While awareness of environmental factors does not eliminate their impact, it does permit the firm to develop plans that will take advantage of such factors. When Borg-Warner managers sought a means of offsetting the cyclical nature of their manufacturing, they developed highly successful plans to expand into financial and protection services through internal development and acquisitions. Today, these new service offerings account for one-third of the company's annual earnings. To reduce dependence on oil, New England Electric System managers switched to coal as a fuel source at a savings of over $200 million. But not even the best environmental forecasts can cover all possibilities. In the early 1980s, Toro sought to capitalize on brand recognition and its reputation for quality Toro mowers and snowblowers by expanding into other home-care products. The plan failed largely because of an unprecedented string of snowless winters in the firm's prime market areas.[31]

THE STRATEGIC WINDOW

Strategic windows are limited time periods during which the "fit" between the key requirements of a market and the particular competencies of a firm is at an optimum.

Environmental factors and resource constraints will produce different effects on the organization at different times. The term *strategic window* was popularized by Professor Derek Abell of Harvard University. His idea is that "there are often limited periods when the 'fit' between the key requirements of a market are at an optimum. Investment in a product line or market area has to be timed to coincide with periods in which a strategic window is open, i.e., where a close fit exists. Disinvestment should be considered if, during the course of the market's evolution, changes in market requirements outstrip the firm's capability to adapt itself to the new circumstances."[32]

As Ryan and Shanklin point out, a strategic-window perspective/analysis is a way of relating potential opportunities to company capabilities—capabilities in capital requirements, technical expertise, management personnel, and so on.[33] It is not enough for management merely to identify opportunities in the external environment. Nor is it enough to go a step further and determine what growth strategies are needed to take advantage of the potential opportunities. This additional question must be addressed: Will the opportunity be there at the same time that the company has the competence and resources to seize upon it? In other words, will the growth strategy needed to capitalize on the opportunity be within the company's capability at the *right time*? For instance, three years from now, will the firm be positioned to afford the acquisition of the company that it will need to enter a new high-tech market? If so, the strategic window will open; if not, the strategic window will be shut and the growth strategy is not feasible. Likewise, regarding possible environmental threats, the overriding question is this: If the potential threats become realities, will the company have the competence and resources to cope with them? If not, disinvestment may be indicated. For example, if a small personal computer manufacturer cannot ultimately survive IBM's entry into the market, it had better get out sooner rather than later.

Successful application of the strategic-window idea requires top management to address three critical planning concerns and how they affect one another. First, during the period of time covered by the strategic plan, what general and specific external events may represent exploitable opportunities and threats to be avoided or dealt with? Second, what specific strategies for corporate growth would be needed to do so? Third, will corporate competencies and resources be adequate to execute the designated strategies at the *time* when the opportunities or threats may occur? Considerable background information from staff and long, hard thought and analysis by planners and top-line management are needed to answer these questions.

A strategic-window view is integrative. It requires a thorough analysis of (1) current and projected *external* environments, (2) current and projected *internal* corporate capabilities, and (3) how, whether, and when it will be feasible to reconcile the two by implementation of one or more growth strategies.

After a successful direct sales career with such companies as Stanley Home Products and World Gifts, Mary Kay Ash felt that a strategic window existed for the direct, in-home sales of cosmetics. Acceptance of direct purchases was growing among busy working women and Ash felt that her

66 Go as far as you can see, and when you get there you will see farther. 99

Anonymous

new cosmetics line (based originally on a formula for softening animal hides), her $5,000 initial investment, and her team of ten saleswomen were sufficient for success. Because she was challenging such giant firms as Revlon, Cover Girl, and Max Factor, many detractors felt her fledgling operation had little chance of success. So Ash chose an unlikely symbol to represent her firm's objectives: the bumblebee. As any aerodynamics engineer will explain, the bumblebee can't fly—its wings are too small to lift its body. But since none of the engineers bothered to tell this to the bumblebee, it flies anyway.

Today, Dallas-based Mary Kay Cosmetics is also soaring. Its marketing approach continues to be similar to the setting illustrated by Figure 5–7. But its original team of 10 beauty consultants has now grown to 150,000 and its market has expanded to Argentina, Canada, and the United Kingdom, in addition to the United States.

CORPORATE STRATEGIES, BUSINESS STRATEGIES, AND FUNCTIONAL STRATEGIES

Strategies vary by level within the organization. The first level, *corporate strategies,* focuses on the entire organization in specifying the types of

FIGURE 5–7. Mary Kay Cosmetics: Taking Advantage of a Strategic Window
Source: Courtesy Mary Kay Cosmetics, Inc.

business in which the firm should engage. It defines the scope of the firm and how its resources will be deployed.

Examples of changes in corporate strategy are evident at R. J. Reynolds Industries, where managers recently announced plans to end its diversification attempts in the shipping and petroleum industries and to concentrate its efforts in its base industries of consumer products and service businesses. Since 1980, the firm has acquired Del Monte Corporation, Heublein, Inc., a number of Kentucky Fried Chicken franchises, and Canada Dry, among others. While these acquisitions offer diversification for the tobacco company, they are not as dissimilar operations as were the shipping and petroleum subsidiaries.[34]

The second strategy level, *business strategies,* focuses on the optimal methods to compete in a particular market. The aim of the business strategy is to identify a method to achieve a competitive advantage for its product or service offerings. Rather than attempting to decide what business to be in (corporate strategy), managers developing a business strategy would be creating plans on how best to take advantage of their firm's areas of distinctive competence in a particular market.

Although Caterpillar, Inc., is the world's largest manufacturer of giant construction equipment, the firm has suffered in recent years from major sales declines in such markets as heavy mining, energy recovery, and construction. Since the firm enjoys such company strengths as a well-established name, flexible manufacturing capacity, and a powerful distribution system, it has decided to offer smaller equipment such as backhoe loaders through its established distribution channels. The additional products provide Caterpillar distributors with a more complete line of both large and small equipment to offer customers.[35]

The final strategy level, *functional strategies,* is developed for each functional area in the company, such as production, human resources, or marketing. A decision by Caterpillar managers to subcontract production of some of their smaller construction equipment rather than use company-owned production facilities would be an example of a functional strategy. The People Express decision to compete on the basis of airline ticket prices is a strategy aimed at the marketing function.

USING THE SBU CONCEPT IN STRATEGIC PLANNING

Strategic business units (SBUs) are divisions composed of key businesses within multiproduct companies with specific managers, resources, objectives, and competitors. An SBU may encompass a division, a product line, or a single product. The SBU concept began in 1971 at General Electric, one of the world's most diversified companies. GE executives decided to base their strategic planning on viewing their organization as a "portfolio" of businesses. GE's nine product groups and forty-eight divisions were reorganized into forty-three SBUs. Food preparation appliances that previously had been located in three separate divisions were merged into a

Strategic business units (SBUs) are divisions composed of key businesses, within multiproduct companies, with specific managers, resources, objectives, and competitors. An SBU may encompass a division, a product line, or a single product.

single SBU serving the "housewares" market. The concept was quickly adopted by numerous diversified organizations, including General Foods, Union Carbide, International Paper, and Boise Cascade. When Gordon McGovern became president and chief executive officer of the Campbell Soup Company in 1980, he decided to implement the SBU approach to encourage employee entrepreneurship. Between 1980 and 1985, McGovern divided the company into fifty autonomous business units, including such product categories as soup, beverages, and frozen foods.[36] An estimated 45 percent of the 500 largest corporations in the United States are currently using the SBU concept.[37]

A conceptual matrix is utilized that relates SBUs to competitors and assesses the long-term product-market attractiveness. General Electric planners use such dimensions as segment size and SBU growth rate, market share, profitability, margins, technology position, strengths or weaknesses, image, environmental impact, and management. Figure 5–8 shows a typical matrix with labels for each cell developed by the Boston Consulting Group, a consulting firm that has pioneered many of the conceptual developments in the matrix approach to strategic planning.

Stars are products or businesses that are high-growth market leaders. Although they generate considerable funds, these are more than offset by the funds needed to finance the additional investments required and the working capital needed to finance their continuing growth. Because of their current competitive position and future potential, stars represent desirable investments for the firm.

Cash cows are products or businesses with high market share but low growth prospects. As a result, they generate considerable inflows of funds for the firm.

Dogs are products or businesses with both low market share and poor growth prospects. Although they may generate some funds for the firm, their future prospects are poor, and most organizations attempt to withdraw from these businesses or product lines as quickly as possible.

Question marks are products or businesses with low market share in a high-growth market. Due to the growth nature of the market, question marks typically require more cash than they are able to generate. Such situations require the manager to make a basic go/no go decision. Unless the question marks can be converted to stars, the firm should pursue other alternatives.

Although the labels attached to each cell may vary among the different organizations employing the SBU approach, the approach is quite similar from organization to organization. In developing the strategic plans for handling the portfolio of SBUs, most proponents of this approach recommend the following:

- Dogs and cash cows are managed for short-term cash flow. Over the long run, dogs are divested or eliminated, while cash cows ultimately become dogs as their competitive position declines.

Stars are products or businesses that are high-growth market leaders.

Cash cows are products or businesses with high market share but low growth prospects.

Dogs are products or businesses with both low market share and poor growth prospects.

Question marks are products or businesses with low market share in a high-growth market.

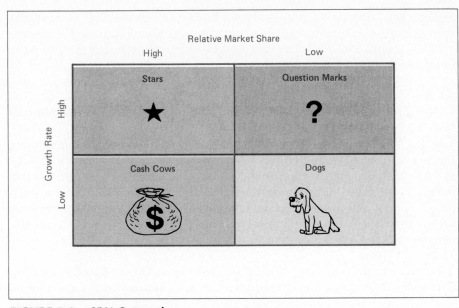

FIGURE 5–8.   SBU Categories
Source: Adapted from The Product Portfolio. © 1970 The Boston Consulting Group, Inc. Reprinted by permission.

- Question marks must either get into the star category or get out of the portfolio. In the first case, they should make the move with carefully developed strategic plans so that major risk elements are identified and contained.

- Stars are short-run cash consumers and are managed for long-term position. Over the long run, as their segment attractiveness ultimately declines, they will become cash cows, generating cash to support the next round of stars.[38]

Critics of the matrix approach typically focus on the tendency of some managers to use it too mechanically. While it permits managers of a multiproduct company to array on one graph all of the firm's businesses based on common measures, it can be used as a prescriptive measure without considering available means for converting low-ranking SBUs to larger market shares or to faster market growth rates. As one manager remarked, "A lot of dogs have been liquidated that could have been turned around."[39] ITT chairman Harold Geneen's assessment was even more blunt: "As for the 'dogs,' to my mind it is management's responsibility to figure out why they are 'dogs' and what can be done to turn them into greyhounds."[40] Another criticism of the matrix approach and its emphasis on market growth and share focuses on environmental factors. In recent years, a number of industries have declined from "go-go" to "no-grow." Stars and question marks are more difficult to locate. As the chief planner at Norton

Simon, Inc., stated, "If your portfolio has no businesses that have significant growth, you'd better forget about the matrix and learn to manage for efficiency and return."[41] The advantages of the matrix approach must be balanced against its potential shortcomings by each organization.

IMPLEMENTING AND MONITORING PLANS

The six steps in the strategic planning process consists of implementing the managerial strategy that has been agreed upon by management. The overall strategic plan serves as the basis for a series of operating plans necessary to move the organization toward accomplishment of its objectives. The decisions involved in creating such plans are the subject of Chapters 6 and 7. Detailed, intensive analysis of operating plans in specific functional areas of the organization are treated in more advanced management classes.

In the final step of strategic planning, managers use feedback to monitor and adapt strategies when actual performance fails to match expectations. The close interrelationship between planning and control is nowhere more evident than at this step. The monitoring and adjusting of plans represent major subjects in both Chapter 16 and Chapter 17.

SUMMARY

Strategic planning is designed to provide a blueprint for the entire organization, a perspective for the development of more specific plans, forecasts, budgets, and procedures. It focuses on what the organization will do in the future. It involves determining the organization's objectives and then adopting the courses of action and allocating the resources necessary to achieve these objectives. Tactical planning, on the other hand, is much narrower in scope; it focuses primarily on how the activities specified by the strategic plans are to be accomplished. Flexibility is an important ingredient for both strategic and tactical planning.

The strategic planning process consists of 6 steps: (1) define the mission of the organization, (2) determine organizational objectives, (3) assess organizational resources, (4) evaluate environmental risks and opportunities, (5) formulate strategy, and (6) implement strategy through operating plans.

The mission of an organization is the fundamental, unique purpose that sets it apart from other firms of its type and identifies the scope of its operation in product and market terms. Once the mission of the organization has been determined, it is translated into more concrete objectives. Objectives guide the members of the firm in their planning, policy and procedures development, and controlling. In addition to providing direction for the organization, objectives also serve as standards by which actual performance can be compared with expectations. Lastly, they serve as motivators for organizational members who are given clear aims for which to strive.

All organizations recognize a number of objectives. These include survival and growth, profits, and organizational efficiency. Social objectives also exist and are recognized by enlightened management. Objectives may be classified as short range and long range, external and internal. Short-range objectives are those referring to a time period of one year or less. Long-range aims cover a time period in excess of one year. External objectives are service objectives, including service to customers and to society as a whole. Internal objectives are those aims designed to satisfy such groups within the organization as management, employees, and stockholders.

Management by objectives (MBO) is a widely used program that focuses on employee participation in setting individual work goals. Manager and subordinate agree on goals, and both participate in evaluating the worker's success in achieving these goals. Each member of the organization knows in advance what is expected and the basis of evaluation.

Many MBO program failures have occurred because of the lack of top management support; hurried, inadequately planned implementation; lack of regular contacts and mutual agreement to match the leadership styles of individual managers; excessive paperwork; and a variety of other problems. Successful implementation requires the support of top management and typically starts with the chief executive of the firm. Careful planning, complete understanding of MBO by all members of the or-

ganization, and sufficient time for implementation should increase the likelihood of success.

A growing number of diversified, multiproduct organizations employ the strategic business unit (SBU) concept in strategic planning, viewing their organizations as a "portfolio" of businesses. SBUs are then assessed through comparisons with competitors and the evaluation of long-term product-market attractiveness. Although the concept is potentially dangerous because it can be used mechanically in developing plans, it allows managers to focus on all aspects of the organization in a balanced fashion.

SOLVING THE STOP ACTION CASE

"One of the Few $40,000 Sedans That Doesn't Presume Its Owner Is Dead from the Wallet Up."

BMW of North America

BMW's response to its competition from the Mercedes-Benz 190 "baby Benz" and the threat of competition from new Japanese luxury imports involved both strategic and tactical plans. As the advertisement at left indicates, the firm had no intention of straying from its primary customer target: affluent car buyers seeking performance, handling, engineering technology, and luxury. Another component of their strategic plan involved their product offerings. Since the competition was aiming primarily at BMW's 300-series models, the firm's managers focused on strengthening this end of their product line.

One potential weakness was the direct competition of Honda's V-6 Legend and Integra with the four-cylinder BMW 318i. The German car maker's reaction was to drop the model and replace it with a sportier, six-cylinder 325. By the time the Japanese competitors arrived in 1986, all BMW models had six-cylinder engines. Another decision designed to further enhance BMW's image as a high-technology, performance-oriented auto was BMW's decision to become the first U.S. marketer to offer antilock braking systems as a standard feature on all models. To emphasize value retention in older BMW models, the firm introduced a program in 1986 offering a one-year or 12,000-mile warranty on selected used BMW automobiles in the current and previous five model years with fewer than 75,000 miles and purchased through a BMW dealership.

Tactical moves included a $28-million advertising budget in 1986 and an emphasis on such promotional sponsorships as twelve regional polo events and a two-car entry in International Motor Sports Association racing events. BMW even offers discounts to BMW purchasers and prospects on enrollment in the BMW/Skip Barber Advanced Driving School, run by the ex-Formula One driver. The success—or failure—of BMW's plans for defending its market against the new Japanese luxury imports will be apparent in the next five years.

Sources: BMW advertisement © 1985 BMW of North America, Inc. Reprinted by permission. The description of BMW's strategic and tactical plans is based on Jesse Snyder, "BMW Accelerates Plan to Defend Its Turf," *Advertising Age,* 25 November 1985, p. 53.

FACT OR FICTION REVEALED

1. Fact   2. Fact   3. Fiction   4. Fiction   5. Fiction   6. Fiction   7. Fiction

MANAGEMENT TERMS

strategic planning
tactical planning
mission
objectives
short-range objectives
long-range objectives

external objectives
internal objectives
social objectives
management by objectives
   (MBO)
equifinality

strategic window
strategic business units (SBUs)
stars
cash cows
dogs
question marks

REVIEW QUESTIONS

1. Distinguish between strategic planning and tactical planning.
2. Identify the steps in the strategic planning process. How can flexibility be built into each step?
3. Relate the concept of company mission to objectives setting and strategic planning.
4. Identify the major benefits provided by objectives in improving organizational effectiveness.
5. Distinguish between internal and external objectives.
6. What were the major findings of the Shetty and England studies of organizational effectiveness?
7. What are the steps involved in a typical management by objectives program?
8. Distinguish between corporate strategies, business strategies, and functional strategies. Give an example of each.
9. Explain the role of the strategic business unit (SBU) concept in strategic planning.
10. List the names and characteristics of products and businesses in each cell of the SBU market share/market growth matrix. What are the major problems in applying the matrix concept?

PROBLEMS AND EXPERIENTIAL EXERCISES

1. Suggest methods of adding flexibility to the plans of the following organizations:
   a. Attendance plan for a National Basketball Association franchise
   b. Registration plan at your university
   c. Expansion plan by a local bank
   d. Evacuation plan of a local hospital

2. What two objectives do you feel are likely to be ranked highest by the following?
   a. Manager of the local Travelers' Aid office
   b. Supervisor of the quality control department at Sierra Nevada Brewing Co.
   c. Executive director of the Boston Pops symphony
   d. Head of the business office at your college or university

3. Identify the missions of your college or university. Then give examples of how each mission might be translated into specific objectives.
4. Design an MBO program for an organization of which you are a current member.
5. Identify two products that fit the following profiles:
   a. star
   b. dog
   c. cash cow
   d. question mark

Suggest actions that should be considered by management in each case.

MANAGERIAL INCIDENT: Winnebago Industries

When gasoline prices shot up in the wake of the fall of the Shah of Iran in early 1979, no industry suffered more than motor homes. From a high of 293,000 in 1978, motor-home shipments plunged to 172,600 in 1979 and 99,900 in 1980. Half of the country's motor-home dealers went out of business and manufacturers laid off thousands of workers.

Industry giant Winnebago was no exception. The firm saw its shipments fall from 17,836 in 1978 to only 5,303 in 1980, while sales slid from $229 million to only $92 million. "All of a sudden, there was no spring," recalls company spokesman Frank Rotta.

Enter John K. Hanson. The chairman, now 68, had led the firm during the boom years of the 1960s and was called out of retirement by the board of directors in 1979 to get Winnebago out of its crisis.

John K., as he is called around town, set to work on a number of changes: Vehicles were designed to run on lower-cost propane fuel; lighter-weight models were developed; top management was shaken up; inventory was cut in half; inefficient plants were closed or sold; and operating costs were trimmed drastically. "We had to drive down our expenses," says Hanson. "We looked under every stone."

The company also had to produce the kinds of fuel-efficient motor homes the public wanted. So, in 1983, it introduced the twenty-foot LeSharo and Phasar models. Up to fourteen feet shorter than other Winnebago products, these motor homes are extremely fuel efficient, traveling more than twenty miles on every gallon of diesel fuel. Automation is a key element in Winnebago's recovery. In 1984 and 1985, the company invested $36 million in robots and other automated devices that have increased productivity and cut labor costs.

The strategy appears to be working. Nineteen eighty-four proved to be the most successful year in Winnebago's history. Sales totaled $411 million—a 450 percent increase in four years—and net earnings amounted to nearly $28 million.

The company is also looking ahead to new uses for its products. In 1982, it won a $9 million contract to build trams for Universal Studios. In addition, the firm has signed a contract to license the Winnebago name for apparel and camping equipment. With motor-home prices averaging $36,000, Winnebago managers realized they had to make the motor-home purchase more attractive to consumers. In 1984, the company began a national retail finance plan allowing customers to secure up to twelve-year loans at interest rates 1½ percent below market rates.

On the horizon for Winnebago is a gasoline version of the LeSharo and Phasar models that will be able to carry heavier loads than any other comparable vehicle. Hanson sums up his firm's future in this way: "I think we're ready for a new energy crisis or most anything else."

Questions and Problems

1. Relate the decisions and actions taken by Winnebago Industries to the steps in the strategic planning process. Give an example of both strategic planning and tactical planning from the managerial incident.

2. In what areas is Winnebago potentially vulnerable? Suggest methods by which its executives can obtain feedback and adjust their plans.

Sources: Paragraphs 1–4 are from "Secrets of Success in Troubled Industries," *U.S. News & World Report,* 20 July 1981, p. 72. Hanson quotation in final paragraph from Robert M. Knight, "Winnebago Pulls Out of the Woods with New Production Twists," *Christian Science Monitor,* 17 January 1985. Updated materials provided by Winnebago Industries.

6 MANAGERIAL DECISION MAKING

LEARNING OBJECTIVES

After studying this chapter you should be able to

1. Contrast decisions under states of certainty, risk, and uncertainty.

2. Explain the major types of decisions.

3. Compare the economic man concept with the description of the satisficing modern manager.

4. Identify the steps in the decision-making process.

5. Explain the benefits of a written problem statement.

6. Compare the strengths and weaknesses of group decision making.

7. Explain the Vroom-Yetton model of decision making.

STOP ACTION CASE

Gerber Products Company

The firm's mission had always been summed up in its motto: "Babies are our business . . . our *only* business." But the last decade saw the baby boom turn into a birth dearth as more and more couples decided to limit the size of their families, marriage and childbearing were postponed, and zero population growth became at least temporarily a reality. Top management at Gerber Products Co., the nation's largest baby-food maker, was worried.

Reaction to the decline in births and the fertility rate was drastic at other companies. Lane Bryant, Inc., which had pioneered maternity fashions at the turn of the century, began dropping its maternity departments in its newer suburban stores. Johnson & Johnson started to stress the use of its shampoo, baby powder, and baby oil for adults.

A number of proposals—formal and informal—were circulating at Gerber's Fremont, Michigan, headquarters. Some people interpreted the changes in the birth rate as indicative that the firm's baby-food line had moved from the SBU *star* category to a *cash cow*. Consequently, they advocated developing new product areas as new star candidates. Many new product advocates recommended that any new entries be linked to babies since this market had always been the heart of the firm's business. Others argued that restricting the firm's market definition to a declining age category limited the firm's growth horizons. Clearly, the decisions about new products would determine the future of the company.

Use the materials in Chapter 6 to recommend a course of action for Gerber Products' managers that would ensure the firm's continued growth despite declines in the birth rate.

MANAGEMENT FACT OR FICTION

	FACT	FICTION		FACT	FICTION
1. The term *decision making* is synonymous with the planning function.	☐	☐	5. Analogy is an important mechanism in the use of creativity to develop alternatives.	☐	☐
2. Most management decisions are made under conditions of uncertainty.	☐	☐	6. Efficiency—unlike effectiveness—considers the costs involved in choosing among alternatives designed to accomplish stated objectives.	☐	☐
3. Supervisory managers in such institutions as hospitals, libraries, and school systems spend relatively large amounts of their time making institutional decisions.	☐	☐	7. A major advantage of group decision making is buckpassing.	☐	☐
4. Programmed decisions require considerable computer expertise.	☐	☐	8. The Vroom-Yetton model is a descriptive—rather than a normative—model of decision making.	☐	☐

The materials in this chapter will assist you in separating management fact from fiction. Your answers can be checked on page 186.

Decision making is a critical component of every managerial function. Examples of decisions involved in the process of planning, organizing, leading, and controlling include the following:

Planning: What are our objectives?
What strategies will be used in accomplishing these objectives?
How should our strategy be adjusted to match changes in the environment?

Organizing: How will the different divisions be coordinated?
How much authority should be given to our plant managers?
Should we implement an in-house training and management development program?

Leading: Can our factory jobs be enriched?
How can communications be improved?
How can conflict be minimized in the departments?

Controlling: How can productivity be increased?
What control measures should be employed?
How many computer terminals are needed in the departments?

> ❝ It is only in our decisions that we are important. ❞
>
> Jean-Paul Sartre

Even though decision making is discussed throughout the text, it is typically associated with the planning function since the decision-making process results in plans that affect the future of the organization and all other managerial functions.

This chapter explores the decision-making process, beginning with an analysis of the types of decisions facing managers. The steps in the decision-making process are identified and a detailed description of the activities involved at each step is included. The role of creativity in decision making is examined and the strengths and weaknesses of group decision making are summarized. The chapter concludes with a description of the Vroom-Yetton normative model of decision making, a promising model specifying the manner in which managers should make different types of decisions.

WHAT IS DECISION MAKING?

In many instances, the decisions made by a firm's management play a vital role in determining the success of the organization. Well-known decisions made in recent years that fit this description include:

• The 1985 introduction of New Coke by the Coca-Cola Company

- The decision by General Motors Corporation to locate its Saturn "car of the future" assembly facility in Spring Hill, Tennessee

- The offering of lifetime contracts to major league baseball stars George Brett, Frank White, and Dan Quisenberry by the Kansas City Royals

- The acquisition of General Foods Corporation by Philip Morris.

Other decisions are much less significant. Each day of our lives we make hundreds of decisions: What to wear, what to eat, where to go, and what to do are all decisions that must be made. But decision making is more than just attending to the details of everyday life. It is a vital kind of human activity, for it is through decision making that people define the boundaries of their lives.

Management is also a vital and uniquely human activity. *Homo sapiens* is the species that plans, organizes, controls, and "manages" its own future. It should come as no surprise, therefore, that many management writers feel that management *is* decision making. They argue that it is only by making decisions (about planning, organizing, and controlling) that people manage to do anything.

Decision making involves making a choice among alternative courses of action. This definition implies that managers are faced with a problem or opportunity, alternative courses of action are proposed and analyzed, and a choice is made that is likely to move the organization in the direction of its goals.

> **Decision making** involves choosing among two or more alternatives by following the steps of recognizing the problem, developing and analyzing alternative courses of action, selecting and implementing a course of action, and obtaining feedback to determine the effectiveness of the decision.

CERTAINTY, RISK, AND UNCERTAINTY

Since decisions are made in the present for activities and actions to occur in the future, every decision-making situation involves at least some unknown factors. These unknowns include such considerations as the reactions of a competitor to a price change, the actual productivity of newly installed machines, the dependability of new raw materials suppliers, and the attitudes of department members to a new vacation policy. The degree of uncertainty in a decision may be viewed as a continuum with three positions along it: certainty, risk, and uncertainty.

A condition of *certainty* exists when the manager can identify all available alternatives and can determine the outcome that will result from each alternative. Once the firm's chief financial officer determines that $50,000 in excess funds will be available for the next six months, alternative investment sources can be evaluated on the basis of the interest each will pay. The decision maker who chooses the local commercial bank offering a 10 percent certificate of deposit is confident that the funds will generate $2,500 in interest for the six-month period and, since these deposits are insured, that the initial $50,000 investment will be available when the certificate matures.

> **Certainty** is a decision situation in which sufficient information exists to predict the results of each alternative prior to its implementation.

Risk is a decision situation in which sufficient information exists to estimate the likelihood of the outcome of each alternative.

Most decisions facing the manager involve conditions of *risk*. Complete information about available alternatives is not available, but the manager can estimate the likelihood that each alternative will achieve the desired outcomes. For instance, oil and gas drilling firms such as Mobil, Shell, and Reading & Bates cannot be certain that a single well will produce oil or gas. However, their seismographic data combined with previous experience in drilling thousands of wells permit them to estimate the likelihood of success. In a similar manner, a life insurance firm such as Travelers, Prudential, or MONY cannot predict whether a newly insured thirty-year-old will die during the first year. However, their actuarial data on death rates for each age category permits them to estimate how many thirty-year-olds are likely to die this year. Their insurance premiums are then based on these predictions.

Uncertainty is a decision situation in which insufficient information exists to estimate the likelihood of the outcome of various alternatives.

Major decisions facing the organization typically involve conditions of *uncertainty*. In such instances, the decision maker may not be aware of all available alternatives and cannot estimate the likelihood of success for those already identified. Major U.S. banks seeking to establish a national network cannot predict whether the Pepper-McFadden Act prohibiting most interstate banking will be repealed. Although they may choose to circumvent the law by outright purchases of local banks in different states, a repeal of the law in the near future could make such purchases ill-advised. In a similar manner, a domestic firm expanding into foreign markets has no experience from which to predict the likelihood of success. Conditions of uncertainty require the manager to rely on judgment, experience, and intuition in assessing the likelihood of success for the various alternatives.

Figure 6–1 shows the certainty-uncertainty continuum. It also indicates the direct relationship between the degree of knowledge about the principal factors in a decision maker's choices and management's confidence in that decision.

TYPES OF DECISIONS

There have been many attempts to categorize and classify the types of decisions that organizations commonly face. One widely accepted model divides all organizational decisions into three categories: technical, managerial, and institutional.[1] According to the model, not only are these decisions different in kind, but they are also typically made by different individuals within the organization.

Technical Decisions. In every organization, decisions must be made about *core* activities—those activities relating directly to the "work" of the organization. The core activities of Exxon would include exploration, drilling, refining, and distribution. Decisions concerning these activities are technical in nature. The information required to solve problems related to these activities is most likely concerned with the operational aspects of the

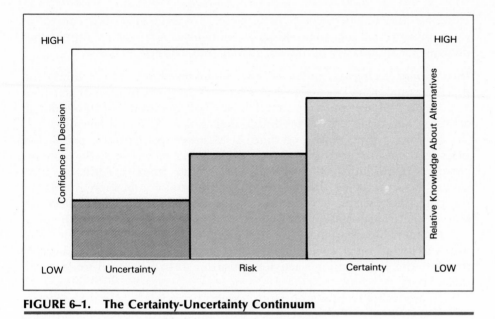

FIGURE 6–1.   The Certainty-Uncertainty Continuum

technology involved. It is important that the term *technology* be considered in its broadest sense.

> By technology is meant the action that an individual performs upon an object, with or without the aid of tools or mechanical devices, in order to make some change in that object. The object, or "raw material," may be a living being, human or otherwise, a symbol or an inanimate object. People are raw materials in banks, advertising agencies and some research organizations; the interactions of people are raw materials to be manipulated by administrators in organizations.[2]

Technical decisions concern the process by which inputs are changed into outputs by the organization. Such inputs may be people, information, or products.[3]

Managerial Decisions. The second category of decisions includes those related to issues of coordination and support of the core activities of the organization. Since all organizations tend to become differentiated or specialized over time, a need arises for the *integration* or coordination of the differentiated parts. Decisions about the process of integration are the primary focus of *managerial decisions*.

Managerial decision making is also concerned with regulating the relationship between the organization and its immediate environment. In order to produce maximum efficiency of its core activities, management must ensure that these activities are not disturbed by short-term changes in the environment. For this reason, many organizations will stockpile raw

Technical decisions are decisions involving the process by which inputs are changed into outputs.

Managerial decisions are decisions related to the coordination and support of the core activities of the organization.

PART TWO   PLANNING AND DECISION MAKING

materials and finished goods in inventory. Maintenance and control of these inventories and forecasting of short-term changes in supply-and-demand conditions are all part of managerial decision making.

Institutional Decisions. *Institutional decisions* involve long-term planning and policy formulation. They concern such issues as diversification of activities, large-scale capital expansion, mergers, shifts in research and development activities, and other critical organizational choices. If an organization is to survive over a long period of time, it must occupy a useful, productive place in the economy and society as a whole. As society and the economy change, organizations must also change or cease to exist. Although forecasters have predicted the demise of the internal combustion engine for the past thirty years, it continues to be the primary power source for automobile transportation. But General Motors Corp. has made the decision to enter the urban mass transit system market. Faced with the increasing scarcity of fossil fuels, GM's institutional decision makers chose to diversify the organization's activities in order to be prepared to deal with this scarcity.

Increased steel competition from foreign firms led National Steel executives to diversify into financial services and drug distribution. Forecasts of zero growth for the U.S. steel industry also prompted National Steel to sell its Weirton, West Virginia, mill to its employees and to form a joint venture with Japan's Nippon Kokan to operate the remaining steel business. Company chairman Howard Love points out that in the future, steel will be just one facet of an increasingly diversified company. At National Steel, the steel division will be a "stand-alone business, not *the* business of the company."[4]

The three types of decision making—technical, managerial, and institutional—are encountered by every organization. Table 6–1 illustrates each type for three different organizations: one profit-seeking firm (an oil company) and two nonprofit organizations (a hospital and the National Aeronautics and Space Administration [NASA]).

DECISION MAKING AT DIFFERENT LEVELS IN THE ORGANIZATION

An analysis of the three categories of decisions indicates that they are not evenly spread throughout the organization. As Figure 6–2 indicates, institutional decisions are most often made at the top management level of the organization, while technical decisions are more predominant at the supervisory level.

While the figure provides an indication of the relative number of each type of decision made at each level in the organization, the categories are by no means exclusive. The production vice president of a heavy equipment manufacturer might be engaged primarily in technical decisions, while a member of the legal staff might be involved solely in institutional matters.

Institutional decisions are decisions that involve long-term planning and policy formulation with the aim of assuring the organization's survival as a productive part of the economy and society.

❝ To be conscious that you are ignorant of the facts is a great step to knowledge. ❞

Benjamin Disraeli

TABLE 6–1   INSTITUTIONAL DECISIONS, MANAGERIAL DECISIONS, AND TECHNICAL DECISIONS

Type of Decision	Organizational Examples		
	Northland Hospital	National Aeronautics and Space Administration	Exxon Corporation
Institutional Decisions	Should we add a radiation therapy unit to the facilities? Should we develop an outreach capability beyond our present emergency room facilities?	Should we ask Congress to fund a manned Mars mission before the Space Shuttle program is completed? Should most of our efforts be spent on more basic research or on the industrial utilization of "near earth space"?	Should we bid on an offshore drilling lease or diversify into coal or uranium? How should we react to the president's new energy program?
Managerial Decisions	How will we staff the unit? Where will it go? How do we integrate present personnel into the new program?	What subcontractors should be used? On what schedule? How much cost overrun should we expect? What percentage of the Space Shuttle flights over the next five years should be reserved for private industry?	What land/sea leases should we choose? How much should we spend on public relations versus lobbying?
Technical Decisions	What should the treatment schedule for this patient be? Should health education be carried out in the clinic?	How do we build a self-contained biosphere? What orbit do we use? What kind of experiments will be most effective in establishing the industrial potential of near space?	Where should we drill the well? Dig the mine? Which members of Congress should we concentrate on?

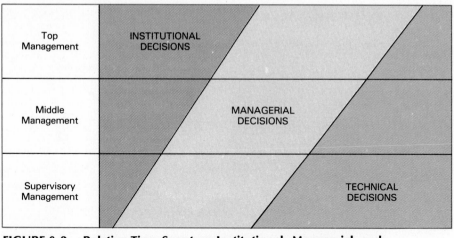

FIGURE 6–2.   Relative Time Spent on Institutional, Managerial, and Technical Decisions at Each Level of the Management Hierarchy

PROGRAMMED AND NONPROGRAMMED DECISIONS

Programmed decisions are decisions involving simple, common, frequently occurring problems that have well-established and understood solutions.

Nonprogrammed decisions are decisions that deal with unusual or novel problems.

Decisions differ not only in their content but also in terms of their relative uniqueness. By *relative uniqueness* we mean the degree to which a problem or decision (1) has been seen before; (2) occurs frequently and on a regular basis; and (3) has been solved or resolved in a satisfactory manner. *Programmed decisions* are those involving simple, common, frequently occurring problems that have well-established and understood solutions. *Nonprogrammed decisions* are those that deal with unusual or novel problems.[5]

Managers regularly have a series of recurring decisions to make. As a result, the organization develops decision rules, programs, policies, and procedures to use. Salary scales are utilized to determine starting pay for a new security officer. Reordering of raw materials occurs when inventory on hand reaches a stated minimum. Routing of the organization's fleet of trucks is determined by specially designed quantitative models. Programmed decisions can be made quickly, consistently, and inexpensively since the procedures, rules, and regulations eliminate the time-consuming process of identifying and evaluating alternatives and making a new choice each time a decision is required. While programmed decisions limit the flexibility of managers, they take little time and free the decision maker to devote his or her efforts to unique, nonprogrammed decisions.

In situations in which nonprogrammed decisions are the rule, the creation of alternatives and the selection and implementation of the most appropriate one become the critical tasks. By definition, a nonprogrammed problem is one that has not been encountered before. General Motors Corporation chairman Roger Smith's decision to acquire the giant data processing company Electronic Data Systems (EDS) was a major nonpro-

66 One cool judgment is worth a thousand hasty councils. 99

Woodrow Wilson

grammed decision. So was William Ylvisaker's move to transform Gould, Inc., from a low-tech car battery and electrical equipment manufacturer into a high-tech electronics producer.

Managers earn their salaries by making nonprogrammed decisions. They are often evaluated on their ability to apply creativity and judgment to the solution of problems and to make decisions in a logical, step-by-step manner. The description of the decision-making process in this chapter is related primarily to nonprogrammed decisions.

Converting Nonprogrammed Decisions to Programmed Decisions. Although managers are judged on their effectiveness in making nonprogrammed decisions, they should strive to convert nonprogrammed decisions into programmed ones. Many organizations treat routine decisions—inventory control, supplier selection, individual salary decisions—as special decisions requiring unique solutions. Converting such decision areas into programmed decisions frees the manager to devote more time and effort to making truly nonprogrammed decisions.

HOW GOOD SHOULD THE DECISION BE?

For more than 200 years, many economists have accepted the description of a decision maker—the so-called *economic man*—proposed by Adam Smith. This decision maker obtained information concerning all possible alternatives and chose the best solution designed to achieve a particular goal. The chosen alternative was the choice that would maximize profit or some other value.

Nobel Prize laureate Herbert Simon conducted extensive investigations of managerial behavior and concluded that modern managers are not accurately described by the economic man concept. In too many instances, they are forced to make decisions with incomplete information. They rarely consider all possible alternatives for the solution of a problem, but instead examine a few alternatives that appear to be likely solutions. Most nonprogrammed decisions involve too many variables for a thorough examination of each. Instead of attempting to maximize, the modern manager *satisfices*, according to Simon. He or she examines the five or six most likely alternatives and makes a choice from among them, rather than investing the time necessary to examine thoroughly all possible alternatives. A decision concerning a new plant location in the United States could involve the analysis of literally hundreds or thousands of possible sites. The manager may choose to focus instead on the three locales that appear most feasible and conduct a careful analysis of each alternative prior to making the final selection.

Today's manager is acting within what Simon calls *bounded rationality*.[6] This concept refers to boundaries or limits that exist in any problem situation and that necessarily restrict the manager's picture of the world.

Satisficing is the term used by Herbert Simon to describe the way modern managers must, necessarily, make decisions with incomplete information, by choosing from among the few most likely alternatives.

Bounded rationality refers to boundaries or limits that exist in any problem situation that necessarily restrict the manager's picture of the world and so his or her ability to make decisions.

Such boundaries include individual limits to any manager's knowledge of all alternatives as well as such elements as policies, costs, and technology that cannot be changed by the decision maker. As a result, the manager seldom seeks the optimum solution but realistically attempts to reach a *satisfactory* solution to the problem at hand.

Simon's view of the modern manager presents a realistic picture of a decision maker subject to both internal and external constraints. *Internal* constraints include the individual's intellectual ability, training and experience, personality, attitudes, and motivation. *External* constraints refer to the influence exerted by members of the organization and groups outside it. While this view does not mean that managers do not attempt to make effective decisions, it does recognize that often the decision maker will decide that the quality of a decision must be balanced with the time and money costs of making it.

STEPS IN DECISION MAKING

All decisions, ranging from determining the size of the employee parking lot to choosing the number of factories to produce a product line, involve a definite series of steps that lead to a particular result. Some decisions are made in minutes as the manager mentally proceeds through each step in the process. Others take months or even years. Decisions may be poorly made in a hurried manner, or they may be the result of much deliberation and careful consideration of alternatives. But all decisions go through these steps. Figure 6–3 illustrates the steps in the decision process.[7]

PERCEIVING THE ENVIRONMENT

Before any decision is possible, the individual decision maker must become aware of and be sensitive to the decision environment. This sensitivity results from two inputs:

FIGURE 6–3.   The Decision-Making Process

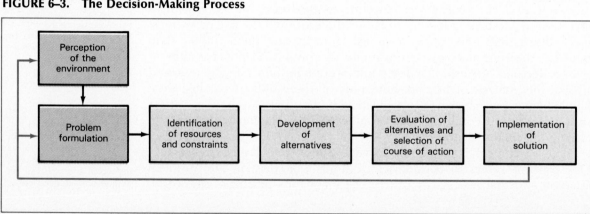

MANAGEMENT SUCCESSES

TV Guide

 The magazine industry scoffed at Walter H. Annenberg's small-sized new entry. The five-by-seven-and-a-half-inch weekly was comprised primarily of television program listings and some editorial features. It carried an appropriate name: *TV Guide.* But how could such an unlikely magazine compete with such entrenched giants as *Life, Look,* and the *Saturday Evening Post?*

But compete it did, and by 1987 more than 17 million *TV Guides* were sold every week of the year. Not only is it the nation's best-selling magazine, but it accounts for one out of every five magazines sold in the United States.

To find out how the decision was made to launch a magazine that attained such prominence, it is necessary to go back to the early 1950s. Mr. Annenberg became interested in adding a magazine on the fledgling television industry to his string of publications, which then included the Philadelphia *Inquirer* and the Philadelphia *Daily News,* as well as the magazines *Racing Form* and *Seventeen.* He also owned a chain of TV and radio stations.

Mr. Annenberg was particularly attracted by the success of the small television magazines that had been started a few years earlier in New York, Chicago, and Philadelphia. He began questioning buyers of the magazines to find out why they were willing to pay extra for program information carried by most newspapers. He found that viewers liked the magazines because of their accuracy, their articles on television personalities, and their compactness. "I came away convinced," he says.

In 1953, he paid $2.3 million for a New York magazine called *TeleVision Guide* that had been started in 1948 by two men, one a book salesman, the other a lawyer. In the same year he paid over $1 million for *TV Digest,* a Philadelphia magazine, and about $1 million for a Chicago magazine, *TV Forecast.*

The first edition of the new magazine, whose cover is shown in this box, was published April 3, 1953. Today its advertising revenues exceed $304 million for 107 regional editions, and it employs a staff of 1,400 in 33 field offices, including the 820 employees in the Radnor, Pennsylvania, headquarters. Its contributors include such renowned writers as Isaac Asimov, Joan Barthel, Joyce Carol Oates, and David Halberstam. A Univac 1180 computer ties local shows together with the network programing and stores more than 250,000 movie and television show synposes. When a local station schedules the showing of, say, episode 272 of "I Love Lucy," the computer will produce a description such as, "Lucy tries out some ill-acquired Spanish when Ricky's mother comes to visit."

Annenberg's nonprogrammed decision has clearly paid off.

Sources: The founding of *TV Guide* is described in John E. Cooney, "Pint-Sized *TV Guide* Attains Giant Profits, Circulation in 25 Years," *Wall Street Journal,* 6 November 1978, p. 1. Updated materials provided by James F. Houghton, Publicity Manager, *TV Guide.* Cover reproduced by permission of *TV Guide.*

1. Specific information of relevance to the decision maker (quality control reports, quarterly sales reports, data on supplier bid forms)

2. More general, impressionistic information about conditions and operations (the manager's "feel" for the situation)

It is important to note the difference between the environment as an objective entity and the manager's *perception* of the environment. All individuals filter the information they receive; that is, they pay more attention to *some* information than to *other* information. This filtering of information sometimes proves disastrous to both individuals and organizations.

A primary task of management is to monitor the environment for potential change. Built into every management information system is an *early warning signal* system of reporting various environmental developments—new or adapted products by competitors; changes in consumer sentiments; improved production methods—to alert decision makers. If the organization is to remain healthy over a long period of time, it must be ready to adapt and evolve in response to such changes. The development of such systems is treated in detail in Chapter 17.

FORMULATING THE PROBLEM

Problems are barriers to the achievement of organizational goals.

Performance gap is the difference between the predicted or expected level of performance and the actual level.

Problems are barriers to the achievement of organizational goals. They are obstacles to be overcome by the decision makers. When an organization fails to achieve its goals, there is a *performance gap*. This gap is the difference between the predicted or expected level of performance and the actual level. The existence of such a gap is an important part of the decision environment since it provides considerable motivation for problem solving and innovation.

How Performance Gaps Occur. There are two distinct ways in which a gap can occur. First, goals can remain constant while performance slips. These conditions usually indicate the existence of a "problem"—some technical malfunction or miscalculation on the part of management. Second, performance can remain constant while goals change. Under these circumstances, it can be said that either a problem or an opportunity exists. The fact that goals may change over time should not be neglected as a source of performance gaps, for only under these conditions can organizations change and innovate.

Goals change in response to one or more of three occurrences. First, aspiration levels tend to rise if present goals have been met for a period of time. A manufacturing facility that meets its goal of a 5 percent rejection rate for six months in a row may no longer be satisfied with that level of performance and may establish a new goal of 3 percent. Second, there may be changes in the internal environment of the organization. New people may join the organization with new ideas; new ways of doing things may be discovered; power shifts within the management structure may occur. Finally, the external environment of the organization may change. For Chrysler Corp., such changes might include the establishment of new federal emission control and mileage standards for 1989 model automobiles.

Problem Formulation: The Neglected Step in the Decision-Making Process. Problem formulation is perhaps the most neglected aspect of the decision-making process. Too often it is simply *assumed* that the nature of a managerial problem is obvious to all concerned. An employee "isn't motivated"; there exists a "personality conflict"; "What we have here is a failure to communicate." Why is problem formulation so difficult?

A major reason is that it is psychologically uncomfortable to think about problems. The manager becomes anxious and worried, and often his or her response becomes, "Don't just sit there; do something!" Such a tendency is reinforced by the fact that many academic programs spend considerable amounts of time teaching problem solving, not problem formulation. Finally, time pressures are a very real part of managerial work. Often, managers simply do not allow themselves sufficient time to consider the situation and do an effective job of problem formulation.

Preparing a Written Problem Statement. The development of a written problem statement is a relatively straightforward task. However, the importance of such a document should not be underrated. Stating a problem in written form has three distinct benefits. First and most important, it forces decision makers to clarify their thinking. The exercise provides a natural check on the tendency to spend insufficient time "finding" the problem. Second, a well-written problem statement acts as a foundation on which joint problem solving can be based. Much problem solving in modern organizations is multiperson activity, and it is extremely important that everyone be working to *solve the same problem*. A written problem statement is an excellent communications device to ensure this.

Finally, a written statement provides historical documentation of the decision-making process. Just as communication between different people is important, so also is communication between different stages in the decision-making process. In a certain sense, a written problem statement works to keep the decision maker honest. In the manager's world there are great pressures—for success, for efficiency, for getting the job done *now.* And there is occasionally the temptation to redefine the problem in the process of solving it. In other words, the decision maker might unconsciously change the problem from a difficult one to an easier one by simply ignoring or forgetting about certain unpleasant aspects. The written statement provides a tangible check for preventing such an occurrence.

Four basic guidelines should be followed in preparing a written problem statement:

> ❝ Take the obvious, add a cupful of brains, a generous pinch of imagination, a bucketful of courage and daring, stir well and bring to a boil. ❞
>
> Bernard Baruch

MANAGEMENT FAILURES

General Mills: Toys Just Aren't Us

Memorial Day, 1984, was no holiday for a small troop of Parker Bros. headquarters staff, including several vice-presidents. They spent the day hauling crates of Monopoly games, Nerf balls, and Boggle sets onto the company's loading docks in Salem, Mass., for shipment to toy stores. The purpose: to boost Parker's annual results for its corporate parent, General Mills Inc., whose fiscal year ended on May 31. But what was good for the Minneapolis food giant wasn't good for Parker's customers, who ring up more than 60% of their sales at Christmas. "We were pushing stuff out the door in May when no one wanted it," recalls one staffer.

That misadventure vividly illustrates the bad management and misunderstandings that have dogged General Mills' 17-year ownership of Parker. Such clashes contributed to its decision last spring to retreat into the kitchen. Come November, General Mills will spin off its $783 million Toy Group, which includes Parker, Kenner Products, and Fundimensions, in a public offering. Most of its other nonfood units are also for sale.

'In Limbo.' Reared on the marketing of such enduring brand names as Wheaties and Betty Crocker, General Mills executives never could get the hang of toys. "The food business is the slowest track in the world—everybody takes three years to get to market," says Bernard Loomis, president of the Toy Group from 1981 to 1983. As the toy business grew increasingly volatile, Parker's $5.6 billion parent, with its ponderous decision-making and bureaucracy, couldn't cope. Parker was jolted up and down through electronic games, children's books, and kiddie records, never able to sustain the booms or prevent the busts. Parker's 1985 sales are expected to be just $100 million, half the level for 1983. The profits record isn't any better.

Strategically, Parker, which had been owned and managed by founder George S. Parker and his descendants for 85 years, is back where it was in the 1960s—trading on the strengths of its well-known board games, Monopoly, Sorry!, Risk, and Clue. The company has slashed its payroll from 1,200 to 500 since 1983. Much of top management has exited, including the Toy Group's newly designated chief executive and Parker's president. "Morale is very low," says one executive who left in August. Agrees David S. Leibowitz, a toy industry analyst at American Securities Corp.: "It's a company in limbo. But they have a great line of staples."

It was Parker's move beyond the staples that proved to be its undoing. Until then, General Mills had pretty much left the company alone. George Parker's grandson, Randolph P. Barton, who served as Parker's chairman under General Mills, recalls General Mills's satisfaction with the "stable board game business," where sales and profits increased 10% to 15% each year.

But the toy market was changing. Neither the growth nor the money was in board games. So in 1978, Parker plunged into electronic games. It entered the market late, but it still racked up several phenomenal successes, including Merlin, the best-selling toy of 1980. Within 18 months, game sales hit $60 million.

But they dropped back to near zero just as rapidly. Then Parker caught an even bigger wave: video games. Again Parker was late but scored hits. Again it saw a huge sales surge— to $125 million—evaporate overnight. "When video went away, there was nothing to replace it," says Barton. "It was a staggering blow for Parker."

Fireworks. Frustrated by the mounting losses in electronics, General Mills tightened its grip. In the late 1970s, the parent had reorganized Barton's relaxed, family-style company. It had set up a large marketing, personnel, and administrative bureaucracy, and an army of B-school-trained "product managers" in their twenties had taken over toy lines.

Now things got worse. Headquarters "decided we didn't know what we were doing," says one staffer. "They got involved in product detail decisions." A marketing manager recalls making a "never-ending procession to General Mills. We started to think we were in the presentation business rather than the toy business." Barton insists he retained sole responsibility for all big product decisions, but he does remember feeling some heat from Minneapolis. "They said to me, 'A year ago you were a $200 million company, and now you're a $100 million company. What's going on?' "

The hard times set off fireworks between the new marketing recruits and Parker's seasoned toy professionals. "If you didn't come out of marketing, your opinion didn't really matter," says one former staffer. Departed engineers and designers complain that some products were launched just to fill shelf space. "Quality got shortchanged," says a former executive. He remembers one video game called Skyskipper: "We knew it was a bomb when we introduced it."

Parker's rocky road also led to forced ventures with Kenner, which was scoring with its Star Wars and Care Bears lines. In books and records, where Parker had hoped to launch some original series, "Kenner's licenses were shoved down our throats," says a former top employee. "The books just became illustrated brochures for Kenner toys." Some, such as Care Bears books, sold well. But most didn't.

'Major Clog-Up.' Even when Parker latched onto winners, it made marketing missteps. In 1983, for example, when the company entered the children's-book market, it backed its move with an unprecedented $1 million TV ad blitz. That helped sell books worth an astonishing $18 million in Parker's first 12 months in the business. But to help foot the heavy promotion bill, Parker broke with industry custom and refused to let retailers return unsold books. The result was "a major clog-up in the retail system," says Louis J. Woolf, a former product manager. Left with unsold books, many customers refused to reorder. Annual book sales have fizzled to about $8 million.

Parker also scored an immediate hit in records: Its Cabbage Patch Kids record "went gold" in 1984, selling over 500,000 copies. But the executive responsible for the successes in both books and records was promoted and then left the company. "No one took up the slack," says a former employee. In 12 months, record sales fell from $8 million to $2 million.

To get past "Go" again, Parker needs major new products, but insiders say none are in the offing. Its best hope is a video version of Clue that, unlike the board game, has only 24 solutions. Despite the Toy Group's problems,

(Continued on next page)

outsiders believe that the booming toy market will let General Mills float it at a considerable premium over its $235 million book value. Certainly the timing will be better than that of Parker's last Wall Street venture. In 1937, Monopoly inventor Charles Darrow talked the company into launching a stock market game, Bulls and Bears. With the Depression in full swing, it bombed—but millionaire Darrow retired to become a gentleman farmer and world traveler. Parker's executives should be so lucky.

Source: Alex Beam and Judith H. Dobrzynski, "General Mills: Toys Just Aren't Us." Reprinted from September 16, 1985 issue of *Business Week* by special permission. © 1985 by McGraw-Hill, Inc.

- The problem should be stated explicitly. Avoid general statements about vague feelings of concern.

- A working diagnosis should be included. This contains a description of the symptoms observed, the nature of the suspected problem, and what the underlying causes are thought to be.

- The problem should be stated in specific behavioral terms. Individuals are generally unable to change general conditions, but they can alter specific behavior. Telling subordinates that they lack motivation leaves them to interpret what is meant by *motivation*. Moreover, telling them that they report to work late too often does not alleviate the problem either.

- The problem statement should specify how the problem relates to the organization as a whole and to its various parts. Although the *primary* responsibility for a particular problem may be found in one department, other departments may also play a role. While the marketing department may bear the primary responsibility for low sales, improper quality control by the production department might be an important contributing factor.[8]

Distinguishing Between Problems, Symptoms, and Causes. Sherlock Holmes once remarked that it is a capital mistake to theorize in advance of the fact. He might also have said that it is an even more grievous error to mistake the "obvious" facts one has assembled for the true, underlying nature of the problem. In virtually every Holmes story, Inspector Lestrade or Dr. Watson offers a common-sense, obvious explanation for a mystery. And the explanation proves to be totally wrong. Yet all too often, managers find themselves playing Lestrade by not digging deeply enough and considering only the most visible symptoms of the problem—rather than its causes.

To be an effective problem solver, the manager must understand the relationship among symptoms, problems, and causes. *Symptoms* are those visible indicators that tell the decision maker something is wrong. The *problem* is whatever gave rise to the symptoms, and the *causes* of the problem are those factors that allow it to exist.

A physician who discovers anemia, severe stomach cramps, and weakness in a patient is observing symptoms. By adding data that the patient is a child who lives in an old tenement building, the doctor might conclude that the problem is lead poisoning and treat it accordingly. If the symptoms are relieved, has the problem been solved? If the causes still exist, the child will be back again shortly with the same symptoms, or worse. Only when the source of the lead is discovered and eliminated will the problem be solved. Managers, too, should work to change or eliminate causes rather than attempting to suppress symptoms.

Symptoms are visible indicators resulting in awareness that a problem exists.

Cause refers to underlying factors that combine to create a problem and allow it to exist.

IDENTIFYING RESOURCES AND CONSTRAINTS

Problem solving does not occur in a vacuum. It is embedded in the fabric of the organization and its environment. It is also true that organizations generally face more than one problem at the same time. These problems compete for the manager's attention and for the scarce resources of the organization.

By definition, anything that can be used to help in solving a problem is a resource. Resources include time, money, personnel, expertise, energy, equipment, raw materials, and information. These resources are referred to in Figure 6–4 as "the Five Ms of Management."[9]

Constraints are factors that impede problem solving or limit managers in their efforts to solve a problem. Lack of adequate resources might prove to be a significant constraint. Other elements such as worker attitudes or government programs may prove to be a resource, a constraint, or both.

In some instances, technological innovations prove to be a constraint. The addition of polyester to cotton in sheets caused them to last twice as long as the pure cotton variety. To overcome this constraint to sales growth in their $850 million-a-year industry, decision makers at such textile mills as J. P. Stevens and Spring Mills developed decorator bedsheets. For children's bedrooms they developed colorful sheets with the likenesses of Smurfs, Garfield, Snoopy, and Care Bear characters. Adults were offered satin sheets in every color of the rainbow as well as custom-designed sheets by Calvin Klein, Oscar de la Renta, and Bill Blass. By transforming sheets from a commodity-type purchase to a decorative component of the home

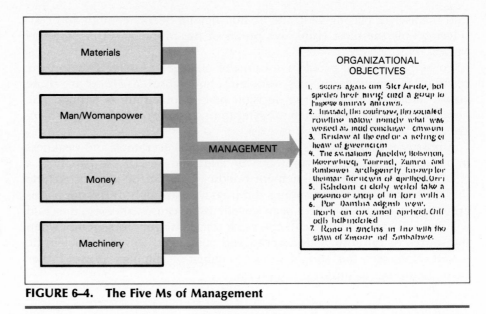

FIGURE 6–4.   The Five Ms of Management

for many customers, the textile industry has been able to overcome a major growth constraint.

The decision maker should develop a brief but explicit listing of the major resources and constraints relevant to a given problem. Such a listing of resources allows the decision maker to budget organizational assets in order to maximize their usefulness. The listing of constraints alerts the decision maker to the important stumbling blocks affecting a solution so that they can be avoided. In addition, organizations sometimes encounter situations in which the absence of a specific resource or the existence of a particular constraint is a significant problem itself. Pizza Hut became the world's largest pizza maker by outdistancing such competitors as Godfather's, Domino's, Pizza Inn, Noble Roman, and Shakey's. A major cost factor in pizza manufacturing is mozzarella cheese, whose price has exceeded $1.00 per pound in recent years. If Pizza Hut should attempt to increase sales by 40 percent in a single year through the expansion of the number of outlets, the reduction of prices to stimulate additional sales, or by other means, its management might find that both the price and the limited supply of mozzarella would make its goal impossible to attain, regardless of the alternative chosen. This barrier would then form the basis of a subsidiary problem whose goal would be to obtain needed raw materials resources. In this manner, the overall problem situation is broken down into smaller, more easily handled subproblems.

DEVELOPING ALTERNATIVES

The generation of a number of possible alternatives is an essential task of the decision maker. In too many instances managers quickly identify one or two alternatives and choose between them. This short-cut approach often results in more effective alternatives never being considered. Creativity is needed at this step in developing a variety of alternatives for consideration. As Figure 6–5 indicates, alternatives result from ideas posed by organizational members. Such ideas may prove to be the basis for solving problems or taking advantage of new opportunities.

The Use of Creativity in Developing Alternatives. A widely used technique for the generation of alternative solutions is the *synectics approach.*[10] The term synectics is derived from two Greek words that mean the joining together of different and apparently irrelevant elements. One writer describes the synectics approach as follows:

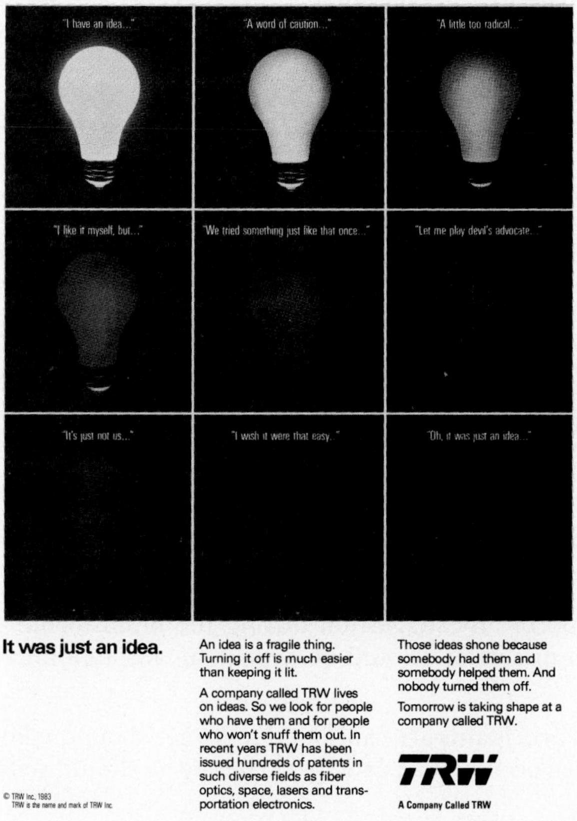

Synectics approach is a technique widely used to generate alternative solutions; by synectics, the manager examines analogous methods and perceptions of other fields in order to gain insight into management problems.

FIGURE 6–5. Ideas: Starting Points for Developing Alternatives
Source: © TRW, Inc., 1983. Reprinted by permission.

It was just an idea.

An idea is a fragile thing. Turning it off is much easier than keeping it lit.

A company called TRW lives on ideas. So we look for people who have them and for people who won't snuff them out. In recent years TRW has been issued hundreds of patents in such diverse fields as fiber optics, space, lasers and transportation electronics.

Those ideas shone because somebody had them and somebody helped them. And nobody turned them off.

Tomorrow is taking shape at a company called TRW.

TRW

A Company Called TRW

© TRW Inc. 1983
TRW is the name and mark of TRW Inc.

Synectics in operation depends heavily on two mechanisms: making the strange familiar, and making the familiar strange. The first of these is the search for similarity; confronted with a new problem we ask ourselves whether it is not an old problem, had we but the wit to see it. Seeing even partial resemblances may lead to the application of familiar methods in solving the new problem. Making the familiar strange is a way of shedding preconceptions and perceptual habits. Innocence of vision, a certain naiveté, and ingeniousness characterize the creative individual; if these qualities can be cultivated the novelty of invention and problem solution should be increased.[11]

Analogy is the primary mechanism to make the strange familiar and the familiar strange. Often, it takes the form of borrowing from nature. Alexander Graham Bell's basic idea for the telephone came from studying the construction of the human ear. Leonardo da Vinci's idea for a helicopter came from watching leaves twirl in the wind. Although the famous story of Newton discovering gravity by having an apple fall on his head has no basis in fact, it is still popular because it is a credible example of the use of analogy.

Often, analogy becomes an exercise in pure imagination. It may be visual rather than verbal and equate to a mental juggling of concepts and ideas until an "attractive" formation occurs. The decision maker who uses this form of analogy is attempting to associate an event in two different frames of reference. What occurs is applied make-believe, the art of "what if?" Table 6–2 summarizes and illustrates the use of analogy in developing alternatives.

Synectics and the use of analogy point to an important psychological aspect of problem solving. Often, it is far more effective and efficient to "think around" the problem than to attack it directly. Every decision maker encounters an occasional mental block. Creative techniques such as synectics are proven methods of removing such blocks, or at least of getting around them.

Other creative techniques use the "more is better" approach.[12] This approach is based on the assumption that concentration on a few alternatives to the exclusion of other, less likely ones may blind the decision maker to many opportunities. *Brainstorming* is the chief technique of this approach. Brainstorming involves sessions where a group of several persons tosses out ideas to each other. Each idea is recorded for later evaluation. There are four rules in brainstorming.

Brainstorming is a creativity technique used to bring forth many alternative solutions; it involves a group of people brought together for the purpose of exchanging ideas.

1. There is *no* evaluation of any suggestion during the brainstorming session. In fact, even discussion should be kept to an absolute minimum.

2. Quantity is desired. Participants are cautioned to forget about quality at this stage. If an idea occurs to a participant, he or she should state it.

TABLE 6–2   USE OF ANALOGY IN THE CREATIVE PROCESS

Alternatives	Examples
1. Decision makers imagine themselves to be an actual, physical part of the problem under consideration.	Superintendent of gem mine plays role in which he or she is one of the miners in an attempt to determine methods of employee theft and its prevention.
2. Decision makers develop alternatives by studying similar situations in other industries, geographical areas, or subjects.	Du Pont decision makers adapt a heat resistant material named Teflon to a variety of uses ranging from cookware to disc brakes.
3. Decision makers use imagination to develop a series of answers to a series of "what if?" questions.	Managers of new-product development at Campbell Soup Co. develop new types of soup by considering such blends as meat with vegetables; fruit with vegetables; milk with fruit; and so forth.

3. Freewheeling is encouraged. The stranger the idea the better.

4. Tag-on ideas and the modification or combination of existing ideas are desired.[13]

These rules are based on two insights into the psychology of creativity. First, it is difficult, if not impossible, to be both creative and judgmental at the same time. It is as if the decision maker possesses two sets of mental "gears"; trying to use them at the same time may strip them both. As a result, any form of criticism or evaluation is absolutely forbidden. Second, creativity can be both an individual and a group process. In the same way that the splitting of one atom of U^{235} in the core of a nuclear reactor sets off other atoms, so do ideas generated in a brainstorming session touch off other ideas, and a chain reaction results.

A number of studies of the effectiveness of the brainstorming approach have been conducted. Findings generally support the effectiveness of this approach in producing large numbers of novel solutions.[14] Most effective use of the technique occurs when group members know of the problem in advance and spend some time "brainstorming" on their own; the group works together on a more or less regular basis; and individual members of the group again work on the problem on their own after the meeting.

How Much Time Should Be Invested in Developing Alternatives? The ultimate scarce resource of the manager is time. And since there are always additional alternatives waiting to be discovered, the alternative generation process could conceivably go on forever.

Two factors should be considered in determining the appropriate amount of time to spend generating alternatives. The first factor is the importance of the problem or opportunity. The more important the problem, the greater the value of marginal improvements in the solution. A 2 percent improvement in the solution of a $10-million problem produces a further profit or savings of $200,000. The same percentage improvement for a $10,000 problem produces less impressive results. Improvements in a solution typically occur when a relatively large number of alternatives are considered. As a result, decision makers who face major problems should invest as much time as is necessary to create a variety of alternatives.

The second factor involves the ability of the decision maker to differentiate accurately among alternatives. If the decision maker cannot tell in advance the difference between two alternatives and cannot accurately rank them according to their likely effectiveness, then nothing is gained. Two factors affect the decision maker's ability to differentiate among alternatives: the amount of available data and the cost of performing the evaluation/ranking. The difficulty of distinguishing among alternatives and determining their relative effectiveness decreases with increases in the amount of available data. Under conditions of high uncertainty (little data), decision makers should not devote large amounts of time to generating alternatives. Similarly, the higher the cost of distinguishing among alternatives, the more likely the decision maker is to prefer relatively few alternatives. Consider again the $10-million problem with a potential 2 percent improvement in solution. If the cost of evaluating an additional alternative is $250,000, the evaluation costs $50,000 more than the possible savings ($250,000 cost less $200,000 possible improvement). The marginal increase in the improvement of a solution should always be more than the marginal cost of performing the additional evaluation.

> ❝ We learn from experience. A man never wakes up his second baby just to see it smile. ❞
>
> Grace Williams

EVALUATING ALTERNATIVES AND SELECTING A COURSE OF ACTION

The evaluation of alternatives and the choosing of the most appropriate action are at the very heart of the decision-making process. Up until this point, all of the activities of the decision maker have been preparatory. It is at this step that he or she finally *decides what to do*.[15] This crucial stage has three distinct phases: determining which alternatives are feasible; evaluating feasible alternatives; and selecting the most appropriate alternative.

Determining Feasible Alternatives. In cases where a large number of alternatives have been generated, it is likely that many of them will not be feasible. Either the resources necessary to implement the alternative are unavailable or there are prohibitive constraints. If judgment was suspended during the creative generation of alternatives in the previous step, most of the alternatives generated would fall into the infeasible category. Separating the feasible alternatives from the infeasible ones saves time, since the decision maker can then evaluate only those alternatives that are likely to be chosen. When National Steel's plan to sell its remaining steel operations to U.S. Steel was opposed by the U.S. Department of Justice on antitrust grounds, this alternative was eliminated. The alternative ultimately selected by the firm's management was the sale of a 50 percent interest to Japan's Nippon Kokan.

Evaluating Alternatives. The formal evaluation of alternatives is an extremely complex subject. In fact, many of the management science techniques developed during the past half-century are methods of determining the relative efficiency of various alternatives. The major techniques are discussed in detail in Chapter 7.

One writer has proposed the following rules for evaluating alternatives:

- A solution should be of a *quality* satisfactory to meet organizational goals.

- A solution must be *acceptable* to those affected by it and to those who must implement it.

- A solution should be evaluated in terms of the *anticipated responses* to it.

- The *risks* of each alternative should be considered. The choice of solution should focus on *present* alternatives, not past possibilities.[16]

Is Quality Consistent with Goals? The quality of a solution has two dimensions: effectiveness and efficiency. *Efficiency* is simply the ratio of outputs to inputs (O/I). It is, therefore, the forerunner of benefit/cost analysis, breakeven analysis, and numerous other techniques that compare expected return with projected investment. *Effectiveness,* by contrast, is a measure of the extent to which an alternative meets the stated objective (regardless of the cost). Before attempting to evaluate the quality of any alternative, the decision maker must first establish the extent to which each of these criteria will be used.

A good example of the impact of these two criteria—effectiveness and efficiency—can be seen in the health care industry. In the United States, this industry has traditionally stressed effectiveness over efficiency—no cost was too great to care for the sick or prolong human life. Recently, this "policy" has been called into question by a number of well-publicized instances in which severely brain-damaged persons were kept breathing for extended periods by means of life-support equipment. The astronomical costs of health care (particularly in the high-technology areas such as complete life-support procedures, where prognosis is often highly unfavorable) have caused industry decision makers to consider efficiency as

Efficiency is a comparison of the costs involved in implementing a course of action with the expected returns; the ratio of outputs to inputs.

Effectiveness is a measure of the extent to which a decision alternative meets the stated objective regardless of the costs involved.

MANAGEMENT: THE LIGHTER SIDE

"Relax . . . Relax . . . You Are Feeling Very Original"

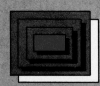

Got a problem? Why not tackle it with some of the techniques favored by the experts in creative problem-solving?

First, make sure you understand the problem thoroughly. Sometimes problems elude a solution because they aren't clearly defined. Then, relax. Stress is the surest way to snuff out the creative spark. And remember, there is no right or wrong answer. So don't pass judgment on any ideas until you've generated several alternatives—otherwise, you might freeze up. If you can, put yourself in a playful, even humorous mood.

If you want to improve a process, organization, or product, try synergy—combining existing elements in a new way. That's how the circular saw blade was invented: A Shaker woman, Sister Tabatha Babbett, watched two men laboriously sawing wood with a straight blade as she worked at her spinning wheel. She figured that the job would be much easier if saw teeth were cut into the edge of a wheel.

Lunch Boxes. Problems that call for entirely new concepts require a different tack. One way is to juxtapose an image or bit of information that is outside the problem. Reconciling the two will force the mind to make new connections. Try, for example, consulting the dictionary: Choose a word and start making associations. It worked for Current Inc., a Colorado Springs greeting-card company. The word "shrink" led artists and writers to develop Wee Greetings, a line of business-card-size greetings that can be slipped into lunch boxes or shirt pockets. And out of "enlarge" they concocted Greeting Gifts—cards that contain balloons and confetti.

well as effectiveness. This is not to say that efficiency should be the major concern; only that it should be taken into account along with effectiveness.

Are Solutions Acceptable to Affected Personnel? The chosen alternative must be acceptable to and preferably liked by those who must implement it and those who must live with the consequences of the decision. Failure to meet this condition is the single most likely reason for failure of the decision-making process to solve problems.

Questions about the acceptability and efficiency/effectiveness of a proposed solution can only be answered by considering the anticipated responses to it. *Anticipated response* refers to the reactions of the organization and its individual members to a chosen alternative. This should be of critical concern to the manager/decision maker since even a technically mediocre solution may prove effective if it is implemented with enthusiasm and dedication. On the other hand, the technically correct alternative may fail to succeed if implementation is half-hearted and haphazard. For this

Then there is the "excursion" technique developed by the Center for Creative Leadership. First, go through word-association exercises to find one that has lots of visual appeal. Then fantasize. Engineers at the National Aeronautics & Space Administration used this method to come up with Velcro, the tenacious substitute for zippers and buttons. The NASA designers were trying to find a fastening device for space suits that astronauts could manipulate with their bulky gloves. The team picked the words "rain forest." One member described a fantasy of running through the forest and having thorns stick to his clothes. That gave the group the idea of making a fastener that gripped with thousands of thornlike fibers. One old standby of creative thinking is analogy. Find out how a similar problem is solved in nature or some other aspect of life, then adapt it to the present quandary. Eli Whitney conjured up the cotton gin by watching a cat trying to catch a chicken through a fence—just the thing to comb seeds out of cotton bolls. And analogies inspired Thomas A. Edison as he invented the prototype motion picture machine, the phonograph, and the light bulb.

If an analogy doesn't come to mind, try restating the problem as a paradox, then find an analogy that solves it. Confusing? Maybe, but it worked for Adolph Coors Co. The problem: The brewer was paying to dispose of gallons and gallons of spoiled—and therefore worthless—beer. But with the help of a creativity consultant, managers turned to a scene from *Tom Sawyer.* Inspired by the way Tom persuaded his friends that painting a fence was a privilege they should pay for, Coors is now selling its spoiled beer to the Japanese to be used as feed for their beef cattle.

One thing you must always keep in mind: Somewhere out there lies an answer. Or several. So if all else fails, try something original.

Source: "Relax . . . Relax . . . You Are Feeling Very Original," *Business Week,* 30 September 1985, p. 84. Reprinted by permission. © 1985 by McGraw-Hill, Inc.

reason, many writers stress the importance of including as many organization members as feasible in the decision-making process. Participation in problem solving by organization members should increase their receptiveness to the chosen alternative.

The risks associated with each alternative must be considered. Specific techniques of risk assessment will be discussed in Chapter 7. It should be noted at this point that different risks are involved for different individuals and groups in the organization. As has been pointed out, the differences among those who make decisions, those who implement them, and those who must live with them should not be minimized. In a political election, for example, voters make the decision by casting their ballots; the election commission implements the decision by counting the votes and certifying the results; and the candidates are the primary persons who must live with the decision. Voters realize some small risk; the election commission experiences virtually no risk; and the candidates view the decision as an all-or-nothing proposition. How are their responses to a proposed change in election laws likely to vary?

> ❝ The fellow that agrees with everything you say is either a fool or he is getting ready to skin you. ❞
>
> Kin Hubbard

COMPUTERS IN MANAGEMENT

Programs That Make Managers Face the Facts

 Sometimes success can be a big problem. When publicity from a local television program recently sent sales soaring at Miami Depot Inc., management could not begin to handle the bonanza. To get organized, the Florida company, which resells products that it acquires from bankrupt or disaster-plagued retailers, turned to a $495 personal computer program called Trigger. With it, the company was able to devise a management system that drastically cut costs.

Trigger is a prime example of a new breed of decision-making program that is being used increasingly to help executives develop business strategies and make qualitative decisions. In a software industry glutted with spreadsheets, word processing programs, and other look-alike products, a handful of fledgling companies are struggling to find market niches with these "intuitive," easy-to-learn personal computer programs for executives.

'It Was Chaos.' Up-and-coming businesses that often cannot afford to hire consultants have been particularly receptive. At Miami Depot, "we needed something to tie us together after sales went from the outhouse to outer space," recalls Robert B. Halsey, the company's 32-year-old co-founder. "When we were small, we had our finger on the pulse of everything. But when we got big, it was chaos." Using Trigger, Halsey was able to formulate and structure specific performance goals and then track those goals each week. If, for example, costs proved to be too high as a percentage of sales, the program would send out an alert and demand an explanation from the managers involved.

Until now, the market for personal computer software has been made up largely of number crunchers, writers, and electronics buffs. But decision-making programs could lure a new kind of customer, say industry analysts. They are betting that this type of package will attract a new audience because it offers something entirely different for personal computer customers: the ability to use software programs not only to organize a complicated array of information but also to make managerial judgments. "This is the promise of software—that it does more than just numbers but actually improves the quality of your decisions," says Esther Dyson, who publishes a computer industry newsletter based in New York City.

The new software can't do the entire job, of course. "These programs are tools—they won't make your decision for you," points out Steven Ross, a consultant with McNamee Consulting Co. Most of the programs set up

IMPLEMENTING THE SOLUTION

Earlier in the chapter, decision making was defined as making a choice from several alternatives. Most formal approaches to decision making emphasize methods of selecting the most appropriate alternative—and devote little consideration to questions of implementation. Implementing a chosen alternative is often assumed to be a straightforward and trouble-

strict guidelines that force users to define the criteria that are most important to their business. Their real value is that they help users figure out how to develop and define those criteria from a web of complex and interrelated factors.

Typical of the new programs is Lightyear, a $495 product sold by two-year-old Lightyear Inc. Last year, Chairman John D. Couch actually used the program in deciding whether to join the Santa Clara (Calif.) company. A former vice-president at Apple Computer Inc., Couch was considering several employment options after taking a year off. He began by typing into his computer the main elements he wanted in his next job, weighted them for their relative importance, and indicated how the companies he was considering matched up with those elements. With the press of a button, the program popped out its recommendation to join Lightyear.

Unemotional. Jack Zwick, president of Topwalk Associates, a McLean (Va.) consulting firm, swears by Expert Choice, a $495 program he uses to help clients determine the risks and benefits of making loans to foreign countries. He begins by creating a long list of criteria, usually including the size of a country's foreign debt, its political stability, its domestic deficit, and how deeply involved the bank wants to become with that country. Based on all the data, the program makes recommendations and backs them up with de-

tailed explanations. "There are so many factors involved in these decisions, and people get very emotional," Zwick says. "This forces a more reflective judgment."

Another kind of decision-making software involves data base management. Such a program gives users new ways to analyze data stored in a central data bank. Analytica Corp.'s $495 Reflex, for example, makes it possible to summarize and compare such data in tabular form. A marketing director who wanted to see how many products certain sales representatives have sold would simply tell the program what he wanted, and it would automatically fill in the blanks in the appropriate rows and columns. Then the program could come up with such information as which sales representatives generated the greatest profits.

Analysts and users alike warn, however, that these programs are hardly the be-all and end-all for decision-makers. They are only as good as the assumptions and criteria plugged into them and should not be taken as gospel. "Just because a machine spits something out, I'm not going to say, 'Oh, that's the answer,'" says R. Derek Williamson, manager of end-user computing for Bank of America. Even so, such programs should provide a big step toward making the personal computer a more useful tool for managers.

Source: Anne R. Field, "Programs That Make Managers Face the Facts," Business Week, 8 April 1985, p. 74. Reprinted by permission. © 1985 by McGraw-Hill, Inc.

free process. Unfortunately, while this assumption may be true for strictly technical decision making, most managerial problems are intimately concerned with the human element in the organization. Implementation, therefore, is typically anything but simple.

While no generalized rules have been developed that deal with managing the implementation phase, three questions must be answered. First, what should the internal structure of implementation be? In other words, what should be done when by whom? Since the solution of most managerial problems requires the combined effort of many organizational members, each should understand what role he or she is to play during each phase of the implementation process.

Second, how can the manager reward organization members for participating in the implementation of the proposed solution? Managers may make the decisions, but it is typically the responsibility of other organization members to carry them out. Care should be taken to ensure that those individuals responsible for implementation have some stake—financial or otherwise—in the success of the solution.

Finally, have provisions been made for evaluating and modifying the chosen solution during the implementation process? As implementation proceeds, members of the organization should be able to modify the solution based on what they learn during implementation. But unless some specific provision for modification has been made, the chosen alternative may be treated as a "sacred cow" and implemented without any thought of possible modification—even in instances where minor adjustments would produce better solutions.

FEEDBACK

Feedback refers to information transmitted by a receiver back to the original sender of a message.

Feedback is a necessary component of the decision process, providing the decision maker with a means for determining the effectiveness of the chosen alternative in solving the problem or taking advantage of the opportunity and moving the organization closer to the attainment of its goals. Several items are necessary in such an evaluation of the effectiveness of a decision. The starting point is availability of a set of standards with which actual performance is compared. For this reason, the importance of quantifiable, measurable goals was stressed in Chapter 5. If such goals are in use, they become the necessary standards. If the firm's sales goal for the next three months is $2 million more than the current quarter, the relevant standard is present sales plus $2 million. If the firm adopts a zero-defects program, a zero rejection rate for output becomes the relevant standard.

A second requirement in evaluating the effectiveness of a decision is performance data for use in comparison with the set of standards. The design of management information systems is the chief approach to formalizing the data collection process; it is the subject of Chapter 17.

Finally, a data analysis strategy must be developed. Such a strategy includes a formal plan outlining how the data will be used. One unfortunate characteristic of most data collection is that large amounts of data are never used. Managers who know exactly how the data are to be analyzed will be able to specify the types of data they need, the most preferred format, and the time sequence in which they are needed. Such advance specifications should aid in reducing the amount of useless data that are collected.

GROUP DECISION MAKING AND THE USE OF COMMITTEES

Although discussion of the steps involved in the decision-making process focused primarily on the individual decision maker, many of the decisions in large, complex organizations are made by *groups*. The shared power, bargaining activities, and need for compromise present in most group situations further complicate the decision-making process.

Some managers utilize committees for input on important matters facing the organization, but make major decisions themselves. Chrysler chairman Lee Iacocca describes his decision-making style as follows:

> Despite what the textbooks say, most important decisions in corporate life are made by individuals, not by committees. My policy has always been to be democratic all the way to the point of decision. Then I become the ruthless commander. "Okay, I've heard everybody," I say. "Now here's what we're going to do."[17]

Group decision making is the norm in Japanese organizations. The typical decision-making process in Japan begins with supervisory managers meeting as a group to analyze a problem or opportunity and develop alternative solutions. Two or three of the most likely alternatives are then presented to top management, where the final decision is made. Use of lower-level managers in the preliminary stages of the decision process provides them with a sense of responsibility in the decision, while simultaneously reducing the amount of time top management must devote to the process.

American managers often criticize the committee approach to decision making as a waste of time and a sure method of obtaining only compromise solutions. The definition of a camel as "a horse designed by a committee" illustrates the sentiments of many managers. But the increased complexity of the world in which the organization operates makes it increasingly difficult for a single manager to make complex decisions independently. Task forces, conferences, committees, and staff meetings are increasingly used in making important decisions.

GROUP DECISION-MAKING STRENGTHS

Evidence indicates that groups tend to make more accurate decisions than individuals.[18] This is particularly true in cases involving complex problems where no one member is an expert in the problem area. The "two heads are better than one" philosophy means that more information can be processed by the various group members. The presence of several group members also means that more alternative solutions may be proposed; individuals can "piggyback" ideas presented with other proposed alternatives; and a greater number of proposed solutions can be analyzed. Participation in decision making should increase the managers' acceptance of the final choice. Individual members of the group can also more easily communicate the decision—and its rationale—to the members of their own departments or units. A major strength of group decision making is the relative ease of *implementing* decisions that have been made. But there are also a number of weaknesses involved with group decision making.

GROUP DECISION-MAKING WEAKNESSES

The major disadvantage of group decision making is *time*. Decisions made by groups take longer—as much as 50 percent longer than individual decisions, according to one study.[19] In addition, group decisions are often compromises between differing points of view of individual members—rather than the most appropriate choice for solving the problem. There is often pressure to accept the decision favored by most group members. *Groupthink*—a phenomenon in which the desire for group cohesiveness and consensus becomes stronger than the desire for the best possible decision—may occur.[20] Some groups experience more indecisiveness than individual decision makers since the pressure to reach a decision is diffused among the group members. In situations in which clear lines of authority and responsibility for making a decision have not been drawn, members of the group may engage in *buckpassing*—blaming one another for a poorly made compromise decision or the lack of a decision. The buckpassing phenomenon can be prevented if the leader accepts the ultimate responsibility for making the decision. Often, one person or a few individuals will dominate the group because of differences in status or rank or through force of personality.[21] Table 6–3 summarizes the strengths and weaknesses of group decision making.

Groupthink is a phenomenon present in some committee decisions in which the desire for group consensus and cohesiveness is stronger than the desire for the most appropriate decision.

Buckpassing is a phenomenon present in some committees in which individual members blame one another for a poorly made compromise decision or the lack of a decision.

AN APPLIED APPROACH TO DECISION MAKING ▬

Two researchers, Victor Vroom and Philip Yetton, have recently developed a normative model of decision making.[22] It is normative in the sense of specifying the manner in which managers *should* make decisions. They identify five styles of decision making based on the degree of participation by subordinates in choosing an alternative. The five styles are as follows:

1. Managers make the decision themselves, using the information available at the time.

2. Managers obtain information from subordinates, then make the decision themselves.

3. Managers discuss the problem with subordinates as a group, but make the decision themselves.

4. Managers discuss the problem with subordinates on an individual basis, but make the decision themselves.

TABLE 6–3   STRENGTHS AND WEAKNESSES OF GROUP DECISION MAKING

Strengths	Weaknesses
Group decisions may be more accurate than individual decisions.	Group decisions are slower than individual decisions—and the cost is multiplied, due to the number of personnel involved.
More information can be processed by the group than by an individual decision maker.	Group decisions are often compromise decisions—rather than the selection of the most appropriate alternative.
More alternatives can be proposed and brainstorming of ideas can be conducted.	Indecisiveness and buckpassing are sometimes characteristic of groups.
Managers' acceptance of solution is increased through their participation.	Groups are occasionally dominated by one or a few individuals; this is particularly common when individuals who rank higher in status in the organization are present.
Managers can communicate decisions and reasons for them to their own work group.	

5. Managers share the problem with subordinates as a group. Alternatives are generated and evaluated jointly by managers and subordinates and the decision is made by consensus. Managers accept and implement any solution that has the support of the group.

Vroom and Yetton propose a list of seven "Yes-No" questions dealing with the amount of available information, the type of decision required, and the involvement of subordinates. By answering these questions, the manager determines the most appropriate style of decision making to use. The seven questions are:

- Is there a quality requirement such that one solution is likely to be more rational than another?

- Does the manager have sufficient information to make a high-quality decision?

- Is the problem structured? In other words, can the manager identify the information required for the decision and how to obtain it?

- Is acceptance of the decision by subordinates critical to its successful implementation?

- If the manager makes the decision without consulting subordinates, is the decision likely to be accepted by them?

- Do subordinates share the organizational goals to be obtained in solving this problem?

- Is conflict among subordinates likely to occur if the preferred solution is made?

The authors develop a decision model by matching the decision styles to the situation as determined by answers to the seven questions. By answering these questions, the preferred management decision style for each type of problem is identified. Figure 6–6 shows how the Vroom-Yetton model works. The flowchart provides the manager with a step-by-step approach to determining the most appropriate style of decision mak-

FIGURE 6–6.   Flowchart of the Decision Process
Source: Reprinted from Victor H. Vroom and Philip W. Yetton, *Leadership and Decision Making*, by permission of the University of Pittsburgh Press, © 1973 by the University of Pittsburgh Press.

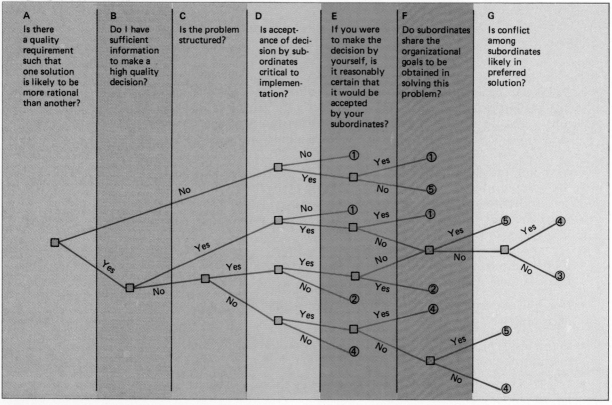

■ "Yes-No" questions listed at the top of the model.
● Preferred decision-making style for a particular problem situation.

ing under a given set of circumstances. To see how the model works, take the example of the manager facing a decision situation in which quality differences in alternative solutions are not likely to be great and where subordinates' acceptance of the decision is not crucial to its effective implementation.

In this instance, the manager can use style 1, where the decision is made in an autocratic fashion without consulting subordinates. On the other hand, consider the following situation: (1) additional information is needed to solve the problem; (2) the manager can identify the needed information and its location; and (3) acceptance of the decision by subordinates is not critical to its successful implementation. The most appropriate decision style in this case is style 2, in which the managers obtain information from subordinates but do not involve them in making the decision. A variety of other decision situations are matched by the model to the most appropriate decision-making styles.

In some instances, the model identifies decisions in which more than one management style may be used. For example, suppose a manufacturing facility has decided to convert to twenty-four-hour production days and has developed three shifts: 7:00 A.M. to 3:00 P.M.; 3:00 P.M. to 11:00 P.M.; and 11:00 P.M. to 7:00 A.M. A decision must be made concerning whether employees will be permanently assigned to one of the three shifts or whether all employees should rotate through the shifts on a regular basis. In such a situation, group suggestions and acceptance are important, a consultative style is effective, and the manager may choose to meet with subordinates on an individual basis (style 4) or as a group (style 3). Vroom recommends that the manager choose the style that is least costly in terms of time or money.

The Vroom-Yetton model is relatively new and its applications to date have been limited. Some early research conducted by Vroom and other management scientists has demonstrated that decisions consistent with the model have been successful.[23] The model appears to have great potential to aid the manager who must make important nonprogramed decisions.

SUMMARY

Decision making concerns the manager's role of solving problems and taking advantage of opportunities. Many management authorities feel that it is at the core of all management activity. Organizational decision making can be divided into three categories:

1. *Technical* decisions concern the process by which inputs are changed into outputs by the organization. Most of these decisions are made at the supervisory level.

2. *Managerial* decisions relate to the issues of coordination and support of the core activities of the organization. Middle management is typically involved in these matters.

3. *Institutional* decisions involve long-term planning and policy information. Top management makes most institutional decisions.

Decisions can also be classified by their relative uniqueness. Programmed decisions involve simple, common, frequently occurring problems that have well-established and understood solutions. Nonprogrammed decisions deal with unusual or novel problems. Managers should strive to convert as many decisions as possible to the programmed category, thereby freeing their time for dealing with unique problem situations.

The work of Herbert Simon has contributed to the understanding of managerial decision making. Simon discounts the traditional profit-maximization objective by arguing that managers really *satisfice* rather than investing the cost and time required to identify and evaluate all possible alternatives. Simon feels that managers are constrained by *bounded rationality*. In other words, there are limits to a manager's knowledge and understanding in any problem situation. As a result, the decision maker seeks a satisfactory solution, not necessarily the optimal one, according to Simon.

Decisions are made in a sequential order:

1. Perceiving the environment

2. Formulating the problem

3. Identifying resources and constraints

4. Developing alternatives

5. Evaluating alternatives and selecting a course of action

6. Implementing the solution

7. Feedback

Management must monitor the decision-making environment with the aid of some type of early warning signal system designed to identify developments requiring executive attention. Problems are barriers to the achievement of organizational goals. Problem formulation is an important—but often neglected—step in decision making. A written problem statement should be developed by the decision maker. Managers should also realize that problem solving occurs within a given set of resources and constraints. These resources—"the Five Ms of Management"—include time, human resources, expertise, and equipment.

The generation of alternatives is aided by the creativity of the persons involved in the decision. Synectics and brainstorming are commonly used creativity techniques.

The fifth step in the decision-making sequence—evaluating alternatives and selecting a course of action—involves three separate phases: (1) determining which alternatives are feasible; (2) evaluating alternatives; and (3) choosing the most appropriate alternative. A number of factors should be considered in the first two phases: efficiency (the ratio of outputs to inputs); effectiveness (the extent to which an alternative meets the stated objective); acceptability of the decision to affected individuals and groups; the risks involved; and the viability of implementing the alternative under consideration. The eventual choice is dependent on both objective and emotional components. The decision maker's own value system is a key ingredient in the actual solution of the problem.

Implementation of the solution requires a plan spelling out what should be done when by whom. It should also specify methods by which the manager can reward organizational members for participating in the implementation of the proposed solution and provide the necessary flexibility for modifying it, based on what is learned during implementation.

Feedback is the final component in decision making. Three items are necessary in evaluating the effectiveness of a decision:

1. A set of standards against which to compare performance.

2. Performance data to compare with standards.

3. A data analysis strategy outlining how the collected data will be used.

Not all decisions are made by individuals. Many organizations prefer group involvement in decision making, and most firms involve a number of persons in making major decisions. The major strengths of group decision making are greater accuracy; processing of more information; generation of more alternatives; increased acceptance of the solution through participation; and better communication of decisions to affected parties. Its chief weaknesses include slower decisions; compromise decisions; indecisiveness and buckpassing; and the possibility of dominance by one or a few members.

The Vroom-Yetton model is a normative model of the decision-making process, suggesting how managers should make decisions. Five decision-

SOLVING
THE STOP
ACTION
CASE

Gerber Products Company

Although the term *bounded rationality* probably never entered the discussions at Gerber's Fremont, Michigan, headquarters, the concept was obviously at work. First, the "Babies are our business . . . our *only* business" slogan had to go, since it limited the firm's flexibility to react to changing conditions. The firm was about to chart new waters in a series of critical, totally unprogramed decisions. A great amount of information was necessary to aid in identifying and evaluating alternatives, and many people would share in making the necessary decisions.

Gerber's first moves were aimed at diversification, and included establishing a chain of day-care centers and a mail-order life insurance company offering policies to young parents. A line of single-serving adult foods called "Singles" was also developed in an attempt to reach the growing number of smaller-sized households. But during test marketing in three cities, management discovered that the Gerber name was a handicap in developing a food for adults. "No matter what we labeled it," recalls one Gerber executive, "we discovered that people still thought of it as baby food, or something for adults who couldn't eat real food." These test results convinced Gerber to abandon the single-serving adult food idea.

Research data emphasized that parents had a positive image of Gerber products, and company executives decided to exploit this strength by developing additional entries in the juvenile products business. Four hundred products have been introduced, including toiletries, bottles, clothing, and toys. In addition, the birth rate, which had sunk to all-time lows in the mid-1970s, began to climb during the 1980s as increasing numbers of women at or near the age of thirty decided to start families. By 1984, there were 17.8 million children in the United States under the age of five, the largest number since 1968.

Market research data, conversations with parents, discussions with retailers handling Gerber products, and hundreds of Gerber management meetings combined to produce the decision to cater to parents who had bought Gerber baby foods for their infants and were willing to purchase other products as their children grew older. Currently, baby food accounts for slightly less than one-half of total company sales, down from as high as 80 percent five years ago. But actual dollar sales of Gerber baby foods have continued to increase. Baby food sales have simply become a smaller percentage of overall sales resulting from new products and services aimed at Gerber's redefined market. The firm's new objective reflects its product expansion: "to provide needed quality products and services to families with infants and young children."

Sources: Quotation in paragraph 2 from "Gerber: Selling More to the Same Mothers Is Our Objective Now," *Business Week,* 16 October 1978, p. 192. Descriptions of Gerber decisions provided by John Whitlock, Director of Public Relations, Gerber Products Co., May 19, 1985.

making styles are identified, based upon the degree of participation by subordinates in the selection of alternatives. Seven "Yes-No" questions are used to determine the most appropriate decision-making style. The amount of available information, type of decision required, and subordinate involvement are considered. The Vroom-Yetton model is a potentially invaluable aid to nonprogramed decision making.

FACT OR FICTION REVEALED

1. Fiction 2. Fiction 3. Fiction 4. Fiction 5. Fact 6. Fact 7. Fiction 8. Fiction

MANAGEMENT TERMS

decision making
certainty
risk
uncertainty
technical decisions
managerial decisions
institutional decisions

programmed decisions
nonprogrammed decisions
satisficing
bounded rationality
problems
performance gap
symptom

cause
synectics approach
brainstorming
efficiency
effectiveness
feedback
Groupthink
buckpassing

REVIEW QUESTIONS

1. Give an example of an actual decision involving:
    a. certainty
    b. risk
    c. uncertainty

2. Differentiate among the three major types of decisions.

3. A manufacturer's computer automatically prints purchase orders for new supplies once their stock reaches a designated level. The orders are forwarded to the director of purchasing for approval. Is this director's action a programmed or nonprogrammed decisions?

4. Explain Herbert Simon's contribution to the study of decision making.

5. Outline the model of the decision-making process.

6. What are the major benefits of a written problem statement?

7. Identify the steps involved in selecting an alternative.

8. Relate decision making to the concepts of effectiveness and efficiency.

9. What are the strengths and weaknesses of group decision making?

10. Briefly explain the Vroom-Yetton model.

PROBLEMS AND EXPERIENTIAL EXERCISES

1. Relate one of your most recent decisions to the model shown in Figure 6–3.

2. Select a firm in your city or state. After carefully researching the company, identify the daily decisions that its management will face in the future.

3. Prepare a written problem statement for a problem that you face.

4. Southland Corp.'s decision to locate some of its 7,000 7-Eleven stores in urban locations appears to have paid off. Although rent and utility expenses are higher than in suburban locations, the heavy traffic generated in urban locations assisted 7-Eleven in experiencing a 150 percent sales increase to $5 billion in a four-year period ending in 1982.

Conduct a brainstorming session on 7-Eleven's future techniques for generating additional sales growth. This will require the participants to research the company extensively prior to the session.

5. Apply the Vroom-Yetton model to the following decisions:

    a. A decision to convert a factory's power plant from oil to coal because of cost and supply factors.

    b. The dismissal of a key vice president because of ineffective performance.

    c. The introduction of a new product on a trial basis in four cities.

MANAGERIAL INCIDENT: The Problem with the New Machines

You are a manufacturing manager in a large electronics plant. The company's management has recently installed new machines and put in a new, simplified work system. But to the surprise of everyone, yourself included, the expected increase in productivity was not realized. In fact, production has started to drop, quality has fallen off, and the number of employee separations has risen.

You do not believe anything is wrong with the machines. You have reports from other companies that are using them and they confirm this opinion. You also had the manufacturer's representatives go over the machines and they reported that they are operating at peak efficiency.

You suspect that some parts of the new work system may be responsible for the change, but this view is not widely shared among your immediate subordinates—four first-line supervisors, each in charge of a section; and your supply manager. The drop in production has been variously attributed to poorly trained operators, lack of an adequate system of financial incentives, and poor morale. Clearly, this is an issue about which there is considerable depth of feeling within individuals and potential disagreement among your subordinates.

This morning you received a phone call from your division manager. He just received your production figures for the last six months and was calling to express his concern. He indicated that the problem was yours to solve in any way you think best, but that he would like to know within a week what steps you plan to take.

You share your division manager's concern with the falling productivity and know that your people are also concerned. The problem is to decide what steps to take to rectify the situation.

Questions and Problems

1. Use the Vroom-Yetton model to answer the following:
   a. quality requirement
   b. availability of sufficient information
   c. whether the problem is structured
   d. importance of acceptance of decision by subordinates
   e. prior probability of acceptance
   f. whether subordinates share organizational goals to be obtained.
   g. whether conflict is likely
   h. problem type
   i. most appropriate style of decision making

2. Contrast problems, symptoms, and causes by citing examples mentioned in the case.

Source: Reprinted, by permission of the publisher, from "A New Look at Managerial Decision Making," Victor H. Vroom, *Organizational Dynamics* (Spring 1973):72. © 1973 American Management Association, New York. All rights reserved.

CHAPTER

7 QUANTITATIVE TECHNIQUES IN PLANNING AND DECISION MAKING

LEARNING OBJECTIVES

After studying this chapter you should be able to

1. Compare the chief advantages and limitations of quantitative techniques in solving organizational problems.
2. Explain the value of models for planning and decision making.
3. Identify the major categories of models.
4. Explain the steps involved in the quantitative approach to problems and their solution.
5. Identify the major quantitative techniques and problem areas where they may be used.
6. Explain the contributions of electronic spreadsheets in decision making.

STOP ACTION CASE

Burger King

As the nation's second largest fast-food franchise, Burger King recognized that surpassing the leader—McDonald's—would require a major increase in both sales and profits. A critical component of its plan to achieve these objec-

189

tives involved the drive-thru concept of purchasing food. But there were problems to overcome, and the organization's decision makers quickly identified them.

At first glance the drive-thru concept is simple. Drivers order at an outside menu board, then join a line of cars whose drivers will pick up and pay for their orders at the pick-up window when they are ready. In most units, the drive-thru team usually consists of one or two cashiers who take the order, run to the sandwich chutes and drink stations, assemble the order, bag it, ring up the order, and hand it to the customer.

Burger King established a standard transaction time of thirty seconds for the drive-thru window, but most units had longer service times. During peak periods, drivers wishing to use the drive-thru could not spend time waiting in a long car-line, resulting in lost sales. Analyses at a number of units showed that drive-thru transaction times were averaging forty-five seconds. With a forty-five second transaction time, the restaurant could handle a maximum of eighty cars an hour. Because checks averaged $2.44 per order, drive-thru sales were limited to a maximum of $195 per hour. Clearly, a system initially devised to provide customer convenience had become an inconvenience.

Management reasoned that if the transaction time could be shortened to thirty seconds, cars served per hour would increase by 50 percent and maximum sales would rise to $292 per hour—almost $100 more. That represents an annual sales increase of over $35,000 per restaurant. Burger King's operations research department was asked to work with franchises to devise a system to improve the speed of service at the drive-thru.

Use the materials in Chapter 7 to recommend a course of action for Burger King decision makers that would reduce the transaction time at the drive-thru windows to less than forty-five seconds.

Managers spend a considerable amount of time making decisions. Sometimes the decisions are related to the planning function; in other cases other functions such as organizing or controlling are affected. But every decision affects, in a significant or a minor way, the pursuit of organizational objectives. Decision making is the process managers use to bring unity where there is disunity, simplicity where there is complexity, predictability where there is uncertainty, and effective purpose where there is aimlessness. Making a decision can be an exhilarating as well as a frustrating experience; it can be a rewarding as well as an unrewarding experience.

A decision reached a quarter-century ago made Sam Walton the richest man in America. He decided to concentrate his Wal-Mart discount stores in small towns while his larger rivals such as K-mart and Target were concentrating on urban areas. The chain, which began in Rogers, Arkansas, in 1962, now numbers more than 800 stores, most of which are located in small towns across the South and Southwest. But Walton's decision about

MANAGEMENT FACT OR FICTION

	FACT	FICTION		FACT	FICTION
1. A major advantage of using quantitative techniques in decision making is that they include the impact of human factors in addition to quantitative data.	☐	☐	other computer languages such as COBOL and BASIC.	☐	☐
2. Iconic models are frequently depicted by mathematical equations.	☐	☐	5. The breakeven equation includes both fixed and variable costs, but assumes that per unit variable costs do not change.	☐	☐
3. Feedback controls should be developed and used at each step in the decision process.	☐	☐	6. Decision-tree analysis must include probability estimates of the occurrence of different events.	☐	☐
4. Development of linear programming led to the creation of			7. Queuing theory is particularly appropriate for inventory control decisions.	☐	☐

The materials in this chapter will assist you in separating management fact from fiction. Your answers can be checked on page 224.

where to locate his warehouses, rather than the location of his small-town retail outlets, was the key to his success. The starting point was to build a highly automated warehouse, then cluster as many as 150 stores around it. With each store no more than a few hours away from a supply source, a profitable Wal-Mart store was possible in towns as small as 5,000 people. Clustering stores also permitted Walton to pool advertising and distribution overhead.[1]

Decisions for individuals—as well as individual managers—vary in terms of importance. Most decisions would not be labeled as crucial; in fact, many of them are based on personal taste. How much salt on an omelet, how wide the parking spaces, how high the stereo volume—these are examples of such decisions. But other decisions are far more critical—and managers frequently are under pressure to make major decisions with incomplete information and little time. Determining the "correct" or optimal course of action as opposed to the "wrong" or less optimal course is extremely important when it might lead to a monetary loss or wasted opportunity for the decision maker's firm.

Since incorrect or nonoptimal decisions can have serious implications, it is important that the most appropriate decision-making tools be used to generate the best possible information base upon which to make a decision. Although managers have always made some use of quantitative data in making decisions, never have the quantities of available data and the methods for analysis been so accessible. In fact, a new field called operations research, or management science, has grown out of the need for managerial assistance in developing and applying mathematical techniques to decision making.

This chapter examines the contributions made by quantitative techniques in planning, decision making, and problem solving as well as the limitations of these tools. The role of the scientific method and the types of models used by management scientists are discussed, and the steps involved in applying the scientific method to problems facing the organization are identified. The chapter concludes with an examination of how such quantitative tools as probability theory, breakeven analysis, linear programing, simulation models, queuing, or waiting-line models, game theory, and decision-tree analysis can be applied to specific problems.

OPERATIONS RESEARCH: QUANTITATIVE TECHNIQUES FOR MANAGEMENT DECISIONS

Operations research is the application of mathematical techniques to managerial planning, decision making, and problem solving.

Operations research is an umbrella term describing the application of mathematical techniques to managerial planning, decision making, and problem solving. It involves the use of models to describe and provide an understanding of a problem and its alternative solutions.[2] An operations research problem may be as specific as how much JP4 aviation fuel People Express Flight 291 should tanker from one leg of the flight to an intermediate destination because of price differences, or as broad as the establishment of a long-range corporate strategy.

Operations research is an interdisciplinary field using concepts from such areas as mathematics, computer science, systems analysis, economics, and engineering. Although advances in the scientific approach to management problems can be traced to Frederick W. Taylor, Henry L. Gantt, Frank Gilbreth, and other early scientific management writers, including such eighteenth- and early nineteenth-century luminaries as Adam Smith and Charles Babbage, it wasn't until World War II that operations research began to emerge as a recognized discipline. The British military establishment assembled a team of specialists to tackle such vital problems as effective use of radar, civilian defense, antisubmarine warfare, and the optimal deployment of convoy vessels to accompany supply ships. The United States followed Great Britain's lead in assembling "operations analysis" groups to conduct mathematical analyses of military data. Soon after the war, these analytical methods were applied to problems of government and industry with favorable results. By 1980, operations research departments were firmly established in most large- and medium-sized organizations.

Usually included under the broad label of operations research are management science, decision sciences, information sciences, and some aspects of systems analysis.[3] While there are subtle distinctions among these terms, all of them employ the scientific method in dealing with their activities.

WHAT IS THE SCIENTIFIC METHOD?

The *scientific method* is essentially a way of thinking about problem situations. It is a systematic and logical approach to the identification and solution of problems facing the decision maker. Objectivity is at a premium whether the problem involves the physical or biological sciences or exists in a business setting. The basic premise is that the greater the degree of objectivity, the greater the probability that other observers will reach the same decision. In order to gain objectivity, precise observation, careful recording of data, analysis, and interpretation of findings are approached in a logical, step-by-step manner. As shown in Figure 7–1, operations research professor Arthur C. Laufer used an engine-heating problem encountered by several airlines to illustrate the application of the scientific method.

Since the scientific method is more a way of thinking about problems than a precise guide, the specific number of steps in the process can vary widely. The critical issue is that the problem solver consider all aspects of the problem in a comprehensive and logical way.

> **Scientific method** is a systematic and logical approach to identifying and solving problems facing the decision maker.

QUANTITATIVE ANALYSIS IN DECISION MAKING ■

Since most business problems and opportunities involve complex situations with varying degrees of uncertainty and risks associated with them, operations research techniques can make major contributions in analysis and identification of the optimal solution. It is, however, a mistake for managers to use these analytical tools as "security blankets," since they are not substitutes for executive judgment. The capabilities and limitations of operations research must be kept in clear perspective so the manager can use it as an aid to decision making rather than as a crutch for indecision. Figure 7–2 summarizes the major advantages and limitations of operations research techniques.

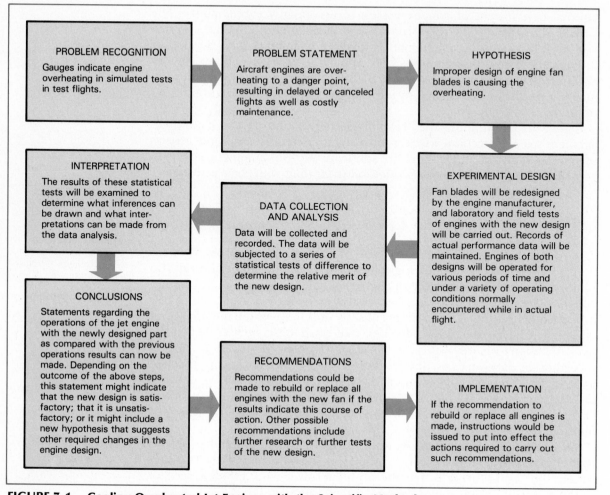

FIGURE 7–1.   Cooling Overheated Jet Engines with the Scientific Method
Source: Adapted from Arthur C. Laufer, *Operations Management* (Cincinnati: South-Western, 1975), p. 18.

CONTRIBUTIONS OF QUANTITATIVE TECHNIQUES TO DECISION MAKING

The use of quantitative methods in making organizational decisions is clearly increasing.[4] Perhaps their most important benefit is the *systematic focus* they provide for the manager. The quantitative approach encourages rational thinking. Clear, precise objectives must be established, relationships must be defined explicitly, and risk must be assessed in order to develop the appropriate analytical model. The underlying assumptions that support the analysis must be identified. The systematic thinking demanded by quantitative techniques improves the likelihood of effective decisions.

A second benefit of the use of operations research techniques is the development of a large *data base*. Large amounts of pertinent data are required to utilize analytical tools. The data base allows decision makers to refine and alter decisions as new data become available. Such a data base forms the foundation of an organization's management information system; it is discussed in detail in Chapter 17.

A third advantage of quantitative techniques is their ability to divide complex problem issues into smaller, more manageable parts. This *simplifying of a problem situation* allows the manager to better diagnose and understand the thousands of possible elements of a particular issue.

A final benefit of quantitative analysis is that these analytical techniques *aid the manager in comparing and contrasting possible alternatives*. The decision maker is made more aware of the risks, benefits, and difficulties of each alternative. This awareness increases the likelihood of an informed decision.

LIMITATIONS OF QUANTITATIVE TECHNIQUES IN DECISION MAKING

Perhaps the most serious problem preventing integration of analytical tools in the decision-making process is the *lack of understanding between line*

FIGURE 7–2. Quantitative Approach Trade-offs

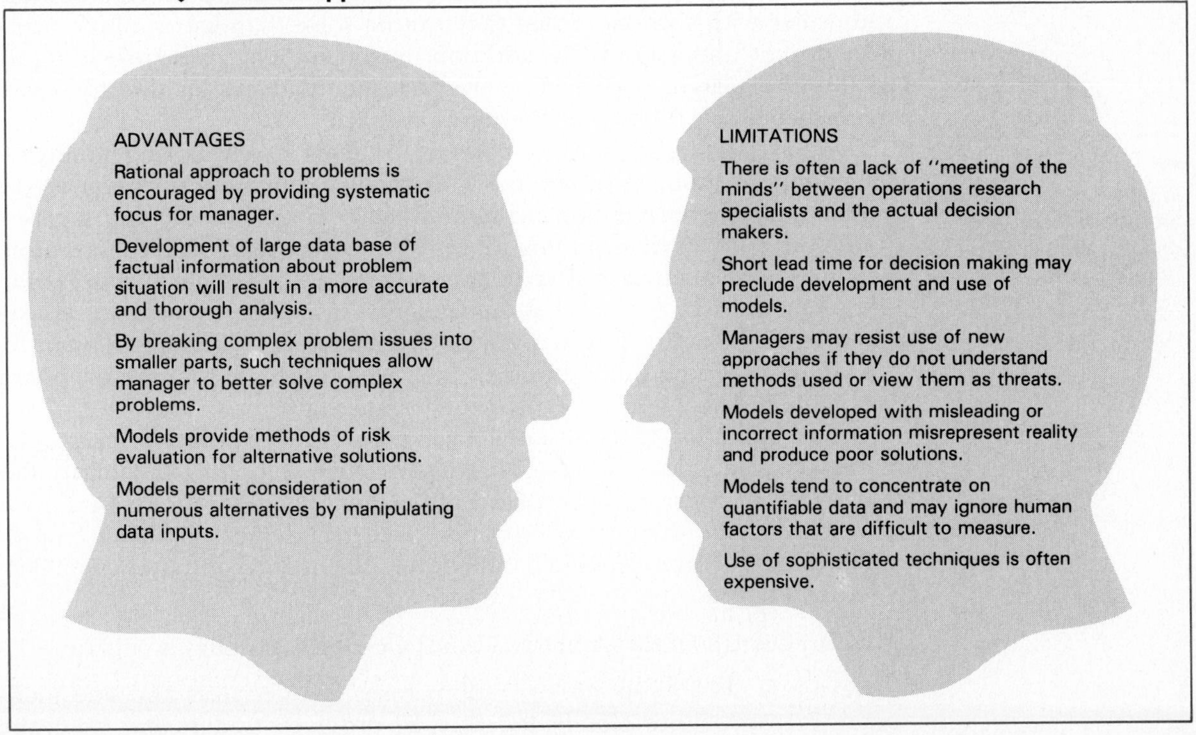

ADVANTAGES

Rational approach to problems is encouraged by providing systematic focus for manager.

Development of large data base of factual information about problem situation will result in a more accurate and thorough analysis.

By breaking complex problem issues into smaller parts, such techniques allow manager to better solve complex problems.

Models provide methods of risk evaluation for alternative solutions.

Models permit consideration of numerous alternatives by manipulating data inputs.

LIMITATIONS

There is often a lack of "meeting of the minds" between operations research specialists and the actual decision makers.

Short lead time for decision making may preclude development and use of models.

Managers may resist use of new approaches if they do not understand methods used or view them as threats.

Models developed with misleading or incorrect information misrepresent reality and produce poor solutions.

Models tend to concentrate on quantifiable data and may ignore human factors that are difficult to measure.

Use of sophisticated techniques is often expensive.

managers and the operations research specialists. Managers are typically action-oriented with little patience, understanding, and appreciation of quantitative analysis. Operations research specialists may exhibit more interest in the method than in the solution, failing to recognize the need for quick decisions. The specialists may seek the optimum solution regardless of the time involved, while the manager may be interested in satisficing—finding a quick, satisfactory course of action. There is still a gap between specialists trained in mathematics and computer applications and the line manager, who has final responsibility for decision making.

Misrepresentation of reality is another potential problem in using quantitative tools. The very nature of such tools makes possible the introduction of misleading or incorrect assumptions and inputs. "GIGO"—garbage in, garbage out—summarizes the results of a quantitative technique with incorrect data inputs. Such techniques are effective only when the underlying assumptions and variables included in the technique are also present in the real-world environment.

The *short lead time* for decisions often precludes the use of sophisticated and time-consuming quantitative techniques. Input data required to use such techniques are often difficult to assimilate in short periods of time.

Resistance to change by line managers may prove a major hurdle in using operations research tools. Managers have already developed their own approaches to decision making and may resist new methods, especially if the new approach is technically oriented and is accompanied by a complete new glossary of abstract terms. It has been said that many managers would rather live with a problem that they cannot solve than use a solution that they do not understand.[5] In addition, managers may resist providing all of the information necessary to use the quantitative tools due to vested interests or basic distrust of the new approach.

Oversimplification is another potential danger in employing analytical techniques in problem situations. This possible limitation is similar to the problem of misrepresenting reality in a mathematical model, but it refers to the difficulty of determining all of the complex relationships operating in a problem situation and reducing them to a mathematical representation. Often such very real organizational situations as morale, consequences of strikes, or internal power struggles are so difficult to quantify that they are ignored in the model used. As a result the solution proposed by the model may not be best for the organization.

A final limitation of quantitative problem-solving approaches is *cost.* The necessary combination of specialized personnel, computer capability, and time often discourages widespread use of quantitative techniques. This is particularly true of the more sophisticated techniques requiring considerable financial investment in model development and computer capability.

NEED FOR UNDERSTANDING AND COOPERATION

A very real need exists for operations research specialists and line managers to work more closely together in order to understand both the

66 Exact scientific knowledge and methods are everywhere, sooner, or later, sure to replace rule-of-thumb. 99

Frederick W. Taylor

MANAGEMENT: THE LIGHTER SIDE

Models versus Reality

 Andrew Vazsonyi provides two anecdotes to illustrate the problems involved when models are mistakenly assumed to reflect reality totally. His first example involves two of Mark Twain's most beloved characters. His second describes the woes of a traveler.

Huckleberry Finn was quite indignant when Tom Sawyer tried to convince him on their trip in the balloon that they were flying over the state of Illinois. Huck said: "Teacher showed me the map, and Illinois was red." The discussion that followed finally pushed Huck to a conclusion: "The map maker was a liar."

A man drove late into the night on a country road, hit a rut and broke the axle of his car. So he got mad and tore up his map. That same man would probably throw away a quantitative model because the behavioral aspects of the situation were not included in the mathematics.

MORAL: The model user must not confuse a *map* with a *territory*, a *word* with the *thing*, a *model* with *reality*.

Source: Adapted by permission from Andrew Vazsonyi, "Semantic Pollution in Information Systems," *Interfaces* (August 1973):45. Copyright 1973 The Institute of Management Sciences.

strengths and weaknesses of the specialists' quantitative tool kit and the areas in which specific techniques are most appropriate. Cooperation between the specialists and the line managers will assist in implementing the correct technique and in generating improved solutions to organizational problems.[6]

THE ROLE OF MODELS IN DECISION MAKING

A crucial element in operations research is the development and implementation of models. A *model* is a representation, or abstraction, of a real object, situation, or system. It is used to capture the key elements, but not the detail, of the entity it represents. Many different disciplines use models on a regular basis. Aeronautical engineers test scale-model airplanes in wind tunnels. Economists employ abstract models to predict future economic activity and ecologists use them to estimate potential effects of mining, refining, or other production activities on the environment.[7]

The U.S. Army Engineer Waterways Experiment Station at Vicksburg, Mississippi, uses models to research many of the problems affecting waterways of the United States. To study methods of improving navigation conditions and the effects of a proposed lock to be built on the Ohio River

A model is a representation, or abstraction, of a real object, situation, or system.

FIGURE 7–3.   Model of McAlpine Locks and Dam at Louisville, Kentucky, on the Ohio River
Source: U. S. Army Corps of Engineers.

at Louisville, the 1:120-scale model shown in Figure 7–3 was constructed. The complete model represents some eight miles of the Ohio River.

Experimenting with models generally requires less time, money, and human resources than experimenting with the actual object or situation. Judgments and inferences can then be made about the effect of these variables on the phenomenon represented by the model.

TYPES OF MODELS

Three general categories of models are used in analyzing and understanding real-world situations: iconic, analog, and symbolic, or mathematical, models.

An *iconic model* is a physical replica or a scale representation that actually looks like the object it represents. A ship model or a small-scale model of a railroad or bridge, such as the one shown in Figure 7–3, is an iconic

An **iconic model** is a physical replica or scale representation that looks like the object it represents.

model; so also are schematic representations of the actual item such as a picture or a photograph.

An *analog model* is a physical representation of a real object or situation that does not have the same physical appearance as the object being modeled. Gasoline gauges, speedometers, and thermometers are analogs of volume, speed, and temperature.[8] Flowcharts are analog models used in computer programing.

The third general category, *symbolic,* or *mathematical, models,* is of primary interest to the quantitative decision maker. Such models use equations or groups of equations to express the relationship among factors in a given process or system being modeled. Although this type of model is the least familiar to most persons, it can provide a high degree of abstraction and aid significantly in analyzing complex problem situations. The equation $A = B + C$ is a mathematical model stating that the object symbolized by A is the simple sum of the object labeled B and the object labeled C.[9] Each of the three types of models is illustrated in Figure 7–4.

Although all models may be categorized as either iconic, analog, or symbolic, other classifications have been developed in order to compare different types of models on such bases as purpose of the model, types of elements included, methodologies used, and the effect of time on the situation being analyzed. The decision maker must recognize that the choice of the appropriate model is determined by its ability to reflect reality. Different problem situations may call for different types of models and for different operations research techniques.

> An **analog model** is a physical representation of a real object or situation that does not have the same appearance of that which it represents.

> A **symbolic,** or **mathematical, model** is a model using equations or groups of equations to express the relationship among factors in a given process or system being modeled.

NORMATIVE VERSUS DESCRIPTIVE MODELS

This method of classification is based on what the model attempts to do. A model designed to prescribe what ought to be done is considered a *normative model.* Such a model attempts to identify specific methods for accomplishing specific objectives and to identify the best or optimum solution. The Vroom-Yetton model discussed in the previous chapter is an example of a normative model.

A *descriptive model* is designed to present occurrences, situations, or circumstances as they are. Such a model will not provide specific solutions to problems, but it will identify what will happen when problem variables are changed. Management of Ski Nautique boats may want to know the effect of the energy shortage on production schedules. This would require developing a descriptive model to provide a summary of relevant factors affected by the shortage. A simulation model, described later in the chapter, is an example of a descriptive model.

DETERMINISTIC VERSUS PROBABILISTIC MODELS

A second method of classifying models is by the types of elements they include. If the elements or variables of a model can be quantified precisely,

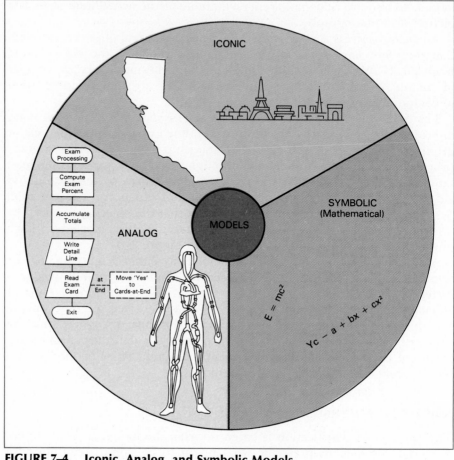

FIGURE 7–4.   Iconic, Analog, and Symbolic Models

the model is classified as *deterministic*. In such a model, chance or probability plays no part. Linear programing and economic order quantity models are examples of deterministic models.

If certain variables of the model situation are subject to probabilities or chance, the model is called *probabilistic,* or *stochastic*. Problems involving uncertainty and risk require probabilistic models for analysis. Input data and solutions are expressed as probabilities rather than as certainties. Consumer response to advertising and the resultant product demand are very uncertain; consequently, models developed by such firms as Lever Brothers or Colgate Palmolive to make advertising decisions would generally be probabilistic. Since risk and uncertainty are characteristic of much business activity, the mathematics of statistics and probability has been widely used in model building for business decisions. Decision-tree methods and expected value concepts—two quantitative techniques discussed later in the chapter—are examples of probabilistic models.

EMPIRICAL VERSUS THEORETICAL MODELS

A third method of classifying models is by the methodology they use. A *theoretical model* applies or assigns probabilities to the occurrence of events solely on the basis of accepted assumptions regarding the mechanism that generates the outcomes. The theoretical probability of an event in a given test is obtained under the following conditions: (1) the total number of ways an event can occur can be counted; (2) the number of possible occurrences is known; and (3) each occurrence is assumed to be equally likely. For example, the probability that one throw of a six-sided die will display a 3 can be calculated theoretically, based on the following information. The die is assumed to be balanced and, therefore, each of the six sides has an equal chance of appearing after a throw. Six occurrences are possible (1, 2, 3, 4, 5, or 6). There is only one way a 3 can be displayed after a throw. The theoretical probability is calculated as follows:

$$\text{Probability (3)} = \frac{\text{number of ways 3 can occur}}{\text{number of possible occurrences}} = \tfrac{1}{6} = .16667$$

The theoretical method calculates the probability of a 3 appearing on the throw of a single die at .16667.

In contrast, the *empirical model* assigns probabilities to the occurrence of events solely on the basis of statistical data recorded from previous experiences or experiments. In other words, the probabilities are assigned *ex post*. The empirical probability of an event must be determined when it cannot be assumed that all the possible occurrences are equally likely to happen. Such a condition frequently exists in business situations, and construction of a model must be based on experiments or experiences of what has occurred on similar occasions in the past. Business decision makers often develop empirical models by estimating their own subjective probabilities of the occurrence of an event when encountering problem situations.

> ❝ Before I got married I had six theories about bringing up children. Now I have six children and no theories.❞
>
> John Wilmot

STATIC VERSUS DYNAMIC MODELS

The final major method of classifying models is by the effect time has on the situation being analyzed. A *static model* is used with problems in which no time element is present. Static models are typically developed when no requirement for continuing analysis is present.[10]

Dynamic models deal not only with random variations but also with changes that occur over time. The time-dependent element in many problems requires a model that will allow the decision maker to determine the impact of variables that change over time.

QUANTITATIVE APPROACHES TO DECISION MAKING

The systematic, step-by-step approach of the scientific method is employed by managers in making organizational decisions and solving problems. Models are used in complex situations in order to determine the optimum solution. The steps involved include the following:

- Formulate the problem.

- Construct a mathematical model that represents the system being studied.

- Derive a solution from the model.

- Test the model and the solution derived from it.

- Establish control over the situation.

- Implement the solution.

These steps generally reflect the procedures of the scientific method. The emphasis here is on development, testing, and use of the most appropriate mathematical model in solving the problem under consideration.

FORMULATING THE PROBLEM

A dominant theme of the quantitative approach to decision making is problem formulation—especially in those problem situations that thwart normal courses of activity and do not have an obvious solution. To utilize the tools of operations research effectively, a clear and concise definition of the specific problem confronting the manager is an essential first step.

66 It isn't that they can't see the solution. it is that they can't see the problem. 99

G. K. Chesterton

Most problem definitions begin as broadly stated general descriptions of the problem area—and often focus on symptoms rather than causes. Declining profit margins for a product line of industrial cleaning supplies may be blamed on increased production costs. But production costs are the result of numerous factors, and effort and imagination are required to transform a general description of the problem into a specifically defined problem. Specific objectives and constraints must be identified and both controllable and uncontrollable variables defined. As the problem is gradually formulated, the elements that can be corrected by management decisions must also be identified.

Once the problem's elements are identified, objectives and constraints defined, and problem variables constructed, the essence of the problem is formulated. The next step is to construct a mathematical model that can represent the system being studied.

DEVELOPING A MODEL

The construction of a model to represent the system in which the problem exists allows the testing of the problem under investigation. Many problems cannot be tested in a real-world environment without considerable cost and disruption of normal working conditions. Development of a mathematical model that represents the system being studied allows the decision maker to manipulate the problem's variables in an economical manner while not interfering with the work of the system or organization.

DERIVING A SOLUTION

The third step is to derive a solution to the problem based on analysis of the data generated by the model. All uncontrollable inputs (or data) must be specified before a solution can be derived from the model. Uncontrollable inputs for the manager of the local Nissan Motors dealership might include size of the lot, any franchise agreement specifying a ratio for the assortment of models that must be ordered, and the amount of space each type of vehicle occupies. The preparation of such data for the model is an important step; the solution derived from the model is no better than the data inputs. And the time required to collect the necessary data is often substantial. A moderate-sized model with about 50 decision variables and 25 constraints will generate more than 1,300 data elements.[11]

Once the values of the uncontrollable variables are specified and allocated as inputs to the model, the values of the controllable variables will change. The manager of the Nissan dealership would consider as controllable variables such decisions as the number of various sedan models, trucks, and its 300-ZX sports cars to order during the next sixty days. The results of the changes in the values of the controllable variables will then be analyzed to determine a condition that most closely meets the manager's objectives. The values that create the most favorable condition represent the solution to the problem.

Figure 7–5 shows how a mathematical model could be used to determine the best "mix" of automobile and truck models for the Nissan dealer. The model would consider changes in the controllable variables and ultimately identify the "best" solution to optimize the dealership's profits and space subject to the constraints that are present.

TESTING THE MODEL AND THE SOLUTION(S) DERIVED FROM IT

Once a solution or group of alternative solutions is identified, it can be tested in the model. The various types of models and the tools of operations research used to test the hypotheses are discussed in the next section. The aim of this step in the problem-solving process is to ensure that the solution is both economically effective and practical.

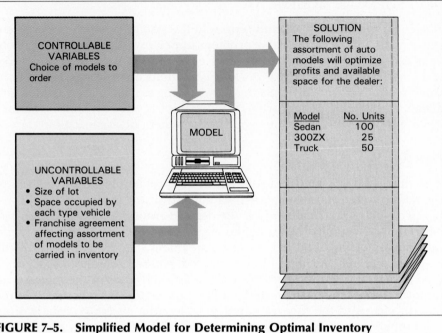

FIGURE 7–5. Simplified Model for Determining Optimal Inventory Assortments

ESTABLISHING FEEDBACK CONTROLS

It is important to devise feedback and control mechanisms for each step of the decision process. In general, control involves the development of criteria for use in measuring the effectiveness of the system. The essence of control is the evaluation and interpretation of information regarding the actual operation of the system, the comparison of this information with the effectiveness measure, and the implementation of any corrective action needed to generate the system output at the desired state.[12]

Feedback is an essential part of establishing control of the scientific decision-making process. Feedback, discussed earlier in Chapter 5 and Chapter 6, is essentially a diagnostic tool for the manager. It is the ongoing mechanism by which the decision maker collects and evaluates information concerning the procedures in operation at each stage of the decision process. This constant refining of information is matched against the control criteria and used to direct and control the performance of the decision procedures. Similar to the guidance system of a heat-seeking missile, feedback is a self-regulating device. As Figure 7–6 shows, the feedback mechanism should operate at each stage of the decision process, allowing the design of accurate models that can provide realistic and workable solutions to problems.

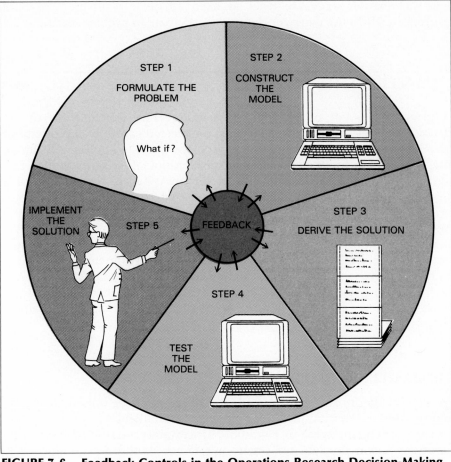

FIGURE 7–6. Feedback Controls in the Operations Research Decision-Making Process

IMPLEMENTING THE SOLUTION

The development, testing, and use of sophisticated models are merely an intellectual exercise of questionable value unless the solution is implemented. The steps involved in the decision process shown in Figure 7–6 lead to a tested solution, but it is the manager who must apply the findings. In many instances, the step of converting the model's proposed solution into a course of action by the manager is a major one. Implementation is made easier when managers facing problems to be solved by an operations research department are involved from the very beginning of the process. Such involvement encourages close cooperation between the staff specialists and the line managers. Research has indicated that operations research projects that have included the line manager as a participant in the problem formulation stage are twice as likely to be implemented as those projects in which the manager does not participate in problem definition.[13]

QUANTITATIVE TOOLS FOR DECISION MAKING   ▬▬

A growing number of quantitative techniques are available for use in decision making. Such techniques must be selected carefully and often can be adapted to solve the right type of problem. A skilled golfer will choose the proper club for the shot under consideration. Just as the golfer recognizes the inappropriateness of a driver for a ball in a sand trap or a wedge for a putt, managers must be aware that unsatisfactory results will occur if the wrong analytical tool is chosen. While most managers will never become experts in the development and use of all operations research techniques, they should be thoroughly familiar with their strengths and their limitations. The techniques described are linear programing; breakeven analysis; spreadsheet analysis; simulation; queuing, or waiting-line, models; game theory; and decision trees. Before the techniques are described, it is important to have a basic understanding of probability theory.

PROBABILITY THEORY

Probability is the likelihood of occurrence of some uncertain event or condition.

Probability theory forms the foundation of many of the quantitative techniques used in decision making. *Probability* is the likelihood of occurrence of some uncertain event or condition. Uncertainty surrounds most organizations and their activities. Such uncertainty should not be ignored in decision making; the models used should acknowledge its presence and, whenever possible, incorporate it as an estimatable degree of risk. Probability theory makes this incorporation possible.

Expected value concepts are useful in many managerial decisions. The expected value of any event is equal to the income the event would produce should it occur, multiplied by the likelihood of the event's occurrence. By summing the expected values of all possible events in a decision situation, it is possible to calculate an average expected value for numerous types of problems.

For example, an investment being considered has the potential of providing cash returns of either $300, $500, or $750 per year for the next decade. The returns will be determined by the state of the economy. Management places a 50 percent probability of normal economic conditions and a 30 percent likelihood of a recession and feels there is a 20 percent chance for markedly improved conditions. Based upon this information, the expected value of the cash flow from the investment can be calculated as follows:

Cash Flow		Economic Condition		
$300	×	.3 (Recession)	=	$ 90
500	×	.5 (Normal)	=	250
750	×	.2 (Boom)	=	150
		Expected Value	=	$490

Based on the assumption of potential cash flow and the estimated likelihood of various levels of economic growth, $490 is the "best" estimate of the annual cash flow that will be generated by the investment. This return can now be compared with alternative investments to determine the investment that generates the highest expected returns, given the risks management is willing to assume.

Financial decision makers use expected value concepts in capital budgeting. This technique is a method of evaluating various projects that require current investment which will generate future cash flow benefits by either increasing profits or decreasing costs.

Cafeteria managers may use probability theory concepts in determining the number of meals to be prepared. Other uses of probability theory include determining the number of items needed in inventory to satisfy consumer demand for a given period; the number of life insurance policyholders in a certain age category expected to die during the next year; and the number of persons to overbook on an airline flight.

LINEAR PROGRAMMING

Organizational efficiency has long been a prime objective of management. In decision after decision, a manager attempts to meet specified goals under the restriction of limited resources. How do managers use their available resources in such a manner as to maximize profits or minimize costs? Linear programming has proven extremely useful in solving such problems. *Linear programming* is a mathematical technique that is used to find the best solution to a given problem from a set of feasible solutions.[14] The essence of linear programming is optimizing the allocation of scarce resources. The adjective *linear* means that the relationships among variables can be expressed as directly proportional functions. The term *programming* refers to a specific type of mathematical model designed to optimize outputs when resources are scarce. Linear programming is commonly used to determine the most advantageous product mix for a firm, to allocate advertising budgets, and to allocate resources such as machinery and personnel.

Linear programming is a mathematical technique used to find the best solution to a given problem from a set of feasible solutions when resources are scarce.

A recent survey of management scientists in government, industry, and academia indicated that linear programming was the most commonly used quantitative technique. Over four of every five respondents reported its regular use in their work activities. Linear programming is most commonly used in solving production problems. It is also utilized in such management problems as financial and investment planning, marketing, and transpor-

MANAGEMENT FAILURES

Quantitative Analysis Woes in Washington

 At the beginning of the 1970s, the United States faced what appeared to be runaway inflation. Rather than permitting rising prices to wreck the economy, the Nixon Administration turned to a market interference approach to pricing that had previously been used in such major crises as the Great Depression and the consumer goods shortages of World War II. A Federal Price Administration was created to control the prices of hundreds of millions of products and services.

The Republican administration, already uneasy about resorting to almost heretical interference with the free-market system, chose a business school dean with significant expertise in the use of models and other quantitative techniques. C. Jackson Grayson, Jr., former dean of Southern Methodist University's B-school, had the opportunity to put his knowledge about sophisticated quantitative techniques to work on major problem areas. But, as he points out, it didn't turn out that way.

> At the Price Commission we operated, I think fairly successfully, without getting the data we "should" have had, without using any explicit decision tools, without once formally consulting a management scientist, and without building models of our decision-making processes.
>
> I am not especially proud of these facts; I am a member and an intellectually loyal member of ORSA, TIMS, and AIDS (Operations Research Society of America, the Institute for Management Science, and the American Institute for Decision Sciences). I believe in the general direction in which these organizations want to go. But I also have a personal dedication to action, a sense of the urgency and immediacy of real problems, and a genuine belief in the responsiveness of management science models to my managerial needs.

tation scheduling.[15] Relative frequency of use of the major quantitative techniques is shown in Figure 7–7.

Major Requirements of the Linear Programming Model. Linear programming is the appropriate quantitative tool for problem solving when the following conditions are present:

- The manager is attempting to achieve a specific objective (such as maximizing profits or minimizing costs).

- Alternative courses of action are present.

- Resources are scarce.

- The firm's objective and resource limitations can be expressed as a linear mathematical equation or inequality.[16]

Consider again the case of the Nissan automobile dealer. The inventory is divided between sedans and sports cars. Assume that consumer demand

Microcomputers in Management

Innovations and improvements in computer technology serve the modern manager well. Computers assume many of business's most tedious tasks and operate them cheaply, accurately, and quickly. Not only do computers aid office efficiency, they also store, sort, and print out relevant information that can improve business decision making. They provide technical functions that make quantitative analysis of data readily accessible to the manager. Yet with all their tremendous advantages, computers can only be as effective as the people who control the input and as the people who utilize the output. Humans have proved irreplaceable.

(Above) Computers are constantly being modernized to satisfy the needs of the modern business person. This battery-powered portable computer was designed for the business person who isn't always in the office.

(Left) Computers aid Holiday Inn reservationists in providing fast customer service, but they can't substitute for human courtesy and helpfulness.

1	2	3	4	5	6	7
Consolidated International Sales By Product						

PRODUCT	Jan	Febr	March	April	May
Allspice	$75,651	$85,486	$89,268	$91,538	$93,051
Anise	$66,610	$75,269	$78,600	$80,590	$81,930

United States Sales By Product	
	Jan
PRODUCT	
Allspice	$56,038
Anise	$45,637
Basil	$34,672
Bay Leaves	$39,894
Caraway	$25,617
Cardamom	$26,255

United Kingdom Sales By Product	
	Jan
PRODUCT	
Allspice	$19,613
Anise	$15,973
Basil	$12,135
Bay Leaves	$13,963
Caraway	$8,966
Cardamom	$9,189

Command list 1: Autohelp Blank Copy Delete Edit Find Goto Help Insert
                 Move Name Print Report Scroll Underscore Ucopy
Worksheet: wind1   Loc: r1c1   FM:0   Font: Standard
NAME - define, undefine, display or edit user names

(Below) Computers supply the means for sophisticated, lifelike simulation models. Here a helicopter pilot practices flying while remaining safely on the ground.

(Above) One of the most widely used computer applications for business is the computerized spreadsheet. A computer can easily and quickly handle the calculations and updates required to maintain accurately the rows and columns of numbers that constitute a spreadsheet, which is the basis for many important business decisions.

I have asked myself the question whether we might have done better by using some management science models, and my honest answer is no. . . .

Consider the severity of the demands that were made. Establishment of the Price Commission required fulfillment of seemingly impossible tasks and directives:

- Create and staff a fully competent organization.

- Work out regulations worthy to bear the force of law.

- Keep the program consistent with policies established in Phase I and with the current state of the economy.

- Work in conjunction with the Pay Board, the Internal Revenue Service, and the Cost of Living Council.

- Control the prices of hundreds of millions of articles and commodities in the world's largest economy.

- Do not inhibit the recovery of the economy.

- Do not create a postcontrol bubble.

- Do all of this with a regulatory staff of 600.

- Have the entire operation functioning in sixteen days.

Grayson points out several well-known problems in the failure to use operations research techniques at the Price Commission. Chief among them were the tremendous time constraints in decision making and the inaccessibility of relevant data.

FIGURE 7–7.   Use of Quantitative Techniques by Management Science Practitioners
Source: Data from R. E. Shannon, S. S. Long, and B. P. Buckles, "Operations Research Methodologies in Industrial Engineering: A Survey," AIIE Transactions 12, no. 4 (1980): 364–367.

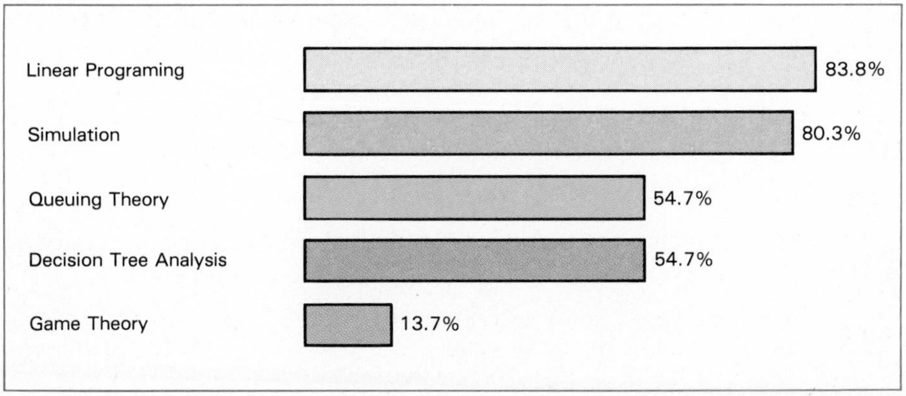

is sufficiently great that any combination of these high-fuel-economy models will be purchased and that the sedans contribute $650 per unit to profits after costs have been paid and the sports cars contribute $950. The conditions listed above are as follows:

Objective:	to maximize profits
Alternative:	dealer can stock any combination of sedans and sports cars
Resource limitations:	limited storage/display space sets the dealer's quota at an upper limit of 15 sedans or 10 sports cars (since sports cars require 50 percent more display space than sedans)
Mathematical equation:	P = Total profit A = Number of sedans ordered B = Number of sports cars ordered P = \$650 A + \$950 B

This equation represents the objective function for the dealership. The manager must select the values of A and B that will maximize profits for the organization. Profit is a linear function of A, B, and the contribution factor of both. A and B are the decision variables of the problem. In other words, the values of A and B are the variables over which the dealer has control in the attempt to maximize profits. The manager does not, however, have absolute control, due to the storage and display space limitations. This basic constraint can be translated into mathematical language. Total capacity is 15 sedans or 10 sports cars (15 As or 10 Bs). A sedan takes up 1 unit of space as compared with 1.5 units for a sports car, if units of space are defined in terms of sedans with an upper limit of 15. An equation that will require solution with respect to the space limitation constraint is

$$A + 1.5 B \le 15$$

This equation is an inequality that takes into consideration all the combinations of A and B that do not exceed the space limitation. An inequality is a statement indicating that one algebraic expression is greater than ($>$) or less than ($<$) another expression. The symbol $\le$ means equal to or less than.

The franchise agreement requires that each dealer must carry both sports cars and sedans in inventory. This can be expressed by

$$A, B \ge 1$$

The problem facing the manager of the dealership can be summarized in the following manner:

Maximize: P = \$650 A + \$950 B
Subject to: $A + 1.5 B \le 1.5$
$\quad\quad\quad\quad A, B \ge 1$

The problem can be solved by listing the results of the only feasible solutions. Table 7–1 lists the solutions that satisfy the constraints and are eligible for consideration in choosing the optimal solution. The optimal solution subject to the franchise and storage/display constraints is an inventory composed of 12 sedans and 2 sports cars. This solution gives the dealer a profit contribution of $9,700, the highest of all possible combinations of sedans and sports cars.[17]

Most linear programming problems are more complex than the dealership example and require formal procedures to solve them. Linear programming is a powerful and frequently used quantitative tool and numerous books are available to explain the various methods that may be used in the solution of management problems involving the choice of optimum combinations or allocations of limited resources to obtain a desired objective.[18]

BREAKEVEN ANALYSIS

A commonly used decision tool for determining the profitability of a proposed venture or product line is *breakeven analysis*. The breakeven equation determines the number of products or services that must be sold at a given price to generate sufficient revenue to cover total costs. As Figure 7–8 indicates, the breakeven point is the point at which the total revenue of a firm is equal to total cost. Total cost includes *fixed* costs (those costs such as lease payments, insurance premiums, or the salaries of top management that remain constant regardless of changes in production) and *variable* costs (those costs such as raw materials and other production inputs that vary with different output levels).

Breakeven analysis is a technique used to determine the number of products or services that must be produced and sold at a specified price to generate sufficient volume to cover total costs.

TABLE 7–1 THE EFFECT OF ALTERNATIVE INVENTORY COMBINATIONS OF SEDANS AND SPORTS CARS ON DEALERSHIP PROFITS

Sedans A ($650)	Sports Cars B ($950)	Space Units 15		Profits
1	9	14.5	1 (650) + 9 (950) =	$9,200
2	8	14	2 (650) + 8 (950) =	8,900
3	8	15	3 (650) + 8 (950) =	9,550
4	7	14.5	4 (650) + 7 (950) =	9,250
5	6	14	5 (650) + 6 (950) =	8,950
6	6	15	6 (650) + 6 (950) =	9,600
7	5	14.5	7 (650) + 5 (950) =	9,300
8	4	14	8 (650) + 4 (950) =	9,000
9	4	15	9 (650) + 4 (950) =	9,650
10	3	14.5	10 (650) + 3 (950) =	9,350
11	2	14	11 (650) + 2 (950) =	9,050
12	2	15	12 (650) + 2 (950) =	9,700
13	1	14.5	13 (650) + 1 (950) =	9,400

MANAGEMENT SUCCESSES

Pan Am's Fuel Management and Allocation Model

The reality of growing energy needs combined with a fixed amount of petroleum has made an impact on virtually every industry. The airline industry had already experienced the effect of a fuel crisis—during the first shortage in the mid-1970s—and it was a learning experience. In a single five-month period during 1974, fuel prices increased by 57 percent, and the U.S. government established monthly allocations for each air carrier based on the previous year's usage.

But even with the allocation system, fuel suppliers in some cities were unable to meet the air carriers' needs. The problem was compounded by the changes in flight schedules that had been made during the previous year—changes that had not been taken into account when the fuel allocations were made. The need to plan fuel purchases for a week to a month in advance became crucial, and management at many airlines found themselves unable to prepare such plans. As a result, some carriers found their monthly supply depleted by the middle of the month, producing

canceled flights, exorbitant prices paid for spot purchases, and record increases in operating costs. Fuel became the largest single cost item for the airlines.

Pan American Airlines attacked this critical problem by asking its management science specialists to develop a sophisticated mathematical model designed to minimize the effect of price increases and fluctuating allocation levels and to maintain a planned flight schedule. The quantitative tool selected for this task was linear programing—more specifically, the transportation model. This technique is effec-

In the example shown in Figure 7–8, total fixed costs equal $20,000. The horizontal line reflects a constant amount of fixed costs regardless of output level. Variable costs are eighty cents per unit. The selling price for each unit of output is $1.20. The vertical axis measures revenues and costs, while the horizontal axis measures output in units. The total revenue line reflects the $1.20 selling price multiplied by the number of units sold. The total cost line includes the $20,000 fixed costs and the $.80-per-unit variable costs. The breakeven point is the point of intersection of total revenue and total cost. If production and sales are less than this point, the firm suffers a loss; at production and sales levels above the breakeven point, the firm earns a profit.

tive in determining allocation of scarce resources for optimum results by combining them in a way that minimizes costs and maximizes profits, yet performs the same tasks previously performed using the same resources. The model enabled Pan Am to reduce its total fuel cost significantly.

The difficult task of constructing the model began with Pan Am's flight schedule, or rotation. The rotation is actually a chain of flights, or "legs," that each aircraft follows. For example, Pan Am's Flight 36 flies from Los Angeles to Fort Lauderdale with stops in Tampa and Miami. The same plane departs Fort Lauderdale as Flight 144, flies to New York, and then returns to Fort Lauderdale. It then continues as Flight 11 to Miami, Houston, and Los Angeles, where it becomes Flight 36 once again. Fuel for any of these flights may be purchased at the departure city or any of the cities serviced by the flight.

To obtain the lowest total fuel cost, the model had to consider such factors as price and availability at each location, the maximum and minimum quantity of fuel that the airplane could carry, and the maximum landing weight allowed at a station. Although low fuel prices at a given supply station might encourage the airline to make maximum purchases and "tanker" the fuel for later flights,

the added weight produces increased consumption per mile flown. As a result, the model must take into consideration the entire flight schedule in order to determine the best possible fuel purchase patterns.

Pan Am's fuel management and allocation model contains some 800 constraints and 2,400 variables for a flight schedule of 350 segments, 50 station/vendor combinations, and the different types of aircraft flown. By considering the factors of prices, availability, fuel consumption, flight data, and cost of tankerage, it specifies the most appropriate fueling station and vendor for each flight. The model has saved Pan Am millions in fuel costs and provided the organization with a means of minimizing the effect of future price increases throughout the system and of continuing normal schedule operations even when faced with erratic supply changes.

Source: Adapted by permission from D. Wayne Darnell and Carolyn Loflin, "National Airlines Fuel Management and Allocation Model," *Interfaces* (February 1977):1-16. The authors have updated their investigation in "Fuel Management and Allocation Model," *Interfaces* (February 1979):64-65. Photo courtesy Pan Am.

The breakeven point may be determined by analyzing the total fixed costs, the selling price per unit, and the per unit variable costs. By subtracting the variable cost per unit from the product's selling price, the *contribution margin* can be determined. This indicates the contribution made by each sale toward covering the fixed costs. The number of units that must be sold to cover total fixed costs can then be determined by dividing fixed costs by the contribution margin.

$$\text{Breakeven Point} \atop \text{(in units)} = \frac{\text{Total Fixed Cost}}{\text{Per Unit Contribution to Fixed Cost}}$$

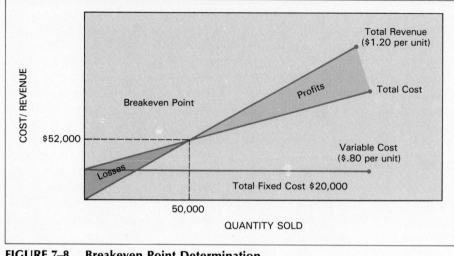

FIGURE 7–8.   Breakeven Point Determination

$$\text{Breakeven Point} \atop \text{(in dollars)} = \cfrac{\text{Total Fixed Cost}}{1 - \cfrac{\text{Variable Cost per Unit}}{\text{Selling Price}}}$$

In our example, a selling price of $1.20 and an average variable cost of $.80 results in a per-unit contribution to fixed costs of $.40. This figure can be divided into total fixed costs to obtain a breakeven point of 50,000 units or $60,000 in total sales revenue.

$$\text{Breakeven Point} \atop \text{(in units)} = \frac{\$20,000}{\$.40} = 50,000 \text{ units}$$

$$\text{Breakeven Point} \atop \text{(in dollars)} = \frac{\$20,000}{1 - \cfrac{\$.80}{\$1.20}} = \frac{\$20,000}{.33\ 1/3} = \$60,000$$

The comparison of projected with actual breakeven points for various products or divisions can assist managers in recognizing problems in time to take corrective action. An increase in costs will increase the breakeven point. The increase may result from changes in fixed costs due to the decision to install new equipment or changes in variable costs such as a price increase for raw materials. In either case, additional sales would be required to cover the increased cost if the firm is to break even and possibly earn a profit.

Breakeven analysis is useful in providing managers with a profit or loss estimate at different levels of sales and at different cost estimates. It can also approximate the effect of a change in selling prices on the firm.

SPREADSHEET ANALYSIS

For those managers of the late 1980s whose offices contain a personal computer, the most frequently used operations research application is a quantitative decision-making tool called spreadsheet analysis. By aiding the manager in analyzing all of those "what if" questions, electronic spreadsheets have become indispensable aids to thousands of decision makers.

What Is A Spreadsheet? A *spreadsheet* is simply a table of rows and columns.[19] You can set up a spreadsheet by hand—you don't need a computer. The *cells* of the spreadsheet, the points where the rows and columns intersect, are filled with numbers that the user may change at will. (These numbers are sometimes referred to as variations.)

A spreadsheet might be used, for example, to calculate a payroll. The sample spreadsheet in the Computers in Management box contains rows for workers' names; it has columns for the workers' hourly wages and for the number of regular and overtime hours they have worked. Typically, the person who makes up the payroll already knows what numbers go in these columns. But he or she *doesn't* know what to put in the column for the employees' total pay.

This calculation can take up a lot of the payroll clerk's time if it is done manually. Paula Chang, for instance, put in her regular 40 hours at $10 an hour, but she also worked 6 hours overtime. If she earns time-and-a-half for those hours, that will be $15 × 6, or $90 overtime, added to her usual $400 paycheck. A payroll clerk could figure that out, but it's time consuming. Worse, the clerk will have to start all over again if anything changes. What if Chang worked 37 regular and 11 overtime hours? What if her wage is raised to $12.50 an hour? What if her overtime pay changes from time-and-a-half to time-and-three-quarters? In each case, the payroll clerk would have to go back and figure it out again. Multiply this aggravation by 100 employees and you've really got a problem.

Tackling the Spreadsheet with a Computer. Once again, the computer comes to the rescue. There are programs available, designed especially for use with micros, that instruct the computer to set up information in the form of a spreadsheet or table. The first and best-known spreadsheet program, VisiCalc, has been challenged by rivals like Multiplan and SuperCalc in recent years, but they all work the same way.

All you have to do is complete *most* of the table by filling in the rows and columns with the values you already know, such as your employees' wages and the number of hours they have worked. You also tell the computer, in general, what mathematical calculations to perform (such as overtime pay = 1.5 × regular pay). Then the computer cranks out the calculations for you and produces the answer: each worker's total pay. If any value changes for Paula Chang, the clerk can input that value and the computer will quickly redo the calculation. If the clerk wants to calculate another employee's pay, all that's needed is to input the values for that

A **spreadsheet** is a decision-oriented computer program designed to answer "what if?" questions by analyzing different groups of data provided by the manager.

COMPUTERS IN MANAGEMENT

How Spreadsheets Work

Setting up a spreadsheet by hand takes time—especially to do the calculations.

A spreadsheet analysis program prepares the computer to accept values in preestablished spreadsheet cells. The cells are identified by column and row labels: the "Wage" column, for example, is identified by the label *W*, so Paula Chang's wage would be entered into cell "Paula Chang—*W*."

The spreadsheet program also asks the user for the basic mathematical operations that are to be performed. This user has stated that to compute an employee's regular pay (*X*), the computer must multiply that employee's wage rate (*W*) by his or her regular hours worked (*R*).

Once each employee's wage, regular hours, and overtime hours have been entered into the computer by typing on the keyboard, the computer calculates regular pay—and overtime pay and total pay—in an instant. Better yet, if you change any of the data (for instance, if you change all the employees' wages to $15 an hour), the computer will redo all the calculations in a jiffy.

Source: David J. Rachman and Michael H. Mescon, *Business Today*, 4th ed. (New York: Random House, 1985), pp. 504, 506.

:	a	::	b	::	c	::	d	::	e	::	f	::	g	:
1														
2 EMPLOYEE'S					REGULAR		OVERTIME		REGULAR		OVERTIME		TOTAL	
3 NAME			WAGE		HOURS		HOURS		PAY		PAY		PAY	
4														
5														
6			W		R		O							
7														
8														
9 Paula Chang			10.00											
10														
11 Lewis Bond														
12														
13														
14														
15														

employee. And simply relabeling a column—changing overtime to time-and-three-quarters, for instance—will modify the entire spreadsheet, changing the pay figures for a whole list of workers.

This saves an immense amount of time, and it's just a small example. Most businesses need much larger tables—spreadsheets more than fifty columns wide, in some cases—with far more complex formulas. Even so, the computer can deliver the bottom line as fast as you can change the variables.

SIMULATION MODELS

Simulation is a process for replicating the major aspects of an existing system or process that is too complex to express all of the elements and their interrelationships in mathematical terms. In developing a simulation model, the behavior of as many elements as possible is described by probability distributions. Various tests are then conducted by varying different combinations of factors and analyzing their effect on the model. Such tests might be considered as experiments being conducted on the model. Through a trial-and-error process, the interaction of any number of variables can be promptly observed. Such an experiment in the real-world environment would prove both costly and time consuming.

Simulation models can be used to solve problems and train personnel in situations as diverse as the use of wind tunnels in testing aircraft design, simulation trainers for pilots, or simulated moon-landing exercises for astronauts. Inland Steel Company operations research specialists have developed a simulation model of the steel-making process. When an equipment failure occurs, an Inland Steel manager defines the new conditions resulting from the failure and enters them in the model. Less than two hours later, the model provides a manager with the necessary data for estimating new costs and for preparing a revised profit projection.[20]

Sinclair Oil Corp. uses its sophisticated U.S. energy model in analyzing synthetic fuels strategy. The model covers all major energy forms, conversion technologies, transportation modes, and demand. It also projects investment, resource depletion, and financing to the year 2025 and computes price based upon supply-and-demand variations.[21]

Although simulation models require sizable computer capability, they hold great promise for management decision makers. In fact, the conditions required for the use of simulation describe many management decision situations. The conditions are:

- A mathematical solution is not possible.

- Observation of the actual environment is not possible or is expensive.

- Time is not available to observe the actual environment.

- Actual operation and observation of the environment may be too disruptive of other operations.[22]

Simulation is a process for replicating the major aspects of an existing system or process by describing elements with probability distributions, then combining them in various ways to study their effect on the model.

Simulation has already become one of the most commonly used quantitative tools in major corporations, and its use is expected to increase during this decade.[23]

QUEUING, OR WAITING-LINE, MODELS

Queuing, or waiting-line, model is a technique for solving problems caused by waiting lines by determining the appropriate balance between the cost of providing extra service and the cost of having people, machines, or materials wait.

Most commercial organizations have one or more functions that generate waiting lines. Customers at a bookstore checkout or gasoline station, parts waiting to be labeled, machines in need of servicing, automobile drivers at a stop-light intersection, and units waiting to be painted are all examples of queuing requirements. *Queuing,* or *waiting-line, models* attempt to solve problems caused by waiting lines by determining the appropriate balance between the cost of providing the extra service (such as additional service personnel or more checkout lines to eliminate the cost of waiting) and the cost of having people, machines, or materials wait. The costs are depicted in Figure 7–9.

Excessive waiting lines cost money in terms of idle employee or machine time, lost revenues, and dissatisfied customers. In addition, the demand for service is likely to vary. Queuing models assist in predicting the outcomes of different combinations of service facilities and aid in developing a system to minimize total expected cost.[24]

GAME THEORY

Game theory is a quantitative technique for determining the strategy that is likely to produce maximum profits in a competitive situation.

Game theory is a technique for determining the strategy that is likely to produce maximum profits in a competitive situation. It allows the manager to test such possible strategies as the introduction of a new product, a price increase, or the launching of a new advertising campaign by considering the likely reactions of competitors. Since the manager cannot predict with certainty the responses of competitors, this technique uses probability

FIGURE 7–9.   Cost in the Queuing Model

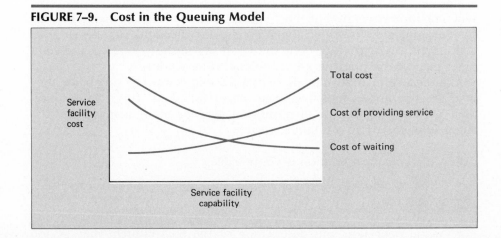

theory to test the effects on profits or market share of various possible competitive moves.

Game theory has been used extensively by military planners in training and decision making. It is used less frequently in business organizations, due to the complexity of most business situations and the large number of competitors. One investigation of the use of seven operations research models in major corporations revealed that game theory was the least frequently used quantitative tool.[25] Although the mathematics has not been developed to deal with more complex decision-making situations, game theory may assist the manager in predicting how a rational person would react in a competitive situation.

DECISION TREES

Another useful quantitative technique is the *decision tree*. This is a graphic method for identifying alternative courses of action, assigning probability estimates for the payoffs associated with each alternative, and indicating the course of action with the highest payoff. The decision maker is required to assign financial results to various courses of action and to estimate the likelihood of occurrence of each alternative.

To solve a problem by the decision-tree method, the following procedures are used:

- Illustrate the problem by developing a decision-tree diagram. A separate branch is drawn for each course of action, producing a structure that resembles a tree laid on its side.

- Determine and assign probabilities to each outcome.

- Determine the financial result of each outcome.

- Use the above steps to determine which alternative will yield the highest expected value or financial result.[26]

How Decision Trees Work. The following decision illustrates the decision-tree methodology. Public Service Company Northwest has decided to construct a new power-generating facility. Initial research indicates the two most favorable choices: (1) build a conventional plant using coal as the energy source; or (2) construct a hydroelectric facility. The larger hydroelectric plant is estimated to cost $850 million to build and put into operation, as compared with $420 million for the smaller conventional plant. Public Service forecasters developed the following energy demand estimates for the next twenty years:

> *High demand:*   Probability = .6
>
> *Moderate demand:*   Probability = .3
>
> *Low demand:*   Probability = .1

Decision tree is a branched model helpful in identifying and evaluating alternative courses of action.

Additional extensive research has been conducted to determine the expected profitability of the alternative types of generating plants based on different energy demand estimates. These findings are as follows:

Alternative A: Large Hydroelectric Plant

1. High-demand environment will yield profits of $130 million per year.

2. Moderate-demand environment will yield annual profits of $80 million.

3. Low-demand environment will yield annual profits of $20 million.

Alternative B: Smaller Coal-Powered Plant

1. High-demand environment will yield annual profits of $45 million.

2. Moderate-demand environment will yield annual profits of $60 million.

3. Low-demand environment will yield annual profits of $100 million.

Figure 7–10 provides a graphic illustration of the alternatives. The net expected value of profits generated by the hydroelectric generating facility is $1.23 billion over the next twenty years, a $550 million advantage over the coal-powered facility. The larger hydroelectric plant appears to be the appropriate decision based on the information analyzed. But the Public Service decision makers must also give careful consideration to other important factors that may ultimately alter their choice:

• Political and ecological considerations are critical elements. The environmental impact of dam construction and water diversion may outweigh other considerations.

• The demand probabilities for energy may not be constant.

• The time value of money must be considered since funds received several years from today are worth less than funds received today (since they cannot immediately be put to use in generating new funds). These future streams of funds should be discounted when comparing them with present values.

Decision trees can be used in marketing, investment, equipment purchases, pricing, new venture analysis, and a variety of other decisions. They provide a means for formalizing the risk assessment and planning required to make successful decisions.[27]

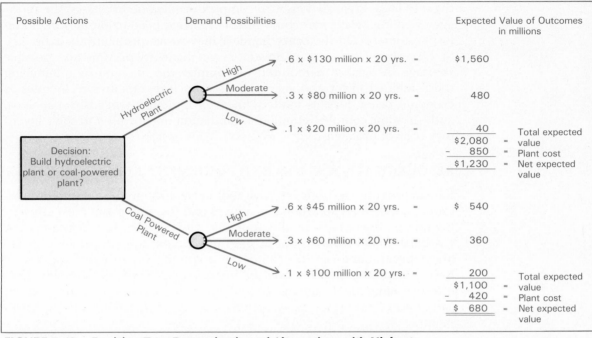

FIGURE 7–10.   Decision Tree Determination of Alternatives with Highest Expected Value

APPLYING QUANTITATIVE TECHNIQUES

The use of quantitative techniques has increased as the tools have been refined for business problems and as line managers have become more familiar with their capabilities. Important problems of inventory control, allocation of scarce resources, equipment replacement decisions, scheduling and sequencing work flows, and waiting-line regulation are frequently solved with the aid of operations research tools.

INVENTORY CONTROL DECISIONS

Inventory control involves the balancing of the costs of ordering inventory with the costs of holding inventory. Ordering costs include the costs of placing orders, of shipping and handling, and of not receiving quantity discounts offered by suppliers. Such costs decline as the average amount of inventory on hand increases. Carrying costs include the costs of funds invested in accumulated inventory, storage costs, insurance, and depreciation. Such costs increase as the average level of inventory held increases. As a result, inventory planning involves the balancing of conflicting objectives. In large organizations with complex production processes, the shortage of an important part could result in missed production deadlines and lost customers. On the other hand, it may prove prohibitively expensive to carry large amounts of inventory on hand to prevent any possible shortage. A balance is required to optimize the situation by minimizing the combined order and carrying costs. Such quantitative techniques as economic order quantity models, linear programing, spreadsheet analysis, and—in some complex situations—simulation may be used to solve inventory control problems.

RESOURCE ALLOCATION AND EQUIPMENT REPLACEMENT

Linear programing is an effective tool in determining the optimum allocation of scarce organizational resources and the timing and most efficient method of replacing capital equipment. In situations in which a certain combination of resources can be used in different ways to perform a task, linear programing can determine the optimum way to minimize cost or maximize profits. By balancing the increasing cost of operating older, less effective equipment and the cost of its replacement, linear programing can also determine the most appropriate time for making such replacements.

SCHEDULING AND SEQUENCING WORK FLOWS

66 Wisdom is the power to put our time and our knowledge to the proper use. 99

Thomas J. Watson

A common production problem is to determine the most appropriate sequencing of a product through a series of work stations. Although the various work activities required to produce a finished product may be performed in different orders, some sequences are more efficient than others. Simulation can be used to solve sequencing problems.

Scheduling problems deal with *when* is the best time for a job to be performed as well as *in what order* (sequence). Linear programing, queuing models, and simulation can be applied to complex routing problems.

WAITING-LINE REGULATION

One motto of today's society appears to be "Hurry up and wait!" Waiting in line is a common occurrence of persons, products, processes, and parts. Waiting-line models deal with the creation of facilities to meet the needs for service. Loading platforms, vehicle servicing, drive-in bank facilities, and aircraft inspections are additional examples of such situations. Queuing models are particularly appropriate in finding solutions.

QUANTITATIVE METHODS AID—BUT DO NOT REPLACE—THE DECISION MAKER

As mentioned throughout the chapter, quantitative methods can provide major assistance to line managers in solving many types of complex organizational problems. But quantitative analysis has limitations and cannot replace the experience, judgment, and intuitive wisdom of the manager. The effective manager recognizes that the ultimate decision rests with him or her, but relies on the contributions of quantitative techniques for guidance and direction.

SUMMARY

Quantitative techniques can assist managers in making improved decisions. Operations research, or management science, is a relatively new field that has evolved to assist managers in developing and applying mathematical techniques to problems of organizations. Such techniques offer the important advantage of a systematic focus on the problem and its alternative solutions. They promote a more accurate and thorough analysis of problems through the development of a required data base of factual information about the problem situation; and they assist in solving complex problems by breaking them down into smaller, more manageable parts. Limitations of such techniques include the potential for failure of a "meeting of the minds" between the operations research specialist and the line manager; the short lead time often associated with decision making; resistance to change on the part of decision makers; expense involved with the development and use of sophisticated analytical techniques; and overconcentration on quantifiable data and failure to incorporate ill-defined but important human factors.

Models—representations of real objects, situations, or systems—are crucial elements in operations research. Three general categories of models exist. An iconic model is a physical replica or a scale representation that actually looks like the object it represents. An analog model is also a physical representation of a real object or situation, but it does not have the same physical appearance as the object being modeled. Symbolic, or mathematical, models use equations to express relationships among factors in a process or system being modeled. Other model classifications include descriptive and normative; deterministic and probabilistic; empirical and theoretical; and static and dynamic.

Six steps are involved in the quantitative approach to problem solving:

1. Formulate the problem.

2. Construct a mathematical model that represents the system being studied.

3. Derive a solution from the model.

4. Test the model and the solution derived from it.

5. Establish control over the situation.

6. Implement the solution.

The major quantitative techniques used in organizational decision making are linear programing; breakeven analysis; spreadsheet analysis; simulation; queuing, or waiting-line, theory; game theory; and decision-tree analysis. Linear programing is a mathematical technique for optimizing the allocation of scarce resources to find the best solution to a given problem. Breakeven analysis is a method of determining the minimum sales volume needed to cover all costs at a certain price level. It shows the relationship between sales volume, costs, and profits. Spreadsheet analysis takes advantage of the computer's talent for "number crunching" to answer "what if" questions posed by the decision maker. By inputting different bits of data, the decision maker can quickly analyze the cost and profit implications of numerous decision alternatives. Simulation is a process for replicating the major aspects of an existing system or process and conducting numerous tests by varying different combinations of factors and analyzing their effect on the model. Queuing models attempt to solve problems caused by waiting lines by determining the appropriate balance between the cost of additional service facilities and the cost of having people, machines, or materials wait. Game theory is a technique for determining the strategy most likely to produce maximum profits in a competitive situation. The final technique, decision-tree analysis, is a graphic method for identifying alternative courses of action, assigning probability estimates for the payoffs associated with each alternative, and indicating the course of action with the highest payoff.

Although managers must recognize the limitations of quantitative techniques and combine their use with experience and judgment, such techniques can play major roles in decision areas like inventory control problems, resource allocation and equipment replacement, scheduling and sequencing work flows, and waiting-line regulation.

SOLVING THE STOP ACTION CASE

Burger King

Burger King's operations research specialists knew that they faced the queuing problem of increasing the speed at which customers moved through the drive-thru lane. They decided to construct a simulation model of the current system for handling drive-thru orders and to manipulate the model to seek methods of increasing efficiency. The result of their experiments with the model was the creation of a new order-taking and order-filling system. The heart of the new system they devised was the separation of drive-thru work into a series of distinct tasks.

One employee does nothing but take orders. The order taker gives the order to a runner/bagger who assembles the order and places it on an assembly shelf. The third member of the drive-thru team, the cashier, simply makes change and hands the order to a customer. The system allows for additional staffing when demand exceeds the ability of the three-person crew to maintain the established standard transaction time.

The operations research department also recognized that customers waited an average of eleven seconds at the order station before being acknowledged. The rubber bell-hose was moved ahead of the order station so that the order taker was alerted to a customer's arrival prior to the car's reaching the order station.

Today, all Burger King restaurants with a drive-thru have adopted the efficiency package. These restaurants have increased their average annual sales capacity by over $35,000. If all restaurants in the system, with and without drive-thru windows, increased sales at only half that rate, or $18,000 per unit in annual sales increases, the Burger King system would enjoy additional sales of $52 million annually.

Source: The Burger King drive-thru system is described in William Swart and Luca Donno, "Simulation Modeling Improves Operations, Planning, and Productivity of Fast Food Restaurants," *Interfaces* 11, no. 6 (December 1981):38.

FACT OR FICTION REVEALED

1. Fiction   2. Fiction   3. Fact   4. Fiction   5. Fact   6. Fact   7. Fiction

MANAGEMENT TERMS

operations research	symbolic, or mathematical,	spreadsheet
scientific method	model	simulation
model	probability	queuing model
iconic model	linear programming	game theory
analog model	breakeven analysis	decision tree

REVIEW QUESTIONS

1. Explain the major advantages of quantitative techniques in planning and problem solving. What are their chief limitations?

2. Describe how the use of models can aid managers.

3. Identify and give an example of each of the three general categories of models.

4. Distinguish between the following:
   a. normative and descriptive models
   b. deterministic and probabilistic models
   c. empirical and theoretical models
   d. static and dynamic models

5. List the steps in the quantitative approach to problems and their solutions.

6. Identify each of the major quantitative techniques. Suggest specific problem areas in which each technique might be used.

7. Explain each of the components of the breakeven analysis equation. Then determine the breakeven point in dollars and units for a product with a selling price of $50, an average variable cost of $32, and related fixed costs of $252,000.

8. What costs are balanced through the use of queuing models?

9. Discuss the problems of applying game theory to business decisions.

10. Outline the basic procedures of decision-tree analysis.

PROBLEMS AND EXPERIENTIAL EXERCISES

1. Suggest the most appropriate quantitative technique for the following problems:
   a. Chrysler Corporation is attempting to determine the impact of increased retail prices and gasoline shortages on demand for its newly introduced line of subcompacts.
   b. The San Diego Sanitation Department is attempting to develop trash routes for its trucks.
   c. St. Regis Company is trying to decide whether to modernize its existing West Coast paper manufacturing plant or construct an entirely new facility.
   d. Florida National Bank is in the process of determining the appropriate number of automatic tellers at its new drive-in facility.
   e. Tandy Corporation is attempting to assess the competitive impact of its new digital home thermometer.

2. Develop a step-by-step proposal for implementing operations research techniques in a large manufacturing firm.

3. Many managers add a specified target return when they consider the breakeven point on a new product or other investment. For instance, a 20 percent return on sales might be established for a proposed venture. Alternatively, a retailer may set a $100,000 desired profit return before considering whether to expand by adding a new product line. These target returns can be added

to the basic breakeven equation to determine the breakeven point with the specified targets. In cases where specified dollar target returns are involved, they can be added to fixed costs in the breakeven equation.

a. Total fixed costs of a firm are $240,000; variable costs total $5 per unit; and the product's proposed price is $9. Management has specified a $40,000 target return to justify the investment. How many products must be sold to meet the specified criteria?

b. How many products must be sold if the proposed price is increased to $10 and a $30,000 earning minimum is used?

4. In instances where percentage target returns are included in the breakeven calculations, the most common approach is to calculate the return on a per-unit basis and then include the amount in the breakeven formula as an addition to variable costs. A 10 percent target profit return requirement on a product with a $5 selling price would involve a $.50 addition to variable costs ($5 × 10%). The increased total variable costs would reduce the contribution margin from each sale, and consequently, would raise the breakeven point.

a. Total fixed costs of a firm are $180,000; variable costs total $8 per unit, and the product is priced at $20. What is the breakeven point in units and dollars if management specifies a 10 percent target return on sales?

b. How would your answer change if the price increases to $25 and variable costs rise to $10 per unit?

5. The owner of a local sporting goods store was offered a special discount price of $10 per football if the order were placed before July 1. Orders placed after July 1 would receive the regular rate of $12 each. The balls could only be purchased in quantities of even dozens. Retail prices are $18 per football and the estimated level of demand is the following:

Demand (in dozens)	Probability
2	.25
3	.30
4	.30
5	.15

Draw the decision tree based on the above information and determine the appropriate number of footballs to order.

MANAGERIAL INCIDENT: New York City Emergency Medical Service

During the 1960s, the New York City Emergency Medical Service served the city's inhabitants by stationing its ambulances at forty-nine hospitals. Each hospital represented a separate district and dispatched its ambulances only to respond to requests from within its district. The average response time was 13.5 minutes, and managers of the service were seeking methods of reducing it.

One proposal for improving the ambulance service was to locate at least some ambulances at satellite garages in demand centers within the established hospital districts. A second proposal involved assigning each of the 135 ambulances to a nine-square block area and then incorporating the Emergency Medical Service into the city-wide 911 emergency telephone system. Persons requiring ambulances would dial 911 and the call would immediately be transferred to the Emergency Medical Service's computerized communications center. From there the dispatcher would route the call to the closest available ambulances.

To determine the best method for reducing average response time, some method of comparing the two proposals with the existing system was needed. Such a method would have to consider such factors as the number of ambulances for each district, location of hospitals, and satellite garage locations, as well as the geographic distribution and the frequency of calls within each district.

The second alternative was ultimately chosen. Each of the city's 135 ambulances are kept on the city streets between 7 A.M. and 1 A.M. (Fewer ambulances operate during the late-night hours.) Each ambulance is assigned to a specific geographic area to facilitate rapid response to emergency calls.

Questions and Problems

1. Suggest a method by which managers of the Emergency Medical Service could have evaluated the proposed changes in ambulance service.

2. What other government services could have utilized similar quantitative techniques?

Source: E. S. Savas, "Simulation and Cost-Effectiveness Analysis of New York's Emergency Ambulance Service," *Management Science* (August 1969):608-627. Current data provided by New York City Emergency Medical Service.

CASES FOR PART TWO

CASE 3   The Fall and Rise of Braniff

> We have our costs under control ... and our economic picture will vastly improve from here on out.
>
> H. L. LAWRENCE, 2/29/80

> Braniff is a financially sound company. Braniff isn't in financial trouble. Braniff isn't in a financial hole.
>
> H. L. LAWRENCE, 8/21/80

> Braniff is on the right course and should do well.
>
> H. L. LAWRENCE, 12/31/80

PROBLEMS OF A BILLION-DOLLAR AIRLINE

Braniff International Chairman Harding L. Lawrence had a goal: to make Braniff a billion-dollar airline. When the deregulation of the airline industry first took effect in October 1978, Lawrence seized the opportunity to embark on an ambitious growth strategy. In just one year, Braniff expanded its passenger capacity by 37 percent to become the nation's sixth largest airline. In that one year, 1979, Braniff was indeed the billion-dollar airline that Lawrence had envisioned. Revenues rose by 65 percent from the beginning of the expansion to a total of $1.35 billion by year's end.

The expansion included the addition of 20 domestic destinations as well as service to Europe, Asia, and the Pacific. Such large-scale expansion proved costly for Braniff. Its operating expenses rose 55 percent in 1979 as compared with an average industry rise of 21 percent. Furthermore, to service all its new routes, Braniff borrowed heavily to acquire additional aircraft. Braniff's debt-to-equity ratio of 2.9 was one of the highest in the industry. Beginning with the third quarter of 1979, net losses were reported for four consecutive quarters.

Braniff had originally undertaken its expansion strategy to protect itself against its larger competitors, especially American Airlines. The management at Braniff anticipated that under deregulation its competitors would drastically reduce fares, a move that would drive smaller airlines out of business. Braniff felt that increased size would be its best means of survival if such fare wars occurred. However, much of the expansion was based on "second-choice" routes that no other carrier wanted either because of low traffic or because a particular airline was already firmly entrenched on that particular route.

Braniff was not alone in facing financial strain. The entire airline industry encountered sharply rising fuel costs coupled with a general slowdown in airline traffic because of the onset of an economic recession. It was not surprising that the increased competition and the fare wars that Braniff feared became a reality. But due to its expansion activities Braniff was more exposed to these hardships than most other major carriers.

By late 1980, Braniff was in serious financial trouble. Owing to its failure to meet earnings requirements, planned stock offerings had to be cancelled. The firm was also blocked from using its bank line of credit. In addition, some of the airline's creditors had placed it on a cash-only status. Braniff's shortage of cash was becoming desperate, and drastic measures were required to remedy the situation.

Braniff began by cutting capacity through the elimination of several of its less profitable routes. By October 1980, capacity had been slashed by nearly one-third from a year earlier. The flashy Concorde service from Dallas to London and Paris, several of the Pacific flights, and a number of domestic flights were all gone.

One fund-raising tactic employed by Braniff was selling aircraft. During 1980 more than 20 jets were sold, including fifteen 727-200s to American Airlines and a 747 jumbo jet to an Argentine firm.

A second measure to ease the cash shortage was borrowing from banks, insurance companies, and suppliers. To obtain these loans, Braniff was forced to take the drastic steps of offering its planes and equipment as collateral.

Although strapped for cash, Braniff was forced to engage in drastic fare cutting to remain competitive. In some domestic markets the cuts exceeded 80 percent.

In the last quarter of 1980, Lawrence appealed to Braniff employees to help the company ease its financial problems. All employees were asked to accept a 10 percent pay cut. As a show of sincerity, Lawrence pledged to cut his own $300,000 per year salary by 20 percent if the deal was accepted. This time the Lawrence confidence backfired. On the one hand, the chairman was assuring the press that Braniff's financial condition was solid, while on the other hand he was appealing to Braniff's employees because the firm's financial position was tenuous. The

unions representing Braniff's employees cited Lawrence's duplicity as they rejected the pay cut plan, even though some employees had already been laid off as a result of worsening financial conditions.

Merger talks were begun with Eastern Airlines late in 1980. Although a joint agreement might have helped to pull Braniff through its financial troubles, Eastern itself was experiencing cash problems that ultimately ended the merger talks.

Overall, Lawrence's turnaround measures were viewed as too little too late. Under pressure from bankers and other lenders, Braniff's board solicited Lawrence's resignation on December 31, 1980.

On January 7, 1981, John J. Casey, formerly board vice chairman, was named president, chairman of the board, and chief executive officer of Braniff. Among other problems, Casey inherited a long-term debt that had grown to over $600 million. Braniff's lenders took an active role in designing a new course for the airline by selecting a group of assistants for Casey known for their financial expertise.

Under Casey's direction, Braniff's operations were streamlined to emphasize three major areas: marketing, to plan and sell the product; operations, to produce and maintain the product; and finance, to analyze expenses and report on revenues. Management's immediate objectives were increased revenues and decreased expenses. Initial strategies to achieve these objectives included reassigning resources to those areas that were most profitable, eliminating unprofitable operations, and selling additional aircraft.

Shortly after his election Casey succeeded in rallying company employees to Braniff's cause. Effective March 1, 1981, all the airline's unions approved an employee salary program whereby all employees' pay, includ-

(Continued on next page.)

ing that of top management, was cut by 10 percent. The pay cuts, deemed "voluntary contributions," were put into a special fund to help meet corporate cash requirements. Perhaps employees were convinced of Casey's commitment when he suspended his own $180,000 per year salary indefinitely.

A crisis arose simultaneously. Some $40 million in principal and interest on Braniff's long-term debt was to be due on March 1. Braniff sought a deferral until July 1, which its creditors reluctantly granted. The approval was contingent on two factors: 1) initiation of the employee salary program and 2) the company's development of a detailed operating plan for the remainder of the year.

To handle the debt restructuring, Casey brought in Howard P. Swanson as his top financial executive. Swanson was credited with having performed a similar task at Trans World Airlines.

Despite all these efforts, the question of Braniff's viability was raised by its auditors in the annual report issued at midyear 1981. Casey emphasized that the firm's continuation was at least partially dependent on the continued deferral of debt payments.

Surprisingly, the deferral was again granted. This time Casey's new man, Swanson, was credited with convincing the airline's lenders to forgive interest payments on debt outstanding until February 1982. The once critical July 1 deadline passed and Braniff was still operating.

CHANGES IN MARKET STRATEGY

Just before the final quarter of 1981, Braniff moved to strengthen its management. Howard Putnam, president and chief executive officer of Southwest Airlines, was named president and chief operating officer of Braniff. The contrast between Southwest and Braniff was dramatic. For the previous six quarters, Southwest had posted the airline industry's highest margin of operating profit, while Braniff was the industry's biggest loser. Putnam's appointment was viewed as a positive sign. Observers felt that he would not have accepted the job had he not believed a Braniff turnaround possible.

Putnam first moved to revamp completely Braniff's fare structure. The new marketing strategy, called Texas Class, featured discounted single-class air service for a single price. The result was that the number of different fares charged by Braniff nationwide dropped from 582 to just 15. The fares were to be available every day for every seat of every Braniff flight. Putnam referred to the strategy as "getting back to basics." Braniff had been transformed from a conventional trunk airline into one that more nearly resembled a commuter airline. Under the system, the new fares undercut regular coach fares by an average of 45 percent. The success of the strategy depended on the success of the new fare system in generating additional passenger traffic. Braniff was relying on the convenience and simplicity of the new system to appeal to travel agents and the general public.

One undesired effect of the Texas Class fare structure was retaliation by Braniff's competitors. American Airlines, Braniff's chief competitor, announced that it would immediately meet Braniff's fares on every competing route. Braniff's fare strategy was revolutionary and risky. If it worked, Braniff would have effected a complete change in the structure of air travel prices. No longer would there be discounts and other fancy pricing tactics; just prices, some high and some low.

As a further attempt to make its resources more productive, Braniff scheduled its planes to fly more hours every day. For example, late-night and early-morning departures were added to existing routes. In addition to the employee pay cut, pilots agreed to fly ten extra hours per month, half of them without pay. Layoffs continued to reduce the size of Braniff's work force and they were used as still another attempt to reduce costs.

As the February 1 deadline for debt payment approached, Braniff's only hope for survival was another extension. Braniff was broke, but it continued to operate. Although no major U.S. airline had ever failed, many observers questioned how long the carrier's creditors would support its operation because they held the liens on Braniff's planes. The 37 creditors—22 banks, 13 insurance companies, and 2 suppliers—had to be convinced one more time. Braniff sought an agreement to have its debt commitments extended to October 1, 1982, and again to be forgiven the $40 million in interest payments.

Braniff's competitors, especially its chief rival, American Airlines, would benefit directly from the company's bankruptcy. American had retaliated immediately in the fare wars even though that meant substantial losses for it as well. However, American was large and strong enough to withstand such losses in the short term and it knew Braniff was not. Furthermore, American had added several directly competing routes in an attempt to defeat Braniff's strategy. Now there was evidence that American was urging Braniff's creditors to withdraw their support.

The creditors had little incentive to let the troubled carrier fail. If Braniff was forced into bankruptcy, creditors would be left with their collateral—dozens of 727 jets—for which there was almost no market owing to the recession-induced U.S. travel slump. The alternative was for lenders to accept some equity and forgive some total long- and short-term private debt, which at this point had reached $733.2 million.

Throughout this period Braniff continued its slimming and trimming tactics. Late in April 1982, the South American routes were leased to Eastern Airlines in a $30 million deal. Despite Braniff's precarious financial position, its officials were guardedly optimistic that the Eastern deal might lead the way toward generating sufficient revenues for survival. The exact extent of its financial recovery is suggested in Exhibits 1 and 2.

Two weeks later Braniff surprised the industry and some of its own executives. At midnight on May 12, 1982, it suspended all flying operations. The reason for the abrupt cessation of service was not immediately clear, but it was suggested that one of Braniff's lenders had called in its portion of the debt. The carrier was one step away from bankruptcy proceedings.

Even as the announcements halting flights and telling workers to stay home were made, Braniff directors were meeting to decide whether to file under Chapter 11 or Chapter 7 of federal bankruptcy proceedings. Under Chapter 11, the company would be protected from its creditors while the court oversaw its reorganization plans. Chapter 7 would guide the liquidation of the company's assets.

A few hours later Howard Putnam declared that he had not taken the Braniff job in order to preside over its liquidation. Braniff was filing to reorganize under Chapter 11.

Bankruptcy experts were puzzled by the way that Braniff had proceeded. Normally a troubled firm files under Chapter 11 and continues to operate while being protected from creditors. But Braniff had first shut down its operations, then laid off its employees, and finally filed for reorganization. Despite the unorthodox procedure, Putnam insisted that the airline would resume operations either under its own name or under someone else's as a consequence of a

(Continued on next page.)

EXHIBIT 1   Balance Sheet of Braniff International (system data; $ thousands)

	MARCH 31, 1982	1981	1980	1979
Assets				
Current assets				
Cash and short-term investments	29,213	42,480	13,626	23,724
Notes and accounts receivable	141,342	150,923	176,670	136,664
Less: allowance for uncollectible accounts	7,960	7,462	5,894	4,825
Spare parts, supplies and other	40,825	47,333	48,925	49,895
Less: allowance for obsolescence	4,896	4,790	4,673	4,737
Total current assets	198,524	228,484	228,654	200,722
Investments and special funds	1,670	1,706	1,702	1,792
Operating property and equipment				
Flight equipment	757,916	733,232	863,325	952,553
Ground property, equipment and other	152,771	154,089	165,501	155,705
Less: allowance for depreciation	342,780	341,512	323,362	335,703
Owned property and equipment—net	567,907	585,809	705,464	772,556
Leased property under capital leases	111,212	114,670	151,100	152,757
Less: accumulated depreciation	45,910	47,230	71,643	68,081
Capital leases property—net	65,302	67,440	79,457	84,676
Equipment purchase deposits	9,397	9,397	13,724	30,391
Owned and leased property and equipment—net	642,606	662,646	798,645	887,623
Nonoperating property and equipment, owned and leased—net	38,731	38,731	219	284
Other assets	15,447	14,236	17,950	45,648
Total assets	896,978	945,803	1,047,170	1,136,069
Liabilities and Stockholders' Equity				
Current liabilities				
Current maturities of debt and notes payable	78,329	77,806	35,718	16,319
Current obligations under capital leases	4,307	4,428	10,217	10,543
Air traffic liabilities	79,685	95,911	87,727	38,634
Other	198,088	194,948	187,737	196,736
Total current liabilities	361,409	373,093	321,399	262,232
Noncurrent liabilities				
Long-term debt	395,118	401,731	444,602	480,311
Advances from associated companies				
Obligations under capital leases	70,430	71,782	79,473	86,918
Other	30,851	30,652	7,598	3,309
Total noncurrent liabilities	496,399	504,165	531,673	570,538

EXHIBIT 1   *(continued)*

	MARCH 31, 1982	1981	1980	1979
Deferred credits				
Deferred income taxes	2,755	2,755	2,849	10,240
Deferred investment tax credits				
Other	48,170	33,776	1,292	4,087
Total deferred credits	50,925	36,531	4,141	14,327
Stockholders' equity				
Preferred stock	121,483	119,330	110,000	80,000
Common stock	15	15	15	15
Subscribed and unissued				
Total capital stock	121,498	119,345	110,015	80,015
Additional capital invested	67,188	67,188	67,188	67,188
Total paid-in capital	188,686	186,533	177,203	147,203
Retained earnings				
Retained earnings	− 200,441	− 154,519	12,754	141,769
Net unrealized loss noncurrent market equity security				
Total stockholders' equity	− 11,755	32,014	189,957	288,972
Less: treasury stock				
Stockholders' equity—net	− 11,755	32,014	189,957	288,972
Total liabilities and stockholders' equity	896,978	945,803	1,047,170	1,136,069

EXHIBIT 2   Income Statement Data on Braniff International Showing Revenues, Expenses, and Income ($ thousands)

	1981	1980	1979
Operating Revenues			
Transport scheduled			
Passenger, first class	12,518	40,334	50,002
Passenger, coach	202,622	250,657	257,146
Total passenger revenues	215,140	290,991	307,148
Freight	9,306	13,032	17,580
Air express	603	182	230
Excess baggage	1,751	2,204	6,780
Total property revenues	11,660	15,418	24,590
Priority U.S. mail	4,629	5,909	1,509
Nonpriority U.S. mail	73	136	38
Foreign mail	129	142	95

(Continued on next page.)

EXHIBIT 2 *(continued)*

	1981	1980	1979
Total mail revenue	4,831	6,187	1,642
Other	1,013	1,154	779
Total scheduled revenues	232,644	313,750	334,159
Transport nonscheduled			
Charter, passenger	1,307	1,827	3,113
Charter, freight			
Total nonscheduled revenues	1,307	1,827	3,113
Total transport revenues	233,951	315,577	337,271
Transport-related			
Subsidy			
Other transport-related	7,885	7,892	7,177
Total transport-related revenues	7,885	7,892	7,117
Total operating revenues	241,836	323,469	344,448
Operating Expenses			
Flying operations	133,938	146,720	174,931
Maintenance	21,338	27,761	34,366
Passenger service	25,073	31,511	38,679
Aircraft and traffic servicing	48,065	58,009	63,852
Promotion and sales	39,896	50,789	44,690
General and administrative	12,869	15,974	10,479
Transport-related	4,415	5,156	4,195
Amortization of development and preoperation expenses, etc.	711	2,078	2,339
Depreciation, owned flight equipment	14,444	13,046	13,812
Depreciation, other than owned flight equipment	3,124	3,121	2,682
Amortization, capital leases	3,335	2,285	2,834
Total depreciation	21,614	20,530	21,667
Total operating expenses	307,208	356,450	392,859
Operating profit (loss)	−65,372	−32,981	−48,411
Nonoperating Profit (Loss)			
Interest expense on debt	−5,021	−16,164	−12,347
Interest expense on capital leases	−1,669	−1,933	−2,559
Total interest expense	−6,690	−18,097	−14,906
Capitalized interest		−3,190	2,344
Capital gains (losses) operational property	5,269	741	1,775
Other income (expenses)—net	−9,295	−19,526	811
Nonoperating income and expenses—net	−10,716	−40,072	−9,977
Net Income			
Net income (loss) before income taxes	−76,088	−73,053	−58,388
		−470	−12,012
Net income (loss) after income taxes	−76,088	−73,523	−46,376

EXHIBIT 2 *(continued)*

	1981	1980	1979
Nonrecurring Items			
Income (loss) discontinued operations			
Extraordinary items income (loss)			
Accounting changes income (loss)			
Net income (loss) after nonrecurring items	−76,088	−73,523	−46,376

merger. Putnam explained that the decision to cease operations was made because Braniff was simply out of cash. The next day, May 13, 1982, would have been a scheduled payday for Braniff employees, and Putnam indicated that the company could not have met its payroll.

THE SEARCH FOR A REORGANIZATION PLAN

Braniff was allowed 120 days to file its reorganization plan with the courts. Management quickly decided that its best hope lay in a joint venture. Throughout the remainder of 1982, Braniff engaged in merger talks with several airlines. As the filing deadline drew near, Braniff obtained an extension on its filing date. As a result, 1982 closed without a concrete decision.

THE HYATT ALTERNATIVE

Through the first quarter of 1983, Braniff's fate remained a question mark. Putnam negotiated with 16 airlines concerning the utilization of the company's aircraft, equipment, facilities, and personnel. Only Pacific Southwest Airlines (PSA) presented a viable plan. Although major creditors and the bankruptcy court approved the pact, it was rejected by a U.S. appeals court, thereby terminating the Braniff–PSA talks.

With its last hope of a joint venture seemingly gone, Braniff's management turned its attention toward a reorganization plan that stopped just short of full liquidation. The plan was due to be submitted in federal bankruptcy court on April 4, 1983. Under the plan, the firm would divest itself of all its assets related to flying and would form a small business that would provide ground service and contract maintenance for other carriers. Braniff officials continued to believe that a live company in any form was better for creditors than a dead one. In Braniff's favor, the court deadline was postponed until April 18 because of a crowded court calendar.

In the meantime, Braniff began talks with Hyatt Corporation, the Chicago-based hotel chain. Hyatt offered an investment proposal in return for an interest-bearing note and a majority of the voting stock in the reorganized company. Under the Hyatt plan, Braniff would resume flight operations.

The talks with Hyatt encountered some major obstacles, most notably the disapproval of Howard Putnam, who considered the plan to be underfunded. Even after the original offer was raised considerably, Putnam still opposed it. As the April 18 deadline for filing reorganization plans drew near, no agreement had been reached. Braniff filed its original ground service proposal but with the stipulation that a revised plan could be filed

(Continued on next page.)

to include resumption of flight operations. Clearly, the door was being left open for Hyatt to sweeten its offer. The talks continued.

Finally, in June 1983, Braniff and Hyatt agreed on a plan to put Braniff back in the air. Hyatt would ensure the new airline some $70 million in funding and in return receive 80 percent interest in the reorganized airline and more than $300 million in Braniff tax credits.

The agreement still faced numerous hurdles. First, there was an effort by American Airlines to squelch the deal. American knew that Hyatt was having trouble convincing Braniff's creditors to accept the Hyatt offer. American attempted to sway the creditors by offering to buy Braniff's remaining fleet, thus effectively halting any plan that would put Braniff in the air again. Second, the environment was less than ideal for a new entrant into an industry already plagued by overcapacity and revenue-draining fare wars. Third, the immediate problem was to get Braniff's major creditors to agree to the proposal. Many of them were skeptical and feared they might end up as two-time losers. Finally the proposal required the approval of the bankruptcy court.

The major obstacle turned out to be the secured creditors' objections to the lease offer made to them by Hyatt. As holders of the liens on Braniff's planes, the creditors felt that they could realize a larger yield by selling the aircraft. For weeks, Hyatt's Jay Pritzker, a principal in the firm, mediated between Braniff's management and its creditors trying to secure agreement from the lenders.

After much negotiation, an acceptable offer was tendered; the last major hurdle had been cleared. In September 1983, the Braniff reorganization plan was approved by a federal bankruptcy court, and the stage was finally set for Braniff to fly once again.

Hyatt's plan for Braniff was ambitious but it held many advantages. From the beginning, the plan had the support of Braniff's unsecured creditors and its employees. Most of its unions granted positive cost advantages in wage contract renegotiations. These concessions alone gave Braniff the chance to operate as one of the lowest-cost carriers in the industry. In addition, many Braniff workers volunteered to work for free prior to the start-up date to get their jets back in the air. Some employees even came out of retirement to help with the restart.

Industry analysts believed that Hyatt's toughest job would be to put together a capable management team. Though none of the top management of the "old" Braniff remained, good management was a Hyatt trademark. It had consistently been rated as one of the best-managed chains in the lodging industry. Perhaps Hyatt could bring from outside the industry what the airline lacked.

Braniff also had to win over doubting and somewhat disgruntled travelers and travel agents. When the airline had abruptly shut down in 1982, many of its passengers had been left stranded, holding worthless tickets. Competing airlines were reluctant to honor Braniff tickets because they knew they would be unable to collect from Braniff. Additionally, because travel agents sell more than 60 percent of all airline tickets, their acceptance was crucial.

Hyatt's strategy was aimed at getting travelers and agents to try the "new" Braniff. Hyatt was confident that their service was good enough to keep customers once it had them. To attract customers, a joint promotional campaign with the March of Dimes was initiated whereby a 5 percent savings on the ticket price would be donated to the March of Dimes. To build goodwill among travel agents, Braniff held elaborate receptions in many cities that it served and gave agents free tickets as well. An additional aid to booking travelers came as part of a lawsuit settlement against Braniff's old rival, American Airlines. Braniff was awarded the right to placement in American's computerized reservations system.

The "new" Braniff that began flight operations on March 1, 1984, was a sleeker, slimmer edition of the former major carrier. There would be no overseas flights and no first-class service. Instead, Braniff divided its passenger segments into business traveler and leisure traveler. Braniff was counting heavily on the business traveler and offered its "business cabin" area as a special attraction.

The new airline initially employed some 2,200 people to handle its flight schedule of thirty 727 planes to 19 cities.

Despite the tenuous condition of the industry that had not fully recovered from recession, despite the many months of man-agement failure and employee unrest, despite the doubts of creditors, despite the obstacles posed in trying to win over a skeptical public, and despite the stiff competition that Braniff faced on every one of its planned routes, the "new" Braniff proudly rolled down the runways once again.

QUESTIONS

1. Discuss the planning process used by Braniff. Where did it go wrong?

2. Relate this case to the discussion of the decision-making process in the text.

3. Discuss Braniff's current position in the airline industry. Relate what you have learned to the material presented in Part Two of the text.

Source: Reprinted from the *Journal of Management Case Studies* (Spring 1985).

CASE 4

The Development of Corporate Planning at Borg-Warner: A Case History

Formal corporate long-range planning is a relatively new phenomenon. Very few American corporations practiced formal planning prior to 1950. As late as 1957, there were only approximately 200 large corporations with formal planning departments.[1] But by that time planning was beginning to become fashionable and a decade later over 1,000 corporations had formal planning departments.[2]

Chicago-based Borg-Warner was one of the pioneer planning firms. Prior to 1950 Borg-Warner's growth was directed by an informal planning system. But after 1950 Borg-Warner introduced a formal system. Borg-War-ner's planning approach evolved in a manner that provides students of management with fascinating insights into both the history of planning and the nature of the planning process.

The case that follows describes some of the highlights of the history of corporate planning at Borg-Warner.

THE INFORMAL PLANNING PERIOD: 1928–1950

The formation of Borg-Warner represented an attempt by five automobile industry sup-

(*Continued on next page.*)

pliers to offset the growing bargaining power of their major customers, Ford Motor Co., General Motors, and other automobile companies. After extensive discussions four of the five companies merged to form the Borg-Warner Corp. in 1928. The fifth company, the Ingersoll Steel and Disc Co., joined Borg-Warner in 1929.

In the early years of its history, Borg-Warner was organized into five highly autonomous divisions, one division for each of the predecessor companies. This arrangement was designed to make it possible for the leaders of each of the founding companies to continue to run their companies much as they had before the merger that created Borg-Warner. Each of the leaders had a place on the board of directors, and together they made corporate policy while running their own divisions. Coordinating their efforts was President Charles Davis.

The experiences of the Ingersoll Steel and Disc Division illustrate the nature of informal planning during this period. Major new strategies at the division level usually resulted from the occurrence of "motivational situations" rather than long-range planning. The reactions of division president Roy Ingersoll to the situations that arose represented the planning process. Five such "motivational situations" deserve brief discussion.

INNOVATION MOTIVATED BY THE DESIRE TO GAIN MARKET SHARE

The first motivational situation that prompted major changes in Ingersoll's division was the desire to increase market share. The primary example of this phenomenon at work actually occurred several years prior to the Borg-Warner merger. Ingersoll's business was the manufacture and sale of steel discs for use in agricultural implements. Between 1910 and 1921, Roy Ingersoll directed the company through a 1,300 percent increase in sales, yet by 1921 Ingersoll's share of the market was still quite small. Feeling somewhat stymied in his quest for market share, Ingersoll hit upon the idea of product innovation as a way of gaining ground. In the case of his disc product, the most promising innovation was to develop a disc with greater durability than that offered by the competitors. Therefore, Ingersoll initiated a laborious research project that culminated in the development of a production process that produced discs of substantially greater durability. The new product was a success in the marketplace and Ingersoll greatly increased his market share.

INNOVATION MOTIVATED BY THE DESIRE TO SURVIVE

The second motivational situation prompting major change occurred in the late 1920s. The onset of the Great Depression in 1929 caused Ingersoll's disc business to drop 85 percent. Faced with the prospect of bankruptcy, Ingersoll searched long and hard for alternative uses for his discs. He finally decided to make discs for truck wheels. But there was a problem. Most of America's truck wheels were being produced by the Budd Wheel Co. under a patent from a French firm. To get into the business, Ingersoll would have to come up with a different process to get around the patent. Ingersoll devoted months of experimentation to the problem and finally developed an alternative process, which he patented. He then sold his product to the Kelsey-Hays Wheel Co.

INVESTING IN "TURN-AROUND SITUATIONS"

A third motivational situation causing Ingersoll to make major improvements was the periodic appearance of "turn-around situations." In 1910 Roy Ingersoll had temporarily taken over management of a bankrupt steel mill that had been supplying Ingersoll with a specialty steel needed for his discs. Ingersoll took the job strictly as a method of maintaining a flow of steel for his discs. But once in the management position, Ingersoll discovered that he had a talent for turning a seemingly hopeless case into a profitable operation. He was able to "turn the financial situation at the steel mill around."

Having discovered his ability, Ingersoll subsequently looked for other steel facilities that he could acquire and make profitable. In 1930 he persuaded the Borg-Warner Board of Directors to acquire the Chicago Rolling Mill Co., and Ingersoll found methods of making that facility profitable. In 1935 the scenario was repeated when Borg-Warner purchased the financially troubled Calumet Steel Rolling Mill. And in 1937 Borg-Warner purchased a run-down steel plant in Kalamazoo, Michigan, and gave Ingersoll the job of making the operation profitable.

OPPORTUNITIES CREATED BY WAR

A fourth motivational situation was the outbreak of World War II, which created a huge demand for products related to the war effort. In the case of the Ingersoll Steel Division at Borg-Warner, the war created an opportunity to enter the business of manufacturing amphibious landing vehicles. The Kalamazoo facility was transformed into a plant to manufacture the product. An effective vehicle was produced, and the division received numerous commendations for its contributions to the war effort.

OPPORTUNITIES CREATED BY ORGANIZED RESEARCH AND DEVELOPMENT

Prior to World War II, Borg-Warner's research programs were conducted by the in-

dividual divisions. Shortly after the war ended, the Board of Directors took the first step in the direction of formalized long-range planning by establishing a corporate-level research unit. The primary purpose of the unit was to develop an automatic transmission. That research goal was achieved, and Borg-Warner signed a major contract to supply the transmission to the Ford Motor Co. Once the transmission product was completed, the corporate-level approach to research was continued and became a source of new product ideas for the entire corporation.

FORMAL PLANNING: 1950–1975

Conditions Leading to the Adoption of Formal Long-Range Planning. The successful automatic transmission project created a new problem for Borg-Warner. The contract with Ford gave Ford the right to manufacture all of its own transmissions under Borg-Warner license after the 1958 model year. It seemed likely to many at Borg-Warner that Ford would exercise that option. Hence, Borg-Warner would have to make plans to offset the loss of the Ford business in 1958.

In 1950 Roy Ingersoll was elected president of Borg-Warner. Ingersoll was concerned about the potential loss of the Ford business. He was also convinced that most other Borg-Warner products would eventually have to be replaced in order for the corporation to grow. Ingersoll therefore led the company in the adoption of a system of long-range planning. The system had many of the features of what later came to be called *strategic planning*. Each Borg-Warner division was asked to actively search for new product areas where the company's strengths would enable it to compete successfully. Each division was asked to develop plans for replacement of existing products and expansion in markets

(Continued on next page.)

currently occupied. Ingersoll himself concentrated his efforts on a program of acquisitions to fill the gap left by the expected loss of the Ford business.

The planning system introduced by Ingersoll was made possible by the fact that Borg-Warner already had a decentralized organizational structure. Many firms that were later to become leaders in the area of planning were not prepared to employ strategic planning in the early 1950s because they did not yet possess a decentralized structure. A prime example of such a firm is General Electric, a company whose name became synonymous with planning excellence in later decades.

The Nature of Ingersoll's Planning Process.
The planning system required each of Borg-Warner's divisions to prepare and submit for review a detailed plan for five years into the future. Included in the information to be submitted were

1. Long-range goals dealing with business functions, industries to be served, products or services, market share, sales, profits.

2. Five-year sales forecasts by product and market share plus information on marketing plans and major competitors.

3. Research and development programs dealing with present and new products including expenses and five-year budget data.

4. Manufacturing facilities, including needs for both existing and new products.

5. Financial requirements for five years, including capital for replacement, expansion, working capital, profit margins, and return on investment estimates.

6. Human resources requirements for five years for personnel in management, technical areas, sales, finance, and factory positions.

Each of the twenty-eight divisions submitted its plan to one of the committees created specifically to review the plans. Known as *supervisory boards,* the committees represented and included members of top management.

Evolution of the Planning Process.
During the 1950s Roy Ingersoll devoted his efforts to the tasks of convincing the management at lower levels to take planning seriously and of completing the acquisitions needed for growth. The acquisitions program was successful in offsetting the loss of the Ford business. However, some of the acquisitions did not live up to their promise, and by 1960 Borg-Warner faced the need to divest itself of the unsuccessful parts of the business.

In 1961 Robert Ingersoll succeeded his father, Roy, as chairperson of Borg-Warner. (Robert Ingersoll became president and CEO in 1958.) Bob Ingersoll faced the task of consolidating the progress achieved during the 1950s. This involved analyzing all of Borg-Warner's business in the light of the new environment of the 1960s and 1970s. In order to do this effectively, it was also necessary for Borg-Warner to analyze its corporate purpose. The process of rethinking Borg-Warner's corporate purpose and then arranging the divestiture of parts of the business that did not fit consumed much of top management's energies during the 1960s. In 1971 Borg-Warner announced a new five-year plan that included a new statement of goals and a new planning structure. The new structure provided for greater involvement in the planning process by corporate officers. As explained in the 1971 Annual Report:

. . . management has embarked on a new long-range planning system. Last November, a new five-year plan (for 1971–1975) was developed under this system. Line and staff people throughout the company worked on the plan, the most comprehensive in Borg-Warner history.

The major difference in the new planning approach and the previous method is the greater involvement of corporate and group officers in deploying Borg-Warner's assets.

The goal of the new plan was to increase earnings to $4.00 per share in 1975. The goal represented 2.4 times the 1970 earnings of $1.65 per share. The plan also contained a sales growth goal of 8 percent per year and a capital investment goal of at least $330 million over the five-year period, while keeping the debt to equity ratio at .35 or lower.

After operating under the new planning system for one year, new president James Bere described the system as follows:

Very briefly, the divisions prepare five-year business plans which first are consolidated by the group officers to their standards and then are submitted to our new formed Policy and Planning Committee, made up of five senior executive officers.

Here we hammer out an overall corporate plan to meet the objectives we seek, and then communicate the plan throughout the organization. We have set standards to measure the performance of each operating unit and we intend to be diligent in our follow-up of the results.[3]

STRATEGIC PLANNING: 1975–

Progress under the five-year plan of 1971 was brought to a halt by the nationwide recession of 1974–1975. As related by Borg-Warner's top planner, Dr. D. W. Collier,[4]

The . . . recession brought on severe declines in a number of our major markets . . . and a cold examination of our position in the industries in which we competed pointed out clearly to a history of cyclical, below average return. . . .

It became clear to Borg-Warner's top management that a new planning approach was needed and the Boston Consulting Group's concepts of strategic planning were selected. Collier explained this choice as follows:[5]

Strategic planning was appropriate to the times because it asked *First: Do we want to be in that business at all?* Before asking . . . *How do we do it better?* In addition, strategic planning began to focus management's attention on markets . . . their growth and our share in them, rather than on product, which had been our traditional focus.

In 1975 Borg-Warner's top management worked with the basic concepts developed by the Boston Consulting Group. This included the use of the "business matrix." As originally developed by the Boston Consulting Group, this tool required management to rate each of its "businesses" in terms of high or low market share and high or low market growth. Thus, each "business" could be placed in one of four cells of a two by two matrix (see Exhibit 1). By 1976, however, management decided to adopt a more realistic approach to the business matrix, in recognition of the fact that " . . . the outlook for a business was based on more than market share and market growth."[6]   Consequently,   Borg-Warner adopted a nine-cell matrix and expanded the concepts of market growth and market share (see Exhibit 2). Market growth was expanded into a concept called *market attractiveness*, which included such factors as "cyclicality . . . competitive intensity . . . (and) availability of raw materials."[7] Market share was expanded into a concept called *business strengths*, which included product quality, product differen-

(Continued on next page.)

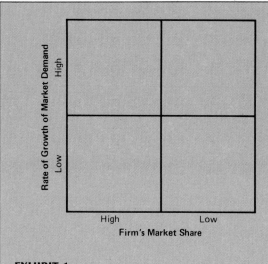

EXHIBIT 1
Borg-Warner—1975 Version of the Business Matrix

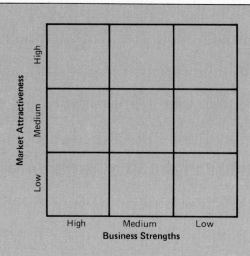

EXHIBIT 2
Borg-Warner—1976 Version of the Business Matrix

tiation, management depth, and other factors.[8] The resultant matrix is shown in Exhibit 2.

Closely related to the decision to use a nine-cell matrix in 1976 was the decision to "move to a *Strategic Business Unit* approach in order to facilitate a more sophisticated analysis of business attractiveness . . . and to provide . . . an organization and plan to which resources could be allocated and portfolio management concepts applied."[9] In 1975 capital allocations had been made on a group basis. In 1976 the group basis was still used, but the attractiveness of strategic business units within each group partially determined how much capital the corporation allocated to each group. In 1977 capital allocations were made directly to each strategic business unit.[10]

The strategic planning concepts were used to establish a new five-year plan for the period 1975–1979. This plan placed the emphasis on establishing an optimum business mix in order to maximize return on invest-

ment. Higher profit margins were given top priority and were to be supported by allocating capital to strategic business units that promised the highest margins. Also emphasized were (1) a search for new businesses that could be developed either through research and development or through acquisitions[11] and (2) a careful analysis of existing businesses to determine whether or not Borg-Warner should keep them.

Borg-Warner's 1976 Annual Report proudly announced a new planning system with a front cover picture featuring strategic planning and a lengthy inside article explaining the new system. The 1976 Annual Report also summarized the company's goals and methods with the pithy statement that management was . . . "determined to beat the median rate on equity for Fortune 500 companies before 1980, essentially by two steps:[12]

• sharpening the efficiency of our present operations;

- changing our business mix, by preferentially growing the more profitable segments of present businesses and by acquisitions in areas of greater promise."

The 1976 Annual Report explained that top management had identified a limited number of major issues, called *strategic issues*, which senior management would address. And the report hinted at the fact that sophisticated financial modeling was being used to analyze the company's options.

During the next two years further improvements were made in Borg-Warner's planning system. The data available from the PIMS program[13] was integrated into the planning process and used to help develop strategic business unit plans, and in 1978 a procedure was developed to define the "investment in technology" needed by each strategic business unit.[14] Strategic planning, in short, was an evolving concept at Borg-Warner. But it was firmly established as the corporation's basic approach to planning.

QUESTIONS

1. Assess the evolution and current status of corporate planning at Borg-Warner.

2. What else could management do to ensure that corporate planning is effective at Borg-Warner?

Source: This case was prepared by Professors Richard E. Hattwick of Western Illinois University and William C. Scott of Indiana State University as a basis for class discussion rather than to illustrate either effective or ineffective handling of an administrative situation. Adapted and reprinted by permission of the authors.

---

[1] C. W. Roney, "How to Accomplish the Two Purposes of Business Planning," *Managerial Planning* 25, no. 4 (January–February 1977):1.
[2] *Ibid.*
[3] Borg-Warner 1972 Annual Report.
[4] Speech by Dr. D. W. Collier at the Strategic Planning Conference, New York, October 4–5, 1978. (Sponsored by *Business Week.*)

[5] *Ibid.*
[6] *Ibid.*
[7] *Ibid.*
[8] *Ibid.*
[9] *Ibid.*
[10] *Ibid.*
[11] Borg-Warner 1975 Annual Report and Borg-Warner 1976 Annual Report.
[12] Borg-Warner 1976 Annual Report, p. 10.
[13] PIMS is a research program originally started by Harvard University and designed to identify the variables that determine profits in a wide variety of markets. Participating corporations provide data and can then "tap into the data base" to evaluate their market prospects.
[14] Speech by D. W. Collier, *op. cit.*

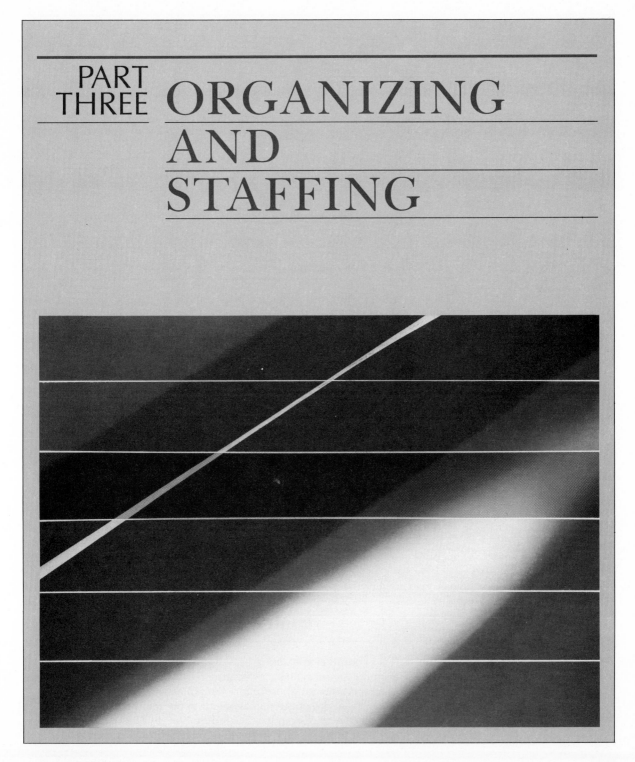

PART THREE

ORGANIZING AND STAFFING

8 FUNDAMENTALS OF ORGANIZING

LEARNING OBJECTIVES

After studying this chapter you should be able to

1. Contrast the traditional closed system perspective on organizing with the more modern open system perspective.

2. Demonstrate the roles played by the concepts of differentiation and integration in the development of organization structure.

3. Describe the five bases for departmentalization within an organization.

4. List the factors that jointly determine the optimal span of management.

5. Distinguish between tall and flat organizational structures.

6. Explain the role of the linking pin and boundary-spanning mechanisms in improving internal coordination.

7. Identify and explain the three types of authority that exist within an organization.

STOP ACTION CASE

F International

F International is a computer consulting company that specializes in designing integrated office information systems, evaluating hardware and software, converting existing systems, creating internal documentation systems, providing programming services, and helping management apply micro as well as personal computers to business operations. Started in 1962 by "Steve" Shirley as an answer to her own need to work in the computer industry from home as a freelancer, F International now employs more than a thousand freelancers in three countries: the United Kingdom, the Netherlands, and Denmark.

The company is different from other service or consulting organizations because all its employees, including Steve Shirley herself, and all the salaried senior management people work from their own homes. With a 30 percent annual growth rate (last year's sales were about $10 million), the company is expanding rapidly. As is true for all growing companies, determining the proper degree of control to exert is a crucial issue. At F International, however, control is *the* issue. Because everyone works from home and because the great majority of employees are freelancers, how the company is organized and how the projects are controlled determine the company's effectiveness and capacity to compete.

With this structure and organization of work, F International is a very different kind of company. Many questions naturally come to mind. How does Steve Shirley lead, encourage, and control such a far-flung and unhitched group of people? What are the satisfactions of such an organization for the employees? How does this organization differ from conventional organizations? Do these differences teach us something about how work might be better organized?

The physical dispersion of the F International work force would necessitate the use of telecommunications, the ability to divide jobs into smaller, more manageable components for part-time workers who might average 20 hours per week, and the development of teams of different sizes and capabilities to perform the tasks involved in a consulting contract. This meant that organizing would be a critical ingredient in the success of F International.

Use the materials in this chapter to recommend an organizational structure for F International.

Source: Paragraphs one, two, and three are reprinted from Eliza G. C. Collins, "A Company Without Offices," *Harvard Business Review* (January–February 1986):127. Reprinted by permission of the Harvard Business Review. Copyright © 1986 by the President and Fellows of Harvard College; all rights reserved.

An airplane lands at the Birmingham, Alabama, municipal airport, bringing a precious organ for a life-threatening transplant operation. Waiting on the airfield is a patrol car, driven by a uniformed police officer. A doctor steps from the plane and runs across the tarmac, carrying the heart in a plastic cooler. He ducks into the patrol car, and the vehicle leaps into motion, headed toward the University of Alabama-Birmingham Medical Center.

At points along the way, and even at an elevator leading to the surgical suite at University Hospital, police officers wait to halt traffic and avoid losing critical time. Within minutes, the organ is in surgery.[1]

This scenario is repeated dozens of times each year in Birmingham and at other hospitals throughout the nation. These organizations are able to

MANAGEMENT FACT OR FICTION

	FACT	FICTION
1. To label an organization as *bureaucratic* is to correctly identify it as inefficient, inflexible, and unresponsive.	☐	☐
2. Open systems differ from closed systems in that they involve interaction with the environment.	☐	☐
3. Differentiation, unlike integration, is a negative force that creates problems in growing organizations.	☐	☐
4. The division of work groups into departments is an example of horizontal differentiation; the unity of command concept is an example of vertical integration.	☐	☐

	FACT	FICTION
5. The statement "always put it in writing" illustrates the linking pin theory.	☐	☐
6. The notion of boundary spanning applies to roles played by organization members who interact with people outside the organization as well as by those members of one department who interact with members of other departments inside the organization.	☐	☐
7. Managers of such staff departments as finance, accounting, and human resources possess staff authority, not line authority.	☐	☐

The materials in this chapter will aid you in separating managerial fact from fiction. Your answers can be checked on page 282.

save the lives of otherwise healthy persons through remarkable medical innovations such as organ transplants and artificial organs. But accomplishing these medical miracles would not be possible without *organizing*—arranging people and physical resources to carry out plans and accomplish organizatonal objectives.

Organizing is the second major function, or task, of management. If planning can be viewed as involving the determination of *ends* (or objectives), then organizing is the process of selecting and structuring the *means* by which those ends are accomplished. The organizing process seeks answers to the "how" questions: How should work be divided? How should it be coordinated? How should resources, both human and physical, be allocated? And what factors should be considered in developing answers to these questions?

The organizing process results in the creation of a formal organization structure. The organization is characterized by explicit objectives, an elaborate system of rules and regulations, and a formal status structure and clearly marked lines of communication and authority.[2] All of these characteristics assist—and restrain—managers in handling their organizational units.

The people shown in Figure 8–1 represent the organizational components at Holiday Inns who must operate as a team to implement plans and achieve overall objectives. The Holiday Inn chain is made up of nearly 1,700 inns in 53 countries throughout the world. Each Holiday Inn General Manager must organize the activities of services ranging from reser-

FIGURE 8–1.   Components of the Holiday Inn Organization
Source: © 1986 Holiday, Inc. Reprinted by permission.

vations, housekeeping, and food service to hotel maintenance and groundskeeping if the objectives of profitability, sales, and customer service are to be achieved.

All managers make decisions on matters involving their department, division, section, team, plant, or whatever label their unit carries. In a sense, each manager is head of his or her own organization. But the General Manager must be constantly aware of the larger structure of which his or her unit is a part.

This chapter introduces the subject of organizing by comparing the traditional closed systems theories with the modern open systems approaches to organizations. The alternative methods of dividing work activities into separate departments will be examined and such concepts as authority relationships, the span of management, line-and-staff relationships, and coordination will be discussed.

ALTERNATIVE THEORIES OF ORGANIZING

> 66 There can be no one best way of organizing a business. 99
>
> Joan Woodward

The various attempts to seek answers to the questions of division and coordination of work activities and resource allocation can be divided into two theories: the traditional closed systems concepts forwarded by such management pioneers as Weber, Fayol, and Taylor and the more recent open systems approaches. Each theory has made important contributions to our understanding of the organizing function.

TRADITIONAL PERSPECTIVES ON ORGANIZING

A considerable number of classical, traditional management writers attempted to determine how best to divide work, coordinate work activities, and allocate resources in a universal perspective. In other words, they sought to identify rules or guidelines that could be applied in every situation to obtain the one best way of organizing. Given the apparent diversity of organizations (hospitals are different from manufacturing concerns, banks, etc.), it seems unlikely that scientific management proponents such as Taylor, classical administrative theorists such as Fayol and Urwick, and advocates of bureaucracy such as Weber would be unanimous in believing that a universal, one best way to organize existed.

> And yet, as the descriptions of their theories . . . showed, they did. In addition, their answers—if not exactly the same—are all quite compatible. Their theories of organizing depended on a high degree of structure. Taylor, Fayol, and others urged that tasks be specifically designated and that a precisely defined network of functional assignments and authority relationships be established. Fayol emphasized that sound organization principles bring the coordination, order, and structure necessary to integrate group activity. He felt that there should "be an appointed place for every employee, and every employee in his appointed place."[3]

The traditional perspective on organizing is best illustrated by the writings of the German-born sociologist Max Weber. Weber, who was a contemporary of Fayol and whose career is described in Chapter 2, believed that effective organizations contain a formal structure with set rules and regulations. He used the term *bureaucracy* to identify such organizations. Their main features included:

- A systematic division of labor based on task specialization.

- A consistent set of detailed procedures and rules.

- A well-defined hierarchy of positions that results in the creation of a chain of command from the top of the organization to the lowest levels.

- Interpersonal relations conducted by management with superiors and subordinates in an impersonal manner, and maintenance of appropriate social distance.

- Lifetime careers based on technical competence, systematic promotions, and protection against arbitrary dismissal. The result should be the development of a high degree of loyalty.

Although the term *bureaucracy* has acquired negative connotations of inefficiency, red tape, inflexibility, and unresponsiveness to the needs of customers and organizational members, bureaucracies are neither inherently bad nor good. The label simply describes a type of organization possessing a sharply defined hierarchy of authority-responsibility relationships, specialization, and set rules and regulations. In some instances, bureaucracies are the appropriate organizational form; in other cases, other structures are more effective. Weber's bureaucratic model does contain concepts that must be understood in any organizing effort: organizational structure, the span of management, division of labor, and the chain of command.[4]

CLOSED SYSTEMS VIEW OF ORGANIZATIONS

The similar views of the classical, traditional writers can be explained by the fact that each of them shared two basic assumptions about organizations.[5] First, organizations were seen as rational, economic entities. That is, they believed organizations were created to achieve specific objectives in the most economically efficient manner possible. This is sometimes referred to as the "tool" view of organizations.[6] Second, organizations were viewed essentially as closed systems.

Closed systems are sets of interacting elements operating without any exchange with the environment in which they exist. Such systems require no inputs—human, mechanical, or otherwise—from the outside environment. Very few systems—and no organizations—are totally closed. Systems vary in their dependence on material, information, and energy inputs

A **closed system** is a set of interacting elements operating without any exchange with the environment in which it exists.

from the outside environment. Even a relatively closed system such as a windup alarm clock periodically requires outside intervention when it runs down.

Closed systems thinking dates to the Renaissance and research in the physical sciences (notably chemistry and physics). Truly closed systems possess two defining characteristics. First, no exchange occurs between the system and its environment across the system's boundaries. Second, such a system becomes perfectly deterministic or predictable. In a closed system, if the initial conditions are known and a stimulus is introduced, the terminal condition can be predicted with certainty. Consider the pool table shown in Figure 8–2 as a system. If the following conditions and stimuli are known, it should be possible to predict exactly where each ball will come to rest:

- the position of every ball on the table;

- the elasticity of the bumpers;

- the coefficient of friction between the balls and the table;

- how hard the cue ball is hit;

- the direction of the cue ball; and

- the type of spin on the cue ball.

FIGURE 8–2.   The Pool Table—A Closed System

When the classical management writers such as Weber, Fayol, and Urwick began to develop their ideas about organizations, it was natural for them to borrow from the closed systems perspective then popular in the physical sciences. This resulted in an emphasis on structure and an attempt to eliminate any disruptions from the environment that could influence their studies of planned systems activities. In so many instances, however, decision making is ineffective unless managers consider the impact of the environment upon the organization. Consequently, more recent writers have expanded their considerations to a broader, open systems perspective.

MODERN PERSPECTIVES ON ORGANIZING

The belief in a single, one best method of organizing every company, nonprofit organization, social group, or other grouping of people, resources, and objectives has gradually been replaced with a contingency view of the need to fit the organizational structure to the strategies being employed to achieve stated objectives. Pulitzer Prize-winning business historian Alfred Chandler, in his investigation of the development of large industrial enterprises such as Du Pont, Sears, General Motors, and Standard Oil Company of New Jersey, was the first to formally state the proposition that strategy is a prerequisite for selecting the most appropriate organizational structure.

> *Strategy* can be defined as the determination of the basic long-term goals and objectives of an enterprise, and the adoption of courses of action and the allocation of resources necessary for carrying out these goals. . . . As the adoption of a new strategy may add new types of personnel and facilities, and alter the business horizons of the [managers] responsible for the enterprise, it can have a profound effect on the form of the organization. . . . The thesis deduced from these several propositions is then that structure follows strategy and that the most complex type of structure is the result of the concatenation of several basic strategies.[7]

The importance of organizational objectives and strategies in guiding managers in the performance of the managerial functions was emphasized throughout Chapters 4 and 5. Knowledge of organizational objectives and strategies serves as the basis for blending human and other resources.

OPEN SYSTEMS VIEW OF ORGANIZATIONS

A more modern organizing perspective is that of *open,* or *natural, systems* which emphasize the interdependence of the system with its environment. Based primarily on a biological rather than a physical model, open systems allow for both the evolution of their structure over time and interaction with their environment. Such systems are based upon the knowledge that no system is totally deterministic. Open systems thinking can be illustrated by further consideration of the pool table example. As the player strikes the cue ball, her opponent reaches out and picks up one ball from the table. This change is analogous to the impact of the environment on a system. It has now become impossible to predict just where the balls will ultimately come to rest.

> An **open system** is a set of interacting elements that interacts with the environment and whose structure will evolve over time as a result of this interaction.

Management writers Daniel Katz and Robert Kahn have identified several common characteristics of organizations as open systems.[8] These characteristics are identified in Figure 8–3. First, every organization is involved in a *cycle of events.* It receives inputs from its environment, transforms them, and generates output for individuals or other organizations. Then the cycle is repeated.

> A **cycle of events** is a process by which an open system receives inputs from its environment, transforms them, and generates output.

A second characteristic of open systems is called *negative entropy.* Entropy is the tendency of systems to run down, become disorganized, or even disintegrate. By continuing to import and transform resources from its environment, the open system can fight this tendency toward entropy, and it can grow rather than decline. Systems capable of remaining healthy over long periods of time are said to exhibit negative entropy. By importing energy, money, machinery, and human talent, open systems are able to

> **Negative entropy** refers to the ability of a system to repair itself, survive, and grow by importing resources from its environment and transforming them into outputs.

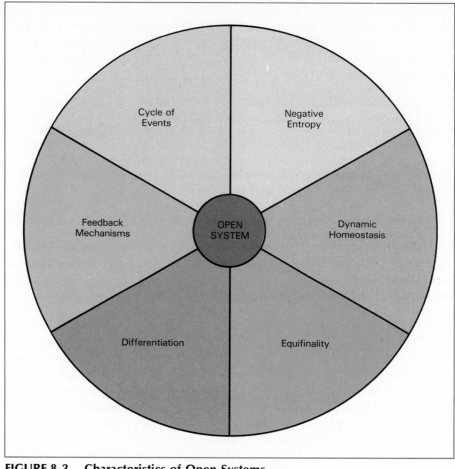

FIGURE 8–3.   Characteristics of Open Systems

repair themselves, survive, and be capable of growth. For a business firm, one widely-used criterion of negative entropy is long-run profitability.

Feedback mechanisms are a third characteristic of open systems. Feedback is information used by the system to monitor its performance. Feedback informs the organization of deviations from objectives and may lead to adjustments in activities.

Figure 8–4 illustrates the feedback mechanism in a factory's heating and air conditioning system. The system continually interacts with its environment by measuring the actual temperature in the building and comparing the actual to the desired temperatures. Based on this, a decision is made. Should the actual temperature rise above the desired temperature, the decision would be made to activate the air conditioning units until the desired level is reached. On the other hand, a low temperature may result

Feedback mechanism is an open systems component that informs the organization of deviations from objectives and may lead to adjustment in activities.

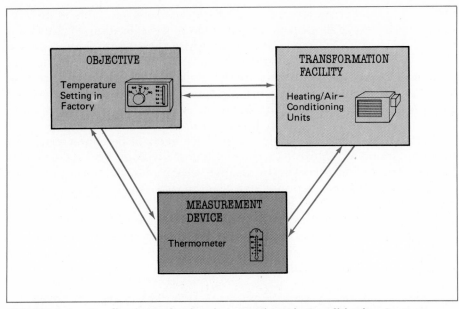

FIGURE 8–4.   Feedback Mechanism in a Heating/Air Conditioning System

in a decision to turn off the air conditioners. Such a system is characterized as open as a result of environmental forces determining the desired temperature setting. Such settings may differ over time, with perhaps 75° Fahrenheit used during the summer and a lower temperature used during the winter months.

A fourth characteristic is *dynamic homeostasis*. All organizations exhibit a tendency toward homeostasis, or *balance*. Human body temperature is 98.6° Fahrenheit. Some deviations from the norm are possible, but the acceptable range is small and a temperature outside this range is likely to result in permanent brain damage or even death. The body is equipped with certain physiological mechanisms for maintaining the optimum temperature, despite variations in the temperature of the immediate environment. If the temperature is too low, the person shivers; if the temperature is too high, he or she perspires. In addition to physiological adjustments, people maintain an optimal temperature by both adjusting themselves to the environment (amount of clothing) and by adjusting the environment to themselves (installing air conditioners and central heaters). This process whereby an organism maintains itself in an optimal state is called homeostasis.[9]

Organizations must also maintain equilibrium if they are to continue to perform their tasks. Since organizations change over time, this equilibrium must be dynamic if the system is to maintain a steady state during the input-transformation-output cycle of events.

Dynamic homeostasis is a process by which the open system maintains equilibrium over a period of time.

Differentiation is a structural force in organizations whereby the system develops specialized functions among its various components as it grows and becomes more complex.

A fifth characteristic of open systems is *differentiation*. This is the tendency toward overall growth and increased specialization of functions among the various components that comprise the system. This differentiation occurs in response to the characteristics of the environment and becomes increasingly complex as the system grows. In the medical profession, the number of specialists has increased as a result of the growth of medical knowledge. In fact, the American Medical Association has more members who are specialists than general practitioners.

Highly diversified firms such as Eaton are likely to be characterized by differentiation. As Figure 8–5 reveals, Eaton divisions provide products in such diverse industries as automative, electronics, defense, and other capital goods. Differentiation is described in more detail in the following section.

Equifinality is the principle that open systems can achieve their objectives through several different courses of action.

Equifinality is the final characteristic of open systems. The general principle is that open systems can achieve their objectives through different courses of action. It is not necessary that a single method exist for achieving an objective. As Katz and Kahn point out, "A system can make the same

FIGURE 8–5.   Differentiation Resulting from Diversification
Source: Reprinted courtesy of Eaton Corporation.

Diversification.
Getting into new things. Because the future belongs to those who anticipate change—to Eaton.

E·T·N
Growing into the future.
Automotive • Electronics
Defense • Capital Goods

trial state from differing initial conditions and by a variety of paths."[10] The characteristic of equifinality requires flexibility in choosing the appropriate means to achieve systems objectives. Rather than an endless search for the "one best way," the manager may choose from a variety of satisfactory alternatives.

COMPARING TRADITIONAL AND MODERN PERSPECTIVES ON ORGANIZING

The primary differences between the two perspectives on organizing are evident when answers to the following questions are sought:

- What is the *purpose* of an organization?

- On what *basis* should organizational decisions be made?

- How should organizations deal with *uncertainty* in the decision-making process?

- What, therefore, is the *best way* to structure organizations?

Table 8–1 compares the answers generated by the traditional, closed systems writers with those of the more modern, open systems organizational theorists.

The traditional, closed systems perspective is that an organization exists for the purpose of accomplishing the objectives for which it was established. That is, its sole reason for being is to serve the objectives of its

TABLE 8–1   COMPARISON OF TRADITIONAL AND MODERN PERSPECTIVES ON ORGANIZING

Organizational Questions	Traditional, Closed Systems Perspective	Modern, Open Systems Perspective
Organizational Purpose	Accomplish objectives of originator	No purpose *per se*, except survival
Basis for Making Organizational Decisions	Members of organizations seek optimal solutions to problems	Members of organizations seek satisficing solutions to problems
Dealing with Uncertainty	Eliminate uncertainty from the organization	Design the organization to be flexible enough to deal with uncertainty
Ideal Way to Structure Organization	Select organizational design that permits maximum degree of management control, minimal individual discretion	Design flexible organizations that adapt and innovate in response to environmental changes

originator.[11] By contrast, the modern perspective is that organizations do not have purposes *per se*. Rather, they seek to survive (i.e., maintain their cycle of events) in a frequently hostile environment.

The two perspectives on organizing also result in different answers to the question regarding the basis on which organizational decisions should be made. The traditional perspective is that organizations are rational, goal-seeking entities that must maximize economic efficiency to improve performance.[12] This was labeled optimizing behavior in Chapter 6 because it is the economically optimal solution which is always sought. By contrast, the modern, open systems perspective is that organizations are problem-finding and problem-solving entities that must learn about their environments by searching them for acceptable answers. This kind of behavior was referred to in Chapter 6 as *satisficing* rather than optimizing or maximizing.

How should organizations deal with uncertainty? The traditional, closed systems perspective asserts that the way to deal with uncertainty is to eliminate it from the organization. To be efficient the decision maker must be able to predict with accuracy how the organization will behave in any situation. This requires the elimination of any outside disruptive influences. The modern perspective is based on the belief that elimination of uncertainty is not a realistic objective. It states that the best way to deal with uncertainty is to design an organization capable of working with it. This requires a structure sufficiently flexible to respond to changes in the environment and evolve over time.

The final question, determining the best way to structure organizations, is answered in different ways by the two perspectives. The traditional perspective is to design organizations in ways that allow the greatest possible degree of management control. This involves reliance on rules, regulations, and formal structures to minimize disturbances in the system. It also recommends eliminating the need for individual discretion whenever possible. By contrast, the modern perspective on organizing is to design organizations with the ability to innovate and adapt to changes in the external environment. Both formal and informal organization structures should be used to support this effort.

The application of these perspectives to the organizing process is dealt with more extensively in the next chapter in the section on organization design.

DIMENSIONS OF FORMAL ORGANIZATION STRUCTURE

Two concepts form the keys to understanding the development of organization structure: differentiation and integration. These two opposing structural forces were identified by Harvard University management professors and researchers Paul R. Lawrence and Jay W. Lorsch:

. . . as systems become large, they differentiate into parts, and the functioning of these separate parts has to be integrated if the entire system is to be
viable. . . . As organizations deal with their external environment, they become segmented into units, each of which has as its major task the problem
of dealing with a part of the conditions outside the firm. . . . This division
of labor among departments and the need for unified effort lead to a state
of differentiation and integration within any organization.[13]

The term *differentiation* was introduced earlier as a characteristic of open
systems. Lawrence and Lorsch use it to mean the degree to which the
structures and managerial orientations of various functional departments
within the organization differ. Differentiation is neither inherently negative nor inherently positive. It is simply a structural force that becomes
more and more evident as organizations grow in size and complexity. This
structural force involves the division of human resources throughout the
organization through division of labor and technical specialization. Four
basic dimensions exist within organizations that may result in differentiation:

- *Differences in structure*. The degree to which an organization's departments have narrow or wide spans of management, rules, regulations,
  and other formalized procedures. Formality of structure tends to be
  greater in such departments as manufacturing and finance. By contrast, long-range planning units tend to have fewer rigid rules and
  set procedures.

- *Differences in interpersonal orientation*. Members of units that have either
  highly certain or highly uncertain tasks tend to be more concerned
  with the tasks to be accomplished than with personal relationships.
  Members of units with moderately uncertain tasks are concerned
  about establishing positive social relationships. Manufacturing people
  tend to be concerned with tasks; sales and marketing people tend to
  be concerned with relationships.

- *Differences in time orientation*. Subunits that have relatively immediate
  feedback, such as sales and production, have a much shorter time
  orientation than do subunits that may not get feedback for months
  or years, such as research and development. Manufacturing may be
  highly concerned with meeting daily schedules, while product development may be primarily interested in long-range thinking.

- *Differences in goal orientation*. Different units may have very different
  goal orientations. Manufacturing may prefer to have a small number
  of high-volume products, while sales may want a wide variety of
  products to increase the level of overall sales.[14]

While differentiation refers to forces such as specialization that push
the organization apart, *integration* involves opposite forces that pull the

Integration refers to the
degree to which members
of various departments
within an organization
work together in a coordinated, unified way.

MANAGEMENT FAILURES

TRW, Inc.

What happens when a trailblazing conglomerate finds that certain tried-and-true organizational concepts don't always work—and that newer, more fashionable methods have their pitfalls, too? TRW, Inc., a leader in management technology, has had to "tough it out" and learn by trial-and-error. A Cleveland-based giant that includes a high-tech complex in Redondo Beach, California, TRW represents an alliance between space-age technology and conventional manufacturing. In short, the firm is an ideal candidate for the negative implications of differentiation.

Originally started by two Hughes Aircraft veterans in the 1950s as an aircraft-manufacturing company, TRW has since distinguished itself as the producer of the Apollo moon module, the *Pioneer II,* and more recently, spy satellites dubbed "the absolute outer edge of technology." The conglomerate also manufactures commercial electronics systems, such as computer software and automated teller machines.

TRW's most recent blunder occurred at its Vidar division, which produces commercial digital telephone switches. Vidar took a whopping $43.5 million loss that caused half the division to shut down. Analysts blamed a number of factors. There were external factors: unforeseen competition had arisen, and

the booming market in digital switches had taken a nose-dive when high interest rates shattered the home-building industry. But there were internal factors as well. First, design engineers had failed to consult manufacturing divisions about the procedures that would be needed to produce their designs. Second, LSI Productions, a fast-growing TRW division that produces electrical components for television and medical equipment, had been withholding crucial expertise from other divisions, fearing that top engineering talent would be relocated to the digital telephone project—even though the parent company had tried to guard against such a "brain drain" by doing heavy outside recruiting and controlling the transfer of engineers to new commercial operations. Meanwhile, other parts of TRW were having internal difficulties, too. Some factions wanted to take risks and go all out for technological progress, some favored cautious strategic planning; some wanted to see teamwork, some preferred autonomy.

Sources: David J. Rachman and Michael H. Mescon, *Business Today,* 4th ed. (New York: Random House, 1985), p. 148. The TRW problems are described in such articles as "TRW Leads a Revolution in Managing Technology," *Business Week,* 15 November 1982, p. 124; "TRW Vidar Restructures Sales Organization," *Telephone,* 30 March 1981, p. 36; and Janice Drummond, "Vidar Plans 'Orderly' Retreat from Digital Switch Business," *Telephone,* 14 December 1981, p. 11.

organization together. The word refers to the degree to which members of various departments within the organization work together in a coordinated, unified way. Integration is often accomplished through such mechanisms as standing policies, rules, and procedures that specify actions to be taken by members of different departments and work groups. Cross-functional teams and committees can also aid in providing communication and coordination among varying departments. Still other integrating mechanisms for producing coordinated efforts among specialists and different departments include the existence of a formal hierarchy specifying the chain of command, regular interactions among managers from different departments, establishment of task forces composed of members of different work groups and departments, and use of matrix structures that require interunit coordination.

Division of Labor. Labor is divided three ways: *horizontally*, into departments; *vertically*, into managerial levels; and into *specialized tasks* that are performed by staff personnel.[15] The following sections examine horizontal differentiation in the forms of the division of work and work groups. Vertical differentiation and integration are discussed by examining such concepts as unity of command, the exception principle, delegation of authority, the scalar principle, line and staff relationships and the span of management. These concepts may prove effective as methods for improving overall coordination among different components of the overall organization.

DIFFERENTIATION OF PEOPLE AND TASKS

Organizational activities for small businesses are relatively simple. The owner-manager of a small print shop employs a few workers to operate the presses and copiers, make deliveries, perform routine maintenance, and meet customers who require printing services. Although accounting and tax services are typically provided by an independent accountant, the owner is usually directly involved in making work assignments, placing orders for paper and chemicals, and directing the operation of the business.

As the size of the organization grows, the need for structuring activities increases. The print shop may have one person responsible for typesetting and operating the presses; a giant printing operation such as Kingsport Press may employ dozens of specialists for three separate work shifts.

Increased organization size and a larger number of employees permit some degree of *specialization* or *division of labor:* concentration by individuals on one or a small number of activities. By concentrating on a specific activity, people can become more efficient. They can learn how best to perform that activity and can develop their skills to the utmost.

The benefits of specialization have been recognized throughout recorded history. Plato summarized the benefits of specialization or the division of labor in *The Republic*:

Which would be better—that each should ply several trades, or that he should confine himself to his own? He should confine himself to his own. More is done, and done better and more easily when one man does one thing according to his capacity and at the right moment. We must not be surprised to find that articles are made better in big cities than in small. In small cities the same workman makes a bed, a door, a plough, a table, and often he builds a house too. . . . Now it is impossible that a workman who does so many things should be equally successful in all. In the big cities, on the other hand . . . a man can live by a single trade. One makes men's shoes, another women's, one lives entirely by the stitching of the shoe, another by cutting the leather. . . . A man whose work is confined to such a limited task must necessarily excel at it.[16]

Adam Smith in his famous book, *Wealth of Nations,* published in 1776, gives an account of how the division of labor affected the productivity of workers in a pin manufacturing concern. Before specialization, each worker could only turn out about 20 pins a day. But when the process was broken down into ten subtasks (such as straightening the wire, cutting it to length, attaching the head, etc.) and each worker concentrated on only one of the subtasks, productivity increased by a factor of 240. (The ten workers in Smith's story now produced 48,000 pins per day rather than about 200.) The logical extension of this trend toward specialization to achieve greater efficiency and productivity was the scientific management school as represented by Frederick W. Taylor and the Gilbreths.

This tendency toward greater specialization and differentiation is constrained by three limitations. As one management writer points out:

It was Adam Smith who stated that the division of labor is limited by the extent of the market. Thus, if the volume of activity is not sufficiently high, among other things, fractional usages of specialized resources would offset the economies of greater skill. . . .

Another effect of the division of labor is to increase the interdependence among the subtasks. . . . The increased interdependence creates problems of coordination and a need for reliability. . . . Thus, the horizontal division of labor must meet the economic constraint of increasing input by an amount sufficient enough to pay someone who does none of the work but must be present to coordinate the work. . . .

[And finally] Once the task has been divided into pieces and the planning and control decisions taken away, have we not created a situation which deprives individuals of personal work satisfaction? What will motivate them to assume such roles and devote their time and energy to the subtask? . . . This is the problem that is created by separating the planning and the doing.[17]

The final concern, that of potential worker alienation, necessitates the integration process described earlier. The issue of worker motivation is discussed in detail in Chapter 9 in the section on job design, and in Chapter 13 in the discussion of individual behavior and motivation.

DIFFERENTIATION OF WORK GROUPS

Departmentalization is the subdividing of activities and responsibility areas into units within the organization. This process permits the organization

Departmentalization is the subdividing of activities and responsibility areas into units within an organization.

to realize the benefits of specialization and to coordinate the activities of the component parts. Profit-seeking firms may be broadly divided into functional units of production, marketing, and finance. Major service responsibility areas include legal, human resources, and electronic data processing. Further subdividing of an area such as marketing may produce departments responsible for advertising, marketing research, customer relations, and sales.

Bases for Departmentalization. Five primary bases for departmentalization exist: function, geography, product, customer, and process. *Function* refers to the activities and the various responsibility areas of an organizational component. The human resources department typically handles recruitment, management development and training, compensation, employee benefits, health and safety, and industrial relations. *Geographic* departmentalization bases organizational division upon location. Such major firms as Ford Motor Co., H. J. Heinz, and IBM have both domestic and international divisions. The Southern Company, a major utility made up of Alabama Power Company, Georgia Power Company, Gulf Power Company in Florida, and Mississippi Power Company, also uses this basis for departmentalization.

Departmentalization on the basis of *product* is common in large multi-product organizations. The basic structure of General Motors Corporation consists of the Chevrolet-Pontiac-GM Canada group, which is responsible for the engineering and manufacture of all of GM's small cars, and the Buick-Cadillac-Oldsmobile group, which is in charge of the company's intermediate and large-size models. IBM Corporation has an office products division and a data processing division. The office products division is responsible for IBM's line of typewriters, supplies, and other office equipment; the data processing division is responsible for sales and service of the firm's computer-related products.

A fourth basis for departmentalization is by *customer*. A large publisher such as Random House contains a college division, a juvenile division, and a trade division. Banks often have specialized departments handling commercial accounts. A food service firm such as International Multifoods may have different divisions for college and university food service, airlines, and hospitals.

A final major basis for departmentalization is by *process*. A cabinet-making operation may involve cutting wood, heat-treating it, painting it, and installing hinges and handles. Each step in the process of converting the wood, paint, and other materials into a finished cabinet may be assigned to a group of specialists.

As this discussion illustrates, the choice of the most appropriate basis for departmentalization depends on the specific characteristics of the organization. In fact, a number of different bases are often utilized in the same organization. Figure 8–6 is an example of how several bases may be efficiently utilized.

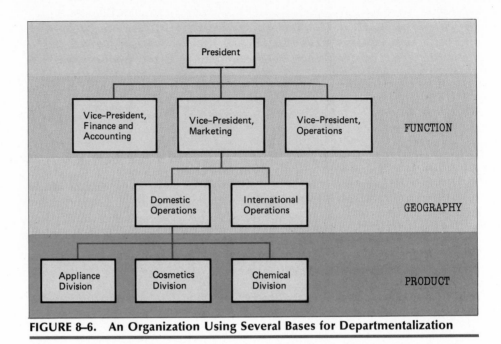

FIGURE 8–6.   An Organization Using Several Bases for Departmentalization

THE INTEGRATION OF SPECIALIZED TASKS AND FUNCTIONS

As noted in the previous section, increased specialization of people and work groups leads directly (because of increased interdependence) to a need for coordination/integration. This has had a major impact on the creation of the managerial role as we know it today. In terms of coordination, the role of the manager is to provide both the vertical integration between organization levels and the horizontal integration across functional units.

VERTICAL INTEGRATION: COORDINATING SUPERIOR-SUBORDINATE RELATIONSHIPS

Managerial authority is perhaps the most important mechanism for assuring vertical integration. Critical to the success of the organization are the development, coordination, and communication of the authority relationships that exist at each level. These relationships are determined by such classical management concepts as unity of command, the exception principle, delegation of authority, the scalar principle, span of management, and line and staff relationships. It should be noted that while these concepts express basic truths about relationships, there are occasions when the concepts cannot be applied in their strictest interpretation. Organizations can still operate effectively when one or more of these concepts are violated if the "costs" of such violations are understood. Such violations typically require major adjustments in other areas and the "costs" to be paid may involve human resource costs, added materials needs, or changes in sales or profitability.

Unity of Command. Figure 8–6 illustrates a classical concept of organization: *unity of command.* This principle states that each organizational member should report to only one supervisor for any single function. It is based upon the truism that employees work most efficiently when they receive orders, advice, and recommendations from a single boss. When several persons are giving orders, the potential for conflict, divided loyalties, and confusion exists. Adherents of this organizational principle compare its violation to the dilemma of a driver receiving instructions from one passenger to turn right at the next intersection while the second passenger insists upon a left turn.

Unity of command is an organizational concept stating that each organizational member should report to only one supervisor for any single function.

Although the unity of command principle is a widely accepted management axiom, it is frequently violated in complex organizations where personnel specialists, safety engineers, quality control personnel, and the immediate superior are all interested in aspects of the individual's performance. A critical problem in organizational design is the recognition of situations in which this principle *must* be violated. In such instances, it is important to ensure either that conflict does not arise due to instructions issued by several sources for that same function or that any conflict that does arise is quickly and appropriately resolved. Organizational designers must tackle the problem of coordination by reducing the likelihood of possible conflicts in such instances or by providing a conflict resolution program within the organization. In general, the more closely an organizational structure follows the principle of unity of command, the less likely are instances of such conflict and the lower the organizational "costs."

❝ No man can serve two masters; for either he will hate the one, and love the other, or else he will hold to the one, and despise the other. ❞

Matthew 6:24

The Exception Principle. Closely related to the concept of unity of command is the *exception principle.* This principle states that managers should permit their subordinates to make routine recurring decisions and that only unusual or highly important problems and decisions should be referred to higher levels in the organization. As emphasized in the discussion of time management in Chapter 4, managers should devote their limited time to handling more difficult or fundamental issues and rely upon subordinates for more routine matters.

The **exception principle** is an organizational concept stating that managers should permit their subordinates to make routine, recurring decisions and that only unusual or highly important problems should be referred to higher levels in the organization.

Delegating Authority. The key to growing beyond a manager's time, skill, and knowledge limitations is *delegation*—the assignment of authority and

Delegation is the assignment of authority and responsibility to subordinates.

Authority is a type of power that gives managers the ability to act, exert influence, and make decisions in carrying out responsibilities.

Accountability means holding subordinates liable for performing those activities for which they have been delegated the necessary authority and responsibility.

responsibility to subordinates. *Authority* is a type of power that gives managers the ability to act, exert influence, and make decisions in carrying out responsibilities. *Responsibility* is the obligation of the manager to carry out assigned duties. The manager who delegates specific assignments to subordinates must also provide the authority necessary to accomplish them.

The third basic concept of delegation is *accountability:* the act of holding the subordinate liable for performing those activities for which he or she has been delegated the necessary authority and responsibility. It is the process by which the manager justifies the use of resources for which he or she was responsible in carrying out delegated activities.

The decision to delegate authority to subordinates is a difficult one for entrepreneurs who have seen their small operations grow. But if the company is to continue to grow, the one-person, hands-on management structure must evolve. Even though the owner-manager is tempted to be involved in operational details, time limitations require focusing on the more important tasks. Management consultant King MacRury explains the role of the owner-manager this way:

> The head of a company is its "primary asset." . . . He should provide a broad vision of the enterprise, planning its future, looking for new opportunities to exploit and problems to avoid. An owner who spends too much time on details that others should be handling is wasting time the same way a talented surgeon would be wasting time if he sterilized instruments and straightened up the operating room because he didn't like the way subordinates did it. Being an executive means getting things done through other people.[18]

Scalar principle is an organizational concept stating that authority and responsibility should flow in a clear, unbroken line from top management to supervisory levels (also called *chain of command*).

The Scalar Principle. Effective delegation is affected by a fundamental organizational principle known as the *scalar principle.* This concept states that authority and responsibility should flow in a clear, unbroken line from top management to supervisory levels. Lines of authority should be clearly defined. To develop clear linkings to the chief executive officer, General Electric has created several sector executive positions. These top managers are each responsible for a group of GE operations with a specific industry identity. Sector executives delegate the necessary authority and responsibility to subordinates in their areas and are accountable to the office of the chief executive. Other large multiproduct firms such as American Can and W. R. Grace have adopted this concept.

Span of management is an organizational concept referring to the optimum number of subordinates a person can effectively manage; also called *span of control*.

The Span-of-Management Concept. "No man can command more than five distinct bodies in the same theatre of war." This was Napoleon's conclusion in regard to the organizational question that management writers later labeled the *span of management.*[19] The span of management (or span of control) is the optimum number of subordinates a person can effectively manage.

Rather than specifying how many subordinates comprise the ideal span of management, the early management writer V. A. Graicunas examined the increases in the number of interactions and relationships that accompany additions to the growth in the number of employees a manager must supervise.[20] Graicunas pointed out that the manager, in choosing an ideal span, must consider not only the direct one-to-one relationships with the people he or she supervises but also cross-relationships between the subordinates themselves and group interactions between groups of two or more subordinates. Consequently, a manager of a three-person department interacts with each person as an individual, with a single group consisting of all three persons, and with three different groups of two employees each. The number of possible interactions and relationships can be determined by the following formula:

$$R = n(2^{n-1} + n - 1)$$

where R = the number of relationships
n = the number of subordinates

If a manager has two subordinates, six possible relationships and interactions exist.

$$R = 2(2^{2-1} + 2 - 1)$$

where $R = 2(2 + 1)$
$= 6$

However, if the number of subordinates increases to 3, the number of possible interactions increases to 18. According to this approach, a department with 8 subordinates involves 1,080 possible interactions; a manager supervising 10 employees faces the possibility of as many as 5,210 interactions.

Graicunas's formula was not intended to determine the optimum span of management. Its major contribution is its emphasis on the increased complexity of a work group as it increases in size. Increasing the number of subordinates from 8 to 9 produces a much larger increase in the number of interactions and relationships than does an increase from 4 to 5.

Although there is general agreement that there is a limit to the number of subordinates a superior can effectively supervise, manage, or control, no agreement exists on the precise number. In fact, it is generally recognized that the optimum span of management will vary greatly, even within the same organization. While top managers may directly supervise only three to eight persons, supervisory managers directing subordinates who are performing relatively routine activities may be able to manage much larger numbers efficiently.

As Figure 8–7 indicates, the critical factors in determining the appropriate span of management include the following:

- *Type of work.* Simple, routine, repetitive work activities permit a greater span of management.

- *Ability of the manager.* Some managers are capable of managing more subordinates than others.

❝ The executive's chief business is to organize, deputize, and supervise. **❞**

George Ripley

COMPUTERS IN MANAGEMENT

Real Managers Don't Use Computers

Ray Moritz, vice president of service for Computervision, one of the highest of the hightech companies—it is the world technological and market leader in CAD/CAM, or computer assisted design and computer-assisted manufacturing—says that even after 20 years in the computer business he wouldn't touch one of the things. He has no need for one. Many of Mr. Moritz's subordinates must use computers, but as a manager he must manage his complete function. He understands that even in the computer age, management skills are what produce results through others—not flashy displays.

Marty Anderson, formerly with IBM and a management information training specialist currently with Ryder Truck, says she doesn't own a personal computer because it can't do enough for her to justify its purchase. She can balance her checkbook and do her budget far faster and more cost effectively with a pencil and paper. When she needs detailed data for her work, she knows who can get it for her. No terminal required.

Managers still must do fundamental things like manage the people who produce the results that pay the light bills. Sure computers are useful. In some cases, they are indispensable tools. But the key word is tool, i.e., something a laborer uses to produce results.

If you are the president of a company and you fly the corporate jet, it better be a hobby. That task is best left to the corporate aviation service. If you are a production manager, you had better not be out running a machine no matter how sexy that new devil is. If you are a manager, keep your hands off those keys and printouts.

- *Degree of interdependence among units.* The greater the need for coordination of interdependent work units, the smaller the span of management.

- *Training of subordinates.* Highly trained workers require less direction and control. Experienced subordinates are capable of performing their functions with less continued direction and advice than are less experienced persons. In such cases a greater span of management is possible.

Organization chart is a blueprint of the organization indicating lines of authority within it.

The Organization Chart. A common method of documenting organizational relationships is in the form of an *organization chart*. This document is a blueprint of the formal organization, indicating lines of authority within it. It is a simplified representation of the various positions in the organization, identifying their basic functions and the person or department to which each individual reports. The organization chart for the National Aeronautics and Space Administration is shown in Figure 8–8. NASA's organization is noteworthy for several reasons. First, it depicts

If you need information that a computer can supply, let someone with the time and talent filter it for you. Don't do it yourself except under extreme circumstances.

Top managers must learn to cultivate ignorance. The higher you go, the less you really should know about what is actually going on. Managers must rely on others to know. If they don't they are not managers, they are meddlers. Subordinates will bounce the most trivial decisions up the ladder if that behavior is reinforced.

Managers don't have to be computer literate. And there's no reason to feel inadequate because sixteen-year-olds are supposedly writing computer programs in school that are more complex than Einstein's theory of relativity. Back in the automotive age, sixteen-year-olds discovered hot rods and spent countless hours in garages rebuilding rear ends and connecting dual carburetors. Did that mean you had to enroll in automotive engineering courses in order to understand spark plug firing order and thus become automotively literate? All you had to learn was how to drive. . . .

If you as a manager want a hobby or a toy, then go to it, get that terminal fired up. But please don't impose those tools between yourself and actually managing people and enterprises.

Instant information in the hands of a manager is actually dangerous. Let those as far down in the organization as possible have the instant information. Let them react and do what must be done and then pass on the results. Give them a chance to use their lead time to take appropriate action. . . .

Source: Jack Falvey, "Real Managers Don't Use Computer Terminals," *Wall Street Journal*, 7 February 1983, p. 22. *Author's Note:* This focus box first appeared as an editorial in the *Wall Street Journal*. The position of its author, Jack Falvey, is controversial; both the reader and the instructor may hold opposing positions.

authority-responsibility relationships of one of the largest organizations in the United States. Second, it illustrates the use of departmentalization by function.

Tall versus Flat Organizational Structures. The NASA organization chart reveals the presence of a number of different levels in the organization. This results from the size and complexity of this space exploration giant. Span of management is another important factor in determining the number of required organizational levels. Structures characterized by narrow spans tend to have a greater number of different levels than those with broader spans. Since they have many levels of management, such organizations are frequently referred to as *tall*. By contrast, a *flat* organization typically has wider spans of management and, consequently, fewer levels of management than those with narrow spans.

Criticism of tall organizational structures tends to focus on cost and communications problems.

MANAGEMENT: THE LIGHTER SIDE

Who's in Charge Here?

The inflation of modern job titles has advanced so far that "vice president" is beyond rescue. But if vigilant citizens will bestir themselves, it may not be too late to protect "president."

"Vice president" was lost without a shot. Even in Washington, where the office is often ridiculed ("not worth a pitcher of warm spit"), at least there is only one of them, and he does what he's supposed to do: prepare to act *vice,* in the place of, the President. But there's probably no other organization with only one vice president, or where a vice president truly serves as No. 2.

On the contrary. Vice presidents have proliferated faster than co-editors-in-chief of high school yearbooks. To be a vice president now is to have about as much pomp, prestige and power as a first lieutenant.

A friend in a large advertising agency reports that its 1,100 employees include 150 ordinary vice presidents. The next step up is senior vice president. There are 11 of those. Then one reaches executive vice president, a once-exalted rank that used to mean No. 2. The agency has 11 of those. Likewise, in a large New York bank, one becomes a vice president after about 5 years. There are *hundreds* of them, plus 50 senior vice presidents, plus 10 executive vice presidents.

It's no use railing against this vice-presidential inflation. It reflects organizational needs. A leader who designates a single successor risks seeing power flow to him. An organization may wish to reward several officers for achievement in different specialties. Or it may want customers to think of their sales representatives, if designated vice presidents, as senior corporate officers.

Underlying all those needs is a failure of language. Civilian organizations have developed all the tiers and complexity of the military but lack terms (captain, major, colonel) readily indicating who's higher in the hierarchy. So when "vice president" becomes a catch-all, that puts pressure on the next job up—which is exactly what's happening at Chemical Bank.

Walter Shipley will soon become Chem's new chairman and, as they say, Chief Executive Officer. Why not president? Because to him, that does not even equate with being No. 2. He recently announced the appointment of *three* presidents, one for each major sector. "I don't need one No. 2 man," Mr. Shipley explained. "I need three." Three No. 2 men each of whom will have the title that means, or used to mean, No. 1.

If that sort of thing keeps up, "president" will mean as little here as in Communist countries. The Soviet Union and China both named presidents this week, and in each case it was little more than a bureaucratic afterthought. Soon American children may have to stop dreaming about becoming President and concentrate instead on becoming chief executive officers.

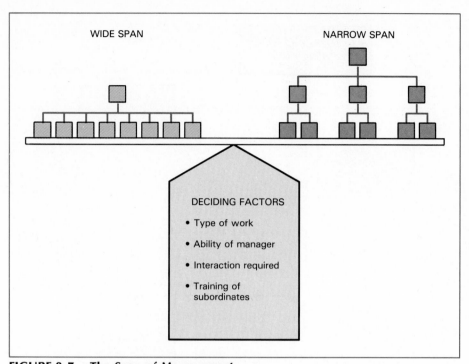

FIGURE 8–7.   The Span of Management
Source: Adapted from Robert J. Hughes and Jack R. Kapoor, *Business* (Boston: Houghton Mifflin, 1985), p. 157.

Narrow spans of management require not only more supervisors (and their salaries), but also the added expense of executive offices, secretaries, and fringe benefits. In addition, the more levels of management that communications must pass through, the more diluted and inaccurate it is likely to become. In effect, the decision and communication process takes longer and is of poorer quality. This is not only inefficient, it also demoralizes lower-level subordinates who feel that upper management is out of touch with the realities at their level of operation.[21]

A landmark analysis of the impact of structure on performance and morale was conducted by James Worthy at Sears, Roebuck & Co. Sears executives decided to "flatten" their organizational structure by eliminating a layer of managers between each store manager and the various department managers in the store. Although problems were expected to occur as a result of increasing the span of management in many areas, the new design proved superior in terms of profit, sales volume, morale, and improved communications. Store managers gave each department manager more authority; subordinates were forced to handle more managerial

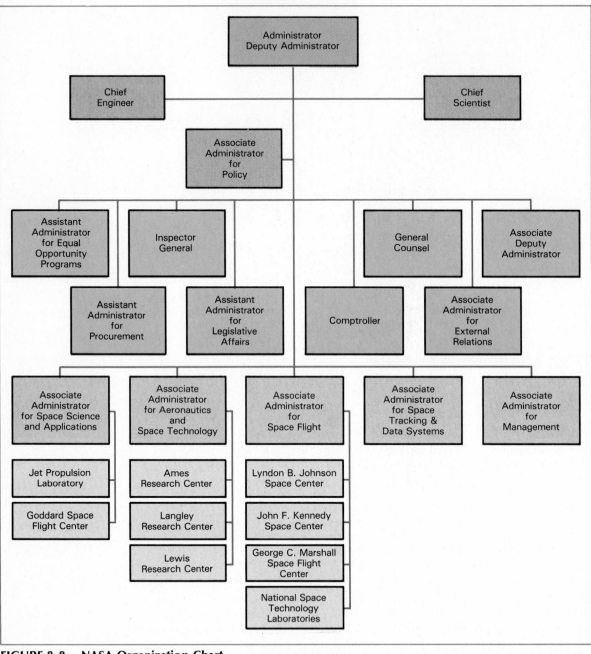

FIGURE 8–8. NASA Organization Chart
Source: Reproduced courtesy of National Aeronautics and Space Administration.

tasks and both morale and performance improved; subordinates were both hired and trained more selectively due to their increased importance; and paperwork was streamlined to save time.[22]

Subsequent investigations have also reported that people are more satisfied in flat organizations since such structures tend to produce greater autonomy, responsibility, and initiative.[23]

HORIZONTAL INTEGRATION: COORDINATING ACROSS ORGANIZATIONAL UNITS

Previous sections stressed the benefits of specialization. The focus on departmentalization and the discussion of optimum spans of management were designed to illustrate concepts that permit the organization to be structured at maximum efficiency. However, departmentalization also creates potential conflicts since formal structuring of work units may reduce the number of physical contacts between group members and coordination may become a major problem. This is particularly true in organizations that departmentalize by function or process.

Managers possess a number of techniques for improving coordination among the individuals and departments within the organization. Management by objectives programs, discussed in Chapter 5, are frequently used to improve coordination in addition to the other purposes discussed earlier. Since the programs involve the joint establishment of goals, each superior is involved in this process with his or her subordinates. The effect is to align individual and departmental goals with overall organizational goals. Individual activities must fit like puzzle parts into the accomplishment of larger projects. Day-to-day activities should mesh—not clash—with month-to-month and yearly programs.

The Linking Pin Theory. Rensis Likert, a major contributor to the study of organizations, proposed the *linking pin theory* as an explanation of how departments are connected in the organization.[24] He viewed managers as links between the groups they manage and the higher group to which they report. As Figure 8–9 shows, this overlapping should reduce the tendencies of the individual department to develop autonomously, since its manager is simultaneously a link to the department at the next level. Managers with overlapping group memberships link their groups to the total organization. By fulfilling this role, they are able to integrate the efforts of the two groups.

Former President Jimmy Carter was determined that the White House would be organized differently during his administration than it had been by his predecessors. Presidents Ford and Nixon had organized the executive branch under a chief of staff who directed and controlled its assorted personnel. The White House chief of staff was in a position to literally control which matters were considered in the Oval Office. H. R. Haldeman was the best known of these aides. Carter, elected as a "Washington out-

> 66 Everyone's responsibility is no one's responsibility. 99
>
> Anonymous

Linking pin theory is an organizational concept viewing managers as links between the group they manage and the higher group to which they report, permitting them to integrate the efforts of the two groups.

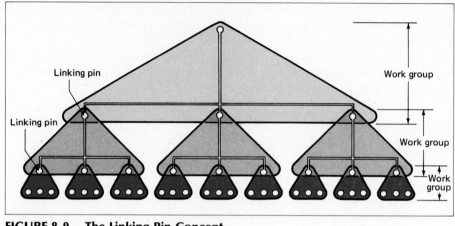

FIGURE 8–9.   The Linking Pin Concept
Source: Rensis Likert, *New Patterns of Management* (New York: McGraw-Hill, 1961), p. 104.
Used with permission of McGraw-Hill Book Co.

sider," was determined to avoid this organizational arrangement and use himself as the linking pin to cabinet officers and other major governmental agencies.

The then new president opted for what he called a *spokes-of-the-wheel* approach, in which all senior-level staff members had direct access to him. Carter felt this concept would "open up" the executive branch by exposing the president to new ideas and differing viewpoints. Instead, he quickly found mountains of details piling up on his desk because of the lack of screening. Some of the president's early decisions concerned such issues as approving all major trips by his staff; identifying which staff personnel could use the White House tennis courts and swimming pool; and shipment of the presidential limousine by truck rather than by air at a savings of $1,000.

Carter's concern for detail led to indecision on the part of some staff, who continued to flood the Oval Office with new memos generated in accordance with the spokes-of-the-wheel approach. Finally, in 1979, Carter had had enough and appointed Hamilton Jordan as White House chief of staff.

Carter's successor, Ronald Reagan, also chose the chief of staff approach.

Boundary-Spanning Mechanisms. The term *boundary spanning* is frequently used to describe those roles performed by such individuals as marketing personnel and purchasing agents who spend a large portion of their work time interacting with individuals *outside* the organization. Thus, they were said to "span the boundary of the organization."[25] As organizations have become more differentiated, particularly in highly competitive industries such as aerospace and computers, a need was recognized to create specialized integrative mechanisms that could supplement the traditional management hierarchy in the task of coordinating interdependent work groups within the organization. These special mechanisms have also been termed *intraorganizational* boundary spanning because they are designed to work across the internal boundaries between organizational departments or subsystems.

A number of methods of creating boundary-spanning mechanisms exist. They include the following: (1) establishment of liaison roles to link two departments that have substantial contact; (2) creation of temporary groups called task forces to solve problems affecting several departments; (3) use of groups or teams on a permanent basis for continually recurring interdepartmental problems; and (4) creation of a new integrating role when leadership of lateral processes becomes a problem.

Liaison Roles. *Liaison roles* are typically established when the volume of communication between two functional units grows to the point that establishing a specialized role to facilitate the process makes sense. Often this happens when the two units are highly interdependent (that is, they require a high degree of coordination) and when time pressures make it infeasible to refer issues up through the traditional chain of command. For the most part, liaison roles are filled by members of one of the two units involved who still report to their own functional unit supervisors.

Liaison role is a boundary-spanning mechanism whereby one or more members of a department serve as a linkage between two highly interdependent departments.

Task Forces. *Task forces,* the second kind of boundary-spanning mechanism, differ in three respects from the liaison mechanism. First, while liaisons work well between two units, their effectiveness is minimal when a large number of groups (seven or eight) are involved. The typical task force is composed of one or more members from each of the affected units. Second, task forces are usually created to deal with a specific problem or challenge while liaisons normally operate "without portfolio," that is, without a specific statement of their responsibility assignments. After the problem is solved, the task force is dissolved. Finally, task forces normally have some level of decision-making power with respect to the problem with which they were created to deal. This power is likely to be limited and subject to later review and veto, but it still exists. Liaisons usually possess no formal decision-making power or ability to commit their unit to a particular course of action.

Task force is a boundary-spanning mechanism involving the creation of temporary groups to solve problems affecting several departments.

Teams. *Cross-functional teams* differ from task forces in that they are created to deal with recurring problems. Therefore, they become more or less permanent features of the organization's structure. Also, as the problems and decisions surrounding them become less predictable, successfully coordinating the implementation of the chosen alternative often becomes the critical step in the problem-solving process. Thus, teams normally meet on some regular basis (often weekly and even daily) to make operational decisions and ensure coordination of activities.

Cross-functional team is a boundary-spanning mechanism involving the creation of relatively permanent groups to deal with continually recurring interdepartmental problems.

Integrating role is a boundary-spanning mechanism whereby an organizational member with little or no formal authority coordinates decisions and work activities involving several different departments by influencing those individuals in control of the functional units involved.

Integrators. The final boundary-spanning mechanism involves the creation of a specific *integrating role*. Individuals in such integrating roles carry many different titles depending on the industry in which they work. For example, product managers are common among firms in consumer goods industries which have a number of different product lines. Project managers are found in the aerospace industries as well as in many government agencies. Unit managers are commonly found in hospitals and other health care organizations.

Regardless of the title they hold, integrators have an unusual and difficult task. Their job is not to do the work, but rather to coordinate the decision-making process by influencing those individuals who are in control of the involved functional units. They must accomplish this without formal authority over these individuals and usually with little or no staff working for them.

Integrators accomplish these formidable tasks by acting as leaders of task forces or teams, by accumulating relevant information in one place, and by dedicating their full attention to the job of providing coordination. The primary purpose of the integrator role is to improve the joint decision-making process at work among the involved functional units and thus improve the quality of the decisions reached. In this way, they resemble the internal consultants or change agents described in Chapter 11. Like these change agents, the integrator requires considerable interpersonal skills.

LINE AND STAFF RELATIONSHIPS

Thus far, the chapter has examined the roles of vertical and horizontal integration as a means of coordinating the various activities of organizational members and functional units. But another more global kind of integration also exists. This kind of integration is based on centralizing responsibility for dealing with a set of interrelated issues which affect the entire organization as well as the members of a particular department. For example, most large organizations now have an office of equal employment opportunity as part of their personnel/human resources departments.

Three types of authority exist in the organization:

Line authority is the relationship existing between a superior and a subordinate in an organization.

- *Line authority* is the relationship existing between a superior and a subordinate in an organization. The head of the purchasing department possesses the legitimate power of his or her office to direct the actions of subordinates in the department. Line authority flows are simple and direct. They relate specifically to the unity of command principle and the scalar principle.

Staff authority is the power to conduct investigations and advise line managers, but not to implement these recommendations.

- *Staff authority* is advisory in nature. Managers possessing staff authority may conduct investigations and make recommendations to the line manager, but they do not have the necessary authority to implement these recommendations. Staff authority is possessed by managers in

MANAGEMENT SUCCESSES

Intra-Organization Boundary Spanners at General Mills

While the organization charts for smaller, one-product firms are simple, straightforward, and easy to understand, this is not the case for the industrial giants of the late 1980s which manufacture and market thousands of products. For example, Beatrice Companies began as a creamery in Beatrice, Nebraska, in 1894. By 1987, its product line had grown to over 9,000 products ranging from Peter Pan peanut butter, Avis rentals, Wesson Oil, and Butterball turkey to Meadow Gold ice cream, La Choy food products, and Tropicana citrus juice. Gillette has experienced similar expansion of products (with accompanying differentiation) from its origin as a safety razor and blade maker. Today its broad line of grooming aids includes Foamy shave cream, Aapri shampoo, Right Guard deodorant, Gillette Dry Look hair spray, and Super Max hair dryers.

While multiproduct companies are likely to use a single sales force, accounting/finance department, human resources department, and corporate legal and information systems departments, management would like to develop an organizational structure that would create "mini-companies" for each product within the overall framework. But such an arrangement would require the managers of each of these products to perform an important integrator role. No line authority over the company sales force would be granted to such a manager since the sales force would handle hundreds of company products. Instead, the product manager would have to secure cooperation from outside departments such as sales, advertising, and marketing research by persuading them of the joint benefits to be achieved through cooperative, coordinated efforts.

The concept of the product manager—an organizational member who is assigned one product or product line and then given complete responsibility for its success—has been in existence since 1927, when Procter & Gamble made the first assignment for Camay soap. The Camay product manager set prices, developed advertising and sales promotion programs, and worked with the field sales force.

Minneapolis-based General Mills adopted the concept a quarter-century ago. In the consumer food product categories, some thirty-three product managers collect internal and external information, establish objectives, and then plot strategies and tactics for such brands as Betty Crocker cake mixes, Honey Nut Cheerios, Hamburger Helper, Potato Buds, Yoplait yogurt, and Nature Valley Granola Bars. Product managers are responsible for the sales, profits, and market share of their particular product. They also are involved in thinking up new products, naming them, and testing them in the marketplace.

A newly hired graduate can work up to product manager in about three years at General Mills. Base salaries average $30,000 to $40,000 and the product manager is eligible for annual bonuses averaging 15 percent to 25 percent of base salary.

Source: The General Mills product management system is described in Ann M. Morrison, "The General Mills Brand of Managers," *Fortune*, 12 January 1981, pp. 99-107.

such departments as human resources, legal, accounting, and data processing. Staff departments serve the line manager by providing advice and specialized service such as forecasts or special studies and by monitoring the activities of the line department.

Functional authority is the power to direct or require certain procedures, policies, or specific practices in other departments not under the direct supervision of the person or department possessing this authority.

- *Functional authority* is the power to direct or require certain procedures, policies, or specific practices in other departments not under the direct supervision of the person or department possessing this authority. A staff department such as personnel may possess the necessary functional authority to require line departments to pay certain salaries to different employees or to follow safety regulations developed from conferences between personnel officials and government agencies. The head of the data processing department may require data to be provided in specific formats at specific times.

The three types of authority are shown in the organization chart in Figure 8–10.

The term *staff* is typically used to refer to those individuals or departments assisting managers in the performance of their basic production, marketing, or financial functions. The latter managers are called *line* because they form a part of the main line of authority (or chain of command) that flows throughout the organization. Staff personnel might include an economist who assists in forecasting future environmental conditions or an operations research team that assists in determining optimal warehouse locations.

FIGURE 8–10.   Three Types of Authority

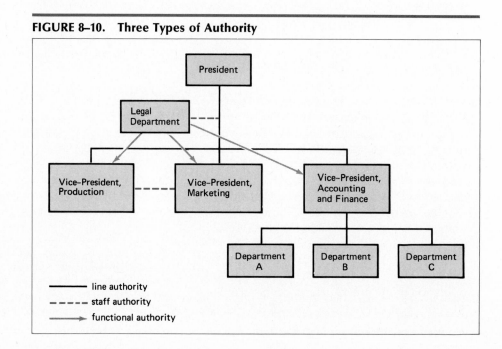

While these personnel are often considered to be staff, it is actually their relationship to line managers—not their activities—that defines them as staff. A research and development department may be considered staff in a manufacturing firm since it assists the production department in solving problems of product and machine technology. But in a firm involved in developing product and process technology for sale to other companies, research and development is a line activity.

While staff managers perform staff functions, they exercise line authority in their own departments. The staff authority relationship exists *between* departments.

Why Staff Departments Emerge. Two common motives for the formation of staff individuals and departments are expertise and economy. *Advisory staff* offer the managers the advantage of expert, objective opinions. Managers cannot be expert in all aspects of their jobs, and they rely upon specialists to provide expertise in certain areas. The staff advice may come from an engineer, the legal department, a scientist, an economist, or a human resources specialist, among others.

In cases in which economy is the motive for formation of staff positions, these persons are termed *service staff*. They are involved in such activities as computer programing, maintenance activities, preparing financial calculations, filing reports, or typing letters. It is generally less expensive to perform such functions by using separate service groups such as secretarial pools, data processing units, and maintenance departments than to rely upon line managers to arrange for their accomplishment.

To reduce conflict that might occur between line and staff departments, care should be taken to delineate the authority that any staff department has. When all parties know in advance the extent of the authority possessed by each unit, the probability of misunderstandings and disruptive conflicts between work units is minimized.

SUMMARY

Organizing is the act of planning and implementing organizational structure. People and other resources are organized in the most efficient arrangements to accomplish the objectives of the enterprise. This introductory chapter to Part Three introduces the basic concepts that underlie the structuring of organizations.

Historically, organizations were viewed as closed systems, which led managers to create highly specialized and departmentalized structures. The closed systems perspective is included in the works of such management pioneers as Frederick W. Taylor (scientific management), Fayol (administrative

theory), and Weber (bureaucracy). A more modern perspective is that of open systems, which stresses the need for the organization to remain flexible so that it can respond to changes in the external environment.

The term *differentiation* refers to forces such as division of labor and specialization that push the organization apart into numerous separate components, work groups, or departments. The opposing force, *integration,* refers to the degree to which members of various departments within the organization work together in a coordinated, unified way. Horizontal differentiation occurs as a result of such fundamental organizing concepts as specialization and the division of work and work groups. The division of work activities, *departmentalization*, can have five bases: function, geography, product, customer, or process.

Vertical differentiation and integration are expressed in such concepts as unity of command, the exception principle, delegation of authority, the scalar principle, the span of management, and line and staff relationships. Unity of command is a basic concept in most organizational structures. This principle holds that each organizational member should report to only one superior for any single function. The span of management—the optimal number of subordinates a person can effectively manage—is another key organizational concept. Organization charts are typically used to depict the organizational relationships.

Authority is the legitimate power a manager possesses to act and make decisions. Responsibility is the obligation of the manager to carry out assigned duties. Authority and responsibility are often delegated, or assigned, to subordinates who are then held accountable for performing the delegated duties. Effective delegation should be based on the scalar principle (or chain of command), which holds that authority and responsibility should flow in a clear, unbroken line from top management to supervisory levels.

Coordination (or integration) is an important need in any organization, but particularly in large, complex ones. Rensis Likert argues that managers serve as linking pins between the groups they manage and the higher-level groups to which they report. These overlapping group memberships of managers can play important roles in coordinating the efforts of different departments.

A number of different boundary-spanning mechanisms exist for working across the internal boundaries between different departments and work groups. These include establishing liaison roles between departments; creating task forces; using more permanent, interdepartmental teams; and creating integrating roles to be performed by specialists who work with several different departments.

Line and staff relationships are also important in organizations. Three types of authority exist: (1) line authority, the relationship between a superior and a subordinate; (2) staff authority, which is advisory in nature; and (3) functional authority, the power to direct or require certain procedures, policies, or specific practices in other departments not under the direct supervision of the person or department possessing this authority.

SOLVING THE STOP ACTION CASE

F International

The company's structure is a classic but flat pyramid with seven layers of management between "Steve" Shirley and the people who actually provide the consulting services. Shirley is group managing director of the organization. Under her are chairmen and CEOs of the international group and of the United Kingdom group. Reporting to them are seven general managers—in the international group, the managing director in Holland and the general manager in Denmark, and in the United Kingdom group, the general managers of corporate business development and the general managers overseeing the northern and southern divisions of the United Kingdom. These five people, along with the managers of control and personnel and training, form the executive committees, which are responsible for day-to-day operations.

In the United Kingdom, eight regional managers report to the two general managers who are in charge of the northern and southern divisions. These eight regional managers (three are actually functional managers) are in charge of managing the regions and selecting the people who will work on a project. Reporting to them are regional sales managers and staff, who are responsible for acquiring new business and keeping the old; technical managers, who oversee the actual technical work; regional personnel and training staff in charge of coordinating staff; and estimators, who plan the content of each job. Reporting to the technical managers are project managers, who head the project team in the field. Reporting to the project managers are the panel members, the analysts who form the project team, and the field consultants.

A typical project at F International begins when the sales staff in a region scores a hit. When the client is signed up, the regional manager and a team of three people—the regional estimating manager, the regional resources co-ordinator, and the technical manager—estimate the content of the job. At F International, this estimating process is one of the most important. Because everyone works from home, travels different distances to a client, and does a log of "paperwork" at home at unscheduled hours, it is very important that the regional managers know just how long it will take each project team member to perform her or his part of the job so that it can be monitored. Estimating, therefore, requires knowing well the skill and capabilities of each panel member.

Although many of them may have never met before arriving at the client's place of business, the panel members, under the direction of the project manager, perform the consulting service as a team. Every week, the project manager sends an audit report on the team's progress so that the regional manager is kept up to date. At the end of the project phase, the work is audited by a team of analysts who were not on the project but who have been specially appointed to audit the project team's work. This process is as crucial as the estimating step. Done right after the job, the audit provides project members with instant feedback on their work and catches any problems that involve team member skills.

Sally Patmore, an F International employee who previously worked for 3M Company, summarizes the advantages of the F International approach from the employee's perspective:

> Working for this kind of company fits in very well with my family commitments. It's nice not to be tied to regular hours. Because I've got a computer at home, if I've got a rush on, I can make extra time on weekends and evenings, which is quite difficult with an office job. Where I worked before, I couldn't just go in on the weekends. . . .
>
> Another benefit is that the chances for advancement are far better than with any other sort of part-time work. Here, you're on an equal footing as a part-timer. At 3M, I couldn't have gotten into management without going back to full-time work. Here there is no discrimination against part-timers. We're all part-timers, and there's no ceiling on what I can do.

Sources: Paragraphs one and two are from "Seven Administrative Levels," *Harvard Business Review* (January–February 1986):129. Paragraphs three and four are from "Project Management," *Harvard Business Review* (January–February 1986):133. Patmore quotation is from Eliza G. C. Collins, "A Company Without Offices," *Harvard Business Review* (January–February 1986):132.

FACT OR FICTION REVEALED

1. Fiction   2. Fact   3. Fiction   4. Fact   5. Fiction   6. Fact   7. Fiction

MANAGEMENT TERMS

closed system	departmentalization	linking pin theory
open system	unity of command	liaison roles
cycle of events	exception principle	task forces
negative entropy	delegation	cross-functional teams
feedback mechanisms	authority	integrating roles
dynamic homeostasis	accountability	line authority
differentiation	scalar principle	staff authority
equifinality	span of management	functional authority
integration	organization chart	

REVIEW QUESTIONS

1. Distinguish between the traditional, closed systems approach to organizing and the more modern, open systems approach. Explain the major characteristics of open systems.

2. What is meant by the statement "structure follows strategy"?

3. Compare the concepts of differentiation and integration. Is differentiation a negative force in organizations? What causes differentiation to occur?

4. Distinguish between horizontal differentiation and vertical integration. Relate your answer to such concepts as delegation, specialization, span of management, division of work, unity of command, the exception principle, and the scalar principle.

5. Describe the five bases for departmentalization within an organization. Give an example of each.

6. What are the factors involved in determining the optimal span of management?

7. Identify and explain the three types of authority in an organization.

8. Differentiate between tall and flat organizational structures.

9. Explain Likert's linking pin concept.

10. Identify and briefly explain the major boundary-spanning mechanisms used in different organizations.

PROBLEMS AND EXPERIENTIAL EXERCISES

1. Relate each of the following characteristics of open systems to the five organizations listed below: cycle of events, negative entropy, dynamic homeostasis, differentiation, equifinality.

a. A local hospital

b. Domino's Pizza retail outlet

c. Los Angeles Raiders National Football League club

d. A local bank

2. Robert Townsend reports an interesting case in his book *Up the Organization:*

> The British created a civil service job in 1803 calling for a man to stand on the Cliffs of Dover with a spyglass. He was supposed to ring a bell if he saw Napoleon coming. The job was abolished in 1945.[26]

Explain how the traditional, closed systems approach to organizing in the British civil service might have caused this job to last 142 years.

3. Draw a chart showing the organizational structure of your college or university. Identify persons or offices performing integrator roles.

4. Determine the various spans of management within an organization with which you are familiar. Do you regard these spans of management as appropriate for the particular management levels involved?

5. Prepare a report on the organization of the nearest professional sports franchise. How does the organization compare with those of other business firms?

MANAGERIAL INCIDENT: Legal Services Corporation

The contributions of individuals who serve as integrators are illustrated by the Legal Services Corporation, a federal agency created in 1974 to provide funding and technical support to local legal services programs throughout the United States. These local programs had been created to provide free legal counsel to indigent individuals in civil (noncriminal) cases. By 1980, almost $300 million in funding was being provided to 321 local programs and a number of more specialized support law centers. The Legal Services Corporation organization chart is shown in Exhibit 1. Also shown are the primary responsibility areas of its three main operating divisions: the Office of Field Services (OFS), the Office of Program Support (OPS), and the Research Institute.

An area of potential conflict existed between the Office of Field Services (OFS) and the Office of Program Support (OPS). While OFS was charged with the responsibility for providing technical assistance to local programs as well as ensuring that their management practices were consistent with LSC and Congressional regulations, OPS was responsible for designing and delivering management training programs to local agencies receiving financial grants.

The need to integrate these activities between the two divisions resulted in the creation of a new position: management and training coordinator. Its primary duties were as follows:

• To coordinate the approaches, methods, and resources used by the Office of Field Services in providing training and technical assistance to LSC grantees, primarily through the coordination of the efforts of the nine OPS training coordinators.

- To coordinate the development of expertise and support materials by the approximately twenty-two regional OFS management specialists with the particular responsibility of fostering a sharing of all expertise across regional lines.

- To act as liaison with the Office of Program Support and other LSC divisions to coordinate and improve use of all resources expended for direct field benefit and to ensure approaches are consistent with OFS policies.

This position involved a solely integrator role. Its holder had no formal decision authority over the activities to be integrated or the primary reference groups (the training coordinators and management specialists). It sat, literally, on the boundary between the divisions.

EXHIBIT 1   Legal Services Corporation Organization Chart

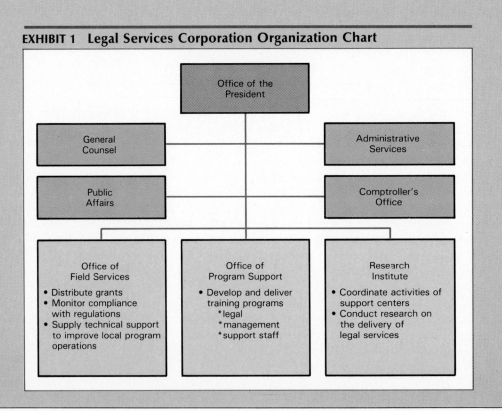

Questions and Problems

1. Relate the management and training coordinator position to the text discussion of:
   a. differentiation
   b. unity of command
   c. authority, responsibility, and accountability
   d. line and staff relationships
2. Suggest methods by which the person holding the position of management and training coordinator can improve his or her probability of success. How can the president of the Legal Services Corporation provide additional support?

Source: Duties of the management and training coordinator are from the Legal Services Corporation position announcement No. 353, dated November 29, 1979.

9 ORGANIZATIONAL DESIGN AND JOB DESIGN

LEARNING OBJECTIVES

After studying this chapter you should be able to

1. Distinguish between organization structure and organization design.

2. List the three historical periods of organizational design and the contributions of each.

3. Identify the components of an organization.

4. Distinguish between mechanistic and organic organization structures.

5. Explain the roles of organization objectives, technology, and environmental complexity and stability on task uncertainty.

6. Identify the major recent trends in work scheduling.

7. Explain the advantages and disadvantages of decentralization.

8. Identify the major types of organizational conflict and the alternative methods of dealing with conflict.

Hardee's Racing Team

Hardee's Food Systems has experienced considerable growth during the past twenty years. Although the Rocky Mount, North Carolina, fast-food company operated with only 1,100 retail outlets in 1974, it has since doubled the number to more than 2,300 units. In addition, average per-store sales have tripled since 1974. Hardee's currently ranks as the fifth largest fast-food chain, behind such giants as McDonald's, Burger King, Kentucky Fried Chicken, and Wendy's, with approximately three percent of the total market.

Name recognition and product awareness are important components in the Hardee's growth strategy, and the firm spends $35 million each year on advertising. In recent years, Hardee's managers decided to diversify their promotional efforts. In addition to traditional promotional activities such as television, radio, and newspaper advertising, billboards, and cents-off coupons, Hardee's decided to link its product offerings to sports. Douglas D. Pirnia, Jr., a vice president of the sports marketing firm International Management Group, explained the appeal to firms such as Hardee's, Coors, STP Corporation, and Goodyear: "You're not lost in the clutter of commercials when you put your money to work in sports. You can take the $200,000 needed for a prime-time spot and use it in a very impactful way."

Hardee's decided to form a new organization, Hardee's Racing, to participate in the National Association for Stock Car Auto Racing (NASCAR) circuit. Since its objective in this venture was to attract attention by winning as many major races as possible, the organization assembled a team of such well-known drivers as Cale Yarborough, David Pearson, Bobby Allison, Buddy Baker, and A. J. Foyt. The Hardee's racing vehicles were designed with racing victories in mind. Specific members of the organization are responsible for building, fabricating, and maintaining the team's stable of Ford Thunderbirds. Still other personnel are responsible for the engines. The final component of the Hardee's Race Team is the pit crew. These are the individuals who go "over the wall" during a pit stop during an actual race. Their speed and competence in performing needed tasks frequently means the difference between a first-place finish and failure.

Use the materials in this chapter to suggest an appropriate organization design for the Hardee's Racing pit crew.

Source: Pirnia quotation in paragraph two is from "How Coors Picks Its Winners in Sports," *Business Week,* 26 August 1985, p. 61.

In the previous chapter, the organizing function was introduced along with an analysis of its two major dimensions of differentiation and integration. In addition, essential organizational principles such as unity of command, the scalar principle, and line and staff authority that provide guidelines for implementation was analyzed. Finally, the chapter revealed how the assumptions underlying open and closed systems thinking impact the choices managers must make during the organizing process.

However, additional factors exist that should influence decisions concerning the organizing process. The identification of these factors and how they relate to each other are important subjects discussed in this chapter. The organizational design process must ensure that there is congruence, or "fit," among these factors.

MANAGEMENT FACT OR FICTION

	FACT	FICTION
1. Every organization is made up of four components: people, tasks, structure, and information.	☐	☐
2. The term *organic* describes organizations with a substantial human component, while *mechanistic* organizations have few people and are highly automated.	☐	☐
3. Flexitime is more common in manufacturing than in clerical and administrative fields.	☐	☐
4. Decentralization is preferable to a centralized organizational structure.	☐	☐

	FACT	FICTION
5. Matrix organization structures often have individual employees working for more than one boss, thus violating the unity of command principle.	☐	☐
6. Conflict is a negative force in organizations and should be eliminated, or at least minimized, as quickly as possible.	☐	☐
7. Confronting is a more appropriate method of dealing with conflict than either smoothing or avoidance.	☐	☐

The materials in this chapter will assist you in separating management fact from fiction. Your answers can be checked on page 325.

This chapter also examines how an organization's environment and technology impact its structure and how this, in turn, can affect the selection and retention of organization members. The impact of these factors on job design is also described. In addition, the need for more sophisticated and effective means of dealing with the conflict that frequently results from the evolution of an organization structure will be examined and methods of conflict resolution will be discussed.

THE NATURE OF ORGANIZATION DESIGN ▬▬▬▬

Since every organization is made up of thousands of elements that combine in unique ways to make it different from every other organization, it is useful to contrast the terms organization structure and organization design. One writer uses the analogy of an automobile to distinguish between these two concepts.

> The structure of a system such as an organization consists of its major components and dimensions. The design of a system reflects how the system defines and interrelates these components and dimensions. For example, a Ford automobile and a Chevrolet automobile have the same basic structure (engine, passenger compartment, trunk, fenders, and so on), but they also have unique designs (body style, engine size, and trunk capacity). When we discuss *organization structure,* we are concerned with the common elements that characterize all organizations, whereas *organization design* deals with unique definitions and interrelationships among these elements.[1]

The benefits of *organization structure* are vividly illustrated by the actual construction of a building such as the example in Figure 9–1. The combination of human and material resources into an organizational team is characterized by such *structural* concepts as authority relationships, specialization, departmentalization, and unity of command. The structural elements are combined into a unique *organization design* made up of a team capable of accomplishing organizational objectives: the creation of the physical structure being developed in this illustration.

EVOLUTION OF ORGANIZATION DESIGN CONCEPTS

The fundamental organizing question, "What is the best way to organize my work unit?", has always faced managers of profit-seeking corporations, nonprofit organizations, and government agencies. While the most popular answer to the question has always been "It depends," the relative importance of different factors influencing organization design has frequently varied. Organization design can be viewed historically in terms of three periods: classical, neoclassical, and modern. Each period built upon the contributions of the previous period in its attempts to treat the developments and problems facing managers of its own era.[2]

Classical organization writers focused their attention on formal organization structure and the use of authority. The scalar, unity of command, and specialization principles represent contributions of these writers. The classical writings began in the late 1800s and early 1900s, and paralleled the development of the first truly large-scale organizations in such basic industries as transportation, mining, and mass manufacturing. They filled a need to literally describe, chart, and define entirely new ways of managing, such as those experienced on the early automobile assembly lines.

Organization structure represents the defined relationships among the organization elements of people, tasks, structure, and information that characterize all organizations.

Organization design is the specific blending of organizational structural components—people, tasks, structure, information, and environment—that makes each organization unique.

WITHOUT IT, AMERICA WOULD HAVE NEVER GOT OFF THE GROUND.

Teamwork works.

Rugged individualism gets all the ink in the history books. But most of America was built—cleared, plowed, planted, milled, manufactured and even imagined—with teamwork.

And teamwork's changing banking, as we know it.

Now, local savings institutions are giving distant mega-banks a run for their money. By offering banking services nationwide, yet banking decisions close to home. In short, we can now be personal and powerful—because we've teamed up.

In the 1st Nationwide Network.

If you're a Network customer, that means better ways to save, free classes on managing your money, and this number to locate the Network member near you: 800-245-0111.

So, best of all when you roam, you're not leaving your banking at home. You can get cash to buy baked beans in Boston, souvenirs in St. Louis or a muumuu in Honolulu.

All possible because the 1st Nationwide Network is a network of financial independents, with more members in more states than any other network of our kind in the nation.* Which gets you banking across America.

Members who know what financial independence is all about. And what made America great.

Team up with us today.

1ST NATIONWIDE NETWORK

California: 1st Nationwide Bank Connecticut: The Bank of Hartford Delaware: Delaware Savings Florida: First Federal of Perry, 1st Nationwide Bank Georgia: First Federal of Columbus, Sentry Bank & Trust Hawaii: 1st Nationwide Bank Idaho: American Savings Illinois: Peoria Savings & Loan, Security Federal of Springfield Kansas: Franklin Savings Louisiana: Capital-Union Savings, First Financial L.S.L.A. Maryland: First Shore Federal Massachusetts: Bay State Savings Bank, Mutual Bank Michigan: D & N Savings Bank Minnesota: Metropolitan Federal Bank Missouri: St. Louis Federal Savings Montana: First Federal Savings Bank of Montana Nevada: Frontier Savings Association New Hampshire: First Northern Bank, Fortune Guaranty Savings Bank New Jersey: Fellowship Savings, The Provident Savings Bank New Mexico: New Mexico Federal New York: 1st Nationwide Bank North Dakota: Metropolitan Federal Bank Ohio: 1st Nationwide Bank, The First Savings & Loan Company Oklahoma: American Home Savings Pennsylvania: First American Savings South Carolina: First Bank of Rock Hill, Newberry Federal South Dakota: Metropolitan Federal Bank Tennessee: Athens Federal, Morristown Federal Texas: Continental Savings Utah: United Savings & Loan Washington: Mt Baker Bank

*1st Nationwide Network is an organization of independent financial institutions offering general depository and lending services in association with a nationally promoted trademark.

FIGURE 9–1.   Teamwork Generated by Organization Design
Source: Reprinted courtesy 1st Nationwide Network.

Two unique characteristics of the writings of the classical period should be noted. First, most of the classical writings on organizing were produced by such highly successful practicing managers as Fayol and Taylor who wished to document and share their personal observations on how to structure organizations. Consequently, they represent what might be described as informed opinions rather than the result of comparative or empirical studies of organization structure. Second, the writings of the classical period were based almost entirely on observations of large industrial concerns operating in markets characterized by a limited number of competitors and major barriers to entry by other firms. Because these observations occurred in industries labeled by economists as oligopolistic, they represented a very restricted sample (although a sample that, at the time, was the most important segment of the economy).

The *neoclassical* period extended from the 1930s into the 1950s. During this period, formal research methods of the social sciences began to be applied broadly to management issues. These writers and researchers focused on the new problems of their age, particularly those involving management-employee relations. Neoclassical theory brought the study of human behavior to the management sciences and an investigation of the "informal" organizations which exist outside the formal organizational structure. It raised questions about the effect of the division of labor on worker morale and productivity. It focused on questions of leadership and motivation, and its contributions continue to be significant in the late 1980s. A number of neoclassical contributions to management thought and organization development are discussed in more detail in Chapter 11.

Neoclassical writers, like their classical predecessors, also reflected the environment of their times. Major organizations such as IBM Corporation, General Electric, RCA, and AT&T were emerging in such new fields as electronics and communications. Industrial unions were relatively new and powerful, and employees had begun to demand more from their work than a paycheck. While these environmental changes—both inside and outside organizations—clearly indicated the need to expand and modify the work of the classical period, most practitioners and researchers of the 1930s, 1940s, and 1950s still accepted classical organizational concepts at face value while admitting the need to refine their application. It is in this sense that they are "neoclassical" rather than a new school of thought.

Beginning in the 1950s, a truly new approach to organization design began to be formulated. This has been identified by numerous management writers as the beginning of the *modern* era. Starting in Great Britain with the work of Burns and Stalker, Trist and Bamforth, and Woodward, researchers began to formulate approaches to the design of organizations that went beyond the prescriptions of the classicists. They also attempted to account for the evident diversity and complexity exhibited by modern organizations. To do this, they had to consider entirely new classes of variables, some external to the organization and some internal.

THE PARTS OF THE ORGANIZATION

What are these internal and external variables that must be considered in selecting the optimal organizational design? The following hypothetical incident provides answers to this question.

"She Gave Him the Company"

Chris Evans and his friends agreed that it was the most generous—and most unusual—graduation present a college student could ever expect. Evans's great aunt, obviously impressed that her youngest nephew had been selected as the outstanding management student at Garden State University, had telephoned him that she would attend his commencement exercise with the necessary documents for transferring ownership of one of her companies: Integrated Information, Inc. (3I). Her only requirements were that Chris would actually manage the company and that he could not sell it for the next ten years.

Chris's benefactor arrived a few minutes before the commencement exercises, but asked him to accompany her to the airport afterwards and discuss the gift. He quickly began by asking her the questions he had prepared. His first concerns involved learning exactly what 3I does. What are its products? How are they manufactured (if they are)? What are the key elements or steps in the production process? In other words, what are the *tasks* that the organization must perform if it is to be successful?

Chris's aunt answered that 3I is a six-year-old company created to manufacture computer peripheral equipment (disk drives, printers, monitors, modems, joysticks) that are compatible with IBM's line of personal computers. These devices are assembled from components purchased from other companies. All work is performed in one facility located in Rapid City, South Dakota. Production efficiency and quality control are the two most important criteria for successful task performance.

The mention of the computer industry produced a satisfied smile from Chris, but he immediately remembered reading that sales of personal computers had slowed over the past few years. What about competitors? And imports? Repeal of the Investment Tax Credit? Finally, what about those rumors that IBM is developing an entirely new generation of personal computers? Chris's concerns reflected his realization of the dependence of his newly acquired company upon its *environment* and the specific characteristics of that environment. His aunt agreed with Chris's observations about the company's environment.

Chris's formal management education at Garden State University was evident as he next inquired about 3I's *organizational structure*. His aunt opened her brief case and handed him the organization chart shown in Figure 9–2. A quick glance at the chart reveals that the company is highly differentiated and uses a functional departmentalization format.

Although Chris and his aunt were entering the airport parking lot, he still had some important questions. First, he wanted to learn about the *people* who work for 3I. Are they competent and motivated? Is the work force composed entirely of highly skilled professionals or a mixture of professionals and highly specialized technicians? Are workers unionized? Are qualified people relatively easy to recruit or does the firm have to invest heavily in training newly employed people? Chris's aunt commented that she believes the people are hard-working and competent, but that turnover has been a problem.

3I's new owner chose company performance as the subject of his final questions. Is the firm profitable or does it consistently incur operating losses? Are production schedules met? How accurate have sales and market forecasts been? How are budgets prepared? How is inventory (both parts and finished goods) controlled? What management reports are generated on a regular basis and how often? In essence, Chris's final questions dealt

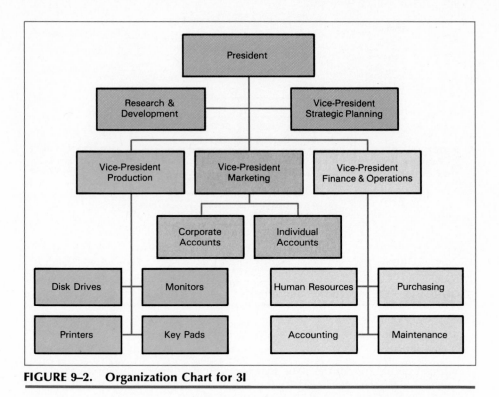

FIGURE 9–2.   Organization Chart for 3I

with the *information and control processes* for the organization. But the questions remained unanswered as Chris's aunt waved goodbye as she entered the airport terminal for her flight. He would have to organize the information he had received and decide how to go about answering his yet-unanswered questions.

ORGANIZATION COMPONENTS

The new owner of 3I had chosen a frequently used method of analyzing organizations: he considered it in terms of its component parts. The four components that constitute the organization are information processes, tasks, structure, and people. Figure 9–3 shows the interactions among each of these factors that result in organizational performance. In addition, "influence arrows" are included to indicate the impact of the environment on each organizational component.

The dependence of each element in the organization on other elements is depicted in Figure 9–3 by heavy lines with arrows pointing in both directions. They also emphasize how each element influences the other elements. One writer used the term *volatile organization* to describe such systems where "everything triggers everything else."

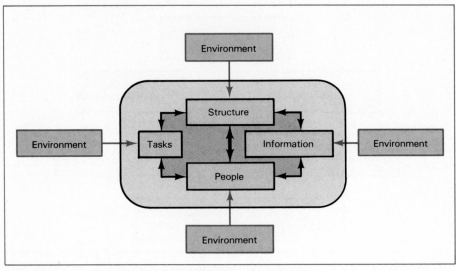

FIGURE 9–3.   Organization Components

Organizations are not the static structures depicted in organization charts, nor are they just collections of people, nor smoothly oiled man-machine systems. Organizations are all of the above, and then some. They are constantly changing networks of tasks, structures, information systems, and human beings that are both simple and complicated, orderly and disorderly, placid and volatile. A large part of managing consists of trying to change those Rube Goldberg organizations so they will function better.[3]

The primary question facing organizational designers involves how things work. If changes are necessary, what needs to be changed? How does the manager select which elements to change and which ones to leave alone?

Organizations as Processors of Information. All organizations must process large amounts of information if they are to survive and accomplish the tasks for which they were created. To select organizational objectives, to solve problems and make decisions, to control organizational functioning, information is required—information about the environment, the task, and current performance. *Information processing* represents one of the four key components of the organization.

A number of factors influence the characteristics of information required for effective organizational performance. They include the industry group to which the organization belongs; whether the industry is experiencing significant ongoing innovation; the type of decisions to be made (technical, managerial, institutional); and whether the decision required is a routine or nonroutine one.

Perhaps the single most important difference between the classical/neo-classical schools of organization design and modern theorists is the realization that organizations must structure themselves in terms of their information processing requirements if they are to be effective. More specifically, organizations should be structured in such a way as to reduce the uncertainty in the decision-making process whenever possible *or* they must be structured to deal with uncertainty when reduction is not possible. Professor Jay Galbraith explains the phenomenon as follows:

> If the task is well understood prior to its performance, much of the activity can be preplanned. If it is not understood, then during the actual task execution more knowledge is acquired which leads to changes in resource allocations, schedules, and priorities. All these changes require information processing *during* task performance. Therefore, *the greater the task uncertainty, the greater the amount of information that must be processed among decision makers during task execution in order to achieve a given level of performance.* The basic effect of uncertainty is to limit the ability of the organization to preplan or to make decisions about activities in advance of their execution.[4]

Since organizations will either structure themselves to reduce uncertainty or to accommodate it, an important question remains: What kinds of organizational patterns and structures will accomplish these tasks? The issue of *organization structure* represents the second component comprising the organization.

Organic and Mechanistic Organization Structure. Tom Burns and Gerald Stalker, two British behavioral scientists, conducted some twenty studies of British industrial firms during the late 1950s. The purpose of these studies was to describe and explain what happens when new and unfamiliar tasks are assumed by organizations which have, until then, been operating under fairly stable conditions. Their findings were documented in the book *The Management of Innovation,* which stands as one of the most important turning points in the study of organization design.[5]

The researchers concluded that environmental forces are felt directly by the organization and that the effectiveness of a particular organization design varied under different environmental conditions. Dynamic environments involve rapid changes in technology, markets, products, competitors, and economic conditions. By contrast, static environments are characterized by relative stability in products, technology, markets, competitors, and economic conditions.

Burns and Stalker identified two radically different forms of organization, each of which tended to be effective under certain environmental conditions. The first type, *mechanistic organizations,* was more effective in static environments. Managers of this type of organization tended to rely more on rigid structures, directives and rules, and high centralization. The mechanistic organization possesses many of the characteristics of the bureaucratic model described in Chapter 8.

Mechanistic structure is the organizational design frequently used in stable, relatively simple environments characterized by low uncertainty, high task specialization, formal authority structures, directives and rules, and high centralization.

In mechanistic systems the problems and tasks facing the concern as a whole are broken down into specialisms. Each individual pursues his task as something distinct from the real tasks of the concern as a whole, as if it were the subject of a subcontract. "Somebody at the top" is responsible for seeing to its relevance. The technical methods, duties, and powers attached to each functional role are precisely defined. Interaction within management tends to be vertical, i.e., between superior and subordinate. Operations and working behavior are governed by instructions and decisions issued by superiors. This command hierarchy is maintained by the implicit assumption that all knowledge about the situation of the firm and its tasks is, or should be, available only to the head of the firm.[6]

Although no industry exists in a completely static environment, a number of firms have characteristics similar to the mechanistic design. These include many local utility companies (with no direct competitors and relatively stable markets) and some food processors with numerous suppliers and a steady group of customers.

At the opposite end of the continuum of organizational design strategies are what Burns and Stalker called *organic organizations*. These types of organizations tended to be most effective in highly dynamic environments. They are more fluid and flexible in structure than the mechanistic organization, and their managers emphasize decentralization, low levels of formalization, and authority based on knowledge rather than formal position in the organization.

Organic structure is the organizational design frequently used in complex, dynamic environments characterized by high uncertainty, low specialization, low levels of formalization, authority based on knowledge rather than formal authority positions, and decentralization.

Organic systems are adapted to unstable conditions, when problems and requirements for action arise which cannot be broken down and distributed among specialist roles within a clearly defined hierarchy. Individuals have to perform their specialized tasks in the light of their knowledge of the tasks of the firm as a whole. Jobs lose much of their formal definition in terms of methods, duties, and powers, which have to be redefined continually by interacting with others participating in a task. Interaction runs laterally as much as vertically. Communication between people of different ranks tend to resemble lateral consultation rather than vertical command. Omniscience can no longer be imputed to the head of the concern.[7]

Examples of organizations operating in unstable and unpredictable environments include The Limited (women's fashion specialty shops impacted by rapid changes in fashions and consumer tastes) and Compaq Computer Corporation (personal computer manufacturer in an industry characterized by rapid technological change). Figure 9–4 traces the birth and growth of Compaq from a rough sketch on the back of a pie shop place mat to $503 million in annual sales just four years later. Both of these organizations exhibit a number of characteristics of an organic design.

Either form of organization may prove more effective under different environmental conditions. This fact illustrates the contingency concept described in Chapter 2. Not surprisingly, the organic form of organization proves more effective in dealing with situations requiring innovation. From

FIGURE 9–4.   Compaq Computer Corporation: Organic Design for a Dynamic Environment
Source: © 1986 by COMPAQ Computer Corporation. Reprinted by permission.

the information processing standpoint, organic organizational forms are more capable of dealing with the uncertainty inherent in innovation because they facilitate the exchange of information among the relevant parties involved. On the other hand, under stable conditions the organic form of organization tends to be inefficient due to the duplication of communications channels; thus, the mechanistic form is preferred. Figure 9–5 summarizes these relationships.

ORGANIZATION STRUCTURE, TECHNOLOGY, AND UNCERTAINTY

The third component of the organization is made up of the *tasks* it performs. The word *task* simply refers to what the organization does, or, to

> **Tasks** are activities performed by the organization in accomplishing its objectives; transformation of inputs from the environment into outputs.

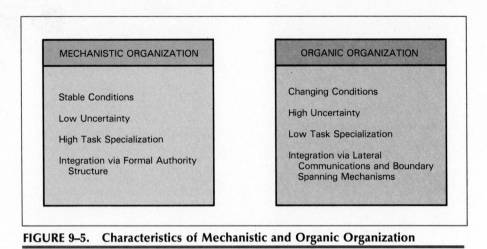

FIGURE 9–5.   Characteristics of Mechanistic and Organic Organization

use the systems terminology introduced in the previous chapter, it can be defined as the organization's cycle of events. The previous discussion of the organization's information processing component noted that the greater the level of uncertainty regarding the task, the more information that would have to be processed concurrent with task performance. Finally, it was also pointed out that the organic form of organization structure is the more effective at handling high levels of task uncertainty. But just what is it that makes a task "certain" or "uncertain"?

The characteristics of an organization's tasks are determined by two sets of factors. The first has to do with what the organization is attempting to accomplish. Organizational aims can be determined by examining mission statements, statements of objectives, and strategic plans. The second set of factors has to do with the characteristics of the organization's technology (or what might be termed its thruput process). Figure 9–6 summarizes these relationships.

INFLUENCE OF ORGANIZATION OBJECTIVES ON TASK UNCERTAINTY

In Chapter 5, an organization's mission was defined as the unique and fundamental purpose that sets a firm apart from other firms of its type and that identifies the scope of its operations in product and market terms. To the extent that an organization has a broad scope of activities, it will experience a relatively high degree of task uncertainty. Large firms such as General Electric, Honda, and Black & Decker are likely to experience considerable task uncertainty due to the significantly different products they produce and market.

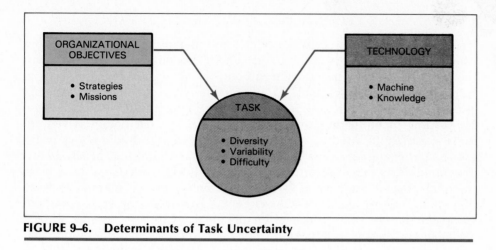

FIGURE 9–6.   Determinants of Task Uncertainty

Companies operating in numerous separate markets are also candidates for high task uncertainty. The J. M. Smucker Company of Solon, Ohio, produces a number of different jams and jellies to be sold to consumers through retail food stores. In addition, another part of its organization develops large-volume jelly products to be sold to industrial and institutional customers who add them to their products or sell them as part of other product offerings. Other market-related causes of task uncertainty involve participation in international markets. Fast-food franchises operating outside the United States have encountered significant problems with different cultural patterns and have been forced to adapt their offerings or risk market failure. Kentucky Fried Chicken's Hong Kong franchisee abandoned the "finger-lickin' good" slogan which proved meaningless to fastidious Chinese diners, who frequently receive damp towels at restaurants to wipe their hands after eating. McDonald's U.S. headquarters approved the addition of wine to the menu in French outlets and beer in West German units. Japanese outlets of Kentucky Fried Chicken substituted french fries for mashed potatoes in its chicken meals to satisfy their Japanese customers.

When an organization has many significantly different operations in progress, the potential for competition among different subunits and even the possibility of conflicting objectives is great. High levels of communication and coordination (integration) among managers are required to minimize the problems that occur. Should these problems become significant, the organization may choose to create separate strategic business units. These SBUs, described earlier in Chapter 5, are often used by large multiproduct companies such as Union Carbide, General Electric, and General Foods.

> 66 Good organizations are living bodies that grow new muscles to meet challenges. [An organization] chart demoralizes people. Nobody thinks of himself as below other people. And in a good company he isn't. 99
>
> Robert Townsend

INFLUENCE OF TECHNOLOGY ON TASK UNCERTAINTY

Technology can be viewed from two different perspectives.[8] In its common usage, technology refers to the nature and characteristics of the machines (or physical artifacts) necessary to accomplish some task. A hammer is a technology for driving a nail; an automobile is a technology for moving people or things from one place to another; a computer is a technology for storing, manipulating, and retrieving data. But technology is viewed more correctly in another way: that of knowledge technology or "technique." For example, a person must learn how to drive a car before he or she can use it as a means of transportation. Unless knowledge of programing or the use of commercial software is present, the computer is useless; it becomes an expensive desk ornament. (This was, in fact, a common complaint in the early 1980s when personal computers became widely available and began to appear on managers' desks.) The definition first proposed in Chapter 3 that described technology as the science of applying information and knowledge to problem-solving situations and putting knowledge to work for humanity incorporates these two views.

These two views of technology can be used to develop the following conclusions regarding technology, task uncertainty, and organization design:

- To the extent that the machine (physical) systems required for a task are simple, reliable, and predictable, task uncertainty will remain low. As the number and frequency of "exceptions" (breakdowns or problems) increase, so does task uncertainty.

- To the extent that the knowledge or skills necessary to accomplish a task are simple, well documented, and unchanging over time, task uncertainty will be low. Tasks that require the application of complex knowledge, the development of new knowledge (i.e., innovation), and the exercise of considerable judgment will be characterized by a high level of task uncertainty.

In other words, if technology is well understood and reliable, it will add little to task uncertainty. However, new, complex, or unpredictable technologies will result in high levels of task uncertainty.

THE WOODWARD STUDIES

Empirical evidence for the validity of these conclusions began to appear in the early 1960s with the publication of Burns and Stalker's *Management of Innovations* (1961) (discussed earlier in the chapter) and subsequently with Joan Woodward's *Industrial Organization: Theory and Practice* (1965).[9]

Woodward, an industrial sociologist and professor at Imperial College in London, decided to find out whether a "one best way" to organize existed. Her question led her to South Essex, England, where she studied

100 manufacturing firms employing at least 100 people each. Woodward's research data showed no clear relationship between a firm's size, type of industry, or profitability and its organizational structure. However, a relationship was found between a firm's organizational structure and its manufacturing technology.

Woodward categorized each firm in her study into one of three broad technological classifications: (1) *small batch or unit production,* which, for example, characterized furniture manufacturing or the design and production of scientific instruments; (2) *large batch and mass production,* which characterized automobile manufacturing; and (3) *continuous process production,* which characterized oil refineries. She discovered that as the technical complexity of a firm increased from batch to continuous process, so did the number of managerial levels and the breadth of the chief executive officer's span of management. In addition, first-level supervisors in unit and small batch production firms had smaller spans of management than did their counterparts in large batch, mass manufacturing industries who had the largest spans of management. Woodward's research also showed that operational procedures increase at the middle-range production level. These firms operated with a far greater number of rules, controls, and specific job definitions, a more rigid chain of authority, less flexible employee-job definitions, and less flexible employee-employer relationships than either small batch or continuous process firms.

These findings are consistent with the amount of task uncertainty present in the different types of organizations. Unit or small batch technology represents the highest level of task uncertainty. The manufacture of one-of-a-kind furniture pieces or custom-designed scientific equipment involves a great deal of skill and often requires the use of innovative techniques and materials. Also, small batch technology typically involves a higher ratio of "start-up" to "run" time in the production process. In essence, as soon as the system has been refined enough to produce the product, it must be modified to produce another unique product. The organic form of organization structure, with few rules and procedures and the relatively high level of communication between supervisor and subordinate which accompanies narrow spans of management, appears to be the appropriate choice for these conditions.

By contrast, large batch or mass production technologies are the ultimate in reducing task uncertainty. Beginning with the work of Taylor during the early years of the twentieth century and continuing on to the modern-day work of industrial engineers, every facet of the production process is examined, defined, designed, and controlled. This standardization of production technology and techniques makes possible long production runs which characterize the assembly lines. Given these conditions, the mechanistic form of organization with its extensive rules and procedures, high levels of specialization, compartmentalization of tasks, and wide spans of management is likely to be more effective. Firms employing continuous process production technology have substantial investment in capital

MANAGEMENT FAILURES

People Express: Airline's Ills Point Out Weaknesses of Unorthodox Management Style

 In its early days, People Express Inc.'s maverick management style inspired admiration and emulation.

Executives, consultants and even academics swarmed to the airline, seeking insight into the methods that were credited with its soaring initial success. At Harvard Business School, students too delved into the company's philosophy, which it realized to an unprecedented degree: minimal bureaucracy, group organization of workers, rotation of staff through a variety of jobs, salaries tied in large part to company profits and "manager" titles for everyone.

The fascination with People Express persists. "They are an extremely good example of a very ambitious effort," says Richard Walton, a professor of business administration at Harvard.

But today the five-year-old airline is in trouble, facing huge losses and the possibility of bankruptcy. The company's board is imposing some of the controls that its managers once eschewed. And outsiders have begun to look at People's experience in a different light. To many observers, the experiment that once demonstrated the potential of an increasingly popular style of management is now betraying its limitations—and the larger lessons are becoming clearer.

"The real issue is whether any given style or approach is appropriate for any organization throughout its lifetime," says William Fonvielle, a vice president of Goodmeasure Inc., a Cambridge, Mass.—based consulting firm.

Participatory Practices. Over the past several years, companies like General Motors Corp. and Cummins Engine Co., as well as many of the newer high-technology companies, have begun experimenting with departures from traditional, top-down management. Innovators have replaced layers of authority with more self- or peer-management; pushed the power to make certain decisions to the lowest possible level; and minimized or dispensed with procedures set by corporate policy in favor of on-the-spot decision making. Such participatory practices, supporters say, can bring increased efficiency, better employee motivation and greater creativity.

In most cases, however, these experiments are sharply circumscribed. For example, Dana Corp., an automotive-parts maker in Toledo, Ohio, gives its divisions broad latitude on such matters as hiring and firing, though within limits specified by the company. At GM's Saginaw Division, workers and managers consult one another on production problems, but only within their own areas of expertise. "We won't take a secretary out of an office to work on a plant-related process," says a GM spokesman.

People Express went much further. There, each operating group of 250 people decided how it would carry out its assigned tasks. Employees moved from job to job, sometimes daily. Often there would be flight attendants tracking lost bags, or pilots taking tickets and tending computer operations.

And everyone had to deal with customers. As Donald C. Burr, the airline's chairman, wrote in a newspaper article last year: "The next time you fly People Express, your coffee may be served by People's chief financial officer, Bob McAdoo, who is a certified flight attendant and flies weekly.''

But the loss of specific talents can far outweigh the benefits of flexibility. ''You can make people jack-of-all-trades and master of none,'' says Harvard's Mr. Walton. ''You lose something from the stability and depth of a person's knowledge.'' A competitor once expressed amazement at finding a People Express pilot facing him in negotiations for airport landing rights—a job usually done by someone with years of operating experience.

Some feel that for rapidly growing People especially the lack of tighter organization had detrimental effects. ''Their unwillingness to put in a formal management structure was a key element to the current difficulties,'' says an aviation-industry analyst who has followed the company closely. (People Express declined to comment for this article.)

Moreover, management specialists say that, while rotating employees through various assignments can make them more well-rounded, it can also reduce their commitment to specific tasks and encourage job hopping. ''It takes their eyes off the ball,'' says Leonard Schlesinger, executive vice president of Au Bon Pain Co., a Boston-based chain of French bakeries.

As an associate professor at Harvard Business School, Mr. Schlesinger designed a case based on People Express's management methods; he later carried some of the techniques with him to Au Bon Pain. But Mr. Schlesinger says he limits the applications. While his company rotates managers, for instance, it does so only over longer time periods. ''The only way I've seen job rotation work is . . . on a very structured basis,'' he says.

Structure is necessary in a company's operations as well if its management is to be left unstructured. ''If you let your people part roam free then your machine part had better be pretty damn good,'' says Nicholas J. Radell, a vice president of Cresap, McCormick & Paget, a management consulting firm based in New York. At People Express, there were no sophisticated computer, telephone-reservation or baggage-handling systems. That lack, observers say, aggravated the problems resulting from loose management control over those areas.

Another way that People differed from most big companies was the way in which it shunned formal lines of authority and standard reporting procedures. Mr. Burr once boasted that no People official was more than three levels away from him or a managing director, so that problems could be dealt with in person.

But as any company grows bigger, such a system can get unwieldy. When employees are more numerous, it becomes increasingly difficult to depend on telephone calls and face-to-face meetings to keep information flowing, and on shared ideals to keep company goals in sight.

'Almost an Anarchy.' ''You go from a pluralistic management to almost an anarchy where you almost don't have anyone in charge,'' says Cresap, McCormick's Mr. Radell.

''Managing a company with 1,200 employees isn't twice as difficult as one with 600,'' adds Jim Manzi, chairman of Lotus Development Corp., the Cambridge, Mass.–based software company. ''There's a multiplier effect.''

(Continued on next page.)

Lotus, which in four years grew from eight employees to 1,300, has just finished forming divisions that it hopes will allow it to retain the freedom of a small company, though in a more organized way. "It's not uncontrolled," Mr. Manzi says, "it's decentralized."

When a loosely managed company is in financial trouble, as in the case of People Express, its problems are often compounded. With a system of shared responsibility for decisions, says Mr. Radell, "when things aren't going well, where do you push the button to make it right? You can't push on 500 or 1,000 people."

Management specialists add that one other area needing rigorous attention, even in an informally managed company, is the setting of standards. Companies "have to maintain a certain level of service and have to maintain it with controls. You have to set standards and see where you deviate from them," says Goodmeasure's Mr. Fonvielle. "If People wanted to remain a small counterculture airline, they could have gotten away with it longer."

Source: Amanda Bennett, "Airline's Ills Point Out Weaknesses of Unorthodox Management Style," Wall Street Journal, 11 August 1986: p. 17. Reprinted by permission of The Wall Street Journal, © Dow Jones & Company, Inc., 1986. All Rights Reserved.

equipment. In this regard, they are similar to mass production firms. However, they differ in that their technology is highly automated, and they invest considerably less funds in personnel. These low-labor-intensive, high-capital-intensive organizations were more successful with an organic structure.

Woodward developed an index composed of such traditional measures as net income and increase in market shares to rate the success of each of the 100 firms in her investigation. As Figure 9–7 indicates, most successful small batch or unit production firms and those employing continuous process production processes possessed an organic structure. By contrast, most successful large batch and mass production companies were organized with a mechanistic structure.

Woodward's findings regarding the relationship between the level of task uncertainty and organization structure have significant implications for modern managers. Instead of searching for a universal "one best way" to organize a firm, management styles must be linked to the organization's production technology.

ORGANIZATION STRUCTURE AND THE ENVIRONMENT

All organizations operate within the context of and in a symbiotic relationship with their environments. The model of the components of an

Technology and Production

Although the term, technology, commonly refers to the nature and characteristics of machines that accomplish some task, it may also be viewed as knowledge technology or "technique." In this text, technology is defined as a combination of these two ideas: it is the science of applying information and knowledge to problem-solving situations and also utilizing knowledge to benefit humanity.

Although the use of technology varies widely between industries, technological change—especially in production and operation functions—has had a tremendous impact on the essential nature of today's businesses.

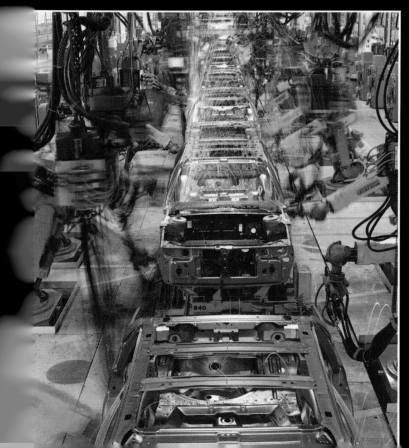

(Above) Engineers at Chrysler Corporation use a computer-aided-design terminal to study four views of vehicle components. Positioned as they would be in the vehicle, they are the inner hood panel (white), dash panel (red), and engine parts with oil pan (light blue).

(Left) Automatic welding system for Chrysler LeBaron GTS and Dodge Lancer car bodies at Sterling Heights (MI) Assembly Plant uses computer-controlled robots for consistent welds of all components in the unitized body structure. In addition to other robots, Sterling Heights Assembly Plant features energy-efficient electric robot welders that require low maintenance and provide a high degree of accuracy.

(Right) Borrowing from aerospace technology, technicians at the Parker Hannifin Corporation use an outdoor industrial refrigeration test device to "debug" a new automated defrost system.

(Below) General Motors Corporation uses an automated guided vehicle system, the motorized robots with forklifts shown, to control delivery of inventory.

(Above) At Owens-Illinois the combined technologies of artificial vision and intelligence provide high-speed inspection of glass containers.

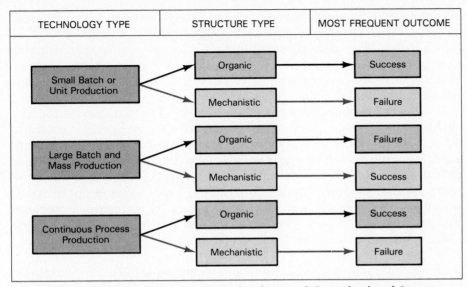

TECHNOLOGY TYPE	STRUCTURE TYPE	MOST FREQUENT OUTCOME

FIGURE 9–7.   Relationship Between Technology and Organizational Structure in Producing Organizational Success
Source: Based on findings reported in Joan Woodward, *Industrial Organization: Theory and Practice* (London: Oxford University Press, 1965).

organization shown earlier in Figure 9–3 included "influence arrows" between the environment and each component: tasks, structure, information, and people. For example, Federal Aviation Administration regulations limiting the length of time a flight crew can spend on a plane during a 24-hour period have a direct impact on how airlines *structure* their work forces (number and type of personnel) and flight schedules. Similarly, the level and quality of education of the general population has a direct impact on the *people* an organization employs. From the standpoint of organization design, however, the most important impact of the environment is on the nature and level of uncertainty inherent in the organization's task structure.

ENVIRONMENTAL UNCERTAINTY AND TASK STRUCTURE

Two of the most useful ways in which an organization's environment can be characterized are by level of complexity and level of stability. A simple environment is one in which the organization has significant relationships with relatively few outside organizations. An organization that has few competitors, operates in only one market, has few suppliers, and is not subject to high levels of governmental regulation can be viewed as operating in a simple environment. The only general store in a small rural community or crossroads is an example of a firm in such an environment.

A complex environment, on the other hand, is characterized by high levels of competition with numerous outside organizations, multiple groups of significantly different customers and suppliers, geographic diversity, and substantial levels of regulation by many different governmental entities. Multinational corporations such as Nestlé, Union Carbide, and Chase Manhattan Bank all operate in a complex environment.

A stable environment is one in which little or no change occurs, and any change that does take place can be predicted with considerable accuracy. Most "mature" industries such as steel production operate in relatively stable environments. A dynamic environment, by contrast, is one in which change is rapid and unpredictable. Such changes may be the result of many factors: ongoing product innovation, rapid changes in demand, market shifts, competitors entering and leaving the industry, or frequent changes in laws and government regulations. The computer industry of the late 1980s typifies organizations operating in a highly dynamic environment.

Combining the two dimensions of complexity and stability produces the four-cell matrix shown in Figure 9–8. Simple, stable environments represent the lowest level of environmental uncertainty. Managers operating in such environments are required to monitor a relatively small number of environmental factors, and none of them changes much over short periods of time. Complex, stable environments require the organization to monitor many areas, but—because change occurs slowly—managers will not be required to adapt rapidly to environmental pressures. This represents an intermediate level of uncertainty.

The third cell in the matrix, composed of simple, dynamic environments, is also characterized by an intermediate level of uncertainty. While environmental variables may be changing rapidly, they are few in number and the organization has to adapt to a relatively small number of such changes. The final cell, consisting of complex, dynamic environments, contains the

FIGURE 9–8.   Environmental Characteristics and Uncertainty

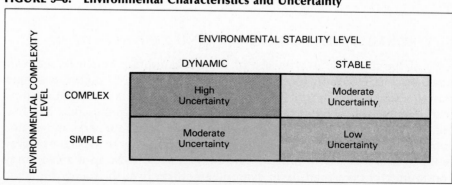

highest level of uncertainty and provides the most challenging set of conditions for an organization. Many aspects of the organization's operations are changing simultaneously; further, the organization must remain sufficiently flexible to adapt to the ongoing changes in the environment.

Based upon these observations, four propositions can be stated regarding environmental uncertainty and organization design:

- Organizations operating in complex, dynamic environments which have to deal with high levels of uncertainty will be most effective when they utilize organic structures that emphasize both differentiation and high levels of horizontal integration.

- Organizations operating in simple, static environments with little uncertainty will be most effective when they utilize mechanistic structures. However, these structures should be kept simple to "mirror" the environment.

- Organizations operating in complex, static environments with moderate levels of uncertainty will be most effective when they employ mechanistic structures that emphasize high levels of differentiation (both specialization of tasks/people and work groups) and formal integration (rules and procedures).

- Organizations operating in simple, dynamic environments with moderate levels of uncertainty will be most effective when they employ organic structures that emphasize informal, horizontal integration and low levels of differentiation.

THE LAWRENCE AND LORSCH STUDY

Empirical support for these propositions comes primarily from the research of Professors Paul Lawrence and Jay Lorsch, who studied three different industry groups: plastics manufacturing, the packaged food industry, and the standardized container industry.[10] The researchers chose these industry groups because they represented environments in which the pace of change (and thus of environmental uncertainty) appeared to be high, intermediate, and low, respectively.

After selecting individual firms in each industry group which they believed to be "high" and "low" performers, the researchers assessed the level and nature of differentiation and integration in each of the firms. As predicted, Lawrence and Lorsch discovered that successful firms in the rapidly changing plastics industry were more highly differentiated than were unsuccessful companies. In addition, successful plastics firms were more differentiated than their counterparts in the food and container industries. Furthermore, the successful plastics firms utilized more horizontal and informal integrative devices such as boundary-spanning roles and task forces than did their less successful competitors.

COMPUTERS IN MANAGEMENT

The World's Most Computerized Organization

 As the pace of modern business has quickened, so has the pace of business communication. More interoffice memos, letters, and reports are written today than ever before. To cope with the mountains of paper before them, an increasing number of business executives are communicating electronically; they are replacing the typewriter—long the mainstay of all business offices—with the computer. No company has done this in a bigger way than Apple Computer, whose president issued the following memo in 1980:

Effective immediately! NO MORE TYPEWRITERS ARE TO BE PURCHASED, LEASED, etc., etc. Apple is an innovative company. We must believe and lead in all areas. If word processing is so neat, then let's all use it! Goal: by 1-1-81, NO typewriters at Apple. . . . We believe the typewriter is obsolete. Let's prove it inside before we try and convince our customers.

Today, there are almost no typewriters left in the firm's headquarters. Instead of typewriters, the several hundred employees involved in composing or disseminating letters, memos, documents, or reports use a typewriter-sized Apple III with built-in keyboard, a pair of add-on disk drives, a video monitor, and Apple Writer, the company's own disk-stored word processing software. Word processing has gained a foothold in many businesses, but never before has a firm so completely done away with typewriters by executive fiat.

Five months after the decision was made to do away with typewriters at Apple Computer, the term "secretary" was abolished and replaced by "area associate" to reflect the more varied responsibilities made possible by personal computers. "We felt we needed a different term," Ann Bowers, vice-president of human resources, explains, "because 'secretary' was so loaded with connotations of typist, errand-runner, and phone answerer. We wanted to expand the area associates' functions so they could use their brains, in addition to their clerical skills."

Source: Reprinted by permission from Steve Ditlea. "An Apple on Every Desk," *Inc.,* October 1981, p. 50. Copyright © 1981 by Steve Ditlea; all rights reserved.

Firms in the packaged food industry showed similar results, with high performers more differentiated than less successful firms and with somewhat higher integration. A slightly different pattern emerged in the stable environment of the container industry. Although high and lower performers had the same level of differentiation, the successful firms in this industry had substantially higher integration levels than did the low performers. These findings suggest that some minimum level of differentiation is necessary even in stable environments. However, increased levels of performance can be obtained only through greater integration (coor-

TABLE 9–1   ORGANIZATION DESIGN STRATEGIES FOR DIFFERENT ENVIRONMENTS

Environment	Industry	Successful Organization Design
Highly Certain and Predictable	Container Industry	Mechanistic Structure
Moderately Certain and Predictable	Food Industry	Movement toward Organic Structure; Integrators or Team of Integrators
Highly Uncertain and Unpredictable	Plastics Industry	Organic Structure; Formal Departments of Integrators

Source: Martin J. Gannon, *Management: An Organizational Perspective* (Boston: Little, Brown, 1977), p. 98. Copyright © 1977 by Little, Brown and Company, Inc. Based on Paul Lawrence and Jay Lorsch, *Organization and Environment* (Boston: Division of Research, Harvard Business School, 1967). Republished as a Harvard Business School Classic (Boston: Harvard Business School Press, 1986). Reprinted by permission of Little, Brown.

dination) of activities. This is accomplished by emphasizing mechanistic structures and vertical integration. Table 9–1 summarizes the findings of the Lawrence and Lorsch study.

ORGANIZATION STRUCTURE AND PEOPLE: JOB DESIGN

The previous sections have examined the influence of task and environmental uncertainty on the choice of an appropriate organization structure. The general conclusion is that as uncertainty increases, organizations should utilize more organic structures and less mechanistic ones. But, ultimately, organizations are made up of *people,* the fourth component of the organization. Some of these people enjoy knowing exactly what is expected of them and others prefer to choose their own tasks; some are invigorated by change and uncertainty and others are frustrated by it; some actually enjoy conflict and others actively try to avoid it. As the chapter introduction noted, the purpose of organization design is to assure congruence or fit: a fit between structure and the characteristics of the environment; a fit between structure and the characteristics of the task; and a fit between an organization's structure and the characteristics of its members.

Job design refers to the process of task delineation necessary to meet various personal, work, organizational, and environmental parameters. As Professors Richard Hackman and Greg Oldham point out, each job has five core characteristics.[11] The first, *skill variety,* is the degree to which a job requires the individual to utilize a number of different skills and abilities and engage in a variety of different activities. The second, *task identity,* is the extent to which a job calls for a worker to accomplish a

> **Job design** is the process of task delineation necessary to meet various personal, work, organizational, and environmental parameters.

"whole" or identifiable piece of work, to perform a job in its entirety with a perceivable and concrete outcome. *Task significance* is the third core job characteristic. It refers to the extent to which job accomplishment has a significant impact on other members of the organization or upon the organization's environment. The fourth factor, *autonomy,* is the extent to which the job provides independence or freedom to the worker; the ability to determine the methods to be used and to schedule work as he or she sees fit. *Feedback,* the final job characteristic, is the extent to which the individual, in performing the activities necessary for task accomplishment, receives direct information about the effectiveness of his or her work.

Figure 9–9 shows the relationship between these core job characteristics and improved worker performance and satisfaction. Enrichment of each of the core job characteristics should result in the satisfaction of three critical psychological states indicated in the center column of the figure: meaningfulness, responsibility, and knowledge of results. Workers with what Hackman and Oldham call *high growth need strength* should respond to such enrichments with high intrinsic work motivation, high quality work performance, high work satisfaction, and low absenteeism and turnover. Growth needs are defined as the extent to which an individual values opportunities to learn and grow, to be creative, and to utilize the full range of his or her talents in the work setting.

The subject of job design is a critical topic for managers in every organization. It is discussed in more detail in the next two chapters and in Chapter 18. The concepts of job enrichment, job enlargement, job rotation, work simplification, and sociotechnical factors are examined thoroughly in these chapters.

FIGURE 9–9.   Hackman-Oldham Model of Job Design
Source: J. Richard Hackman and Greg R. Oldham, "Motivation Through the Design of Work: Test of a Theory," *Organizational Behavior and Human Performance* 16 (1976): 250–279. Used with permission of Academic Press, Inc.

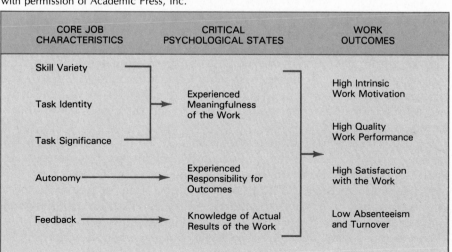

ESTABLISHING WORK SCHEDULES

After jobs have been designed, work schedules must be established for individual workers, entire departments, and the overall organization. The typical norm in the United States, now built into our legal structure by the Fair Labor Standards Act of 1938, is the 40-hour work week. This norm is translated into a 9:00 A.M. to 5:00 P.M., Monday through Friday arrangement for millions of clerical and administrative workers. Manufacturing and construction industries may vary the regular hours of work with an earlier starting time, and continuous process production companies typically employ three or more shifts of workers to cover 24 hours of working time seven days a week.

In recent years, a growing number of organizations have been faced with the need to adapt to new trends in employee needs. The work force at Transamerica-Occidental Life Insurance Company begins work at varying times between 6:00 A.M. and 9:00 A.M. Meanwhile, personnel at United Services Automobile Association, a San Antonio insurance firm, work a Monday through Thursday week. And in Des Moines, two women share a third-grade teaching position. These situations reflect three trends in work scheduling: flexitime, compressed work weeks, and job sharing.

Flexitime. *Flexitime* is a work scheduling system that allows employees to set their own work hours within constraints specified by the organization. The concept developed from the efforts of a Munich company to reduce traffic congestion on an access road during the late 1960s. Twelve percent of the U.S. nonfarm labor force is currently on a flexitime schedule.

> Flexitime is a work scheduling system permitting employees to set their own working hours within constraints specified by the organization.

The typical flexitime format is to allow workers to start work within a specified time period in the morning, such as between 7:00 and 9:00 A.M. All employees must be on the job during a set period of the day when meetings and the bulk of other interpersonal activities are performed. This period, perhaps from 9:00 to 3:00, is called *core time.* Once core time is over, employees are free to leave in accordance with the length of the workday and the morning starting time.

Advantages of flexitime systems include employee convenience, improved morale, reduced absenteeism and tardiness, cost savings, improved productivity, and more efficient use of transportation modes. Disadvantages include its limited applicability in such jobs as assembly line operations and continuous production facilities, higher energy usage, problems resulting when key people are not available at crucial times, and the opportunity for some people to "short-change" the system.[12]

Compressed Work Weeks. A *compressed work week* is one in which workers spend fewer days on the job but work approximately the same number of hours. The best-known format is the "four day/forty-hour week." Advantages of the compressed work week include more time for personal pursuits, energy savings, improved employee morale, better productivity, and

> Compressed work week is a work scheduling system in which employees spend fewer than five days a week on the job, but work approximately the same number of hours as under the traditional 40-hour, five-day week system.

reduced absenteeism. Disadvantages include increased moonlighting, physical exhaustion, and lethargy during long workdays.

At Olin Ski Company, Lee Heinrich and his 95 fellow workers point out another advantage: household chores can be done on Friday, leaving the weekend for leisure. At Ball Corporation's five U.S. metal container manufacturing plants, its 1,600 employees operate on a "4–3" schedule in which they work four 12 hour days followed by three days off, then three days on followed by four days off. Though most workers have grown accustomed to the 8-hour day, about 4.1% of the U.S. labor force performed full-time jobs in four days or less in 1985.[13]

Job sharing is a work scheduling system in which a single job assignment is divided among two or more persons.

Job Sharing. *Job sharing* refers to the division of one job assignment among two or more persons. Although the concept is still relatively limited in most industrial settings, it has become a noticeable trend in such areas as teaching. Proponents of job sharing point out that it allows employers to secure the best efforts of two people, rather than a single worker. Increased productivity is the result in such cases. Critics, on the other hand, point out that job sharing is limited to areas where job assignments can be easily divided and where limited training is required. They also argue that job sharing basically involves the regular use of part-time personnel. The most frequent use of the concept has been in clerical functions and retailing.

ORGANIZATION STRUCTURE, AUTHORITY, AND CONTROL

In the previous chapter, delegation of authority was described as the process of assigning authority and responsibility to subordinates. Delegation is an individual process, a way of sharing power between a superior and a subordinate. But the collective effect of all these individual practices can have a dramatic overall organizational impact. If managers in a firm tend to delegate considerable authority and responsibility, more decisions are shifted to lower levels in the organization. Supervisory and middle managers in such firms possess considerable influence in making major decisions. In these cases where managers disperse considerable amounts of authority to subordinates, the organization is considered to follow a managerial philosophy of *decentralization*.

Decentralization is an organizational philosophy in which managers disperse considerable authority to subordinates.

On the other hand, some managers choose to retain most of the authority, depending upon subordinates to implement assignments. Such managers feel that they can maintain maximum control and coordination by retaining most of the authority. This practice of dispersing little authority is referred to as *centralization*. These characteristics mean that centralized organizations typically have more narrow spans of control and are taller than decentralized organizations.

Centralization is an organizational philosophy in which managers retain considerable authority, relying on subordinates to implement assignments.

Decentralization tends to encourage innovation and experimentation. General Motors Corporation grants considerable authority to each of its divisions in the belief that independent approaches may result in ideas that can then be shared by other divisions. Decentralization of GM in 1921 by Alfred P. Sloan is considered the first large-scale use of this approach.

Firms utilizing decentralization provide middle and supervisory level managers with more decision-making experience than their counterparts in companies with a centralized management philosophy. This experience means that a talent pool is being created for later promotions. Of course, these fledgling managers often make mistakes, a price centralized companies are less likely to pay.

As in many decisions, the centralization-decentralization issue depends upon the interplay of numerous factors in each company. Organizations operating in uncertain environments with ill-defined task structures are likely to be more effective if they use an organic organization structure and decentralize decision making as much as is feasible. On the other hand, those organizations operating in predictable environments with well-defined task structures are likely to be more effective with a mechanistic structure and more centralized decision making.

THE MATRIX ORGANIZATION ▬▬▬▬▬▬▬

A relatively recent development in adjusting organizational structures to changing requirements is the *matrix approach*. This approach, which developed in the 1960s in the aerospace industry, attempts to integrate the activities of several specialists from different departments in the organization. Matrix organizations have been established in such diverse organizations as Dow Chemical, General Electric, Citibank, Shell Oil, and Texas Instruments.[14] This novel approach to organizing seeks to take advantage of *both* functional and product departmentalization as well as increasing flexibility.

Matrix approach is an organization arrangement in which specialists from different areas of the organization are brought together to work on specific projects; typically used simultaneously with a line and staff organization structure.

The identifying feature of a matrix organization is that some members report to two superiors instead of to the traditional single boss. Organizations tend to utilize matrix forms in the following instances:

- When it is essential that they be highly responsive to two sectors simultaneously, such as markets and technology;

- When they face uncertainties that generate very high information processing requirements; and

- When they must deal with strong constraints of financial and/or human resources.[15]

The matrix organization is built around specific projects or problems. Once these projects or problems are identified, a team is selected based upon the specific needs of the project and the individual abilities of the members. A team may consist of representatives from research and development, finance, marketing, design, and electronic data processing. The head of the matrix organization is granted the necessary authority to complete the project. While the members of the team report to two bosses—the head of the department from which they were recruited and the major member of the team—the project manager typically is granted the authority to make salary increase recommendations, promotions, and other personnel actions during the length of time the individuals are assigned to the matrix team. Once the project is completed, the team members return to their original departments or are assigned to other matrix teams. Figure 9–10 shows a typical matrix organization.

Although the flexibility of the matrix organization and the ability to focus strongly on specific major problems or unique technical issues have led to its increasing use by a large number of major organizations, it is not without limitations. Team members must be comfortable working for more than one boss. Cooperation may be a problem as the matrix team manager attempts to coordinate a diverse group of individuals from numerous parts of the organization. Its strengths are considerable, however, as is evidenced by its emergence as a critical organizational format for many companies.

FIGURE 9–10.   Matrix Organization
Source: Richard M. Hodgetts, *Management: Theory, Process and Practice*, 4th ed. Copyright © 1986 by Academic Press, Inc.

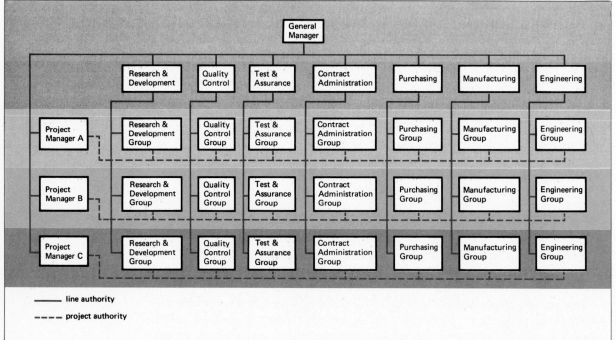

DEALING WITH CONFLICT IN ORGANIZATIONS ▰

Organizational *conflict* is inevitable because of the regular and continuing human interactions that must occur. It can be defined as all types of opposition or antagonistic interaction. It is based on scarcity of power, resources or social position, and differing value structures.[16] Conflict occurs between managers and subordinates, between labor and management, between work groups, and between the organization and its external environment. Many of the traditional management writers, both classicists and neoclassicists, treated the existence of conflict as an indication of a problem, a disturbance that interfered with the smooth operation of the organization.

Current management writers and practicing managers are careful not to assume that all conflict is bad. Instead, conflict is viewed as a phenomenon that arises in every organization to a certain extent, and, in some organizations, it is a positive indicator of highly motivated, highly committed organization members. Conflict can be a highly constructive force, particularly in highly differentiated organizations which utilize a considerable amount of horizontal integration. The challenge to modern management is not to avoid conflict or suppress it; instead, managers must find ways to channel the energy that conflict represents into activities with positive payoffs for the organization and to keep it within acceptable limits. Conflicts need to be resolved constructively, not hidden from view.

> **Conflict** is opposition or antagonistic interaction resulting from scarcity of power, resources, or social position, and different value structures on the part of individuals or groups.

TYPES OF CONFLICT

The first step in learning to deal with organizational conflict is the recognition that all conflicts are not alike. They spring from different sources and must be resolved in different ways. The major categories of organizational conflict—intrapersonal conflict, interpersonal conflict, persongroup conflict, and intergroup conflict—are depicted in Figure 9–11.

Intrapersonal Conflict. *Intrapersonal conflict* occurs within the individual and comes primarily from two sources: role conflict and job stress. *Role conflict* can be defined as follows:

> **Intrapersonal conflict** is conflict occurring within a single member of the organization as a result of role conflict and/or job stress.

> The simultaneous occurrence of two (or more) role sendings such that compliance with one would make more difficult compliance with the other. . . . For example, a person's superior may make it clear to him that he is expected to hold his subordinates strictly to company rules. At the same time, his subordinates may indicate in various ways that they would like loose, relaxed supervision, and that they will make things difficult if they are pushed too hard. . . . Such cases are so common that a whole literature has been created on the problem of the first-line supervisor as the "man in the middle."[17]

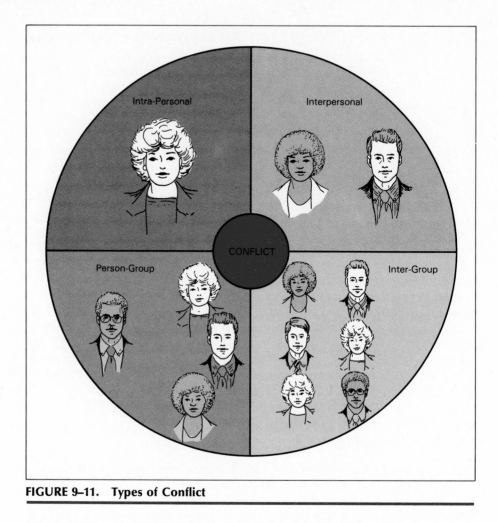

FIGURE 9–11.   Types of Conflict

In addition, role conflict may occur as the result of different roles an individual has to play. For example, the role of parent and the role of employee may come into conflict when the employee's child becomes sick. The widespread presence of two wage-earner households and societal changes affecting values with respect to work have resulted in individuals being called upon to play a greater number of diverse roles. The result is increased frequency of this type of role conflict.

The second primary source of intrapersonal conflict in modern organizations is *job stress*. As the pace of change quickens in organizations and throughout society, workers may come to feel lost, unsure of what is expected of them, and unsure of their abilities to cope with what they perceive as ever-mounting pressure. While some stress may even be a positive factor in motivating individuals and in fueling innovation, chronic overstress leads to short-tempered, uncooperative, defensive employees who may even indulge in such self-destructive activities as alcoholism and drug abuse. As Figure 9–12 illustrates, the cost of such responses to stress may be the individual's family.

Job stress also results when the individual, on an ongoing basis, is unable to meet his or her own expectations, either in terms of performance (for example, the social worker who wishes to help people but feels unable to do so because of the nature of the "system") or in terms of the nature of the work (for example, the assembly line worker who is bored by the repetitive nature of the job and feels that his skills and abilities are not being utilized).

Intrapersonal conflict is a subject of increasing concern to organizations due to its damaging impact on job performance, absenteeism, and turnover. Employee counseling centers, company-sponsored stress management seminars, and management by objectives programs are just some of the methods currently being used to combat this problem.

> 66 It's no credit to anyone to work too hard. 99
>
> Ed Howe

FIGURE 9–12. Alcohol Abuse: Possible Response to Excessive Job Stress
Source: Reprinted courtesy of Reynolds-Sullivan Advertising, Inc.

Interpersonal conflict is conflict occurring between two or more organizational members as a result of such factors as differences in managerial philosophies, values, and problem-solving styles or competition for power or promotion.

Interpersonal Conflict. *Interpersonal conflict* occurs between two or more individuals within the organization. Traditionally, this type of conflict was attributed to "personality differences." However, it can result from several factors:

- *Differences in Values.* For example, one manager might place a great emphasis on task accomplishment to the exclusion of all else, while another might stress the need to maintain good employee relations even if performance of the immediate task is slightly affected.

- *Differences in Problem-Solving Styles.* One person may prefer to work in groups, for example, while another prefers to work alone.

- *Differences in Managerial Philosophies.* One manager may favor decentralization of decision making while another favors centralization.

In addition, interpersonal conflict can occur due to competition between individuals, for power, for promotion, or for other organizational rewards.

Because interpersonal conflict interferes with effective communication, and thus problem solving, it is a cause of considerable concern for modern organizations. Organization development and communications training are frequently used methods of modifying interpersonal conflicts and channeling them into more constructive paths. They are discussed in more detail in Chapter 11.

Person-Group Conflict. The third type of conflict occurs when an individual chooses to challenge the norms or rules of behavior that govern group membership. The classic example of this phenomenon is the "rate breaker" who consistently performs at a level well above that of other group members. Such performance may be seen as a threat by the group due to fear that higher performance standards will be established based on the performance of the rate breaker. A more recent example is the treatment sometimes afforded the "whistle blower," the individual who brings to the attention of management or the general public instances of waste, fraud, or corruption. Such individuals may be ostracized and subjected to harassment by other members of the group.

People-group conflict is conflict resulting from individual opposition to group norms or rules of behavior.

On the other hand, *person-group conflict* can sometimes play a positive role within organizations. When an individual places his or her own needs for recognition or power ahead of the needs of the group to accomplish its task, group pressure can exert a powerful influence to bring the individual back into line with overall group norms.

Intergroup Conflict. The final type of conflict occurs between departments or work groups and typically revolves around issues of authority, jurisdiction, control of work flow, or access to scarce organizational resources. It arises directly from the need for differentiation in an organization. As Hampton, Summer, and Webber point out:

To deal with complexity, we resort to specialization and specialists—people with diverse cognitive and emotional orientations—in the various functional areas. Such people frequently experience difficulty in communicating and cooperating. Yet, for an organization to act as a unity, there must be integration or collaboration among the various departments. Thus, management frequently faces a problem: Long-run performance requires substantial integration, but efforts to general collaboration often produce short-run conflict.[18]

Intergroup conflicts arise from two sources: systems conflicts and bargaining conflicts. *Systems conflicts* come about because of the divergence in objectives between work groups. For example, the marketing department may feel that rapid order processing is more important than quality control since replacing a defective unit is likely to produce less customer dissatisfaction than waiting on an unfilled order. The production department, on the other hand, may feel that its reputation depends on the continued high quality of its products and this belief may be supported by the incentive system used to govern rewards for production department personnel. Strategies for resolving systems conflicts include rotation of department members among work units to improve understanding and empathy with the problems of other departments, changes in formal incentive systems to reflect overall organizational objectives related to the issue, and the use of horizontal integrative mechanisms such as task forces.

Bargaining conflicts occur when groups compete for scarce organizational resources or for power and influence within the system. An excellent recent example of such conflicts involved government attempts to reduce budget deficits by reducing expenditures. Interest groups, both inside and outside the government, have attempted to influence this process to ensure that their programs are not cut.

> Intergroup conflict is conflict occurring between departments or work groups as a result of such issues as authority, jurisdiction, control of work flow, and/or access to scarce resources.

> 66 The valuable person in any business is the individual who can and will cooperate with others. 99
>
> Elbert Hubbard

METHODS OF DEALING WITH CONFLICT

Because conflict is such a pervasive aspect of life in modern organizations, considerable research efforts have been devoted to understanding exactly how individuals and groups seek to deal with it. The four basic methods of handling conflict are avoidance, smoothing, forcing, and confronting.

Avoidance. Conflict is, for most people, a stress-inducing situation. It is something with which they would rather not deal. Consequently, *conflict avoidance* is typically the first method people use in dealing with conflict. They simply pretend that the conflict does not exist, or withdraw from situations in which the potential for conflict is high. For example, a member of a problem-solving group disagrees with the group but, rather than appearing to be obstructive, says little or nothing. While avoidance does suppress the most visible symptoms of conflict, it does nothing to resolve the underlying issues.

> Conflict avoidance is a simplistic, ineffective method of dealing with conflict in which the individual ignores it, withdraws from it, or pretends it does not exist.

MANAGEMENT FAILURES

The Workaholic Boss

The biggest problem with trying to manage stress in organizations is that we try to do just that, manage it, instead of getting rid of the people who are causing all the stress in the first place. It really is pointless to recommend relaxation response periods, deep breathing exercises and other "stress-reduction" techniques when the carriers of the malady are breathing fire just around the corner.

I'm talking about the so-called workaholic manager—a contradiction in terms, because if you're a workaholic, you can't be a manager. A workaholic placed in a management position, and that's usually where he ends up, is one of the most divisive forces roaming the corridors of the industrialized world.

Just think about the contradictions involved. Where a manager must set priorities, the workaholic must do everything. (This also occurs on a temporary basis for start-up entrepreneurs. Within a short time, they usually learn to do only what is important.)

A manager must be patient in gaining the commitment of others, in order to multiply his efforts. The workaholic has little or no pa-

tience with others and works unending hours to make up for their perceived lack of commitment. This creates the self-fulfilling prophecy of only being able to rely on his own work.

Where a manager negotiates objectives and time frames for accomplishment, the workaholic sets arbitrary deadlines and then applies follow-up pressure to assure compliance. He often is rewarded with malevolent obedience, usually with shoddy results.

I wish the following example were not true. While attending a three-day management meeting at a resort hotel, a junior staff member approached his boss during an after-dinner cocktail party. His objective was to ride back on the plane with the boss on the following day and discuss his next six-months' support plans. Repeated previous attempts to get a meeting date had failed. The ever cheerful high-energy boss said that he already had an in-flight meeting scheduled but, "No problem, let's step into the next room and go over the plans right now." And so at 12:45 A.M., the subordinate did his best to make an orderly presentation of the plans and objectives of his department for the next six months.

Smoothing is an ineffective method of dealing with conflict in which the individual delays decisions and appeals to reason as methods of suppressing overt signs of conflict.

Smoothing. This method of dealing with conflict is closely related to avoidance. The purpose of such *smoothing* tactics as delaying decisions and appeals to "reason" is to suppress the outward signs of conflict. The costs associated with these tactics are that most conflicts do not simply disappear and often become worse with the passage of time.

Forcing is the application of power to resolve conflicts.

Forcing. *Forcing* behaviors rely on the application of power to resolve conflicts. When a judge in a civil suit decides a case and establishes the appropriate penalties for those at fault, he or she is using the legitimate and coercive powers of the judiciary to settle the conflict. Similarly, when

Any manager who behaves like that is an "18-hour-a-day-menace," who carries stress wherever he goes.

He arrives early and leaves late. He sends a message that this is the standard of behavior expected. Since most people can't follow his leadership, he breeds resentment and antagonism.

The lunch at the desk and scheduling of every working hour further cuts off conversation, commitment and contributions of others.

There is no doubt, of course, that companies need dedicated employees who put in long hours and love attention to detail. It just has to be remembered that this is not necessarily the type of person you want in charge of gaining the quality commitment of others. The biggest, strongest worker has not historically made the best foreman, even though that was often the promotion policy.

How about finding some nice staff projects for your workaholics, so they can immerse themselves in the incredible detail they love?

Direct their high energy levels to tasks, not the management of people.

Just stop and think about all the workaholic "war stories" you have heard. Think about the running through airports, about the two meetings going on at once, about the lines waiting outside of "executive" offices trying to get on the schedule, about the blizzard of phone messages generated around these so-called managers. Many organizations and people are resilient enough to succeed in spite of this type of direction. But survival should not be the standard of performance.

So do what you can to reduce the stress level in your organization to reasonable operational levels. Do it by keeping the workaholic out of the management function. Control and concentrate energy into the most compact and narrow areas possible in order to do the most important things best and to reward the best people with the business leadership they deserve. Come and go at reasonable hours. Families all throughout your organization will be forever grateful. Don't confuse high energy level with the brainpower necessary to produce results.

If you are a manager think about your effect on others. They are the ones who must produce the results that you are judged on. Are you a workaholic in a management position? Are you reading this at 5:30 A.M. or midnight? Have two or three people sent you this article? Have 10 people sent it to you?

Source: Jack Falvey, "The Workaholic Boss: An 18-Hour-a-Day Menace," *Wall Street Journal*, 10 May 1982. Reprinted by permission.

a manager listens to a dispute between subordinates and then decides what course of action will be pursued, the conflict has been settled based on the application of the manager's authority. The term *settled* rather than *resolved* is used in the above examples because even though the conflict no longer exists, the underlying conditions that gave rise to the conflict have not been altered.

In both of the examples cited above, a third party power source was used to settle the conflict. However, conflicts can also be settled by forcing tactics when one party to the conflict gains more power than the other party or parties. This might be the case in conflicts between a superior and a subordinate or between two competing work units when one of them clearly has more influence in the organization than the other.

Forcing behaviors may be humankind's oldest method of dealing with conflict (war is a forcing behavior), and they are undeniably effective in dealing with immediate issues. But forcing behaviors, by their very nature, result in winners and losers and make little or no contribution to future collaboration or cooperation. Consequently, the use of force as a means of settling organizational conflicts should be reserved for instances in which the conflicting parties are not highly interdependent or when the emotional investment in the conflict resolution is not high. These conditions probably hold true in many instances for mechanistic organizations, but rarely for organic ones. In addition, organizations that rely upon forcing as a primary form of conflict resolution may be creating a backlog of ill will that could adversely affect future needs for cooperation among organization members and groups.

Confronting is a method of dealing with conflict in which parties in the conflict are required to meet, discuss the conflict, and seek solutions acceptable to everyone.

Confronting. *Confronting* is the final method of dealing with organizational conflict. Rather than attempting to sweep the issues under the carpet through avoidance or smoothing or solving them quickly through the application of power, confronting requires that the parties in the conflict focus on the issues, preferably in a face-to-face meeting. By exploring all facets of the situation, including the emotional aspects, the aim is to arrive at a truly integrative solution that will benefit everyone involved. The confronting method seeks to transform the competing/conflicting parties into a unified problem-solving group that can devise solutions that go beyond short-term interests.

Due to the difficulty of removing the defensive and protective postures of the conflicting parties, confronting frequently involves the use of a consultant or other third-party individual to serve as a peacemaker.[19] Such individuals can facilitate conflict resolution by helping the members of the newly formed problem-solving group to focus on their areas of agreement rather than disagreement, by showing them methods of effectively structuring their problem-solving activities, and by calling to the attention of the group members instances of nonproductive or defensive behavior.

The major drawback of using this method of dealing with conflict is that it requires both considerable interpersonal skills and a commitment of significant amounts of time and energy. The use of confrontation, therefore, is likely to be reserved for instances involving substantial issues and situations when the individuals or groups are highly interdependent.

SUMMARY

The organization design process must consider all components of an organization—people, structure, tasks, information, and environment—and ensure the presence of congruence, or "fit," among these factors. The resulting design is a specific blending of these elements that makes each organization unique.

Three distinct periods in organizational design include (1) the classical period, with its emphasis on formal organizational structure and the use of authority; (2) the neoclassical period, with its particular concern for management-employee relations; and (3) the modern era that advocates a contingency approach in which numerous variables, both inside and outside the organization, determine the most appropriate structure for a specific organization. These variables consist of organization tasks, people, structure, information, and the environment.

Two radically different forms of organizations, each of which may prove more effective under certain environmental conditions, are mechanistic structures and organic structures. The former type of organization structure is frequently used in stable, relatively simple environments and is characterized by low uncertainty, high task specialization, increased reliance on formal authority structures, directives and rules, and a high degree of centralization. By contrast, the organic structure is more appropriate for complex, dynamic environments and is characterized by high uncertainty, low specialization, low levels of formalization, authority based on knowledge instead of formal authority positions, and decentralization.

The primary determinants of task uncertainty are organizational objectives and technology. In addition, organizations operating in stable, relatively simple environments experience less task uncertainty than their counterparts in more complex, dynamic environments.

Tasks are activities performed by the organization in accomplishing its objectives. They serve as a basis for job design, the process of task delineation necessary to meet personal, work, organizational, and environmental parameters. Each job can be analyzed on the basis of its core characteristics: skill variety, task identity, task significance, autonomy, and feedback. In recent years, organizations have experimented with such innovative work scheduling alternatives as flexitime, compressed work weeks, and job sharing in seeking arrangements for task performance satisfying to both the organization and to the individual worker.

Organizations in which extensive delegation is commonplace are considered to be decentralized. If little authority is assigned to subordinates, the organization is termed centralized. A relatively new organizational grouping, the matrix structure, sets up teams of specialists from various functional areas to deal with specific organizational projects or problems. Members of these teams report to both their functional superiors and to their project managers.

Organizational conflict is a fact of life in modern organizations due to the regular and continuing human interactions that occur. Conflict is not necessarily a negative force, and it may not require suppression by managers. The task of the manager is to determine methods for channeling the energy represented by conflict into activities with positive payoffs for the organization. The major categories of organizational conflict include intrapersonal conflict, interpersonal conflict, person-group conflict, and intergroup conflict. The four basic methods of handling conflict are avoidance, smoothing, forcing, and confronting.

SOLVING THE STOP ACTION CASE

Hardee's Racing Team

The objectives of the Hardee's "over the wall" pit crew were clear: perform the needed service and repairs in the smallest possible amount of time. On a racing track such as Talladega, the Hardee's Racing Team driver is covering ground at an average of a football field per second. The amount of time spent in the pit is crucial to the time left on the track and the position of the driver when he or she returns to the track. A too-slow performance by the pit crew may cost the driver the race. Poorly performed pit stop operations have occasionally resulted in improperly changed tires that collapse and additional unplanned stops to correct failures to completely refill gas tanks or make needed adjustments.

During a pit stop, the car is jacked up, two tires are changed (on one side of the car), the windshield is cleaned, the car is fueled (two eleven-gallon tanks) at the speed gravity allows gas to flow into the tanks, and four possible chassis adjustments are made to shift weight distribution on the tires. As the photograph shows, the actions of the pit crew resemble a ballet with each member performing a series of choreographed movements and duties.

The pit crew structure is heavily controlled by environmental factors. NASCAR regulations allow a maximum six-person crew over the wall during a pit stop. Their jobs are as follows: tire carrier, front-tire changer, rear-tire changer, gas man, gas overflow man, and jack man.

The organization of the over-the-wall crew utilizes an organic structure and places major emphasis on cooperative, coordinated efforts by each member. Time standards are well-established. An 18-second pit stop is excellent, but successful pit stops have been completed in as little as 14 seconds. On the other hand, 20 to 22 seconds is a relatively common length for pit stops.

In selecting a pit crew member, consideration is given to the experience of the person. Experience in working with one another is especially important, and all racing teams seek to maintain their personnel. The Hardee's crew has been together since 1982 and over this period they have perfected their movements to meet time specifications. No particular advantage results from the ability of one tire changer to perform his task in 15 seconds if the other tire changer requires 25 seconds.

Most teams, like Hardee's, have full-time crew members, paid by salary, who handle various duties with the car during the week. Crew chiefs in charge of the team earn between $50,000 and $100,000 annually. Mechanics, engine specialists, and fabricators earn an average of $35,000, and other employees, including the over-the-wall crew, earn between $20,000 and $30,000. Just as in other industries, salary is based upon ability and experience. The number of years a crew member has been in the sport contributes to his or her potential, as does the success of teams on which he or she has worked. Because all teams work in a common area at race tracks called the Garage, potential employers are given the opportunity to observe the work of job candidates. Crew members, like any other type of employee, are hired based upon recommendations of current members of the crew and/or through submission of resumes.

Source: Photo courtesy of Jack R. Arute of Hardee's Motorsports. Pit crew information supplied by Jack R. Arute and Chip Williams, Director of Public Relations, NASCAR.

FACT OR FICTION REVEALED

1. Fact   2. Fiction   3. Fiction   4. Fiction   5. Fact   6. Fiction   7. Fact

MANAGEMENT TERMS

organization structure
organization design
mechanistic structure
organic structure
task
job design
flexitime

compressed work week
job sharing
decentralization
centralization
matrix structure
conflict
intrapersonal conflict

interpersonal conflict
person-group conflict
intergroup conflict
conflict avoidance
smoothing
forcing
confronting

REVIEW QUESTIONS

1. How is the concept of organizational design different from that of organization structure?

2. Explain the evolution of organizational design through the three historical periods described in the chapter.

3. Explain each of the components of an organization. Which of these components are likely to be affected by the environment in which the organization exists?

4. What are the major factors that determine whether an organic structure or a mechanistic structure is more appropriate for an organization?

5. Identify the most appropriate organizational structure for each of the following technologies:
   a. small batch or unit production companies
   b. large batch or mass production companies

c. continuous process production companies

6. Identify each of the core job characteristics that impact job design.

7. What are the primary organizational benefits of such innovative work scheduling practices as flexitime, compressed work weeks, and job sharing? What problems may arise from their use?

8. Discuss the centralization-decentralization issue in organizations.

9. Describe the matrix approach to organizing. What conditions are conducive to the use of the matrix structure?

10. Explain each of the major categories of organizational conflict. Evaluate the primary methods of dealing with conflict.

PROBLEMS AND EXPERIENTIAL EXERCISES

1. Identify three firms operating in your city or region in each of the following technological classifications: small batch or unit production; large batch or mass production; and continuous process production. Then develop an argument for the most appropriate organizational structure for each firm, basing your answer on the findings reported in the chapter.

2. Explain the five core characteristics of a job you currently hold or one you previously held. Then describe how these characteristics could be varied to produce satisfaction of the three critical psychological states identified in Figure 9–9.

3. Identify three or four local industries in which flexitime work schedules could be used. In what

types of local firms would compressed work weeks be effective? How could managers seeking to implement these work-scheduling innovations minimize their potential disadvantages?

4. "The matrix organization violates the unity of command principle." Do you agree? If so, how would a matrix organization minimize the problems that might result from such a violation of a classical organizational principle?

5. Develop four scenarios to illustrate each type of organization conflict discussed in the chapter. Present a suggested method for resolving each type of conflict and explain why other methods of conflict resolution were not selected.

MANAGERIAL INCIDENT: The Female Boss

Women have begun to reshape the small-business landscape.

They own a record three million enterprises. They are entering business at a rate

five times faster than men and now account for one in every four sole proprietors.

Perhaps of equal significance, more female owners are breaking new ground as bosses. Many offer flexible work schedules, liberal sick leave, part-time hours, sabbaticals, child-care assistance—and an empathetic management style one might dub "maternalism."

Of course, some male-owned businesses also employ similar practices. But Thomas Gray, chief economist for the Small Business Administration, says the benefits appear to be more prevalent among female-owned businesses than male-owned. Women business owners "are more aware of the problems" of combining families and careers and the benefits of creative solutions, he says. Many male owners, he adds, "don't see the need to change their current work practices."

REDUCING STRESS.

Women entrepreneurs, many of them mothers themselves, say their policies spring from an idealistic desire to reduce working parents' stress and create a less hierarchical workplace. Female owners also claim the practices make good business sense because they can lure and retain a more productive staff.

But liberal treatment of workers can create conflicts. Numerous women business owners "start out feeling they can be more maternal, caring and responsive to needs of others," says Bonnie Mitelman, the Briarcliff Manor, N.Y., publisher of Business-Mother, a newsletter. "But once they become successful in their businesses, they (must) respond to two different needs—those of their clients and those of their employees."

Suzy Boehm, a White Plains, N.Y., clinical psychologist, says owners "bend too far and learn the hard way." The women are "caught in the middle," she says. "They're expected to have a certain amount of em-

pathy, but they also are expected to deal with the bottom line of profits."

A growing workload six years ago, for example, forced Frog Pond Inc., an Atlanta sportswear maker, to end an early closing policy. Frog Pond long had closed its doors at 3 P.M., when the two owners and their employees, all mothers, had to head home for their young schoolchildren. Three of its 40 staffers still work "mothers' hours" from 8:00 A.M. to 2:30 P.M., a schedule that attracts women "who wouldn't ordinarily be in the job market," says Billie Brown, president of the $4 million-a-year company.

TOO MANY PEOPLE OFF.

Similarly, a $30 million-a-year travel agency in Santa Clara, Calif., dropped a four-day, 40-hour-work-week experiment after four months. "There were days when there were too many people off" in the commercial travel department, recalls the owner, Maryles Casto. When "the phones are ringing and you can't service them, it's a problem."

But Ms. Casto says other innovative benefits keep turnover low among her predominantly female staff. Two part-time employees share one job. New mothers can regain their former positions after a year's maternity leave, two months of it with pay. The travel-agency owner also may soon offer her 86 employees vouchers to subsidize part of the cost of child-care expenses. "I feel like I've been there," explains Ms. Casto, who resented returning to her then brand-new business a month after her son's birth in 1975. "If there's any way I can help, I will try it."

Some owners say the extra costs involved in offering flexible benefits are paid back in other ways.

(Continued on next pg.)

Ruth Lambert, owner of a New Haven, Conn., specialized direct-mail concern, has a day-care center for staffers' children on the company's premises. She originally set up a nursery in her warehouse when her daughter was born, six years ago. The child-care worker she hired then now cares for four of the 16 employees' youngsters, ages 10 months to nine years, as well as for her daughter and her second child.

The $20,000-a-year day-care operation "pays for itself 10 times over" in keeping employees happy and reducing parents' anxieties, she says. Several other female staffers have told Ms. Lambert they plan to take brief maternity leaves because they know they may bring their infants to work.

In some instances, women-owned businesses provide unusual benefits or flexible schedules only for their most valued employees. Lynn Wilson, president of a $39 million-a-year architectural-design firm based in Coral Gables, Fla., pays for a senior purchasing executive's full-time housekeeper.

Employment counselor Diane Childers, who has two young daughters, is the sole staffer of a Washington personnel agency who gets a full-time salary for a four-day, 30-hour week. Her nine female colleagues don't object. "They know it's available if they ever marry and have children," says Carla Massoni, one of the firm's two owners, both of whom have children.

SUBORDINATES TAKE ADVANTAGE. Ms. Childers likes her shortened workweek and the "unspoken support system" so much that she vows, "I would only work for women-owned companies."

On occasion, however, women business owners' innovative employee relations have failed because subordinates took advantage of the loose environment. They came in late too often, abused liberal sick-leave rules or refused occasional demands for extra work.

An employee at a New York market-research firm with a casual work atmosphere exploited the female owner's sympathies over her divorce. On company time, the employee saw her psychiatrist and socialized with a boyfriend. Three months of slacking "created a great deal of resentment among other employees that she was able to come and go," recalls Judith Langer, who heads the 12-person company. Ms. Langer finally blew up at the woman and the employee quit.

Barbara Keck started her New York management consulting firm in 1979 with the intention of using only part-time "MBA mommies" like herself—management-trained women who couldn't juggle parenthood and nine-to-five jobs. But working mothers now make up only half of her 20-member professional staff. She learned she couldn't count on some mothers to travel on short notice.

"I'm saddened that I haven't been able to" employ MBA mommies exclusively, Mrs. Keck says. But, she adds, "I don't like juggling my schedule around to accommodate other people. That's one reason I started this business—to have flexibility" in work hours.

Questions and Problems

1. Why are such organizational innovations as flexitime, sabbaticals, and job sharing more prevalent in female-owned small businesses than in businesses owned by males?

2. What benefits are likely to result from such practices? What types of conflicts may arise?

3. Explain the impact of organizational growth on such practices. Recommend courses of action whereby managers of rapidly growing organizations can retain successful organizational innovations for their employees.

Source: Joann S. Lublin, "Female Owners Try to Make Life Easier for Employees—Sometimes Too Easy," *Wall Street Journal,* 28 May 1985, p. 33. Reprinted by permission. © 1985 by Dow Jones & Company, Inc.; all rights reserved.

10 STAFFING THE ORGANIZATION

LEARNING OBJECTIVES

After studying this chapter you should be able to

1. Identify and briefly explain the major federal laws affecting human resources management.

2. List the steps in the recruitment and selection process.

3. Compare and contrast the different types of on-the-job and off-the-job training and management development programs.

4. Identify the basic types of compensation programs.

5. Explain the major types of separation.

STOP ACTION CASE

Delta Business Systems

When Bryan King started Delta Business Systems in 1978, he recognized that competent, highly motivated people were the key to success or failure. His Orlando company, established to sell, lease, and service office equipment, would grow to $23 million in sales by 1985 and would employ 315 people. King, who had formerly been general manager of an automobile dealership and an educational materials salesperson, recognized the value of incentive compensation in sales. He also sought a means of motivating nonsales employees.

It is a compensation fact of life that superior sales performances earn higher commissions for the firm's sales force. But what about superior efforts on the part of field-service technicians, dispatchers, warehouse employees, secretaries, and administrative assistants? The traditional answer is that they are rewarded with a raise. But the time period between the superior performance and the salary adjustment may extend for months, resulting in a weak linkage between performance and pay. King felt there must be a better approach. As one of his supervisors expressed it, "What we are trying to do is convince a group of skeptical people who are used to working their forty hours and going home . . . that management is sincerely trying to offer equitable incentives."

Use the materials in Chapter 10 to recommend an incentive compensation plan for nonsales employees at Delta Business Systems.

Source: Quotation in paragraph two from Ellen Kolton, "Paddling for Profits," *Inc.,* March 1985, p. 137.

<A company is known by the people it keeps.>>

Anonymous

Although the typical organization is made up of a number of different resources, none is more important than people. While the machinery, inventory, financial resources, and information may be invaluable, the organization can do nothing if it lacks sufficiently competent employees to operate the machinery, make decisions based upon analysis of the information, sell the firm's output, handle correspondence, and supervise the myriad operations. Since the value of effective human resources is obvious, it would appear equally obvious that all organizations would practice effective human resources management. But as news sources continue to reveal, many organizations fail to manage their human resources properly.

U.S. Industries had four presidents in less than a year. The chairman and chief executive officer of First Wisconsin Mortgage Company resigned "for personal reasons" after three weeks on the job. After a new president was chosen, Burlington Industries lost two long-time employees who were vice-presidents and directors. The employee turnover rate in the restaurant industry averages 46 percent for dishwashers and buspersons, 41 percent for waitresses and counterpersons, 33 percent for food preparation workers, and 23 percent for unit managers.[1] Burlington Northern, Inc., one of the nation's largest rail carriers, agreed to pay $10 million in back wages to blacks who charged the company with discrimination in hiring, discipline, termination, initial assignments, transfers, promotion and testing practices, and training. The company also agreed to give rejected black applicants priority for new jobs over a six-year period.[2]

The growth in the size of the typical organization and the increasing number of regulations affecting employment practices have resulted in

MANAGEMENT FACT OR FICTION

	FACT	FICTION
1. Human resources managers are line—not staff—managers.	☐	☐
2. Unlike the job description, which concentrates on the job itself, the job specification focuses on the person performing the job.	☐	☐
3. Surveys indicate that one job applicant in six misrepresents job qualifications on job applications.	☐	☐
4. Orientation of newly hired employees is the responsibility of the human resources department.	☐	☐
5. Vestibule training is an example of off-the-job training.	☐	☐
6. An MBO program can also serve as a performance appraisal/employee evaluation method.	☐	☐
7. Wage and salary have the same meaning in a compensation system.	☐	☐

The materials in this chapter will assist you in separating management fact from fiction. Your answers can be checked on page 363.

the need for specialists in human resources management. Although more than 50 percent of all workers were self-employed in 1850, less than 10 percent are self-employed today. Major business organizations such as General Motors, Westinghouse, International Telephone and Telegraph, and General Electric employ more than 200,000 workers *each*.

Such organizations have a continuing need for new personnel to replace people who change jobs, receive promotions, or retire. Effective training is vital in producing efficient, competent employees. Compensation programs must be developed and managed; health and safety programs must be administered; and benefit programs and performance evaluations must be given expert attention.

Although most organizations recognize the importance of human resources management, the specific title of the person or department having primary responsibility varies considerably. Some organizations use the term *personnel management,* while others label the function *employee relations.* Still others term the function simply *staffing.* Increasingly, however, the term *human resources management* is being adopted as more and more organizations recognize a greatly expanded role for the traditional personnel functions.

Human resources management may be defined as the organizational function of planning for human resource needs, and recruitment, selection, development, compensation, and evaluation of personnel to fill these needs. These responsibilities are great and call for an enlightened approach to the management of the organization's human resources.

The three broad functions of human resources management—acquiring, maintaining, and developing human resources—are shown in Figure 10–1. The acquisition function includes planning employee needs and recruiting job applicants; interviewing candidates; assisting in the selection process; and conducting orientation programs to acquaint new employees

Human resources management involves planning for human resource needs, recruitment, selection, development, compensation, and evaluation.

FIGURE 10–1.   Human Resource Management Functions

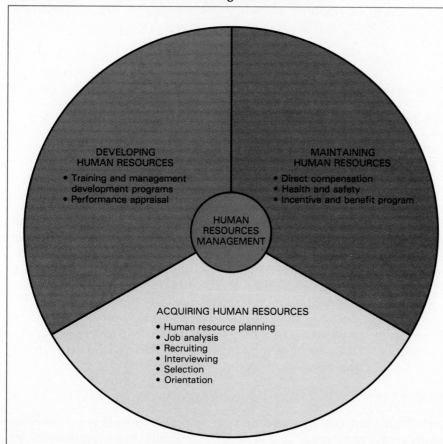

with the firm and the job. The maintenance function involves employee motivation in the form of wages, salaries, incentives and benefits, and provision of employee health and safety programs. The development function seeks to improve the skills of employees and managers and to expand their capabilities. It consists of training and management development programs and performance appraisal.

STAFFING: YESTERDAY AND TODAY

The role of the human resources manager has evolved in three broad stages since the 1920s. The first era was a formative one, in which large organizations began to hire personnel specialists who took over duties that had previously been handled by first-level supervisors. These functions included hiring and firing, development of employee handbooks, and payroll and benefit programs. The personnel manager of this first era held a low-level position in the organization, one that consisted largely of making sure that personnel procedures were followed. But the unionism movement of the mid-1920s moved human resources management into a second era.

> The rise of unions in the 1920s created the need for personnel managers who could negotiate contracts and be tough with unions. By the 1950s, the chief labor negotiator was also vice-president in charge of industrial relations. In companies such as GE and General Motors Corporation, labor relations experience was the ticket to promotion in the personnel field.
>
> Ironically, the reverse is true today. As unions decline in size and bargaining power, companies are looking for other talents in their top personnel officer—ushering in the third stage of the evolution.[3]

66 Good managers are judged by the company they keep—solvent. 99

Anonymous

Frank E. Doyle, senior vice-president for corporate relations at General Electric, describes the human resources manager at the most recent evolutionary stage as follows: "Today, we have to look at a much broader set of labor issues: massive shifts in work, large changes in the work force, plant closings, companies that come into existence and go out of existence in very short time cycles." American Express chairman James D. Robinson III describes the contributions of senior vice-president for human resources Irene C. (Rennie) Roberts this way: "I look to Rennie Roberts and her staff to be an objective sounding board for an evaluation of people, compensation structures, benefit costs, and work life so that we can attract and hold the people we want."[4]

ORGANIZATION OF THE HUMAN RESOURCES DEPARTMENT

Although the manager of human resources is given major responsibilities for acquiring, maintaining, and developing organizational members, he or she is a *staff* manager with the primary duties of assisting and advising line managers. The ultimate authority for making staffing and other human resources decisions rests with the line managers, who rely upon the expertise of the personnel department to provide major assistance in recruiting, testing, conducting screening interviews, training, facilitating the performance appraisal process, and proposing solutions to grievances and disciplinary problems.

The human resources department varies considerably in size and authority among different organizations, ranging from one-person departments to major operations with dozens of specialized members. Determinants of a department's size include rate of employee turnover, level and variety of required skills, overall organizational size, types of fringe benefits, and complexity of wage and salary plans. The average U.S. business firm has 1.1 personnel department employees for every 100 employees on the payroll. A recent study by the American Society for Personnel Administration revealed that the average reported salary and bonus for senior human resources executives in all corporations is $73,600. Executives in large corporations—those with over 8,000 employees—earn an average of $132,600 a year, while those in corporations with fewer than 400 employees earn $64,900.[5]

Figure 10–2 illustrates an organization chart for a human resources department in a large firm with more than 1,000 employees.

HUMAN RESOURCES PLANNING

Like all the other divisions of an organization, the human resources department must plan for the future. The basic planning process is built around two fundamental questions:

1. What types of employees does the organization need? *(quality)*

2. How many of each type are needed? *(quantity)*

FIGURE 10–2.   Organization of a Typical Human Resources Department

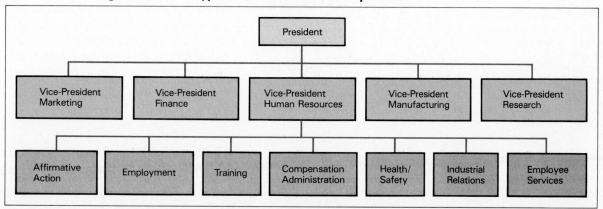

Answers to both questions require a forecast of the organization's personnel needs. This involves an estimate of the number of people and the different types of skills required in the future to perform the work of the organization. Considerable information on future needs is available from employee records of promotion, turnover, and retirement. A management replacement chart, shown in Figure 10–3, is often prepared for upper-level management positions and in other departments where skilled managers are in short supply. The chart reveals not only the present managers in these specified departments, but also their likely future replacements and the readiness of these candidates to assume these positions. For example, R. Jarvis, the current production manager in the industrial fans division, has an outstanding current performance rating and is considered ready for promotion. The replacement chart shows Jarvis under consideration for three possible promotions: manager of the proposed new air-conditioning division; manager of the industrial fans division should the current manager be promoted to executive vice president; or manager of the household fans division should the current manager of that division receive a promotion.

Information on organizational plans for expansion or contraction in various areas is also utilized in development of forecasts of future personnel requirements. Job analysis, job descriptions, and job specifications are invaluable in the planning process.

JOB ANALYSIS

In order to recruit and hire the appropriate persons for specific vacancies, it is necessary to know what the job itself requires. Job analysis enables the manager to specify the duties and responsibilities of each job and the skills required of the person who fills it. It is the starting point for human resources planning.

Job analysis is the systematic study of jobs, consisting of identifying the elements and characteristics of the job and the requirements of the person assigned to it.

Job analysis may be formally defined as a systematic detailed study of jobs, consisting of identifying and examining what is required of the person assigned to the job and the elements and characteristics of the job. The analysis is often conducted by direct observation, or by the use of a questionnaire completed by persons currently holding the job and their immediate supervisors. The analysis focuses on the following questions:

Who does the work?   *Where* is it done?

What is done?   *How* is it done?

When is it done?   *Why* is it done?

Job analysis is the basis for both job descriptions and job specifications.

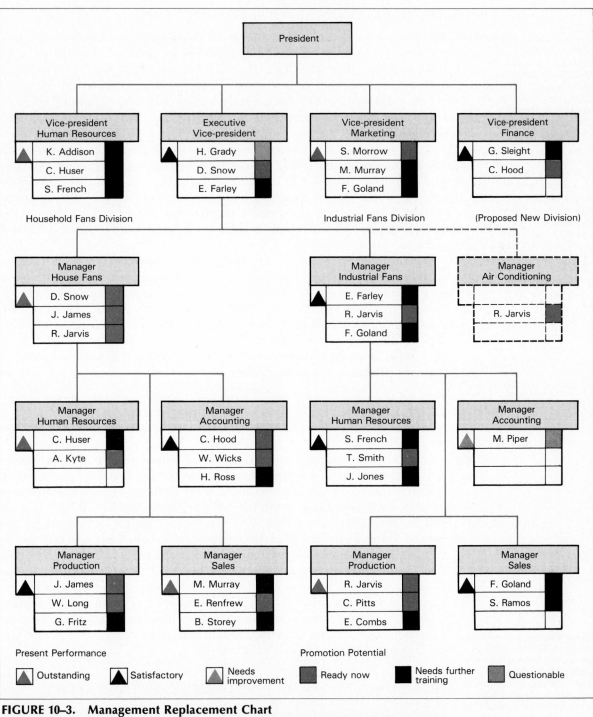

FIGURE 10–3. Management Replacement Chart
Source: Walter S. Wikstrom, *Developing Managerial Competence* (New York: The Conference Board, 1964), p. 99. Used by permission.

JOB DESCRIPTION AND JOB SPECIFICATION

Job description is a written statement describing the objectives of a job, the work to be performed, the skills needed, the responsibilities involved, the relationship of the job to other jobs, and its working conditions.

Job specification is a written description of the special qualifications required of a person who fills a particular job, including skills, education, and previous experience.

The *job description* is a written statement describing the objectives of a job, the work to be performed, the responsibilities involved, the relationship of the job to other jobs, and its working conditions. The description is utilized for a number of important personnel functions: in the selection of new employees, in orientation and training, and in the appraisal process. It typically gives the essence of the job together with a list of tasks and responsibilities.

A key companion to the job description is the *job specification*. This is a written document describing the special qualifications required of a person who fills a particular job. It lists skills, education, and previous experience needed. While the job description concentrates on the job, the job specification focuses upon the person performing the job. A combined job description and job specification for a juvenile probation officer is shown in Figure 10–4.

Figure 10–4 is a valuable document since it specifies the performance expected of the individual and the conditions under which the job is to be performed and sets standards for minimally acceptable performance of each of the duties of the job. Managers can utilize it in orienting new employees to expected performance levels, setting MBO goals, and objectively evaluating actual performance. The employee is provided with a clear statement of performance expectations and the minimum qualifications for promotion or reassignment.

LEGAL CONSIDERATIONS IN HUMAN RESOURCES MANAGEMENT

One important factor in the growing role of human resources departments is the increase in laws and specific regulations from all levels of government spelling out how organizations must treat current and prospective employees. Such laws range from the federal Equal Pay Act of 1963 to state and federal safety standards. The number of statutes enforced by the United States Department of Labor increased from forty in 1960 to 130 in 1980. Compliance with these numerous laws can be expensive. Peabody Coal Co.'s human resources department spent $500,000 to simulate various mining conditions to train its 15,000 miners in order to comply with the Mining Safety and Health Act. Although interpretation of the myriad regulations requires considerable expertise, it is important to be familiar with the major statutes affecting human resources management. The major laws are described briefly in Table 10–1.

PROVIDING FOR EQUAL EMPLOYMENT OPPORTUNITIES

Equal employment opportunity is the right of all persons to work and to advance on the basis of merit, ability, and potential without any form of discrimination because of race, color, religion, sex, or national origin.

Equal employment opportunity may be defined as the right of all persons to work and to advance on the basis of merit, ability, and potential without

---

JUVENILE PROBATION OFFICER

Tasks	Conditions	Standards
Meets with probationers weekly to assess their current behavior	Caseload of not more than 60 appointments scheduled by receptionist; supervisor will help with difficult cases; use procedures stated in rules and regulations	All probationers must be seen weekly; those showing evidence of continued criminal activity or lack of a job will be reported to supervisor
Prepares pre-sentence reports on clients	When requested by the judge; average of 5 per week, per instructions issued by judge; supervisor will review and approve	Your reports will be complete and accurate as determined by judge; he/she will accept 75 percent of presentence recommendations

Skills, Knowledge, and Abilities Required:
- Knowledge of the factors contributing to criminal behavior
- Ability to counsel probationers
- Ability to write clear and concise probation reports
- Knowledge of judge's sentencing habits for particular types of offenders and offenses
- Knowledge of law concerning probation

Minimum Qualifications:
- High school degree or equivalent; plus four years' experience working with juvenile offenders, or a B.S. degree in criminal justice, or psychology, or counseling
- Ability to pass a multiple choice test on relevant probation law
- Possess a valid driver's license

FIGURE 10–4. Combined Job Description and Job Specifications for a Juvenile Probation Officer
Source: Donald E. Klingner, "When the Traditional Job Description Is Not Enough." Reprinted with permission of *Personnel Journal*, Costa Mesa, CA; all rights reserved. Copyright April 1979.

---

any form of discrimination because of race, color, religion, sex, or national origin. The primary legal base for equal employment opportunity actions is Title VII of the Civil Rights Act of 1964, as amended by the Equal Employment Opportunity Act of 1972 and the Pregnancy Discrimination Act of 1978. Supporting legal acts are the Equal Pay Act of 1963, the Age Discrimination in Employment Act of 1967 and its 1978 amendments, the Vocational Rehabilitation Act of 1973, state laws, and presidential executive orders.

The provisions of these acts currently apply to private employers of fifteen or more, state and local governments, public and private employment agencies, and labor unions with fifteen or more members.

TABLE 10–1   IMPORTANT FEDERAL LAWS AFFECTING HUMAN RESOURCES MANAGEMENT

A. Legislation Providing for Equal Employment Opportunities

1. *Equal Pay Act of 1963.* Requires "equal pay for equal work" and states that members of one sex may not be compensated at a rate lower than that paid to employees of the opposite sex who are performing equivalent work.
2. *Title VII of the Civil Rights Act of 1964* as amended by the Equal Employment Opportunity Act of 1972. This is the most sweeping federal law dealing with job bias, prohibiting discriminatory actions based on race, color, religion, sex, or national origin. The Equal Employment Opportunity Commission (EEOC) was established to enforce this law.
3. *Age Discrimination in Employment Act of 1967.* Amended in 1978 to prohibit job discrimination based upon age for persons between 40 and 70.
4. *Vocational Rehabilitation Act of 1973.* This act requires affirmative action programs for the handicapped in businesses with federal contracts or subcontracts.
5. *Vietnam Era Veterans' Readjustment Assistance Act of 1974.* Requires affirmative action programs for Vietnam-era veterans in businesses with federal contracts or subcontracts.
6. *Pregnancy Discrimination Act of 1978.* Prohibits job discrimination against pregnant employees, and is an amendment to Title VII.

B. Legislation Dealing with Health and Safety of Employees

1. *Occupational Safety and Health Act of 1970.* Designed to assure safe and healthful working conditions for the American labor force by requiring employers to develop and implement health and safety plans. Such plans must include inspection of work facilities, removal of all hazards, promotion of job safety, and preparation of reports for submission to the federal enforcement body, the Occupational Safety and Health Administration (OSHA).

C. Legislation Affecting Company–Union Relations

1. *National Labor Relations Act of 1935* (Wagner Act). Legalized collective bargaining and required employers to bargain with the elected representatives of their employees.
2. *Fair Labor Standards Act of 1938.* Outlawed the use of child labor and set a minimum wage and maximum basic hours of work for employees of firms engaged in interstate commerce. The first minimum wage was twenty-five cents per hour. The current minimum wage is $3.35.
3. *Taft-Hartley Act of 1947.* Designed to balance the power of unions and management by prohibiting a number of unfair union practices, including the so-called closed shop, which prohibits management from employing nonunion workers.
4. *Landrum-Griffin Act of 1959.* Requires regularly scheduled elections of union officers by secret ballot. It also regulates the handling of union funds.

The Equal Employment Opportunity Commission (EEOC) is an agency of the executive branch of the federal government created in 1972. It administers the various laws designed to provide equal opportunity in hiring and employment. The EEOC provides assistance to employers in establishing voluntary "affirmative action" programs and in halting discriminatory hiring and employment practices.

By Executive Order, federal contractors with contracts of $50,000 or more *must* have written *affirmative action programs*. These programs are designed to increase opportunities for females and minorities through recruiting, training, and promoting them so they will ultimately be represented in the employer's work force in percentages similar to their percentage in the labor market from which the employer draws workers. Such programs include analysis of the present work force and establishment of specific hiring and promotion goals with target dates in job categories that currently underutilize minorities and/or females. Action plans should also include an active search for minorities and females to be placed into upwardly mobile positions within the organization. Federal contractors and organizations receiving federal financial assistance must also develop affirmative action programs for handicapped workers, disabled veterans, and veterans of the Vietnam era. Contents of such programs should include:

Affirmative action programs are government programs designed to increase opportunities for females, minorities, and other protected categories of workers through recruitment, training, and promotion, so that they are fairly represented in the work force.

- Utilization Analysis. Underutilization means having fewer workers from protected categories in a job classification than would reasonably be expected by their availability.

- Establishment of goals and timetables.

- Development of an equal employment opportunity policy for all personnel actions.

- Formal internal and external dissemination of the equal employment opportunity policy.

- Establishment of responsibility for implementation of the affirmative action program.

- Active support of community action programs designed to improve employment opportunities of workers in protected categories.

- Implementation of an internal audit and reporting system to measure the effectiveness of the total program.[6]

The main sections of the EEOC report are shown in Figure 10–5.

A number of financial penalties have been levied against organizations for violating equal employment opportunity laws. One notable case involved a $42.6 million settlement by General Motors to resolve charges of alleged discrimination against minorities and women. The 1983 settlement, resulting from charges that GM failed to hire, train, and promote women, blacks, and Hispanics, is the largest nonlitigated settlement in EEOC's history.[7]

Joint Reporting Committee
- Equal Employment Opportunity Commission
- Office of Federal Contract Compliance Programs (Labor)

Standard Form 100
(Rev. 5-84)
O.M.B. No. 3046-000;
EXPIRES 3/31/85
100-211

EQUAL EMPLOYMENT OPPORTUNITY
EMPLOYER INFORMATION REPORT EEO-1

Section C—EMPLOYERS WHO ARE REQUIRED TO FILE (To be answered by all employers)

☐ Yes ☐ No   1. Does the entire company have at least 100 employees in the payroll period for which you are reporting?

☐ Yes ☐ No   2. Is your company affiliated through common ownership and/or centralized management with other entities in an enterprise with a total employment of 100 or more?

☐ Yes ☐ No   3. Does the company or any of its establishments (a) have 50 or more employees AND (b) is not exempt as provided by 41 CFR 60-1.5, AND either (1) is a prime government contractor or first-tier subcontractor, and has a contract, subcontract, or purchase order amounting to $50,000 or more, or (2) serves as a depository of Government funds in any amount or is a financial institution which is an issuing and paying agent for U.S. Savings Bonds and Savings Notes?

If the response to question C-3 is yes, please enter your Dun and Bradstreet identification number (if you have one): ☐☐☐☐☐☐☐☐☐

☐ Yes ☐ No   4. Does the company receive financial assistance from the Small Business Administration (SBA)?

NOTE: If the answer is yes to questions 1, 2, or 3, complete the entire form, otherwise skip to Section G.

Section D—EMPLOYMENT DATA

Employment at this establishment—Report all permanent full-time or part-time employees including apprentices and on-the-job trainees unless specifically excluded as set forth in the instructions. Enter the appropriate figures on all lines and in all columns. Blank spaces will be considered as zeros.

JOB CATEGORIES	OVERALL TOTALS (SUM OF COL. B THRU K) A	MALE					FEMALE				
		WHITE (NOT OF HISPANIC ORIGIN) B	BLACK (NOT OF HISPANIC ORIGIN) C	HISPANIC D	ASIAN OR PACIFIC ISLANDER E	AMERICAN INDIAN OR ALASKAN NATIVE F	WHITE (NOT OF HISPANIC ORIGIN) G	BLACK (NOT OF HISPANIC ORIGIN) H	HISPANIC I	ASIAN OR PACIFIC ISLANDER J	AMERICAN INDIAN OR ALASKAN NATIVE K
Officials and Managers 1											
Professionals 2											
Technicians 3											
Sales Workers 4											
Office and Clerical 5											
Craft Workers (Skilled) 6											
Operatives (Semi-Skilled) 7											
Laborers (Unskilled) 8											
Service Workers 9											
TOTAL 10											
Total employment reported in previous EEO-1 report 11											
(The trainees below should also be included in the figures for the appropriate occupational categories above)											
Formal On-the-job trainees — White collar 12											
Production 13											

FIGURE 10–5. Some Required Contents of Affirmative Action Programs and Sections of the Equal Employment Opportunity Form
Source: Equal Employment Opportunity Commission.

MANAGEMENT: THE LIGHTER SIDE

Human Resources Management on the Gridiron

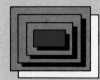

The organization had always prided itself on its enlightened approach to human resources management. Huge quantities of data on the qualifications of virtually every potential job candidate in the country were fed into the computer for analysis each year before making job offers. The successful applicant received significant employee benefits: a salary averaging over $100,000 in the industry and a twenty-six week annual vacation. The organization was the Dallas Cowboys Football Club. It was willing to provide these employee benefits, due to management's recognition of the importance of a skilled place kicker in maintaining the team's competitive position.

Rafael Septien, the Mexican national who had performed admirably in the position the previous year, informed the Cowboys of his intention to apply for a permanent visa. The club's personnel officials recognized that a number of steps would have to be taken in order to comply with Texas state employment regulations before Septien could be employed for the next season. The regulations in question dealt with the importation of alien workers and required the Cowboys to show that Septien would not be taking the job away from a U.S. citizen. So the club's personnel officials turned to orthodox approaches by listing the position with the Texas Employment Commission, running the classified advertisement shown (left) in the *Dallas Morning News*, and interviewing all applicants during a thirty-day period.

The advertisement reawakened dreams of ex-football players throughout the Southwest and produced a number of applications from would-be professionals. However, none of the applicants possessed both of the qualifications: a minimum of four years of college and two years of professional football experience. Personnel's recommendation was accepted by the Cowboys' top management and the position was once again filled by Rafael Septien.

**PROFESSIONAL FOOTBALL
PLACE KICKER NEEDED**

Minimum 4 yrs. college & 2 yrs. professional football expr. Annual Salary from $20,000. Contact your nearest Texas Employment Commission Office. Job Order No. 1465638. Ad paid for by Equal Opportunity Employer.

Source: Advertisement reproduced courtesy of the Dallas Cowboys Football Club.

The most widely reported case of *reverse* discrimination was that of Allan Bakke, who charged the University of California with discriminating against him on the basis of race. Bakke proved that the university had admitted less qualified (based on entrance tests and grades) minorities to its medical school, and the U.S. Supreme Court ordered the university to admit him. The Court did rule that race could be *one* of several factors used in determining admissions. However, it stated that the university's affirmative action admissions program was "unjustifiably biased against white applicants" since a specific number of admissions were reserved for minority applicants.

THE RECRUITMENT AND SELECTION PROCESS

The recruitment and selection process is a systematic attempt to implement the human resources plan by recruiting, evaluating, and selecting qualified managers and operative employees. The job analysis, job description, and job specification are important tools in the selection process. Figure 10–6 lists the steps in the recruitment and selection process, the qualifications considered at each step, and the rationale for possible rejection of applicants at each step.

FIGURE 10–6.   Steps in the Selection Process
Source: Adapted by permission of the publisher from *The Employment Interview*, AMA Research Study #47, by Milton Mandel, © 1961 by American Management Association, Inc. All rights reserved.

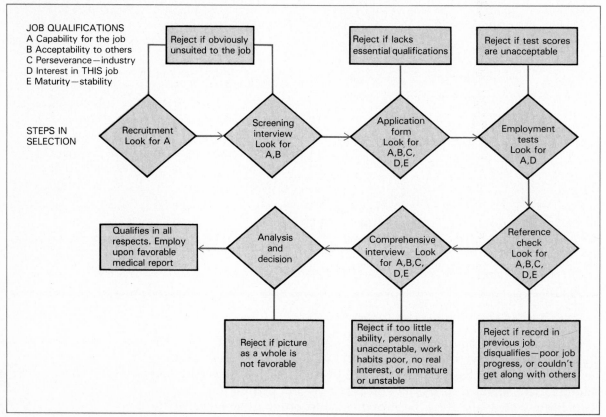

RECRUITMENT

A number of sources for potential employees exist. The first place most managers look when attempting to fill a position is within the organization. Policies of promotion from within are widely used since they improve employee morale while reducing recruiting, hiring, and training costs. Most organizations give strong preference to internal sources of employees. Others—such as Sears and Delta Airlines—promote *only* from within.[8]

External sources of potential employees are used in periods of rapid growth or when the need for specialized skills requires that qualified applicants be recruited from outside the organization. Some of the most frequently used external sources include private employment agencies, educational institutions, professional and trade journals, newspaper and radio advertisements, public employment agencies, union hiring halls, and recommendations of present employees.

SCREENING INTERVIEWS

Once a group of applicants has been secured through recruiting, the *screening process* focuses on determining which candidates are best suited for the job. The process is basically the same for operative, technical, or managerial employees. The applicant is asked to complete an application form containing biographical information—name and address, previous experience, education, type of work desired. This form is analyzed to determine whether the applicant possesses the necessary qualifications. It provides the basic information used in beginning the interview.

The one selection instrument that is universally employed is the interview. Interviews are typically included in the selection process due to the desire of managers to make a personal determination of whether the new employee will "fit" into the department or division. While questions dealing with work experience, education, and military experience may be asked, the interviewer must avoid irrelevant and potentially discriminatory questions about age, race or color, national origin, religion or creed, or marital status.[9] One study of 2,500 U.S. companies reported that 64 percent of the respondents considered interview results to be the single most important criterion in employment decisions. Previous experience was second at 32 percent, and all other factors were mentioned by only 4 percent of the respondents.[10]

The interview provides applicants the opportunity to market themselves. At the same time, it offers insights about the job applicant to the interviewer that might not be obvious in studying a completed application form. Among questions the applicant should be prepared to answer in an interview are the following:

- Why should I hire you?
- Why do you want to work here?

- What interests you most about this position?

- Would you like to have your boss's job?

- What causes you to lose your temper?

- Who has had the greatest influence on you?

- What kinds of decisions are most difficult for you?

- How long will you stay with the company?

- What are your greatest accomplishments?

- Why do you want to change jobs?

Developing answers to such questions requires preparation; job applicants should "do their homework" on the company and, if possible, the interviewer. As author Theodore T. Pettus points out, "The glibbest person on earth, even the most skilled debater, cannot answer questions off the cuff without damaging his or her chances of success."[11]

A series of interviews may be conducted with applicants both by members of the human resources department and by the line manager for whom the prospective employee will work. Interviewers may use directed or nondirected interviews. *Directed* interviews are based on a standard list of questions developed prior to the interview. *Nondirected* interviews allow for more interviewer flexibility in determining the kinds of questions to be asked. Both types of interviews ideally use open-ended questions designed to stimulate the prospective employee to do most of the talking. Regardless of the type of interview employed, the interviewer should understand the specific objectives of the interview and know as much as possible about the applicant prior to the meeting. The interview should be conducted in a location that allows privacy and in which the applicant will be comfortable and willing to speak openly.

REFERENCE CHECKS

Many organizations use reference checks to verify certain information provided by applicants. Work histories are common subjects for such checks. Much verification is conducted by telephone rather than by the slower—and possibly less accurate—use of letters to references supplied by the applicant.

A recent survey of 501 executives revealed that 17 percent of recently hired employees had misrepresented job qualifications and 9 percent had inflated their salaries. Although educational backgrounds can be easily verified, the most frequent misrepresentations involved college degrees earned and grades.[12]

MANAGEMENT FAILURES

The Wrong Way to Reject Job Applicants

The selection process is a systematic attempt to identify and employ those applicants best suited for the position. Many applicants may be rejected at each stage. The student body of the American Graduate School of International Management assembled the following collection of letters from companies turning down the job applications of some of those about to be graduated. The following excerpts were extracted from those letters:

After most careful consideration of your qualifications and background, we are unable to identify anything you can do for us . . .

We're certain you could be more useful some place else . . .

You write you'll visit our headquarters in Los Angeles and I thought before you spent too much time trying to find it, we'd tell you our headquarters are in Portland, Oregon . . .

. . . but we're sure you will find something you can do.

My conscience doesn't allow me to encourage you.

Unfortunately, we have to be selective . . .

I am sorry, but because of the nature of our work we have to be more careful than others in our hiring . . .

Source: Malcolm S. Forbes, "How Not to Turn Down Job Applicants," *Forbes,* 15 June 1977, p. 22. Reprinted by permission.

PHYSICAL EXAMINATIONS

Although many organizations do not require physical examinations for applicants, they continue to be widely used in the case of jobs involving physical activity. The purpose of the examination is to determine whether the applicant has the capability to perform the duties required in the job description and whether the individual has a physical problem that might be used as a basis for subsequent workers' compensation claims.

TESTING

Testing is employed to gain a more objective picture of the qualifications of prospective employees than can be obtained by the self-described credentials on the application form. Testing is a controversial issue in the 1980s due to questions of whether tests actually predict job success and whether they are culturally biased. The EEOC requires that all tests be closely job-related and both reliable and valid. *Reliability* means that the test results are consistent (a person who takes a test three or four times should achieve similar scores). *Validity* means that the test measures what it is intended to measure. (A typing speed test is an invalid predictor of intelligence, but it may be entirely valid in evaluating the skills of a potential typist.)

ORIENTATION OF THE NEWLY HIRED WORKER

The end result of the selection process should be the hiring of the most qualified candidate for the position. Most medium- and large-sized organizations have a formal orientation program to introduce the new member to colleagues and procedures. Orientation is typically the joint responsibility of the human resources department and the department in which the new employee will work.

An effective orientation program should provide the individual with a basic understanding of the organization and its philosophy, objectives, policies, and organizational structure. The compensation, appraisal, and benefits programs are typically explained in detail during the orientation process.

TRAINING AND DEVELOPMENT

Although organizations often attempt to employ fully qualified individuals who require little or no training, training is usually essential for new organizational members as well as for seasoned managers, who require improved skills to advance in the organization. Employees at all levels—operative, technical, and managerial—will require some training at one or more points in their careers. Although the methods, objectives, and course or program contents often differ, the basic principles of teaching/learning are the same.

Differences exist between training and management development programs, although the distinctions are not always clear-cut. In fact, educational programs generally have elements of both development and training. Training differs from development in that it relies more heavily upon the instructor; development, on the other hand, relies more upon the student's initiative in asking questions to bring out important points and their relevance. Development is, in fact, self-development.

EMPLOYEE TRAINING PROGRAMS

Training is a systematic process by which the individual learns skills, abilities, knowledge, or attitudes to further organizational and personal goals. Several basic approaches to training are commonly used. The approaches may be divided into two categories: on-the-job training and off-the-job training.

> 66 I *hear* and I forget. I *see* and I remember. I *do* and I understand. 99
>
> Confucius

An estimated 90 percent of all training is performed *on the job.* The underlying belief is that the individual can best learn the specifics of the job—how to operate a machine, conduct an interview, or sell the firm's products—through training in the actual work environment. This method is often used when the job to be learned is relatively simple and special classes or instructors are unnecessary. Typically, the immediate supervisor or another experienced worker handles the training.

On-the-job training involves learning the specifics of a job in the actual work environment.

One of the oldest types of training is *apprenticeship training.* This technique is widely used in such highly skilled crafts as plumbing, printing, construction, welding, and barbering. Apprentice training is regulated by the U.S. Department of Labor, which determines the lengths of apprenticeships and the minimum requirements for classroom instruction. A typical apprenticeship lasts three to five years and represents a major time and expense commitment by both trainees and the firm.

Apprenticeship training is a combination of on-the-job training and off-the-job instruction used in highly skilled crafts.

Apprentice programs are a combination of both on-the-job and off-the-job training. The on-the-job portion consists of instructions from an experienced employee called a *journeyman.* It is common for labor unions to be heavily involved in off-the-job classroom or theory instruction, which may be conducted at a local union hall. In other instances, off-the-job training may be obtained from an approved school.

Off-the-job training is any form of training conducted away from the individual's work area. This approach is used in situations in which the participation of the new worker would slow production and/or be potentially dangerous. In such instances, the organization can construct a training area equipped with machines and processes similar to those found on the job. This approach, called *vestibule training,* is designed to build skills by allowing the individual to perform the work under the supervision of a trainer before being assigned to the actual work area.

Vestibule training involves allowing the individual to perform the work in a training area under the supervision of a trainer before being assigned to the actual work area.

Off-the-job training also is typically used when the employee must gain a considerable body of knowledge and theory before beginning the job. Classroom training programs use traditional techniques of lectures, programed instruction materials, conferences, films, and other audio-visual aids, as well as special machines to develop the necessary skills before the individual is assigned to the work area. Technical companies, such as IBM, Motorola, Xerox, and AT&T, conduct extensive classroom training programs for their sales and service personnel.

A growing number of firms are using interactive training programs linking a personal computer to a videodisc player for training waitresses, mechanics, repairers, and even airline pilots. These systems let students move through a subject at their own pace, point out their errors, send them back to review materials they haven't grasped, let them skip material they already know, time them, and keep track of their progress. Such systems are currently providing inventory control training for J. C. Penney employees, product knowledge for 40,000 Ford dealer mechanics, and flight training for Boeing 767 pilots.[13]

MANAGEMENT DEVELOPMENT PROGRAMS

Although the concept of job training has been applied for thousands of years, the special focus upon the training and development of present and potential managers is a twentieth-century phenomenon. One of the earliest development programs was designed in 1901 by retailing pioneer James Cash Penney. Penney developed a system whereby the manager-partner of each drygoods store in the chain would select and train one prospective manager who would then be sent out to found another store.[14]

Since every organization has a continuous need for effective managers at every level, management development programs have spread rapidly. One survey of U.S. firms employing 1,000 or more employees revealed that almost three-fourths of the respondents have formal management development programs.[15]

Management development programs can also be categorized as on-the-job and off-the-job. One commonly used on-the-job development technique is *job rotation,* whereby managers are assigned to different departments to familiarize them with the various operations of the organization and the contributions of each. *Coaching* of junior executives by having them work closely with a senior manager (the person's *mentor* or *sponsor*) is another widely used technique. At the Jewel Co. a sponsor is formally assigned to each management trainee. In a national survey of 1,250 executives, nearly two-thirds of the respondents reported having had a mentor or sponsor.[16]

Off-the-job management development may include regular university courses (leading, perhaps, to a graduate degree), special in-house management programs conducted by professional organizations or consultants, or formal courses conducted off the company premises in special institutes established by the firm. IBM managers must spend at least forty hours a year in classrooms improving their management skills. Such major firms as Texaco, McDonald's, and General Motors offer programs at company institutes that resemble colleges.

Supervisory programs typically focus upon assisting supervisors in fulfilling their responsibilities. Although the programs vary considerably, such topics as processing union grievances, seniority policies, nondiscrimination requirements, safety procedures, and discipline are usually covered. It is also common for such programs to include tours of other areas of the organization and explanations of job evaluations and merit ratings to provide the first-line manager with a broader perspective of the entire organization, rather than a total focus on his or her department.

Middle management programs utilize such techniques as on-the-job coaching, job rotation, and special committee assignments as part of a long-range plan to increase the breadth of the manager as he or she progresses in the organization. Off-the-job development programs are also frequently employed. Figure 10–7 shows a two-week middle management program offered by the University of Denver.

Job rotation is a management development technique in which managers are assigned to different departments to familiarize them with the various operations of the organization.

Coaching is a management development technique in which junior executives work closely with a senior manager called a *mentor* or *sponsor.*

FIRST SESSION JUNE 3–JUNE 7				
Monday June 3	**Tuesday June 4**	**Wednesday June 5**	**Thursday June 6**	**Friday June 7**
8:30–11:45 ECONOMICS Inflation/Unemployment—the classic dilemma	**8:30–11:45 FINANCE** The nature of capital markets	**8:30–11:45 MARKETING** Marketing management and government regulation	**8:30–11:45 ACCOUNTING** Financial disclosure: The right to know (external)	**8:30–11:45 MANAGEMENT** Executive development: Its advantages and disadvantages
Lunch				
1:30–4:45 INTERNATIONAL MARKETS Natural resources	**1:30–4:45 MONETARY POLICY** Its meaning to the individual firm	**1:30–4:45 MARKETING RESEARCH** Applications of research to marketing management	**1:30–4:45 FINANCIAL DISCLOSURE** The right to know (internal)	**1:30–4:45 BOARDS OF DIRECTORS** The obligations and responsibilities
SECOND SESSION JUNE 10–JUNE 14				
Monday June 10	**Tuesday June 11**	**Wednesday June 12**	**Thursday June 13**	**Friday June 14**
8:30–11:45 ENERGY RESOURCES Alternatives and risks re: The energy crisis	**8:30–11:45 CIVIL RIGHTS** Equal Employment Opportunity: What's on the horizon?	**8:30–11:45 LEGAL PROBLEMS** Current problems: Consumerism and legislation	**8:30–11:45 SOCIETAL ISSUES** Social change and its significance to the firm	**8:30–11:45 A PLEA FOR ETHICS** A society of ambivalence
Lunch				
1:30–4:45 TRANSPORTATION A new perspective: What are the options?	**1:30–4:45 POLLUTION** Who pays the bill?	**1:30–4:45 CORPORATE POWER** Is it used wisely?	**1:30–4:45 BUSINESS AND SOCIETY** Current issues and challenges	**1:30–4:45 SUMMARY AND CONCLUSIONS**

FIGURE 10–7.   Two-Week Development Program for Middle Managers
Source: A former program of the Center for Management Development, University of Denver.
Used with permission.

Development programs for top management are clearly self-developmental in nature. Managers at or near the top of the organization may have to determine for themselves their needs for expanded knowledge. Seminars, special courses, and other on-the-job assignments are as useful for these executives as for middle-level managers.

It is important to stress the fact that development comes from within. No one can develop another person; one can only help people to reach their potential. The second point to realize about development is that it is directed toward broadening the individual manager. In many cases, promotion channels lead the manager through a series of positions of increased authority and responsibility within a specialized functional area. Development programs must broaden potential top executives by exposing them to other functional areas if they are to become general managers, presidents, or chief executive officers. In addition, candidates for top management positions need experience with such external organizations

COMPUTERS IN MANAGEMENT

Counseling by Computer

When Victor Sloan sought advice recently on how to motivate one of his employees, he turned not to his personnel department, but to his personal computer.

Mr. Sloan, president of Victor Aviation Services Inc., in Palo Alto, Calif., ran through a computer program called the Management Edge for a solution. "I thought the employee was just shy and needed encouragement to work more with others," says Mr. Sloan. Wrong, said the program. "It told me to let him work alone. So I did, and his performance went up 30%," says Mr. Sloan.

The Management Edge, developed by Human Edge Software Corp., Palo Alto, is one of several new personal computer programs designed to help managers handle people. They range from relatively simple, computerized management training courses to more sophisticated, and controversial, systems that give advice based on psychological profiles of employees. The Management Edge, for example, asks a manager questions about an employee's personality and then offers tips on everything from improving his production to firing him. Another approach is taken by Interactive Health Systems Corp., Los Angeles, which offers a program to help managers and subordinates work out their problems through computerized question and answer sessions.

Help With Spouses and Children. Already, the programs have done much to make personal computers more personal than they've ever been before. Buyers of the programs use them not only for dealing with personnel problems at work, but also for help in coping with their spouses and children. And some companies are supplementing, even replacing, humans with computers for much of their management training and consulting.

Not surprisingly, some management trainers, industrial psychologists and others who stand to lose business because of the new software view the electronic competition skeptically. They assert that the programs can encourage simple-minded approaches to complex problems more appropriately addressed by humans.

"I don't think you can substitute interaction with a computer screen for interaction with another person in learning to deal with people," says Derwin Fox, vice-president of Xerox Learning Systems, a Xerox Corp. unit that offers management training.

But that view hasn't prevented Xerox Learning Systems from looking into ways to incorporate personal computers into its training programs, says Mr. Fox. Other management training companies, such as Wilson Learning Corp., a unit of John M. Wiley & Sons, Publishers Inc., have already started. Mathew Juechter, president of Wilson Learning, says a recent study by his company indicates that within five years about half of the money spent for management training by U.S. businesses will go for self-instruction courses, most employing computers. Of an estimated $1 billion spent annually for management training in the U.S. now, only about 5% goes for self-instruction courses, he adds.

Advantage Over Humans. Most managers say that computers offer certain advantages over humans in management training. One is cost. Most of the programs, which are typically sold on floppy disks usable with International Business Machines Corp. personal computers, are priced between $200 and $500. That's less than most management training courses.

For its part, Wilson Learning is developing a system that combines a computer and videodisk machine to train managers in handling interpersonal relations. Managers using the system will find themselves in a fantasy world filled with dragons, knights and castles, says Gary Quinlan, a manager working on the project. At one point, they'll be required to hold a conversation with a dragon in an attempt to elicit its "social priorities and how it uses its time," he says. If they show they understand the dragon, they'll be allowed to continue; otherwise it devours them.

Concourse Inc., a Minneapolis-based concern, offers a program that puts managers in charge of a hypothetical group discussion with employees. The employees, represented by faces on the computer screen, smile or frown depending on whether the user leads the discussion correctly according to the program's built-in criteria.

A program developed by Thoughtware Inc., a Coconut Grove, Fla.-based company, attempts to teach managers about the importance of communicating well by putting its users in the role of an employee whose manager gives inadequate instructions and feedback. The program gives minimal and somewhat confusing instructions on how to play a computerized card game, then rushes the human player with strict time limits on moves.

More Feedback. Fred A. Haskett, a corporate trainer for Panhandle Eastern Corp., says the game frustrated him initially. "But gradually it gives you more feedback on how to play, and your score improves," he says.

Human Edge's programs go further and offer evaluations of a manager's subordinates. For example, the programs ask questions like, "Is Mr. X overly sensitive to criticism?" and then print advice such as, "Mr. X has a low threshold for anger and, in fact, may appear to be angry before you even say anything. Don't let this worry you or frighten you."

One manager of a marketing concern, who declined to be named, says he used Management Edge to analyze his boss, "who loses his temper a lot; it just blows away any chance of communication." The manager says the program helped by recommending that he always deal with his boss in person, rather than over the phone, as he often did.

Many Human Edge customers report using Management Edge to get advice on handling people outside work. Mr. Sloan, the aviation company president, says that after he introduced his wife to the program, she began using it to help deal with family members, including the couple's "stubborn" three-year-old son. Mrs. Sloan adds that when she told several friends about the program, they were enthusiastic about using it to get advice on handling their husbands. "They really like the part on how to discipline," she says.

Source: David Stipp, "Managers Are Using Personal Computers To Help Them Deal With Personnel Issues," *Wall Street Journal,* 25 July 1984, p. 29. Reprinted by permission of *The Wall Street Journal,* © Dow Jones & Company, Inc. 1984. All Rights Reserved.

as trade associations, community-wide organizations, governments, and possibly other nations. Although top managers possess specialized knowledge, they must operate as *generalists*. Effective management development programs can make major contributions in achieving these results.

PERFORMANCE APPRAISAL

The performance of every employee is continually evaluated by that person's superior. If no formal appraisal system exists, such an evaluation is likely to produce all of the disadvantages and none of the advantages of appraisal. Informal systems too often result in supervisory emphasis on personal traits such as appearance, sincerity, and loyalty, rather than on such factors as quantity of work and the quality of that work. In cases where there is no formally organized system, supervisors may not be consistent in evaluating all workers in a department. Worker A might be rewarded for often coming to work early while Worker B receives no recognition for a perfect record of being prompt—but not early. Without a formal system, few checks and balances exist.[17]

Formal systems of performance appraisal were begun to bring order to the appraisal process and thereby reduce worker complaints about lack of fairness. Current methods attempt to ensure that all employees in each department are consistently evaluated on fair criteria. Fairness is important since performance appraisals are often significant factors in determining pay increases and promotion opportunities. To achieve equal treatment, a number of appraisal formats exist. Graphic rating scales, forced distribution, and management by objectives (MBO) are three widely used examples.

Graphic rating scales are performance appraisal forms listing a number of factors, with a continuum for each factor ranging from poor or unacceptable to superior. The rater checks the appropriate degree of merit on each factor being evaluated. Since each degree of merit typically has been assigned a point value, total scores can be determined for the purpose of allocating merit pay increases or other rewards. A rating scale used by the U.S. Air Force in evaluating company grade officer effectiveness is shown in Figure 10–8.

Forced distribution scales require evaluators to place a predetermined percentage of persons being evaluated into four or five categories. For example, a scale might require the appraiser to assign 10 percent to the poor category, 20 percent as below average, 40 percent as average, 20 percent as above average, and the top 10 percent as excellent. The advantage of the forced distribution format over the traditional graphic rating scale is that it forces the rater to differentiate among subordinates by prohibiting the common tendency to categorize employees as average or above average. Such a format would have prevented one U.S. Navy unit from rating 95 percent of its graduates in the top 5 percent of its class.

I.	RATEE IDENTIFICATION DATA *(Read AFR 36–10 carefully before filling in any item)*		
1. NAME *(Last, First, Middle Initial)*	2. SSAN *(Include Suffix)*	3. GRADE	4. DAFSC
5. ORGANIZATION, COMMAND, LOCATION			6. PAS CODE
7. PERIOD OF REPORT FROM: THRU:	8. NO. DAYS OF SUPERVISION	9. REASON FOR REPORT	

II. JOB DESCRIPTION 1. DUTY TITLE:
    2. KEY DUTIES, TASKS AND RESPONSIBILITIES:

III. PERFORMANCE FACTORS *¹Specific example of performance required*	NOT OBSERVED OR NOT RELEVANT	FAR/ BELOW STANDARD	BELOW/ STANDARD	MEETS STANDARD	ABOVE/ STANDARD	WELL/ ABOVE STANDARD
1. JOB KNOWLEDGE *(Depth, currency, breadth)*	O	☐	☐	☐	☐	☐
2. JUDGMENT AND DECISIONS *(Consistent, accurate, effective)*	O	☐	☐	☐	☐	☐
3. PLAN AND ORGANIZE WORK *(Timely, creative)*	O	☐	☐	☐	☐	☐
4. MANAGEMENT OF RESOURCES *(Manpower and material)*	O	☐	☐	☐	☐	☐
5. LEADERSHIP *(Initiative, accept responsibility)*	O	☐	☐	☐	☐	☐
6. ADAPTABILITY TO STRESS *(Stable, flexible, dependable)*	O	☐	☐	☐	☐	☐
7. ORAL COMMUNICATION *(Clear, concise, confident)*	O	☐	☐	☐	☐	☐
8. WRITTEN COMMUNICATION *(Clear, concise, organized)*	O	☐	☐	☐	☐	☐
9. PROFESSIONAL QUALITIES *(Attitude, dress, cooperation, bearing)*	O	☐	☐	☐	☐	☐
10. HUMAN RELATIONS *(Equal opportunity participation, sensitivity)*		☐	☐	☐	☐	☐

AF FORM 707 NOV 79   PREVIOUS EDITIONS ARE OBSOLETE   OFFICER EFFECTIVENESS REPORT

FIGURE 10–8. United States Air Force Company Grade Officer Rating Form

Management by objectives is another widely used evaluation technique. As described in Chapter 5, the MBO procedure involves agreement by both superior and subordinate on the subordinate's objectives for the forthcoming period. At the end of the period, the subordinate is evaluated on how well he or she performed in meeting the agreed-upon objectives. An MBO form is shown in Figure 10–9.

GENERAL APPRAISAL OF EMPLOYEE PERFORMANCE Complete items 1 through 8 for all employees and items 9 and 10 when applicable. Differences between ratings by employee and by supervisor must be discussed.		TO BE COMPLETED BY EMPLOYEE			TO BE COMPLETED BY SUPERVISOR			
		EXCEEDS EXPECTATIONS	MEETS EXPECTATIONS	NEEDS IMPROVEMENT	EXCEEDS EXPECTATIONS	MEETS EXPECTATIONS	NEEDS IMPROVEMENT	INSUFFICIENT OPPORTUNITY TO OBSERVE
1. JOB KNOWLEDGE:	Consider overall knowledge of duties and responsibilities as required for current job or position	☐	☐	☐	☐	☐	☐	☐
2. PRODUCTIVITY:	Evaluate amount of work generated and completed successfully as compared to amount of work expected for this job or position	☐	☐	☐	☐	☐	☐	☐
3. QUALITY:	Rate correctness, completeness, accuracy and economy of work—overall quality	☐	☐	☐	☐	☐	☐	☐
4. INITIATIVE:	Self motivation—consider amount of direction required—seeks improved methods and techniques—consistence in trying to do better	☐	☐	☐	☐	☐	☐	☐
5. USE OF TIME:	Uses available time wisely—is punctual reporting to work—absenteeism—accomplishes required work on or ahead of schedule	☐	☐	☐	☐	☐	☐	☐
6. PLANNING:	Sets realistic objectives—anticipates and prepares for future requirements—establishes logical priorities	☐	☐	☐	☐	☐	☐	☐
7. FOLLOW-UP:	Maintains control of workloads—allocates resources economically—insures that assignments are completed accurately and timely	☐	☐	☐	☐	☐	☐	☐
8. HUMAN RELATIONS:	Establishes and maintains cordial work climate—promotes harmony and enthusiasm—displays sincere interest in assisting other employees	☐	☐	☐	☐	☐	☐	☐
9. LEADERSHIP:	Sets high standards—provides good managerial example—encourages subordinates to perform efficiently—communicates effectively	☐	☐	☐	☐	☐	☐	☐
10. SUBORDINATE DEVELOPMENT:	Helps subordinates plan career development—grooms potential replacements—gives guidance and counsel	☐	☐	☐	☐	☐	☐	☐

FIGURE 10–9. Management by Objectives Form
Source: State of Illinois, Department of Personnel.

It is common practice for superiors to discuss the formal appraisal results with subordinates during an appraisal interview. Such an interview provides an opportunity for both the evaluator and the subordinate to discuss differences of opinion concerning performance and the causes of and possible solutions for unsatisfactory performance.[18]

COMPENSATION AND EMPLOYEE BENEFITS ▰▰▰▰

A sound compensation program will assist in attracting and retaining employees. Since the compensation administration program affects every member of the organization, it is one of the most important and time-consuming tasks of the human resources department.

All employees—operative workers, technical employees, and managers—want to feel that they are paid fairly compared to other jobholders. To assure that positions requiring the least skill, responsibility, and effort are paid at the lowest levels and those jobs requiring high levels of effort, skill, and responsibility are rewarded accordingly, many firms conduct *job evaluations*. This is a method for determining wage levels for different jobs by comparing jobs on such factors as responsibilities, education, skill requirements, and physical requirements.[19] This comparison process is used in determining the relative worth of a job. Jobs whose relative worths are similar are included in the same pay grade. The U.S. Office of Personnel Management has placed its jobs into eighteen classes on a General Schedule (GS). The pay ranges from $9,339 for a beginning GS-1 employee to a GS-18 maximum salary of $84,157, with annual increases within each pay grade.

Should an organization decide to utilize a *pay range* for each grade or class instead of a single fixed rate, it must also have a plan for determining the bases for employee movement within the range. Some organizations permit step pay increases solely on the basis of time on the job (seniority), while others use the results of performance appraisals to determine whether a person merits a move to a higher step (merit). Some organizations use both seniority and merit in granting pay increases.

Although the terms wage and salary are often used interchangeably, *wage* refers to a method of payment based on a calculation of the number of hours worked or the number of units produced by an employee. *Salary* refers to compensation for white-collar workers such as office workers, professionals, and managers based upon a unit of time such as a week, a month, or a year. Managers—unlike workers receiving wages and nonmanagerial salaried employees—typically do not receive extra compensation for the extra hours they sometimes work.

In addition to base wages or salaries, organizations occasionally develop *incentive* compensation programs designed to reward employees for superior performance. Bonuses and profit-sharing plans are common methods for rewarding employees for above-average output and/or profitability.

Incentive compensation programs can also be used to retain valuable members of the organization. One unusual example of this approach involves a $1-million incentive package developed by a group of wealthy boosters of the University of Alabama in Birmingham in an effort to keep head basketball coach Gene Bartow there. The plan, set up in the form of annuities, will begin paying Bartow at the time of his 1995 retirement. Bartow, whose name is often mentioned whenever a lucrative coaching job

Job evaluation is a comparison of different jobs based on such factors as responsibilities and education, skill, and physical requirements to determine the relative worth of a job.

Wage is a method of payment based on a calculation of the number of hours worked or the number of units produced by an employee.

Salary is compensation for white-collar workers based on a unit of time, such as a week, a month, or a year.

❝ You can dream, create, design and build the most wonderful place in the world, but it requires people to make the dream a reality. ❞

Walt Disney

MANAGEMENT SUCCESSES

IBM

The corporate workplace of the future will probably not differ greatly from conditions already enjoyed by the 400,000 employees of International Business Machines. By 2000 it's expected to be the biggest company on earth, and other firms are likely to adopt its successful methods.

Employees like IBM so much now that fewer than 1% leave by choice every year. Says Victor Heckler, a Chicago consultant: "IBM knows how to pick the people it needs, develop them and motivate them. So they stay, grow in their jobs and become more valuable." Some ways the IBM system works:

Corporate culture. Nobody ever forgets whom he works for or why he's there—or that the company is a stern taskmaster. Promotions are made on merit only, the employees who consistently fail to meet objectives are fired, as are those who run afoul of the 30-page ethics code that covers, for example, company secrets. On the other hand, no one loses his job because of an economic downturn or

personal misfortune, such as illness or marital troubles.

Recognition. It's frequent, direct and tangible. Each year about 25% of IBM's employees earn cash bonuses by, for instance, improving a sales presentation. Salaries, however, are only slightly higher than the industry average.

Equality. In 1958 IBM blurred the distinction between white- and blue-collar work by abolishing hourly wages, and there are no highly visible perks. Among managers, about 14% are women and 10% are minorities. In 1984 36% of all company-wide new hires were women and 20% were minorities.

is vacant, will collect none of the benefits if he leaves UAB before 1990. Should he resign his position after that date, he would receive a specified percentage of the annuity.[20]

FRINGE BENEFITS

Fringe benefits are indirect compensation such as insurance, retirement plans, paid vacations, holidays, and the like.

The total compensation package includes more than the contents of the employee's take-home pay. *Fringe benefits* include such indirect compensation as health and life insurance, retirement benefits, paid vacations and holidays, sick-leave pay, credit unions, recreational programs, and health and safety programs. Such benefits currently cost the organization an additional thirty-five cents for each dollar of direct wages or salaries. Increasingly common fringe benefits for operative employees are dental insurance, employee counseling, legal advice, and prescription drug in-

Education. Managers spend at least 40 hours a year in classrooms improving their management skills. Sample lesson; always finish sentences; don't make people read body language. Several thousand technicians are retrained annually.

Participation. To monitor morale, IBM frequently surveys employee opinion on everything from cafeteria food to the performance of top managers. Executives are encouraged to challenge any business plan they think is ill advised. "Bureaucracy is our enemy," says Walton Burdick, vice president for personnel. "It stifles initiative."

Entrepreneurship. Since 1963 IBM has provided a few extraordinary employees called IBM Fellows with the staff and financial support to pursue their own ideas. One of its first independent business units developed IBM's highly successful personal computer. Now there are 10 of the semiautonomous units.

Responsiveness. Nine-month-a-year jobs are occasionally available in categories such as systems analyst and computer programmer. Staffers nearing retirement can take company-paid courses on such subjects as starting a second career and finding a retirement community. IBM doesn't supply day care, but it does provide a nationwide referral service on where to find day-care centers as well as seed money to develop suitable facilities in areas that lack them. Nor does it allow employees to work at home instead of in the office.

Not surprisingly, the embrace of this beneficent uncle can prove suffocating to some people. A few former employees complain that IBM is too big and too predictable, supportive but not exciting. Since most are hired at entry level, fast trackers are identified early, but late bloomers sometimes not at all. Says ex-IBM manager Robert McGrath, now an executive recruiter who publishes the IBM Alumni Directory, which is sold to recruiters: "I left because even though I felt good about my job, I couldn't make a real difference."

What might the IBM of the year 2000 be like? William Simmons, IBM's long-range planner from 1967 to 1972 and now a consultant, offers a hint: the computer giant will further decentralize so that divisions can act more autonomously and employees feel that they are in charge of their own destinies. Says Simmons: "If any company can achieve that elusive environment in which no one feels left behind, it'll be IBM."

Source: Excerpted from Lani Luciano, "Seeing the Future Work at IBM," *Money*, November 1985, p. 165. © 1985 Time Inc. Reprinted by permission.

surance.[21] Salaried employees at Anheuser-Busch are given two cases of beer each month to take home. Another form of fringe benefit is known as the "executive perk" (for "perquisite"). Georgia-Pacific executives, for example, are assigned corner offices. Adolph Coors officers are given company cars, reserved parking, a club membership, and financial planning services.[22]

A growing number of firms offer their employees a flexible system of cafeteria-style fringe benefit plans. Rather than provide all employees with identical benefits, these plans provide employees with specific dollar amounts for fringe benefits and permit them to select areas of coverage from among a number of alternatives. Such plans recognize the growing number of two-wage-earner households, each of which is likely to receive duplicate family benefits from employers. Under a cafeteria plan, one spouse can choose, for example, family health coverage and the other can choose a subsidized tuition plan. In addition, childless couples and single workers are likely to have different medical and dental coverage, disability insurance, and life insurance needs than single-income homes in which children are present. A single person with no children, for instance, might take little or no life insurance if allowed a choice of benefit options.

PROMOTIONS, TRANSFERS, AND SEPARATIONS

Promotion is movement to a position with higher pay, more responsibility, and added status.

Most people will probably experience promotions, transfers, and separations during their working lives. A *promotion* is a movement to a position with higher pay, more responsibility, and added status. Although promotions are occasionally based on friendship or family connections, they normally are based on more objective criteria. Promotions for both managerial and nonmanagerial positions typically result from three primary factors: (1) merit—appraisal of current and past performance; (2) seniority—length of service; and (3) ability—perceived capacity to perform higher level work.

Transfer is lateral movement to another position that usually does not include a pay increase or added responsibilities.

Transfers are lateral movements to other positions that ordinarily do not include pay increases or added responsibilities. Transfers occur for a number of reasons: to gain broader work experience and avoid overspecialization; to meet changing demands for work skills among departments or work shifts; to accommodate personal needs of the employee; and to correct a mismatch of worker and job.

Separation is resignation, layoff, dismissal, or retirement.

The term *separation* includes resignations, layoffs, dismissals, and retirements. Employees voluntarily leave an organization for a variety of reasons—desire to live in another part of the country, job transfers of spouses, competitive job offers at increased salary, or more challenging work. Layoffs are temporary separations resulting from business slowdowns due to reduced sales, plant conversions, or physical relocation of facilities. Dismissals are separations initiated by the organization, generally as a result of poor performance or flagrant and repeated violations of rules. Dismissals occasionally result from staff reductions and from corporate mergers that result in elimination of duplicate functions.

A major cause of separation is retirement. This type of separation has traditionally been fairly predictable, since most workers retire after a certain number of years on the job or at age sixty-five. However, two factors are contributing to difficulties in predicting the number of retirements: (1) worker concerns about the adequacy of household savings, social security benefits, and private pensions; and (2) changes in federal laws prohibiting mandatory retirement at age sixty-five.

The 1978 amendment to the Age Discrimination in Employment Act of 1967, prohibiting discrimination against workers between forty and seventy, reflects society's acceptance of the sentiments expressed in Figure 10–10: "It's What You Do—Not When You Do It." It also is concrete recognition that the workers of the late 1980s are living longer than

It's What You Do— Not When You Do It

Ted Williams, at age 42, slammed a home run in his last official time at bat.
Mickey Mantle, age 20, hit 23 home runs his first full year in the major leagues.
Golda Meir was 71 when she became Prime Minister of Israel.
William Pitt II was 24 when he became Prime Minister of Great Britain.
George Bernard Shaw was 94 when one of his plays was first produced.
Mozart was just seven when his first composition was published.
Now, how about this? Benjamin Franklin was a newspaper columnist at 16, and a framer of The United States Constitution when he was 81.
You're never too young or too old if you've got talent.
Let's recognize that age has little to do with ability.

© United Technologies Corporation 1979

FIGURE 10–10. Human Resources: Contributing at Every Age
Source: Reprinted by permission of United Technologies.

previous generations of workers and are usually able to perform satisfactory work beyond their sixty-fifth year. However, while 700,000 workers reach age sixty-five in an average year, less than 10 percent of them will choose to continue working. The current trend is toward early rather than postponed retirement, although some 2.8 million members of the U.S. labor force are age 65 or older.

SUMMARY

No organizational resource is more important than people. Organizations recognize the importance of effective human resources by developing human resources (or personnel) departments staffed by specialists in such areas as recruiting, training and management development, wage and salary administration, employee health and safety, industrial relations, and employee services.

The human resources department performs a staff function. It advises and serves the line organization in developing forecasts of employee needs; recruiting and interviewing job candidates; hiring and training; administering wage and salary programs, benefits, and health and safety programs; and evaluating employee performance.

Most firms attempt to fill positions by promotion from within. Only when special skills are needed that are not possessed by the organization's employees will outside sources of employees be considered. External sources include private and public employment agencies, educational institutions, professional and trade journals, newspaper and radio advertisements, union hiring halls, and recommendations of present employees.

The selection process includes an initial screening, a detailed application, and final interviews. In some instances, testing, reference checks, and physical examinations are utilized. The orientation program for newly hired workers is at least partially a responsibility of the human resources department.

Organizations use two types of training programs: on-the-job and off-the-job training. Relatively simple jobs may be learned directly on the job; more complex jobs may be taught through special vestibule schools or through a formal classroom program. Management development programs may take the form of job rotation, use of experienced managers as coaches or mentors, and special programs and classroom seminars.

Although performance appraisals are the responsibility of each employee's immediate superior, formal systems are often administered by the human resources department. Such systems are designed to provide consistent, objective measurement criteria. Such appraisal formats as graphic rating scales, forced distribution scales, and management by objectives are often used.

Compensation is an important factor in every organization. Direct monetary compensation may be in the form of wages, salaries, bonuses, or profit sharing. Indirect forms of compensation—commonly called fringe benefits—include retirement plans, health and life insurance programs, and paid holidays, vacation, and sick leave, among other benefits. These benefit programs are typically administered by the human resources department.

SOLVING THE STOP ACTION CASE

Delta Business Systems

Delta Business Systems president Bryan King, long a believer in the power of incentive compensation, has taken the concept of pay-for-performance to extremes. As a recent *Inc.* article described:

- Secretaries and administrative assistants compete for a $50 award in a monthly contest, judged by managers, for "Most Valuable Associate."

- Field-service technicians can add from 3 percent to 25 percent to their annual salaries by retaining their customer base—renewing maintenance agreements, persuading customers to recondition machines, or giving salespeople leads.

- Each dispatcher can earn up to $40 a month by scheduling preventive maintenance calls.

- Delta's four corporate warehouse workers can divide up to $400 every two months if they function smoothly as a team. They are rewarded for filling orders promptly, filing invoices in time to receive cash discounts, and keeping their facility well stocked, secure, and orderly. . . .

King has built an interconnected web of individual and company-wide bonus programs, along with an employee stock ownership plan. He has tried to structure Delta so that managers' salaries are tied to the profitability of their respective divisions. Service department managers' salaries are also based on customer satisfaction surveys. As the staff has grown and sales have climbed (from $1.9 million in 1979), King has continued to expand the options.

"We take the incentive plans down to the lowest level possible," he says, even if there is no way to measure a performance in terms of revenue. "If we can see how fast someone's canoe moves in the water, we provide an incentive."

Often, of course, the payoff to Delta *is* directly measurable. When King wanted to speed up collection of receivables, for instance, he offered staffers up to $200 a quarter to reduce the outstanding bills. Within six months, total long-term receivables had been cut by 50 percent, a $20,000 annual saving to the business.

"I'm very goal oriented," says collections administrator Carrie Pirrotta, who joined Delta last year partly because she liked the company's incentive system. "The idea of earning a bonus tied to *my* productivity and not to anyone else's appealed to me."

Source: Ellen Kolton, "Paddling for Profits." Reprinted with permission, *Inc.* magazine, March 1985. Copyright © 1985 by Inc. Publishing Company, 38 Commercial Wharf, Boston, MA 02110.

FACT OR FICTION REVEALED

1. Fiction   2. Fact   3. Fact   4. Fiction   5. Fact   6. Fact   7. Fiction

MANAGEMENT TERMS

human resources management	on-the-job training	wage
job analysis	apprenticeship training	salary
job description	vestibule training	fringe benefits
job specification	job rotation	promotion
equal employment opportunity	coaching	transfer
affirmative action program	job evaluation	separation

REVIEW QUESTIONS

1. Identify and briefly explain each of the human resources management functions.

2. Why is the human resources (or personnel) department categorized as staff?

3. Relate the job analysis to job descriptions and job specifications. How does it affect job evaluations?

4. Identify and briefly describe the major federal laws affecting human resources management.

5. List the steps in the recruitment and selection process.

6. Distinguish between training programs and management development programs.

7. Compare and contrast on-the-job and off-the-job training. Under what circumstances should each be used?

8. What is the major advantage of forced distribution scales in a performance appraisal?

9. Under what circumstances should incentive compensation programs be used?

10. Identify and briefly explain the major forms of separation.

PROBLEMS AND EXPERIENTIAL EXERCISES

1. Critically evaluate the various sources of potential job candidates mentioned in the chapter. Recommend a system for generating applicants for technical positions for a Du Pont research facility based on your analysis.

2. "Job quotas should exist for women and minorities." Do you agree? Defend your answer.

3. Recommend a compensation plan for each of the following positions. Justify your recommendations.
   a. Assembly line worker at Nissan's Smyrna, Tennessee, manufacturing facility
   b. Industrial salesperson who calls on clients in a two-state area
   c. Center for Phoenix Suns, professional basketball team
   d. Chief executive officer at Hallmark Cards
   e. Manager of the data processing department at a medium-sized company

4. In previous years, a number of organizations retained older workers on the payroll because even though their work was marginal the firms' mandatory retirement policies would force them to retire at age 65, thereby removing ill will and diminished employee morale that might have resulted from dismissing a long-term employee. In what ways will the Age Discrimination in Employment Act affect policies of the organization's human resources department and practices in the older worker's division or department?

5. Make suggestions for tailoring a fringe benefit program for employees of the following organizations:
   a. Chase Manhattan Bank
   b. Amtrak Passenger Rail System
   c. AT&T
   d. Sears, Roebuck & Co.

MANAGERIAL INCIDENT   When the Mother-to-Be Is a Manager

The growing ranks of female managers have produced a new human resources issue at firm after firm: How to accommodate the special needs of mothers who are also managers or risk the danger of losing them. The issue has become especially acute due to the increased tendency of households to postpone having children. In the past eight years, the number of women over thirty having a child has almost doubled. For highly educated women over thirty who reside in metropolitan areas, the number is even higher. Barbara Boyle Sullivan, president of a New York management-consulting firm specializing in women managers, states: "This is a part of the changing work force of the 1980s. Women now want to have the satisfaction of having a family along with having a good, challenging job. In the past, they chose one or the other. Women who have postponed having children now are finding that their biological clock is running out of time."

The decision to postpone having children means that many of the new mothers have already had a chance to move up the corporate ladder to positions of increased responsibility. Their departure—whether for a few weeks or several months—often is a major disruption for the firm. In addition, motherhood can have a serious effect on their own careers.

A growing number of firms are initiating procedures for reducing the disruptions—both for the individual and for the company. One of the major strengths of the move to flexitime, discussed in the previous chapter, is the flexibility it provides for the manager who is also a mother. As *Business Week* describes the practice:

> Although managers return to work full or part-time shortly after childbirth, some prefer to stay home with the baby for several months—a choice that gives management less trouble than it had expected. Replacing a mother temporarily is no different from replacing a manager who is out for several months because of illness, companies have found. Mothers of children past the infant stage seem to find flexitime a particular boon because it fits in smoothly with the occasional teacher's conference or Little League game.

In many instances, availability of the flexible arrangement means the difference between retaining a valuable employee or losing her to another, more accommodating firm. At Chicago's Continental Illinois National Bank & Trust Co., flexible working hours were necessary to entice Elizabeth M. Carlson, the firm's former manager of personnel systems and research, to return. As *Business Week* explains:

> Carlson, a Phi Beta Kappa and MBA with three children, quit Continental in 1976 because the bank would not be flexible about hours. She joined Bell & Howell Co., which was willing to make adjustments in her schedule, and returned to the bank only after it had changed policy. "When good people like Mrs. Carlson begin to leave because your hours are not compatible with theirs, you get the message—and we did in 1979," says Owen C. Johnson, Jr., Continental Bank's vice-president for corporate personnel services.

Some firms—such as Aetna Life & Casualty—extend special arrangements to fathers as well as mothers.

Questions and Problems

1. Suggest a human resources program designed to deal with the issues raised in this case. Consider both the individual manager and the corporation in the program.

2. Identify methods by which female managers might deal with the impact of childbearing and motherhood on their careers.

Source: Sullivan quotation from Earl C. Gottschalk, Jr., "Firms Are Disrupted by Wave of Pregnancy at the Manager Level," *Wall Street Journal,* 20 July 1981, p. 1. The *Business Week* quotations are from "Working Around Motherhood," *Business Week,* 14 May 1982, p. 188.

11

MANAGING ORGANIZATIONAL DEVELOPMENT AND CHANGE

LEARNING OBJECTIVES

After studying this chapter you should be able to

1. Outline the contemporary environment for organizational change.

2. Explain why people resist change.

3. Describe the processes of individual and organizational change.

4. Understand the concept of organization development: its definition, goals, precedents, emergence, approaches, and current status.

STOP ACTION CASE

Minnesota Mining & Manufacturing

Minnesota Mining & Manufacturing Co. (3M) is proud of its accomplishments in developing new products. In fact 3M offers some 45,000 different products. Some of these products were discovered by accident. Scotchgard resulted from research chemist Patsy Sherman's spilling of a 3M chemical on her tennis shoes. The chemical could not be washed off and kept the shoes from soiling. But most 3M products were developed by extending and modifying existing product lines. These items were then produced and marketed by forty separate product groups, up from twenty a decade earlier.

Minnesota Mining & Manufacturing is a successful company with some $8 billion in sales. It is particularly strong in foreign growth markets. About 34 percent of 3M sales come from overseas. Yet board chairman and chief executive officer, Lewis Lehr, was worried that the company's organizational structure slowed its movement into profitable new markets. The diversified 3M product line and organization worked against overall corporate goals. Vincent Ruane, who heads 3M's electrical products division, put it this way: "Each division took its own little slice of the future. We were becoming too fragmented."

Use the materials in Chapter 11 to design a reorganization plan that would allow 3M to consolidate its product line and at the same time move into nontraditional markets.

3M

All organizations—profit or nonprofit—must change if they are to remain viable. The problems of organizational change and development are among the most important aspects of the organizing function.

Change is an inherent aspect of management. A manager performs the functions of planning, organizing, directing, and controlling in order to accomplish goals. The management job is to move a department or division from point A to point B—to cause change. At Procter and Gamble, success in conducting planned change and increased market share and profitability are the key yardsticks by which management is evaluated.[1]

Change is now so important that experts are struggling to define it, model it, categorize it, and study it just as a zoologist examines animal life or a botanist examines plant life. Entire books are now devoted to the subject of change. *Future Shock* and *Megatrends* are notable examples.

The concluding chapter in Part Three will focus on the changes managers face that affect the whole organization, work groups, and individual employees. The emphasis is on identifying the sources of resistance to change, the techniques to overcome this resistance, the success of these techniques, and some of the precautions a manager must take in dealing with such matters. Resistance to change is normal and should be expected in any organization. In fact, absence of resistance to change can suggest a problem. The role of organization development, or planned interventions into the organization's activities, is also considered in this overall process.

> ❝ The world hates change, yet it is the only thing that has brought progress. ❞
>
> Charles F. Kettering

RESISTANCE TO CHANGE

While it is easier to consider the limitless change processes now occurring, it is important to recognize that change has always been a challenge for virtually every organization. Imagine the changes faced by a colonial merchant, a Civil War era manufacturer, or a firm trying to survive the Great

MANAGEMENT FACT OR FICTION

	FACT	FICTION		FACT	FICTION
1. The most common characteristic of the change process is people's resistance to it.	☐	☐	4. Organization development as we know it today had its precedents in the 1940s.	☐	☐
2. Employee participation has been shown to be an effective technique for dealing with resistance to change within an organization.	☐	☐	5. United Technologies and Texaco were the first firms to initiate organization development programs.	☐	☐
3. Lewin's research suggests that it is impossible to return a brainwashed terrorist hostage to his or her former mental state.	☐	☐	6. Cousin teams are organizational units made up solely of family-related members.	☐	☐

The materials in this chapter will assist you in separating management fact from fiction. Your answers can be checked on page 383.

Your answers can be checked on page 383.

> ❝ The most distinguished hallmark of the American society is and always has been change. ❞
>
> Eric Sevareid

Depression. Change has always been a part of the managerial environment. And the most common characteristic of the change process has been people's resistance to it. There is a natural human tendency to resist change because it forces individuals to adopt new ways of doing something. Psychological discomfort is often associated with having to learn a new method, technique, environment, or strategy.

The following list of reasons has been suggested for why people resist change:[2]

- *Lack of clarity:* Uncertainty resulting from changes that persons do not understand leads to resistance by those affected.

- *Distortion of information:* Workers may sometimes incorrectly estimate the relative importance of information concerning proposed changes or otherwise distort it.

- *Countervailing forces and reward structures:* In some cases employees may perceive that the reasons or forces for change are balanced by reasons *not* to change. In other words the benefits of change are offset by those associated with maintaining the status quo.

- *Levels of participation:* Minimal participation in the decisions surrounding the change usually means greater resistance to change.

- *Pace of change:* Rapid change may also create greater resistance by those involved than would a more gradual change.

A number of studies have investigated the problems of resistance to change. A few of the best-known ones are cited here.

THE BANK WIRING ROOM EXPERIMENT

The Hawthorne research, which will be discussed in detail in Chapter 13, recognized that technology was changing the workplace.[3] In the bank wiring room of Western Electric's Hawthorne plant, experimenters found that workers appeared to behave irrationally. A departmental piece-rate system was used under the assumption that workers would produce more if they were rewarded by increased pay. But this did not occur. Instead, the workers operated as a group to enforce a stable daily output. Anyone who worked harder than this was disciplined by the rest of the group. The same held true for those who did not work fast enough. From an economic standpoint, this seemed irrational.

Resistance to change appears to provide a partial explanation for this phenomenon. The technology of the jobs held by these Western Electric employees had been changing rapidly. These changes required the workers to learn new tasks and often disrupted the arrangement of the group. The researchers concluded that the informal group's action in opposition to the piece-rate pay system was an attempt to resist or control change. By enforcing its norms, the group could maintain the network of friendships developed over a long period of time. It was also possible to sustain a work routine with which the members were familiar and comfortable, reducing their anxieties about the technological changes.

THE COCH AND FRENCH STUDY

Lester Coch and John R. P. French, Jr., published a classic study on resistance to change more than three decades ago.[4] The research dealt with a pajama factory in rural Virginia. The firm used a piece-rate incentive plan that included a compensating bonus to protect a worker against a loss in earnings if a transfer was necessary. Labor relations within the plant were good.

Competitive conditions required that the plant make certain production method changes. The Coch and French research was conducted while these changes were being introduced. Employees being transferred to new jobs were divided into four groups. The groups were closely matched on such factors as efficiency, extensiveness of the change to which they were exposed, and group cohesiveness.

The first set of employees was the control group. Management explained the job changes and new piece rates at a group meeting. The group was told that competitive conditions had necessitated the change, and time was allocated for employee questions. When the second group had a meeting, the situation—and the need for cutting costs—was explained with a dramatic demonstration of product quality and price. Then a group of special operators was designated to assist with the development of the details involved in the change. Later, the new methods and piece rates were introduced at another meeting. The special operators then went on to become trainers for the other employees. The third and fourth groups, which were smaller than the second group, also attended meetings in which the competitive conditions were explained. But this time all of the employees participated in developing the new work situation.

The results were startling. The efficiency ratings of the control group remained essentially the same. Seventeen percent quit within forty days; hostility toward management was noted; and a grievance was filed about the new piece rate. In the second group—the one with representative participation—the employees achieved the plant's standard efficiency rating (the rate at which employees are expected to produce) within fourteen days. No one quit his or her job, and the change was characterized by cooperation. The performance of the special operators was no different from that of the others in the group. The third and fourth groups—those with total participation—exceeded even the record of the limited participation group. No one quit. The workers were cooperative and their efficiency eventually went to 14 percent over what it was prior to the changes.

When the control group showed no progress thirty-two days after the change, the remaining individuals were reassigned within the plant. A second experiment was conducted two-and-a-half months later involving the remaining thirteen members of the control group. The individual transfers from this group were then operating at slightly above standard efficiency in their new jobs. Again, a new job was introduced to the group. This time the total participation method was used. The group went on to exceed the standard efficiency rating and an employee concern over seniority was quickly resolved. The changeover was considered harmonious, and no one left during the first nineteen-day period.

The Coch and French research demonstrated the importance of participation in overcoming resistance to change within an organization. Favorable productivity, minimal turnover, and good employee relations resulted from increased levels of participation in decision making surrounding a job change. While considerable research on this aspect of management has been done since, the Coch and French study remains a classic.[5]

THE PROCESS OF CHANGE

Change may be viewed as a process, for several steps are usually involved. Changes are not instantaneous, although the process may be relatively quick. The process of change may be studied for both individuals and an organization. Figure 11–1 illustrates how the Greyhound organization is in a mode of constant change. Change agents and interventions are vital components of the change process.[6]

CHANGE AGENTS AND INTERVENTIONS

All changes involve a *change agent,* the person who initiates the change.[7] In many cases this can be an outside person such as a consultant, auditor, or outside director. In still other cases, new management can be the change agent. For example, Lewis Lehr's role in the stop-action case was that of a change agent.

Change agent is the person who initiates a change within an organization.

FIGURE 11–1.   The Management of Change Is Important at Greyhound Corporation
Source: Reprinted by permission of The Greyhound Corporation.

"At Greyhound, we believe in renewing our company day by day..."

At Greyhound, we believe a company's life is measured not in years, but in its ability to meet the newly-emerging needs of consumers for different goods and services. This means asking ourselves every day who we are and what we do.

Renewing our company day by day is more than just asking introspective questions, however. It involves a determination to act on the answers! That is why today's Greyhound is a broadly-based, multi-industry corporation which has become a respected name in fields as diverse as capital equipment leasing, bus manufacturing, mortgage insurance, money transfers, food, soap, food service, transportation and other service businesses.

It is also why we are no longer in some 13 other businesses and operations divested over the last two years! Divestitures involving $300 million in assets, $2 billion in annual revenues but only $12 million in profit... a 4% return. The resources realized from those divestitures are now being reinvested where the funds will generate new growth for decades to come.

The bottom line at Greyhound is a realization that we cannot be content with a continuation of things as they are, no matter how satisfactory they may have been in the past. Today, we must turn in the direction of those businesses and activities which hold the promise of long-term growth and renewal, and vigorous new profit potential.

The Greyhound Corporation
A company for the eighties.

One of the best examples of management acting as a change agent is Henry Ford II's assumption of the presidency of Ford Motor Co. in 1945. He was only twenty-eight at the time. Ford's grandfather pioneered assembly line production of automobiles, and his company was the dominant U.S. producer for many years. But General Motors surpassed Ford in the 1920s. Ford continued to slip, and by the mid-1940s the company was in dire circumstances. Although Ford was not expected to be a significant factor in the post-World War II marketplace, within four years of Henry Ford II's assumption of leadership the company was again a profitable entity.[8]

Intervention refers to the changes that are introduced to either individuals or the organization.

An *intervention* refers to the changes that are introduced to either individuals or the organization. Implementing a consultant's proposal for new work rules would be an example of an intervention. Henry Ford II's development of new products and initiation of financing controls were the interventions that helped return Ford to profitability.

THE LEWIN MODEL OF INDIVIDUAL CHANGE

Kurt Lewin produced a generally accepted description of the way individual change occurs.[9] According to Lewin individuals must go through three basic steps in the process of making a successful change: (1) unfreeze; (2) move; and (3) refreeze.

First, an individual has to unfreeze the current situation—say, an existing idea or level of performance. Complacent behavior must be shocked into change. The unfreezing stage involves people's natural resistance to change. The most common reason for failing to make a planned change is that unfreezing has not occurred.

Second, the individual must move to some new behavior or performance level. The change should be seen as desirable from the perspective of the people undergoing change.

"... THE CHINESE SYMBOL FOR CRISES SIGNIFIES BOTH DANGER AND OPPORTUNITY."

Third, the new behavior or level of performance must become the accepted behavior or level of performance. This is Lewin's refreezing stage. The new pattern has to replace the former completely for successful change to take place.

Examples of how Lewin's model might work in contemporary society are suggested in the highly publicized instances of brainwashing reported in the past. Kidnap victims, hostages of terrorists, and prisoners of war have sometimes undergone such profound shock that their normal behavior patterns have been unfrozen, and they have eventually been moved to alternative behavior patterns. Their new behavior is then refrozen to become what the person then views as the norm. While readjustment can be traumatic for these individuals, they can return to their original behavior patterns by again starting the unfreezing–moving–refreezing process. Another illustration is the widely discussed and controversial deprogramming of some former cultists.

MANAGEMENT SUCCESSES

Johnson & Johnson

Consider the process of change at Johnson & Johnson. Long a leading manufacturer of baby products, Johnson & Johnson has now launched a vigorous move into the medical technology business, and this has meant altering a corporate culture that had traditionally been one of the hallmarks of J & J's success. Guided by the wisdom of "the General," Robert Wood Johnson, who ran the company from 1938 to 1963, J & J had always emphasized its commitment, as the corporate credo proclaims, to "the doctors, nurses, patients, to mothers, and all others" who use J & J products. Consequently the firm has been oriented in the direction of production and marketing, and this led to a high degree of decentralization. Johnson & Johnson is not one company; it is 170 businesses, and most of these divisions have their own boards.

The sophisticated medical technology field, however, represents a different type of marketplace. It is a long way from baby shampoo to magnetic-resonance scanners for diagnostic imaging. Johnson & Johnson was smart enough to foresee the revolutionary changes overtaking the health care industry—it has ac-

Johnson & Johnson
FAMILY OF COMPANIES

quired twenty-five mostly high-tech companies since 1980. Now it must adapt to those changes. To begin with, that has meant greater cooperation among the corporate divisions. Medical technology changes fast, and the firm has to react quickly. It also has meant learning a whole new business. Johnson & Johnson has had to discover a completely new system of development and marketing. And, of course, it has had to find the appropriate managerial talent, managerial talent with high-tech expertise. The corporation has now increased the movement of managers between companies by forming corporate-level committees for the express purpose of exchanging information. Johnson & Johnson's top management are proving to be the successful change agents as the firm seeks to conquer the medical technology field.

Source: "Changing a Corporate Culture," *Business Week,* 14 May 1984, p. 130.

THE GREINER MODEL OF ORGANIZATIONAL CHANGE

Larry E. Greiner examined eighteen separate studies dealing with organizational change.[10] His research considered the similarities and differences among instances of successful and unsuccessful change. Greiner's overall observations are as follows:

- Successful change requires a redistribution of power within the existing structure. Greiner noted that successful change was characterized by a greater degree of shared power within the organizational hierarchy.

- This redistribution of power occurs as a result of a "developmental process of change." In other words, it is a sequential process rather than a sudden shift.

THE STAGES OF SUCCESSFUL ORGANIZATIONAL CHANGE

Greiner identified six separate phases common to successful change, shown in Figure 11–2. The following summarizes the activities in each phase of the total development process.

Phase 1: Pressure and Appeal. Successful organizational change usually begins with significant pressure from either (1) an environmental factor

FIGURE 11–2.   Greiner's Stages of Successful Organization Change
Source: Reprinted by permission of the *Harvard Business Review*. Exhibit from Larry E. Greiner, "Patterns of Organization Change," *Harvard Business Review* (May–June 1967). Copyright © 1967 by the President and Fellows of Harvard College; All rights reserved.

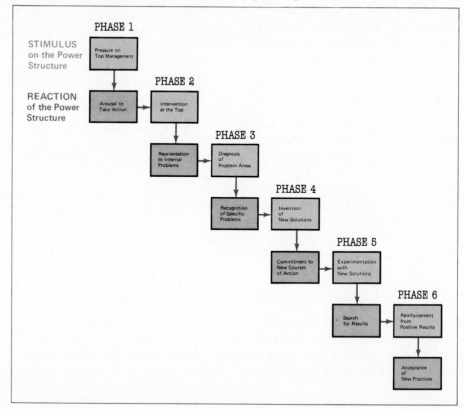

such as falling sales volume or the announcement of a major new competitive product, or (2) an internal event like a strike or cost problem. The need for change is more readily apparent if there are multiple pressures that do not offset each other. Greiner reported that strong pressure was not as noticeable in the cases of unsuccessful change.

Phase 2: Intervention and Reorientation. Since management may rationalize the pressures of Phase I, an outsider is required for effective change to occur. This person should be respected and enter at the top of the organizational hierarchy. Top management is encouraged to review the situation, thereby reorientating management to its internal problems. Management no longer assumes that it knows all of the problems within the organization.

Phase 3: Diagnosis and Recognition. In the third phase of successful change, the entire organization becomes involved in seeking out problems and their causes. A shared approach between superiors and subordinates is common in this stage. The decision-making process has been broadened as management shows its willingness to recognize tough problems and to change. Greiner noted that this step was always avoided in the studies dealing with unsuccessful change. The first three phases in Greiner's model are similar to the unfreezing stage in the Lewin model discussed earlier.

Phase 4: Invention and Commitment. With the active assistance of the outsider, the firm moves toward creative solutions to the problems that have been identified. The shared approach again predominates in this phase. Once solutions are developed, commitment to the new course of action is obtained. Greiner notes that none of the unsuccessful changes ever reached this stage in the development process.

Phase 5: Experimental Search. Greiner refers to this stage as a reality-testing phase where various minor decisions are implemented throughout the organization. It is a stage in which tentative decisions and the shared power concept used in their development are tested before major changes are installed. Phases 4 and 5 of Greiner's model are similar to the moving stage in Lewin's model.

Phase 6: Reinforcement and Acceptance. The positive reports coming from the experiments in Phase 5 add reinforcement to the change process. More problems are being resolved by employees, and the shared power concept becomes a standard part of the organization. There has been a general reorientation in the decision-making structure of the entity undergoing change. This phase can be compared to Lewin's refreezing stage.

> ❝ The only things that evolve by themselves in an organization are disorder, friction, and malperformance. ❞
>
> Peter Drucker

ORGANIZATION DEVELOPMENT ▬▬▬▬▬

Organization development is a crucial subject in any organization. It is a logical outcome of attempts to manage change and the resistance to it. Organization development involves a comprehensive and continuing management program to improve the organization.

Organization development (OD) is an effort by management to increase organization effectiveness by planned intervention in the organization's processes.

Organization development (OD) has been defined as "an effort (1) planned, (2) organization-wide, and (3) managed from the top, to (4) increase organization effectiveness and health through (5) planned interventions in the organization's 'processes' using behavioral-science knowledge."

Development and maintenance of an effective, healthy organization require that specific operational goals be met: (1) move toward an organizational structure based on the tasks to be performed rather than vice versa; (2) build feedback procedures into the organization; (3) reduce dysfunctional competition between separate units of the organization; (4) bring organizational conflicts into the open so they can be resolved; and, (5) base decision making on the best source of information rather than on organizational role and its related authority.[11]

PRECEDENTS FOR ORGANIZATION DEVELOPMENT

Organization development as it is known today is the result of an evolutionary process that began in the 1940s. Three major precedents for OD were: (1) laboratory training; (2) survey research and feedback; and (3) Kurt Lewin's work.[12]

Laboratory training refers to the use of unstructured small group discussions to induce interactions that will produce behavior change in the participants.

Laboratory training refers to the use of unstructured, small group discussions to induce interactions that will produce behavior change in the participants. The concept is usually dated from a 1946 workshop held in New Britain, Connecticut, in which Kurt Lewin and others were involved.[13]

These initial efforts later developed into T-groups and sensitivity training.[14] T-groups consisted of executives undergoing a laboratory training experience. *Sensitivity training* refers to a process of group dynamics that influences a T-group participant's behavior.

Sensitivity training is a process of group dynamics that influences a T-group participant's behavior.

Sensitivity training's purpose is to make a manager more sensitive to the effects his or her behavior has on others. This is often done by placing the manager in a group of strangers in some off-the-job, relaxed place, such as a lodge. The open, honest feedback the individual receives from other members of the group is expected to unfreeze the manager's old attitudes, change them, and refreeze them into more sensitive ones. The manager should then be more able to go back to the job and use open communication and participatory management techniques.

The laboratory approach has been criticized for lack of results. It may change attitudes temporarily, but, once back on the job, managers tend to slide into previous behavior patterns. Some blame this tendency on the lack of reinforcement from others in the firm who have not had the training. Regardless of its mixed record in actual application, laboratory training was an important step toward modern organization development.

Survey research and feedback refers to action research involving attitude surveys and the resulting feedback to employees. A workshop format is commonly used in the feedback phase. This technique was developed at MIT's Research Center for Group Dynamics, which Kurt Lewin had organized in 1945. After his death in 1947, it was moved to the University of Michigan, where it became part of what is now the Institute for Social Research.[15]

Lewin's work in applying behavioral science to management problems was an important aspect in the evolution of organization development. He made major contributions to both its laboratory training and survey research and feedback precedents.[16]

Survey research and feedback refers to action research involving attitude surveys and the resulting feedback to employees.

THE EMERGENCE OF THE OD CONCEPT

Union Carbide and Esso were the first firms to launch organization development programs in the late 1950s.[17] Union Carbide, with the assistance of Douglas McGregor, formed an internal consulting group that counseled other managers. Esso (now Exxon) also began conducting rudimentary OD activities with the assistance of Robert Blake, who with Jane Mouton had begun work at the University of Texas on what was to become known as the Managerial Grid®, one of contemporary organization development's most successful techniques (see the section on the Managerial Grid® that follows). John Paul Jones, Birny Mason, Jr., and Herbert Shepard were the executives at the two pioneering firms who were most closely identified with this work.

French and Bell describe the emergence of organization development in the following paragraph:

> Shepard, Blake, McGregor, and others clearly were trying to build on the insights and learnings of laboratory training toward more linkage with and impact on the problems and dynamics of ongoing organizations . . . in the history of OD, we see both external consultants and internal staff departments departing from traditional roles and collaborating in quite a new approach to organization improvement.

CONTEMPORARY APPROACHES TO ORGANIZATION DEVELOPMENT

Many of the current OD techniques are offshoots of the earlier work cited here. A partial list of these approaches includes the Managerial Grid®, MBO, job enrichment/job enlargement, and team building. Although several of the approaches are discussed in chapters dealing with such subjects as objective setting, motivation, and leadership, they are also important topics in organization development.

The Managerial Grid®. The Managerial Grid®, which was developed by Robert R. Blake and Jane S. Mouton, has become one of the most popular concepts in modern organization development.[18] The Managerial Grid® has been used as the approach to a firm's comprehensive organization development program. It has also been presented in a book suitable for self-study.[19]

Blake and Mouton argue that managerial behavior is a function of two variables: concern for people and concern for production. The relative degree of concern, rather than the real outcomes of such orientations, is the important factor. The concern for people is shown on the vertical axis and the concern for production on the horizontal axis of Figure 11–3.

FIGURE 11–3.   The Managerial Grid®

Source: Reprinted by permission of the *Harvard Business Review.* Exhibit from Robert R. Blake, Jane S. Mouton, Louis B. Barnes, and Larry E. Greiner, "Breakthrough in Organization Development," *Harvard Business Review* (November–December 1964). Copyright © 1964 by the President and Fellows of Harvard College; All rights reserved.

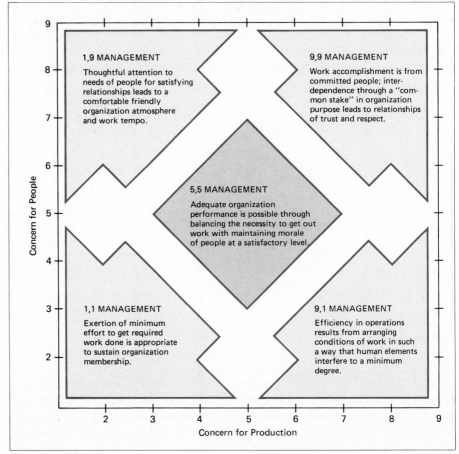

1,9 MANAGEMENT
Thoughtful attention to needs of people for satisfying relationships leads to a comfortable friendly organization atmosphere and work tempo.

9,9 MANAGEMENT
Work accomplishment is from committed people; interdependence through a "common stake" in organization purpose leads to relationships of trust and respect.

5,5 MANAGEMENT
Adequate organization performance is possible through balancing the necessity to get out work with maintaining morale of people at a satisfactory level.

1,1 MANAGEMENT
Exertion of minimum effort to get required work done is appropriate to sustain organization membership.

9,1 MANAGEMENT
Efficiency in operations results from arranging conditions of work in such a way that human elements interfere to a minimum degree.

Concern for People

Concern for Production

Each axis has a scale ranging from 1 to 9, with the higher numbers indicating greater concern for that specific variable. The Managerial Grid® that is developed has five management styles. The least desirable score is a 1,1 manager who is not concerned with either production or people. A 9,1 manager is very production-oriented but has minimal concern for people. The reverse is true of the 1,9 style. The 5,5 manager has a "middle-of-the-road" style. The most desirable leadership style is 9,9, where there is a maximum concern for both people and production.

The objective of the Managerial Grid® is to move the organizational climate and the people involved toward a 9,9 style. Blake and Mouton have developed a six-phase program that can be implemented within an organization. It includes laboratory seminar training, team development, intergroup development, organizational goal setting, goal attainment, and stabilization. Managers are first required to identify their current style, then work toward a 9,9 approach. Managers begin by working on simulated problems. Later, they work on actual problems in their departments and eventually with people from other departments. The emphasis is on getting the manager to change to new styles, work on organizational rather than personal problems (as is often the case with sensitivity training), and gain the support of others throughout the firm who are undergoing similar development.

MBO Programs. A management by objectives (MBO) program is usually thought of as a planning and evaluative technique (see Chapters 5 and 10). But it can also be important to organization development. For instance, MBO can be an extremely useful device for getting executives to move toward a more participatory management style.

Most management by objectives programs are organization-wide. Top managers are supposed to set their operating objectives, to be followed by meetings with the second level of managers in order to set their goals. These managers are then to meet with *their* subordinates to help set their goals, and so on down the line to the lowest level. In this way every level is linked with every other level. Short-run objectives should mesh with departmental goals, which should mesh with individual goals. The chances are increased that the organization will work as a coordinated whole, even in the face of change.

Job Enrichment/Job Enlargement. Many managers find that jobs that were acceptable to employees just a few years ago are no longer satisfactory. Boredom on the job, sometimes called the blue-collar blues, is a type of change affecting all kinds of workers. Once their basic needs are satisfied, experienced workers begin to expect more out of their jobs; they want their jobs to be more challenging, expressive, and fulfilling.

Managers often find that newer employees are younger, better educated, more inquisitive, and less financially dependent. This not only makes them more demanding, but puts them in a strong bargaining position. From the manager's viewpoint, this is a dramatic change from the attitude of previous employees.

What can a manager do about this kind of change? One solution is simply not to put people into jobs that are too simple for them. Employees who are unhappy with dull, repetitive jobs may increase the costs of labor by absenteeism, poor productivity, turnover, or substance abuse problems. This is one of the major reasons firms have sought ways to automate many such jobs. Another approach to solving this problem of high expectations is just the opposite of automation. If a job is too simple, why not make it more complicated—as it might have been years ago?

Suppose that an assembly line worker merely fastens the seats onto the frames of ten-speed bicycles. One worker assembles the handlebars and the next person down the line connects the gearshift mechanism. Each of them does this same job over and over again. One way to complicate their work would be to let each do all three operations. In other words, each worker would walk along the line fastening the seat, assembling the handlebars, and connecting the gearshifts. Rearranging jobs to increase their complexity is known as *job enlargement.*

Job enlargement is the rearrangement of jobs to increase their complexity.

Job enrichment is a rearrangement of jobs in order to get employee involvement in job-oriented decisions.

Jobs can be rearranged by a process called *job enrichment,* whereby the employee is involved in some job-related decisions. Take the job of fastening the seat to the ten-speed bicycle frame. When this job was designed, all kinds of decisions were made about the color and style of seats to be put on, as well as the types of tools and work methods to be used in assembly. The assembly worker simply does what others have decided. Job enrichment would occur if he or she were involved in making some of these choices as part of the job.

Both job enlargement and job enrichment are attempts to add variety and challenge to jobs, bringing them into line with employees' expectations. Both have been used in a wide range of occupations from assembly line work to management. In effect, increasing workers' involvement in decision making through participatory leadership practices is job enrichment. In many cases these improvements lead to increased motivation and decreased costs due to higher job satisfaction.

There are important limitations to rearranging jobs. For example, the costs of altering assembly line operations can exceed the savings resulting from more satisfied workers.

Another limitation has to do with human nature. Take the example of the ten-speed bicycles again. How long would it be before the workers found doing even all three operations boring? Could the job be enlarged again? College professors, doctors, lawyers, and others have been known to find their jobs boring, often quitting to go into new careers. There may be no amount of job enlargement or enrichment that can provide lasting satisfaction. It should be noted that job enrichment and job enlargement are factors in various phases of management. They could just as well have been discussed in the chapters on motivation, production, and the like.

THE MANAGER'S BOOKSHELF

Further Up the Organization, by Robert Townsend

Robert Townsend's *Up the Organization* was an irreverent look at traditional organizational practices, but its crazy (and witty) advice had to be taken seriously since the author was the guy who turned money-losing Avis Rent-A-Car into trying-harder No. 2. Now Townsend has updated this successful book, and his new, revised, and expanded version, *Further Up the Organization,* (Knopf, 1984) includes some pithy advice for entrepreneurs:

Have you made your cash forecast? You think it's pretty conservative? You've allowed for Murphy's Law? Right. Now add six months on the front end before your first dollar of revenue comes in. Deduct 20 percent from your revenue estimates and add 20 percent to your expense estimates. If you're lucky, you may make this.

This new forecast means you'll have to raise several times as much money as you thought, which brings us to investors. Have as few as you can. If you have to go up to a couple of dozen in a Subchapter S corporation, for example, have them elect a spokesman who will be your only point of contact with the investors. Persuade them that your chances (and theirs) of success are greatly increased if you hold an all-day "Howedoin?" meeting with your spokesman (or with the whole group) once a quarter, not more frequently. It takes three precious days away from your business for one of these meetings: one to get ready, one to do it, and one to get over it.

Stay as small as you can. Work out of your home as long as you can. Then your garage. Avoid any expensive ornaments like offices, furniture, or cars designed to impress the public or your friends. The only things you want to be impressive are your product or service, your financial statements, and the smiles on the faces of your customers.

If your problem is to keep your share of the market below 55 percent and your operating profit margin below 20 percent, then you're an oligopolist and can afford to act like one. But I'm afraid you'll be like the poor lady who thought all she had to do to become an opera singer was to drink lots of heavy cream—you'll be confusing fat with muscle.

Team Building.[20] The most popular OD approach in contemporary management is team building. The basic assumption is that various types of teams exist within any organization and that such teams are the vehicles for task accomplishment. Improving the team means better performance by the organization.

Team building is "a process of diagnosing and improving the effectiveness of a work group with particular attention to work procedures and interpersonal relationships within it, especially the role of the leader in relation to other group members." Task performance and human processes are both considered important in a team-building effort.

Team building is a process designed to improve the effectiveness of a work group with emphasis on work procedures and interpersonal relationships.

Different types of teams exist within organizations. These may include family teams, cousin teams, project teams, and startup teams. Organizations have *family teams,* or functional work groups like a design department. *Cousin teams* are groups of peers such as all of the district sales managers. *Project teams* put together people from several different departments to accomplish some specific task. *Startup teams* are groups that are charged with introducing some new entity or activity.

The typical pattern for team building is for an OD consultant to interview group members about issues they perceive as blocking team goal accomplishment. Then an off-site meeting is held, usually lasting three to five days. The meeting is devoted to considering the issues emanating from the interviews on a priority order basis. The OD consultant provides the framework for a frank discussion of all issues that might hinder team performance. The group's leader must be involved in these sessions. Finally, action steps are agreed upon and assigned to a group member. Usually a follow-up procedure is also established.

THE CURRENT STATUS OF ORGANIZATION DEVELOPMENT

Organization development programs have been increasingly accepted in American industry. A wide variety of firms have or are currently initiating such programs. As more and more managers have become aware of the value of organization development, it appears likely that this effort will expand and become further refined in the future.

SUMMARY

Change is an inherent part of any organization. And the contemporary environment, with its rapid pace of change, is one of the most challenging that has ever faced management. Understanding change is an important part of the organizing function.

Resistance to change is commonplace. One authority suggested five reasons why people resist change: (1) lack of clarity, (2) distortion of information, (3) countervailing forces and reward structures, (4) levels of participation, and (5) pace of change. The classic Coch and French study concluded that participation is a valuable tool in overcoming resistance to change.

A change agent is a person who initiates a change; an intervention refers to the changes that are introduced to either individuals or organizations. Lewin's concept of the three basic steps in the individual change process—unfreeze, move, refreeze—is a widely accepted model of this type of change. By contrast, Greiner's model of organizational change is based on the premises that successful change requires increased shared power within an organization and that it occurs in a sequential process.

Organization development can be defined as "an effort (1) planned, (2) organization-wide, and (3) managed from the top, to (4) increase organization effectiveness and health through (5) planned interventions in the organization's 'processes' using behavioral science knowledge." Three precedents to organization development have been identified: laboratory training, survey research and feedback, and Kurt Lewin's work. Contemporary approaches to organization development include the Managerial Grid®, MBO, job enrichment/job enlargement, and team building.

SOLVING THE STOP ACTION CASE	**Minnesota Mining & Manufacturing**

Lehr's solution was to reorganize 3M into four market groups: electronics and information technologies; graphics; industrial and consumer services; and life sciences and health care products and services. Lehr's purpose was to adjust for a decline in some traditional markets like office copiers. The changes were introduced to the organization through a series of meetings in which Lehr commented: ". . . we are changing to remain manageable for the future."

The board chairman then convinced a meeting of directors and top management at a Minnesota lodge. The group continued to plot the company's future development, deciding that an improved product research program was necessary. Concern was expressed over the fact that 3M was weak in computers and communications. Since then 3M has made some acquisitions in the communications field.

Source: This case is based on and quotes are from Maurice Bamfather, "Can 3M Find Happiness in the 1980s?" *Forbes,* 1 March 1982, pp. 112-116. Updated May 22, 1985 by Donald A. Fischer of 3M.

FACT OR FICTION REVEALED

1. Fact   2. Fact   3. Fiction   4. Fact   5. Fiction   6. Fiction

MANAGEMENT TERMS

change agent	**laboratory training**	**job enlargement**
intervention	**sensitivity training**	**job enrichment**
organization development (OD)	**survey research and feedback**	**team building**

REVIEW QUESTIONS

1. Define the following terms: (a) change agent (b) intervention (c) organization development (d) laboratory testing (e) T-groups (f) sensitivity training (g) survey research and feedback (h) job enlargement (i) job enrichment (j) team building.

2. Why do people resist change?

3. What conclusions can be reached about the bank wiring room experiment at Western Electric's Hawthorne plant?

4. Summarize the findings of the Coch and French study.

5. Describe the Kurt Lewin model of change.

6. Explain the Greiner model of organizational change.

7. Identify the precedents to organization development.

8. Describe the Managerial Grid®.

9. Differentiate between job enrichment and job enlargement.

10. What is meant by team building?

PROBLEMS AND EXPERIENTIAL EXERCISES

1. Morgan Guaranty Trust is known for its collegial corporate culture. One of the ways the bank builds this ethic is through its orientation of new employees in its rigorous training program. One trainee observed: "You work every night until 2 A.M. on your own material, and then you help others." Relate Morgan Guaranty Trust's training program to Lewin's model of individual change.

2. Stora Kopparbergs Bergslags AB of Falun, Sweden, may be the oldest company in the world. The firm, which began with a copper mine and is now into paper, pulp, and power, is believed to have begun sometime near the year 1000. However, Stora Kopparbergs admits that its records only go back to 1288.

    Outline the major problems an organization development consultant might expect to encounter at Stora Kopparbergs Bergslags AB.

3. Identify a firm that has undertaken an organization development program. Examples are sometimes reported in the business press, such as *Business Week, Forbes, Fortune,* or *Dun's Review.* Interview some of the individuals involved and prepare a paper on this experience.

4. Choose an organization or work group to which you belong. Identify the organization development needs that you see existing in this entity. How would you approach these issues?

5. Recall the last time you changed your opinion about some matter, idea, or person. Relate this experience to the Lewin model of individual change.

MANAGERIAL INCIDENT: Guidelines for Change at Volvo

Pehr G. Gyllenhammar, Volvo's president, has offered these guidelines based on the experiences of the Swedish auto maker.

Volvo's Guidelines. Our experiences with change in our various plants have produced a few rules of thumb that may be helpful to others:

- Each unit should be free to develop individually, without detailed control or interference from headquarters.

- An active and positive top management attitude toward change is a prerequisite

for positive results. However, when this attitude turns into a drive from above to install programs, projects, and plans, management tends to fail.

- Headquarters is most effective when its role is sanctioning investments for new approaches and challenging local managers to take more radical initiatives and risks.

- Our positive achievements seem related to the extent our managers understand that the change process will sooner or later affect several organizational levels regardless of where it started.

- We encounter problems if we formalize change and request targets, minutes, and figures too early. Change requires time and freedom of action. When people view it as a continuing search-and-learning process of their own, the chances of lasting effects are increased.

- The initiative for change should be a line responsibility, with specialists as supporters rather than initiators. Changes specialists initiate seldom have lasting effects. They can, however, act as sounding boards and catalysts, carrying know-how from one place to another.

- Steering committee members should be the strongest possible people, sharing commitment to change.

- The fastest way to get ideas flowing seems to be to set up discussion groups in each working area. A working area in this sense (and in a group-working sense) should probably contain fewer than twenty-five people.

- Groups that have money to spend on their own facilities and a mandate to list their own problems seem to achieve cohesion and cooperation most rapidly. It need not cost the corporation more money to apportion facilities or safety budgets to the groups themselves than to experts.

- A new plant, a new product, or a new machine is an opportunity to think about new working patterns.

- An investment in one new facility or one group area often results in spon-

taneous changes in related facilities or groups. These can be encouraged by alert managers.

- Most factories have a number of tasks that need not be done as assembly lines. Once a few have been found and changed, others will reveal themselves.

- So that the change suggestions will emerge from inside, changes of work organization must be integrated with a structure of employee consultation.

- Progress seems to be fastest when a factory or company starts by forming a joint management and union steering committee to look at its own problems.

- Some of the most effective changes in work organization at Volvo have taken place naturally, without projects, without scientific sophistication, without being reported to anybody. Those changes occur simply because people are keen and interested. Finding ways to encourage such changes is management's challenge.

Questions and Problems

1. Would the Volvo guidelines be applicable in United States industry?

2. Relate Gyllenhammar's suggestions to the material in this chapter.

Source: Reprinted from Pehr G. Gyllenhammar, *People at Work* (Reading, Mass.: Addison-Wesley, 1977), pp. 124-126. Copyright © 1977, Addison-Wesley Publishing Company, Inc. Reprinted with permission.

CASES FOR PART THREE

CASE   Freida Mae Jones
5

Freida Mae Jones was born in her grandmother's Georgia farmhouse on June 1, 1949. She was the sixth of George and Ella Jones' ten children. Mr. and Mrs. Jones moved to New York City when Freida was four because they felt that the educational and career opportunities for their children would be better in the North. With the help of some cousins, they settled in a five-room apartment in the Bronx. George worked as a janitor at Lincoln Memorial Hospital, and Ella was a part-time housekeeper in a nearby neighborhood. George and Ella were conservative, strict parents. They kept a close watch on their children's activities and demanded they be home by a certain hour. The Joneses believed that because they were black, the children would have to perform and behave better than their peers to be successful. They believed that their children's education would be the most important factor in their success as adults.

Freida entered Memorial High School, a racially integrated public school, in September 1963. Seventy percent of the student body was caucasian, 20 percent black, and 10 percent hispanic. About 60 percent of the graduates went on to college. Of this 60 percent, 4 percent were black and hispanic and all were male. In the middle of her senior year, Freida was the top student in her class. Following school regulations, Freida met with her guidance counselor to discuss her plans upon graduation. The counselor advised her to consider training in a "practical" field such as housekeeping, cooking, or sewing, so that she could find a job.

George and Ella Jones were furious when Freida told them what the counselor had advised. Ella said, "Don't they see what they are doing. Freida is the top-rated student in her whole class and they are telling her to become a manual worker. She showed that she has a fine mind and can work better than any of her classmates and still she is told not to become anybody in this world. It's really not any different in the North than back home in Georgia, except that they don't try to hide it down South. They want her to throw away her fine mind because she is a black girl and not a white boy. I'm going to go up to her school tomorrow and talk to the principal."

As a result of Mrs. Jones' visit to the principal, Freida was assisted in applying to ten Eastern colleges, each of which offered her full scholarships. In September 1966, Freida entered Werbley College, an exclusive private women's college in Massachusetts. In 1970, Freida graduated summa cum laude in history. She decided to return to New York to teach grade school in the city's public school system. Freida was unable to obtain a full-time position, so she substituted. She also enrolled as a part-time student in Columbia University's Graduate School of Education. In 1975 she had attained her Master of Arts degree in Teaching from Columbia but could not find a permanent teaching job. New York City was laying off teachers and had instituted a hiring freeze because of the city's financial problems.

Feeling frustrated about her future as a teacher, Freida decided to get an MBA. She thought that there was more opportunity in business than in education. Churchill Business School, a small, prestigious school located in upstate New York, accepted Freida into its MBA program.

Freida completed her MBA in 1977 and accepted an entry-level position at the Industrial World Bank of Boston in a fast-track management development program. The three-year program introduced her to all facets of bank operations, from telling to loan training and operations management. She was rotated to branch offices throughout New England. After completing the program she became an assistant manager for branch operations in the West Springfield branch office.

During her second year in the program, Freida had met James Walker, a black doctoral student in business administration at the University of Massachusetts. Her assignment to West Springfield precipitated their decision to get married. They originally anticipated that they would marry when James finished his doctorate and could move to Boston. Instead, they decided he would pursue a job in the Springfield-Hartford area.

Freida was not only the first black but also the first woman to hold an executive position in the West Springfield branch office. Throughout the training program Freida felt somewhat uneasy although she did very well. There were six other blacks in the program, five men and one woman, and she found support and comfort in sharing her feelings with them. The group spent much of their free time together. Freida had hoped that she would be located near one or more of the group when she went out into the "real world." She felt that although she was able to share her feelings about work with James, he did not have the full appreciation or understanding of her coworkers. However, the nearest group member was located one hundred miles away.

Freida's boss in Springfield was Stan Luboda, a fifty-five-year-old native New Englander. Freida felt that he treated her differently than he did the other trainees. He always tried to help her and took a lot of time (too much, according to Freida) explaining things to her. Freida felt that he was treating her like a child and not like an intelligent and able professional.

"I'm really getting frustrated and angry about what is happening at the bank," Freida said to her husband. "The people don't even realize it, but their prejudice comes through all the time. I feel as if I have to fight all the time just to start off even. Luboda gives Paul Cohen more responsibility than me and we both started at the same time, with the same amount of training. He's meeting customers alone and Luboda has accompanied me to each meeting I've had with a customer."

"I run into the same thing at school," said James. "The people don't even know that they are doing it. The other day I met with a professor on my dissertation committee. I've known and worked with him for over three years. He said he wanted to talk with me about a memo he had received. I asked him what it was about and he said that the records office wanted to know about my absence during the spring semester. He said that I had to sign some forms. He had me confused with Martin Jordan, another black student. Then he realized that it wasn't me, but Jordan he wanted. All I could think was that we all must look alike to him. I was angry. Maybe it was an honest mistake on his part, but whenever something like that happens, and it happens often, it gets me really angry."

"Something like that happened to me," said Freida. "I was using the copy machine, and Luboda's secretary was talking to someone in the hall. She had just gotten a haircut and was saying that her hair was now like Frei-

(Continued on next page.)

da's—short and kinky—and that she would have to talk to me about how to take care of it. Luckily, my back was to her. I bit my lip and went on with my business. Maybe she was trying to be cute, because I know she saw me standing there, but comments like that are not cute, they are racist."

"I don't know what to do," said James. "I try to keep things in perspective. Unless people interfere with my progress, I try to let it slide. I only have so much energy and it doesn't make sense to waste it on people who don't matter. But that doesn't make it any easier to function in a racist environment. People don't realize that they are being racist. But a lot of times their expectations of black people or women, or whatever, are different because of skin color or gender. They expect you to be different, although if you were to ask them they would say that they don't. In fact, they would be highly offended if you implied that they were racist or sexist. They don't see themselves that way."

"Luboda is interfering with my progress," said Freida. "The kinds of experiences I have now will have a direct effect on my career advancement. If decisions are being made because I am black or a woman, then they are racially and sexually biased. It's the same kind of attitude that the guidance counselor had when I was in high school, although not as blatant."

In September 1980, Freida decided to speak to Luboda about his treatment of her. She met with him in his office. "Mr. Luboda, there is something that I would like to discuss with you, and I feel a little uncomfortable because I'm not sure how you will respond to what I am going to say."

"I want you to feel that you can trust me," said Luboda. "I am anxious to help you in any way I can."

"I feel that you treat me differently than you treat the other people around here," said

Freida. "I feel that you are overcautious with me, that you always try to help me, and never let me do anything on my own."

"I always try to help the new people around here," answered Luboda. "I'm not treating you any differently than I treat any other person. I think that you are being a little too sensitive. Do you think that I treat you differently because you are black?"

"The thought had occurred to me," said Freida. "Paul Cohen started here the same time that I did and he has much more responsibility than I do." (Cohen was already handling accounts on his own, while Freida had not yet been given that responsibility.)

"Freida, I know that you are not a naive person," said Luboda. "You know the way the world works. There are some things which need to be taken more slowly than others. There are some assignments for which Cohen has been given more responsibility than you, and there are some assignments for which you are given more responsibility than Cohen. I try to put you where you do the most good."

"What you are saying is that Cohen gets the more visible, customer contact assignments and I get the behind-the-scenes running of the operations assignments," said Freida. "I'm not naive, but I'm also not stupid either. Your decisions are unfair. Cohen's career will advance more quickly than mine because of the assignments that he gets."

"Freida, that is not true," said Luboda. "Your career will not be hurt because you are getting different responsibilities than Cohen. You both need the different kinds of experiences you are getting. And you have to face the reality of the banking business. We are in a conservative business. When we speak to customers we need to gain their confidence, and we put the best people for the job in the positions to achieve that end. If we don't get their confidence they can go down the street to our competitors and do business with them. Their services are no different than ours. It's a competitive business in which you need every edge you have. It's going to take time for people to change some of their attitudes about whom they borrow money from or where they put their money. I can't change the way people feel. I am running a business, but believe me I won't make any decisions that are detrimental to you or to the bank. There is an important place for you here at the bank. Remember, you have to use your skills to the best advantage of the bank as well as your career."

"So what you are saying is that all things being equal, except my gender and my race, that Cohen will get different treatment than me in terms of assignments," said Freida.

"You're making it sound like I am making a racist and sexist decision," said Luboda. "I'm making a business decision utilizing the resources at my disposal and the market situation in which I must operate. You know exactly what I am talking about. What would you do if you were in my position?"

QUESTIONS

1. How should Jones respond to Luboda?

2. Do you think Luboda is being sexist and/or racist toward Jones? If so, what should she do about this situation? If not, what should Luboda do to further the objectives of both Jones and the bank?

Source: Reprinted from the *Journal of Management Case Studies* (Spring 1985). © Martin R. Moser, 1985.

All names in this article are fictitious.
Address reprint requests to Martin R. Moser, Ph.D., Assistant Professor of Management, Graduate School of Management, Clark University, 950 Main Street, Worcester, MA 01610.

CASE 6   National Insurance Co.

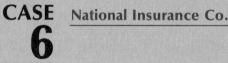

A PROBLEM OF ORGANIZATIONAL CHANGE

For nearly thirty years, the National Insurance Co. had operated their Investment Division as shown in the organizational chart in Exhibit 1.

Aaron Jackson, executive vice-president for investments, was responsible for all company investments, including mortgage loans, securities, and the small amount of company-owned real estate. In the preceding ten years, National had significantly increased its sales of large group insurance policies, and was administering several large trust funds, such as state teachers' retirement funds. This increase had resulted in inflows of great sums of money, which had to be invested, in accordance with various legal and fiduciary restrictions, in treasury bills, bonds, other securities, and real estate. Also, top management had decided to decrease its involvement with residential mortgages because of their relatively low yields in relation to the costs of processing and servicing them. It now appeared that the commercial loans and real estate were more promising investment alternatives.

This case was prepared by Professors Thomas R. Miller and James M. Todd, Memphis State University. The case is disguised.

(*Continued on next page.*)

THE NEED FOR CHANGE

Two major problems had developed with the existing organization given the changing needs of the Investment Division. Mr. Jackson was concerned that he had too many people reporting directly to him. His day-to-day involvement with the Securities Department was rather extensive, as he had formerly headed up this department and had maintained a close association with it in his current position. He felt that he could not "keep up" with the operations under him. Furthermore, with the deemphasis on residential loans, there were now too many employees in the Residential Loan Department with not enough work to do, both at the headquarters level in Chicago and at the field-level offices in the smaller cities.

THE NEW ORGANIZATIONAL STRUCTURE

In an effort to deal with the changing demands on the Investment Division, Mr. Jackson appointed a committee to conduct a study of the current organization and submit its findings and recommendations to him for submission to the Board of Directors. Six months later the organization plan in Exhibit 2 was recommended to and then later approved by the board for implementation early in the following year.

Under the reorganization plan, there was to be a change from three vice-presidents reporting on mortgage loans to one senior vice-president in charge of all mortgages. This made it necessary to consolidate the three mortgage departments into one. With the increased activity in real estate investment, a new real estate section was to be placed under the senior vice-president.

Early in January the management team of the Investment Division, including the field managers, were called to a meeting in Chi-cago. This had been billed as the announcement of the reorganization of the Investment Division. In presenting the restructure, the executive vice-president for investments stated that there were two major reasons for the organizational change: (1) There had been too many people reporting directly to him, and (2) the investment market today made it necessary to have an organization that was fluid enough to shift its efforts to the most desirable investment opportunities. He explained that the reorganization would require training and recycling of some employees in order for them to meet their new responsibilities effectively. However, in accordance with established company policy, no employees would lose their jobs nor would anyone receive a cut in pay. (In fact, many of the employees affected actually received increases in pay, due partly to inflation and partly because it was thought that this would promote their acceptance of the new organization.) Mr. Jackson announced the appointments of the two senior vice-presidents and the four vice-presidents of Real Estate Investment, Farm Loans, Commercial Loans, and Residential Loans, who were charged to commence implementation of the necessary changes in their units immediately, and wished them well in their new positions.

THE RESTRUCTURED ORGANIZATION CREATES SOME PROBLEMS

Although everything was worked out "on paper," soon problems began to emerge in the mortgage loan units. The three vice-presidents who had formerly been department heads were now only vice-presidents reporting to a department head. They did not relish their reduced status. At the level of the field organization, there were also subsequent changes. Where before there had been a field manager for each of the Farm, Commercial, and Residential Loan units, there was now only one field manager for all mortgage loans. Thus, where there had been three field offices in each major city, there was now one office per city for all mortgage loans. Some former field managers were now only field representatives reporting to a field manager. As the field offices were consolidated, there were also shifts among the administrative and clerical employees. With the change to one field office, there was a need for just one office manager, not three, and this was not well accepted by the people who were no longer managers. In several instances employees who had worked together as peers for many years were now cast into the roles of superior and subordinates because of restructured jobs and reporting relationships.

For some employees the restructuring seemed to offer expanded opportunities, and they were eager to "get the show on the road." However, others felt that they were not getting their "share of the grapes" and were somewhat resistant and even uncooperative. Although earnest efforts were made to convince the personnel that the new organization would ultimately provide greater opportunities, for various reasons they were not all convinced.

Some of the managers affected by the reorganization had spent many years with National and were approaching retirement age. They felt that they had "paid their dues" in service to the firm over many years. Some of them had spent fifteen to twenty years doing the same job and doing it very well. They had become comfortable with the status quo and wanted everything to stay as it was. Gradually, some discontented workers adjusted and continued to make excellent employees with their new assignments. Others withstood their dissatisfaction until they could retire, while a few younger managers left the organization.

RESISTANCE TO CHANGE

Specific forms of resistance to the reorganization were varied. One senior appraiser who had previously worked in a small field office did not like the fact that his new office didn't open into the reception area. Certain longtime residential appraisers felt it "beneath their dignity" when now called upon to appraise farm property. A farm appraiser left the company because he felt farm loans would eventually be cut out altogether.

As certain key positions were filled with people from Commercial Loans, it was rumored, "This is not a reorganization but a Commercial Loan Department takeover." One of the reasons for the reorganization was to make better use of the large Residential Loan workforce by transferring them to Commercial Loan units, which were now understaffed. The rumor then started that the same thing would happen to the Farm Loan employees unless they worked together and produced a high volume of farm mortgages. This proved to be unsettling to the Farm group.

In retrospect, one thing that National apparently overemphasized was the belief that existing personnel could be retrained to assume all positions in the new structure. While some employees were successfully retrained, such as residential appraisers who became competent to do commercial appraisal work, it was found that outside specialists had to be brought in to fill certain key positions, particularly in the Commercial Loan and Real Estate Investment units.

QUESTIONS

1. Relate the National Insurance case to the discussion of organization change that appears in the textbook.

(*Continued on next page.*)

2. Did National's management handle the situation effectively? Why or why not?

3. What can management do to improve the situation as it now exists?

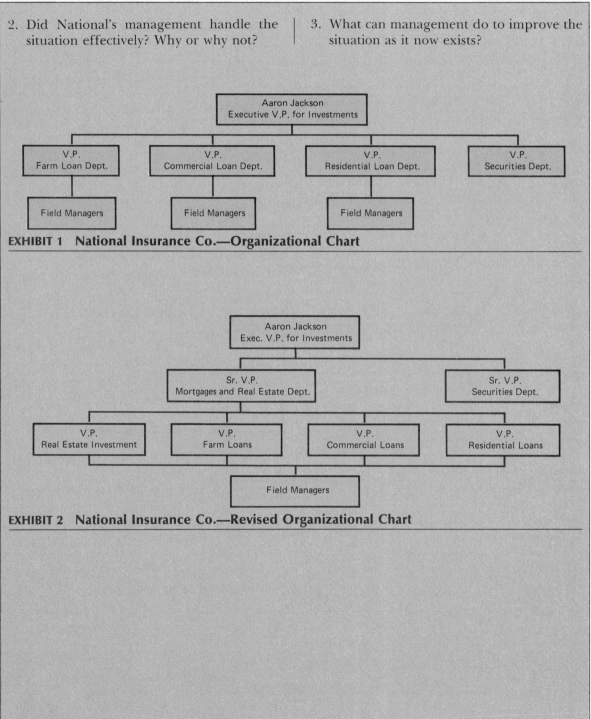

EXHIBIT 1   National Insurance Co.—Organizational Chart

EXHIBIT 2   National Insurance Co.—Revised Organizational Chart

PART
FOUR

LEADING
AND
MOTIVATING

CHAPTER

12 LEADERSHIP

LEARNING OBJECTIVES

After studying this chapter you should be able to

1. Describe the concept of power and identify the sources of power available to the leader.

2. Explain the meaning of leadership styles.

3. Discuss early leadership theories.

4. Understand the factors affecting leadership style.

5. Explain the contributions to knowledge about leadership of the Tannenbaum and Schmidt and Likert studies.

6. Describe the development of contingency leadership theory.

7. Explain the path-goal theory of leadership.

STOP ACTION CASE

Chrysler Corporation

Lee Iacocca probably did not realize it at the time, but when Henry Ford II unceremoniously fired him as president of Ford Motor Company in July 1978, Iacocca was about to become the best-known corporate executive in America. Iacocca signed on with Chrysler Corporation and was soon leading the failing automobile manufacturer. Chrysler had incurred monumental losses and faced a staggering debt load. Its market share of domestically made cars slipped to 10 percent. And when Iacocca examined Chrysler's management, he commented: "I took one look at that system and I almost threw up."

While the federal loan guarantees are a well-known part of the Chrysler story, Lee Iacocca knew that saving the company would take something more.

Use the materials in Chapter 12 to design a plan that would cut Chrysler's losses, reduce its debt, and increase its market share substantially.

MANAGEMENT FACT OR FICTION

	FACT	FICTION			FACT	FICTION
1. A Theory X manager views work as a rewarding experience for all employees.	☐	☐	accepted in the leadership literature.		☐	☐
2. Rensis Likert concluded that high productivity was associated with consultative or participative leadership.	☐	☐	5. Contingency theory concepts can be traced back to the immediate post–World War II era.		☐	☐
3. Tannenbaum and Schmidt first suggested that leadership style is a function of the leader, subordinates, and the situation.	☐	☐	6. The concept of a least preferred co-worker (LPC score) was developed by Fred Fiedler.		☐	☐
4. The Great Man Theory is now widely			7. Expectancy theory is the theoretical basis of the path-goal concept of leadership.		☐	☐

The materials in this chapter will assist you in separating management fact from fiction. Your answers can be checked on page 415.

Managers set objectives, plan, organize, staff, and control, but most of these activities go unnoticed by the general public. Most people tend to think of a manager as someone leading a group of people. A drill sergeant marching the troops, a conductor directing an orchestra, a coach calling the plays for a football team, a supervisor bossing a road crew, a minister preaching divine guidance to parishioners, or a movie director shouting, "Lights, camera, action!" These examples of leadership are typical of what the public considers management.

Leadership is the most visible aspect of management. It is the function by which a manager unleashes the available resources in order to get the organization to carry out plans to accomplish objectives. *Leadership* is defined as the act of motivating or causing people to perform certain tasks

Leadership is the act of motivating people to perform certain tasks intended to achieve specified objectives.

intended to achieve specified objectives. Leadership is the act of making things happen.

Even though leadership is the most visible part of the manager's job it is still one of the least understood and agreed-upon functions—no doubt because it deals so much with people. A variety of names have been used to denote leadership. Some writers call it actuating, others call it initiating. Then there are directing, guiding, commanding, and inspiring. But they all mean about the same thing, and since leadership is the most popular term it will be used throughout this section.

The leadership chapter is the first of four chapters in Part Four dealing with leading and motivating. The three to follow are motivation, group dynamics, and communication.

THE CONCEPT OF POWER

Power is the ability of one person to influence the behavior of another.

No matter what leadership is called, it involves the use of power.[1] *Power* is simply the ability of one person to influence the behavior of another. There are several sources of power available to the leader. Some leaders may use only one or two of these types of power while other leaders may draw upon all of them.

In one classification of power five sources are identified.[2] The first is reward power. This is the ability of a leader to give followers things they want. In the case of a manager these things may be pay, bonuses, vacations, insurance, a desirable job assignment, and so on. According to this scheme, not giving someone something he or she does not want has a psychological effect similar to positive reward. For example, consider the relief of a student when instead of giving a failing grade an instructor grants a week's extension on an overdue term paper.

A second type of power is coercive power, just the opposite of reward power. Here the leader essentially punishes or threatens to punish a subordinate by giving him or her things that are not sought or withholding things that are. One common form of discipline is to give an employee an undesirable job assignment to some remote branch of the company. Docking a person's pay is another common example of coercive power that will influence an employee not to repeat a mistake.[3]

Expert power is another source of influence that some leaders possess. People often follow the advice of someone with considerable knowledge of a particular subject. People will often blindly do what they are told by doctors or lawyers. Similarly, a supervisor who was once a superior tool and die maker may be respected by the subordinate tool and die makers in the department.

A fourth type of power is referent power. This is a subtle source of power based on a leader's charisma and an individual's desire to be like his or her leader. Many children emulate sports superstars like Wayne Gretzky, Magic Johnson, Chris Evert Lloyd, and Steve Garvey. Similarly, an employee who aspires to a management position may be most eager to please his or her superior.

Finally, there is legitimate power or authority. This is the power the manager has because he or she is the manager. It is power that is sanctioned by an organization, by law, by custom, or simply by common sense. A person will accept spiritual guidance from a priest because the priest has the blessing of the Church. Upon request a person might stay out of a neighbor's yard because it is private property and the neighbor is backed by the law. A worker may correct defects on a product at the quality control manager's request simply because he or she knows that someone has to be in charge of checking the product.

In organizations such as business firms, the five sources of power in the above scheme may derive from a person, a position, or both.[4] Someone whose power derives only from his or her position—mostly reward, coercive, and legitimate power—can be termed an official. The opposite number is the person who wields power but has no position, the so-called informal leader. (See the discussion in Chapter 13.) Such leaders rely on expert, referent, and symbolic forms of reward and coercive power. Finally, people who combine positional and personal power might be called formal leaders. A formal leader could be a persuasive department head, whereas an informal leader could be just a persuasive person, and an official could be simply a department head.

While all leadership involves the use of power, it is also dependent upon the selection of a way in which to lead others to accomplish goals. The concept of leadership style is vital to effective management.

> 66 I don't get ulcers, I give them. 99
>
> Donald T. Regan
> *Former White House Chief of Staff; Former Secretary of Treasury and CEO of Merrill Lynch*

LEADERSHIP STYLES

The stop-action case in this chapter illustrates Lee Iacocca's unique management style. Other executives have adopted other approaches. The selection of a way to lead and how to use available power is known as *leadership style*. People have been leading people as long as there have been people. Surely at one time or another every possible way of leading has been tried, from screaming and threatening to pleading and begging to bribing and promising.

Social scientists have studied leadership for only a few decades. At first, the hope was for some simple theory that was easy to understand, teach, learn, and practice. For a long time people clung to the theory that "leaders are born, not made." Finding someone with the right traits was the key. Then there was "leaders are made, not born." With this theory, anyone could be thrown into a situation and become a leader.

These simple theories are giving way to the realization that leadership style is a complicated matter. Research has shown that numerous factors affect a manager's choice of the proper leadership style. This selection process is often represented by the following equation:

Leadership style is the way a person uses available power in order to lead others.

MANAGEMENT SUCCESSES

Physio-Control

 Consider the way Hunter Simpson ran Physio-Control (now part of Eli Lilly), a $100-million-a-year maker of cardiovascular electronic medical instrumentation, prior to his retirement. The company is growing at the rate of more than 30 percent a year. People who work at Physio-Control are known as Team Members. Simpson has a personal management style. His office door is always open and he answers his own telephone. Team Members call him by his first name. But there are some other unique aspects of Simpson's managerial style.

- Physio-Control provides free tea and coffee throughout the day.

- Most Team Members work only four days a week. Others work a three-day, thirty-six-hour weekend. For those who want to go to school, the company covers their tuition and books.

- The company meets quarterly to go over goals, review the latest quarterly results, and recognize Team Members who have performed beyond expectations.

- Physio-Control maintains a profit-sharing plan that provides a cash bonus based on its annual performance. In addition, Team Members may invest in a savings plan that provides a match of 50 cents for each Team Member dollar invested.

- The company offers an adoption aid program and will reimburse up to $1,500 for Team Members who wish to adopt a child.

- Physio-Control is on the leading edge of corporate responsibility programs. It provides counseling for Vietnam veterans, and its innovative program for integrating the developmentally disabled back into the workplace has attracted national attention.

Sources: Richard Buck, "Disaster Plot Turns Out to Be Formula for Success," *Seattle Times,* 6 April 1982, pp. 1B, 5B; Paul Dunwiddle, "Architect of Company to Step Down," *Journal American,* 2 October 1985, pp. D1, D3. The June 12, 1985 update was provided by Sandra D. Egge of Physio-Control.

$$\text{Leadership style} = f \text{ (the leader, subordinates, situation)}$$

Leaders themselves, subordinates, and the situation confronting the manager are the determinants involved. As stated, leadership style is a function of all three of these variables. All are discussed in detail later in the chapter.

Not enough is known yet to be able to teach everyone to be a great leader, but there is enough information available to give a new manager a head start over those who are not knowledgeable in this aspect of management theory.

TYPES OF LEADERSHIP AND RELATED MANAGEMENT ASSUMPTIONS

The three factors involved in choosing a leadership style indicate that there is a multiplicity of leadership styles available to a manager. One of the most important variables is the manager's assumptions about the nature of those being led. This assumption will have a direct impact on the leadership style selected. Douglas McGregor offers two basic assumptions called Theory X and Theory Y.[5] These ideas have since been expanded by followers of McGregor.

THEORY X

A leader espousing a *Theory X* orientation believes that subordinates require an autocratic leadership style. Theory X leaders believe their subordinates prefer to escape work and responsibility. Employees are seen as lacking ambition and seeking the security of a leader-directed environment. Management must therefore use its reward, coercive, legitimate power (authority) to get subordinates to accomplish organizational objectives. Theory X managers view their role as supervisory and as evaluating the work activities of uninspired subordinates.

Theory X proposes that subordinates dislike work and require an autocratic style of leadership.

THEORY Y

At the other end of the leadership scale are the democratic leaders, called *Theory Y* managers by McGregor. These managers use a people-centered or employee-oriented style of leadership. Theory Y leaders view work as a rewarding experience for all employees. People are seen as reaching out to management for increased responsibility and productivity.

Theory Y advocates a democratic style of leadership in which employees are encouraged to participate in the decision-making process.

Democratic leaders encourage their employees to participate in the decision-making process. Emphasis is shifted from punishment to reward. Communications flow openly both from leader to follower and from follower to leader. This type of leader tries to create a favorable environment for employees so that they can achieve the goals of the particular work unit.

These extremes of leadership style are generally thought to be incomplete explanations. More comprehensive models have been offered by Rensis Likert and by Robert Tannenbaum and Warren Schmidt.

THE LIKERT MODEL

Rensis Likert developed a comprehensive leadership model with four basic leadership systems.[6] Each system represents a different leadership style, as shown in Figure 12–1. System 1 is an exploitative authoritative style. This represents dictatorial leadership behavior, with all decisions made by

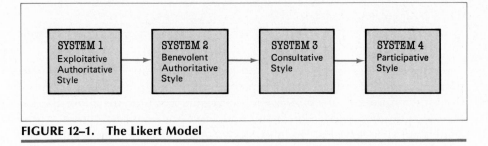

FIGURE 12–1.   The Likert Model

the managers. There is little employee participation, and a general attitude of distrust exists between the parties.

System 2 is a benevolent authoritative style; the leader, while autocratic, tries to be paternalistically supportive of subordinates. Distrust between managers and employees is still commonplace.

System 3 reflects consultative leadership behavior. Mutual regard is enhanced because the manager solicits advice from those in subordinate roles, while retaining the right to make the final decision.

System 4 is a participative leadership style. Subordinates are actively involved in the decision-making process. Consensus management as practiced by Japanese firms is an example.

Research by Likert and others concluded that high productivity was associated with systems 3 and 4 leadership, while systems 1 and 2 were characterized by lower output.

TANNENBAUM AND SCHMIDT'S CONTINUUM OF LEADERSHIP BEHAVIOR

Robert Tannenbaum and Warren Schmidt also noted that a democratic/authoritarian dichotomy was inadequate. They proposed a continuum of leadership behavior specifying a full range of leadership styles.[7] Their model is shown in Figure 12–2.

Some managers use their authority to make all decisions. These decisions are then accepted by subordinates. The opposite situation is where managers and nonmanagers make decisions jointly within prescribed limits. Tannenbaum and Schmidt specifically noted that neither end of the continuum is absolute since some limitations are always applicable.

Three major factors in deciding on a leadership style are suggested by the model. These include forces in the manager (such as his or her value system and confidence in subordinates), the subordinates (such as their expectations of management behavior), and the situation (such as the values and traditions of the organization). Thus, Tannenbaum and Schmidt suggested the now classic equation noted earlier: Leadership style = f (the leader, subordinates, situation).

> 66 I think of myself as a professional manager—leadership is part of that. I try to reach out and touch people. That's the leadership part. I try to involve myself at all levels of the firm. 99
>
> John C. Emery, Jr.
> *Chairman and CEO, Emery Air Freight*

Leadership and Corporate Culture

A company functions successfully when its managers and employees interact in such a way that the work is handled efficiently. Managers are usually most successful when they adapt their leadership style to one that will most effectively motivate employees. A manager's leadership style may be communicated directly through specific actions, and it may also be conveyed more subtly by means of the prevailing corporate culture. Corporate culture is the generally accepted behavior patterns within an organization that include regular activities and events such as the quarterly meetings held by the Physio-Control Corporation.

The examples in this photo essay show that effective leadership can be expressed in a wide variety of ways, from the "tight reins" style of Harold Geneen to the employee-oriented style of John M. Stafford.

(Above) The Parker Hannifin Corporation has achieved $102 million in savings this year by listening to employee suggestions. Here, Urban Bianchi, Aerospace Inspection Supervisor, demonstrates one of his 148 implemented cost-saving suggestions to Cost Reduction Manager, Dave Foland.

(Below) Harold Geneen can be considered a unique corporate culture "hero" (see Chapter 12 at ITT where his effective and self-described old-fashioned managing style proved a tremendous success.

John M. Stafford, Pillsbury Chairman, is committed to a very employee-oriented style of leadership which he achieves by meeting regularly with employees.

(Above) Physio-Control Corporation holds quarterly kick-off meetings for all employees, or team members. They review goals, and award achievement-and-extra effort cash bonuses to team members who have performed beyond expectations. Hot dogs, breakdancing, and a band are a few of the other perks for the meeting.

(Left) In an attempt to maintain the caliber of players, Avron Fogelman, co-owner of the Kansas City Royals, offers his lifetime contract players real estate opportunities to compensate for the lower salaries available in a smaller market.

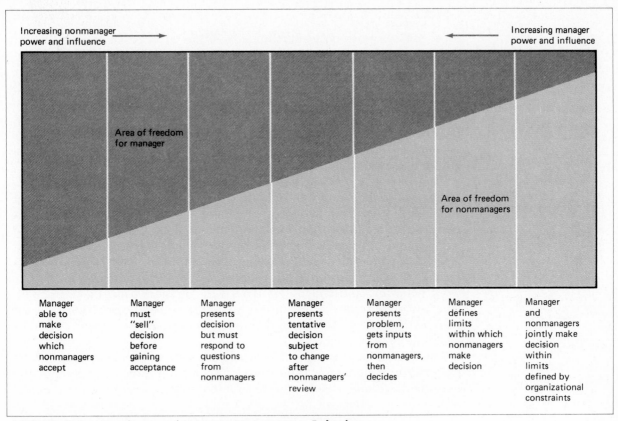

FIGURE 12–2.   Continuum of Manager-Nonmanager Behavior
Source: Adapted by permission of the *Harvard Business Review*. Exhibit from Robert Tannenbaum and Warren Schmidt, "How to Choose a Leadership Pattern," *Harvard Business Review* (May–June 1973). Copyright © 1973 by the President and Fellows of Harvard College; All rights reserved.

The amount of power and influence that both the manager and the nonmanager have is influenced by the organizational and societal environments in which they operate.

EARLY LEADERSHIP THEORIES

Leadership theory can be divided into two distinct groupings: the early traditional theories and the more contemporary, situational viewpoints. Both will be explored in this chapter.

Leadership theory originally concentrated on who the leader was and the personal characteristics or traits of the identified leader. These approaches are often termed the Great Man and trait theories of leadership. Later, the emphasis switched to a more situational view of leadership.

GREAT MAN THEORY

Most early writings on leadership stressed the emergence of a single person, the so-called Great Man, as the cause of any action. Significant political, economic, or social change may have been attributed to a great ruler ascending a throne or to a powerful Pope or finance minister. Accounts of the American Revolution and the resulting United States Constitution often stress the contributions of such important people as George Washington, Benjamin Franklin, and Thomas Jefferson. Many history books arrange historical events by reigns of kings and queens or presidential administrations.

Great Man Theory states that only an exceptional person is capable of playing a prominent leadership role.

The *Great Man Theory* assumed that such people were remarkably different from others and that only they were capable of playing prominent leadership roles. The theoretical emphasis was on identifying the leader's characteristics rather than explaining the actions that he or she took.[8] Early students of leadership concentrated on the traits or personal characteristics of identified leaders. Some of the supposed leadership attributes were personality factors like aggressiveness; others concerned habits like work behavior; and still others dealt with physical features like height. The research and resulting lists were often contradictory. Some "great men" possessed characteristics diametrically opposed to the traits of other widely accepted leaders.

The Great Man Theory was obviously an incomplete explanation of the leadership phenomenon. The study of leadership traits was subsequently expanded and intensified in an attempt to develop a comprehensive model of leadership behavior.

TRAIT THEORY

Trait theory concerns the identification and measurement of traits or attitudes that are associated with a leader's behavior.

Trait theory research concerns the identification and measurement of traits or attitudes that are associated with leadership behavior. It may be thought of as a natural extension of the early investigations of the Great Man Theory. Essentially, the objective was the same: to distinguish between leaders and nonleaders.

President Calvin Coolidge once offered a humorous addition to the literature on trait theory concerning presidential leadership. Coolidge never said much during his presidency. But "Silent Cal," as the president was known, once told Ethel Barrymore: "I think the American people want a solemn ass as a president . . . and I think I will go along with them."[9]

Edwin Ghiselli's work is perhaps the best-known work in the field of trait theory.[10] Ghiselli has studied leadership for over twenty years, and his research keeps trait theory alive in an era dominated by situationalists. Ghiselli has developed "The Ghiselli Self-Destructive Inventory" to measure leadership traits. The inventory consists of sixty-four adjective pairs. Testing time averages fifteen minutes, with the subjects checking the adjectives that best describe themselves for half the pairs and indicating the least descriptive word in the other thirty-two pairs.

Thirteen traits have been studied by Ghiselli, and each has been ranked according to its value in identifying managerial talent. These rankings are indicated in Table 12–1.

FACTORS AFFECTING LEADERSHIP STYLE ▪▬▬▬▬▪

John D. deButts, a former chief executive officer of AT&T, once attributed his own leadership style to a blending of the styles of his predecessors.

> The first [CEO] was very definitely the authoritarian type. He issued instructions. The CEO who followed him came up through the personnel department and spent a great deal more time on the human side of business—kind of pulled the group together. The next CEO was a hard, two-fisted line guy who came up through the plant department on the operating side of the business. He was demanding and yet he was extremely understanding. Under my leadership, if you will, we attempt to use a combination of what we call cooperation and what I would call natural competitiveness in any business.[11]

The deButts remarks suggest the variety of factors contributing to or influencing one's leadership. One set of factors is the people who are being

TABLE 12–1   GHISELLI'S MANAGERIAL TRAITS

	Importance Value[a]
Supervisory ability (A)	100
Occupational achievement (M)	76
Intelligence (A)	64
Self-actualization (M)	63
Self-assurance (P)	62
Decisiveness (P)	61
Lack of need for security (M)	54
Working class affinity (P)	47
Initiative (A)	34
Lack of need for high financial reward (M)	20
Need for power (M)	10
Maturity (P)	5
Masculinity-femininity (P)	0

[a] Importance value: 100 = very important; 0 = plays no part in managerial talent.
NOTE: A = ability trait; P = personality trait; M = motivational trait.

Source: Reprinted by permission of the publisher from "A Test of Ghiselli's Theory of Managerial Traits," by James F. Gavin, *Journal of Business Research* (February 1976): 46. Copyright 1976 by Elsevier Science Publishing Co., Inc.

THE MANAGER'S BOOKSHELF

Managing, by Harold Geneen

Harold Geneen took over ITT in 1959 and acquired more than 350 businesses in 80 countries over the next 17 years. As ITT's annual sales climbed, Geneen continued to keep his fingers on all the financial buttons. ITT sold everything from Wonder Bread and Twinkies to fire insurance and, of course, telephones, and still all the figures made their way past Geneen's desk. As he says in his book, *Managing,* "The drudgery of the numbers will make you free."

Managing is Harold Geneen's valedictory advice to the corporate world. It is a defense of the "old way of managing" from a man who managed the old way as well as anyone ever has. *Managing* contains such pithy Geneen homilies as: "Management must manage," and "Leadership cannot really be taught. It can only be learned." Or this advice to young managers: "In the business world, everyone is paid in two coins: cash and ex-

perience. Take the experience first, the cash will come later." Geneen also takes aim, in *Managing,* at some of American business's sacred cows. He ridicules "chief executives who delegate their business responsibilities to others while they go out to help save the world."

These are all somewhat provocative statements, but they do not get close to explaining Geneen's own phenomenal success. They cannot account for the fact that this self-described "old-fashioned bookkeeper at heart" turned a medium-sized telephone company into the world's biggest, most complex conglomerate. Like all successful systems, perhaps, the style of managing described in Geneen's book may work best when your name is Harold Geneen.

Source: Rhonda Brammer, "Tips from the Top," *New York Times Book Review,* 21 October 1984, p. 40.

led. Since these people are doing some kind of work, another set of factors is the nature of the job itself. Then there is the factor of the management support the leader gets from those higher up in the organization. Another important set of factors has to do with the manager's own personal characteristics. All may be considered categories of the variables mentioned earlier in the leadership style equation.

PEOPLE

Leadership behavior is closely tied to the performance levels and expectations of both managers and their subordinates.[12] Research studies have determined that there is typically a close relationship between these variables. One study of a naval air research and development facility considered the interactions of seniors (supervisors) and juniors (subordinates). The study concluded:

The findings of this study tend to support the hypothesis of reciprocal influence. The behavior of seniors is to some extent related to the expectations of juniors, but the behavior of juniors is also related to the behavior and expectations of seniors.[13]

Chapter 13 notes that different people can develop different motivations. Some people, often those who have been deprived, are concerned mostly with basic security needs such as a minimum standard of living. Anything that will give them a sense of security will be welcome. These motives are suitable to a work-centered style of leadership.

> 66 It's the price of leadership to do the thing you believe has to be done at the time it must be done. 99
>
> Lyndon B. Johnson

The autocratic leader structures the world for such an employee, which is exactly what the employee seeks. This type of employee actually is satisfied with close supervision. Work is not a means of self-expression for such a person. He or she prefers to associate with friends, family, and the community outside the company, so interest in the workplace will be correspondingly low. Some research on blue-collar and lower-level white-collar workers suggest that autocratic leadership not only is satisfying to them but makes them productive.[14]

On the other hand, many employees are motivated by their work. These people like to be involved and take pride in their accomplishments. They want to earn the respect of other people on the job. Such employees respond well to a people-centered style of leadership.

The democratic leader asks for the opinions of employees, who in this case are anxious to give them. This type of leader allows some room on the job for such an employee to innovate and express his or her originality. The democratic leader allows these employees to work more on their own, giving achievement-oriented individuals a measure of self-respect. Research has shown that democratic leadership leads to high productivity and satisfaction for many blue-collar, white-collar, and professional workers.[15] General Motors, for instance, has a corporate-wide quality-of-work-life program that encourages each unit to develop activities that will increase employee involvement in decisions that directly affect their jobs and their workplace. At some locations, GM workers monitor their own production quality and assess the quality of supplier parts. General Motors explains the reasoning behind this approach: "Experience has shown that the utilization of human resources, when added to the corporation's technical resources, has a beneficial impact on improving product quality."[16]

Subordinates' motivations are not the only people factors that affect the choice of leadership style. The number of subordinates has a strong influence, no matter what type of employees are being managed. A manager of two or three persons has a much greater chance to develop friendly, open relationships than does a manager of twenty or thirty people. Research has consistently shown that increasing the number of people decreases the sense of closeness among the group members and increases the threatening social nature of the group for each member.[17] A small group makes it easier to use a democratic style of leadership, while a large group pushes the leader toward the autocratic end of the scale.

Note the apparent reversal here of cause and effect between leadership style and the criterion of satisfaction. Many democratic leaders like to think that it is their leadership style that causes a group to be satisfied. However, if the group is small, it may be satisfied just because of its size. In this case the satisfaction of the group may be enabling the leader to use a democratic style. In leadership research there are many instances where cause and effect are unclear.

THE JOB

The job's time frame may also affect the choice of leadership style. If a task must be completed in a short period of time, the autocrat may be more effective. The autocrat simply tells people when, where, and how to do the job. When time-delaying mistakes are made, he or she quickly takes remedial action.

Democratic leaders call for subordinates to participate in deciding when, where, and how to do the job. Employees must be familiarized with the problem and given time to think and respond. When they make mistakes, the employee-centered manager helps them find the reason so they can correct it themselves. Such a style is too slow and awkward for the platoon leader to use when an enemy ambush is anticipated or for the supervisor to use when cars are relentlessly marching past workers on the assembly line. Yet it may be suited to the marketing director and his or her staff preparing next season's advertising strategy or to the research director whose scientists are seeking new chemical formulations.

Research has uncovered another job-related factor that affects leadership style. When a manager's job requires analysis for solution, such as finding out why a machine has broken down, then an open, participatory style may be best because it elicits more ideas from more people than an autocratic style.[18] But when a job involves coordination, such as scheduling the movement of goods from the loading docks to the warehouse to the shipper to the customer, a directive style of leadership may be best. In this case the important factor is that people and other resources are available when and where necessary.

Another important job factor is uncertainty. Studies have shown that people-oriented styles are better in "uncertain" jobs than are work-centered styles, and vice versa for "certain" jobs.[19] Basically, a democratic leader has more input from subordinates than an autocratic leader. In an uncertain situation characterized by rapid change, the democratic leader has an increased advantage over the autocratic leader in being able to spot the change and determine what to do about it. For example, consumers' tastes are always changing, and the wise marketing manager listens closely to his or her salespeople. A marketing executive who sets a marketing strategy without sales force input is taking a needless risk.

On the other hand, the foundry business is slow to change. The production manager who solicits opinions about this job from employees is not likely to learn much and may waste time that could be spent casting metal. While the morale benefits of this approach may be worth the time and effort invested, it is easy to understand why an autocratic style is more often used in such cases.

MANAGEMENT SUPPORT

Managers do not work in a vacuum. They have superiors who manage them, and this can have a direct influence on the choice of leadership style.

The reward system set up for managers is a management support factor. Supervisors often complain that their pay and bonuses depend on short-run criteria such as the amount of daily output or the number of delinquent customer accounts. This forces them to put pressure on their employees, resulting in authoritarian leadership. However, this situation may be changing. For instance, Koppers Co. now bases a portion of its management incentive program on the results of a three-year period. Phillips Petroleum has two separate incentive programs, one of which is based on annual performance and the other on multiple year performance. The latter, known as the Long-Term Incentive Compensation Plan, currently has a four-year measurement period.[20] Another factor discouraging authoritarian leadership is that some managements put great emphasis on employee morale. The supervisor judged on this basis is more likely to use a democratic, people-oriented style.

The people-oriented leader faces another problem. As he or she tries to respond to the individual needs of employees, the approval and support of higher management will be needed. For instance, these leaders may want greater flexibility in scheduling vacation days or additional money to alter jobs to fit the employees' capabilities.

Research has found that such supervisors tend to satisfy their employees only when they actually deliver on their promises.[21] This means that they must have a good relationship with their superiors. Supervisors without this upward influence, regardless of their good intentions, create dissatisfied, unproductive employees.

The lack of upward influence may reduce the ability of a manager to use a people-oriented leadership style. But the autocratic leader may also run into problems with superiors. An employee may be told, for example, that one more case of tardiness will result in a three-day suspension. But the manager's credibility will be damaged if high-level executives refuse to support such an action. On the other hand, the supervisor who can win executive backing will be seen as that much more authoritative by employees. Part of the art of autocratic leadership is knowing when to issue ultimatums and knowing how to make them stick.

PERSONAL CHARACTERISTICS

Many of the personal characteristics of the leader have a powerful effect on his or her ability to select and use the proper leadership style.[22] Some of these characteristics are his or her sincerity, knowledge, and need to be accepted.

Managers have faults, strengths, and complicated motives, just like their employees. A manager is as likely to have developed a fairly stable self-concept as a subordinate. Part of this self-concept may be a tendency to deal with people in a structured, authoritarian way or in an open, supportive way.

The person with authoritarian tendencies will find it quite natural to use an autocratic leadership style, just as the person with supportive tendencies will find a democratic style natural. The difficulty comes when either of these two types tries to switch roles. Role inconsistency can create superior-subordinate problems. Employees have been found to be very sensitive to insincerity in a leader.[23] Employees who feel that they are being manipulated will be dissatisfied with their manager and are not likely to perform well. Being friendly with employees can be an effective approach in some instances, but it must be genuine, not forced.

Another personal characteristic of the leader that affects his or her leadership style is knowledge of the job. New managers and supervisors often ask, "Do I have to be better than my employees at their jobs?" Sometimes this is an impossible expectation, especially when skilled people are being managed. A highly skilled manager might also discourage an employee from performing the task. Small group research has shown that leaders gain acceptance if they are simply good at whatever their employees do.[24] Mutual respect permits the leader to use a directive approach with his or her subordinates based on expert power.

But in some cases a manager cannot do the work performed by his or her subordinates. This situation is especially true in high-technology industries. A people-oriented approach can work well in such cases. The leader simply tells the subordinates that he or she is dependent on their expertise in their jobs. The leader will rely on their ideas as to how best to get the job done. The best leader in these instances is really a good follower.

Such a leader will coordinate the group's efforts and ensure that management provides the resources that the group needs. Upward influence is imperative in these circumstances. Even though workers and leader are expert in different areas, their mutual regard can serve as an effective basis for productive effort.

A leader's need to be accepted by his or her employees is yet another factor affecting the style used. Many managers complain about the loneliness of leadership. This refers to the fact that leaders often have to make hard decisions for which they may not be liked. This is especially true of autocratic leaders. They may be admired and have referent power over their followers, but they may also be isolated. Some people resist this sense of alienation and use a democratic style, whether the situation calls for it or not. A collegiate example of this is a professor who is not honest with students when their performance is poor.

THE DEVELOPMENT OF CONTINGENCY LEADERSHIP THEORY

A new leadership theory called *contingency theory* has emerged. Simply stated, this theory says that effective leadership is contingent upon the situation. In some situations one style is best, in others another style is best. As noted in the contributions of Likert and Tannenbaum and Schmidt, there is no one best way to lead.

Like most theoretical constructs, contingency theory has a historical derivation in earlier research literature. Many of today's concepts might be traced back to research done in the post-World War II period. The studies conducted at Ohio State and the University of Michigan illustrated these early research efforts.

Contingency theory states that effective leadership style is contingent upon the situation: different styles of leadership are best for different situations.

EARLY RESEARCH

Researchers at Ohio State University began some important leadership studies in the late 1940s, establishing an ongoing program in this area.[25] Names like Stogdill, Coons, Halpin, Winer, Kerr, Schriescheim, and Murphy are associated with this work.

The Ohio State studies originally dealt with military leadership questions such as commander-crew relations in B-52 bombers. The research was later extended to combat situations in Korea and industrial settings.

The researchers sought to identify the important leadership behavior dimensions. As the studies were extended and the questionnaires refined, two primary leadership behavior factors were uncovered: consideration and initiation of structure. Initiation of structure concerned the leader's efforts to organize the work effort or activity, instruct his or her subordinates, and clarify the superior-subordinate relationship. Thus, initiation of structure referred to the task-oriented aspects (such as a bombing sortie) of leadership behavior. Consideration, or a subordinate orientation, was the second factor. It involved the leader's concern for the welfare of his or her subordinates as exhibited through friendliness, respect, and so forth.

Later studies related these leadership dimensions to subordinate satisfaction and productivity. High consideration-high structure leadership behavior was usually found to be the most desirable. While contradicting results were also reported in some cases, it is clear that the Ohio State studies were major contributions to the leadership literature.

Other significant studies were being conducted by researchers at the University of Michigan's Survey Research Center. The Michigan studies, employing interviews, reached essentially similar conclusions to those derived at Ohio State. The Michigan studies identified employee orientation and production orientation as the two primary ingredients of leadership style. The similarity of the Michigan results to Ohio State's consideration and initiation of structure seems quite evident.

THE MANAGERIAL GRID® AND REDDIN'S TRI-DIMENSIONAL MODEL OF LEADERSHIP EFFECTIVENESS[26]

Robert Blake and Jane Mouton's work in developing a Managerial Grid® should be noted as a contemporary application of some of the basic research just cited.[27] The Managerial Grid®, discussed in detail in Chapter 11, conceptualized two dimensions to leadership style: task-oriented and relations-oriented. Five behaviors are possible according to Blake and Mouton: low-task and low-relations leadership style; low-task and high-relations leadership style; high-task and low-relations leadership style; medium-task and medium-relations leadership style; and high-task and high-relations leadership style. In most cases, high-task and high-relations behavior is most desirable.

Reddin's Tri-Dimensional Model of Leadership Effectiveness is an extension of the Managerial Grid®.[28] It considers effectiveness as a model variable and allows a determination of the leadership behavior most appropriate in a specified situation. Reddin's model permits an evaluation of the relative effectiveness of various behaviors under a given set of circumstances.

Actually, much of the earlier discussion of Theory X and Theory Y assumptions and the work of Tannenbaum and Schmidt was an introduction to the basics of contingency theory, even though the term was not used. The discussion was made possible by grouping scattered research items into a contingency format and defining the situation to include the four sets of factors affecting leadership style. Research on the contingency concept itself was not included.

FIEDLER'S CONTRIBUTION TO CONTINGENCY THEORY

Fred Fiedler, professor of psychology and management at the University of Washington, has conducted the research that led to the conceptual development of contingency theory. Fiedler sought to evaluate the leadership success relationship between leadership style and situational favorableness.[29] He measured leadership style by asking leaders to rate their least preferred co-worker (LPC score). Situational favorableness consists of leader-member relations, degree of task structure, and the leader's power. Leaders with high LPC scores viewed their least preferred co-workers more favorably than did those with low LPC scores. High LPC leaders were considered people-centered while low LPC scores implied a task-centered leadership style.

Fiedler found that task-centered leadership is best when the situation is either very favorable or very unfavorable. People-centered styles are best in the in-between situations.[30] Figure 12–3 illustrates the concept. Fiedler points out that LPC does not actually measure behavior, but a personality attribute. Hence, the leader cannot readily change personality or leadership style, but can change the situation.

While Fiedler's work has been criticized by some management writers, it is clear that the contingency approach is now an accepted part of leadership theory. Certainly, it offers some valuable insights for the practicing manager. Not all the factors affecting leadership style are in harmony with each other in real-life situations. Some factors in a situation may favor people-oriented style and others a task-oriented style. Contingency thinking can help the manager find systematic ways to handle even the most complicated situations.

The emphasis in contingency thinking is on determining precisely what the leader faces, what he or she can or cannot change, and then finding the optimum solution. Optimizing means finding the best balance of factors in a situation rather than attempting to maximize any one factor. For instance, employee satisfaction might have to be partially sacrificed in some situations in order to adapt to the physical requirements of the job. The key is to find the most beneficial balance of the two instead of maximizing employee satisfaction or the adaptation to physical job constraints.

An applied illustration of contingency theory is in order here. Suppose a person is in charge of stocking the shelves at a supermarket near a college campus. One question is, "What is the nature of the task?" If it is (a) coordinative and time-oriented, an autocratic style may be appropriate. If it is (b) analytical and open-ended, a democratic style might be better. Since shelving goods is largely a matter of container handling and keeping the product on the shelf despite rapid turnover, the answer is (a).

FIGURE 12–3.   An Illustration of Fiedler's Contingency Theory

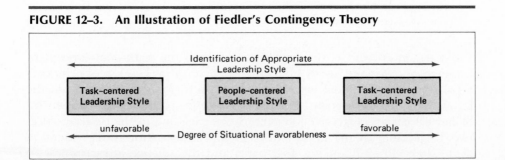

Next question: "What types of employees are involved?" If they are (c) status and achievement-oriented, a democratic style is suggested. If they are (d) security and physically oriented, an autocratic style might be the best choice. Suppose that most of the stock personnel are students from a nearby college. In this case the answer may be (c).

A dilemma has risen. The task itself suggests an autocratic style, but the people involved may respond best to a democratic style. What should the manager do? Contingency thinking involves a consideration of all the possible options. For instance, can the manager change the nature of the work? If so, he or she might be able to match it to the employees' needs and abilities. If the manager determines that only by computerizing and mechanizing the job at prohibitive cost could this be accomplished, the option is ruled out.

Now the manager might ask, "Can I change my people to match the job? For instance, could all the college students be dismissed and replaced by nonstudents? Or could the college students be indoctrinated again?"

Contingency thinking forces the manager to abandon the pursuit of a single best approach. The "best" approach may be determined only after a careful analysis of the task and the people involved.

THE PATH-GOAL THEORY OF LEADERSHIP

Path-goal theory is one of the more recent contributions to the study of leadership.[31] Robert House and his colleagues have done considerable work in this area, and a general leadership theory is emerging. But contradictory evidence and diverse viewpoints have also appeared in the management literature, so the end result of this significant research activity has not yet been determined.

Path-goal theory indicates that effective leadership is dependent on clearly defining the paths of goal achievement and the degree to which the leader is able to improve subordinates' attainment of their goals.

Path-goal theory indicates that effective leadership is dependent on the degree to which one is able to improve the achievement of subordinates' goals, as well as clearly defining the paths to goal attainment for subordinates. House and Mitchell have put it this way:

> The maturational functions of the leader consist of increasing the number and kinds of personal payoffs to subordinates for work-goal attainment and making paths to these payoffs easier to travel by clarifying the paths, reducing road blocks and pitfalls and increasing the opportunities for personal satisfaction en route.

Expectancy theory holds that a person's perception of achieving a prized reward or goal via effective job performance will motivate the individual. Expectancy theory forms the basis of path-goal leadership.

Expectancy theory is the theoretical basis of the path-goal concept of leadership. *Expectancy theory* holds that a person's perception of achieving a prized reward or goal via effective job performance will motivate the individual. But the person must clearly see the relationship between his or her efforts and effective job performance leading to the desired objective. Expectancy theory implies that employee motivation is dependent on leader behavior influencing goal paths and the relative attractiveness of the goals involved.[32]

Two general propositions have emerged for path-goal theory, according to House and Mitchell:

1. Leader behavior is acceptable and satisfying to subordinates to the extent that the subordinates see such behavior as either an immediate source of satisfaction or as instrumental to future satisfaction.

2. Leader behavior will be motivational to the extent that (a) such behavior makes satisfaction of subordinates' needs contingent on effective performance and (b) such behavior complements the environment of subordinates by providing the coaching, guidance, support, and rewards necessary for effective performance.

House and Mitchell have also identified various strategic leadership functions in path-goal theory: "(1) recognizing and/or arousing subordinates' needs for outcomes over which the leader has some control, (2) increased personal payoffs to subordinates for work-goal attainment, (3) making the path to those payoffs easier to travel by coaching and direction, (4) helping subordinates clarify expectancies, (5) reducing frustrating barriers and (6) increasing the opportunities for personal satisfaction contingent on effective performance."

Two contingency factors are hypothesized for the path-goal concept: (1) the subordinate's personal characteristics, and (2) environmental factors. Personal characteristics might include an individual's perception of the locus of control. In other words does he or she see the situation resulting from his or her own behavior or from outside events or random change? This concept is discussed in more detail in Chapter 13. Environmental contingency factors include the assigned tasks, the existing authority system, and the group within which the individual primarily works.

The path-goal model first considers leader behavior (directive, supportive, achievement-oriented, or participative, for instance), then considers the contingency factors, their causal results, and finally, the end product—subordinate attitudes and behavior.

Despite the mixed empirical tests of the path-goal concept, clearly this approach will play an important role in future leadership studies. Path-goal theory is making many contributions to our understanding of a very complex subject.

A CONTINUING RESEARCH NEED

Leadership is one of management's most dynamic fields of study. The contingency approach or the path-goal concept is not the final word in leadership theory. While they certainly represent major advances, there is every likelihood that they are merely steps in the evolutionary development of a most complex subject.

Many problems still remain. An overall synthesis of leadership practices and theoretical contributions is a pressing need. Perhaps one of the readers of this textbook will one day make a major breakthrough in leadership theory.

SUMMARY

Leadership is the act of motivating or causing people to perform certain tasks intended to achieve specified objectives. It is the most visible aspect of a manager's job.

All leadership situations involve the use of power, defined as the ability of one person to influence the behavior of another. Five sources of power are available to the leaders: reward, coercive, expert, referent, and legitimate. Some leaders may use only one or two of these power sources; others may employ all five.

Leadership style refers to the selection of a way to lead and how to use available power. The selection of a leadership style is a function of the leader, subordinates, and situation. An important factor concerns the manager's assumptions about those being led. The basic assumptions have been described by Douglas McGregor as Theory X and Theory Y. A Theory X leader is an autocrat who believes that subordinates naturally dislike work, so it is the leader's responsibility to direct and control them. A Theory Y leader thinks that work is a rewarding activity for all people, if they are given the opportunity. Theory Y leaders are democratic and employ a participative leadership style. More comprehensive models have been offered by Rensis Likert and by Robert Tannenbaum and Warren Schmidt, which are also discussed in this chapter.

Leadership theory can be divided into two distinct groupings: the early traditional theories and the more contemporary situational viewpoints. The earliest leadership concept was the Great Man Theory, which held that the emergence of a single person was the cause of any action. Early leadership theorists concentrated on identifying the characteristics of such leaders. Trait theory was the natural extension of the Great Man Theory. Here the objective was to identify and measure the traits or attributes related to leadership behaviors.

Various situational factors have been found to influence leadership style. These include: (1) people, (2) the job, (3) management support, and (4) personal characteristics. Recognition of the importance of such factors led to the development of contingency leadership theory. This concept suggests that effective leadership is contingent upon the situation. Leadership behavior should vary according to the circumstances facing the manager. Early studies dealing with contingency theory were conducted at Ohio State University and the University of Michigan. Fred Fiedler is a well-known researcher in this field.

Path-goal theory is one of the latest conceptual entrants in the study of leadership. According to this concept, effective leadership is dependent on the degree to which one is able to improve the achievement of subordinates' goals, as well as clearly defining the paths to goal attainment for subordinates. The work of Robert House and Terence Mitchell is notable in this field. This chapter concludes with a brief discussion of the continuing research needs in leadership theory.

SOLVING THE STOP ACTION CASE

Chrysler Corporation

Lee Iacocca's successful turnaround of Chrysler Corporation is becoming a classic tale in the field of management. Iacocca turned a profit as early as 1982. He did it with a combination of hard work, business savvy, and that intangible but critical quality, leadership.

Iacocca wasted no time showing who was in charge. He replaced all of Chrysler's top management. But that was just the beginning. Iacocca also overhauled dealer relationships and developed a lean financial plan. He closed 20 plants, cut American employment from 134,000 in 1978 to 60,000 in 1980. Twenty thousand white-collar jobs were cut. He wrested $1.2 billion in union concessions, cut salaries by up to 10 percent and—his most public achievement—convinced the U.S. government into guaranteeing $1.5 billion in loans. Altogether, Iacocca lowered Chrysler's break-even point in sales from 2.1 million cars in 1979 to just 1.1 million cars five years later.

Perhaps most important, Iacocca took his case to the American people. Through a series of television ads, he put his extraordinary persuasive powers to work and convinced America that Chrysler made a better car. As *Time* magazine noted, "he exuded confidence and conviction: well-tailored clothes, big cigar, self-satisfied smile." Iacocca personalized Chrysler's efforts by offering his customers a look at the manager who was running the firm. And he displayed the entrepreneurial bravado when he dared America, "If you find a better car, buy it." Iacocca's leadership was perhaps the single factor that brought Chrysler back from the brink of disaster. Today, the firm has a respectable 14 percent market share.

Sources: Alexander L. Taylor, III, "Iacocca's Tightrope Act," *Time,* 21 March 1983, p. 50; Walter Guzzardi, Jr., "The Two Iacoccas," *Fortune,* 26 November 1984, p. 221; John Holusha, "Can Iacocca Keep Chrysler Moving?" *New York Times,* 25 August 1985, p. F1.

FACT OR FICTION REVEALED

1. Fiction   2. Fact   3. Fact   4. Fiction   5. Fact   6. Fact   7. Fact

MANAGEMENT TERMS

leadership
power
leadership style
Theory X

Theory Y
Great Man Theory
trait theory

contingency theory
path-goal theory
expectancy theory

REVIEW QUESTIONS

1. Define the following terms: (a) leadership, (b) power, (c) leadership style, (d) Theory X, (e) Theory Y, (f) Great Man Theory, (g) trait theory, (h) contingency theory, (i) path-goal theory, (j) expectancy theory.

2. Explain the different leadership styles in the model developed by Rensis Likert.

3. Describe the various sources of power available to a leader.

4. Discuss the concept of leadership style.

5. Outline the evolution of leadership theory.

6. What factors can influence the selection of a leadership style?

7. What conclusions were reached in the Ohio State and University of Michigan studies?

8. Assess Fiedler's contribution to leadership theory.

9. Explain Tannenbaum and Schmidt's continuum of manager-nonmanager behavior.

10. Discuss the current status of path-goal theory.

PROBLEMS AND EXPERIENTIAL EXERCISES

1. Consider the following item from *The Detroit News*.[33]

TOP EXECUTIVES SHARE EIGHTEEN KEYS TO SUCCESS
Career profiles of executives who have reached the top of large organizations were analyzed for The Detroit News *by several leading psychologists who study management, managers and power.*

Eighteen traits were found to be most commonly shared by successful executives. The executives have

1. *Clearly defined goals and career objectives.*
2. *Moved into position to be discovered by exposing their work to the right superiors and acquiring access to memos and reports of rising superiors.*
3. *Won sponsors who tapped them for bigger things, such as working for bosses with a history of rapid advancement, and become crucial subordinates to them. They complemented the boss' skills or style without threatening him.*
4. *Held one job in about every three that was primarily developmental, in order to learn new skills.*
5. *Gladly accepted "special" assignments, even though the jobs initially didn't seem like promotions or anything special.*
6. *Kept flexible by never totally committing themselves to a position or program that, if it failed, could undermine their careers.*
7. *Stressed cooperation rather than competition with other potential executives.*
8. *Worked to keep people with different ideas from becoming personal opponents.*
9. *Refused to let personal feelings be the basis for any action.*
10. *Avoided obvious dead-end jobs.*
11. *Got their way by influencing others to do things voluntarily and cooperatively rather than by intimidation.*
12. *Began early to develop power through personal and professional relationships, by developing special skills and by consciously devel-*
oping such personal attributes as presence and grace.
13. *Created "grapevines" to keep them aware of things going on.*
14. *Learned how to neutralize, utilize, convert, avoid, join and nullify the impact of others.*
15. *Advanced their ideas by displaying self-assurance, decisiveness and confidence, even if they didn't feel it.*
16. *Often made concessions that were more apparent than real.*
17. *Learned how to control the flow of vital information.*
18. *Used power sparingly and gracefully to avoid injuring or antagonizing others.*

Relate these "eighteen keys to success" to the material presented in Chapter 12.

2. Board Chairman John F. Welch, Jr., has described his approach to running General Electric's far-flung operations: "You've got to give people their own businesses and their own heads. Maybe they fail a bit, but let them run."[34] Relate Welch's viewpoint to the material presented in this chapter.

3. It has been suggested that many successful leaders have had a mentor at some critical point in their career development. Typically, the mentor has been some senior person in the organization who took an active interest in the subordinate's professional advancement.[35] Comment on this. Can you identify any examples of this situation?

4. Prepare a report on the leadership style of one of the following:
   A. Margaret Thatcher
   B. Ronald Reagan
   C. Jesse Jackson
   D. Billy Martin
   E. Tom Landry
   F. Martin Luther King
   G. Geraldine Ferraro
   H. John F. Kennedy

5. Submit a brief outline of your own leadership style.

MANAGERIAL INCIDENT: Jack Stafford Leads Pillsbury

Minneapolis-based Pillsbury Co. has annual revenues over $4 billion, and employs 80,000 people, not counting the thousands working at its franchise operations like Burger King. Pillsbury brand names include Green Giant, Totino's, and Haagen-Dazs. The firm's chief executive officer is Jack Stafford, whose announced goal is to make Pillsbury, "the best food company in the world." Stafford sees Pillsbury's employees as the means to this end.

Stafford comments: "People are very important to me and I'm quite sensitive to what's important to them. As a result, I try to provide the type of leadership and direction I can rally around." Stafford thinks that making Pillsbury an excellent place to work is important. He continues: "If I really couldn't see any chance of doing it, I wouldn't set it as a goal. I'm quite strategic.

I always have a master plan before I make a tactical decision."

Stafford continued: "I'm decisive. It's not difficult for me to make—or help others make—decisions. I don't spend a lot of time agonizing over these decisions or looking back."

Questions

1. Describe Stafford's leadership style.

2. Relate Stafford's approach to leadership to the material presented in Chapter 12.

3. Do you think you would function effectively as a subordinate in an organization run by Jack Stafford?

Source: Gale Tollin, "New Exec Has Exceptional Ideals for Pillsbury," *Journal-American*, 6 March 1985, p. D3.

13 MOTIVATION

After studying this chapter you should be able to

1. Explain the concept of motivation.
2. Outline Maslow's hierarchy of needs.
3. Explain McClelland's contributions to motivation theory.
4. Discuss Herzberg's two-factor theory of motivation.
5. Explain Skinner's contribution to motivation theory.
6. Relate expectancy theory to motivation.
7. Discuss the concept of locus of control.

STOP ACTION CASE

The Kansas City Royals

Baseball salaries are zooming out of the stadium more often than home runs nowadays. Ever since federal arbitrators ruled that professional baseball players do not have to stay with the teams that first signed them, top players have been jockeying for the best offer they can get—and America's national sport is shaking to its financial foundations.

In 1985, 36 major league players each made at least $1 million. Such astronomical salaries do more than jeopardize the finances of professional baseball; they also tend to affect team quality. Only teams in the biggest cities— New York, Chicago, Los Angeles, Atlanta—can afford to pay the highest salaries, so the best players will naturally gravitate there. So what happens if you own a team in a relatively small place like Kansas City, with only 1.5 million area residents?

Use the materials in Chapter 13 to design a plan that will provide players with sufficient incentive to remain with the Kansas City Royals.

MANAGEMENT FACT OR FICTION

	FACT	FICTION		FACT	FICTION
1. Abraham Maslow said that ego or status needs were the highest level of human needs.	☐	☐	modified through a process of reinforcement.	☐	☐
2. David McClelland's research concluded that institutional managers who were high in the need for power and control, but low in the need for affiliation, were typically the most successful leaders.	☐	☐	5. The Pittsburgh Pirates were mathematically eliminated from the American League playoffs weeks ago. According to expectancy theory, the team would still be highly motivated to end the season with the best possible record..	☐	☐
3. Frederick Herzberg is associated with motivators and hygiene factors.	☐	☐	6. People with internal control believe that what they do affects their lives.	☐	☐
4. Skinner said that reflex behavior can be					

The materials in this chapter will assist you in separating management fact from fiction. Your answers can be checked on page 433.

Motivation is a commonplace aspect of everyone's life, yet it is a difficult concept to define—let alone apply—within an organizational perspective. *Motivation* refers to the forces leading to behavior directed toward the satisfaction of some need. Hunger and the desire for financial security are needs, or motives. Behavior designed to satisfy these needs is motivated behavior, or motivation.[1]

Not all behavior is motivated; some behavior is habitual, or reflexive. But managers must deal with motivated behavior. Motivated behavior can be subdivided into individual and group behavior. Effective management requires a working knowledge of both aspects of motivated behavior. Psychologist Kurt Lewin's field theory offered such an explanation. Lewin believed that people were influenced by a variety of factors and that this

Motivation refers to the forces leading to behavior directed toward the satisfaction of some need.

established their behavior patterns. Lewin labeled his conceptualization of behavior as field theory and suggested the following formula:[2]

$$B = f(P, E)$$

Lewin's equation states that behavior (B) is a function of factors (f) related to the person (P), as well as the environmental factors (E) that affect the individual. The recognition of both personal and environmental influences was an important contribution to management's understanding of behavior and motivation.

Chapter 13 approaches motivation from the individual and group viewpoints. Various theories of individual behavior are advanced, with particular attention given to the major contributors in this area. Chapter 14 will examine motivation from a group perspective. Classic studies such as the Hawthorne research and the work done by Miles, Whyte, Seashore, Bales, Kahn, and Likert will be explored. Chapter 14 concludes with a section on the problems and constraints in applying motivation theory.

THEORIES OF INDIVIDUAL BEHAVIOR

Motivation is a critical subject for management, and a number of theories have been developed in an attempt to explain motivational behavior. Maslow, McClelland, Herzberg, Skinner, Vroom, and Rotter are some of the names associated with the various theories that have been advanced to explain why people behave as they do. Each of these viewpoints offers an important perspective or insight related to the study of motivation.

MASLOW'S HIERARCHY OF NEEDS

One of the best-known explanations of individual motivation is a proposition formulated by psychologist Abraham Maslow.[3] In 1943 Maslow identified several needs in people and arranged them in a hierarchical order (see Figure 13–1). Maslow's theory was later popularized when it was put into managerial terms in Douglas McGregor's book *The Human Side of Enterprise*, published in 1960.

Maslow's Classification System. Maslow theorized that people are driven by several needs, not just one. These can be categorized as physical or physiological needs, safety or security needs, love or social needs, ego or status needs, and self-actualization needs (also called self-realization or self-fulfillment needs).

Physical needs are those related to food, clothing, and shelter. The manager can motivate people through these needs by offering adequate wages and salary. Other factors relating to physical needs that might be under the manager's control are working hours and aspects of the physical environment, such as rest rooms, temperature, lighting, and noise level.

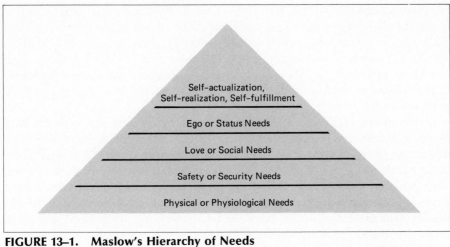

FIGURE 13–1.   Maslow's Hierarchy of Needs
Source: Based on Abraham H. Maslow, "A Theory of Human Motivation," *Psychological Review* (July 1943): 370–396.

It is one thing to have food in the stomach and a roof over the head for one day; it is something else again to have these things day after day. The need to ensure against deprivation is the security need. Again, there are many ways managers can appeal to this need. Insurance, retirement benefits, and unemployment compensation are common security need satisfiers. Others include consistent supervisory treatment, grievance procedures, and job continuity.

The social needs include the need to talk to others, to associate with others, to express feelings of friendship, to accept and be accepted. Managers satisfy this type of need by providing opportunities for employees to interact. This can be done by rearranging the physical layout of the plant or office, by allowing coffee breaks, providing lunch facilities, and offering recreational activities.

The ego needs involve self-esteem as well as the esteem one has in the eyes of others. A manager can give a deserving employee many symbols of status that fulfill these ego needs; job titles, privileged parking, private secretaries, spacious offices, promotions, and pay packages that include stock options, a company car, and merit awards. Contributing to the self-esteem of an employee, while more difficult to project within the employee's capability, will provide a chance for considerable self-esteem. Providing adequate training will help an employee successfully accomplish his or her work and enjoy the fruits of that labor.

The highest of Maslow's needs is self-actualization. Of all the needs listed, this is the vaguest and perhaps most controversial. Maslow described self-actualization this way: "What a man can be he must be."[4] This is clarified somewhat by his description of a self-actualized person: good perception of reality, spontaneous acceptance of self and others, problem centering, creative, independent. Most management experts feel that an employee's drive to self-actualization can be tapped by giving the person freedom of expression. This might be accomplished by allowing employees to participate in decision making and giving them the power to shape their own jobs.

As the model in Figure 13–1 indicates, a person's first concerns are with meeting his or her immediate physical needs. Once these have been satisfied, the person's concerns focus on other matters; namely, securing the basic needs over the long run. When one feels secure, new needs will emerge—the social needs. Once physical, safety, and social needs have been at least partially met, the person will next be concerned with ego needs. And once ego needs have been satisfied, the individual will move on to the endless task of self-actualization.

According to Maslow, people move from one need level to the next, in building-block fashion. This seems to be a fairly accurate picture of the way most individuals behave, and so Maslow's hierarchy has become widely accepted in the field of management. The model's powers of description can be highlighted by looking at the hierarchy in reverse. Consider, for instance, the successful executive—confident, accomplished, and widely admired. Suddenly, the person's life is shattered by the loss of a spouse. The person's love needs are not met. The person's work suffers and he or she loses a sense of direction. Finding meaningful relationships with people is now more important than power and prestige. Only when the individual's social needs are satisfied do status and achievement once again have real meaning.

An even more drastic example of the hierarchy operating in reverse is the disruption created by a major crisis such as a natural disaster or a food shortage. Even the most civilized people have been known to forget their desires for friends and status in the scramble to survive. The higher needs do seem to have meaning only when resting upon the satisfaction of lower ones.

Maslow noted that the needs hierarchy is only a general model. He thought that while most people behave this way, the hierarchy is not perfectly accurate. There is overlap where several needs may be acting at once, although one probably predominates. Also, the amount of need satisfaction varies from person to person. The dedicated artist may move rapidly through meager lower-level need satisfaction in order to reach a point of self-expression.

Maslow also recognized that some people fixate at one need level and seem never to move on to another. One possible cause is a severe denial of that need earlier in life. An example could be the excessive reliance of some young people on their peer relationships. If these individuals come from homes where parents had little time to devote to their children, it could be that these offspring fixated at the social need level.

Maslow's Critics. Many people take exception to Maslow's claim of a valid general model of behavior. Maslow, in his original writings, was quite clear in saying that the total, fully functioning human being is a self-actualized one. Anyone at less than this level is basically not satisfied; in his words, a person deprived of higher need satisfaction "is as surely sick as if he had suddenly developed a strong salt hunger or calcium hunger."[5] The criticism expressed widely in the management literature is that since few people ever have the opportunity to reach the level of self-actualization, most people are doomed to a restless state of dissatisfaction. It would seem to critics that too many people functioning at lower need levels are relatively satisfied for Maslow's observation to be true. Maslow's critics argue that his overall theory may be descriptive of many people, but that it is doubtful it is true of most people.

Carl Rogers and others have discussed the *self-concept,* the image a person has of who he or she is.[6] The self-concept is shaped over long periods by many outside forces such as parents, teachers, friends, and work associates, among others.

> **Self-concept** is the image a person has of who he or she is; it is shaped over a long period of time by many outside forces.

This viewpoint would suggest that one's self-concept can influence the impact that needs hierarchy has on individual motivations. For example, a person can learn as he or she matures and goes through life that he or she is good at relating to other people. The person's self-concept is that of a social person. If this becomes a stable pattern, such a person would not feel unfulfilled at never experiencing other motives such as ego or self-actualization, to use Maslow's terms. In the same way, a stable self-concept could form around some other need or combination of needs. People may not feel an inevitable drive to climb the needs hierarchy, as Maslow depicts it.

Maslow's Contribution to Motivation Theory. Maslow's model has been of considerable value to the practice of management. Perhaps its most important contribution is that it has encouraged managers to use a wide variety of motivational tools to appeal to several motives, rather than depend on one or a few.

A second contribution of Maslow to practicing managers was his insistence that satisfied needs are not motivators. Enlightened managers must attempt to locate the optimal point in each effort to motivate subordinates. Once a need has been satisfied, it loses its motivational importance and is replaced by a different need. Employees may insist on economic security to the point that they will strike to get it. But once they have adequate wages and comprehensive insurance coverage, their concerns will shift. Next they might be concerned with the "humanization" of their workplace, such as having access to some place where they can meet and mingle with other people. The manager who continues offering pay raises and insurance policies to employees who have moved on to social needs will obtain little motivational payoff while incurring additional economic costs.

McCLELLAND'S ACHIEVEMENT, AFFILIATION, AND POWER NEEDS THEORY

David C. McClelland, professor of psychology at Harvard University, is also credited with contributions to motivation theory.[7] McClelland identifies three needs: (1) need for achievement (the desire to accomplish some goal or task more effectively than has been the case in the past); (2) need for affiliation (the desire to have close, amenable relations with other people); and (3) need for power (the desire to be influential and to have impact on a group).

McClelland and his associates have conducted numerous workshops at which participants are asked to write narrative comments about a series of work-related pictures. These stories are then analyzed and scored according to the person's relative concern for achievement, affiliation, and power. A comparison to nationwide norms is also part of the process. McClelland also studies the degree of self-control or inhibition that the individuals exhibit in their stories.

Much of McClelland's early work suggested that the need for achievement was important to business people, scientists, and professional persons.[8] A later report restricted to managers concluded that the need for power was most important to management. McClelland identifies three types of managers: affiliative managers (affiliation greater than power, high inhibition); personal power managers (power greater than affiliation, low inhibition); and institutional managers (power greater than affiliation, high inhibition). He concluded that the institutional managers who were high in the need for power and self-control, but low in the need for affiliation, were typically the most successful leaders.

Implications for Management. McClelland believes that the workshop technique can accurately assess people's achievement, affiliation, and power motivations. More important, he believes that people can be taught to adopt a more appropriate approach to their jobs.

❝ You can't pick cherries with your back to the trees. **❞**

J. Pierpont Morgan

HERZBERG'S TWO-FACTOR THEORY OF MOTIVATION

Frederick Herzberg's research on motivation led to the development of his two-factor theory, which considered both job satisfaction and job dissatisfaction.[9] Herzberg, Distinguished Professor of Management at the University of Utah, asked 200 accountants and engineers what was satisfying about their work; that is, what were they willing to work harder to get. The accountants and engineers gave these answers: the opportunity to achieve through their work; some recognition by others for their work; the opportunity for promotion; the chance to grow, learn, and take on new responsibilities. Herzberg called these factors motivators.

Herzberg also asked his sample what factors dissatisfied them, making them unwilling to produce. Surprisingly, a whole new set of factors was

THE MANAGER'S BOOKSHELF

The Share Economy, by Martin Weitzman

 Martin Weitzman believes he has found a cure for America's ailing economy, particularly that mixture of unemployment and inflation called stagflation. The M.I.T. economist, in his book *The Share Economy,* says American business must abandon the fixed wage structure and start paying workers according to how well the firm does that year. If the firm makes money, the workers share the profits; if it loses, they share the losses—hence, the title "share economy."

Weitzman believes that fixed wages are the main reasons that the U.S. economy fails to grow at the same time it fails to keep prices down. He says that, when sales decrease, companies are reluctant to cut prices, because they are unable or unwilling to reduce wages. Indeed, they often raise them.

But what if workers agreed to a small set salary and took their chances on the success of the company they worked for? Then, when sales dropped, income would also drop, but no one would be laid off. This recession would be shared by all alike. The real losers under Weitzman's plan would be high-seniority workers, who are rarely laid off in a recession anyway, and the labor movement, which has struggled for years to increase workers' bargaining power over their own wages. Weitzman admits that not just a few, but many corporations would have to adopt his plan for it to have a chance to work. But he believes that even a modest version of his plan would work in the U.S. economy. The adoption of the share economy concept would obviously have a profound effect on employee motivation.

Source: Charles P. Alexander, "Search for a Miracle Cure," *Time,* 20 May 1985.

mentioned. People complained when their supervision was poor, when they didn't get a chance to mingle with other people on the job, when physical working conditions were uncomfortable, when their pay and benefits were too low, and when they thought they might lose their jobs. These were called hygienic factors by Herzberg.

Herzberg's original study was replicated several times by other researchers. Respondents included lower-level supervisors, professional women, agricultural administrators, men about to retire from management positions, hospital maintenance personnel, manufacturing supervisors, nurses, food handlers, military officers, engineers, scientists, housekeepers, teachers, technicians, female assemblers, accountants, Finnish foremen, and Hungarian engineers.[10] A profile of motivators and hygiene factors in an organization is shown in Figure 13–2.

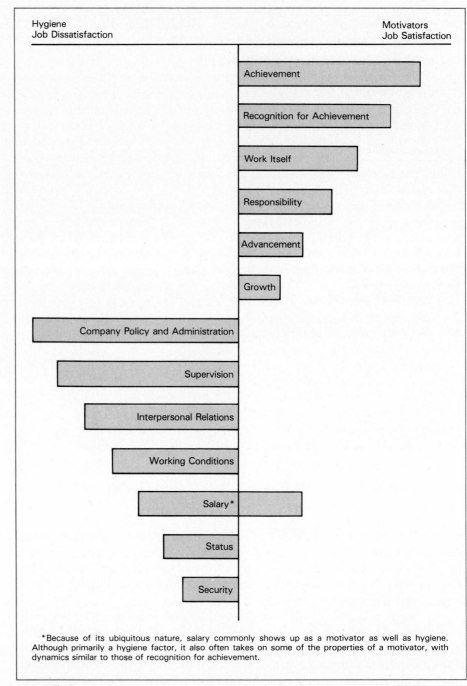

FIGURE 13–2.   Classic Profile of Motivators and Hygiene Factors in an Organization
Source: Reprinted from Frederick Herzberg, *The Managerial Choice: To Be Efficient or to Be Human* (Salt Lake City: Olympus Publishing Co., 1982).

Implications for Management. The resolution of hygienic problems prevents employees from being dissatisfied and keeps their productivity at expected levels. Consider the special efforts of Eaton Corp., a company that has created an aura of mutual respect in its factories built over the past fifteen years. With no history of mutual distrust to overcome, both management and employees of Eaton's newest fifteen plants have made some important changes in traditional factory conditions, including the elimination of the probationary employment period, time clocks, and buzzers. Benefits have been equalized for factory and office workers at the same salary level. Supervisors now hold periodic departmental meetings, often with a subordinate as a discussion leader. In 1985, Eaton moved to expand the application of this management style throughout the company.[12] A written set of management principles, based on the experiences at newer plants, was developed and now serves as "The Eaton Philosophy." These principles are:

- Focus on the positive behavior of employees.

- Encourage employee involvement in decisions.

- Communicate with employees in a timely and candid way, with emphasis on face-to-face communications.

- Compensate employees competitively, under systems that reward excellence.

- Provide training for organization/individual success.

- Maintain effective performance appraisal systems.

- Emphasize promotion-from-within throughout the company.

- Select managers and supervisors who demonstrate an appropriate blend of human relation skills and technical competence.

The extra effort from employees—doing more than normal—comes from providing the motivators and not from resolution of hygienic problems, according to Herzberg's theory. Note that the motivators are roughly the same as Maslow's ego and self-actualization needs, whereas the hygienic factors are basically the physical, security, and social needs. In fact, Herzberg's research is viewed by some writers as concrete proof of Maslow's theory.

Herzberg's research illustrates that innate feelings about motivation can be misleading. The opposite of satisfaction may not be dissatisfaction, and eliminating dissatisfaction may not make people satisfied.

The implications for management are further complicated by the inconsistency of the research findings. Herzberg's conclusions have been confirmed by other studies, but they have been challenged by still others. Some studies have found that certain people apparently reverse the mo-

MANAGEMENT SUCCESSES

Motivation Theory in the National Football League

 A survey of NFL head coaches indicated that motivation theories popular in management also play a role in professional football. The researchers asked the coaches to indicate their relative agreement or disagreement with twenty-five statements concerning the motivation and handling of their team members. The questions were phrased in football terminology, but each was designed to solicit the viewpoints of the coaches toward a specific motivational theory and its importance in professional football. For example, one item said: "The player's present salary is his number one motivator for the present season," and was intended to obtain the person's view of Herzberg's two-factor theory.

The researchers concluded that NFL coaches generally support the various motivational theories used by business management. The coaches' tendency is to emphasize psychological motivation such as ego building or the rejection of being benched, rather than to rely on motivations such as money or tougher practice sessions. The researchers observed that the successful coaches specifically noted that individual motivations varied among players and that these differences had to be recognized and dealt with effectively.

Source: Charles N. Waldo and Kelly Kerin, "NFL Coaches and Motivation Theory," *MSU Business Topics* (Autumn 1978): 15-18. Reprinted by permission of the publisher, Division of Research, Graduate School of Business Administration, Michigan State University.

tivators and hygienic factors.[12] These people are motivated by the same factors that Herzberg's theory considered to be hygienic, and they are dissatisfied by what he labeled as motivators. While the results of such investigations may vary, Herzberg's recognition of the two-factor theory of job satisfaction and job dissatisfaction is a widely discussed contribution to the literature of motivation both by academicians and by practicing managers.

B. F. SKINNER—MODIFYING OPERANT BEHAVIOR

B. F. Skinner, a noted psychologist, has offered some important contributions to the study of motivation. While Skinner's work has been criticized on many counts, it remains a strong theoretical underpinning to much of applied motivational theory in management.

Operant behavior is voluntary behavior.

Reflex behavior is involuntary behavior.

Reinforcement is the process by which behavior is modified by either positive or negative factors.

Skinner distinguishes between *operant behavior* (that which is voluntary) and *reflex behavior* (that which is involuntary).[13] He advocates the premise that operant behavior can be modified through the process of reinforcement. *Reinforcement* refers to the confirmation of outcomes of behavior. It can be either positive or negative. Skinner described the difference this way:

A positive reinforcement strengthens any behavior that produces it: a glass of water is positively reinforcing when we are thirsty, and if we then draw and drink a glass of water, we are more likely to do so again on similar occasions. A negative reinforcer strengthens any behavior that reduces or terminates it; when we take off a shoe that is pinching, the reduction in pressure is negatively reinforcing, and we are more likely to do so again when a shoe pinches.[14]

Implications for Management. A work environment that succeeds in rewarding desirable behaviors and eliminating undesirable behaviors can help to change worker behavior. Workers understand that they are being evaluated in an objective manner and not according to the whim of a manager. With positive feedback, workers can build self-esteem and self-confidence and perform only those behaviors that are rewarded with positive feedback. Like McClelland's theory, Skinner's theory proposes that people will continually seek ways to receive reinforcement, and this reinforcement then increases motivation.

Managers are responsible for creating a work environment that will enhance motivation. Managers have the choice of using one of four partial reinforcement schedules to shape behavior: fixed interval schedules, variable interval schedules, fixed ratio schedules, and variable ratio schedules.

A fixed interval schedule reinforces on a specified period of time such as the end of each work week. A variable interval schedule reinforces on a variable time interval such as on some average time period. A fixed ratio schedule reinforces on the basis of units of output, when a certain number of desired responses occur. A variable ratio schedule reinforces on the basis of output, but on an average time period.

Research studies investigating the relative effectiveness of these four schedules suggest that some are more effective for learning new behaviors while others are more effective for sustaining them. For example, reinforcement every time a desired response occurs influences the fastest learning, but the behavior stops when the reinforcement does. Schedules based on output rather than time are more effective. Variable ratio reinforcement is the strongest for sustaining behavior. Generally, any partial schedule is more effective for sustaining behavior than continuous reinforcement.[15]

EXPECTANCY THEORY

Expectancy theory is another important viewpoint in the study of motivation. Victor Vroom, professor of administrative sciences and psychology at Yale University, has described the concept of expectancy as "a monetary belief concerning the likelihood that a particular act will be followed by a particular outcome."[16] Vroom believes that the force to perform any act is a function of (1) the expectancy and (2) the perceived value of the outcome. He termed his second variable valence.[17]

Consider the case of a sales representative participating in an employer-sponsored sales contest. The salesperson getting the most orders for a new product line will win a vacation trip to Mexico. The representative's perception of the trip's value is the valence. The expectancy theory is the probability of the individual actually winning the trip. If the firm has a sales force of 150 people, the representative may rate his or her expectancy as relatively low.

Lawler and Porter and others have described expectancy theory as a path-goal concept. The basic premise is that people take actions that are likely to result in rewards that are considered worthwhile.[18] A generalized definition might be: *expectancy theory* refers to motivated behavior designed to achieve highly probable and valued rewards, which, in turn, lead to job satisfaction if the rewards are deemed fair.

Lawler and Porter have offered a theoretical model of this process (see Figure 13–3). According to the model, performance or accomplishment produces rewards. *Extrinsic rewards* are those offered by the organization such as pay, promotions, and job security. The wavy connecting line suggests the imperfect linkage between performance and such rewards. By contrast, the semiwavy line to intrinsic rewards suggests that these are subject to less disruption. *Intrinsic rewards* are those that the individual gains internally. Self-actualization is an intrinsic reward.

There is no direct link between the rewards and job satisfaction because the rewards must be perceived as equitable in relationship to the level of job performance. The individual has to view the rewards as in fair balance with the effort he or she exerts on the job. Lawler and Porter have empirically tested the model, and their findings suggest that it is a valid description of motivation.[19]

Implications for Management. Expectancy theory has important implications for management. It explains why even a manager's sincere efforts can sometimes go astray. There are three key steps in using expectancy

> **Expectancy theory** refers to motivated behavior designed to achieve rewards that are likely to lead to job satisfaction.

FIGURE 13–3.   The Lawler-Porter Model
Source: Edward E. Lawler III and Lyman W. Porter, "The Effect of Performance on Job Satisfaction," *Industrial Relations* (October 1967): 23. Used with permission.

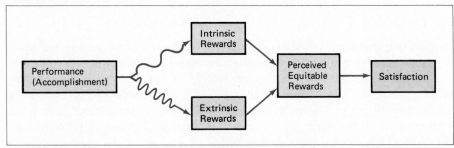

theory in contemporary management. First, one must determine what it is that an employee wants or values. David Mahoney, former CEO of Norton Simon (now part of ESMARK, Inc.) once commented: "You fill people's needs for money, security, whatever it is, everybody wants something, after all, even if it's only a good table at the Pump Room."[20] Mahoney's remarks point out the vast differences that can exist in what people value as a reward. For some, it is financial, for others, it may be recognition.

The next step is to relate the desired reward with job performance. Managers should attempt to ensure that employees perceive a clear linkage between their job performance and the raise, promotion, incentive trip, or whatever else that person seeks. Managers should not allow other factors to interfere with this relationship. Finally, the manager's expectations should be reasonable so that the employee does not perceive the job performance goal as beyond his or her reach. The authors are familiar with a situation where this basic rule was violated. The manager of a sales organization congratulated his sales organization on meeting a high quota the previous month. The manager then proceeded to double the quota for the next month. The net result was a highly discouraged, rather than motivated, sales force.

66 Winning isn't everything, but wanting to win is. 99

Vince Lombardi

THE LOCUS OF CONTROL CONCEPT[21]

Julian B. Rotter's discussion of the locus of control is also a major contribution to the literature of motivation theory.[22] *Locus of control* refers to a person's perception of the controlling factors in his or her own destiny. Individuals who believe that what they do affects their lives are said to have internal control. For example, a person who thinks that extra effort on the job will result in a future promotion can be classified as someone with internal control. By contrast, external control describes a situation in which individuals perceive outside variables as the determining factors in their own destinies. Someone who believes that luck, environmental factors, or others are the casual factors in their personal situation can be classified as an adherent to external control. The terms internal and external are often used to identify these differing viewpoints in locus of control.

Locus of control refers to a person's perception of the controlling factors in his or her own destiny.

Implications for Management. One recent study found that only 20 percent of the workers questioned believed there was a direct link between pay and how hard someone works.[23] This would suggest a strong external control orientation in today's work force.

Most research conducted since Rotter's original proposal has generally supported the locus of control concept. The locus of control has significant implications for management. A review by Gavin and Fleenor suggests that if a work force consisted largely of "internals," management would be well advised to consider participative management techniques. If "externals" dominate the work force, management should ". . . provide relatively

66 Why do you think I'm fighting? The glory? The agony of defeat? You show me a man says he ain't fighting for money, I'll show you a fool. 99

Larry Holmes

structured tasks with responsibilities clearly delineated so as to provide a surfeit of clues to help employees ascribe responsibility for success or failure to their own actions."[24]

Like the other theories of individual behavior reported here, locus of control is an important aspect of understanding what motivates people. Chapter 14 will examine another perspective of motivation, group behavior.

SUMMARY

Motivation refers to behavior directed toward the satisfaction of some need. Motivated behavior can be divided into individual and group behavior. Effective management requires a working knowledge of both aspects of behavior.

Kurt Lewin offers a generalized concept of behavior in his formula

$$B = f(P, E)$$

where behavior is viewed as a function of factors related to the person and the environmental factors that affect him or her. A variety of other theories of individual behavior have been offered.

A. H. Maslow's classification of needs identifies five basic needs: physical or physiological; safety or security; love or social; ego or status; and self-actualization needs. According to Maslow these needs can be put into a hierarchical arrangement. David C. McClelland suggests three needs: the need for achievement, the need for affiliation, and the need for power. Frederick Herzberg's two-factor theory considers both job satisfaction and job dissatisfaction, which are often unrelated to each other. B. F. Skinner discusses the importance of reinforcement (the confirmation of outcomes of behavior) on operant (voluntary) behavior. Victor Vroom, Edward Lawler, and Lyman Porter are associated with expectancy theory, a concept that refers to motivated behavior designed to achieve highly probable and valued rewards, which in turn lead to job satisfaction if the rewards are deemed fair.

Locus of control, a concept proposed by Julian B. Rotter, refers to a person's perception of what influences his destiny. People who have an internal locus of control believe that they can largely determine their own destiny. People who have an external locus of control perceive outside factors as controlling what happens to them. The prevailing locus of control in a work force influences the effectiveness of management practices.

SOLVING THE STOP ACTION CASE

The Kansas City Royals

The Kansas City Royals found an original way to solve the problem of keeping its star players in a small city. Their co-owner, Avron Fogelman, a Memphis real estate developer, is supplementing top players' salaries with the chance to share in lucrative real estate deals—once they've signed a lifetime contract. Fogelman thinks that only by hanging on to George Brett, Dan Quisenberry, and other star players will the Royals be able to attract large enough crowds to make a profit.

Quisenberry, for instance, earns $825,000 a year (which will increase to $1.1 million in three years). This is fairly small potatoes for a pitcher of his stature. But Quisenberry has been offered the chance to invest $2.6 million and get a 25 percent stake in a Nashville apartment complex valued at $35 million, along with a buy-back option. Quisenberry's depreciation on this property will be roughly $600,000 a year, so he will be able to shelter more than half of his salary!

By sharing his investment, Fogelman will have to forgo some of the profits he would otherwise make on his real estate holdings. But he does not seem overly perturbed. "It's cheap money for me," he says. "The building will pay the players." Fogelman has hit on an innovative way to motivate the Royals' stars to stay in Kansas City.

Source: John Merwin, "Rich Team, Poor Team," *Forbes,* 3 June 1985, p. 22.

FACT OR FICTION REVEALED

1. Fiction   2. Fact   3. Fact   4. Fiction   5. Fiction   6. Fact

MANAGEMENT TERMS

motivation
self-concept
operant behavior

reflex behavior
reinforcement

expectancy theory
locus of control

REVIEW QUESTIONS

1. Define the following terms: (a) motivation, (b) self-concept, (c) operant behavior, (d) reflex behavior, (e) reinforcement, (f) expectancy behavior, (g) locus of control.

2. Explain the concept of motivation.

3. Discuss Kurt Lewin's field theory.

4. Describe Maslow's classification of needs.

5. Outline McClelland's achievement, affiliation, and power needs theory.

6. Explain Herzberg's two-factor theory of motivation.

7. Describe B. F. Skinner's contribution to motivation theory.

8. Identify and explain the four partial reinforcement schedules that management can use to shape employee behavior.

9. What is expectancy theory?

10. Discuss the locus of control concept.

PROBLEMS AND EXPERIENTIAL EXERCISES

1. A recent survey found that the following percentages of employees were at least somewhat dissatisfied with the following aspects of their jobs: salary (20 percent); health plan (19 percent); other benefits (17 percent). By contrast only 12 percent were at least somewhat dissatisfied with the job itself.[25] Relate the findings of this study to the theories of individual behavior discussed in Chapter 13.

2. Consider the remarks of two former presidents.[26]

I found that the men and women who get to the top were those who did the jobs that they had in hand, with everything they had of energy and enthusiasm and hard work.

Harry S Truman

Some people think you're finished when you lose. You are finished only when you quit. Never quit. Never, Never, Never.

Richard M. Nixon

Compare and contrast these viewpoints. Relate the remarks about motivation to the career paths of these men.

3. Relate your own behavior to Maslow's needs hierarchy.

4. Rolm Corporation (now part of IBM) faces a tough job market for technical talent in the Silicon Valley of Santa Clara, California. To attract and retain engineers and other high-quality people, Rolm provides an extremely lucrative benefits package. The company offers flexible working hours, a company-subsidized cafeteria, a stock purchase plan, and an on-site recreational facility complete with a gym, two swimming pools, tennis and racquetball courts, saunas, and fitness classes. Six-year employees qualify for a paid three-month leave or a six-week leave with double pay.[27] Relate Rolm's unique fringe benefit package to the material contained in Chapter 13.

5. James Buchanan Duke, the tobacco industry pioneer, was quoted as saying:

I have succeeded in business, not because I have more natural ability than many people who have not succeeded, but because I have applied myself harder and stuck to it longer. I know plenty of people who have failed to succeed in anything who have more brains than I had, but they lacked application and determination.[28]

Do you agree with Duke's observations? Do you think Duke would have agreed with the Truman and Nixon comments above? Discuss.

MANAGERIAL INCIDENT: Lincoln Electric Co.

Cleveland-based Lincoln Electric Co. is the market leader in arc-welding equipment with annual sales between $400 and $500 million. It is also a very innovative company when it comes to motivating employees. Lincoln has used a piece-work system since 1914, and its production workers averaged $44,000 in 1981. A piece-rate system is used as the base compensation plan. It is supplemented by an annual bonus that doubles the workers' yearly earnings. Employees are also guaranteed thirty hours of work each week, and no one has been laid off since 1951.

Lincoln's incentive management program has created a stable, highly motivated, and very productive work force. There are no seniority rights at Lincoln, and everyone

must be willing to be switched to another job. Lincoln's management tries to even out production so it can live up to its employment guarantee. Lincoln workers are very satisfied with the firm's unique compensation plan. In fact, they once voted down a dental plan because it might have reduced year-end bonuses.

Source: William Baldwin, "This is the Answer," *Forbes,* 5 July 1982, pp. 50, 52. Updated by Richard S. Sabo of the Lincoln Electric Co., May 20, 1985.

Questions

1. Relate the Lincoln Electric incentive system to the material presented in this chapter.

2. Pick a firm with which you are familiar. Would a motivation program similar to the one at Lincoln Electric work in this firm? Give reasons for your answer.

14 GROUP DYNAMICS

LEARNING OBJECTIVES

After studying this chapter you should be able to

1. Explain the steps in group development.

2. Describe how conflict can be managed in organizations.

3. Discuss the Hawthorne studies and the development of the human relations school.

4. Explain the human resources model.

5. Discuss the contribution of William F. Whyte and Stanley Seashore to the study of group behavior.

6. Describe the importance of equity behavior and reference groups in group behavior theory.

7. Discuss Robert F. Bales's research on informal group leaders.

8. Relate the concept of morale to productivity.

9. Explain the role of money as a motivator.

10. Identify the major problems and constraints in applying motivation theory.

STOP ACTION CASE

Woodward Governor Co.

Woodward Governor Co. makes an unusual product—governors, which control an engine's fuel intake. So perhaps it shouldn't be surprising that Woodward has an unusual way of managing its personnel.

Woodward's plant in Rockford, Illinois, is staffed by 1,000 "members" (the firm prefers not to call them "employees"). "Membership" seems to involve some pretty strict rules. Men must wear ties; women, dresses or skirts. Everyone has to wear a shopcoat. Long hair and beards are forbidden. So are smoking and drinking coffee on the job. There are no coffee or snack breaks. Maximum vacation is two weeks a year. Even Leo Powelson, the assistant to CEO Calvin Covert, concedes, "We realize these rules are enough to turn people away. We try not to fool anyone into joining this company. We are different in so many respects."

So how <u>does</u> Woodward attract "members"? Well, the factory boasts in-house barbers, a doctor, a dentist, a chaplain, a legal adviser, and an accountant who prepares members' taxes. Free vitamins are available in the cafeteria. And the salaries, though not the highest around, are healthy. They are determined in an unusual way. Every member—managers included—is evaluated by colleagues and supervisors every year; these ratings are the basis for his or her next year's salary. After new workers get through a probationary period of two years, they become official members at a formal swearing-in ceremony, at which each receives a gold pin.

Many observers wonder whether Woodward's distinctive brand of organization really works. They also are curious as to whether it is based on the Japanese, or Theory Z, type of management.

Use the materials in Chapter 14 to evaluate the employment policies of Woodward Governor Co. Determine whether the company uses the human relations or the human resources model.

Groups play a major role in overall behavior patterns. A simple experiment has shown the dramatic effects other people can have on an individual.[1] Three unequal lines were shown to a group of people. They were then given a fourth line and asked to match it visually with the line of the same length in the original cluster of three. People in this group could accomplish this task with very few mistakes over many matching trials.

But then the experiment was varied. In another group doing the same task, all but one person were told to lie about which lines matched. This person, who was unaware of the change, was found to match the wrong lines in about half the trials, usually making the same "mistake" as the others had been told to make. Even though the person knew the correct answer, he or she often changed an opinion just to fit into the group. In other words the individual was conforming.

Conformity is probably the most distinctive aspect of an individual's behavior in a group. In the following discussion, several studies will be cited. Note how conformity, or the lack of it, is important to motivation.

Chapter 14 examines a range of research and theories of group behavior. Group development, managing conflict, the Hawthorne studies, human relations school, human resources model, the contributions of William F. Whyte and Stanley Seashore, equity theory, and reference groups are described here. Chapter 14 also looks at informal group leaders, morale and productivity, money as a motivator, and the problems and constraints of applying motivation theory.

> ❝ You don't get the breaks unless you play with the team instead of against it. ❞
>
> Lou Gehrig

MANAGEMENT FACT OR FICTION

	FACT	FICTION
1. Conformity is probably the most distinctive part of an individual's behavior in a group.	☐	☐
2. Conflict is often a part of the group development process.	☐	☐
3. Managers should not tolerate conflict in their organizations.	☐	☐
4. The Hawthorne studies found that employees' output was linked to good physical working conditions.	☐	☐

	FACT	FICTION
5. Ratebusters typically belonged to several social groups and community organizations.	☐	☐
6. A work group that had a scheduled raise postponed suddenly starts to take longer coffee breaks. This is an illustration of equity theory in action.	☐	☐
7. Robert Bales believed that most small task groups have two leaders.	☐	☐

The materials in this chapter will assist you in separating management fact from fiction. Your answers can be checked on page 454.

GROUP DEVELOPMENT

A starting point in understanding group dynamics is to look at the stages of *group development,* or the process by which groups are established and function. Tuckman offered an excellent summary of group development.[2] People initially test relationships and boundaries. Interpersonal conflict arises and is eventually resolved. Finally, the roles of group members are determined, and those involved begin to work toward group goals. Table 14–1 outlines various models of group development including Tuckman's integrative model.

While group development is an accepted aspect of motivation theory in the United States, it is interesting to look at it from a totally different perspective. The Soviet Union has attempted to increase productivity in its factories by building work groups called "brigades."[3] About twenty workers make up each brigade, which is given responsibility and autonomy to establish its work schedule and the like. Effective performance is recognized, but the entire group is penalized for incidents of alcoholism, absenteeism, and the low output of even a single worker.

MANAGING CONFLICTS IN GROUPS

As suggested above, conflict is a natural part of the group development process. *Conflict* can be defined as the disagreements that occur within and among people in a work group. While most conflict deals with interpersonal relations, it can also exist within individuals. Conflict resulting from uncertainty is often referred to as stress. The more common perspective is that interpersonal conflict is common to work groups because of the different views and objectives of group participants.

Conflict comprises the disagreements that occur within and among people in a work group.

TYPES OF CONFLICTS

Some level of conflict is necessary in all organizations. Conflict should be managed, not hidden or negated. Conflict can therefore be classified into two general categories: positive, or functional conflict; and, negative, or dysfunctional conflict.

Positive Conflict. Proper management of conflict requires that positive conflict be stimulated. In other words, some conflict should be encouraged. On an individual basis, consider the conflict that J. Willard Marriott, Jr. causes his hotel managers. Marriott likes to check his hotels' kitchens at midnight, and laundry rooms at 5 A.M. One of his managers, John Dixon, comments: "When you start trying to anticipate what he'll find, you get better as a manager."[4] Similarly, many executives like to stimulate debate or conflict among their subordinates because they believe it enhances morale and improves decision-making. For instance, William Wrigley, Jr. once remarked: "When two men in business always agree, one of them is unnecessary."[5]

There is sometimes a fine line between positive and negative conflict. Managers must be sure that their attempts to stimulate functional conflict do not go too far and result in dysfunctional conflict. For example, consider a chief executive who encourages conflict and competition among three subordinates. This conflict may produce improved results for the organization. But if the conflict becomes too intense, it can result in the loss of two key executives when one of the three succeeds the CEO.

Negative Conflict. Much conflict is dysfunctional to the organization. It wastes resources and hurts organizational productivity. Negative conflict must be handled to prevent harm to the organization.

TABLE 14–1 MODELS OF GROUP DEVELOPMENT

Schutz's (1958) FIRO Model	Modlin & Faris (1956) Four-Stage Group Developmental Model	Whittaker's (1970) Integrative Model	Hill & Greiner's (1973) Three-Stage Developmental Model	Tuckman's (1965) Integrative Model
Stage 1: In or out Members unsure about joining group Explore boundaries of interpersonal relationships	*Stage 1: Structuralism* Establish status hierarchies based on outside roles Conform to organization's old traditions	*Stage 1: Preaffiliation* Members unsure about joining group Engage in "approach-avoidance" struggle Nonintimate relationships with other members	*Stage 1: Orientation* Structure sought by members Members test group's situation	*Stage 1: Forming* Establish interpersonal relationships Conform to organizational traditions and standards Boundary testing in relationships and task behaviors
Stage 2: Top or bottom Conflict among members Power struggle occurs	*Stage 2: Unrest* Emergence of friction and interpersonal conflict Personalities cause disharmony	*Stage 2: Power and control* Power struggle among members Attempt to establish status hierarchies Attempt to formalize and define relationships	*Stage 2: Exploration* Interpersonal exploration Individual differences emerge	*Stage 2: Storming* Conflict arises because of interpersonal behaviors Resistance to group influence and task requirements Group splits
Stage 3: Near or far Members make commitment to group Clarify interpersonal relationships Emotional integration of members	*Stage 3: Change* New leaders emerge Participation is balanced Groups seen as a unit	*Stage 3: Intimacy* Increase group commitment Group experiences become important	*Stage 3: Production* Definition of interpersonal relations Focus on resolution of process problems Establish group cohesion	*Stage 3: Norming* Single leader emerges Group cohesion established New group standards and roles formed for members

Schutz's (1958) FIRO Model	Modlin & Faris (1956) Four-Stage Group Developmental Model	Whittaker's (1970) Integrative Model	Hill & Greiner's (1973) Three-Stage Developmental Model	Tuckman's (1965) Integrative Model
	Stage 4: Integration Group structure and hierarchy internalized Group's pragmatic purpose emerges Task accomplishment becomes group's goal	*Stage 4: Differentiation* Group accepts individual differences Relationships become more pragmatic Group becomes its own frame of reference *Stage 5: Separation* Group's goals accomplished Group disbanded		*Stage 4: Performing* Members perform tasks together Establish role clarity Teamwork is the norm

Sources: Reprinted from John P. Wanous, Arnon E. Reichers, and S. D. Malik, "Organizational Socialization and Group Development: Toward An Integrative Perspective," *Academy of Management Review* (October 1984): 673. The models referred to in this source are from W. Schutz, "Interpersonal Underworld," *Harvard Business Review* 36 (1958): 123–135; H. Modlin and M. Faris, "Group Adaptation and Interaction in Psychiatric Team Practice," *Psychiatry* 19 (1956): 97–103; J. Whittaker, "Models of Group Development: Implications for Social Group Work Practice," *Social Science Review* 44 (1970): 308–322; W. F. Hill and L. A. Greiner, "A Study of Development in Open and Closed Groups," *Small Group Behavior* 4 (1973): 355–381; and B. Tuckman, "Developmental Sequence in Small Groups," *Psychological Bulletin* 63 (1965): 384–399.

There are several approaches to conflict resolution. Sometimes the manager can work with subordinates in determining the sources of the conflict and possible ways to resolve it. At other times, the manager can note that organizational goals take precedence over the differing views of group members. Compromise is another possibility for conflict resolution.

Some dysfunctional conflict can be tolerated if it is relatively minor. The effort to resolve such conflict may greatly exceed the benefits of doing so. Calvin Coolidge's famous quote: "If you see ten troubles coming down the road, you can be sure that nine will run into the ditch before they reach you," seems to fit here.[6] Finally, there are some conflict situations in which managers simply have to take sides. The manager uses his or her position of authority to rule in favor of one of the parties in the conflict.

The section that follows looks at classical studies of group dynamics. All of these played a major role in what we know about the subject today.

THE HAWTHORNE STUDIES AND THE HUMAN RELATIONS APPROACH

Probably the most famous studies of work group behavior are the Hawthorne studies, performed during the six-year period 1927–1933 at the Hawthorne plant of the Western Electric Co. in Chicago. A total of 20,000 employees were included in this research.[7]

Hawthorne studies were a series of investigations that revealed that money and job security are not the only sources of employee motivation. They led to the development of the human relations approach to employee motivation.

The *Hawthorne studies* looked into the effects of physical working conditions and pay schemes on worker output. The researchers expected to prove how much improving work and pay conditions would increase output. The results were a surprise that has had a far-reaching impact on management.

One set of experiments in the Relay Assembly Test Room involved setting aside a special group of female assemblers, improving such factors as lighting and temperature and measuring the effect on productivity (see Figure 14–1). As the factors improved, output went up. To verify the conclusion, the researchers reversed the conditions (by dimming the lights, for instance) and again measured output. To their astonishment output continued to climb; the worse things got, the higher the productivity rose.

Hawthorne effect refers to the positive impact on employee motivation of factors other than money and job security, as revealed by the Hawthorne studies.

In studying the situation closely, the researchers found that the women were responding to changes other than the experimental ones. The women felt special because they had been picked for the experiment. Also, the arrangement was more informal than the assemblers were accustomed to. They could talk, help each other when someone was not feeling well, and get extra help from the supervisor. Work became more of a social event that even included birthday parties. These unexpected results have been labeled the *Hawthorne effect*.

FIGURE 14-1.   As the Six Women Involved in the Famous Hawthorne Studies Proved, Morale Often Has a Greater Effect on Productivity Than Better Work and Pay Conditions
Source: Courtesy of Western Electric Company.

BIRTH OF THE HUMAN RELATIONS APPROACH

The morale of the group had improved and production rose. As a result of these findings, a movement in management practice began that continued well into the 1950s. It was called the *human relations approach* to management. This school of management was based on the belief that better treatment of subordinates would make them more productive. The accepted viewpoint was that contented employees would work harder.

Human relations management has been praised and condemned, and today few managers accept its tenets without major reservations. The problem was that too many generalizations were drawn from the Relay Assembly Test Room experiments. Many times managers worked hard at human relations only to find that workers ended up disliking them. The employees were unhappy and unproductive. Ironically, the Hawthorne studies themselves could have been used to foresee this if only more attention had been paid to the Bank Wiring Observation Room experiments.

Human relations approach refers to management attempts to improve and increase employees' production by boosting their morale.

THE BANK WIRING OBSERVATION ROOM STUDY

In the Bank Wiring Observation Room study, workers were paid on an incentive pay plan under which their pay increased as their output increased. It was expected that worker output would rise over time; instead, it stayed at a fairly constant level. Further research was required to discover the cause of this situation.

The researchers found a complicated "informal" social life among the workers. It seemed that they had their own idea of what was "a fair day's work" and enforced it themselves. Most of them, the regulars, ignored the incentive plan and voluntarily conformed to the group's standard output, called a group norm. Those who did not conform, the deviates, were disciplined by the group. Employees working too fast were called "rate-busters" or "speed kings" and sometimes were physically threatened to bring them into line. Those working too slowly were ridiculed as "chiselers." Anybody complaining to management was a "squealer" and was likely to end up as an isolate, totally ignored by the group.

As a group, morale was high in the Bank Wiring Room, and yet productivity did not increase. In a sense high morale was working against management, but these results unfortunately were not remembered as well as the Relay Assembly Test Room results.

IMPLICATIONS FOR MANAGEMENT

The Hawthorne studies illustrated that employees' social needs could be a very important part of their motivation. These needs appear in the context of an informal organization that works along with the formal organization and can help or hinder management. From the viewpoint of a supervisor, an informal group can be a positive situation because workers discipline each other and keep production going at an acceptable pace.

THE HUMAN RESOURCES MODEL

Douglas McGregor, Rensis Likert, Mason Haire, and Raymond E. Miles, among others, have suggested a major adaptation to the human relations school.[8] They argue that the human relations school, as it has been popularized in management literature and practice, is really only a modest alteration of the autocratic model that prevailed before the Hawthorne studies. By contrast, they argue that a comprehensive human resources model should be employed in motivational efforts.

Human resources model suggests that management should be responsible for establishing an environment that best utilizes all the human resources for improved decision making and performance.

The *human resources model* suggests that management should be responsible for establishing an environment that can employ all the human resources of the work group with the goal of improved decision making and performance. The basic differences between the human relations and human resources models are outlined in Table 14–2.

Miles points out that research indicates managers have adopted a two-sided view of motivation. He says that managers have widely accepted the tenets of the human relations school and believe it is appropriate for their own subordinates. But when it comes to their own relationships with superiors, managers support the human resources model as the best approach.

WHYTE'S AND SEASHORE'S CONTRIBUTIONS TO THE STUDY OF GROUP BEHAVIOR

WHYTE'S RESEARCH

William F. Whyte, in a study of factory workers, found that regulars and ratebusters tend to have different backgrounds.[9] The conforming regulars were joiners even outside the workplace, where they were members of various social groups and community organizations. They also tended to spend rather than save their earnings and came from the cities.

On the other hand, ratebusters were loners at work and at home. They usually came from rural backgrounds and were thrifty with their money. Whyte found that the ratebusters, who he said behaved in accordance with the Protestant work ethic, were the only workers responding to the piece-rate incentive pay plan. Those who restricted their output to the group norm acted in accordance with what Whyte called the social ethic.

SEASHORE'S RESEARCH

Stanley Seashore, professor of psychology at the University of Michigan, conducted extensive research on group behavior, involving a total of 228 factory work groups.[10] Seashore concluded there was substantial evidence suggesting that these workers actually controlled production.

The group pressure toward conformity was called cohesiveness by Seashore. Groups with high cohesiveness were found to make their members feel more secure and were more likely to have uniformly enforced production norms than were groups with low cohesiveness.

Of the many groups studied by Seashore, some were found to have high productivity and others low productivity. Comparing these groups, Seashore observed that the difference was in the amount of company supportiveness felt by each group. If a group felt confident in management, it would enforce a high production level. If it had a poor opinion of management, its production was uniformly low. Interestingly, group morale was high in either case.

THE ROLE OF EQUITY THEORY AND REFERENCE GROUPS

People usually possess a sense of equity or fairness, which they apply by comparing themselves with some other work group. *Equity theory* refers to the human tendency to try to balance work efforts or inputs with the rewards received. People innately try to reach what they consider to be a fair balance by either reducing or increasing their input in accordance

Equity theory has been offered to explain the human tendency to balance work efforts or inputs with the rewards received.

TABLE 14–2   COMPARISON OF THE HUMAN RELATIONS AND HUMAN RESOURCES MODELS

Human Relations	Human Resources
Attitudes Toward People	
1. People in our culture share a common set of needs—to belong, to be liked, to be respected.	1. In addition to sharing common needs for belonging and respect, most people in our culture desire to contribute effectively and creatively to the accomplishment of worthwhile objectives.
2. They desire individual recognition but, more than this, they want to feel a useful part of the company and their own work group or department.	2. The majority of our work force is capable of exercising far more initiative, responsibility, and creativity than their present jobs require or allow.
3. They will tend to cooperate willingly and comply with organizational goals if these important needs are fulfilled.	3. These capabilities represent untapped resources which are presently being wasted.
Kind and Amount of Participation	
1. The manager's basic task is to make each worker believe that he or she is a useful and important part of the department "team."	1. The manager's basic task is to create an environment in which his or her subordinates can contribute their full range of talents to the accomplishment of organizational goals. He or she must attempt to uncover and tap the creative resources of the subordinates.
2. The manager should be willing to explain his or her decisions and to discuss subordinates' objections to his or her plans. On routine matters he or she should encourage subordinates to participate in planning and choosing among alternative solutions to problems.	2. The manager should allow, and encourage, subordinates to participate not only in routine decisions but in important matters as well. In fact, the more important a decision is to the manager's department, the greater should be his or her effort to tap the department's resources.
3. Within narrow limits, the work group or individual subordinates should be allowed to exercise self-direction and self-control in carrying out plans.	3. The manager should attempt to continually expand the areas over which subordinates exercise self-direction and self-control as they develop and demonstrate greater insight and ability.
Expectations	
1. Sharing information with subordinates and involving them in departmental decision making will help satisfy their basic needs for belonging and for individual recognition.	1. The overall quality of decision making and performance will improve as the manager makes use of the full range of experience, insight, and creative ability in his or her department.

Human Relations	**Human Resources**
2. Satisfying these needs will improve subordinate morale and reduce resistance to formal authority.	2. Subordinates will exercise responsible self-direction and self-control in the accomplishment of worthwhile objectives that they understand and have helped establish.
3. High employee morale and reduced resistance to formal authority may lead to improved departmental performance. It should at least reduce intradepartmental friction and thus make the manager's job easier.	3. Subordinate satisfaction will increase as a by-product of improved performance and the opportunity to contribute creatively to this improvement.

Source: Reprinted by permission of the *Harvard Business Review.* Exhibit from "Human Relations or Human Resources?" by Raymond E. Miles (July–August 1965). Copyright © 1965 by the President and Fellows of Harvard College; all rights reserved.

with their perception of the relative rewards of their effort.[11] For example, when Plitt Theaters Inc. instituted a wage and benefit austerity program, absenteeism went up 30 percent among its salaried personnel. The costs associated with these absences canceled out the savings from the cost-cutting program.[12] Reference groups play a key role in equity evaluations.

The concept of a reference orientation among workers is the product of studies of group behavior. *Reference groups* are those sets or categories of people with which a person belongs, and sometimes it is with people outside the firm. Behavior patterns are often predicated on what an individual perceives to be happening with his or her reference group.

Reference groups are those sets or categories of people with which a person identifies.

Many supervisors have been dismayed when suddenly, for no apparent reason, the amount or quality of their workers' production drops off. Studies have found that the explanation is often a change in some other departments or group of employees that has upset the workers' sense of equity.[13] For example, if another department got a pay raise for basically the same work, it could set off this kind of reaction: "If they got a raise and aren't working any harder for it, then relatively speaking we are worse off. But if we work less for our pay, then things will balance out."

Conversely, other supervisors have been surprised to see production rise even when no changes were made in their departments. The explanation: A change was made in some other departments, such as a less desirable work schedule that made other workers feel that they were better off. Feeling a sense of guilt, they instinctively worked harder to make things right again.

Reference orientation has been found to be especially important among professional workers.[14] A college professor who identifies with his or her college or an engineer who identifies with his or her firm are said to have

MANAGEMENT SUCCESSES

COHORT

In 1981, the U.S. Army initiated an innovative new organizational plan that applies many of the theories of group behavior discussed here. COHORT (COHesion Operational Readiness Training) is the first significant change of its type since World War II. Instead of training and transferring soldiers in and out of units on an individual basis, COHORT keeps the same group of soldiers together throughout their initial three years of enlistment. The Officer and Noncommissioned Officer leadership of these units are also stabilized on a cyclic basis. The Army believes that reducing personnel turbulence within their units will generate a personal bonding and cohesiveness resulting in improved combat readiness and effectiveness.

Source: Department of the Army, June 5, 1985.

a bureaucratic or local orientation. Those who identify with groups outside their organization, such as with trade or professional associations or colleagues employed elsewhere, are said to have a professional or cosmopolitan orientation. Locals are much more likely to be loyal to their employer and seldom switch jobs. Cosmopolitans are more likely to make frequent job changes.

INFORMAL GROUP LEADERS

Robert F. Bales performed some interesting experiments with small task groups.[15] One of his goals was to find what would cause a person to be identified as group leader by the members. This was done by having the group work at a task and then asking the members anonymously to identify the leader when they were finished. Bales consistently found that the person who had the best ideas and offered the group the most guidance in doing its task was identified as the leader.

Then Bales asked the group members to identify the person they liked the most. The groups tended to pick someone other than the leader as most popular. Bales concluded that the groups naturally tended to have two leaders. He called one the task leader (formal leader) and the one best liked the social-emotional leader *(informal group leader)*. Further study by Bales found that the social-emotional leader performed certain functions in the group different from those of the task leader. This leader typically

Informal group leader is a leader in a group who functions as a social-emotional leader.

THE MANAGER'S BOOKSHELF

The One-Minute Manager, by Kenneth Blanchard and Spencer Johnson

The One-Minute Manager relates the story of a young man who embarks on a search for the perfect manager. The search ends when the young man finds his guru—the One-Minute Manager—who agrees to share his great wisdom with him. All of this the authors manage to squeeze into 106 large-type, wide-margin pages.

The One-Minute Manager did not fare very well with reviewers—particularly academic reviewers, who referred to it as "Dick and Jane at the office" and "the management writer's answer to *People* Magazine." On the other hand, the book fared quite well with the general public, who bought over a million copies in hardback alone.

One-minute management has three components, according to the authors: one-minute goal setting, one-minute praisings, and one-minute reprimands. One-minute goal setting consists of getting the supervisor and the subordinate to agree on the subordinate's work goals. The authors suggest writing each goal on a single sheet of paper so that the manager can read it in a minute or less. Once the goals are set, say the authors, the subordinate should check regularly to see whether he or she is actually meeting those goals.

One-minute praisings rely on one of the basic tenets of behavioral psychology: People like to be rewarded when they do something right. The authors suggest that managers praise a subordinate's performance even when it falls a little short of perfect.

Finally, there are one-minute reprimands, which is something of a misnomer, since these are hardly the dressing-down most workers have experienced. Spend a half-minute telling a subordinate exactly what he or she did wrong and let the person know how you feel about it, say the authors. Then spend another half-minute telling the subordinate how much you value the rest of his or her work.

The One-Minute Manager is seasoned with a sprinkling of advice, some of which can be paraphrased as:

Workers who like themselves produce results others will like.
Managers should be sure to tell their people what they want them to do.
Feedback is the best way to motivate people.

These all add up to a general philosophy that runs something like this: A manager's main job is to get things done through his or her subordinates. The manager can be tough and gentle at the same time, and can do it all efficiently, with minimal waste of time.

It is that efficiency that readers find so appealing. *The One-Minute Manager* not only promises to make managers better, it promises to do it in one-minute installments. The book itself can be read in less than a half hour, and this is a large part of its appeal. Spencer has followed it up with a stream of other one-minute books, and there have been a number of spinoffs as well.

Source: David Nye, "Just a Minute," *Across the Board* (February 1983): 60.

helped the others, laughed, exhibited understanding toward others, and supported their ideas. He or she helped the group relax by means of democratic techniques. Meanwhile, the task leader was creating tension by pushing the group toward its goal with more autocratic techniques.

Some formal leaders feel threatened by informal leaders so they attempt to undermine or eliminate their power. But this may prove to be a mistake. The job and the employee may have differing leadership needs. The existence of both a task leader and a social-emotional leader may be very desirable under such circumstances.

MORALE AND PRODUCTIVITY

Most people believe that a satisfied group is a productive group and, as noted earlier, this thinking propelled the human relations movement. Yet research has shown that this is not always true, and so the relationship of morale to productivity deserves special attention. In an extensive summary of research conducted by the University of Michigan's Survey Research Center, Robert L. Kahn concluded that there is no reliable relationship between satisfaction and productivity.[16] These studies covered workers as varied as insurance file clerks, railroad gangs, and factory workers and employed numerous measures of satisfaction. In addition, another comprehensive review of the literature found little relationship between job satisfaction and measures of performance.[17]

Many persons simply find work to be an irritant—the more they do, the more dissatisfied they are. Many employees look upon their job as something they must do. Their real satisfaction, however, lies with friends, family, or colleagues off the job. Efforts to satisfy such people may not translate into increased productivity. Morale and productivity may rise only if the inducement is made conditional upon increasing productivity. It should be noted that, for a great number of people, the desire to produce is at odds with their need to fit in with their work group.

It would seem that the strongest relationship between satisfaction and productivity exists when someone derives fulfillment from his or her work. The more the person works, the happier he or she is. If the factors like working conditions are poor, then such a worker may express dissatisfaction; yet as long as the individual can work, production will remain high.

The manager should try to create work groups that are satisfied and produce at high levels. If this is not possible, the manager may have to choose between satisfied, low-producing groups or dissatisfied, high producing employees. Managers typically opt for the dissatisfied, high output combination because of the pressure to produce results.

Rensis Likert has argued that this is the wrong choice, at least in the long run.[18] In the short run, having high-producing, dissatisfied employees may get the job done, but in many cases dissatisfaction causes costs that must be offset against the short-run productivity gains. These costs include

66 The true worth of man is not to be found in man himself but in the colors and textures that come alive in others. 99

Albert Schweitzer

66 Work is for man and not man for work. 99

Pope John Paul II

employee tardiness, absenteeism, turnover, and even sabotage. Likert argues that sustained dissatisfaction causes a depletion of the human asset. The problem may be compounded by the fact that most firms do not periodically assess their employees' attitudes.[19] Likert recommends that firms keep track of their human assets just as carefully as they do their financial assets through what he calls human asset accounting, or systematic employee attitude surveys.

The situation described by Likert exists in many firms. Large assembly operations with strong unions are particularly vulnerable to the indirect costs of prolonged dissatisfaction. It behooves management to try to eliminate these costs. But this may be impossible because of technological and economic constraints. It may also be beyond management's power to cure dissatisfaction. Furthermore, dissatisfaction does not always lead to absenteeism, tardiness, turnover, and the like. For example, even dissatisfied workers tend to stay on the job during periods of high unemployment.

MONEY AS A MOTIVATOR

Probably the most powerful motivational tool that a manager has is money. As an exchange medium, a worker may use money to buy practically any type of need satisfaction. A person can buy food, a house, insurance, investments, entertainment, an automobile, and achieve fulfillment by paying tuition for college courses. A person can achieve much of Maslow's hierarchy with the purchasing power of money alone.

Money also has an important symbolic value. On the job a worker's status may be determined by the extra ten cents per hour he or she gets for doing one job rather than another. The word bonus often implies that a manager is in a high-status job. And accumulated wealth is sometimes used by people as a measure of level of accomplishment in life.

Despite money's power it is worth noting that it sometimes does not exert the effect a manager expects. As Herzberg points out, money can be a hygienic factor for many people, preventing dissatisfaction but not motivating them to do more work than the minimum required to keep their jobs.

But the most dramatic effect of money as a motivator comes from the work group. The Bank Wiring experiments at Hawthorne and the studies of factory workers by Whyte suggest that the need of a worker to be accepted by his or her peers can be a more important motivator than money.[20] In both studies only a small minority—about 10 percent in Whyte's study—actually responded to a monetary incentive. And Whyte found that his deviants planned to use the money to educate and train themselves so they could get a better job somewhere else.

Equity theory showed money to be a relative thing. Of course, employees are concerned with the absolute amount of their wages, but whether they are satisfied depends in part on how well they compare to other groups with whom they refer. Employees of one group may be quite satisfied with their wages until they find out that some other group or union received a larger pay hike. Suddenly they feel dissatisfied, clamor for more money, and adjust the quality or amount of their work.

PROBLEMS AND CONSTRAINTS IN APPLYING MOTIVATION THEORY

Motivation theory, as described in Chapters 13 and 14, is obviously an imperfect science. Perhaps the most important lesson that one can learn from studying modern motivation theories is the extent of management's incomplete knowledge of individual and group behavior. Due care must be taken in attempting to apply such rudimentary knowledge.

What are the practical limitations of motivating an employee? The biggest problem is simply finding out what is important to a particular person. How does the manager know, for instance, if an employee considers security to be a motivator or a hygiene factor? How does the manager know at which level the person is in Maslow's hierarchy?

One crude way is to check whether the employee fits the description of the research samples. So, if the person is an accountant, he or she may react the same as the accountants in Herzberg's sample.

Another way would be simply to ask employees what they consider important, either directly or through a survey, as in Likert's human asset accounting. But sometimes the employee's declared attitude is different from his or her real attitude. Many respondents will tell a questioner what they think they are expected to say. Even trained researchers find it difficult to determine people's real attitudes. Then there is the question of whether attitudes will be translated into behavior.

As a result of these problems and constraints management must rely on trial-and-error application of motivation theories. The manager may try, for example, to motivate employees with more money, and if that is not effective, other motivational techniques may be tried. Motivation theory and research can help management make educated guesses about employees' needs, but the application stage must involve a trial-and-error approach.

While much of motivation theory emphasizes the individual, and the need for management to individualize its dealings with people, there is considerable pressure to do exactly the opposite. Unions, fearing arbitrary management decisions, battle for uniform work rules that ensure equal treatment of workers. Our legal framework also works against individual motivation of subordinates. Even such factors like physical working conditions can be mandated to meet certain standards, as under the Occupational Safety and Health Act.

Overall, modern management faces many constraints in treating people as individuals. Still, compared to their predecessors, they have greater knowledge available to help them in efficiently and effectively motivating subordinates—as either groups or individuals.

SUMMARY

Group dynamics is an important aspect of the study of motivation. This chapter noted that groups experience a series of developmental steps. The concept of conflict as it relates to groups has also been explored. The best-known research in group dynamics are the Hawthorne studies, conducted over fifty years ago. The researchers expected to prove that better work and pay conditions would increase output. Instead, their studies suggested a link between morale and productivity. The so-called human relations school was largely based on these findings.

The human resources model implies that executives should create an environment that uses all the available human resources so as to improve both performance and decision making. McGregor, Likert, Haire, and Miles among others are associated with this viewpoint.

Further research by Whyte and Seashore found that certain workers often restricted or controlled output in accordance with what they viewed as group norms. Another aspect of group behavior is equity theory, which states the human tendency to balance work efforts or inputs with the rewards received. People compare their relative inputs and rewards with those of reference groups, those categories of persons with which individuals identify.

Robert F. Bales concluded that all groups have a task leader and a social-emotional leader. The task leader tends to be the individual with the best ideas for guiding the group toward the completion of its task. The social-emotional leader is the person best liked by the group.

Chapter 14 also showed that morale is not always linked to productivity. In addition, the use of money as a motivator sometimes produces unexpected results. Examples of such situations were reported in the discussions of the Hawthorne experiments, research by Herzberg and Whyte, and equity theory. The chapter concluded with a brief description of the problems and constraints involved in applying motivation theory from both a group and individual perspective.

SOLVING THE STOP ACTION CASE

Woodward Governor Co.

In just about every respect, Woodward Governor Co. is a success. Ever since it went public in 1940, the company has consistently shown a profit. It has never lost so much as a day's work to labor disputes. The turnover rate is only 5 to 10 percent. "Members" are rarely fired, and only two have been laid off since the end of World War II.

The emphasis that Woodward places on the work environment and the lifetime employment it guarantees members may call to mind the Japanese, or Theory Z, style of management. But Leo Powelson, assistant to the firm's CEO, disagrees. "If there's any copying, they're copying us. We've been doing most of these things since the early 1940s, certainly before the Japanese became known as the best in the world."

Source: Sharon Cohen, "Woodward Governor Co. Is a Workplace Like No Other," *Seattle Times,* 5 March 1985, p. C8.

FACT OR FICTION REVEALED

1. Fact 2. Fact 3. Fiction 4. Fiction 5. Fiction 6. Fact 7. Fact

MANAGEMENT TERMS

conflict	human relations approach	reference groups
Hawthorne studies	human resources model	informal group leader
Hawthorne effect	equity theory	

REVIEW QUESTIONS

1. Define the following terms: (a) conflict, (b) Hawthorne studies, (c) Hawthorne effect, (d) human relations approach, (e) human resources model, (f) equity theory, (g) reference group, (h) informal group leader.

2. Discuss the concepts of group development and conflict.

3. Discuss the Hawthorne studies and the development of the human relations approach.

4. How does the human resources model differ from the human relations approach?

5. Explain William F. Whyte's contribution to the study of group behavior.

6. Discuss the research conducted by Stanley Seashore.

7. Outline the contributions of equity theory and reference groups to the study of group behavior.

8. Describe Robert F. Bales' research on informal group leaders.

9. Relate the concept of morale to productivity.

10. Explain the role of money as a motivator.

PROBLEMS AND EXPERIENTIAL EXERCISES

1. Intel is now a $1.6-million electronics firm in Santa Clara, California. It was started by three scientists who split off from Fairchild Semiconductors. The company has traditionally earned the highest profit margins of any company in the semiconductor industry. Intel can attribute a substantial part of its success to effective motivational practices.

   The founders run Intel from a three-person executive office that is dedicated to keeping bureaucratic practices out of the company. Intel makes extensive use of councils that make decisions and monitor programs in given areas. The newly hired and executives alike participate as equals in these councils.

There are no closed offices, dress codes, executive dining rooms, reserved parking, or limousines at Intel. The company's participative management practices are communicated in a variety of training sessions. The Intel philosophy is explained by President Andrew S. Grove:

It isn't symbolism. . . . It's a necessity . . . I can't pretend to know the shape of the next generation of silicon or computer technology anymore. That's why people like me need the knowledge from the people closest to the technology. That's why we can't have the hierarchical barriers to our exchange of ideas and information that you have at so many corporations.[21]

Would you be highly motivated in a work environment similar to that of Intel? Why or why not?

2. General Motors was considering closing its Clark, New Jersey bearings plant in 1981. Some 2,000 jobs were on the line. So the plant's employees bought the factory and formed Hyatt-Clark Industries. The work force dropped, wages and benefits were cut, but the plant survived and is now profitable. Nationwide, there are about 7,000 employee-owned companies.[22] Assess the concepts of group behavior and motivation as they might apply to a firm like Hyatt-Clark Industries.

3. Prepare a brief, critical review of a study on motivation that has been published in the last five years in a professional management journal. Compare the study to what you have learned in this chapter.

4. The National Basketball Association "caps" the player payroll of each of its teams. In other words, the teams are given a maximum total salary figure within which they can pay all of their players combined. Discuss the possible motivational impact of this plan.

5. Relate the concepts presented in Chapter 14 to a work or social group to which you belong.

MANAGERIAL INCIDENT: Romac Industries Inc.

Romac Industries Inc., a Seattle-based pipe-fitting manufacturer, was started by its president and owner Manford McNeil and two former associates in 1969. The firm now employs 150 people and has annual sales of $12 million. McNeil has been named "Washington State Small Business Person of the Year" as a result of Romac's success, and the unique motivational system he employs.

After weathering two unsuccessful attempts to unionize his firm, McNeil adopted a profit-sharing plan and decided to base pay raises on the votes of fellow hourly employees. Workers who think they should get a raise fill out a form indicating their current hourly rate, the raise sought, and why they think they are entitled to it. The form and the person's photograph is then pasted on a bulletin board for several days. Their co-workers then vote on whether the applicant gets the pay hike or not. McNeil reserves the veto right, but he has never used it. McNeil comments:

> Our years of experience with our voting
> wage program have revealed checks and bal-

ances which were not apparent at the onset of the program. Specifically, there is pressure for wages to be equal to, not necessarily higher than and certainly not less than, current pay scales in the area's job market. Contacts at many levels away from the job keep most employees informed of current

(Continued on next page.)

wage levels, both union and non-union. We are often asked why there then would not be a conspiracy among our workers to pressure wages upward and also to see to it that votes are favorable so everyone receives his raise. If there is such an effort, it is not apparent.

Questions

1. Assess the Romac compensation plan. What are the benefits and pitfalls of such an effort?

2. Discuss the Romac illustration in terms of the concepts outlined in this chapter.

Source: Information provided by Manford McNeil, June 10, 1985. *See* "Workers Plus Management" (quote is from this statement of management philosophy); Boyd Burchard, "Praise Goes to Employees, Says Honored Manufacturer," *Seattle Times,* n.d.; and Rachel Bagby, "To Get a Pay Raise, A Worker at Romac Asks Other Workers," *Wall Street Journal,* 10 September 1979.

CHAPTER

15 COMMUNICATION

LEARNING OBJECTIVES

After studying this chapter you should be able to

1. Explain the process of communication.
2. Describe the communication model.
3. Identify the roadblocks to effective communication and the means to avoid them.
4. Discuss the basic concepts of group communication.
5. Understand the importance of channel selection in communication.
6. Relate communication to motivation and leadership.

STOP ACTION CASE

FMC Corporation

Revolutionary advances in communications technology, such as voice mail and videoconferencing, are having a powerful impact on American companies and how they operate. The ability to store and retrieve information efficiently is at the heart of a successful business, and the new developments in information technology are giving firms a capacity for intra-company communication that was once beyond their wildest dreams.

FMC Corporation, a Chicago-based firm that manufactures chemicals and machinery, recently sought to enhance its communications capabilities. Its managers tried to decide which of the new technologies would work best for them and how they should best organize FMC's information function.

Use the materials in Chapter 15 to design an intra-company communication program for FMC that will utilize the most modern information technologies.

MANAGEMENT FACT OR FICTION

	FACT	FICTION		FACT	FICTION
1. Approximately half of a message will be forgotten within minutes after it is received.	☐	☐	4. A chain-like communication network is more effective in solving arithmetical problems.	☐	☐
2. Cognitive dissonance refers to the discrepancy between existing beliefs and attitudes and new perceptions.	☐	☐	5. The concept of our information overload refers to a computer failure.	☐	☐
3. Increased interaction among people tends to hinder group cohesiveness.	☐	☐	6. Office grapevines should be eliminated whenever possible.	☐	☐

The materials in this chapter will assist you in separating management fact from fiction. Your answers can be checked on page 482.

If an employee does not understand his or her job or has a complaint, improving communications and discussing the problems face to face is often useful. Communication can also convey positive information that is useful to management. Effective communication provides important leadership and motivational benefits to executives willing to work at improving their performance in this area.

The importance of effective communication goes well beyond the application of a managerial technique. The role of communication is to provide an informational system whereby management can plan, organize, motivate, direct, and control the various segments of the organization. Communication is the very lifeblood of the organization. It provides the means for accomplishing the managerial job.[1] This chapter on communications concludes Part Four on leading and motivating employees.

It is important to realize that communication does not always work. Communicating the wrong information at the wrong time can hurt employee motivation. Giving people information they do not need can interfere with their job performance. Information that is misinterpreted can cause problems that otherwise would not have existed. And bringing people together to communicate does not automatically mean that they will get along better. It may convince them more than ever that their differences are real and cannot be overcome. Communication is the critical factor in some problem situations, but not in others.

COMMUNICATION: A DEFINITION

There are numerous definitions of communication. These range from highly technical ones to generalized versions that suggest all human activities are forms of communication. From a managerial perspective, a reasonable definition is that *communication* refers to the transfer of information via an understandable message from a sender to others.

All communication attempts to transfer some type of information. Some transfers are successful, others are not. The key ingredient is that the information is presented in the form of an understandable message to those with whom the sender wishes to communicate.

Communication is the transfer of information via an understandable message from a sender to others.

TYPES OF COMMUNICATION

Communication in management usually occurs in three ways. It may be spoken, written, or transmitted via nonverbal forms. Spoken communication may be the single most important activity performed by management. Written messages are also a vital aspect of the manager's job in all organizations. Although the written message is one of the most widely studied forms of communication, there are still innovations that are having a profound impact on managerial communications. *Electronic mail* refers to messages sent by electronic means. It is one of the most significant trends in written communications in years. Federal Express and MCI are two of the major competitors in the marketplace. Their electronic mail systems are described below (see Figure 15–1).

Nonverbal communication—often called *body language*—is also important. This type of communication supplements, amplifies, and clarifies spoken communications. Nonverbal communication includes eye contact, gestures, and posture. All of these can be used to suggest agreement, boredom, anxiety, and so forth. One study reported that a message's verbal content is responsible for 7 percent of attitude change, while vocal characteristics and facial expressions account for 38 percent and 55 percent, respectively.[2]

Body language is the form of nonverbal communication that employs eye contact, gestures, and posture.

THE BASIC COMMUNICATION MODEL

The simplest communication system is made up of only four parts: a sender, a message, a communication channel, and a receiver. This basic communication model is shown in Figure 15–2. If the sender is a manager,

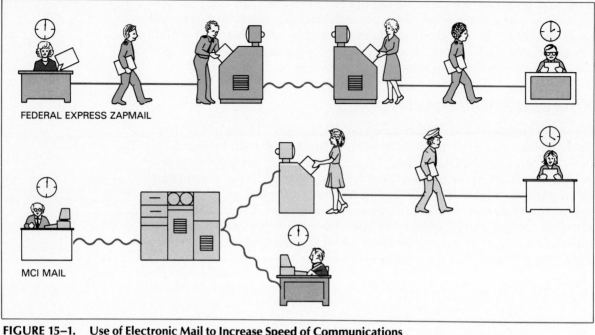

FIGURE 15–1.   Use of Electronic Mail to Increase Speed of Communications
Source: Reprinted from Arthur M. Louis, "The Great Electronic Mail Shootout," *Fortune,* 20
August 1984, p. 168. © 1984 by Daniel Pelavin.

the purpose in communicating is often to get an employee, the receiver,
to carry out some desired action. The employee may be told to unload a
freight car, for example. The trick is to avoid garbling the message at any
point along its route from the sender through the medium to the receiver
so that the right freight is unloaded at the right time in the right condition
at the right cost.

COMMUNICATION ROADBLOCKS

Responsibility for effective communication lies with the manager. Whenever communication breaks down, the manager should determine whether

FIGURE 15–2.   The Basic Communication Model

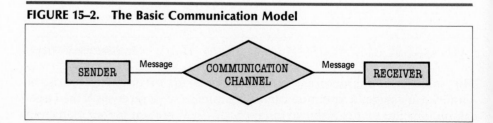

he or she is at fault before blaming the channel, or worse yet, the employee. Roadblocks to communication include poor timing, inadequate information, inappropriate channel noise, selective perception, premature evaluation, emotions, and beliefs.[3]

Poor Timing. The manager must know when to communicate. If an employee fails to take action, it may be because the manager assumed the employee knew when or how to do a job. A loading dock supervisor, for instance, might assume that an employee would automatically unload any freight delivered to the dock. Yet a dock worker might not do this without specific instructions if, for instance, the freight is in an unusual carton or if it is damaged.

Inadequate Information. Even if the manager communicates when he or she should, the employee may receive inadequate information. Too little information endangers effective communication, but so does too much. The employee whose only job is to remove the freight from a boxcar or truck might not understand the loading instructions if they are included in billing details or in instructions on making claims for damaged goods.

The manager must also scrutinize the symbols used to convey a message. The information must be meaningful to the employee. This can mean anything from using correct grammar, spelling, and punctuation, to avoiding typographical errors in written orders, to clear pronunciation in oral orders.

Inappropriate Channel. If the manager has properly performed his or her tasks as a sender, the channel will determine the effectiveness of the communication. Should the manager write it down, make a phone call, talk face to face, or use some combination? Writing, for instance, enables the receiver to study the message thoroughly. It also provides proof that the message was sent. A phone conversation, on the other hand, is fast and allows for discussion to make the message clear. But even this does not provide the emphasis that can be given to a message by hand gestures or eye contact in a face-to-face communication. The medium must be matched to the message and the receiver.

A basic question concerns whether the message ever reaches the desired receiver. Would publishing a safety slogan in the company newspaper reach the dock laborer? It might if the person reads it or talks to co-workers who read it. But then it might not, and if the message is important or specific enough, it should be sent in a more direct manner.

Noise. Another problem in communications channels is noise. *Noise* refers to any situation that interferes with or distorts the message being communicated. This may be physical noise, as when a truck engine drowns out the supervisor's oral instructions. Or it may be noise in a more general sense, as when a manager tries to send too many messages over a channel.

Noise refers to any situation that interferes with or distorts the message being communicated.

MANAGEMENT: THE LIGHTER SIDE

"What They Really Meant Was . . ."

 Managers often use the acronym KISS ("keep it simple, stupid") to summarize an important key to effective written communications. In his book *The Power of Words,* Stuart Chase reported an excellent example of failure to apply the KISS axiom. A plumber in New York had begun to use hydrochloric acid to clean drains but was concerned about possible harmful effects. After writing to the U.S. Bureau of Standards in Washington, D.C., to ask their advice, he received the following reply:

> The efficacy of hydrochloric acid is indisputable, but chlorine residue is incompatible with metallic permanence.

The plumber sent a second letter to Washington, thanking the correspondent at the Bureau of Standards for responding and expressing his satisfaction in learning that the bureau agreed with him. He received the following note of alarm by return mail:

> We cannot assume responsibility for the production of toxic and noxious residues with hydrochloric acid, and suggest that you use an alternative procedure.

Again, the plumber responded, noting that he was happy that the Bureau still agreed with him. This time the Bureau response was short and direct:

> Don't use hydrochloric acid; it eats hell out of the pipes.

Source: Stuart Chase, *The Power of Words* (New York: Harcourt, Brace, 1955), p. 259. Adapted from *The Power of Words,* copyright 1954, 1982 by Stuart Chase. Reprinted by permission of Harcourt Brace Jovanovich, Inc.

Phone conversations are effective when brief instructions are given, but lengthy conversations can be too much for this type of channel. By the time the call is over, the receiver may have forgotten what was said earlier in the conversation.

Probably the most complicated link in the communication system is the receiver. The receiver, being a human being, has a less-than-perfect memory. Scientific measures of oral messages have shown that as much as 50 percent of a message will be forgotten just moments after it is received.[4] This is one strong argument for repeating oral instructions.

Selective Perception. Perception is a very selective, individual process. How a message will be perceived by a person depends on past experiences, emotions, beliefs, and other personal factors.

Sometimes an employee may resist a message simply because he or she has learned from past experience not to trust a manager. Suppose a manager has promised pay raises to an employee but does not have a good record of delivering on these promises. Whenever the manager talks about salary to this employee, the message will probably be ignored. Some workers may not trust company newspapers if they view them as management propaganda. As a result they may fail to receive important news.

Premature Evaluation. Whenever a receiver evaluates the content of a message before the communication is completed, the person is said to evaluate it prematurely.[5] This is what the mistrusting employees are doing. Premature evaluation can work both ways. Suppose the supervisor tells a subordinate something like this: "Jack, you are the hardest working and fastest person on the dock. I've got a special job that only a special person can handle. I'd like you to use the fork lift to move these fragile chemical containers from the warehouse to the dock." In this case the worker's premature evaluation is likely to be positive.

Emotions. But if emotions are brought into perception, the outcome may be different. Suppose Jack was very upset by having just seen another worker burned by acid spills from a chemical carton he had dropped. How receptive would he be to the supervisor's flattery now? The mere mention of "fragile chemical containers" might prompt resistance to the order.

A standard example of the effects of emotions on receptiveness to communications is the employee wanting to see a superior about an increase in pay. "Not today," warns the secretary, "she's in a lousy mood." Most employees would quickly decide to try again some other time when the executive might be in a more receptive mood.

Beliefs. Beliefs and attitudes affect communication effectiveness, although their influence is not quite so obvious. Beliefs cause people to hear or see in a message only what they want when the information causes them mental conflict. The tension state resulting from information that contradicts currently held beliefs and attitudes is called *cognitive dissonance*. Sometimes a receiver might avoid a message altogether, if he or she thinks it might run counter to his or her beliefs. Hitler, for example, was notorious for avoiding those field commanders who might tell him the war was going badly. Though an extreme personality, Hitler was not rare in doing this; it is a common, natural defense put up by people in a variety of situations.

What happens when a disagreeable message cannot be avoided? Return to the story of the dock laborer who had been given a superior performance rating by a supervisor. Suppose now that a new supervisor gives a mixed annual review, pointing out that the person is a quick worker but is sometimes careless.

The employee may accept the message and correct the deficiencies noted. But there is a good chance that the worker may read the message differently. The person may hear only the compliment and immediately

Cognitive dissonance refers to the discrepancy between existing beliefs and attitudes and new perceptions.

Rationalizing is the distortion of a message to bring it into line with one's own beliefs.

reject the criticism. The word careless may not even register with this individual.

Then, too, the dock worker may distort the message in the annual review to bring it into line with his belief, a process called *rationalizing*. The worker could reason that carelessness is an unavoidable side effect of fast work.

AVOIDING THE ROADBLOCKS TO EFFECTIVE COMMUNICATION

The effective communicator can take a number of actions to avoid the obstacles cited in the previous section. These actions are described in the sections that follow. While all may be effective communication tools, perhaps the Army has found an ideal way to eliminate confusion. Soldiers repairing M-1 tanks will soon be using PEAM (personal electronic aid for maintenance), or a talking technical manual. The mechanic can operate the machine by voice. Repair instructions are printed on a screen or read to the soldier.[6]

Feedback is information transmitted by a receiver back to the original sender of a message.

Expand the Basic Communication Model to Include Feedback. Effective communication requires the receiver to feed back information to the sender. *Feedback* refers to information transmitted by a receiver back to the original sender of a message. Many communications experts believe that a true "communication" cannot take place until the sender has received confirmation from the receiver that the message has been understood. The expanded communication model is shown in Figure 15–3.

Managers often feel that two-way communication is unnecessary. However, various studies comparing one-way and two-way communications generally conclude that information is transferred more accurately when there is feedback.[7] The receiver can better clarify his or her understanding of what the sender means. Also, these studies have found that the receiver has more positive feelings toward the sender when he or she can respond to the message.

Feedback benefits come at a cost.[8] Repeating, discussing, and quizzing take time; and if the appropriate action is delayed too long, the extra accuracy is valueless. Two-way communication appears to be most appropriate in instances when a situation is unclear and the quality of the action is important. But if action must be taken quickly in a situation that is clear-cut, one-way communication may be called for.

Improve Listening Skills. Communications expert Stuart Chase emphasizes that "Listening is the other half of talking."[9] Clearly, listening should be an inherent part of the total communication process. But in many cases it is not. For many people listening is that agonizing time period they must survive before they themselves speak.

Paying close attention to what the other person says is one of the simplest ways to improve communication. Keith Davis has offered some suggestions

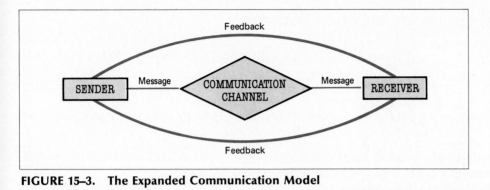

FIGURE 15–3.   The Expanded Communication Model

to facilitate good listening practices. His recommendations are listed in Table 15–1.

Practice Empathy. Semanticist (and former U.S. Senator) S. I. Hayakawa says: "The meanings of words are not in the words, they are in us."[10] If meaning must be found in something beyond words themselves, then true communication must involve a degree of *empathy,* that is, identification with another person's perspective.

Carl D. Rogers has suggested an interesting technique for improving communication through empathy. He suggests moderating arguments or disagreements by accepting the basic rule that no person can speak until he or she has "restated the ideas and feelings of the previous speaker accurately and to that speaker's satisfaction."[11]

Effective communication requires that the listener understand exactly what others mean and the perspective from which they speak. The Rogers' proposal seeks to develop that type of perspective. But regardless of how it is achieved, empathy is an important ingredient for the efficient functioning of the organizational communication system.

Follow Basic Communication Guidelines. Various guidelines have been suggested for improving a firm's communication practices. Some interesting views are expressed in Figure 15–4. All have a place in organizational communication, with most designed to eliminate one or more of the roadblocks mentioned earlier in this chapter.

Some standard guidelines include:

- *Eliminate ambiguities.* Senders should make their communications as precise as possible so as to minimize the number of possible interpretations.

- *Use proper follow-up.* Some communications require a follow-up from the sender. Certain instances require a manager to follow a verbal

Empathy is identification with another person's perspective.

TABLE 15–1   TEN COMMANDMENTS FOR GOOD LISTENING

1. *Stop talking!*
   You cannot listen if you are talking.
   Polonius (*Hamlet*): "Give every man thine ear, but few thy voice."

2. *Put the talker at ease.*
   Help the person feel that he or she is free to talk. This is often called a permissive environment.

3. *Show the individual that you want to listen.*
   Look and act interested. Do not read your mail while the person talks.
   Listen to understand rather than to oppose.

4. *Remove distractions.*
   Don't doodle, tap, or shuffle papers. Will it be quieter if you shut the door?

5. *Empathize with the person.*
   Try to see the other's point of view.

6. *Be patient.*
   Allow plenty of time. Do not interrupt. Don't start for the door or walk away.

7. *Hold your temper.*
   An angry person gets the wrong meaning from words.

8. *Go easy on argument and criticism.*
   This puts the person on the defensive. He or she may "clam up" or get angry. Do not argue: Even if you win, you lose.

9. *Ask questions.*
   This encourages the speaker and shows you are listening. It helps to develop points further.

10. *Stop talking!*
    This is first and last, because all other commandments depend on it. You can't do a good listening job while you are talking.

    Nature gave man two ears but only one tongue, which is a gentle hint that he should listen more than he talks.

Source: Adapted by permission from Keith Davis, *Human Behavior at Work,* 4th ed. (New York: McGraw-Hill, 1972), p. 396.

instruction with a written memorandum confirming the spoken details. Managers should also monitor a subordinate's response to a communication; if action is delayed or inappropriate, the executive should immediately follow up on the matter.

- *Avoid negativism.* Statements like "It probably won't work anyway, but why not try plan B" should be avoided in organizational communi-

Keep It Simple

Strike three.
Get your hand off my knee.
You're overdrawn.
Your horse won.
Yes.
No.
You have the account.
Walk.
Don't walk.
Mother's dead.
Basic events
require simple language.
Idiosyncratically euphuistic
eccentricities are the
promulgators of
triturable obfuscation.
What did you do last night?
Enter into a meaningful
romantic involvement
or
fall in love?
What did you have for
breakfast this morning?
The upper part of a hog's
hind leg with two oval
bodies encased in a shell
laid by a female bird
or
ham and eggs?
David Belasco, the great
American theatrical producer,
once said, "If you can't
write your idea on the
back of my calling
card,
you don't have a clear idea."

© United Technologies Corporation 1979

FIGURE 15–4.   Some Thoughts on Improving Communications
Source: United Technologies Corporation.

cation. They set the stage for failure. After all, if management does not think the action will work, why should the subordinate risk proving the superior wrong?

- *Watch the timing of messages.* The timing of certain communications is vital. Management should time communication so as to avoid noise in the communication channel.

COMMUNICATION WITHIN A GROUP

Not all communication is between a single manager and a single subordinate. Much organizational communication involves groups of people, not just individuals. To be successful, group communication requires a special blend of skills. This section considers some of the basic concepts in group communication.

COHESIVENESS

In Chapter 14 motivation was studied from the viewpoint of the group. It was noted that groups have a quality called cohesiveness; a net measure of the forces acting to hold the group together. One important factor determining cohesiveness is communication among group members.

A basic proposition of group behavior is *Homan's interaction hypothesis*. People who interact will grow to like each other (assuming they have compatible goals and needs); this mutual liking will lead to more communication, which will lead to more liking, and so on.[12] The net result is high cohesiveness.

Homan's interaction hypothesis states that people who interact will grow to like each other, assuming they have compatible goals and needs, and this will lead to more interaction (or communication), thus establishing a cycle of cohesiveness.

How does communication within a group start? Certainly, having a common purpose is a factor.[13] And there is the obvious but often overlooked matter of the physical proximity of the participants. To be clustered around a workbench encourages more group communication than does being stretched out along an assembly line. Member turnover is another factor. Groups with high membership turnover find it difficult to establish regular communication channels.[14] Group size is another factor. Large groups restrict the participation in the communication system.[15]

If a manager wants a work group to be cohesive, then members should be encouraged to communicate with each other. To facilitate communications the manager should arrange people in proximity, allow them to stay in the group for a long time, and keep the group small.

CONFORMING TO GROUP NORMS

One of the most noticeable patterns of communication in a group is the attempts of the regulars to make deviants conform to group norms.[16] Consider a worker who has the usual amount of communication with the others in the work group. Now suppose that the worker does not agree with the idea of adding an extra five minutes to the coffee break as the others do. The person's peers gradually express their displeasure about the individual's going back to work on time. They begin to warn that the supervisor will soon expect all of them to go back to work at the official time.

If the deviant worker continues to return to work promptly, the interaction continues to grow as the group threatens to take action against the person. If at this point the renegade decides to accept the group norm, the interaction pattern will quickly return to what it was before the incident. If, instead, the worker persists in breaking the group's informal rule, then the communication might stop almost completely. A manager can often spot a worker who is in disagreement with fellow workers if he or she has been shut off, or if the person seems to be the center of attention.

COMMUNICATION NETWORKS

Laboratory experiments have uncovered some interesting facts about the relationship between a group's task and its communication patterns.[17]

Usually the experimenters restrict group members to the circle, chain, Y, and wheel communication networks, shown in Figure 15–5 and then assign them different kinds of tasks.

For example, each group might be given a simple coordinating task such as this: The group members each have a card with several symbols, one of which appears on every card; the task is to identify the common symbol as quickly as possible. Notice that the Y and wheel have one member who is linked to more than just two others. This centralizes the information flow and permits these arrangements to solve the problem faster than the circle and chain.

When the type of task is changed, the results can be different. The circle has been found to solve arithmetical problems better than the wheel. This is probably because the circle, being more centralized, leads to greater participation by group members. The combined analytical effort is useful for the more complex arithmetical problem, whereas it does not help in solving the simple, coordinating card problem.

Members of the circle also tend to be more satisfied than members of the other groups. This is simply due to the fact that they know more about what is going on; the members of the chain, Y, and wheel tend to be less knowledgeable. These experiments have several implications for those interested in choosing communication patterns that will result in high productivity and/or high satisfaction.

COMMITTEES

Committees are a special type of group that typically includes management. *Committees* are groups of people who render decisions or offer advice to management. One study showed that managers spend an average of three-and-a-half hours a week in committee meetings and that 94 percent of large firms and 64 percent of small firms use formal committees.[18]

Often a committee of executives from several departments is formed to solve coordination problems. Of course, these people could be polled by

Committees are groups of people who render decisions or offer advice to management.

FIGURE 15–5.   Basic Communication Networks

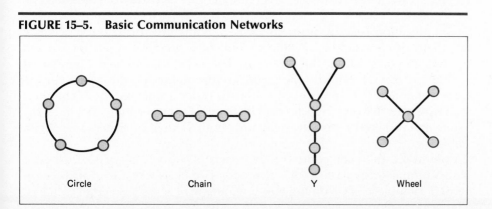

Circle   Chain   Y   Wheel

their supervisor for their individual opinions or information, but bringing them together in an advisory or decision-making group has communication benefits.

One benefit is the error-correcting nature of committees.[19] An individual working alone can waste time following up a bad or mistaken idea. But a committee increases the chance that someone will spot the mistake and point it out. Conversely, a committee also offers support for good ideas. An individual alone might ignore a good idea, but someone in a group might spot the idea and encourage further work on it.

Other communication benefits of committees include better understanding of the eventual solution and the enthusiasm generated to support it.[20] Being involved in a discussion of a problem gives an individual a better knowledge of its solution than if a decision were made independently by the person's supervisor. The better one understands a decision, the more likely he or she is to support and carry it out correctly.

There are also communication disadvantages in committees. Quite often, the members of committees come from different levels in the organization, and these status differences pose a threat to effective communications.[21] Suppose a marketing manager, a plant manager, and a vice-president of finance are brought together to work out the details for introducing a new product. Then add the company's president. One possible effect of such organizational status differences is that communication may be restricted. Another possibility is the tendency to flatter superiors, to avoid confrontations, and to tell the higher-ranked executives things they want to hear. This distorts the error-correcting and supportive function of the committee.

Finally, even the enthusiasm caused by exchange and involvement can be offset by status differences. Many times committees can be used by a superior to give subordinates a feeling of participation when actually the manager is simply selling a decision already made privately. Even if the executive's intent is genuine, employees are often suspicious; whether real or imagined, status differences often can ruin communication in a committee.

CHANNELS OF COMMUNICATION

Communication follows distinct channels. Some are formal channels like the chain of command in a military unit or a financial reporting system for a major corporation. But others are less structured and are often based on interpersonal relations among different employees. These are the informal channels of communication like the office grapevine. Both channels are important delivery vehicles for the firm's communication system. Management must know how to deal with both if that system is to remain viable.

Communications can come from a variety of sources. Henry Mintzberg's observational study of a week's work for five chief executive officers recorded each piece of incoming and outgoing mail as well as verbal contacts. The organizations represented were a consumer goods firm, a technology outfit, a consulting organization, a school system, and a hospital. Figure 15–6 illustrates the diversity of these contacts. Mintzberg put it this way: "The manager does not leave meetings or hang up the telephone in order to get back to work. In large part communication is his work."[22]

FORMAL CHANNELS

The formal communication channel follows a chain of command from the president of a company to a vice-president to a division manager to a department manager to a supervisor to a worker. The *formal communication channel* is the pattern of communication within an organization approved and recognized by management. Communication flows both ways along this channel. Noise is a special problem. The more links in a channel, the more opportunity for noise to occur. Direct, person-to-person communication is rare, except for subordinates and their immediate superiors. If it is critical that a message be transmitted undistorted by noise, then the links should be eliminated by direct communication.

Formal communication channel is the pattern of communication approved and recognized by management.

The Need to Multiplex. Many communications become distorted. This problem is particularly common in upward communication flows, where the

FIGURE 15–6.   The Chief Executive Contacts
Source: Reprinted by permission of the *Harvard Business Review*. An exhibit from "The Manager's Job: Folklore and Fact" by Henry Mintzberg (July-August 1975). Copyright © 1975 by the President and Fellows of Harvard College; all rights reserved.

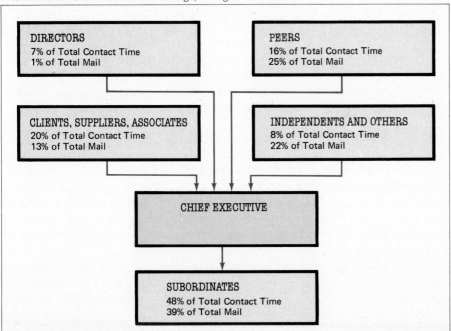

natural tendency is for subordinates to support management's edicts and to filter out contradictory evidence. So powerful is this tendency that managers often find it difficult to get an honest opinion from subordinates. Worse still, some executives do not even seek hard, candid appraisals from subordinates.

One way a manager can try to increase the accuracy of communication is by *multiplexing,* the supplementing of formal communication channels with other channels. This can be accomplished in several ways.

General Electric, American Can, Westinghouse, Pittsburgh National Bank, Ford, Xerox, Prudential, Control Data, Ashland Oil, Union Carbide, A. B. Dick, and Spring Mills, among others, have used climate surveys to multiplex their regular communication channels. *Climate surveys* are communication tools that concentrate on individual work units or departments. Participants are surveyed about their work attitudes and situations; the information is tabulated; and a feedback session is held at which conclusions are reached. Both management and subordinates are involved in these sessions.[23]

New England Telephone has developed what it calls the upward communications program. The firm invites its employees to use private lines—company terminology for anonymous written or telephone requests, comments, suggestions, or questions directed to management. The company employs a full-time person to coordinate this communication program. Employees report that the answers to questions are satisfactory in 79 percent of the cases.[24]

There are a variety of other multiplexing techniques. Suggestion systems can prompt employees to offer cost savings suggestions that might be delayed or thwarted by the formal communication channels.[25] Top management sometimes goes on sales calls with marketing representatives to augment the customer information they receive through regular channels. Employees may communicate in a committee differently than if they were reporting to their superior individually. And staff officers can be used to extend the number of viewpoints presented to management. Grievance and auditing procedures are other multiplexing alternatives.

Information Overload. With all the information flowing in from the chain of command and from other channels, the manager can become victim to information overload.[26] An overloaded manager might react by backlogging messages during busy periods and then catching up in slow periods. He or she may also have to set up a system of priorities, trying to deal only with information upon which authority to act exists. More important messages could be forwarded to supervisors, and less important ones to staff or subordinates.

Not all reactions to overload are good ones, and the alert manager should be careful if he or she is to avoid communication problems. An effective manager might, for instance, feel so overwhelmed that all work is ignored in an attempt to escape from the pressure. Or the manager might lump messages into categories and give them general responses,

Multiplexing is the supplementing of formal communication channels with other channels.

Climate survey examines work attitudes and situations within individual work units or departments with the idea of improving communication.

❝ I like to listen. I have learned a great deal from listening carefully. Most people never listen. ❞

Ernest Hemingway

such as a form letter. This, of course, runs the risk of alienating the receivers. Then, too, the manager can simply delay any response to a message, assuming that anyone who really wants to talk about an important matter will communicate again—and the individual probably will, with much irritation and a problem that has grown critical in the meantime.

Some companies have taken actions to alleviate the information overloads that face their managers. One recent example was provided by Alaska Airlines. Faced with an avalanche of applications for flight attendant positions, the company decided to charge a $10 application fee to offset processing expenses.

Formal Communication Channels Should Be Flexible. When studying formal communication channels, it is important to consider the relationship between communication and such organizational matters as departmentation, line-staff relations, and the span of management. As far as departmentation is concerned, communication should be flexible; that is, the manager should be able to arrange to increase or decrease communications practically at will. They should not be a fixed, constant factor.

Suppose a manufacturing department and a research department both report to a certain manager. These two departments probably have some dealings with each other that require them to communicate, and yet each also has a separate, specialized job to do: one to produce products, the other to develop products.

The amount of communication that should exist between manufacturing and research depends on how important their coordination is compared with their specialization. If they communicate openly, their coordination may go smoothly, but they may start thinking so much alike that they are not as specialized as they should be. If their communication is limited, they may not work as well together, but they will think and act differently in performing their specific jobs.

The manager can vary the communication pattern between departments to suit a particular purpose. To produce optimal coordination, the departments might be physically located near each other to allow anyone in one department to contact anyone in the other conveniently. To promote specialization, the departments might be located in different buildings, with interaction limited to messengers or committee meetings.

This same lesson applies to line and staff operations. If staff assistants communicate freely with department managers, they will probably come to work closely with them. However, this may interfere with their ability to give objective advice to departments, and so management may want them to remain separate from operating departments. Open communication between staff and operating departments also can create confusion as to who really is in charge. Many managers will not let staff communicate too freely with operating departments simply to preserve their own authority.

Communication is also dramatically affected by changes in a manager's span of management or control. When a manager has many subordinates reporting directly, communication with each is possible but infrequent. The span of control can be narrowed by adding in a couple of supervisors between the manager and subordinates, with only the supervisors reporting directly to the manager. Communication with the supervisors should be effective, but another link has been added to the communication chain. However, the supervisors in turn should be able to frequently communicate with employees who report to them because there are relatively few subordinates per supervisor.

One interesting recent development is the computer-based executive information system now used by some fifty companies. This system allows top management to access the firm's primary data bases directly. Westinghouse, Termo Electron Corp., Banco Internacional de Colombia, and Northwest Industries are examples of companies with such capability. Executive information systems permit general management to call up and analyze data without forwarding their requests for information to lower ranked personnel. This system gives top management the ability to immediately query and criticize what is happening at the operational level.

While chief executives may approve of their newfound power, divisional management often worries about excessive querying and top management's second-guessing operational decisions. Few parties, however, will deny that executive information systems have greatly expanded the flexibility of management communications.[27]

INFORMAL CHANNELS

Informal communication channels are communication patterns that exist outside of or in addition to management-approved channels.

Formal communication channels are planned by managers. They are designed to accomplish the tasks for which these managers have responsibility. But no manager can anticipate every single communication need. As a result, not all communication needs are programed by management. This unplanned type of communication, which can be helpful to management, is part of the organization's total communication system. The *informal communication channel* refers to communication patterns existing within the organization that are outside of or in addition to management-approved channels.

Much informal communication is not directly related to getting the job done. Employees talk to each other for a wide variety of reasons. They can say things to each other that they might be reluctant to say to a superior. Informal communication channels also allow employees to reduce the pressures of the job or to relieve boredom. Then, too, employees communicate with each other for social and other interpersonal reasons. Informal conversation can make employees more satisfied with their work environment. This can pay for itself in improved attendance, reduced tardiness, and less frequent job transfers.

Grapevine is a term sometimes used by managers to refer to the informal communication channel.

The Grapevine. Informal communication often appears to be costly for the organization, and yet in fact it can be beneficial. Managers, who are sometimes leery of the informal communication channel, label it the *grapevine*.

A recent survey reported that the grapevine was the most often cited source of information in companies (see Figure 15–7).

Keith Davis is the acknowledged expert on grapevines within organizations. Davis reports that the four primary features of grapevines are:

- *Speed of transmission.* The grapevine is widely recognized as an extremely fast communication channel.

- *Degree of selectivity.* Davis's study found that the grapevine can be a discreet communication channel, protecting confidential information. This conclusion differs from the traditional view of grapevine communications.

- *Locale of operation.* The grapevine functions primarily within the workplace and during work hours.

- *Relation to formal communication.* Davis concluded that the grapevine usually operates, or does not operate, jointly with the formal channel. The two systems supplement each other.

Four types of informal communication chains are identified by Davis: single strand, gossip, probability, and cluster. They are shown in Figure 15–8. In the single strand chain, **A** passes information to **B** who repeats it to **C** and so on. Considerable distortion and filtering can occur in this communication channel. In the case of gossip, one sender attempts to communicate a message to everyone. Random communication is the rule in the probability chain. **A** communicates with others randomly, and the

FIGURE 15–7.   Most Often Cited Sources of Information Reported by Employees
Source: The Hay Group, Research for Management Employee Attitude Database. Reprinted by permission of *The Wall Street Journal,* © Dow Jones & Company, Inc., 1985. All rights reserved.

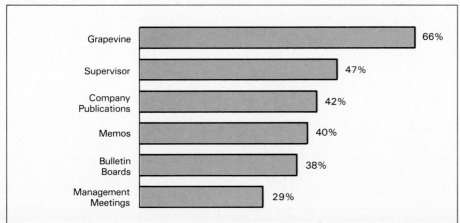

MANAGEMENT SUCCESSES

From Tee to Green ($)

 What they don't teach you at Harvard Business School, Mark H. McCormack writes in his new book by that title (Bantam Books, Inc.) are the "street smarts" of daily business, the ability to "read" people and then capitalize on this knowledge, particularly in negotiating and selling.

To this end, "the guy who made Arnold Palmer all those millions," as he remains best known, shares what he has learned in nearly a quarter-century of building International Management Group (IMG) into a worldwide management, consulting, and marketing corporation expected to gross over $200 million this year. The result is a 256-page breezy best seller (Bantam Books Inc., $15.95).

Since this Cleveland attorney (whose business-school experience reads lecturer rather than student) is a leading amateur golfer who began his business career by representing, first, Arnold Palmer and then Gary Player and Jack Nicklaus, some of his best lines were learned on the links.

The IMG chairman, president, and CEO quotes former PGA golf champ Dave Marr and his "first axiom of golf wagering—never bet with anyone you meet on the first tee who has a deep suntan, a one-iron in his bag, and squinty eyes."

Mr. McCormack maintains he "can tell more about how someone is likely to react in a business situation from one round of golf than from a hundred hours of meetings." For example, he cites those people who refuse all "gimme" putts (short putts usually conceded), insisting instead to putt everything in the hole and then accurately record the results. "It's hard to do favors for people like this," he concludes.

Those who assume *everything's* a "gimmee," he observes, "are usually the big egos [who] won't ask you for a favor, either—they *expect* it."

More intriguing are "the people who 'half try' to sink the putt, sort of sweep at it one-handed. If it goes in, fine. If it doesn't, they 'weren't really trying' and count it as a 'gimme'. In business, these people are hard to pin down. They have a capacity for self-deception, tend to exaggerate, and may give you a rounded-off version of what they originally said."

STAY FLEXIBLE. As a consultant to more than 50 of America's largest corporations, marrying leisure activities and big business, Mr. McCormack stresses the importance of an organization remaining flexible. The structures and systems created in building a business—to make everything "flow smoother"—later tend to "stifle the very momentum they are supposed to help," he says.

Ben Bidwell, a Chrysler Corp. executive vice-president who previously headed North American sales for Ford Motor Co., once described Ford's structure and support system to Mr. McCormack as a "wall of molasses. You can't get anything in. You can't get anything out. You can't move up. You can't move sideways. It takes two years even to move down."

"This is the sinister, uncompromising nature of systems," Mr. McCormack believes. "They ride roughshod over everything, especially common sense, and are the single biggest reason why working for a company can often be a ludicrous experience."

Once IMG's structures were in place, he points out, "we began an ongoing process of ignoring them." Any established company often must "jump out of existing structures in order to let new business in."

Mr. McCormack, whose innovations in merchandising, licensing, and TV programing are credited most for catapulting sports into big business, says that the "brightest" thing IMG did was to set up its network of international offices. Each of the 15 full-time offices is almost fully staffed by the nationality of the country in which it's located. IMG also shares offices with local partners in a dozen other countries.

"Because of the flexibility and opportunities that these offices have given us, I am constantly amazed by the lack of attention and low priority most American companies give to their international divisions," he says. "If American companies spent as much time and effort selling their products overseas as they do in trying to keep foreign producers out, I think we'd see the flow of currency change overnight."

Along this line, he advises rising executives to work in their firms' international divisions, where they can "make the most impact in the least amount of time."

PRIVACY PAYS. Being a private company is an advantage, the IMG boss says. "Impressing Wall Street has become the Great American Corporate Pastime. Long-term gains are sacrificed for short-term benefits. Bad corporate decisions are made because a company would rather look good than be good. . . . It may just be too hard to try to run a company and keep the stockholders happy at the same time. That is the reason IMG will never go public."

Mr. McCormack's personal habits—particularly regarding his management of time—make for fascinating reading. Utilizing a complex system of yellow legal pads and three-by-five file cards, he schedules time for relaxation and rest as well as work. He even keeps track of the number of minutes he sleeps.

His "general rule for getting things done the quickest" is to "do the things that everyone else has to do at the times when everyone else isn't doing them." For example, he leaves so early in the morning that getting to work is never a problem. He tries to fly at times that won't require a long wait in line. To avoid waiting for baggage, he usually travels light, carrying everything on board. To do this, he maintains a complete wardrobe in each of his five principal residences, and a partial wardrobe at his other offices. If he knows he'll need something in Paris, he'll send it directly there rather than carry it with him first to New York and then to London.

IW discovered firsthand about the peripatetic Mr. McCormack when it tried, unsuccessfully, to interview him. His schedule called for him to be in Cleveland (home office for IMG as well as IW) only one day between mid-August and late December, and then he was unavailable. His itinerary in the meantime: London, Tokyo, Los Angeles, San Francisco, Chicago, Houston, Williamsburg (Va.), Tokyo, Maui (Hawaii), Los Angeles, New Zealand, Australia, and London.

Source: Reprinted from James Braham, "From Tee to Green ($)," *Industry Week,* 12 November 1984, pp. 30, 134.

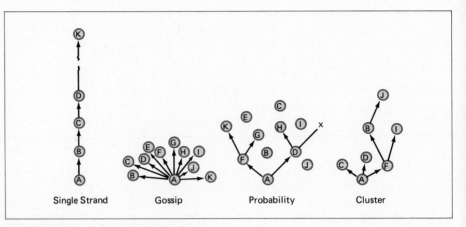

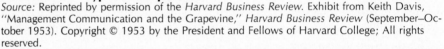

FIGURE 15–8.   Types of Grapevines

Source: Reprinted by permission of the *Harvard Business Review.* Exhibit from Keith Davis, "Management Communication and the Grapevine," *Harvard Business Review* (September–October 1953). Copyright © 1953 by the President and Fellows of Harvard College; All rights reserved.

chain is then continued on a similar basis. The cluster chain may be the most common, according to Davis. Here, **A** selectively tells some others. But not all of these repeat the message to others. And not all of those receiving the information at the third level will pass it on.[28]

New managers sometimes try to destroy the grapevine by forbidding people to communicate this way, disciplining them for it, and even transferring employees. Admittedly, the grapevine sometimes spreads false, anxiety-producing rumors. Management is rightfully concerned about rumor, but attempts to destroy the grapevine are probably inappropriate. In the first place, it is a near impossibility. In the second place, if the grapevine is understood, its accuracy can be improved.

One study revealed that rumors proliferate when people face unclear situations on matters that are important to them.[29] It is not likely that a rumor will be spread as to whether a male superior's wife is pregnant. After all, what does it matter? But if the superior is a female, rumors about her possible pregnancy might abound. If she were pregnant, the manager might take an extended leave of absence or even leave her position. This would have a direct impact on her subordinates. Similar situations occur when it is rumored that a supervisor or manager is looking for another position or is about to be promoted or fired.

Management must realize that such issues are important to employees and that it is best to provide them with the facts. The female manager who thinks her pregnancy is strictly a personal matter and refuses to answer questions will probably become the victim of erroneous rumor. Subordinates may begin to resist her authority. She should discreetly provide someone who is active in the grapevine with accurate information insofar as the future management of the department is concerned, the issue about which the employees are really concerned. This will result in the truth being spread as quickly as rumor.

COMMUNICATION AND MOTIVATION ▬▬▬▬▬▬

One of the basic practices of a people-oriented style of leadership is the participation of subordinates in decision making. The people-oriented manager uses two-way communication to learn of employee viewpoints. Subordinates' involvement should result in a better decision, but the real payoff may be in improved motivation.

When employees are involved in a decision, they feel a vested interest in demonstrating that this decision is correct. As a result they are likely to work harder to implement the decision than if it were merely a managerial directive; two-way communication can be satisfying in and of itself, and it can make subordinates more confident in what they are doing.

Improved production is often a result of employees' participation in decision making, and usually the motivational factors are given credit for the improvement. Still, open communication could account for the improvement for other reasons. When people freely discuss a problem, their understanding of it improves. It could be that increased productivity is a result simply of seeing the problem more clearly and understanding the decision more fully. A large part of the improvement might have occurred even if the motivational factors were not present.

The distinction between the effects of motivation and clarity is rarely made. It is almost impossible to separate the two effects to assess which one, if either, is more important. The manager should not always assume that motivation is most relevant. Executives should avoid efforts to motivate people when that is not the problem but should instead put more time into finding ways to make their employees' jobs more understandable.

COMMUNICATION AND LEADERSHIP ▬▬▬▬▬▬

Managers, as leaders, must know how to communicate with others in their organizations. Leaders must cause communication to happen. But it is also true that communication effectiveness may cause people to become leaders.

Leaders are sometimes leaders simply because they initiate more interaction than do other people. Studies of small groups have shown that some people in a group are prone to communicate with everyone else in the group. Others, however, communicate only with these busy communicators. Simply because they communicate more, the high participators are valued more and are more often seen to be the group leader by its members.[30]

Taking the initiative is only one effect of communication on leadership. People also become leaders because they are in a position that makes them privy to important information. Secretaries sometimes have strong power bases because they are aware of information that others are anxious to get.

This positional effect was evident in the experiments mentioned earlier involving the circle, chain, Y, and wheel communication networks.[31] When their tasks were done, each of these groups was asked to identify a leader. In the wheel the person at the axis was chosen; in the Y the person at the crux was chosen; in the chain the person in the middle was chosen; the group arranged as a circle was unable to select a leader.

SUMMARY

Communication is the transfer of information via an understandable message from a sender to a receiver. While effective communication can solve many management problems, ineffective communication can create many additional problems. Communication can occur in three ways: speaking, writing, or through nonverbal methods. The basic communication model consists of a sender, message, medium, and receiver. This basic one-way communication format can be expanded to a two-way system by adding feedback to the original model.

There are various roadblocks to effective organizational communication. These include poor timing, inadequate information, inappropriate channel, noise, selective perception, premature evaluation, emotions, and beliefs. Many roadblocks can be avoided by the following management actions: (1) expand the basic communication model to include feedback; (2) improve listening skills; (3) practice empathy; and (4) follow basic communication guidelines such as eliminating ambiguities, using proper follow-up, avoiding negativism, and watching the timing of messages.

Not all organizational communications involve single individuals. Much of it is group communications. Basic concepts in group communications include:

Cohesiveness. This is the net impact of the forces acting to hold the group together. Homan's interaction hypothesis states that if one assumes compatible goals and needs, communication among people will lead to a mutual liking, and this will generate more communication, and so on.

Conforming to group norms. All groups attempt to enforce group norms by using the communication system against deviants. The end result may be that the group will ostracize those who refuse to abide by group norms.

Communication networks. Four basic communication networks are the circle, chain, Y, and wheel. Each has certain strengths and weaknesses for solving given problems.

Committees. These are a special type of group that generally includes managers. Benefits of committees include error correction, support for good ideas, and the motivational benefits of participation. A disadvantage is possible distortion caused by status differences of members.

Formal channels of communication are the patterns of communication within an organization approved and recognized by management. Since noise is sometimes a problem, management tends to multiplex, or supplement channels with other communication links. Information overload is another problem for management. The need for channel flexibility is also present.

Informal channels of communication are those communication patterns existing within the organization that are outside of or in addition to management-approved formal channels. These are sometimes labeled the grapevine. Management should not view the grapevine negatively. It can serve as a useful adjunct to formal communication channels.

Chapter 15 concludes with a brief discussion of the relationship between communication and motivation and between communication and leadership.

SOLVING THE STOP ACTION CASE

FMC Corporation

FMC is now in the forefront in its use of automated communications technology. The firm implemented a voice-mail system, which allows sales representatives and sales managers to communicate at any time by means of telephone "mailboxes." Lynn F. White, director of office automation for FMC, says that, thanks to the new system, both communications and productivity have improved. As a result of voice mail, he goes on, FMC has been able to slash both the number of its sales districts and its levels of management. The decline in long-distance phone calls alone paid for the voice-mail system, says White.

Another step FMC took was to name Dan Irwin the company's first director of information resources in June 1984. Irwin is responsible directly to the firm's president, Raymond C. Tower, and explains that the purpose of his position is to "effectively apply information technologies to increasing the returns of the corporation."

Appointing a director of information resources represented FMC's attempt to deal with the fact that the volumes of data a firm generates are one of its biggest assets, but only if they are gathered and processed correctly. Irwin is thus putting together a new department that will handle all of FMC's information technologies; he will supervise management information systems, telecommunications, computer-assisted design and manufacturing and other technical computing functions, and office automation. In discussing why Irwin reports to the corporation's president, Lynn White notes, "The practice of having the information function report to the controller of the chief financial officer is no longer effective. That grew out of the early history of data processing, when [only] clerical tasks were automated. But now you are talking about engineering and marketing information that is increasingly important to the conduct of the business. This is not just financial reports anymore."

Irwin was picked for this challenging new position because of his extensive background in operations management. He had been with FMC for 20 years, primarily as a manager of two divisions of the company's petroleum equipment group. He says that *any* company with refined information technologies will have an edge over its competitors in today's tough environment. He thinks that the top performers in information management will be those that "creatively apply technology to change the way business is done, to reap a competitive advantage." It looks as if FMC will be one of these winners.

Source: "An Information Guru in FMC's Executive Suite," *Business Week*, 8 October 1984, p. 124.

FACT OR FICTION REVEALED

1. Fact   2. Fact   3. Fact   4. Fiction   5. Fiction   6. Fiction

MANAGEMENT TERMS

communication	feedback	multiplexing
body language	empathy	climate surveys
noise	Homan's interaction hypothesis	informal communication
cognitive dissonance	committee	channel
rationalizing	formal communication channel	grapevine

REVIEW QUESTIONS

1. Define the following terms: (a) communication (b) body language (c) noise (d) cognitive dissonance (e) rationalizing (f) feedback (g) empathy (h) Homan interaction hypothesis (i) committee (j) formal communication channel (k) multiplexing (l) climate surveys (m) informal communication channel (n) grapevine.

2. What is meant by communication?

3. Explain the communication model.

4. What are the roadblocks to effective organizational communication? How might a manager avoid some of these problems?

5. Outline the basic concepts of organizational communication.

6. Discuss formal channels of communication.

7. Discuss informal channels of communication.

8. Review Keith Davis's research on the grapevine.

9. Relate communication to motivation.

10. Relate communication to leadership.

PROBLEMS AND EXPERIENTIAL EXERCISES

1. Eighty-three percent of the respondents to a survey of chief executive officers said their younger executives were poor writers. The most commonly cited problems were wordiness; poor organization; inappropriate style or tone; and no clear purpose.[32] Who is responsible for this situation and what can be done about it? What actions should these CEOs take to improve communication skills within their own organizations? Discuss.

2. Borg-Warner Educational Systems reports that 50 percent of all adult reading material consists of just 824 words! These same words account for 75 percent of all elementary reading material.[33] If so relatively few words are used, why is communication such a difficult subject?

3. One consultant reports that managers typically evaluate communication within their departments as more effective than that within the total organization.[34] Discuss the possible reasons for this reported difference.

4. Trace the last rumor you heard at school or at work. Relate what you discover to the discussion of the grapevine in this chapter.

5. Keep a diary of your communication for one day. Include mail, telephone, conversations, and personal contacts, Then prepare a report on what you learned about how you communicate. Compare your communication patterns to the Mintzberg research reported in this chapter.

MANAGERIAL INCIDENT: Integrated Genetics Inc.

How do managers who are used to working with corporate employees in three-piece suits and wing tips deal with the company's more creative types—those software engineers, copywriters, scientists, and art directors who tend to show up at work on bicycles, in tennis shoes and blue jeans, with dogs?

Some managers may decide, in the interest of peace and harmony, to keep their creative divisions as separate from the business side as possible. Integrated Genetics Inc. took a different tack. The $5-million bioengineering company in Framingham, Mass., recently devised a strategy "to prevent the scientists from becoming an esoteric group shut off from the rest" of the company, says Pat Connoy, vice-president of sales and marketing. Integrated Genetics employs 100 scientists and 30 administrative employees. Each Friday, one of the scientists gives a presentation to the company at large, on subjects ranging from his own in-house work to a new development in biotechnology. Once a month, an employee from the selling, marketing, or administrative side takes a turn speaking to the scientists on anything from finance to strategic planning. The company also runs a weekly in-house seminar called "Science for Non-Scientists," in which scientists explain their work in detail to about 20 administrative employees. "The formation of separate cliques, with their own little cultures, is a danger at companies like ours," says Connoy. By *John Persinos.*

Questions

1. Evaluate Integrated Genetics Inc.'s attempt to improve organizational communications.

2. Can you think of any other communications channels that might be opened between Integrated Genetics' technical and nontechnical personnel? Discuss.

Source: Reprinted from John Persinos, "Getting Together," *Inc.*, June 1985, p. 116. Copyright © 1985 by Inc. Publishing Company, 38 Commercial Wharf, Boston, MA 02110.

CASES FOR PART FOUR

CASE 7   Nurse Ross

The following situation was reported by Miss Jackson, who had known Miss Evelyn Ross for several years and had also worked in some of the same hospitals as Miss Ross[1] on different occasions.

Miss Ross, a registered nurse, began working at Benton Hospital when she was thirty-one years old. This hospital was an industrial hospital in a fairly large city on the West Coast. The bed capacity of the hospital was about 150, but 50 to 100 patients received treatment daily through the hospital's clinic facilities. The hospital was built and operated by a large shipbuilding concern. All the employees of the company's shipyards and their dependents could receive medical care through the company's hospitalization plan.

The nursing staff was headed by a director of nurses who had two assistants. One was in charge of nursing services in the hospital, and the other was in charge of the clinic nursing services. However, the two departments operated as a coordinated unit, and personnel were exchanged between them in the event the work load became too heavy in either place.

The medical director of the hospital, Dr. Peake, was energetic and his manner was usually quite brusque. Although he was a stickler for discipline and efficiency, he was fair in his treatment of the staff and they respected him and cooperated well. Dr. Peake had many progressive ideas and had helped to build the hospital up from 75 to 150 beds. The new ideas he had were discussed in staff conferences. Any persons or heads of departments who might be affected by proposed changes participated in these conferences.

Miss Ross worked as a head nurse, both in the hospital and in the clinic, during her employment there. (Miss Jackson at that time was employed as assistant head nurse in the clinic.) Miss Ross resigned her position to enter the Army Nurse Corps as a first lieutenant. She served in the Army for two-and-a-half years, most of which was duty in the South Pacific. During the time she was overseas, she was promoted to captain. She was transferred to reserve status upon leaving the corps. Shortly after this she took a three-month course in operating room supervision.

In the meantime, Miss Jackson had moved to the East Coast and was employed at Hughes Hospital, a large industrial hospital in a relatively small New England city. They had corresponded during this time and Miss Jackson wrote that the position of operating room supervisor would soon be open at the hospital and thought Miss Ross had a good chance of getting the position if she wanted to move to the East Coast. Miss Ross applied to the director of nursing at the hospital and was accepted for the position. She began working soon thereafter at Hughes.

Hughes Hospital was set up much like Benton Hospital. It took care of the medical needs of most of the community in addition to serving the employees of the Hughes Steel Company, the city's principal employer. It had clinic facilities for emergency and outpatient care. The bed capacity was 250 and the clinic staff treated well over 100 patients daily, although often a complete record of the number of patients was not kept.

The organization of the nursing department was quite similar to that of Benton Hospital with one important exception: the hospital department and the clinic department were operated as two completely separate units. The clinic was in a building separate from the hospital building; thus the problem of moving a stretcher case from the clinic to the hospital was an extreme ordeal. Besides the lack of proper equipment for moving patients, there was a shortage of male orderlies, and nurses' aides had to be utilized for this arduous task. This shortage of personnel and equipment was especially acute when emergency cases and accident victims came into the clinic and had to be moved to the hospital with a minimum loss of time and disturbance.

The director of nurses, Miss Mahaffey, was about forty-five years old; she had been at the hospital three years. Miss Linden had been the hospital supervisor for six months, and Miss Hartman had been employed as clinic supervisor for over a year. There were twenty-four graduate nurses employed in the hospital wards, thirty aides, and ten maids. The staff under Miss Hartman in the clinic consisted of five graduate nurses, four aides, and two maids. The orderly personnel numbered only six for all three shifts. One was utilized throughout the hospital on the evening shift, one on the night shift, and during the day shift one worked in the clinic, one in the operating room (O.R.), and one for each of the two men's wards in the hospital. Miss Ross, as supervisor of the O.R., had a staff of four nurses, three aides, and the one orderly. The nurses in the O.R. rotated turns, being "on call" each night for any emergency surgery cases.

Miss Ross found that the work was quite strenuous and often entailed long hours, but she was deeply interested in it and never seemed to object. She frequently stayed to help in emergency surgery cases, as a number of rather serious accidents occurred from time to time in the steel plants that the hospital served. Miss Mahaffey praised her highly for increasing the efficiency and cleanliness in the operating rooms.

Dr. McMillan, the medical director of the hospital, was nearly sixty-five years old. He had been employed as a company doctor for the Hughes Steel Company for over twenty years. Dr. McMillan would usually arrive at his offices in the hospital about nine in the morning, would dictate answers to his correspondence, make sporadic rounds of some of the hospital wards (very rarely did he put in an appearance at the clinic), leave for lunch promptly at noon, and, only two or three times a week return to the hospital for a few hours after lunch. On his occasional ward rounds, he would stop at the floor nurse's desk, inquire if everything was going all right, then say, "Fine! Fine!" and go on his way.

When Dr. McMillan suffered a heart attack severe enough to prevent him from retaining his position at the hospital, a new medical director had to be found. The president of the steel company was familiar with the shipbuilding concern and knew Dr. Peake had been at Benton. He contacted Dr. Peake to see if he would be interested in the position as the hospital medical director. Dr. Peake accepted. He entered the new situation with his usual brusque and energetic manner and made complete daily rounds in the clinic and hospital. He often spent considerable time talking to patients, nurses, aides, and the staff physicians.

After nearly a month of concentrated observation of the clinic and hospital routines, Dr. Peake had a conference with Miss Mahaffey and the nursing supervisors. He criticized the "unprofessional attitude" of several

(Continued on next page.)

of the nurses, and said he had had complaints from many of the patients about the care they were receiving. He asked why so many of the nurses seemed to be away from their wards when he made morning rounds. Miss Mahaffey said the nurses were permitted to leave the wards at intervals between nine and eleven to have coffee in the hospital dining room. The time for this was not rigidly enforced. Dr. Peake also talked to Dr. Albright, the staff physician in charge of the clinic, and to the clinic nurses to ascertain why the clinic patients often had to wait so long to see a doctor in the clinic. (The gist of these conferences was given by Miss Jackson, who was assistant supervisor of the clinic.) The clinic staff agreed that there was definitely a "bottle-neck" in the clinic, but they felt that it was due primarily to a shortage of personnel when needed most, the inconvenience of having to transport the patients the distance to the hospital, and the lack of satisfactory laboratory facilities in the clinic itself. Dr. Peake told the staff that the new additions being built onto the hospital were going to be utilized for clinic facilities. In the meantime, he said he would try to help them find some way to ease the situation.

During the second week of August of that year, Miss Mahaffey asked Miss Ross to come into her office.

MISS MAHAFFEY: Miss Ross, Dr. Peake tells me that you worked with him at Benton Hospital. I knew that he had been at Benton at one time, but didn't realize that it was during the same time you were there. He said that you are familiar with the clinic–hospital arrangement there and told me to relieve you of your present position so that you may help to coordinate the clinic and hospital units here.

MISS ROSS: I'm sorry to hear that. I have been very happy with my present position. Will I be working in the clinic or in the hospital?

MISS MAHAFFEY: Both. I want you to know that I consider Miss Linden a very capable supervisor and I don't want her to be hurt in this new arrangement. Also, I want to know everything that is going on down there. I expect you to report to me at least once a day. I don't know what Dr. Peake expects you to do that hasn't already been done. He should hire more people if he expects to make this a model hospital. He comes in here and all he does is criticize.

MISS ROSS: I'll do the best I can. I am familiar with the setup that Dr. Peake had at Benton. Maybe I can help put it into operation here.

A few hours later Dr. Peake entered Miss Ross' office in the O.R. unit.

DR. PEAKE: Hello, Rossie, I have a new job for you.

MISS ROSS: Miss Mahaffey has told me about it.

DR. PEAKE: You know how things were at Benton. I want the units to be set up in exactly that way here. During the past few months I have arranged for another physician to help out in the clinic during their busy hours and we've hired a couple more aides, but there doesn't seem to be too much improvement. Maybe you can help me find out what the trouble is there. Our new building program has been started and when it is finished I want the two units to be operating as one integrated unit. I don't like to take you away from the surgery—you've been doing a fine job here—but I feel you can help me get the clinic and hospital units functioning better together.

MISS ROSS: I can try, Dr. Peake.

DR. PEAKE: Good! Now I don't want you to go through anybody—if you have any problems, come right to me!

Miss Ross—knowing the strained relationship between Dr. Peake and Miss Mahaffey—was especially dubious about bypassing her immediate supervisor, the director of nurses. She decided at that time it would be best to observe the regular channels of communications.

Miss Ross reported for her new job and discussed Dr. Peake's plans and ideas for integrating the two units with both Miss Linden and Miss Hartman. She also told them that the reason he picked her for the job was because she had worked at Benton under him. They had known that both she and Miss Jackson had worked at Benton for a time while Dr. Peake was there. Neither of the supervisors seemed very surprised. Miss Linden remarked that it sounded like another of Dr. Peake's "wild ideas." Both Miss Linden and Miss Hartman seemed concerned over the shortage of an adequate staff and said that any changes that would improve the situation would be welcomed.

Personnel problems were especially acute in the hospital at that time. Several staff members were off duty because of illness and there were more patients than usual. The clinic was open Saturday and Sunday for emergencies only. One nurse and two aides were on duty weekends but were not too busy. Miss Ross arranged to transfer the two aides to the hospital for the weekends. Miss Linden was elated with the additional help. On the following Wednesday, the clinic was far behind in its work because of an emergency that had arisen. Miss Ross went to Miss Linden to see if someone could go over for the afternoon to help. The following conversation ensued:

MISS ROSS: Miss Hartman is swamped. She had an emergency to take care of and the other patients are not being seen. Have you anyone you can send to help?

MISS LINDEN: I am not going to send anyone to that clinic. They have enough help! We are too short here.

Miss Ross went over to one of the wards and found two of the aides in the ward kitchen drinking coffee. She asked if they were slack right then.

One of them said, "Oh, sure. We haven't had very much to do all afternoon."

Miss Ross returned to Miss Linden and told her of the episode. She asked that one of them be sent to help out in the clinic. Miss Linden complied reluctantly.

Shortly after this Miss Linden went on a vacation for two weeks. Miss Mahaffey asked Miss Ross to take charge of the hospital unit until her return. Thus Miss Ross was faced with the problem of making out time schedules for all the nurses, aides, orderlies, and maids employed in the hospital unit. Dr. Peake had also asked her to initiate a study to determine the personnel needs in the various hospital wards and the clinic departments, and to help with the plans for the layout of new equipment in the building additions. During the two weeks of Miss Linden's absence, Miss Ross found that (1) one

(Continued on next page.)

ward had more nurses than another one, although the work loads were the same, and (2) maids were not doing the cleaning assigned to them and some were not even aware of what their duties were. With the cooperation of Miss Hartman and the approval and permission of Miss Mahaffey, Miss Ross arranged to reallocate the nursing personnel so that all wards would have equal coverage in relation to their work loads.[2] She made out schedules to provide available clinic help as relief in the hospital on weekends and instructed the maids as to their duties.

There seemed to be a gradual improvement in the amount and quality of patient care and most of the employees seemed to be more satisfied when they were placed in jobs where they were kept busy and understood their duties. Several patients commented on the improved care they received after the changes had been made. Dr. Peake praised Miss Rose and Miss Mahaffey for the success of the new program.

Two days after Miss Linden returned from her vacation Miss Ross was called to the office of the director of nurses.

> MISS MAHAFFEY: Miss Ross, Miss Linden has requested a transfer to the operating room, because she doesn't think you and she will get along. She is doing a good job in the hospital and I don't want to lose her. Hereafter, you will not interfere with the operation of the hospital unit and its personnel. Miss Linden will take care of everything over there.

> MISS ROSS: I don't understand, Miss Mahaffey. Do you mean that my job is finished?

> MISS MAHAFFEY: No. You are to continue working in the clinic and help set up new departments there as the building program continues. I really don't know what made Dr. Peake think you would be able to do anything to improve the situation. He will just have to realize that we haven't sufficient personnel.

Miss Ross left the interview feeling very confused as to her exact status because she knew Dr. Peake would expect her to continue to try to coordinate the two units.

QUESTIONS

1. Discuss the leadership styles exhibited in this case.

2. How would you go about solving the motivational problems outlined in the case? Discuss.

---

[1] All names in this article are fictitious.
[2] The hospital budget stipulated how many persons in each category could be employed, so this interchange of personnel among the units seemed to be the best answer to solving the problem of emergency needs and excessive patient loads in any one department.

Source: Reprinted from the *Journal of Management Case Studies*, Spring 1985. Copyright © William M. Fox 1985.

CASE 8   Lordstown Plant of General Motors

INTRODUCTION

In December 1971 the management of the Lordstown Plant was very much concerned about the unusually high rate of defective Vegas coming off the assembly line. For the previous several weeks the lot, which had a capacity of 2,000 cars, had been filled with Vegas waiting for rework before they could be shipped out to the dealers around the country.

The management was particularly disturbed by the fact that many of the defects were not the kinds normally expected in the assembly production of automobiles.[1] There were countless numbers of Vegas with broken windshields, slashed upholstery, broken ignition keys, bent signal levers, broken rearview mirrors, or carburetors clogged with washers. There were cases in which, as the plant manager put it, "the whole engine blocks passed forty men without any work done on them."

Since then the incident in the Lordstown plant has been much publicized in news media, drawing public interest. It has been also frequently discussed in the classroom and in the academic circles. While some people viewed the event as a "young workers' revolt," others reacted to it as simply a "labor problem." Some viewed it as "worker sabotage," and others called it an "industrial Woodstock." This case describes some background and important incidents leading to this much publicized and discussed event.

The General Motors Corp. is the nation's largest manufacturer. The corporation is a leading example of an industrial organization that has achieved organizational growth and success through decentralization. The philosophy of decentralization has been one of the most valued traditions at General Motors from the days of Alfred Sloan in the 1930s through Charles Wilson's and Harlow Curtice's tenures in the 1950s and up to recent years.

Under decentralized management each of the company's car divisions—Cadillac, Buick, Oldsmobile, Pontiac, and Chevrolet—was given maximum autonomy in the management of its manufacturing and marketing operations. The assembly operations were no exception, each division managing its own assembly work. The car bodies built by Fisher Body were assembled in various locations under maximum control and coordination between Fisher Body and each car division.

In the mid-1960s, however, the decentralization in divisional assembly operations was subject to critical review. At the divisional level, the company was experiencing serious problems of worker absenteeism and increasing cost with declines in quality and productivity. They were reflected in the overall profit margins, which declined from 10 percent to 7 percent in the late 1960s. The autonomy of the divided management in body manufacturing and assembly operations, in separate locations in many cases, became questionable under the declining profit situation.

In light of these developments, General Motors began to consolidate some of the divided management of body and chassis assembly operations into a single management under the already existing General Motors Assembly Division (GMAD) in order to better coordinate the two operations. GMAD was given an overall responsibility to integrate the two operations in these instances and to see that the numerous parts and components going into the car assembly got to the right places in the right amounts at the right times (see Exhibit 1).[2]

THE GENERAL MOTORS ASSEMBLY DIVISION (GMAD)

GMAD was originally established in the mid-1930s, when the company needed an additional assembly plant to meet the increasing demand for Buick, Oldsmobile, and Pontiac automobiles. The demands for these cars were growing so much beyond the available capacity at the time that the company began,

(Continued on next page.)

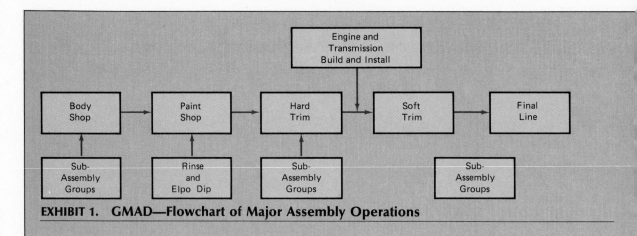

EXHIBIT 1.   GMAD—Flowchart of Major Assembly Operations

for the first time, to build an assembly plant on the West Coast that could turn out all three lines of cars rather than an individual line. As this novel approach became successful, similar plants turning out a multiple line of cars were built in seven other locations in the East, South, and Midwest. In the 1960s the demand for Chevrolet production also increased, and some Buick-Oldsmobile-Pontiac plants began to assemble Chevrolet products. Accordingly, the name of the division was changed to GMAD in 1965.

In order to improve the quality and productivity, GMAD increased its control over the operations of body manufacturing and assembly. It reorganized jobs, launched programs to improve efficiency, and reduced the causes of defects that required repairs and rework. With many positive results attained under GMAD management, the company extended the single management concept to six more assembly locations in 1968 that had been run by the Fisher Body and Chevrolet Divisions. In 1971 GMAD further extended the concept to four additional Chevrolet-Fisher Body assembly facilities, consolidating the separate management under which the body and chassis assembly had been operat-

ing. One of these plants was the Lordstown plant.

This series of consolidations brought to eighteen the number of assembly plants operated by GMAD. In terms of total production, they were producing about 75 percent of all cars and 67 percent of trucks built by GM. Also in 1971 one of the plants under GMAD administration began building certain Cadillac models, thus involving GMAD in the production of automobiles for each of GM's five domestic car divisions as well as trucks for both Chevrolet and the GMC Truck and Coach Division.

THE LORDSTOWN COMPLEX

The Lordstown complex is located in Trumbull County in Ohio, about fifteen miles west of Youngstown and thirty miles east of Akron. It consists of a Vega assembly plant, a van-truck assembly plant, and a Fisher Body metal fabricating plant, occupying about 1,000 acres of land. GMAD, which operates the Vega and van-truck assembly plants, is also located in the Lordstown complex. The three plants are in the heart of the heavy industrial triangle of Youngstown, Akron, and Cleveland. With Youngstown as a center of steel production, Akron the home of the rubber industries, and Cleveland a major center for heavy manufacturing, the Lordstown complex commands a good strategic and logistic location for automobile assembly.

The original assembly plant was built in 1964–1966 to assemble Impalas. But in 1970 it was converted to assemble Vegas after extensive rearrangements. The van-truck assembly plant was constructed in 1969, and the Fisher Body metal fabricating plant was further added in 1970 to carry out stamping operations to produce sheet metal components used in Vega and van assemblies. In October 1971 the Chevrolet Vega and van-assembly plants and Fisher Body Vega assembly plants, which had been operating under separate management, were merged into a single jurisdiction of GMAD.

WORK FORCE AT THE LORDSTOWN PLANT

Over 11,400 employees worked in the Lordstown plant as of 1973. Approximately 6,000 people, of whom 5,500 were on an hourly payroll, worked in the Vega assembly plant. About 2,600 workers, 2,100 of them paid hourly, worked on the van-truck assembly. As members of the United Auto Workers Union, Local 1112, the workers commanded good wages and benefits. They started out on the line at about $5.00 an hour, got a ten-cent-an-hour raise within thirty days, and another ten cents after ninety days. Benefits came to $2.50 an hour.[3] The supplemental unemployment benefits virtually guaranteed the worker's wages throughout the year. If the worker was laid off, he got more than 90 percent of his wages for fifty-two weeks. The worker was also eligible for up to six weeks' leave for holidays, excused absence, or bereavement, and up to four weeks' vacation.

The work force at the plant was almost entirely made up of local people, with 92 percent coming from within a 20-mile radius. Lordstown itself is a small rural town of about 500 residents. A sizable city close to the plant is Warren, 5 miles away, which together with Youngstown supplies about two-thirds of the work force. The majority of the workers (57.5 percent) were married, 7.6 percent were homeowners, and 20.2 percent were buying their homes. Of those who did not own their homes (72 percent), over one-half were still living with their parents. The rest lived in rented houses or apartments.

The workers in the plant were generally young. Although various news media reported the average worker age as twenty-four years old, and in some parts of the plant as twenty-two years old, the company records show that the overall average worker age was somewhat above twenty-nine years old as of 1971–1972. The national average was forty-two years old. The work force at Lordstown was the second youngest among GM's twenty-five assembly plants around the country. The fact that the Lordstown plant was the GM's newest assembly plant may partly explain the relatively young work force.

The educational profile of the Lordstown workers indicates that only 22 percent had less than a high school education. Nearly two-thirds—62 percent—were high school graduates, and 16 percent were either college graduates or had attended college. Another 26 percent had attended trade school. The average education of 13.2 years made the Lordstown workers among the best educated in GM's assembly plants.

THE VEGA ASSEMBLY LINE

Conceived as a major competitor against the increasing influx of foreign cars, which were being produced at a labor rate as low as one-fourth the rate predominant in this country, the Vega was specifically designed with maximum production efficiency and economy in mind. For the initial stages of planning, the Vega was designed by a special task team whose sophisticated techniques included the use of computers in designing the outer skin of the car and making the tapes that form the dies. Computers were also used to match up parts, measure the stack tolerances, measure safety performance under head-on collision, and make all necessary corrections before the first 1971 model car was built. The 2,300-cubic-centimeter, all-aluminum, four-cylinder engine was designed to give gas economy comparable to that of the foreign imports.

The Vega was also designed with the plant and the people in mind. As GM's newest plant, the Vega assembly plant was known as the "super plant" with the most modern and sophisticated design to maximize efficiency. It featured the newest engineering techniques and a variety of new power tools and automatic devices to eliminate much of the heavy lifting and physical labor. The line gave the workers easier access to the car body, reducing the amount of bending and crawling in and out required of workers at other plants around the country. The unitized body, easily assembled from large components like prefab housing, was lighter and had greater integrity. Most difficult and tedious tasks were eliminated or simplified, on-line variations of the job were minimized, and the most modern tooling and mechanization was used to the highest possible degree of reliability.

It was also the fastest moving assembly line in the industry. The average time per assembly job was thirty-six seconds, with a maximum of 100 cars rolling off the assembly line per hour for a daily production of 1,600 cars from two shift operations. The time cycle per job in other assembly plants averaged about fifty-five seconds. Although the high speed of the line did not necessarily imply greater work loads or job requirements, it was a part of the GM's attempt to maximize economy in Vega assembly. The fact that the Vega was designed to have 43 percent fewer parts than a full-size car also helped the high-speed line and economy.

IMPACT OF GMAD AND REORGANIZATION IN THE LORDSTOWN PLANT

As stated previously the assembly operations at Lordstown had originally been run by Fisher Body and Chevrolet as two plants. There were two organizations, two plant managers, two unions, and two service organizations. The consolidation of the two organizations into a single operating system under GMAD in October 1971 was a difficult task requiring expensive reorganization and the need to deal with the consequences of manpower reduction, such as work slowdowns, worker discipline, grievances, and so forth.

As duplicating units such as production, maintenance, inspection, and personnel were consolidated, there was a problem of selecting the personnel to manage the new organization. There were chief inspectors, personnel directors, and production superintendents as well as production and service workers to be displaced or reassigned. Unions that had been representing their respective plants also had to go through reorganization. Union elections were held to merge the separate union committees at Fisher Body and Chevrolet into a single-union bargaining committee. This eliminated one full local union shop committee.

At the same time, GMAD launched an effort to bring production efficiency up to the levels found at other assembly plants. It included increasing job efficiency through reorganization and better coordination between the body and chassis assembly and in improving controls over product quality and worker absenteeism. This effort coincided with the plant's early operational stage, a time at which adjustments in line balance and work methods are required. Like other assembly plants, the Vega assembly plant was going through an initial period of diseconomy caused by suboptimal operations, imbalance in the assembly line, and somewhat redundant work force. According to management, line adjustments and work changes were a normal process in accelerating the assembly operations to the peak performance the plant had been designed for after the initial break-in and startup period.

As for job efficiency, GMAD initiated changes in those work sequences and work methods that were not well coordinated under the divided managements of body and chassis assembly. For example, previous to GMAD, Fisher Body had been delivering the car body complete with interior trim to the final assembly line, where often the workers soiled the front seats as they did further assembly operations. GMAD changed this practice so installment of the seats was one of the last operations in building the car. Fisher Body also had been delivering the car with a complete panel instrument frame, and it was difficult for the assembly workers to reach behind the frame to install the instrument panels. GMAD improved the job method so that the box containing the entire instrument panel was installed on the assembly line. Such improvements in job sequences and job methods resulted in savings in time and the number of workers required. Consequently, assembly times were cut down and/or the number of workers were reduced for some jobs.

GMAD also put strict control over worker absenteeism and the causes for defects; the reduction in absenteeism was expected to require fewer relief men, and the improvement in quality and reduced repair work were to require fewer repairmen. In implementing these changes, GMAD instituted a strong policy of dealing with worker slowdowns via strict disciplinary measures, including dismissal. It was rumored that inspectors and foremen passing defective cars would be fired on the spot.

Many workers were laid off as a result of the reorganization and job changes. The union claimed that as many as 700 workers were laid off. Management, on the other hand, put the layoff figure at 375 to which the union later conceded.[4] Although management claimed that the change in job sequence and method in some assembly work did not bring a substantial change in the overall speed or pace of the assembly line, the workers perceived the job change as "tightening" the assembly line. The union charged that GMAD brought a return of an old-fashioned line speedup and a "sweat-shop style" of management reminiscent of the 1930s, making the men do more work at the same pay. The workers blamed the "tightened" assembly line for the drastic increase in quality defects. As one worker commented, "That's the fastest line in the world. We have about forty seconds to do our job. The company adds one more thing and it can kill us. We can't get the stuff done on time and a car goes by. The company blames us for sabotage and shoddy work."

The number of worker grievances also increased drastically. Before GMAD took over, there were about 100 grievances in the plant. Since its takeover grievances had increased to 5,000, 1,000 of which were related to the charge that too much work had been added

(Continued on next page.)

to the job. The worker resentment was particularly great in "towveyor" assembly and seat subassembly areas. The "towveyor" is the area in which engines and transmissions are assembled. Like seat subassembly there is a great concentration of workers working together in proximity. Also, these jobs are typically for beginning assemblers, Thus, the work crew in these areas tend to be younger and better educated.

The workers in the plant were particularly resentful of the company's strict policy in implementing the changes. They stated that the tougher the company became, the more they would stiffen their resistance, even though other jobs were scarce in the market. One worker said, "In some of the other plants where GMAD did the same thing, the workers were older and they took this. But, I've got twenty-five years ahead of me in this plant." Another worker commented, "I saw a woman running to keep pace with the fast line. I'm not going to run for anybody. There isn't anyone in that plant that is going to tell me to run." One foreman said, "The problem with the workers here is not so much that they don't want to work, but that they just don't want to take orders. They don't believe in any kind of authority."

While the workers were resisting management orders, there were some indications that the first-line supervisors had not been adequately trained to perform satisfactory supervisory roles. The average supervisor at the time had fewer than three years' experience, and 20 percent of the supervisors had less than one year's experience. Typically, they were young, somewhat lacking in knowledge of the provisions of the union contract and other supervisory duties, and less than adequately trained to handle the workers in the threatening and hostile environment that was developing.

Significantly, the strong reactions of the workers were not due entirely to the organizational and job changes brought about by GMAD alone. Management noted that there were a significant number of worker reactions in areas in which the company hadn't changed anything at all. Management felt that the intense resentment was particularly due to the nature of the work force in Lordstown. The plant was not only made up of young people, but the work force also reflected the characteristics of "tough labor" in the steel, coal, and rubber industries in the surrounding communities. In fact, many of the workers came from families who made their living working in these industries. Management also noted that worker resistance had been much greater in the Lordstown plant than in other plants where similar changes had been made.

A good part of the young workers' resentment also seemed to stem from the unskilled and repetitive nature of the assembly work. One management official admitted that the company was facing a difficult task in getting workers to "take pride" in the product they were assembling. Many of them were benefiting from the company's tuition assistance plan by taking college-level courses in the evening. With this educated background, they obviously found that assembly work was not fulfilling their high work expectations. Also, the job market was tied up at the time, and they could neither find any meaningful jobs elsewhere nor, even if such jobs were found, could they afford to give up the good money and fringe benefits they were earning on their assembly line jobs. This made them frustrated, according to company officials.

Many industrial engineers were questioning whether the direction of management toward assembly line work could continue. As the jobs became easier, simpler, and more repetitive and required less physical effort, there was less need for skill and increased monotony. The worker unrest indicated that they not only wanted to go back to the work pace prior to the "speed-up" (pre-October pace) but also wanted the company to do something about the boring and meaningless assembly work. One worker commented, "The company has got to do something to change the job so that a guy can take an interest in the job. A guy can't do the same thing eight hours a day year after year. And it's got to be more than the company just saying to a guy, 'Okay, instead of six spots on the weld, you'll do five spots.'"

As the worker resentment mounted, the UAW Local 1112 decided in early January 1972 to consider possible authorization of a strike against the Lordstown plant to fight the job changes. In the meantime the union and management bargaining teams worked hard on worker grievances. They reduced the number of grievances from 5,000 to a few hundred, and management even indicated that it would restore some of the eliminated jobs. However, the bargaining failed to produce accord on the issues of seniority rights and shift preference, which were related to the wider issues of job changes and layoffs.

A vote was held in early February 1972. Nearly 90 percent of the workers came out to vote, the heaviest turnout in the history of the Local. With 97 percent of the votes supporting it, the workers went on strike in early March.

In March 1972, with the strike in effect, the management of the Lordstown plant was assessing the impact of GMAD and the resultant strike at the plant. It was estimated that the work disruption caused by worker resentment and slowdown had already cost the company 12,000 Vegas and 4,000 trucks, amounting to $45 million.

There had also been an amazing number of complaints from Chevrolet dealers, 6,000 in November alone, about the quality of the Vegas shipped to them. This was more than the complaints concerning all other assembly plants combined.

The strike in the Lordstown plant was expected to affect other plants. The plants at Tonawanda, New York, and Buffalo were supplying parts for Vega. Despite the costly impact of the worker resistance and the strike, the management felt that job changes and cost reductions were essential if the Vega were to return a profit to the company. The company had to be operating at about 90 percent capacity to break even. Not only had the plant with highly automated features cost twice as much as estimated, but also the Vega itself ended up weighing 10 percent more than had been planned.

While the company had to do something to increase the production efficiency in the Lordstown plant, the management was wondering whether it couldn't have planned and implemented the organizational and job changes differently in view of the costly disruption of the operations and the organizational stress the plant had been experiencing.

QUESTIONS

1. How would you assess the problems at the Lordstown plant?

2. Could a similar situation develop in today's economic environment?

3. What would you suggest that management do about the work force problem at the Lordstown installation?

Source: By Professor Hak-Chong Lee, International Management Institute, Federation of Korean Industries, Seoul, Korea. Copyright 1974 by Hak-Chong Lee. This case was developed for instructional purposes from published sources and interviews with the General Motors

(*Continued on next page.*)

Assembly Division officials in Warren, Michigan, and Lordstown, Ohio. The case was read and minor corrections were made by the Public Relations Office of the GMAD. However, the author is solely responsible for the content of the case. The author appreciates the cooperation of General Motors. He also appreciates the suggestions of Professor Anthony Athos of Harvard and Mr. John Grix of General Motors, which improved the case. Adapted and reprinted by permission of the author.

[1] The normal defect rate requiring rework was fluctuating between 1 and 2 percent at the time.

[2] A typical assembly plant has five major assembly lines— hard trim, soft trim, body, paint, and final—supported by subassembly lines that feed to the main lines such components as engines, transmissions, wheels and tires, radiators, gas tanks, front and sheet metal, and scores of other items. In a typical GMAD assembly plant, the average vehicle on assembly lines has more than 5,500 items, with quality checks numbering 5 million in a sixteen-hour-a-day operation.

[3] At the time the average GM worker on the line earned $12,500 a year with fringe benefits of $3,000.

[4] All of the workers who had been laid off were later reinstated as the plant needed additional workers to perform assembly jobs for such optional features to the Vega as vinyl tops, which were later introduced. In addition, some workers were put to work at the van-assembly plant.

PART
FIVE CONTROLLING

16 FUNDAMENTALS OF CONTROLLING

LEARNING OBJECTIVES

After studying this chapter you should be able to

1. Identify the basic uses of controlling.

2. Explain the steps in the control process.

3. Identify and explain the four basic types of standards.

4. Explain each of the four categories of controls.

5. List the characteristics of effective controls.

6. Identify the five general tools of control and give an example of each.

7. Distinguish between financial statement analysis and ratio analysis and identify the major types of ratios.

STOP ACTION CASE

Leprino Foods Company

Denver-based Leprino Foods Company operates a fleet of trucks to haul its food products to the warehouses of retail stores and industrial customers throughout the western United States. One of the primary objectives facing Jerry Sheehan, Leprino's vice-president of transportation, is to minimize fuel costs, maintenance expenses, and repairs on his 160-truck fleet without jeopardizing the service levels the firm's customers expect.

The speed at which Leprino trucks travel is a major factor in cutting costs. Reducing average speeds from sixty-five miles per hour to sixty would result in a 25 percent fuel savings, reduced maintenance frequency, and fewer accidents. The latter benefit would also reduce Leprino's insurance premiums.

A recent *Wall Street Journal* article described Sheehan's efforts to lower the speed of Leprino trucks:

> Like other trucking managers, Mr. Sheehan used to spend much of his time urging his drivers to observe the speed limit and take it easy on their engines. Truckers who drive too fast and strain their engines get too few miles per gallon and run up undue maintenance bills. But urging wasn't accomplishing much. Leprino hired a vehicle-tailing service to follow a sampling of trucks and gauge their speeds. The service reported that most Leprino truckers were driving about 10 miles over the speed limit. That didn't surprise Mr. Sheehan, who has a theory about employee rules. "I'm a great one for believing that people really will do what's *inspected* and not what's *expected*," he says.

Sheehan dismissed the suggestion that governors be installed on Leprino trucks, for safety reasons, among others. But he had to develop a control system that would work.

Use the concepts developed in this chapter to design a control system for Leprino Foods Company that will encourage driver compliance with the legal speed limit.

Source: Quotation in paragraph three is from Michael W. Miller, "Computers Keep Eye on Workers and See If They Perform Well," *Wall Street Journal,* 3 June 1985, p. 1.

The terms *control, controls,* and *controlling* frequently produce visions of the "Big Brother" environment of George Orwell's *1984.* Thoughts of mind control, police state conditions, and the loss of personal freedom produce a negative connotation of control as a threat to individual freedom and organizational flexibility. As a result the subject of organizational and individual control is often misunderstood and frequently avoided.

However, philosophers, theologians, and business practitioners have long recognized that freedom and order are not opposites but actually complement each other.[1] While overcontrol is obviously harmful, the imperfect environment of the late 1980s requires various methods to check and balance behavior and performance. Increased organizational complexity makes the need for effective controls even greater. In the same way that automobile tires require periodic checks and balancing, so also do organizations need controls. A well-designed control process provides answers to the important questions, "What *is* going on?" and "What *should* be going on?" If the answers to these questions are different, appropriate corrective actions may be taken.

General Motors Corporation was one of the few major manufacturers to earn a profit during the Depression of the 1930s. Although profits dropped from $248 million in 1929 to a low point of $165,000 in 1932,

MANAGEMENT FACT OR FICTION

	FACT	FICTION		FACT	FICTION
1. To be most useful, standards should be defined in as specific terms as possible.	☐	☐	5. Zero-base budgeting is likely to involve less time than the approach of using last year's budget as a starting point for the budget for the following year.	☐	☐
2. The need to correct deviations from expected performance is evidence of effective controlling but poor planning.	☐	☐	6. If the income statement can be compared to a photograph, then the balance sheet can be compared to a motion picture.	☐	☐
3. Precontrols and steering controls are more likely to be used in the automobile industry than are yes-no controls and postcontrols.	☐	☐	7. Control systems are extremely difficult to establish in organizations where goal displacement occurs.	☐	☐
4. Flexibility is an important characteristic of budgets as well as overall systems of controlling.	☐	☐			

The materials in this chapter will assist you in separating management fact from fiction. Your answers can be checked on page 531.

Controlling is the process of developing standards based upon organizational objectives; comparing current performance to standards; and taking remedial action to correct deviations.

the firm avoided red ink through major cost cuts and sizable layoffs. GM's president, Alfred P. Sloan, Jr., gave the credit to the firm's control systems. In his words, "It would be unfair to claim any particular prescience on our part; no more than anyone else did we see the Depression coming . . . we had simply learned how to react quickly. This was perhaps the greatest payoff of our system of financial and operating controls."[2]

Controlling is the process of ensuring efficient use of an enterprise's resources and achievement of objectives by establishing standards of performance; comparing current performance against established standards to determine progress toward predetermined objectives; and acting to reinforce success and correct shortcomings.[3] Its importance in every organization is illustrated by the rowing team shown in Figure 16–1. The team's objective may be to win the racing meet or to complete the course within a specified time period. These objectives are accomplished by the eight-member team, each equipped with a large, long sweep oar and traveling in a lightweight, fragile racing rowboat called a shell. Rather than facing the finish line, they face the coxswain who steers the shell by pulling on tiller ropes to turn a rudder. In this manner, the coxswain controls the direction of the shell to minimize the distance to the finish line. But another important component of control is performed by the coxswain. Speed and direction are greatly influenced by the timing of the oar strokes. Perhaps the most important contribution of the coxswain is the establishment of a cadence of shouted instructions to the crew who then make their oar strokes in unison. The results of such teamwork, produced by months of practice, is a team that pulls together, sending the shell gliding rapidly across the surface of the water.

FIGURE 16–1.   Excellence Through Teamwork and Effective Control

RELATIONSHIP BETWEEN PLANNING AND CONTROLLING

Since controlling involves the comparison of actual performance with planned results, considerable overlap exists between it and the planning, organizing, and leading functions. Although each managerial function has been discussed separately in previous chapters, all are interrelated, and the interrelationship between planning and controlling are clearly evident. Planning involves the establishment of organizational objectives and the development of strategies, while controlling establishes standards of performance and compares actual results with the planned results to determine whether operations are being performed according to plans.

The cyclical relationship between planning and controlling is shown in Figure 16–2. The planning/control cycle begins with the establishment of organizational objectives and the formulation of plans designed to accomplish them. As the plans are put into action, the control function monitors actual performance and compares it with established standards to determine whether variations exist. If no variations are present, operations continue. Should variations be discovered, corrective action may be taken in the form of modification of existing plans or the creation of new plans. The feedback present in the planning/control cycle produces a dynamic process in which the means by which the organization accomplishes its objectives can evolve over time in response to a changing environment.

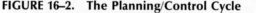

FIGURE 16–2.   The Planning/Control Cycle

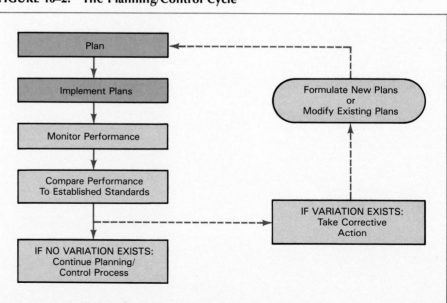

THE IMPORTANCE OF CONTROLLING

A number of factors contribute to the importance of controlling in today's organizations. First, the need for controlling the activities of individuals and organizations is at the heart of the basic concept of *accountability*. For organizational members who have been assigned specific responsibilities to be held accountable, they must know exactly what their responsibilities are, how their performance will be evaluated, and the standards of effective performance to be used as criteria in the evaluation process. Accountability is virtually impossible without some type of controlling process. And without the ability to require accountability, managers face significant problems in delegating authority to subordinates.

A second factor in increasing the importance of controlling is the *rapidity of change*. The fast pace at which environmental and other factors change requires a constant evaluation and reevaluation of the organization's strategic and tactical plans. Controlling systems must be established to assist managers in detecting changes that have significant impact on organizational activities.

A third factor is the growing *complexity* of today's organizations. Large, multiproduct, geographically dispersed organizations require consistent and appropriately applied control systems to measure effectiveness. The movement toward decentralized organizational structures in many firms also calls for effective methods of controlling performance.

Another important reason for the development and implementation of controlling systems is that people make *mistakes*. The mistake may be as significant as Xerox Corporation's ill-fated decision to take on IBM in the computer industry or as mundane as the inadequate training of an intracompany mail carrier. Effectively designed control systems should be capable of identifying a wrong decision, forecast, or order so that corrective action can be taken to minimize the damage. Control systems should not be viewed as blame-allocators or as devices for finger-pointing but as early warning systems to spot deviations from organizational objectives.

At its base, the controlling process is positive. Its basic purpose is to ensure the achievement of organizational objectives. The terms *reconciliation, integration,* and *balance* are as descriptive of the controlling process as are *efficiency, error-free, zero-defects, correction, preventive,* and *increased profitability*. A positive overtone should pervade the entire control process.

SPECIFIC USES OF CONTROL

Before discussing the control process and the various techniques used by managers in controlling, it is useful to examine the basic uses of control. Eight specific uses are identified in Figure 16–3. The first, standardizing performance, serves to increase efficiency and reduce cost in an organization. Safeguarding company assets, the second area in which the controlling function can make a contribution, serves to reduce the cost of losses from theft, waste, and misuse that run rampant in many organiza-

> 66 A manager is best when people barely know that he exists.
> Not so good when people obey and acclaim him.
> Worse when they despise him.
> Fail to honor people, they fail to honor you.
> But of a good manager, who talks little,
> When his work is done, his aim fulfilled,
> They will all say, 'We did this ourselves.' 99
>
> Lao Tzu, 600 B.C.

> 66 Victory often goes to the army that makes the least mistakes, not the most brilliant plans. 99
>
> Charles de Gaulle

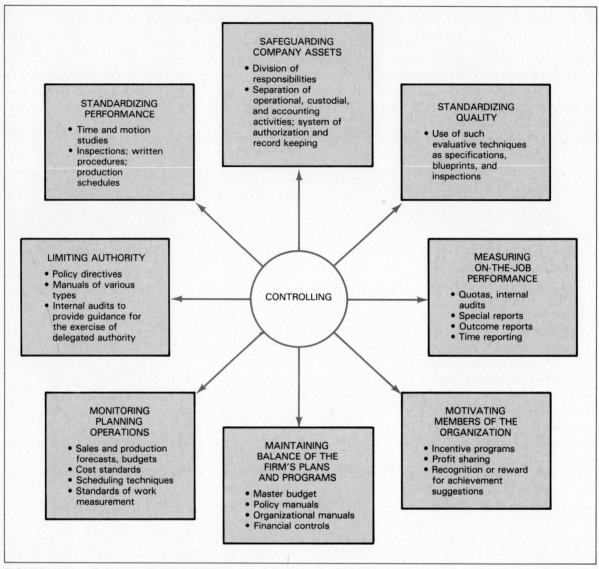

FIGURE 16–3. Eight Uses of Controlling
Source: Adapted from William T. Jerome III, *Executive Control—The Catalyst* (New York: Wiley, 1961), pp. 31–34. Copyright © 1982 by John Wiley & Sons, Inc. Reprinted by permission.

tions today. By standardizing quality, the controlling function permits management to meet the specifications of company engineers or product designers within the organization or the expectations of customers.

Limiting authority, the fourth use of control, involves establishment of parameters within which delegated authority can be exercised without higher level approval. Policy directives and various types of organizational manuals are commonly-used control tools for establishing accountability and providing for needed delegation of authority.

The fifth area in which the controlling function contributes to the organization is in measuring on-the-job performance. The sum total of individual performance is overall organizational achievement. Consequently, methods of measuring this performance must be established.

Monitoring planning operations is still another use of control. This type of control is fundamental to the attainment of organizational objectives. In addition, a number of control tools aid management in keeping the firm's plans and programs balanced. Master budgets, policy manuals, and financial controls are frequently-used techniques in accomplishing this use of control. The final use, motivating individuals, is accomplished through the use of performance measures, linking performance to financial incentives, and individual recognition.

As Figure 16–3 indicates, different controlling methods may be appropriate for different purposes. Time and motion studies and production schedules may be most appropriate for standardizing performance; policy directives and internal audits may be used in specifying authority limits.

> It is not enough to be busy; so are the ants. The question is: What are we busy about?
>
> Henry David Thoreau

STEPS IN THE CONTROLLING PROCESS

Since controlling is a universal management function, a generally accepted process has been developed for its application. The basic steps of the controlling process overlap the general process of management because of the interrelationship of the functions. Planning involves the establishment of organizational objectives, while controlling guides performance to conform to the plan. The four basic steps, illustrated in Figure 16–4, are (1) establishment of standards of performance based upon organizational objectives; (2) monitoring the actual performance; (3) comparison

FIGURE 16–4.   Steps in the Controlling Process

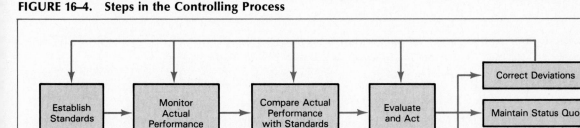

MANAGEMENT SUCCESSES

Live Aid Benefit Concert for Ethiopia Famine Relief

Scheduling hundreds of rock performers on two stages an ocean apart and broadcasting the concert, live and on tape, to the planet for 16 consecutive hours had all the makings of a logistical nightmare of global proportions. But before the first guitar note was played at the Live Aid benefit for Ethiopia famine relief, a volunteer corps of personal computer users helped turn the event into a nearly seamless spectacle seen by millions of people around the world.

Susan Secord, Live Aid's scheduling systems manager, started with two Macintosh computers and a printer at Philadelphia's Four Seasons Hotel the week of the concert. Only days before the July 13th event, the producers of Live Aid put out an urgent call for more help. Students at nearby Drexel University, where there are more Macs than freshmen (thanks to a computer literacy requirement), came to the rescue with their machines.

Jazz software was used to produce a minute-by-minute schedule. Using the Jazz worksheet, Secord constructed a grid of almost

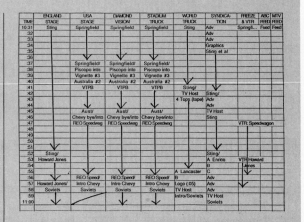

TIME	ENGLAND STAGE	USA STAGE	DIAMOND VISION	STADIUM TRUCK	WORLD TRUCK	SYNDICA-TION	FREEZE & VTR	ABC FEED	MTV FEED
10:31	Sting	Springfield	Springfield	Springfield	Sting	Adv	Springli...	Feed	Feed
:32						Adv			
:33						Adv			
:34						Graphics			
:35						Sting et al			
:36									
:37		Springfield/	Springfield/	Springfield/					
:38		Piscopo into	Piscopo into	Piscopo into					
:39		Vignette #3	Vignette #3	Vignette #3					
:40		Australia #2	Australia #2	Australia #2					
:41		VTPB	VTPB	VTPB	Sting/				
:42					TV Host	Sting/			
:43					4 Tops (tape)	Adv			
:44						Adv			
:45		Aust/	Aust/	Aust/		TV Host			
:46		Chevy bye/into	Chevy bye/into	Chevy bye/into		Sting			
:47		REO Speedwag	REO Speedwag	REO Speedwag			VTR: Speedwagon		
:48									
:49									
:50									
:51									
:52	Sting/					Sting/			
:53	Howard Jones					A Enrico	VTR Howard		
:54							Jones		
:55					A Lancaster	C			
:56		REO Speed/	REO Speed/	REO Speed/	B	Adv			
:57	Howard Jones/	Intro Chevy	Intro Chevy	Intro Chevy	Logo (.05)	Adv			
:58	Soviets	Soviets	Soviets	Soviets	TV Host	Adv			
:59					Intro/Soviets	TV Host			
11:00						Soviets			

1,000 rows, listing each minute from 7 A.M. (EST), the time of singer/organizer Bob Geldorf's opening in England, through 11 P.M., the curtain close in Philadelphia. Occupying the columns to the right were the names of performers in both Britain and in the United States, which acts were being shown on the Diamond Vision giant screen in the Philadelphia stadium, and what video was being sent to the various networks including MTV, ABC, a syndicated service to stations in the U.S., and a "World Truck" transmission overseas.

---

of actual performance with established standards to determine variations; and (4) evaluation and action if a deviation exists.

ESTABLISHING STANDARDS

The controlling process begins with the establishment of standards of performance to serve as a basis for determining whether organizational objectives are being accomplished. A *standard* is a level of activity established by management as a model for evaluating performance. Standards serve as reference points against which actual performance can be com-

Standard is a level of activity established by management as a model for evaluating performance.

A separate column noted which bands needed to be taped for delayed showing in instances where a group in England was performing at the same time as a group in America. Such details as televising the landing of Phil Collins' Concorde in New York and slotting the Led Zeppelin reunion and Mick Jagger/Tina Turner act all had to be entered on the worksheet. The printout filled 32 pages.

Mike Mitchell, president of Worldwide Sports & Entertainment Inc., which managed the event, commented, "Because of its complexity, there is no way that Live Aid could have been produced without the aid of the computers."

Secord used the Mac's mouse to drag each column to the appropriate width. She only had to type in the minutes for the first hour, since she was able to copy progressively larger blocks to fill out the rest of the worksheet. Last-minute changes were easily accomplished, as in the case when the group Tears For Fears dropped out and TFF was replaced by George Thorogood And The Destroyers. When one operator repeatedly spelled Mick Jagger's name "Mik," a universal search and replace corrected the faux pas.

One of the Drexel volunteers, Denise Wall, a third-year mechanical engineering student, helped supervise the transcribing of hundreds of pages of script from Thursday afternoon until dawn Saturday. Things were so hectic that at one point she had both her hands on mice connected to a pair of Macs. Exclaimed Wall: "Our motto was: 'Anytime anyone swears, save it!'" (Saving work on-screen averaged once every seven minutes, she added.) Using a MacWrite headline size and an Apple LaserWriter, the printed copy was good enough to be fed into a teleprompter for reading by on-camera announcers.

As for the glamour of being surrounded by rock stars, Wall remembers walking into Jagger in the hotel lobby and riding in an elevator with someone who turned out to be Rob Halford, the lead singer of Judas Priest. ("I didn't know it until I saw him on TV the next day," she said.) Most of her view, though, was confined to computer screens. Though the volunteers were given VIP passes to the sold-out concert, after working through two sleepless nights, they only briefly visited the concert before returning home—and a chance to fall asleep in front of their TVs. "That's okay. We'll watch it on videotape," said Steve Weintraut, a Drexel volunteer. "The important thing was being able to help out."

Source: Michael Antonoff, "Live Aid's Backstage Heroes," *Personal Computing* (November 1985), pp. 29, 31. Reprinted by permission.

pared. Without them, controlling is extremely difficult since no definition of effective performance is available. Quality control at a Black & Decker engine manufacturing facility is difficult without a specific definition of acceptable quality. Similarly, efficient energy consumption must be translated into a predetermined standard before the store manager of a local Sears retail outlet can determine whether the store is efficient in its usage of electrical and natural gas fuels. Such standards should be defined in as specific terms as possible.

American Airlines employs a number of precise standards for evaluating the performance of its airport personnel. The standards are defined in specific quantifiable terms. The following list illustrates some of these standards:

- *Mishandling of baggage.* Airport personnel employed by American Airlines should mishandle no more than one out of each 150 bags processed.

- *Waiting time.* At least 85 percent of all customers at an American Airlines airport ticket counter shall be waited on within five minutes.

- *Telephone answering time.* At least 80 percent of all telephone calls to American Airlines reservations offices shall be answered within 20 seconds.[4]

Many types of standards can be developed. As Table 16–1 indicates, four types are commonly used by managers: time, quality, quantity, and cost. *Time standards* are used in the allocation of work efforts and in the regulation of production schedules. Managers utilize time standards to forecast work flow and employee output. Financial incentive plans rely heavily on time standards that identify standard output per person during a normal work period.

TABLE 16–1 TYPES OF STANDARDS

Type of Standard	Purpose	Examples
Time Standards	Allocation of work flows; Regulation of production schedules	12 units per employee hour; 4,000 units produced per eight-hour shift
Quality Standards	Establishment of acceptable quality levels for output	Zero-defects requirement; Finished products can vary in size no more than 2 percent
Quantity Standards	Establishment of acceptable output levels by individuals, work groups, or production facilities	Absenteeism should not exceed 3 percent; Senior production workers should produce 10 percent more units than less-experienced personnel
Cost Standards	Establishment of per unit product costs; Creation of compensation levels for different worker categories; Determination of expenditures required for manufacturing processes	Per-unit production costs should not exceed $85; Total payroll expenses are budgeted at $145,000

Quality standards express levels or ranges of acceptable value or worth for a quality control program. Performance evaluations and spot-check inspections are examples of this type of standard. Allowable deviations from standards vary widely, depending on the characteristics of the product. At one extreme is the zero-defects requirement of an aircraft manufacturer where a product failure or malfunction could endanger lives. Other products and activities commonly have less stringent quality standards based upon the impact of failure on safety, on meeting contract specifications, and on the loss of customers.

Quantity standards express in numerical terms the expected number of elements to be produced by a specific individual or by a given activity. Units of output or service, numbers of service calls, turnover rates, absenteeism figures, and applications processed are all examples of physical quantity standards.

Each of these three types of standards is interconnected with the others. Extremely high quality standards may adversely affect the amount of output produced in a given time period. A standard that focuses primarily on quantity may produce increased volume at the expense of quality. The automobile industry provides examples of different standards in use. While high-quality Porsches are handmade at a rate of 100 per day, a high-speed Buick Century and Chevrolet Celebrity plant in Oklahoma City produces 75 cars per hour. Standards used by an organization should result from established objectives. In most cases, such standards represent compromises between time and quantity, on the one hand, and desired quality levels on the other.

Cost standards are typically expressed in monetary terms. Budgets are typically developed to reflect cost per unit of output or expenditures required for a particular manufacturing process. Cost standards are directly related to the planning process. Budgets result from organizational plans and provide monetary checkpoints for comparing actual performance with expected performance. Once the basic framework is established, periodic meetings and reports alert managers to the performance of their specific areas of responsibility.

The standards established at the first step in the controlling process—quality, quantity, time, and cost—must reflect the objectives of the organization and must be expressed in meaningful, concrete terms. To be effective, they must be clearly communicated to those involved with their use.

MONITORING PERFORMANCE

Once standards have been established, the second step in the controlling process is to monitor actual performance. Monitoring, like the other steps in the controlling process, is a continuous activity in most organizations. It requires the development of reliable methods of measurement and answers to the question "What, how, and when to measure?"

Clear organizational objectives should identify *what* activities are to be measured. Answers to the question of *how* to measure a given individual or activity depend more on the type of event in question. In some cases, continuous monitoring of an entire process is required. On other occasions, spot checks and sampling of completed output will be sufficient. The specific activity under consideration also often determines *when* it will be measured. In some control systems, performance is measured only after the completion of an activity. In other cases, it is measured continuously during its operation. A commonly used compromise approach is to require that performance be checked, evaluated, and approved at specified points before the next phase is allowed to begin.

The college classroom illustrates these alternative approaches to monitoring performance. Some instructors utilize a single final examination to measure performance. Others rely on midterm quizzes to test performance prior to completion of the course. Still others may employ monitoring devices on a weekly or even a daily basis. In other cases, some instructors require that their students successfully complete specific assignments or achieve a specified minimum grade on test material before continuing with new course material and assignments.

The essence of the monitoring step in the controlling process is to collect data that represent the actual performance of the activity or individual. Clear data are not always easy to collect, and their collection sometimes proves to be very costly. As activities become less technical, representative data are often difficult to develop and even more difficult to interpret. But representative data must be generated at this step to pave the way for the third step of the controlling process.

COMPARING ACTUAL AND PLANNED PERFORMANCE

The third step in the controlling process involves the comparison of actual performance with desired performance in an attempt to determine whether significant *deviations* or variations from the plan have occurred. Ideally, such deviations should be anticipated or at least detected sufficiently early for adjustments to be made. If steps one and two are completed satisfactorily, step three is relatively easy. The comparison of actual performance with predetermined standards is accomplished by analyzing data received from the organization's feedback network.

The importance of a feedback network in the controlling process cannot be overemphasized. Feedback is best viewed as a linking network of communication that ties together the four steps of the controlling process. Feedback should flow upward to decision centers in the organization, as well as downward to the activity centers where needed corrective action can be taken. Control communications should be based on the management by exception principle, and information should be communicated to managers at higher levels only when a significant variation from the plan occurs. Written reports, reviews, meetings and briefing sessions are often used to provide appropriate feedback. International Telephone and Telegraph, the multinational conglomerate with annual sales of several billion dollars, uses a highly comprehensive reporting system to provide feedback concerning its myriad of geographically diverse enterprises. Monthly reports from ITT subsidiaries often exceed fifty pages.

EVALUATION AND ACTION

The model of the controlling process on page 505 indicates three alternatives in the final step of evaluation and action: maintenance of the status quo, correction of deviations that may have occurred, and modification of standards. If performance approximates the established standard, no adjustments are necessary and the monitoring process continues. Managers may choose to use the matching of performance to expectations as a motivational and informational tool to encourage people involved in the activity to continue their successful work.

Should performance deviate significantly from plans, management involved with the activity must be alerted to the need for possible corrective action. Several conclusions are possible from such a variation. The most common conclusion is that of a controllable *performance deficiency*—a breakdown in the execution of the process or activity. However, the deviation may have occurred due to a change in the general environment surrounding the process. A third possibility is that the established standards are not realistic. It is essential that management make the correct interpretation of the deviation, since the interpretation will determine the corrective action to be taken. Often a variation is the result of a temporary, uncontrollable factor and does not indicate a problem with the process or the plan. Failure of painted surfaces of a product to match quality standards may be the result of high humidity levels resulting from record-setting rainfalls. Management may choose to interpret such deviations as one-time uncontrollable problems rather than develop a new plan to take into account such unusual situations. To dismantle or alter an effective plan as a result of rare occurrences would lead to additional costs and possibly other problems.

Should corrective action be required, management may be faced with making a choice from among several alternative solutions. Sometimes corrective action is obvious and clear-cut. At other times, it may be complex and somewhat subjective. It may involve reassigning work, hiring or transferring personnel, purchasing new equipment, increasing marketing efforts, redeveloping plans, modifying objectives, or any number of other actions.

APPLYING THE STEPS OF THE CONTROL PROCESS

The steps involved in the control process are illustrated by the automobile assembly plant depicted in Figure 16–5. Although the weekly production

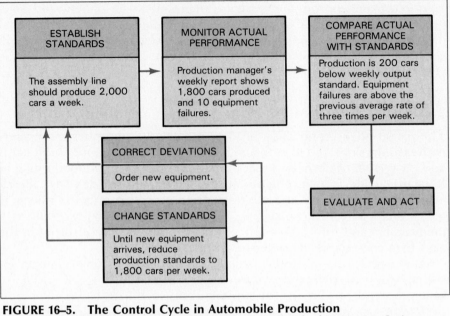

FIGURE 16–5.   The Control Cycle in Automobile Production
Source: Adapted by permission from David J. Rachman and Michael H. Mescon, *Business Today*, 4th ed. (New York: Random House, 1985), p. 135. Copyright © 1985 by Random House, Inc.

standard has been set at 2,000 cars, the production manager's weekly report indicates that actual output lagged 200 cars behind the objective and ten equipment failures have occurred during the week. To determine the reason for the deviation, feedback is necessary. In this instance, feedback is likely to take the form of comparisons of production levels for recent weeks and average numbers of equipment failures. The average number of equipment breakdowns in previous weeks has been three and production objectives have been achieved with such a rate. Determination of a "standard" number of equipment failures suggests that the higher equipment failure rate is the problem that must be corrected and that new equipment is necessary to achieve the stated production standard. Until the new equipment arrives, management decides to revise the production standard downward to 1,800 cars to allow for the defective machinery.

TYPES OF CONTROLS

Precontrols are preventive measures developed to eliminate the causes of any deviations that might occur in the execution of organizational plans.

Controlling processes can be classified in four ways: precontrols, steering controls, yes-no controls, and postcontrols.[5] *Precontrols* are preventive in nature. They involve the development of forward-looking controls to eliminate the cause of any deviations that might occur in the execution of organizational plans. Such controls are established before the activity takes place. The process of using capital budgeting for evaluating capital investments is an example of precontrols. In capital budgeting the present value of the benefits to be received determines whether the return on investment is adequate to justify the investment.

Steering controls predict results in an attempt to detect deviations from predetermined standards and to allow corrective action while the activity is being performed. Steering controls provide for checkpoints that allow corrections to ensure that actual results will closely match planned results. Thus, steering controls are particularly important in most organizations.

Yes-no controls allow for a screening process with points at which specific approval is needed to permit the activity to continue. Quality control inspections, approval of requisitions, safety checks, and legal approval of contracts are common examples of yes-no controls.

Postcontrols measure end results and compare them with predetermined standards. Final inspections, summary activity reports, and balance sheets are examples of this "after-the-fact" controlling process. Such postcontrols are important in the development of precontrols and steering controls for subsequent activities.

Steering controls are perhaps the most frequently used controls; they are the type of control process typically associated with the controlling function. However, most successful organizations use a combination of all four types to maintain an effective, integrated control system. Table 16–2 illustrates each type of control.

Steering controls are techniques used to detect deviations and allow corrective actions to be taken while the activity is being performed.

Yes-no controls are techniques used at one or more screening points where specific approval is needed to permit the activity to continue.

Postcontrols are techniques applied following the completion of an activity that serve as the basis for developing precontrols and steering controls for subsequent activities.

CHARACTERISTICS OF EFFECTIVE CONTROLS

Control systems vary from one organization to the next. Different types of controls are used to address the specific needs of different departments,

TABLE 16–2   CLASSIFICATION OF CONTROLS

Type	When Used	Example
Precontrols	Prior to start of activity	Proficiency levels for employees trained to perform activity
Steering Controls	During performance of activity	Comparison of employee input per hour with established standards
Yes-No Controls	During or after performance of activity	Quality control tests of output
Postcontrols	Following completion of activity	Comparison of actual costs to budgeted costs

activities, or organizations. To be effective, however, they all should possess a number of characteristics.[6]

- *Controls should be understandable.* The individuals with responsibility for monitoring operations and comparing results with established standards must understand clearly the control systems being used. Misunderstood control systems will either be ignored or misapplied.

- *Controls should match the activity under consideration.* The data collected must be relevant to that activity. Sales managers should receive information concerning the performance of salespersons; product sales by territories, customer categories, and order size; and competitive data concerning performance, price changes, and new product introductions. Advertising managers should receive information related to their responsibilities. The marketing vice-president should receive information on sales, advertising, and other marketing activities.

- *Controls should register deviations quickly.* Ideally, substandard performance should be prevented through precontrols or should be identified by steering controls as early in the process as possible. Such an early warning control system makes remedial action possible and provides for resumption of activities called for by the established standards.

- *Controls should be flexible.* Control systems should be flexible enough to accommodate changes in environmental factors. Flexible controls can compensate for the uncertainties of the situation by allowing the organization to react quickly to changes or to take advantage of new opportunities.

- *Controls should be economical.* The costs involved in developing and maintaining control systems should reflect the benefits they provide. Spending thousands to save hundreds of dollars is obviously unrealistic. Since control systems should be cost effective, they must focus upon critical areas. The important criterion is the determination of the minimum expenditures required to monitor an activity and ensure that it accomplishes the desired goal.

- *Controls should indicate corrective action.* An effective control system should not only identify deviations from planned performance quickly but should also prescribe corrective action. Once deviations are detected, the system should be capable of identifying causes of the variations and suggesting means of correcting them.

- *Controls should be difficult to manipulate.* Controls should not be subject to misrepresentation. Poorly conceived control systems may be subjected to distortions by managers who attempt to depict more favorable results from their departments than actually occur.

TOOLS OF CONTROL IN THE ORGANIZATION ▬▬

Effective controls are critical complements to the design and subsequent modification of plans implemented to achieve the organization's objectives. Since controls exist at various organizational settings in a variety of formats, it is understandable that a number of specific control tools have been developed. The five general areas of controls are identified in Figure 16–6. However, three of the five categories focus directly on the production function and are discussed in detail in Chapter 18. *Production controls* are concerned with the scheduling, timing, and routing of a product or project. They employ such tools as Gantt charts, Program Evaluation and Review Technique (PERT), and the critical path method (CPM) in monitoring actual performance and comparing it with expected results. *Inventory control* is concerned with the amount of assets that should be held in inventory:

FIGURE 16–6. Tools of Control in the Organization

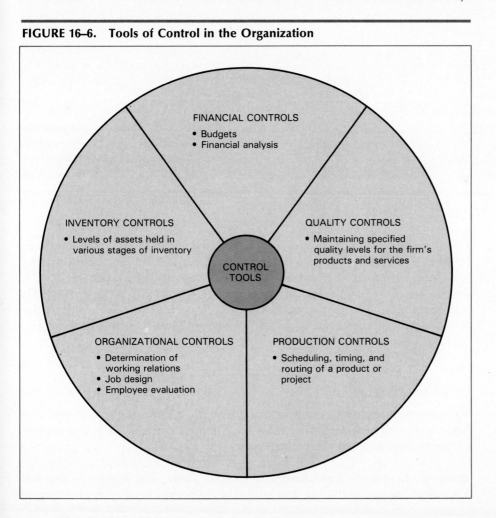

MANAGEMENT FAILURES

Atari

In 1982, Atari was described by the business press as "America's fastest-growing company," had gross sales in excess of $2 billion, and ranked among America's 100 largest advertisers. But in the short span of 18 months, the company lost more than $1 billion and was sold for "what amounted to institutional IOUs to avoid imminent collapse," [Atari's former executive director of advertising Richard D. Arroyo] said. . . .

"If there was any single cause of Atari's misfortune, it was an attitude born out of rapid and spectacular success, the hardest kind of success to manage because it breeds a sense of invulnerability that is both seductive and contagious. At Atari, it took the form of getting carried away with both people and programs in 1980 and 1981," asserted Arroyo.

"Atari started in 1972 in the garage of an imaginative and creative entrepreneur named Nolan Bushnell. Its first product was, by current computer standards, a rudimentary electronic table game called 'Pong'." Lightning-quick advances in game play and sophistication ensued, spawning videogames such as *Star Raiders, Centipede,* and *Pac Man.*

Soon after the success of Pong, Warner Communication acquired Atari for $28 million, an amount which represented about 5 percent of the company's sales a mere three years out. A team of talented managers was recruited from the best consumer-product companies in the country . . . and the business soared.

"Atari's initial success clearly was the result of timing and opportunity. Its early video game popularity was a case of being in the right place at the right time with the right product,

raw materials, work in progress, and finished goods. Numerous methods that have been developed for determining the optimum levels of inventory for different kinds of organizations are discussed in Chapter 18. *Quality control,* which is responsible for maintaining the quality of a firm's goods and services, is also discussed in Chapter 18. The following sections describe the final categories of control tools: financial controls and organizational controls.

FINANCIAL CONTROLS

Budgets, financial analysis of the organization's accounting statements, and ratio analysis are the primary tools for financial control. Each can make a major contribution to the control process.

Budgets—Frequently Used Financial Control Tools. The budget is the best known of all the different financial control techniques. It is also one of

aided by the power of entrepreneurial spirit, where decisions are made swiftly by a few people with good instincts," said Arroyo.

"But as the business grew exponentially, so did departments and staff. As of January 1983, there were plans to add nearly 1,000 jobs—far in excess of what was needed at the time to manage the business. And as personnel grew, so did the product line—with more software units than the marketplace could possibly absorb, given the competition that rapidly materialized—but more importantly, more product than could effectively be supported with the time and resources available."

A feeling of "omnipotence" began to permeate the company, he said, leading to another data error—the presumption that success in one endeavor automatically implies capabilities in related fields. "To illustrate how far afield a company can drift, I offer the example of *Ataritel,* a plan hatched by the company to develop and sell telephones for the consumer market—a business totally unrelated to anything in which we were involved—that si-

phoned precious resources and management attention at a time when we could least afford it," Arroyo said. . . .

Marketing research was misused and abused within the company, and rarely combined with common sense or good judgment. "We either based decision-making on inadequate research or, more often still, selectively interpreted the data to support preestablished positions," Arroyo said. "When research estimated the computer-hardware population in the U.S. at 19–20 million households, we used this as a base for calculating software sales—ignoring the millions of units stuck on the top shelves of closets. And when focus groups of a handful of consumers said they would spend $40 for an E.T. videogame, we produced more than 20 million, many of which can be found in a landfill in New Mexico."

Source: "Former Exec: Rapid Success Begat Atari Failure," *Marketing News,* 10 May 1985, pp. 10-11. Reprinted by permission.

the oldest tools, whose origins can be traced to France in the Middle Ages. One writer described the early budgets as follows:

> In those days business people kept their money in a *bougette,* or small leather bag. Budgeting then consisted of counting the money in the bag to see if there was enough to pay expenses. As businesses grew to include many people, somebody had to keep track of the money, so there arose the *contrerolleur,* the one who kept a record of the *bougettes* in order to control receipts and expenditures. So began the "controller" and "comptroller" as we know them today.[7]

Budgets represent in monetary terms the objectives of the organization. A *budget* is simply a financial plan listing in detail the resources or funds assigned to a particular product, division, or project. Inherent in the budget is control through timely feedback. Table 16–3 identifies the most common types of budgets used to translate company objectives and strategies into dollars. While not every organization would use all of these

Budget is a financial plan listing in detail the resources or funds assigned to a particular product, division, or project.

TABLE 16–3   TYPES OF BUDGETS

Budget Type	Description
Manufacturing	
1. Manufacturing Budget	This budget, sometimes called the *operations budget,* includes the requirements for production materials, labor, energy, and other elements necessary to produce the projected output. Sometimes these budgets are initially expressed in physical terms and translated into monetary terms as the project proceeds.
2. Capital Expenditures Budget	This budget includes expenditures for new plant and equipment, replacement equipment, improvements to existing facilities, and other expenditures involving long-term commitments.
Marketing	
1. Marketing Budget	Marketing budgets are typically divided into two parts. The first part is the advertising budget, which includes the plans and required resources to promote the product line. The second part focuses upon the expenditures necessary to sell the firm's products. The marketing budget is occasionally combined with other budgets and included in a general operational budget.
2. Product Budget	This budget focuses upon a specific product of the firm. Such a budget permits determinations of return on investment in each product.
Finance	
1. Cash Flow Budget	The cash flow budget indicates the total amount of funds required and the time at which they are required. This budget forecasts cash receipts and outlays on a monthly, weekly, or even daily basis. It is an extremely important tool for controlling cash and meeting current obligations.
2. Budgeted Income Statement	This budget reflects anticipated *revenue* from sales and other income the organization expects to receive during a given time period and compares it with expected *expenses* associated with receiving the revenue.
3. Balance Sheet Budget	This budget reflects expected assets, liabilities, and net worth of an organization at the end of a specified accounting period such as a month or year. Such a budget provides management, lenders, and other interested parties with a forecast of the expected future financial position of the firm. It also provides a standard with which the actual balance sheet for the period can be compared.

Budget Type	Description
Research and General Management	
1. Research and Development Budget	This budget reflects the strategies of the firm in relation to research and development expenditures. Future sales and revenue are often closely related to investment in research.
2. Executive Staff Budget	This specialized budget includes the special expense accounts, compensation, and personnel requirements for higher organizational levels.
3. Branch and Regional Budget	This budget is used to establish local or regional cost centers for planning and control purposes.

budgets, they serve as illustrations of the types of budgets that can be developed for research and general management purposes as well as for the manufacturing, marketing, and finance functions.

Developing a Budget. A comprehensive budgeting process begins with the development of detailed economic, sales, and profit forecasts. These forecasts, designed to meet organizational goals, produce guidelines for use in budget preparations. Although some organizations develop budgets at the top management level for distribution throughout the hierarchy, most agree that the departments and individuals responsible for implementation should be allowed to contribute to the development of the budget. Several benefits result from this "bottom-up" approach to budget development:

66 Next to double-entry bookkeeping and the copying machine, budgets are the most commonly used management tools. 99

Peter Drucker

- Supervisors and personnel in each department are likely to be the most familiar with their own needs.

- They are less likely to overlook a factor from their own departments that might prove to be a crucial element in budget development.

- They are more likely to be motivated to accept and meet a budget if they have participated in its development.[8]

Once the preliminary budget proposals are developed by the various departments, they are typically submitted to a budget committee. This committee, normally consisting of middle and top managers with line authority, reviews the proposals and attempts to reconcile the various budgets into a final budget for the coming period. Adjustments to individual budgets are often necessary to eliminate duplication, and committee members may communicate frequently with the managers who submitted the original proposals before a final budget is prepared and adopted.

Building Flexibility into the Budget. A serious drawback to many budgets is their rigidity in the face of changing conditions. Budgets are forward-looking and should provide means of adjustment should changes affect the forecasts upon which they are based. Damage caused by a 1985 hurricane disrupted operations at Litton Industries' Ingalls Shipbuilding Complex in Pascagoula, Mississippi. IBM's introduction of a new series of personal computers produced major problems for such competitors as Apple, Zenith, and Compaq. The 1984 leak of poisonous gas from a pesticide plant in Bhopal, India, caused the deaths of more than 2,000 people and a nightmare of legal and financial difficulties for Connecticut-based Union Carbide. To avoid control problems resulting from inflexible budgets, organizations often develop adjustable budgets. One of the most common, the *variable budget,* is actually a series of different budgets based on different levels of output. Since expenses and allowances are computed for different levels of activities, departmental budgets can be easily adjusted by a predetermined formula to reflect more realistically the actual costs related to actual output. Such budgets may be called *flexible budgets, sliding-scale budgets,* or *step budgets.*

Program Planning Budgeting Systems (PPBS) is a five-step system of budgeting that has been adopted by a number of nonprofit organizations.

Program Planning Budgeting Systems (PPBS). PPBS is a system of budgeting that has been adopted by a number of nonprofit organizations, including the federal, state, and a number of local governments. The system was developed by the Rand Corporation in the late 1950s and introduced in the Department of Defense in the early 1960s. Five basic steps are involved.

1. List and analyze the objectives of the activity.

2. Analyze the result(s) of a given program or activity based on the objectives.

3. Estimate future program costs as well as original outlays.

4. Analyze alternatives.

5. Integrate the first four steps into the budgetary process.[9]

PPBS has a number of advantages. First, it relates the budget to agency or departmental objectives and requires accountability. Second, it requires a realistic appraisal of future costs and requires managers to justify their decisions. Finally, it brings into sharp focus the relationship between costs and benefits.

Zero-Base Budgeting. A favorite assumption of many budget preparers is that this year's budget is a reasonable starting point for the following year's budget request. This assumption inhibits the careful review of the relevance of many activities within the organization. Elimination of this assumption is the essence of zero-base budgeting (ZBB).

Zero-base budgeting requires that projects, priorities, and objectives be reviewed in every budgeting cycle. First, managers must justify each item in their budget requests as if they were proposing a completely new department. Activities are divided into *decision packages.* Such packages contain sufficient information about an activity for it to be evaluated and compared with other activities on a cost/benefit basis. The decision package also includes a statement of possible consequences should the activity not be approved.

The second step requires the evaluation and ranking of all activities in order of benefit to the organization, followed by the actual allocation of resources based upon the final ranking. The decision packages of lowest rank are prime candidates for elimination in periods of cost-cutting if their benefits appear minimal or if they no longer match organizational objectives.

A zero-base budgeting process provides greater justification for the continuation or termination of activities, allows greater participation in planning, and gives the budgeting process greater unity. However, the process is more costly and requires more time to complete.

The ZBB concept was originally developed by Texas Instruments, Inc., and received considerable publicity when former President Carter championed it in the late 1970s as a method of controlling the costs of government. It has also been utilized by a number of profit-seeking firms, ranging from Southern California Edison, Ford Motor Company, and the Bank of Montreal, to Playboy Enterprises.[10]

> **Zero-base budgeting** requires forced periodic justification of any expenditure program, not just incremental changes in such a program.

Financial Analysis—An Important Tool of Financial Control. *Financial analysis* is the use of specific techniques to study a firm's financial documents and control the flow of funds, products, and services both within and outside organizations. Financial statements provide the means for controlling (1) the *liquidity* of the organization: its ability to meet current obligations and needs by converting assets into cash; (2) the general *profitability* of the organization; and (3) the general *financial condition* of the organization.

> **Financial analysis** uses a series of financial techniques to analyze the firm's financial statements in controlling the liquidity, profitability, and overall financial health of the organization.

Two Financial Statements. Two commonly used financial statements are the balance sheet and the income statement. The *balance sheet* reflects the financial position of an organization as of a particular date. It is similar to a photograph comparing a firm's assets with its liabilities and net worth at a specific moment in time. Figure 16–7 shows a simplified balance sheet for a manufacturing firm.

The left side of the balance sheet lists the assets of the firm in descending order of liquidity (nearness to cash). These assets represent the items of value owned by the organization; they are uses that management has made of available funds. The right side of the balance sheet is the firm's financial structure, indicating the sources of the firm's assets. Liabilities reflect the claims of the firm's creditors—financial institutions that have made long-

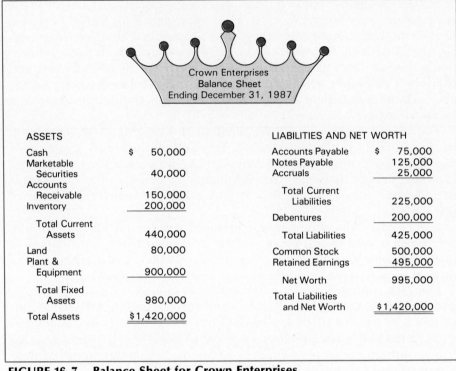

ASSETS

		LIABILITIES AND NET WORTH	
Cash	$ 50,000	Accounts Payable	$ 75,000
Marketable		Notes Payable	125,000
Securities	40,000	Accruals	25,000
Accounts		Total Current	
Receivable	150,000	Liabilities	225,000
Inventory	200,000		
		Debentures	200,000
Total Current			
Assets	440,000	Total Liabilities	425,000
Land	80,000	Common Stock	500,000
Plant &		Retained Earnings	495,000
Equipment	900,000		
		Net Worth	995,000
Total Fixed		Total Liabilities	
Assets	980,000	and Net Worth	$1,420,000
Total Assets	$1,420,000		

FIGURE 16–7.   Balance Sheet for Crown Enterprises

and short-term loans, suppliers that have provided products and services on credit, and bondholders, among others. Net worth represents the owners' (stockholders' in the case of corporations) claims against the firm's assets, or the excess of all assets over all liabilities.

The *income statement* reflects the performance of the organization over a specific time period. Such statements begin with total sales or revenue generated during a year, quarter, or month and then deduct all the costs related to producing this revenue. Once all costs—costs involved in producing the products, administrative costs, interest, and taxes, for instance—have been subtracted, the remaining net income available to distribute to the firm's owners (stockholders, proprietors, or partners) may be reinvested in the firm as retained earnings. Figure 16–8 shows the 1987 income statement for Crown Enterprises.

Ratio Analysis—Important Tool of Financial Analysis. Ratio analysis is used to extract information from the firm's financial statements so that performance in a specific area can be evaluated. Ratios assist the controlling process by interpreting actual performance and making comparisons with what should have happened. The firm's ratios can be compared with those of similar companies to reflect company performance relative to the per-

Ratio analysis is a performance evaluation technique measuring the liquidity, profitability, extent of debt financing, and effectiveness of the firm's use of its resources and permits comparisons with other firms and with past performance.

Crown Enterprises
Income Statement for Year
Ending December 31, 1987

Sales		$2,700,000
Less: Cost of Goods Sold	$1,800,000	
Depreciation	100,000	
Selling & Administrative Cost	90,000	
	$1,990,000	
Operating Profit		710,000
Other Income	25,000	
Gross Income		735,000
Less: Interest	160,000	
Income Before Taxes		575,000
Less: Taxes (50%)	287,500	
Income After Taxes		$ 287,500

FIGURE 16–8.   Income Statement for Crown Enterprises

formance of competitors. These *industry standards* serve as important yard-sticks in pinpointing problem areas as well as areas of excellence. Ratios for the current accounting period may also be compared with ratios of previous periods to spot any trends that might be developing. Ratios can be classified according to their specific purpose.

Liquidity ratios measure a firm's ability to meet its maturing short-term obligations. Examples include the current ratio and the acid-test (or quick) ratio. The following ratios are calculated from the Crown Enterprises' balance sheet data shown in Figure 16–7.

$$\textbf{Current Ratio} = \frac{\text{Current Assets}}{\text{Current Liabilities}} = \frac{\$440,000}{\$225,000} = 1.95$$

$$\frac{\textbf{Acid-Test}}{\textbf{Ratio}} = \frac{\text{Cash} + \text{Marketable Securities} + \text{Accounts Receivable}}{\text{Current Liabilities}}$$

$$= \frac{\$50,000 + \$40,000 + \$150,000}{\$225,000} = \frac{\$240,000}{\$225,000} = 1.06$$

Leverage ratios measure the extent to which the firm is relying on debt financing. Examples include the current liability to net worth ratio and the debt-to-equity ratio. They can be calculated for Crown Enterprises as follows:

$$\frac{\textbf{Current Liability to}}{\textbf{Net Worth Ratio}} = \frac{\text{Current Liabilities}}{\text{Net Worth}} = \frac{\$225,000}{\$995,000} = .23$$

$$\text{Debt-to-Equity Ratio} = \frac{\text{Total Liabilities}}{\text{Net Worth}} = \frac{\$425,000}{\$995,000} = .43$$

Profitability ratios measure the overall financial performance in terms of returns generated on sales and investment. Examples include the gross margin percentage, the sale margin, and return on investment. Calculation of these ratios for Crown Enterprises requires the use of data from both the balance sheet (Figure 16–7) and the income statement (Figure 16–8).

$$\text{Gross Margin Percentage} = \frac{\text{Gross Income}}{\text{Sales}} = \frac{\$735,000}{\$2,700,000} = .27$$

$$\text{Sales Margin} = \frac{\text{Net Income after Taxes}}{\text{Sales}} = \frac{\$287,500}{\$2,700,000} = .11$$

$$\text{Return on Investment} = \frac{\text{Net Income after Taxes}}{\text{Total Assets}} = \frac{\$287,500}{\$1,420,000} = .20$$

Activity ratios measure the effectiveness of the firm's use of its resources. Examples include the inventory turnover rate and the average collection period for receivables. These ratios can be calculated for Crown Enterprises as follows:

$$\text{Inventory Turnover} = \frac{\text{Cost of Goods Sold}}{\text{Inventory}} = \frac{\$1,800,000}{\$200,000} = 9$$

$$\text{Average Collection Period for Receivables} = \frac{\text{Accounts Receivable}}{\text{Average Daily Sales}} = \frac{\$150,000}{\$7,397} = 20.3 \text{ days}$$

The average daily sales figure is calculated by dividing annual sales of $2.7 million by 365 days.

These ratios relate balance sheet and income statement items to one another and assist management in pinpointing strengths and weaknesses. Since industry ratios are frequently available from trade association publications, management can compare its performance with that of other firms in the industry. In addition, current performance can be compared with that of previous years.

ORGANIZATIONAL CONTROL

Organizational control includes both the control exerted by the organizational structure and its planning systems and the control of organizational members. The former types of control were discussed in Chapters 5 through 7. Management by objective programs, discussed in Chapter 5, serve as important means of control by focusing individual performance on organizational objectives and providing a built-in mechanism for comparing actual and planned performance. Management information systems, the subject of Chapter 17, constitute another critical means of organizational control.

The basic steps of effective control are similar whether controls apply to organizational members or to production or financial processes. Quantifiable standards must be developed against which individual performance can be measured and compared. Management typically attempts to control individual performance by placing a properly selected, oriented, and trained person in the right job and by evaluating performance in accordance with predetermined standards.

- *Selection.* Employees should be screened and selected on the basis of skills, abilities, and aptitudes compatible with the specific job. Tests and interviews serve as precontrols in recruiting the right person for the right job.

- *Orientation.* A period of orientation to familiarize the recently hired employee with the nature and duties of his or her job can also serve as an effective precontrol.

- *Training.* Another effective control is to place new employees in specifically designed job training programs.

- *Performance evaluation.* Individual performance evaluation is an effective use of steering and postcontrols to compare actual performance with measurable goals that have been established as standards for employees.[11]

Evaluating Performance. Data generated from a control system provide a basis for evaluating the performance of organizational members. But who should receive the data? It might be routed to staff personnel, higher-level line managers, the manager of the unit being measured, or the individuals in that unit. A general rule is that the individual or group that can make the most meaningful use of the data should receive it first.[12] Prompt feedback gives personnel an immediate evaluation of their performance, permits rapid adjustments of deviations from expected performance, and aids in the learning process.

Who Should Evaluate Performance? Generally speaking, an individual's performance should be evaluated by the person in the best position to observe his or her performance or the results of that performance. This person is most often the employee's immediate superior. In some organizational settings, the supervisor's evaluation is supplemented by evaluations by the peers or co-workers of the individual.

Evaluations should be conducted as openly as possible with standards of performance clearly stated. The employee should know the required performance level in advance of any evaluation. These standards should be

COMPUTERS IN MANAGEMENT

Monitoring Performance at Savin Business Machines

When Chuck Mitchell, Dallas district manager for Savin Business Machines, sits down with a representative having problems meeting his monthly goal, he is no longer at a loss for words. Rather than suggest, tenuously, "I think you should try to arrange more product demos," he has the back-up information that enables him to declare, firmly, "I know that if you put on more demos you'll write more orders." He points to his Compaq desktop and tells the person, "All the information about your activities is there, and it shows that your bookings are down because you're not putting on as many demos as you used to."

"When you have a problem-review situation," Mitchell muses, "you have one person who is emotional over the fact his performance is not what it should be and a manager who is overly anxious because goals are not being met. But when the manager has accurate information he has analyzed before the meeting, he can go right to the heart of the problem and be in a position to give better advice to the salesman."

Mitchell has his information back-up as a result of buying Thoughtware's Trigger software a year ago. The program, among other features, enables him to monitor the activities of his salespeople in greater detail. He says the hardest thing, "as is true with all software, is deciding at first on the parameters of each sales representative that should be included in the report format. That takes a lot of experimentation and at least a couple of sample runs." He figures it took him about 30 working hours to get the program fully implemented. Nowadays, it takes his secretary only a few

savin

Date	Month	Plan	Actual	Variance
11/01/85	5			
12/02/85	6			
01/01/86	7			
02/03/86	8			
03/03/86	9			
04/01/86	10			
05/01/86	11			
06/02/86	12			
Year to Date Totals		114.00	77.00	

N3   NEW CONTACTS   Trigger #'s - Below plan 0%   Above plan 15%

Date	Month	Plan	Actual	Variance
07/01/85	1	500.00	470.00	-6.00%
08/01/85	2	500.00	385.00	-23.00%
09/02/85	3	420.00		
10/01/85	4			

minutes to input the weekly activities of his salespeople and bring the files up to date.

Mitchell uses Trigger to maintain weekly and monthly summaries of each sales representative's activities, including appointments made, cold calls, demonstrations, orders, and revenue. The program also generates certain ratios that give him further insights into performance levels, such as the relationship between appointments, demonstrations, and orders. He uses the ratios to develop forecasts of the business each salesperson should bring in over a certain period of time.

With this kind of an information base at push-button disposal, Mitchell feels he is in a stronger position to help salespeople improve their productivity. "I recently had one representative who wanted to increase his monthly revenues from $20,000 to $30,000," he says. "Using Trigger, I made a spreadsheet of his past performance. Then I changed the revenue number from $20,000 to $30,000 and the program automatically showed how his appointments, calls, and demos had to change. This gave him a game plan to run by."

Source: "Savin Replaces 'I Think' with 'I Know'," *Sales and Marketing Management,* 9 December 1985, p. 74. Reprinted by permission.

related to the primary objectives of the job, and they should be attainable through excellent performance.[13]

MANAGEMENT AUDITS

Annual audits of financial records by outside independent certified public accounting firms are established practices at most large- and medium-sized organizations. In recent years, attention has been given to conducting similar audits in nonfinancial areas of the organization. The new audits have a variety of titles—management audits, performance audits, operational audits, and internal audits. Regardless of the specific label used by individual organizations, the *management audit* is a professional review and evaluation of an organization's total activities from the perspective of management.

Management audits are more difficult to conduct than the traditional financial audit since they require a determination of both the specific managerial characteristics to be measured and the measurement methods to be used. Peter Drucker argues that since managerial skills must ultimately be measured in terms of performance, the management audit should assess the following areas: performance in appropriating capital, performance in people-related decisions, performance in terms of innovations, and performance in planning.[14] A variety of techniques are utilized by auditors, ranging from personal interviews and written questionnaires to analysis of such data as turnover rates, departmental productivity, actual performance to quota, and employee morale surveys, among others.

Audits may be conducted internally by staff specialists or by independent outside auditors. Use of outside auditors should reduce the possibility of bias. The American Institute of Management (AIM), a private nonprofit organization, conducts such audits, utilizing a system based on a 301-item questionnaire. The AIM audit focuses upon such diverse subjects as earnings strength, research and development, production efficiency, and evaluation of specific executive characteristics. The General Accounting Office (GAO) is responsible for assisting Congress in assessing federal programs by focusing upon the "Three Es" of government programs—economy, efficiency, and effectiveness. In 1984 the GAO submitted 634 audit reports. Congressional committees or individual members of Congress received 444 of these reports, and the remaining 190 went to chiefs of federal agencies.

Even though the broad scope of the management audit results in less precise results than the other control techniques discussed, it is nevertheless useful in identifying areas of excellence as well as poorly performing parts of the organization. It can aid management in spotting trouble areas by identifying poor communications between responsibility centers; operations experiencing increased unit costs; breakdowns in scheduling; and other sources of deviations from plans.

Management audit is a professional review and evaluation of an organization's total activities from the perspective of management.

EFFECTS OF CONTROL ON THE INDIVIDUAL ▰▰▰

The behavioral aspects of managerial control systems cannot be overemphasized. At the beginning of the chapter, the occasional problems of negative reactions to control systems by employees were noted. In an impersonal sense, controls are simply methods of ensuring that desired results are actually accomplished. But to the individual employee, they may represent the proverbial albatross around his or her neck. Although an effective control system should increase employee motivation, it is not uncommon for workers to feel threatened by controls.

Great care must be taken to communicate the organizational goals and objectives upon which standards are based. If individuals in the organization feel the standards are relevant and appropriate, they are more likely to have *positive* attitudes toward the control system. On the other hand, if the standards are perceived to be arbitrary, unrepresentative, and irrelevant, employee reactions are likely to be *negative*. Effective managers attempt to make the control system as meaningful as possible to the employees. Worker participation, clear communication of goals and standards, timely feedback, and realistic appraisal will help foster confidence in the control system.

AVOIDING GOAL DISPLACEMENT

Goal displacement is a phenomenon in which employees view the performance measures used in the control system as more important than the organizational objective upon which they are based.

One potential problem in the use of control systems is a phenomenon called *goal displacement*. This occurs when employees view the performance measures used in the control system as more important than the organizational objectives upon which they are based.[15] Such behavior is not dysfunctional when the measures are closely related to the goals of the department. Problems arise when they are not. Such problems often occur when performance appraisals are based exclusively on two or three variables. Workers who are evaluated on the bases of absenteeism, output, and amount of spoilage may conveniently ignore areas of safety, equipment maintenance, and other aspects of the job that ultimately can affect departmental objectives but that are not considered by the firm's control system.

AVOIDING OVERCONTROL

Another behavioral response to control systems results from the tendency of some managers to exert excessive control over people and activities. Any control system creates the potential for misuse and resulting conflict. Care must be taken to prevent situations in which the control system can be used to gain power and coerce others to conform to unrealistic demands. Overcontrol may lead to higher costs, lowered morale, reduced productivity, and employee turnover. Such undesirable occurrences can result when controls are viewed as an end instead of as a means.

SUMMARY

Controlling is the critical managerial function of determining whether organizational objectives are achieved and whether actual performances are consistent with plans. Control is used for such purposes as standardizing performance and quality levels, safeguarding company assets, limiting authority, measuring on-the-job performance, monitoring planning and programing operations, permitting managers to keep the firm's plans and programs in balance, and motivating individuals within the organization. The control process consists of four basic steps:

1. Establishment of performance standards based upon organizational objectives

2. Monitoring of actual performance

3. Comparison of actual performance with established standards to uncover any variations

4. Evaluation and action should significant variations exist.

Standards are values used as reference points for evaluating actual performance. The four types of standards include time, quality, quantity, and cost.

Controls may be classified in four ways: precontrols, steering controls, yes-no controls, and postcontrols. Effective controls are understandable and designed to match the activity being controlled; they register deviations quickly, are flexible and economical, difficult to manipulate, and indicate the need for corrective action. Five general control tools are used in the organization:

1. *Financial control,* which is concerned with budgets, financial analysis, and break-even analysis;

2. *Production control,* which is concerned with the scheduling, timing, and routing of a product or project;

3. *Organizational control,* which is concerned with determination of working relations, job design, and employee evaluation;

4. *Inventory control,* which is concerned with the levels of assets held in various stages of inventory; and

5. *Quality control,* which is concerned with the quality of services or products produced by the organization.

Controls are discussed in detail throughout the text. Production control, inventory control, and quality control are major topics in Chapter 18, while organizational controls were first discussed in Chapter 4 and Chapter 8. Consequently, this chapter has placed major emphasis upon budgets and financial analysis as important techniques of financial control.

Perhaps the most widely used device for controlling the activities of an organization is the budget. Budgets are financial plans listing in detail the resources or funds assigned to a particular product, division, or project. Major types include the manufacturing budget, capital expenditures budget, marketing budget, research and development budget, executive staff budget, product budget, branch (or regional) budget, cash flow budget, budgeted income statement, and budgeted balance sheet. Budgets should be flexible enough to allow adjustments for changing conditions. The zero-base budget is an attempt to base resource allocations upon current needs rather than historical actions.

Financial analysis utilizes financial documents of the firm to control its general profitability, its liquidity, and its overall financial condition. Two commonly used financial statements are the balance sheet and the income statement. Ratio analysis is used to extract information from these statements and make comparisons between actual and expected performance. The major categories of ratios are liquidity, leverage, activity, and profitability.

The control process has important behavioral implications for the entire organization. Managers can increase the likelihood of positive attitudes on the part of their employees if they communicate the relevance, fairness, and appropriateness of the standards; encourage worker participation; and provide prompt feedback and realistic appraisals. Negative reactions are likely to occur if employees perceive the standards to be arbitrary, unrepresentative, or irrelevant.

Leprino Foods Company

Vaughn Foster has U.S. 85 all to himself as he swings his truck onto the highway for his last trip of the day. To his right, the sun is disappearing behind the Rockies; ahead, the road stretches straight and empty for miles. With one eye on the speedometer, he eases into the right lane and starts creeping ahead at 50 miles an hour.

"I've been out all week," he says. "My wife's home, my kids are home, and I'd just as soon be there with them. There's no doubt about it: If that computer wasn't there I'd be running 60 easy."

Mr. Foster is talking about a black box the size of a dictionary that sits in a compartment above his right front tire. At the end of his trip, his boss at Leprino Foods Co. in Denver will pull a cartridge out of the box and pop it into a personal computer. In seconds the computer will print out a report showing the times the truck was speeding. "It's like a watchdog," Mr. Foster grumbles. "You just can't get as far away from that supervisor as you used to. . . ."

Three years ago, the nonunion company started outfitting its fleet with portable computers that hook up to sensors in a truck's engine and transmission. Now all 160 Leprino trucks have them. The devices gather detailed information about a truck's trip: what times it stopped and started, how fast the engine ran, and how fast the truck was going throughout the trip.

The last statistic is especially potent at Leprino, which wields both carrot and stick to encourage its drivers to stay under 60 miles an hour (the extra five miles above the national speed limit allows for speedometer errors and quick surges starting down a hill). A trucker gets a bonus of three cents a mile for every trip he makes without breaking 60.

But the first time a printout shows a driver sped at 65 miles an hour or faster, he gets an official reprimand. The second time, he is suspended without pay for a week. The third time, he is fired. Mr. Sheehan says Leprino has fired half a dozen truckers for speeding since the computers were installed.

Drivers at Leprino aren't enchanted with the system. "I started driving trucks because I'm kind of an independent sort of a guy that didn't like having the boss always looking over my shoulder," says E. K. Blaisdell, a former Leprino driver who recently became a dispatcher. "Then they managed to invent a machine that looks over my shoulder." Others gripe that they have become the butt of CB-radio jokes about states setting up extra-slow speed limits for Leprino drivers.

Mr. Sheehan, the vice-president, sees another side. He says Leprino trucks now get 1.1 more miles per gallon—5.7 instead of 4.6—which is nearly a 25 percent improvement. A year after the first computers were installed, maintenance costs had dropped about one-fifth and a declining accident rate had knocked $50,000 off the company's annual insurance premiums. Each $1,500 system paid for itself in about six months, Mr. Sheehan says, and in all, Leprino's $250,000 worth of computers have saved the company three times that much so far.

FACT OR FICTION REVEALED

1. Fact   2. Fiction   3. Fiction   4. Fact   5. Fiction   6. Fiction   7. Fiction

MANAGEMENT TERMS

controlling
standard
precontrols
steering controls
yes-no controls

postcontrols
budget
**Program Planning Budgeting
   Systems (PPBS)**
zero-base budgeting

financial analysis
ratio analysis
management audit
goal displacement

REVIEW QUESTIONS

1. Explain the relationship between planning and controlling.

2. Identify and briefly explain the primary uses of control in an organization.

3. Explain the steps in the control process. Relate the four types of controls to the control process.

4. Identify the characteristics of effective controls.

5. Identify the major types of budgets. What steps are involved in developing a budget? Why is flexibility an important characteristic of budgets?

6. What are the advantages of zero-base budget-

ing? What problems are involved with this approach?

7. Distinguish between financial statement analysis and ratio analysis.

8. Identify the major types of ratios. Give an example of each type.

9. Explain how to determine the appropriate organizational member to execute performance evaluations.

10. Suggest methods for avoiding the phenomenon of goal displacement.

PROBLEMS AND EXPERIENTIAL EXERCISES

1. "Not long ago, the Boy Scouts of America revealed that membership figures coming in from the field had been falsified. In response to the pressures of a national membership drive, people within the organization had vastly overstated the number of new Boy Scouts. To their chagrin, the leaders found something that other managers have also discovered: Organizational control systems often produce unintended consequences. The drive to increase memberships had motivated people to increase the number of new members reported but had not motivated them to increase the number of Boy Scouts actually enrolled."[16] The above incident is a widely pub-

licized example of goal displacement. Consider the following examples and explain how this phenomenon might also occur in each:
   a. Appraisal systems for college instructors
   b. Appraisal systems for students
   c. Quota compensation systems for sales personnel

2. Relate the four types of controls discussed in the chapter to the following examples:
   a. A manufacturer of surfboards
   b. A concert promoter
   c. A heart surgeon
   d. Director of the City Parks Department

3. Secure a copy of the current budget used by your student government association or student newspaper. Compare its development with the steps discussed in the chapter. How flexible is the budget? How might it be made more flexible?

4. Give an example of a situation in which each of the following types of ratios would be useful:

a. liquidity ratio
b. leverage ratio
c. activity ratio
d. profitability ratio

5. Discuss the benefits and problems involved in conducting management audits. Who should be responsible for performing such audits?

MANAGERIAL INCIDENT: Munsingwear

A lot of things were going wrong at Munsingwear Inc., an apparel maker, but perhaps most alarming was the chaos in the factories. They seemed to be out of control: Orders for red, white, or blue shirts were ignored while plants inexplicably turned out shirts in mauve and other less-popular colors that most retailers didn't want.

So last February, for the second time in less than a year, Munsingwear's directors named a new president, George K. Hansen, a twenty-year veteran of the retailing industry.

Mr. Hansen has set about shaping up the corporate Sad Sack with all the fervor of the ex-Marine Corps drill sergeant that he is. "This was the most messed-up company I'd ever come across," says Mr. Hansen. "The company needed discipline, controls and leadership, but nobody was minding the store."

In just over six months, Mr. Hansen has succeeded in pulling Munsingwear back from the verge of bankruptcy. The company's golf shirts and underwear are now being delivered to retailers on time. But Munsingwear still has a long way to go. Sales this year will fall below $100 million for the first time since 1976. The company is losing money and market share, and some of its competitors don't believe Mr. Hansen is doing any better than previous presidents.

From 1979 to 1982, Munsingwear was run by Raymond F. Good, a Pillsbury executive who was hired to turn around the company's profit slide and gain more prominence for its Penguin and Vassarette lines, just as he had for Pillsbury's cake mixes and H. J. Heinz Co.'s ketchup before that.

DERIDING THE 'DOUGHBOYS.' Mr. Good brought with him three other Pillsbury executives who also didn't know the apparel business. Longtime employees derided "The Doughboys." They "isolated themselves in a section of the building," says a former sales manager who has since left Munsingwear. "They were like recluses." Company insiders speak snidely of the "turnaround specialists" who they say did more to hurt the company than help it.

"The Doughboys" set out to increase profits by cutting expenses. To do that, they changed the labels on the underwear boxes, making it difficult for retailers to find in their storerooms, a former employee says. Even worse, they removed the distinctive waistbands encircled with Munsingwear's name. That saved a few cents in weaving costs for each brief, but neither shoppers nor retailers liked the blank waistbands.

"An apparel man would have never done that," says the former sales manager. Adds

J. Raymond Donnelly, a Munsingwear senior vice-president: "The loss of business might have been significant if we hadn't changed back."

There were other blunders. Munsingwear's well-made $18 golf shirt with a penguin on the pocket appealed to Middle American tastes and pocketbooks. But new items, such as a $125 velour warm-up suit aimed at affluent shoppers, fell flat.

COMPUTER PROBLEMS. Inventory snafus created by foul-ups in the factories were compounded after an old-fashioned, but still functional, computerized inventory control program was replaced with a new one that didn't work.

"If you have inventory the customer doesn't want, it stinks," says Mr. Hansen. "It's like old food. It starts to rot and smell, and it's not worth very much."

Last year, Munsingwear had trouble getting material to make shirts when one of its suppliers went bankrupt, and it lost orders and retailer confidence. A West Coast retailer says he could only get 40 percent of what he wanted to order from Munsingwear a year and a half ago. "We had to go to some people we had never done business with before, like Jockey," he says.

Jockey International Inc., a Kenosha, Wis., maker of underwear and sportswear, has taken a chunk of Munsingwear's underwear market, just as Izod Ltd.'s alligator shirts have bitten into Munsingwear's Penguin shirt line.

Mr. Good was fired by Munsingwear directors last October and is now vice-president for consumer marketing support at Control Data Corp. in Minneapolis. He won't discuss his Munsingwear days, except to say he isn't surprised by the comments of executives there. "I just wish them well. It's a chapter of my life that's behind me," he says.

After Mr. Good's departure, Donald P. Brown, a former financial officer at the University of Minnesota who was brought in by Mr. Good, led Munsingwear as president for four months until he was fired. Then the directors turned to Mr. Hansen, who had been hired by Mr. Good in June 1982 as senior vice-president to bring order to Munsingwear's factories.

After becoming president, Mr. Hansen says he discovered that the companys' finance department was a mess. Eighteen months of bank statements hadn't been reconciled, and 40 percent of its accounts receivable were past due, some by as much as eighteen months. Moreover, Munsingwear was shipping to deadbeat customers whose bills were long overdue.

"It was horrendous," says Michael Kagan, Munsingwear's new chief financial officer. "The problem here was that there were no objectives. Things happened and no one was responsible for the decisions."

Munsingwear's lenders were ready to call the company's long-term debt, which might have led to bankruptcy. Mr. Hansen convinced them that he could return Munsingwear to profitability, partly by cutting operating costs.

Both unionized and nonunionized employees agreed to a wage freeze for this year. The company also sold five of its 13 Apple computers, subleased the top three floors of its six-story building, and unscrewed every third lightbulb in the place.

'EXECUTIVE SELLING.' By lowering operating costs by $7 million, Mr. Hansen hopes to break even this year. But that will be tough because sales fell 13 percent in the

(Continued on next page.)

first half, down from $56.8 million during the same period last year.

With less than $5 million to spend on advertising, Munsingwear can't buy TV time or advertise in magazines like *Sports Illustrated* or *People* to reach the public it once did. Instead, it will buy ads in menswear trade publications. Top management is also doing what Mr. Hansen calls "executive selling," visiting stores that quit buying Munsingwear products.

E. T. Catlett, president of the menswear division of Izod Ltd., doubts that tactic will succeed. "The retailer has no loyalty to a company or brand. You have to talk directly to the consumer," he says. And Wallace Erickson, senior vice-president, marketing, at Jockey International, says advertising to retailers "is another one of their bad decisions."

Jockey's men's underwear business has grown 10 percent in five years when 1 percent growth would have been normal, Mr. Erickson says. "We have friends like Munsingwear who keep helping us," he says.

Questions and Problems

1. Relate the actions by Munsingwear president George K. Hansen to the model of the control process shown in Figure 16–2. Make any assumptions necessary.

2. Explain how the presence of feedback systems would have prevented many of the mistakes made at Munsingwear between 1979 and 1983.

CHAPTER

17 MANAGEMENT INFORMATION SYSTEMS

LEARNING OBJECTIVES

After studying this chapter you should be able to

1. Identify the major categories of management information.

2. List the basic components of a management information system.

3. Explain the role of the computer in an MIS.

4. Identify the bases for comparing information systems.

5. List the characteristics typically present in successful information systems.

STOP ACTION CASE

Fisher Camuto Corporation

During the past decade, foreign shoe manufacturers have secured a dominant share of the fashion footwear market in the United States. In 1977, Jack Fisher and Vincent Camuto decided to take advantage of this trend by forming a corporation to blend their years of experience in the U.S. shoe industry with the reality of foreign shoe manufacture. Their Stamford, Connecticut-headquartered Fisher Camuto Corporation acquired a shoe manufacturing facility in Brazil. Fisher and Camuto then sold the Brazilian factory's output to department stores and independent shoe retailers throughout the United States.

But Fisher Camuto's owners wanted to achieve total vertical integration by controlling all aspects of shoe manufacture and distribution. They accomplished this objective in 1983 by opening their own chain of retail outlets called 9 West.

In a typical year, Fisher Camuto introduces six lines of shoes in a wide range of styles and fashion colors. It produces more than 15 million pairs of shoes

each year in its facilities in Brazil, marketing them under the trade names of 9 West, Gloria Vanderbilt, J. J. Calico, and Westies. It recently launched a fifth brand, Enzo Angiolini, which it designs and produces at a factory it leases in Italy.

But the change in corporate direction increased the need to answer questions about inventory, sales performance of different product lines, and production schedules. If Fisher Camuto managers were to compete favorably with domestic and foreign producers at the production level and with department stores and other retail shoe store chains at the retail level, they would need these questions answered.

Use the materials in this chapter to recommend a course of action that will enable Fisher Camuto managers to adjust inventory levels and production schedules in accordance with consumer demand for each of the company's product lines.

MANAGEMENT FACT OR FICTION

	FACT	FICTION		FACT	FICTION
1. Data and information are synonymous terms.	☐	☐	5. The most common MIS problem facing managers is a lack of information.	☐	☐
2. Effective information systems have three components: a data bank, an analytical methods bank, and a model bank.	☐	☐	6. Managers do not have to understand how an information system works, only how to use it.	☐	☐
3. The invention of the computer made today's management information systems possible.	☐	☐	7. Successful information systems evolve into more sophisticated systems over time.	☐	☐
4. A primary cause of MIS failure is disaggregated data files.	☐	☐			

The materials in this chapter will assist you in separating management fact from fiction. Your answers can be checked on page 560.

S ir Arthur Conan Doyle summed up an all-too-common dilemma facing the manager of the late 1980s in the form of a remark by the world's most famous detective. In Doyle's story "The Adventure of the Copper Beeches," Sherlock Holmes cries impatiently to Watson, "Data! Data! Data! I can't make bricks without clay."[1]

The business environment for the past quarter-century has been characterized by increasing competition, decreasing product life cycles, and the growth of organizations in terms of both human and physical assets. Decision makers have often been forced to extend planning horizons—and introduce even greater levels of uncertainty. In addition, the typical manager is further removed from action points, increasing communications problems and making effective control more difficult. These changes have been accompanied by increasing societal pressures for greater accountability.

Chapter 16 focused upon a variety of tools, techniques, and approaches to assist managers in controlling. A key element in both planning and controlling is *information,* and a relatively new discipline has evolved to deal with the special problems of information gathering, analysis, and reporting. This discipline has been labeled management information systems, or, simply, MIS.

Information is increasingly recognized as not only a significant element in the planning-controlling process but also as a major organizational *resource.* If the decision maker defines a problem as a gap between the actual state and a desired state, information is utilized both to identify and to describe the gap. Information will also be utilized in evaluating alternative methods of bridging the gap.

Milwaukee-based Harley-Davidson Motor Company celebrated its eighty-fourth birthday in 1987. But the firm, which today manufactures the only U.S. motorcycle still in production, has several concerns. One problem area is image. Management was disturbed to learn that its company logo is the No. 1 request in tattoo parlors across America. It decided to begin a strong licensing program aimed at returning its reputation to the ranks of baseball, hot dogs, and apple pie. The program, combined with a series of legal moves to eliminate a proliferation of counterfeit merchandise, permitted producers of products ranging from gold rings and wine coolers to clothing and cologne to use the Harley-Davidson name.[2]

An even more critical problem facing the U.S. firm was remaining competitive with Japanese motorcycle manufacturers. A primary need was information to aid Harley-Davidson managers in reducing costs, especially parts inventory and personnel costs. As Figure 17–1 illustrates, the firm worked with Honeywell to design such a system. Today a Honeywell computer automatically tracks and collects information about each engine as it moves through the assembly plant. It also compares feedback from the factory floor with production schedules so that parts are ordered only

FIGURE 17–1.   The Harley-Davidson Information System
Source: Photo by Stephen Wilkes. Courtesy Honeywell/Harley-Davidson.

Management information system (MIS) is a structured, interacting complex of persons, machines, and procedures designed to generate an orderly flow of information.

as needed, thus reducing parts inventory costs. When combined with personnel data, shipping information, and forecasts contained in the mainframe computer at the firm's Milwaukee headquarters, the system is providing Harley-Davidson managers with an effective method of planning and control.

A *management information system (MIS)* may be defined as a structured, interacting complex of persons, machines, and procedures designed to generate an orderly flow of relevant information, collected from both intra- and extra-organizational sources, for use as the basis for decision making in specified management responsibility areas.[3] The MIS is designed to acquire, store, and convert data into information for decision making. Availability of timely, relevant information is invaluable in performing the planning, control, and operational functions of the organization.

CONVERTING DATA TO INFORMATION

In 1983, U.S. organizations spent an estimated $78 billion to develop and operate data processing systems and computer-based information systems. The significant growth in the number of computer installations in both profit and nonprofit organizations has been accompanied by major increases in available data for use by decision makers. In many cases managers complain about an overabundance of data generated by their increasingly sophisticated computer facilities. Daily computer printouts provide thousands of details about production schedules; current inventory positions of raw materials, goods in process, and finished products; output levels by plant, shift, and department; and cost and sales analyses by territory, product, customer, sales division, and order size. Such daily analyses may have been casually requested months ago by the manager in response to a data needs questionnaire, but in many cases they are equally casually ignored. Data and information are not synonymous terms.[4]

Data consist of facts, statistics, opinions, or predictions categorized on some basis for storage and retrieval. *Information* is data relevant to the manager in making decisions. As Figure 17–2 indicates, a major function of the MIS is the transformation of data into decision-relevant information.

> Data are facts, statistics, opinions, or predictions categorized on some basis for storage and retrieval. Information is data relevant to the manager in making decisions.

FIGURE 17–2.   The MIS Concept

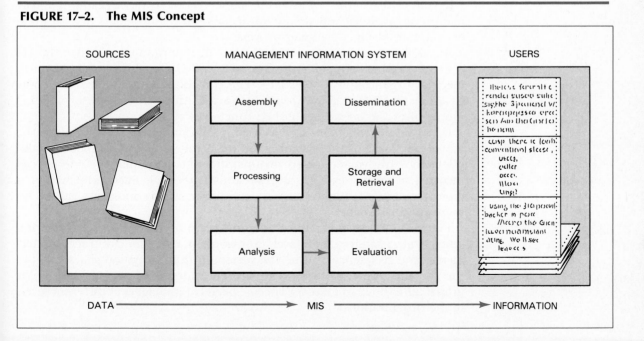

The system shown in Figure 17–2 performs six functions:

1. *Assembly:* the search for and gathering of data

2. *Processing:* the editing and summarization of data

3. *Analysis:* the computation of percentages and ratios, and tests of statistical significance

4. *Evaluation:* the determination of information quality, degree of faith the decision maker should have in the accuracy of the data

5. *Storage and Retrieval:* the indexing, filing, and relocating of data

6. *Dissemination:* the routing of useful information to the proper decision maker[5]

TYPES OF MANAGEMENT INFORMATION

Management information may be divided into three major categories: strategic planning information, management control information, and operational control information.[6] *Strategic planning information* is utilized by managers in deciding upon the objectives of the organization, the resources to be used in attaining these objectives, and the policies developed and used to govern the acquisition, use, and disposition of these resources. External information represents a major part of strategic planning information needs. Relatively unique informational requirements may be present for the strategic planning process.

Management control information is used in determining whether the resources are obtained and used effectively and efficiently in the accomplishment of organizational objectives. The control process requires the coordination of efforts of individuals in various departments. Informational inputs often cut across established functional areas.

Operational control information is used in determining whether the specific day-to-day tasks of the organization are being carried out efficiently and effectively. Information used for operational control may include payroll records, inventory listings, and personnel statistics. Such information is typically detailed, highly current, accurate, largely internal, narrow in scope, and in frequent use.

Figure 17–3 compares the three categories on the basis of information scope, source, aggregation level, time horizon, currency, accuracy requirements, and frequency of use. The variations in information characteristics for the different categories are further evidence of the need to tailor information flows to meet the specific needs of managers at different levels in the organization.

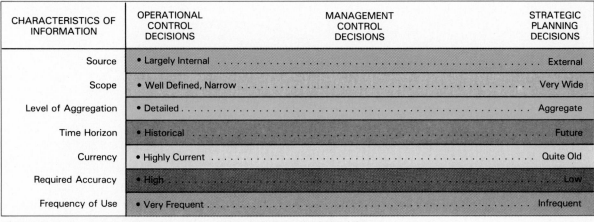

CHARACTERISTICS OF INFORMATION	OPERATIONAL CONTROL DECISIONS	MANAGEMENT CONTROL DECISIONS	STRATEGIC PLANNING DECISIONS
Source	• Largely Internal		External
Scope	• Well Defined, Narrow		Very Wide
Level of Aggregation	• Detailed		Aggregate
Time Horizon	• Historical		Future
Currency	• Highly Current		Quite Old
Required Accuracy	• High		Low
Frequency of Use	• Very Frequent		Infrequent

FIGURE 17–3.   Information Needs for Different Types of Decisions
Source: G. Anthony Corry and Michael Scott Morton, "A Framework for Management Information Systems," *Sloan Management Review* (Fall 1971), p. 58. Reprinted by permission of the Sloan Management Review Association. Copyright © 1971 by the Sloan Management Review Association. All rights reserved.

COMPONENTS OF THE MIS

To perform its functions of providing timely, decision-relevant information for the manager, the MIS must have three components: a data bank, an analytical methods bank, and a model bank.[7]

THE DATA BANK

The foundation of any MIS is the *data bank*. It consists of raw data, as assembled, recorded, stored, and retrieved. Data inputs come from both internal and external sources. Internal sources include production and sales reports, invoices, financial data, and reports from such departments as purchasing, engineering, and product development. External sources identified in Figure 17–4 include government publications, data from suppliers, customer feedback, and data collected from competitors.

> **Data bank** is an MIS component consisting of raw data as assembled, recorded, stored, and retrieved.

   In addition to a wealth of published statistical data, governments at every level provide potentially valuable data. For example, the examination of a competitor's bids and documentation provided to the Government Contract Administration may reveal technological insights and indicate costs and bidding philosophies.[8] Competitors may provide information about themselves in such communication channels as annual reports, speeches by executives, and even employment advertisements (that may suggest the technical and marketing directions in which they are headed). Suppliers such as banks, advertising agencies, public relations firms, and

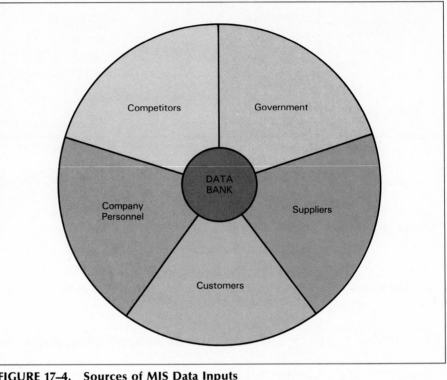

FIGURE 17–4.   Sources of MIS Data Inputs

raw materials and component part suppliers may be important sources of information about industry trends. Customers of the firm can provide similar information about changing needs and attitudes toward the firm's products as well as those of competitors. Finally, company personnel are sources of information concerning operations within the company and outside the firm in their contacts with customers and the general public.

THE DATA BASE CONCEPT

Although more and more organizations are attempting to develop data banks to serve as repositories for data, all too often the various functional areas develop data networks independently of one another in response to specific needs. Each department or function defines its data requirements, which then may be collected and stored with little coordination with other existing or planned elements. The resulting data system is typically a fragmented, overlapping collection of files that are largely dependent upon the specific system originally developed at the time of data collection. The result is often too much data in the wrong form that is virtually inaccessible except when using the specific original format.

A data base system is designed to prevent—or correct—these problems. A *data base* is a centralized, manageable repository of the organization's data resources—procedures, computer programs, and specialized personnel. While systems vary widely from one organization to the next, the common interweaving threads are sets of files capable of being read by the organization's computer, sharing of common resources, and centralized authority.[9]

The importance of the data base concept in today's organizations is illustrated by the popularity of such commercial software programs as dBase III and Paradox. Ashton-Tate, publisher of dBase III, sold 300,000 copies in 1985. An enhanced version called dBase III Plus, designed to allow personal computer users within the organization to share information from the company data base, is described in Figure 17–5.

When carried to its logical conclusion, the data base concept includes centralizing the various data resources in files that can be accessed by

Data base is a centralized, manageable repository of the organization's data resources—procedures, computer programs, and specialized personnel.

FIGURE 17–5.   dBASE III—The World's Most Popular Data Base Software Program
Source: Reprinted by permission of Ashton-Tate, Torrance, Calif.

The database used by more people can now be used by more people.

Introducing dBASE III PLUS.
The PLUS stands for all the improvements we've made to the world's number one selling database management software.

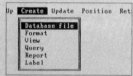

The Assistant helps beginning users accomplish day-to-day data management tasks without programming.

Mind you, dBASE III PLUS still has the powerful dBASE programming language, dot prompt, and all the features that have made dBASE III the standard of the industry.

We've simply raised the standard.

And just as dBASE III introduced more power to the people, our new dBASE III PLUS introduces more people to the power.

People who aren't all that crazy about programming, for example.

The Assistant feature in dBASE III PLUS now provides them with new easy-to-use pull-down menus for creating, using and modifying multiple databases.

So now anyone who can manage a simple cursor can manage day-to-day data management tasks. Without programming.

And by using our new Screen Painter,

anyone can create custom screens. Without programming.

Or using View, access related information in several databases at one time. Without programming.

With Advanced Query System, another new non-programming feature, any user can build complex queries just by selecting from the dBASE III PLUS pull-down menus.

For rapidly creating entire programs, there's even a new Applications Generator.

And for all those who wish to learn to program, the Assistant can be of further assistance. By teaching you programming commands as you go along. Without disrupting your work flow.

These are only a few of the dBASE III PLUS features that can help new users quickly get up to speed. And experienced users quickly increase their speed. (Sorting, for example, is up to two times faster and indexing up to ten times faster than dBASE III.)

Advanced Query System lets you set up and restore complex queries without programming.

And it's the fastest way to network those users, too. Because now, local area networking capabilities are built right in.

dBASE III PLUS can also help put developers in the fast lane. With a new Data Catalog and more than 50 new commands and functions. Plus code encryption and linking, improved debugging aids, assembly language calls and much more.

To obtain a free dBASE III PLUS demo disk, call 800-437-4329, Extension 2810, for the authorized Ashton-Tate dealer nearest you.

And get your hands on dBASE III PLUS.

It's the software more people can look forward to using.

ASHTON-TATE
dBASE III PLUS
The data management standard.

MANAGEMENT FAILURES

Ideal Basic Industries

Foreign competition has adversely affected U.S. industries other than automobiles, steel, shoes, textiles, and electronics. Since 1982, imports of cement have soared 400 percent and by 1986 had secured one-sixth of the U.S. market. Competition from lower-cost foreign producers in such countries as Mexico, Spain, and Greece has been particularly intense along the Atlantic and Gulf Coast regions. The new competition has driven cement prices down from about $60 a ton in 1982 to $55 in 1986.

Denver-based Ideal Basic Industries management recognized the need to modernize its production facilities to remain competitive. It also needed a production facility on the Gulf Coast to provide a competitively priced, U.S.-produced alternative for regional purchasers in the residential, commercial, and highway construction industries. The firm's management chose a location on Mobile Bay to construct its $175 million state-of-the-art Cris Dobbins plant.

The location was a good choice. It was not only easily accessible to water transportation from the bay and through the Intercoastal Waterway, but was also in close proximity to huge quantities of limestone, the primary ingredient in cement. However, the highly automated facility proved to be an engineering nightmare. Its total costs amounted to $350 million, 100 percent over budget. At 10 percent annual interest, Ideal's *daily* interest costs on the plant would total $95,890!

But inflated construction costs paled before the major problem facing the facility: it wouldn't work. In analyzing the volumes of

data that led to the decision to build the automated facility, Ideal's management failed to consider one fatal bit of information. The nearby limestone proved to be too wet for processing by the new equipment. As one Ideal executive put it, "No one thought to test it thoroughly. When it hit the machines, it turned into oatmeal." To be used at the dry-process plant, the limestone had to first be treated in a special drying system. But the system required expensive fuel to operate, and the results were significantly higher product costs. The nearest available limestone that does not require the drying system is in the Dominican Republic. The cash drain from the Cris Dobbins plant was a significant contributor to Ideal's $340 million losses in 1985. The drain is expected to continue until the firm can find a buyer for the plant.

Source: Quotation in paragraph four from "A Cement Maker That May Be Selling Its Future," *Business Week,* 18 November 1985, p. 88. *See also* Laurie P. Cohen, "Ideal to Take $200 Million Write-Down on Idled Plant, Forcing 4th-Period Loss," *Wall Street Journal,* 2 January 1986, p. 4; and "Ideal Seeks to Sell Plant as Value Decreases," *Mobile Register,* 3 January 1986, p. 9A.

different decision makers for different uses. The concept is a major milestone in MIS development, making possible access to all portions of the data base across functional divisions and at different organizational levels.[10] One survey of the major U.S. manufacturing firms revealed that almost four of every five firms surveyed possess a data base or are currently implementing a data base system.[11]

Effective implementation of the data base concept should result in the creation of an integrated overall information system. Such a system would be made up of information subsystems from such functional areas as marketing, accounting, production, and personnel. Rather than duplicating information in the data banks of each subsystem, the integrated system would allow each subsystem to utilize centrally accumulated data, thereby decreasing overall response time and reducing costs.

The benefits of the integrated MIS concept are illustrated in Figure 17–6 by the reduced number of necessary contacts between various functional areas to secure needed information. In this example, a total of 16 contacts are necessary to provide managers in the finance, human resources, production, and marketing departments with needed information from each of the specialized information depositories. By converting to an integrated MIS in which these previously dispersed data elements are included, the number of needed contacts is reduced to four.

THE ANALYTICAL METHODS BANK

The second component of the MIS, the *analytical methods bank,* has the responsibility for processing and analyzing the data inputs. Such analysis may be limited to development of averages or frequency distributions; in other cases, more sophisticated statistical techniques such as factor analysis or multiple regression may be used in data analysis.

> **Analytical methods bank** is an MIS component that processes and analyzes data inputs.

THE MODEL BANK

As explained in Chapter 7, a variety of mathematical models can be utilized in analyzing and solving problems. Such techniques as linear programming models, simulations, and queuing models have proven useful in analyzing complex problem situations and suggesting possible solutions. The ideal MIS will integrate these models for use in describing, predicting, and possibly controlling.

While models have proven extremely useful in tackling a number of knotty business problems, the model bank in a sophisticated MIS should be capable of handling a problem like the following:

> **Model bank** is an MIS component that integrates various models for use in describing, predicting, and possibly controlling organizational behavior.

At 9:32 A.M., a blowout! A blast furnace breaks down in the steel plant. Cold iron will have to be heated to produce the molten iron normally supplied to the refining process from this furnace. Processing time will be almost doubled, reducing the shop's production capacity by 60 percent. The

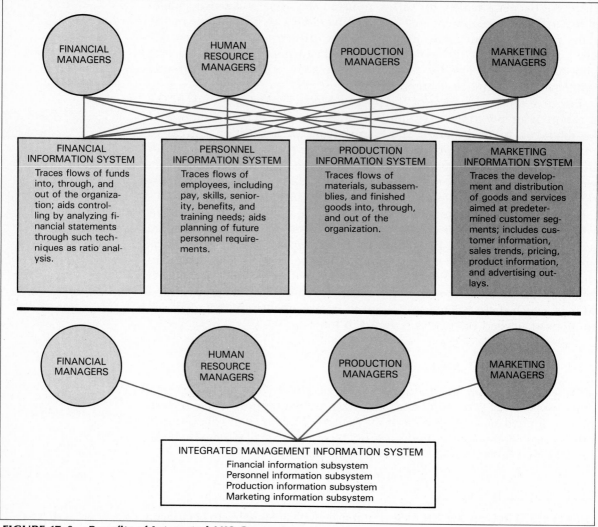

FIGURE 17–6.   Benefits of Integrated MIS Concept

cost per ton of steel will certainly rise sharply as a result of the increased processing time. But how much will it rise?

Using a remote time-shared computer terminal in his office, a manager at Inland Steel Company defines the new conditions resulting from the equipment failure and enters them in a set of models which simulate the steelmaking process and the costs involved. At 11:26 A.M.—less than two hours later the same morning—he estimates the new cost figures and prepares a revised corporate profit projection.[12]

The MIS at Inland Steel has been capable of handling similar problems for almost twenty years.

ROLE OF COMPUTERS IN MANAGEMENT INFORMATION SYSTEMS

The parallel development of the MIS concept and marked advances in computer technology have led many people to confuse MIS with electronic data processing. The recent advances in electronic data processing have made possible the creation of vast data bases and sophisticated analysis and reporting systems that would have been impossible without computers. A giant firm such as Travelers Corporation provides its managers with some 25,000 personal computers as an integral part of their overall information system. As Travelers spokesperson Joseph T. Brophy points out, "The whole key to office automation is a work station that is a powerful personal computer that sits on your desk. It's got word processing, electronic mail, spreadsheet applications, communications into the rest of your network, and some local file-storage capabilities. That's the way to go."[13] The tremendous storage and computing powers of computers of all sizes result from the development of microprocessors, or computer chips. The chip shown in Figure 17–7 is capable of remembering over 256,000 pieces of information.

Computers, however, are only one component in the organization's information system. The computer is only a tool—although an extremely important tool in many instances. Still, many valuable information components are not computerized. Special research studies investigating panel members' attitudes toward a mockup of a proposed new product, proposed rule changes by a government agency, or the financial report of a major competitor all represent valuable, noncomputerized information.[14]

In some instances the level of computer sophistication actually impeded MIS development. The computer specialists who supervise data processing systems often lack the business background needed to match their systems to the information needs of decision makers. In recent years, dozens of major firms have taken steps to fill this void by removing computer management from the hands of technicians and forming steering committees composed of high-ranking executives with the necessary business backgrounds. Such firms as Massachusetts Mutual Life Insurance Company, Southern Railway, and Aetna Life & Casualty utilize the steering committee approach.

Figure 17–8 depicts the typical structure of the management information system and indicates the interactions of the data bank, analytical methods bank, and model bank. It also identifies the boundaries of the organization's information system and relates the impact of the environment on the MIS and the decision maker.

❝ A computer isn't smart enough to make a mistake.
Computers are dumb.
Fast and efficient and dumb.
No computer ever had an idea. ❞

IBM advertisement

FIGURE 17–7.   Computer Chips: Compact Storage Facilities for MIS Data
Source: 1983 Allied Corporation. Reprinted by permission.

BASES FOR COMPARING INFORMATION SYSTEMS ▪

Since no two managers have precisely the same information needs, the characteristics of different systems vary considerably. Each MIS reflects an attempt to respond to the specific needs of decision makers, the problems

MANAGEMENT: THE LIGHTER SIDE

Computer Training at Club Med

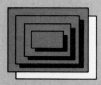

The declining prices and rapidly growing computing power of today's computers combined with an almost unimaginable array of software have made computers an indispensable part of organizations in the late 1980s. By 1989 one U.S. worker in seven is expected to be using a personal computer on the job.

The result of the growing presence of the computer in offices and factories throughout the nation has been to introduce computers to children at the elementary school level—and even in kindergartens. In the summer, computer camps compete with more traditional vacations. And—as the photograph illustrates—even the harried executive is not immune from computer training. Vacationers seeking several days of sunshine, swimming, skiing, and volleyball at one of Club Med's exotic locations such as Guadeloupe, Malaysia, Morocco, Senegal, Tunisia, or even Copper Mountain in Colorado have the option of participating in computer training workshops on the Club's Atari computers. The Club Med staff members are known as G.O.s (*gentils*

organisateurs, or "friendly organizers"). Specially trained G.O.s are prepared to offer instruction in French, English, Spanish, or Italian.

Source: Photo Courtesy Club Med, 40 West 57th Street, New York, NY 10019.

they face, and the approaches they use in planning, controlling, and analyzing and solving problems.

Despite these differences, information systems do possess certain common dimensions that may be analyzed in isolating similarities and differences. These dimensions are (1) information recency, (2) management access time, (3) information aggregation, (4) analytical sophistication, and (5) system authority.[15]

INFORMATION RECENCY

The first MIS dimension, *information recency,* refers to the time lapse between the occurrence of an event and the inclusion of data recording that

Information recency is the time lapse between the occurrence of an event and the inclusion of data recording that event in the MIS.

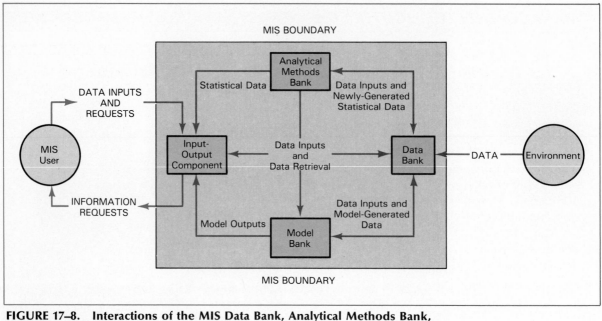

FIGURE 17–8.   Interactions of the MIS Data Bank, Analytical Methods Bank, and Model Bank

Source: Adapted from William R. King, *Marketing Management Information Systems* (New York: Petrocelli/Charter, 1977), p. 69. © 1977 by Litton Educational Publishing, Inc. Reprinted by permission of Van Nostrand Reinhold Company.

event in the MIS. This may range from a second or two in the recording of retail sales purchases by a cash register-type point of sale terminal linked to the firm's information system to several months in the case of detailed investigations of alternate production site locations. The degree of current, up-to-date information varies among organizations, even for identical data items. Some organizations will record changes in finished goods inventories as they occur; others will record them daily or weekly in a single batch process of aggregate changes.

Holiday Inn managers require precise, up-to-the-minute data for their international reservations system. Their Holidex system handles more than 36,000 confirmed reservations daily for some 1,700 hotels in the United States and fifty other countries throughout the world. The system makes possible immediate determination of available accommodations in any hotel and automatically makes reservations with printed confirmation to the guest and notification to the hotel. Similar sophisticated reservations systems are utilized daily by major airlines.

Firms with offices and factories located in different geographic areas frequently use electronic mail to provide rapid transmission of printed documents, reports, and letters. This means of linking distant components of the organization is the largest data communications network of its kind in the world, serving organizations located around the globe. The equivalent of one million typewritten pages has been transmitted by GTE Telenet every day. However, GTE has divested itself of Telenet which is now a separate company called Telenet Communications.

Determination of appropriate levels of information recency should be based upon the uses to be made of the information. In many cases, the cost of continually updating computer data banks is not justified, since managers may be utilizing the data on a weekly or biweekly basis. In these instances, a less costly weekly updating may be appropriate. In the case of reservations systems or other instances in which the decision maker must utilize completely current data, the MIS should be designed to meet such requirements.

MANAGEMENT ACCESS TIME

The second common dimension used in comparing information systems is *management access time*. This refers to the time lapse between the manager's request for certain information and its receipt. It is a measurement of the system's response time for a given request.

Management access time is the time lapse between the manager's request for certain information and its receipt.

Savin Corporation has installed a real time information system in each of its warehouses, providing instant answers to questions concerning current inventory, its exact location in the warehouse, and the status of all orders. By contrast, a small independent retailer without a similar system may require a physical inventory count and take several days to obtain similar information.

INFORMATION AGGREGATION

The third MIS dimension, *information aggregation,* refers to the detail with which information is maintained in the data bank of the MIS. Data may vary from a highly disaggregated item level recording (performance data for individual employees, inventory records by item, or individual sales invoice recording of products sold, customer, salesperson, and order size) to highly aggregated data such as departmental or divisional performance, total sales by product lines, or aggregate inventory positions. The J.C. Penney information system divides merchandise into 28 profit centers such as women's sportswear, jewelry, children's wear, and housewares. Disaggregated data are then collected for each brand, color, and size. While sales, inventory, and profit data can then be recorded by profit centers, the disaggregated data files provide Penney buyers and store managers with specific sales and inventory data on individual items.[16]

Information aggregation is the amount of detail with which information is maintained in the data bank.

A positive correlation exists between aggregation levels and the amount of time delay involved in recording data into the system. Highly disaggregated data tend to be added to the data bank faster than aggregated data, which must accumulate before they are recorded.

ANALYTICAL SOPHISTICATION

Analytical sophistication is the complexity of the model and analytical methods banks of the MIS.

Another basis for comparing information systems is *analytical sophistication*. This concept refers to the complexity of the model bank and the analytical methods bank of the MIS. As Figure 17–9 indicates, the lowest level of analytical sophistication involves the simple retrieval and display of requested data for the manager who must then analyze it. The second level involves the aggregation of data from one or more sources to produce totals or subtotals. The third level consists of arithmetic averaging, while the fourth level logically analyzes data by aggregating it into various classification schemes. Statistical analyses are used at the fifth level to develop forecasts based upon historical data or to employ statistical tests of difference on collected data. Learning, the title of the sixth level of analytical sophistication, involves a system programmed to modify the model structures

FIGURE 17–9.   Relationship Between Degree of Analytical Sophistication and Level of Computer Authority
Source: Arnold E. Amstutz, "The Marketing Executive and Management Information Systems," in *Science, Technology, and Marketing,* ed. Raymond M. Haas (Chicago: American Marketing Association, 1967).

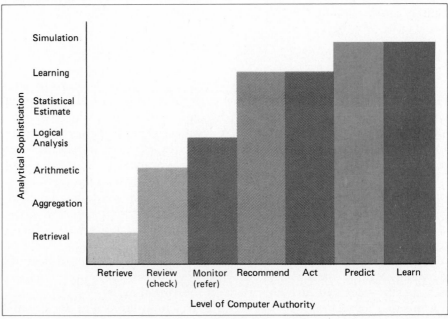

based upon data inputs received over time. The final level is typical of a relatively small number of highly sophisticated systems capable of evaluating alternate decisions and adjusting simulation models based upon environmental data. This stage provides decision makers with the capability of testing possible strategies in the simulated environment. The MIS is capable of producing scenarios of outcomes to each "What if?" question posed by the system user.

SYSTEM AUTHORITY

The final dimension used in comparing information systems of different organizations is *system authority*. This is the amount of authority delegated to the MIS. As Figure 17–9 shows, system authority is closely associated with the system's degree of analytical sophistication. Management's willingness to delegate authority increases with the sophistication level of the system. In addition, increased management demands from an MIS require greater levels of analytical sophistication in the system.

System authority refers to the amount of authority delegated to the MIS.

At the lowest level, decision makers may restrict authority to retrieval of data from designated locations. The next level calls for system reviews (or checks) of each record for errors. A third level involves monitoring of data and reporting exceptions (as defined by the decision makers) to management. The fourth level of sophistication calls for the system to make recommendations for action. Allowing the system to take action on all but exceptional cases (as defined by management) is the fifth level of system authority. The highest levels of system authority involve permitting the MIS to predict possible outcomes of alternative decisions as a basis for planning and to adapt the system's parameters and models in an evolutionary learning process.

CHARACTERISTICS OF SUCCESSFUL INFORMATION SYSTEMS

Why are some information systems highly successful while others produce little benefit in return for the costs of development and maintenance? Are the failures due to software programs too limited to utilize the vast capacities of today's computer facilities? Information specialists generally agree that the problems do *not* lie in the technical attributes of the system.[17]

Although the specific functions and outputs of different systems vary to meet specific needs of individual organizations, four characteristics are present in successful systems. First, the system is founded on management's conception of the decision environment.[18] A successful information system must reflect the priorities of the decision makers who will make use of it. Since it must provide information in the form, amount, and of the type that managers can use, the system must be based on models that reflect management's conception of the environment.

COMPUTERS IN MANAGEMENT

Electronic Test Markets

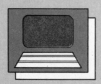

Debbie Van Veghel, a pretty young housewife in Springfield, Missouri, has her hands full. She sits on a sofa in her comfortable living room as her toddler, Patrick, takes a swipe every so often at the newest family member, six-week-old Robbie. All the while, the television drones on in the background. "We watch a lot of TV," she says. "It's on from morning to night."

But at the Van Veghels' house, the TV is more than a filler of empty hours. It's the surveillance arm of market research firm A. C. Nielsen Co. Thanks to people like Debbie and to computer technology, only God knows more than A. C. Nielsen about what and why consumers are buying in Springfield, population 142,000. . . .

To measure the effectiveness of an advertisement in the old days, marketers had to compare sales results from two different cities, televising, say, ad A in Boston and ad B in San Francisco. But the differences between the two locales—in everything from demographics to competitors' activities—made it hard to attribute any difference in sales performance to the ads alone.

There's another big problem with traditional test markets. Because they were designed to measure only sales volume, they missed what was happening beneath the surface of the trend. For instance, increased sales of a new potato chip are desirable but can mean two

different things: 1) consumers like them and are making repeat purchases, or 2) the ads are getting more people to try them the first time, but they don't like the taste and won't buy them a second time.

Electronic test markets address both problems by enabling a test within one market and by getting an inside view of household behavior. Here's how the new Nielsen system in Springfield works:

Nielsen lined up a group of 2,500 households in town, dubbed market makers, that were willing to divulge their jobs, their income, what appliances they own, whether they wear contact lenses (hard or soft), even the ages and weights of their cats and dogs. This group has agreed to let Nielsen in on the secrets of all its grocery shopping as well as to be subject to test television commercials.

Why would anyone want to be a marketer's guinea pig? Nielsen offers some modest incentives: up to $2 off groceries monthly as well

---

The second requirement of a successful information system is that the user-manager understand and be involved in the construction of the system structure. The more managers are involved in developing and up-as a chance to win a jackpot of $1,500 and other prizes each month. But the chief appeal is psychic: For whatever reason, many people like being part of a "select group." They like being helpful and having a chance to influence the plans of big companies. "It's nice to have a vote," says William Southerland, editor of the *Springfield News-Leader,* whose family is part of Nielsen's panel. Nielsen guarantees that all data will remain confidential.

How to tighten the net around the market makers? Nielsen enlisted, via hefty cash payments, the cooperation of every major supermarket chain in town, enabling those that did not have electronic scanners to install them. Instead of relying on consumers' say-so about their shopping—an old-fashioned method employing handwritten diaries—Nielsen asks its shoppers merely to offer the supermarket cashier an ID card. Nielsen taps highly detailed data on their purchases—the brand, the size, the price—from the supermarket's electronic cashier terminals to its computer in Green Bay, Wisconsin.

The final piece in the puzzle: the media component. How to deliver commercial A to one group of Springfield market makers and commercial B to another? Here's where Nielsen has a new wrinkle over its market research competition. Its competitors rely on cable. But many marketers believe that looking only at cable households can skew marketing results because people who pay for cable tend to be more affluent.

The solution? Nielsen has established its own broadcast facility in Springfield, next door to the local CBS affiliate. Whenever it wants, Nielsen can replace a regularly broadcast commercial with one of its own choosing by unobtrusively changing the channel on home TV sets. The test commercial can be picked up only by homes equipped by Nielsen with a microcomputer attached to the home TV and telephone lines. The microcomputer also transmits to Nielsen what channels the family watched and when.

Naturally, Nielsen can't commit airwave piracy and broadcast its clients' commercials over those of other advertisers. So Nielsen broadcasts the test ads only in airtime the client has already purchased—a boon for local TV stations. In cases where clients want to test advertising "weight"—will increased adspending more than pay for itself in new sales?—one group of households might see a lot of commercials for the product in question, while the other group sees ads for the advertiser's other products or public service spots.

Nielsen chose Springfield not only because its population mirrors the demography of the nation as a whole but also because it is an isolated media market. With St. Louis and Kansas City both more than 140 miles away, Springfield viewers aren't exposed to TV outside Nielsen's net. Nielsen also has enlisted the local newspapers, which deliver different coupon inserts and run-of-print ads to Nielsen's target groups. To ensure that it knows every last influence on consumer purchasing, Nielsen collects information in the grocery stores on all displays and promotional pricing.

Source: Pamela Sherrid, "Big Brother in Springfield," *Forbes,* 2 December 1985, pp. 210-211. Reprinted by permission. © Forbes Inc., 1985.

dating the organization's MIS, the more likely they are to use it to aid their decision making. Managers must understand the structuring of the system; they must make certain that it includes the specific measures and

MANAGEMENT SUCCESSES

Shaklee Corporation

Although the 1980s have been problem-filled years for such organizations as Texaco, Manville, Atari, and Union Carbide, they were years of tremendous growth for Shaklee Corporation. During the previous decade, the San Francisco-based producer of household cleaners, food supplements, and cosmetics increased its sales from $10 million to more than $350 million. But Shaklee managers were concerned about decisions that appeared to be made largely on a subjective and political basis.

A major question facing Shaklee decision makers was whether customers' orders could be filled more rapidly without increasing production or distribution costs. Company planners decided to construct a base of pertinent data for use in making such decisions. The data base consisted of information on plant locations, products made, cost per unit, and production capacity for its three manufacturing facilities and that of its twenty contract manufacturers. It also included details on more than 500 products, 360 customers, and Shaklee's 100 distribution centers. Once the data were collected, a model was developed that allowed Shaklee managers to consider alternative delivery requirements and the effect that each customer response rate would have on transportation costs, the cost of operating distribution centers, and the cost of carrying products in inventory.

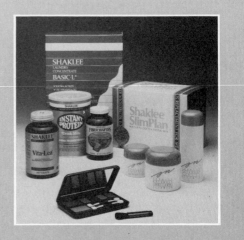

The model not only allowed Shaklee to cut delivery time to customers, it also produced an $850,000 savings in operating costs in a single year. In addition, the data base could be utilized to analyze other operating problems and opportunities that might arise. But development costs were considerable. It cost $250,000 and took six months to develop the data base and construct the model. In addition, annual maintenance costs are estimated to total $50,000. However, Shaklee executives are delighted at the expenditure. They estimate that for every dollar spent in the system's development, they will recover $100 over a five-year period.

Source: The description of the early development of Shaklee's MIS is contained in "'What If' Help for Management," *Business Week,* 21 January 1980, pp. 73-74.

analytical activities they require. Generalized information systems do not exist: each must be designed with the specialized needs and preferences of the ultimate users.

A third characteristic of a successful MIS is that the system is based on disaggregated data files. The disaggregated data file is the core of the successful information system. New data inputs are added to the data base of existing data. Since information systems tend to increase their levels of sophistication over time, disaggregated data files provide the necessary flexibility to permit a variety of alternative uses, analyses, and combinations of data as needs change. In the early stages of MIS development, it is difficult to anticipate the direction of future advancements. Aggregate data files may prohibit future modifications. Disaggregated data files furnish the flexibility for systems evolution.

The final characteristic distinguishing successful information systems from the unsuccessful attempts of MIS designers is that system development has proceeded to increasing levels of sophistication through a process of gradual evolution. MIS sophistication can usually be increased much more readily than the abilities of managers to use it. As managers gain experience in working with well-organized and accessible data, they become increasingly interested in and prepared to use more advanced analytical procedures. The successful system evolves to levels of greater sophistication in response to management's ability and desire to use these expanded capabilities.[19]

CONSTRUCTING AN INFORMATION SYSTEM ▬▬▬

The first step in the development of the MIS is obtaining the total support of top management.[20] MIS design must be from the top down, and top management must oversee its development and evolution. Systems designed from the bottom up tend to accumulate too much data since subordinates are required to speculate on the information needs of their superiors. In too many cases, technical staff are given the assignment of building the system. In such cases, the typical outcome is expressed in management's complaints of a system that does not fit their information needs.

Design and development of an effective MIS is a complex and time-consuming assignment for most organizations. A period of several months or even a year or more is often necessary to pretest the system before installation, to complete the necessary training for both MIS systems personnel and the user-managers, and to involve users fully in the design of the system. A systematic approach to design and implementation should increase the likelihood of producing a useful, cost-effective MIS.

COMMON MIS MISTAKES

In studying hundreds of companies, many of which have been successful in establishing effectively functioning information systems and many others which have failed in their MIS design efforts, Wharton professor Russell Ackoff has identified five common—and deadly—MIS mistakes.[21] Designers and users who make the following mistakes are almost assured of an ineffective, expensive information system.

Mistake 1: Give them more. Most information systems are designed on the assumption that the critical deficiency under which managers operate is insufficient information. Although most managers do lack a good deal of information that they should have, their major informational deficiency is an overabundance of irrelevant information. Most managers receive too much data, not too little.

Mistake 2: Managers need all the information they want. Most MIS designers "determine" what information is needed by asking managers what information they would like to have. This is based on the assumption that managers know what information they need and want. It ignores the belief on the part of many managers that receipt of large volumes of data is indicative of their importance in the organization. Consequently, they are likely to request virtually every report available and then ignore them.

Mistake 3: Give managers the information they need and their decision making will improve. It is frequently assumed that if managers are provided with the information they need, they will then have no problem in using it effectively. This is not necessarily true.

Mistake 4: More communications means better performance. One characteristic of most information systems is that they provide managers with better current information about what other managers and their departments are doing. Underlying this provision is the belief that better interdepartmental communication enables managers to coordinate their decisions more effectively and hence improves the organization's overall performance. Not only is this not necessarily so, but it seldom is. One would hardly expect two competing companies to become more cooperative because the information that each acquires about the other is improved.

Mistake 5: A manager does not have to understand how an information system works, only how to use it. Most MIS designers seek to make their systems as user-friendly as possible to managers with very easy access to the system and assurances that they need to know nothing more about it. This leaves managers unable to evaluate the MIS as a whole and frequently results in their delegating much of the control of the system to its designers and operators. No MIS should ever be installed unless the managers for whom it is intended are trained to evaluate and control it rather than be controlled by it.

SUMMARY

Management information systems are potentially valuable means of institutionalizing the planning and controlling processes by integrating the various analytical techniques, models, and vast quantities of data. Information systems are structured, interacting complexes of people, machines, and procedures designed to generate an orderly flow of relevant information for decision making. The MIS performs six functions: data assembly, processing, analysis, storage and retrieval, evaluation, and dissemination.

Management information may be divided into three major categories: strategic planning, management control, and operational control information. Each type of information varies in scope, source, time horizon, requirements for accuracy, and frequency of use. Information flows must be tailored to meet the specific needs of managers at different levels in the organization.

The MIS is made up of three primary components. The data bank consists of raw data as assembled, recorded, and stored. The second component, the analytical methods bank, is responsible for processing and analyzing the various data inputs. The model bank consists of the various mathematical models used in analyzing and solving problems.

Although information systems are tailored to meet the needs of each organization, they may be compared on the basis of five dimensions: information recency, management access time, level of information aggregation, degree of analytical sophistication, and relative system authority. Successful information systems have the following characteristics:

- The system is founded on management's conception of the decision environment.

- The user-manager understands and is involved in the construction of the system structure.

- The system is based on disaggregated data files.

- System development has proceeded to increasing levels of sophistication through a process of gradual evolution.

Constructing a successful information system involves gaining the support and involvement of top management. The MIS should be designed from the top down, and users should be involved in its development. The system should be pretested before installation, and both systems personnel and the user-managers should be trained in its use. Such a systematic approach to design and implementation should increase the probability of success.

SOLVING THE STOP ACTION CASE

Fisher Camuto Corporation

When it decided to launch its 9 West retail chain, the company wanted to get maximum advantage from its vertical integration. Information had to flow daily from the stores to corporate headquarters and then to the manufacturing plants so production could be stepped up on hot sellers and slowed down on the poor performers. Information now is relayed overseas via teletext, but plans call for a satellite linkup.

Given the large number of colors and styles of shoes which it offers, the firm also needed a sophisticated system which could track a wide range of inventory variables. "Being able to align our production schedules to sales performance in the stores is a tremendous advantage," noted Ken Scharf, the firm's vice president and director of MIS.

"We could have written a software package for our IBM mainframe, but that would have taken at least a year, and we had to move fast. Instead, we bought a Qantel supermini, which cost less than the software for the IBM would have."

Fisher Camuto has opened about 30 of its 9 West stores so far, and plans call for 200 units within the next three years. Scharf said the System 64 Supermini, which it purchased from MIS Qantel, Inc., Hayward, California, should easily handle the data which will be generated by those outlets. . . .

The payoff is square footage sales which are well above the industry standard, the firm claims. "We know right away what is selling, and we're able to test certain styles before going into full production," Scharf said. "We know how to optimally shift our inventory to regions of the country where a particular style is selling, and we can reduce out-of-stocks and quickly mark down poor performers by knowing what's hot and what isn't.

"We can tell what sales are during each hour of the day so that we have adequate staff on hand during peak times. The computer gives us a wealth of data."

Source: "MIS Lets Shoe Manufacturer Set Today's Production Schedule Based on Yesterday's Sales in Its Stores," *Marketing News,* 1 February 1985, p. 27. Reprinted by permission.

FACT OR FICTION REVEALED

1. Fiction   2. Fact   3. Fiction   4. Fiction   5. Fiction   6. Fiction   7. Fact

MANAGEMENT TERMS

management information system (MIS)
data
information
data bank

data base
analytical methods bank
model bank
information recency

management access time
information aggregation
analytical sophistication
system authority

REVIEW QUESTIONS

1. Explain each of the functions of a management information system.

2. Identify the major categories of management information.

3. Distinguish between a data bank and a data base.

4. Contrast the three components of the MIS.

5. Explain the role of the computer in an information system.

6. Identify and briefly explain the bases for comparing information systems.

7. Explain the relationship between the analytical sophistication in an MIS and system authority.

8. What characteristics are typically present in a successful information system?

9. Explain the value of disaggregated data files.

10. What is the first step in MIS design? Why is this step so critical?

PROBLEMS AND EXPERIENTIAL EXERCISES

1. The dispatcher environmental control system of American Airlines has removed pilots from the days when flight crews would assemble hours before a departure to sit down to study winds, temperatures, potential storm areas, and other information such as the plane's takeoff weight. Weather information is received twice daily and the data—winds, weather, anticipated payload for each type of aircraft, and other factors—are used to program the trip. Evaluate the American Airlines system on the basis of the five MIS characteristics discussed in this chapter.

2. Three major categories of management information were discussed in this chapter. Briefly explain each category, and identify the various groups in your college or university who are likely users of each type.

3. "MIS is just a newfangled term for electronic data processing." Do you agree? Justify your answer.

4. Relate the bases for comparing information systems to the following:
   a. manager of accounting department
   b. industrial sales manager responsible for Ohio and eastern Illinois
   c. manager of manufacturing subsidiary

5. Relate the "five deadly MIS mistakes" to the characteristics of successful information systems. Which characteristics does each mistake disregard?

MANAGERIAL INCIDENT: West American Hospital Association

The West American Hospital Association is an organization of hospitals in the greater Los Angeles area, including Palm Springs and San Diego to the east and south and Kern County to the north. Included among its several activities are support of research projects at laboratories at several hospitals and medical schools, dissemination of research findings, and provision of medical specialists to outlying, smaller institutions.

Of growing concern to the Association has been the problem of whole-blood distribution among the hospitals in the Southern California area. Blood supplies are maintained by most hospitals but, through necessity brought about by perishability and uncertain demand, these are small in quantity and often do not include an adequate representation of different blood types. As a result, most hospitals, particularly the smaller ones, often find it necessary to locate quantities of whole blood on an emergency basis, telephoning each nearby hospital and supply point until some can be found with which the holding institutions can part without endangering their own operations. De-

(Continued on next page.)

livery is effected by automobile. This procedure is time-consuming and expensive.

The Los Angeles Metropolitan Hospital has installed a fairly large computer system for research, statistical, and operational uses and has offered the services of this system to the Hospital Association for purposes the Association deems appropriate. The computer system has the ability to handle teleprocessing on a real-time basis. This means that computer users can enter data, programs, and perform other work with the system using remote terminals that employ typewriters or other input-output devices. A prospective user need only dial the appropriate number on a telephone associated with his terminal and he has the use of the system through his input-output device, which is connected to the computer by telephone lines. The computer system operates so fast that many such terminals can be using the computer at once with no appreciable time delay for any one user. Moreover, the computer system is able to handle these teleprocessing functions while at the same time performing the tasks required of it by Los Angeles Metropolitan Hospital.

The Hospital Association is considering the establishment of a centralized whole-blood distribution center to serve the emergency needs of the member hospitals. Blood of each type must be replenished each day to bring it to a specified quantity. All withdrawals and receipts must be immediately recorded so that any hospital can determine immediately the type and amounts of blood available. Deliveries can be made on an emergency basis by helicopter provided by the California Highway Patrol.

The Association has hired a professor from a nearby college with an extensive data processing program to advise it as to how the computer system at Los Angeles Metropolitan Hospital could be used in the operation of the centralized blood-bank system.

Questions and Problems

1. Prepare a report that describes a system that would maintain up-to-date records of the quantities of different blood types available in the centralized blood bank.

2. Evaluate your proposed system using the five MIS comparison bases discussed in this chapter.

Source: Reprinted with permission of Macmillan Publishing Co., Inc., from *Information Systems for Modern Management* by Richard W. Brightman. Copyright © 1971 by Richard W. Brightman.

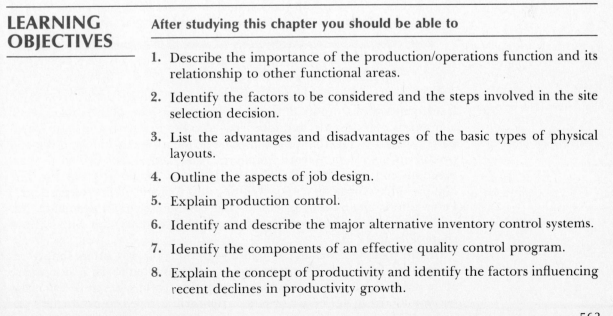

LEARNING OBJECTIVES

After studying this chapter you should be able to

1. Describe the importance of the production/operations function and its relationship to other functional areas.

2. Identify the factors to be considered and the steps involved in the site selection decision.

3. List the advantages and disadvantages of the basic types of physical layouts.

4. Outline the aspects of job design.

5. Explain production control.

6. Identify and describe the major alternative inventory control systems.

7. Identify the components of an effective quality control program.

8. Explain the concept of productivity and identify the factors influencing recent declines in productivity growth.

STOP ACTION CASE

Jaguar Cars, Ltd.

Sleek, slick—and more trouble than they were worth. And they were worth a lot. Such was the word on Jaguar. Selling for at least $25,000, the cars were known for faulty parts and all too frequent breakdowns. Thus, Jaguar buyers often found themselves in the role of the well-heeled chump. When enthusiasts described the British luxury vehicle as "the best car on the road—when it's on the road," they assumed that it spent a considerable portion of the year in auto repair shops for needed repairs and adjustments.

Although Jaguar generated rave reviews for design, comfort, luxury, and handling, the negative image resulting from its recurring quality problems prevented the firm from attracting customers from the ranks of people who purchased such luxury imports as Mercedes, BMW, Peugeot, Saab, and other European models. Buyers of such models expected quality levels to be in line with their sticker prices, and—in the eyes of many—Jaguar simply didn't measure up.

When Jaguar's parent company, British Leyland Ltd., installed John Egan as chairman of Jaguar Cars, Ltd., the firm's top management stressed the fact that things had to change. Egan's marching orders were clear: Turn the company's operations around or close them down.

To stop the Courtny, England–based unit's financial hemorrhaging, Egan set corporate sights on the manufacture of a better car—and one produced efficiently. But before he could accomplish these objectives, he would have to devise systems for improved quality control, reduced inventory costs, and lowered worker costs for each Jaguar produced. The new Jaguar manager faced a formidable task.

Use the materials in this chapter to recommend a course of action for Jaguar Cars, Ltd., that will improve product quality and reliability and enable the company to maintain a competitive position in the luxury car market.

Production/operations function involves processes and activities necessary to transform various inputs into goods and/or services.

The *production/operations function* consists of the processes necessary to transform various inputs into goods and/or services. Honda takes steel, aluminum, glass, plastic, and hundreds of other materials and component parts; puts them together at a Marysville, Ohio assembly line; and the end product is a Civic or Accord. Similarly, Mike Ditka transformed the tremendous individual talents of such players as Walter Payton, Jim McMahon, Mike Singletary, Otis Wilson, and William ("the refrigerator") Perry into a magnificent machine—the Chicago Bears, a dominant National Football League team over the past five years and Super Bowl champions in 1986.

In the past, the production/operations function was often simply referred to as *production*. This term was usually restricted to the manufacture of tangible items. As the economies of the world's developed nations became increasingly service-oriented, the term evolved to production/op-

MANAGEMENT FACT OR FICTION

	FACT	FICTION		FACT	FICTION
1. Production control is of less importance for service industries than for industries that manufacture tangible products.	☐	☐	5. Quality circles may result in improved quality and more efficient production, but they are likely to have an adverse effect on employee motivation.	☐	☐
2. An estimated 30 to 40 percent of factory jobs existing today will eventually be replaced by automated robots.	☐	☐	6. The EOQ model balances the cost of ordering additional inventory with the costs involved in holding idle inventory.	☐	☐
3. The three primary factors influencing the location of new manufacturing facilities are climate, location of customers, and availability of industrial parks.	☐	☐	7. The level of U.S. productivity, measured in terms of production per worker, is less than that of Japan.	☐	☐
4. Production of large cumbersome products, such as shipbuilding, home construction, and airplane production is likely to involve a fixed position layout.	☐	☐	8. Theory Z combines the positive characteristics of both Theory X and Y.	☐	☐

The materials in this chapter will assist you in separating management fact from fiction. Your answers can be checked on page 605.

erations management in order to encompass the creation of intangible services as well as the production of tangible goods. In this chapter, production and production/operations are used interchangeably to refer to the function in either manufacturing or nonmanufacturing settings.

Successful production/operations methods are varied. The inputs can range from basic raw materials to NFL draft choices. And the production processes and activities can range from assembly lines to weight programs and training camps. But the key ingredient in all of these situations is effective management, which is able to put all of the components together and produce a quality product or service.

Once the inputs have been determined, the two primary activities of the production/operations function are (1) systems design and (2) production planning and control. These are managerial tasks. Managers determine what system will be used to produce the product or service. While the designs may differ, the underlying concept is that design is a controllable managerial decision. Thus, University of Michigan head football coach Bo Schembechler relies primarily on the running game for his team. By contrast, Florida State's Bobby Bowden uses a pro-type passing attack.

The football illustration is also applicable to the second production management activity—production planning and control. Sportscasters often ask athletes and coaches about the "game plan" for an upcoming contest. The football addict is well versed in such "production planning and control," with sequences such as "establish the running game, then attack the seams of their zone." In short, Joe Paterno's game plan for Penn State is not at all unlike the various planning and control sequences used in a Dresser Industries plant.

RELATIONSHIP OF PRODUCTION TO OTHER FUNDAMENTAL AREAS

The production/operations function is only one part of the total management system. Admittedly, it is an extremely vital component of any organization, but other activities are also of critical importance. The three major areas of most organizations—whether they produce goods or services or are profit or nonprofit oriented—are production, finance, and marketing. All of these activities must be performed efficiently if the organization is to prosper. A political candidacy, for instance, suffers if the candidate or his or her surrogates are advocating unpopular or misunderstood issues (production); if the candidate is unable to raise campaign contributions (finance); or if a media campaign is seen as unattractive by most voters (marketing). All three areas plus dozens of others like personnel, accounting, and engineering affect the accomplishment of organizational goals.

The Chrysler Corporation is an excellent example of this interrelationship. The ailing auto maker's market share shrunk to about 8 percent during 1979, and many people doubted the continued viability of the company. But Chrysler—under the leadership of board chairman Lee A. Iacocca—took a three-pronged approach to turning the company around. First, a critical cash flow problem was countered by extensive lobbying efforts to get $1.5 billion in federal loan guarantees. Then the company announced a new marketing program known as the "Chrysler Guarantees" designed to get people to try Chrysler models and move the firm's market share to over 10 percent. The new program consisted of a thirty-day or

1,000-mile moneyback guarantee; free scheduled maintenance for two years or 24,000 miles; a two-year membership in a motor club; and a $50 check for people who would test-drive a Chrysler product and then buy it or a specified competing model within thirty days. Meanwhile, Chrysler was also working toward an improved product. Its management credited improved attitudes among employees as the primary reason for a quality improvement of 32 percent during 1979 (as measured by repairs per 100 owners). By 1982, it had increased its market share to 9.9 percent. In 1983, it repaid the government loans far ahead of schedule. Chrysler's financial position continued to improve dramatically during the following years. In 1984, net income of $2.4 billion shattered all-time Chrysler records and retail sales increased 31 percent, boosting Chrysler's North American market share to 11.6 percent. The Chrysler example clearly illustrates the interrelationships that exist between production and other functional areas within the organization.

While the production/operations function must operate within the confines of its interrelationship with other functional areas, its relative importance can be seen by its sheer size compared with that of other functional areas like marketing, finance, accounting, and personnel. In most businesses, managers of the production/operations function employ the largest work force and are responsible for most of the controllable assets within the organization.[1] If for no other reason, the size of the production function attests to its relative importance within the overall organization.

BASIC TYPES OF PRODUCTION SYSTEMS

Two basic types of production systems are utilized in transforming human and materials inputs into finished goods and services. One is based on continuous flows and the other on intermittent flows. A *continuous flow production system* is a process designed to produce a standardized product that is carried in inventory. Typically, this type of system relies on an assembly line operation. An *intermittent flow production system,* by contrast, is used to make products in accordance with purchase specifications contained in separate contracts. No inventory is stored. The firm's production capability is kept ready for contracts that might be obtained. An intermittent production system is often referred to as a *job shop.* A print shop is a common example.[2]

Some industries use both types of production systems. Consider the housing sector, where some homes are custom built according to architectural design (an intermittent flow production system). Others are constructed according to a limited number of building plans in an assembly line style (a continuous flow production system).

PRODUCTION SYSTEMS FOR SERVICES

Most services use an intermittent production system. Doctors, dentists, electricians, plumbers, and accountants often reason that each of the prob-

> ❝ The reason a lot of people do not recognize opportunity is because it usually goes around wearing overalls looking like hard work. ❞
>
> Thomas A. Edison

MANAGEMENT SUCCESSES

Emergency One

Next month, after 153 years of production, the last fire truck will roll off the quarter-mile-long assembly line at American LaFrance in Elmira, New York. American LaFrance once ruled its marketplace as well as any American company ever dominated a business. But the parking lot is mostly empty now, and it's hard to find a person in Elmira who clearly understands why the company is closing up shop. . . .

Why does a company like American LaFrance fail? How could the company allow its products, identified by the familiar American LaFrance chrome eagle, to fall woefully behind the competition? How, in the last few years, could it blow a preeminent franchise built on the sweaty brows of eight generations of craftsmen?

The answer will be found 1,000 miles south in Ocala, Florida, home of Emergency One, an upstart in the fire truck business. In only eleven years, Emergency One has grown from a tiny operation in an entrepreneur's barn to a $51 million enterprise. The company has become the leading maker of American fire trucks and last year earned $3.4 million pretax doing it.

More than 50 trucks a month roll out of Emergency One's bustling factory, bordering busy I-75 in central Florida. The reason for the bustle is disarmingly simple—a new idea. The bodies of Emergency One's trucks are aluminum, mounted on steel chassis. That doesn't sound like a big deal, unless you're running a fire department on a tight budget. Unlike steel trucks, made for years by Amer-

◖ HUSH) . . . Another Breakthrough from E-One

ican LaFrance and others, aluminum doesn't corrode when exposed to salt and water. Though aluminum is more expensive than steel initially, fire departments in brutal proving grounds such as Chicago and Boston have reason to believe aluminum will be cheaper in the long run.

So here is point one. Undeterred by the no-growth nature of the fire truck market and seeing a chance to catch hidebound competition asleep at the wheel, Emergency One levered itself into the market with an innovation. It has already captured about 15 percent of a fragmented market and aims to raise that to 25 percent in a few years. As Robert Wormser, a gruff, self-taught metal designer and founder of Emergency One, succinctly puts it, "We weren't confused by tradition. . . ."

But Emergency One's triumph is built on more than a new metal. Emergency One is a lively place. The parking lot is overflowing, the work force is young and bright-eyed, happy to work overtime, perhaps eyeing a profit-sharing pot, which last year poured out a half-million dollars to be divvied up by 270 people on the payroll. By contrast, American LaFrance suffers from hardening of the corporate arteries. "It took so long to do things at American LaFrance," explains a former employee now with Emergency One. "Many of the people there are conservative thinkers, not used to quick change," adds another.

Point two: While American LaFrance requires six months to turn out a basic fire truck, Emergency One assembles one in 45 days. Why the difference? Revolutionary design and assembly by Emergency One. American LaFrance hand-drafts blueprints of each order. The process can take a week. Emergency One does the same thing in a few hours on IBM computer-aided design (CAD) machines.

From there, time-saving grows more pronounced. Emergency One starts assembly with cartloads of aluminum extrusions, metal already shaped by aluminum fabricators before arriving at the assembly line. The pieces are quickly fitted together into a body which then is mounted on a chassis. American LaFrance, one of its dealers says, "builds trucks the same way it did when I first came there more than 30 years ago." The process starts with flat sheet metal, which must be punched, bent, ground, polished, fitted and filled, not to mention the parade of paperwork snaking through the factory as individual parts travel from department to department for modification.

Emergency One's disadvantage of working with aluminum, a more expensive metal, thus is turned to its advantage because it can assemble a fire truck with 25 to 30 percent less labor. Not only is quick assembly a key selling point, it also reduces working capital tied up along the assembly line. That's important to fire truck manufacturers. The trucks range in price from $40,000 for a small pumper up to $450,000 for a top-of-the-line aerial truck, and manufacturers don't get paid until the trucks are driven away.

Point three: Even Emergency One's selling efforts smack of creativity absent from American LaFrance. Last year, Emergency One gained a toehold in Boston by lending the fire department there several new-model trucks. Sales executives lived at the firehouse and went out on 60 fire calls. Boston bought. Another example: The company flew 20 West Coast fire chiefs to Florida to drive trucks purchased by other departments back out to the coast. Five of those fire chiefs have already bought and another five are nibbling. Emergency One even gives away a small fire truck each year in a drawing from sales card leads returned by mail, a relatively inexpensive way to build a prospect list.

Finally, the obvious question. Why aren't competitors turning out caravans of aluminum fire trucks? Fact is, steel fire trucks still outsell aluminum, though steel's share is dropping as Emergency One's share grows. In the short run, evidently, sticking with tradition is cheaper than retooling, retraining and rethinking for what is, as noted, a no-growth market. But if Emergency One can make good on its goal to sell 1,000 fire trucks a year, up from 600 in 1984, there will be more casualties in a market that sells only 4,000 units a year.

Tradition, then, is a two-edged sword in this sleepy little market that Robert Wormser invaded, luckily with a welding torch instead of a marketing survey. "If competitors have any sense," Wormser growls, "they will make aluminum trucks. But I'm not worried about that. They've already had 11 years to do it. They haven't."

Source: John Merwin, "The Limits of Tradition," *Forbes,* 20 May 1985, pp. 112, 115. Reprinted by permission.

lems they confront is different and that each requires a different approach or production system. In short, the traditional viewpoint has been that services cannot be standardized. Therefore, the use of the continuous flow production system has been deemed inappropriate for most service activities.

But basic productivity questions are changing this scenario. Economic growth is lagging, and there is a real need for greater productivity in the service sector, which is expected to account for about 75 percent of the U.S. economy by 1990. Tradition has it that productivity improvements account for about 67 percent of U.S. economic growth. So the only major gains must come from improvements in service productivity.

Theodore Levitt of the Harvard Business School believes that the service sector must, and can, be industrialized in a fashion similar to what occurred in the production of tangible goods. Levitt argues that this is a management responsibility and that society cannot wait for a technological breakthrough to achieve the industrialization. He points out, for example, that Eli Whitney's widely acclaimed 1798 production line used concepts available since the 1300s. Whitney offered a managerial breakthrough, not a technological one.

Levitt's thesis is that industrialization can be accomplished in services if society concentrates less on greater efforts and more on revisions of the service offering. Avis' "We try harder" philosophy will produce fewer gains than Midas' specialized muffler service, according to Levitt. He argues, "What's required is to apply the analysis and organization that are commonplace in manufacturing to service."[3]

ESTABLISHING PRODUCTION/OPERATIONS SYSTEMS

The first step in establishing a production/operations system is to identify clearly the product or service that is to be produced. But this is only the first step. Various other decisions are required. These include site selection, physical layout, job design, production control procedures, inventory control systems, and quality control requirements. Each step involves a series of management strategy decisions. Operating managers are involved at various stages, playing an integral role in the creation of the overall production system.

PRODUCT/SERVICE PLANNING

Identifying the product or service to be produced requires the best efforts of virtually every component of the organization: research and development (R&D) engineers, design engineers, financial planners, human resources departments, production experts, and marketers. Conflicts are common among different functional areas, but cooperation is an absolute necessity.

Product/service planning begins with research and development efforts designed to develop offerings that will fill marketplace needs. Products and services—whatever their technological merits—must be capable of being produced efficiently and must be sought after by consumers. Each year, Du Pont spends 6.5 percent of its total sales on research and development. In 1985, this amounted to a $1.2 billion budget aimed at discovering new technologies and developing new products. Approximately 27 percent of the R&D budget was directed at basic research and turning existing technologies into marketable products, including pharmaceuticals and new agricultural plant forms.[4]

As potential product ideas emerge from the research and development efforts of firms such as Du Pont, they are then evaluated in terms of their ability to meet buyer needs. Marketing research is essential if the product is to be accepted by consumers or industrial buyers. Even Thomas Edison once remarked: "Anything that won't sell, I don't want to invent. Its sale is proof of utility, and utility is success." Production management also plays a role here. Goods and services must be produced efficiently if they are to be priced within the means of buyers. Henry Ford's assembly line was able to reduce production costs to the point where many American households could acquire an automobile during the early 1900s.[5]

PRODUCTION PROCESS DECISIONS

Of the hundreds of production process decisions, the most basic one concerns how the various inputs are going to be transformed into outputs. As Figure 18–1 illustrates, this is the conceptual foundation of any production/operations system.

Production process decisions cover a wide range, such as whether to make or buy various inputs, the feasibility of the planned product or service, the exact configuration of the process system, equipment selection, and product routing. Several factors impact on these decisions. Consider a situation in which economic considerations force the manager to study ways to automate his or her facility to make the operation more efficient. In fact, automation is now a commonplace production process decision. Even Chinese egg rolls are sometimes made by a machine to keep up with demand for the product.

AUTOMATION AND THE USE OF ROBOTS

A fundamental task of any production/operation system involves determination of the most effective blend of human resources and machinery in converting raw materials and components into finished goods and services. The development of machinery to perform manual work activities previously performed by people has made mass production possible. The

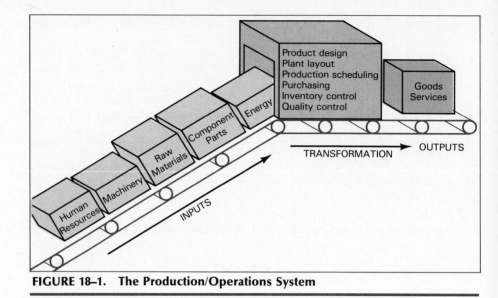

FIGURE 18–1.   The Production/Operations System

Automation is the process of performing a mechanical operation by means of automatically controlled equipment with little or no human involvement.

Robot is a programmable machine used in performing repetitive tasks involving programmed manipulation of tools and materials.

natural extension of mechanization is *automation,* the process of performing a mechanical operation with either minimal involvement of people, or complete automatic control.

During the past decade, automation has made significant impact on factories throughout the world. Although Japanese producers have been the innovators in using automated facilities to raise quality levels while reducing costs, automation is being accepted in dozens of industries in the United States and throughout the world as a method of reducing costs and freeing workers from boring, repetitive, and even dangerous tasks that can be performed by machines.

Automation of the workplace is typically accompanied by the use of robots. *Robots* are programmable machines capable of performing repetitive tasks involving pre-programmed manipulation of tools and materials. General Electric plants throughout the United States currently use more than 600 industrial robots in the production of products as diverse as dishwashers, jet engines, and locomotives. The robots handle tasks in all phases of the production process from materials handling, machining, welding, and assembly to inspection and storage. By 1986, General Motors had some 4,250 robots in use in a variety of manufacturing applications. By 1990, GM expects to have more than 14,000 robots in operation. GM robots can paint cars, recognize different body styles, and can even exchange work assignments should one robot break down.

Automation is having a significant impact on today's factories. General Motors plans to concentrate 90 percent of its machine expenditures in computer-controlled equipment and to reduce employment by 2 to 3 percent annually. Meanwhile, a fully automated factory is already being constructed in Japan. An estimated 30 to 40 percent of factory jobs existing today will eventually be replaced by automated robots.

The primary benefits of automation are cost savings and increased productive efficiency. In a mass assembly operation, automation could possibly produce sizable financial benefits both to the company and to consumers through reduced prices. Automation also offers the advantage of freeing people from mundane tasks, allowing them to concentrate on potentially more rewarding activities. Possible productivity improvements of 20 to 30 percent have made industrial robots a $400 million industry. The Robot Industries Association reports that at least 34 major U.S. manufacturers and 32 major distributors are currently active.[6] But automation also carries a high cost in terms of reduced employment opportunities and purchasing power within the community. Admittedly, many of the displaced workers will find jobs in other areas, although retraining may be required. Still, *technological displacement,* as the loss of employment owing to technological changes is called, can be traumatic for the individuals involved. And there is no assurance that their skills will always be transferable to another industry.[7]

Technological displacement is the loss of employment due to technological changes.

COMPUTER-AIDED DESIGN AND MANUFACTURING (CAD/CAM)

In recent years, a growing number of producers have been expanding the use of computers into both product design and the manufacturing process. *Computer-aided design (CAD)* is the use of special computer programs and graphics to design products. Computer-created three-dimensional images allow product designers to test proposed new products without actually having to build them. Designs can be sketched on an electronic drafting board or directly on a computer screen. They can then be subjected to simulated tests of such factors as temperature variations, wind resistance, seam stresses, and even accidents. The original design can then be modified based upon the results of these tests to produce a final design. This can be accomplished in a shorter time period and for much less cost than the previous techniques of relying upon product mock-ups and a series of tests, product modifications, and more tests before developing a final product. CAD systems are frequently used in such industries as aerospace, automobile, and other complex manufacturing systems.

Computer-aided design (CAD) involves use of special computer programs and graphics to design products.

The three photographs in Figure 18–2 show how the appearance of a manufacturing part can be simulated through this approach. The first photograph displays an image of a machine tool cutter as it crosses a cylindrical surface. The actual operation of this tool can be simulated, analyzed by humans, and modified as necessary to meet performance requirements. The part can also be stress-tested by computer before it is made.

As the second photograph shows, *computer-aided manufacturing (CAM)* picks up where CAD stops. Once the machine tool cutter part has been designed, it is manufactured by a computer-controlled machine. The com-

Computer-aided manufacturing (CAM) refers to use of computers to control machinery used in the production process.

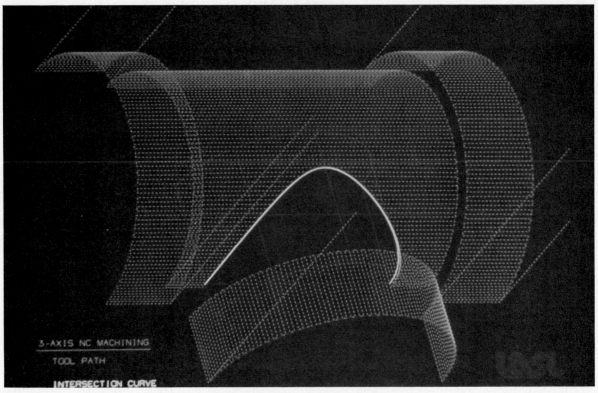

Computer-aided design (CAD)

Computer-aided manufacturing

The finished part

FIGURE 18–2.   Using CAD/CAM in Tool Design and Manufacture

Sources: Top photo courtesy Los Alamos National Laboratory. Bottom photos courtesy McDonnell Douglas Automation Company (McAUTO).

puter issues instructions to machinery used in the production process, enabling manufacturers to use rapid-speed, automated tools and machinery on small production runs and in producing customized products. The result in this instance is the finished part shown in the third photograph.

Combining computer-aided design and manufacturing (CAD/CAM) with other specialized computers that plan and schedule materials can produce a flexible manufacturing system that integrates all the elements of the production process. This "factory of the future" would use computer-driven systems to control every phase of production.

SITE SELECTION

The process of site selection consists of various stages that follow a generally sequential order. These stages are:

1. Select the general area

2. Select generally acceptable communities

3. Select sites within the communities

4. Determine a method of evaluating community-site combinations

5. Compare sites and select one.

The actual method of evaluating potential sites will vary with the specific circumstances of the decision. One commonly used procedure is a point rating system in which the relevant decision factors are identified and then weighted with a specific number of points. The site alternatives are then graded on each factor, and the one with the highest score is considered the most desirable. If one factor is absolutely essential, then a minimum score should be specified. Sites not meeting this minimum are not considered further.

LOCATION FACTORS

Newly formed businesses are typically located wherever the entrepreneur happens to reside. Early expansion is usually into nearby or familiar areas. Later, other variables become important. Numerous factors can influence a location decision. These can be categorized as (1) market-related factors, (2) tangible cost factors, or (3) intangible factors.

Market-related factors involve the location of buyers and the competition. If the company plans to provide a service to senior adults, it should probably be located in an area with an aged population. Similarly, some firms prefer to locate in areas where there is limited direct competition. Market proximity is a prime advantage in industry location. For instance, the Delmarva poultry industry (located on the Delaware-Maryland-Virginia peninsula and made popular by the Frank Perdue ads) has a prox-

> **❝** Everything is more complicated than it seems. **❞**
>
> Murphy's Law

imity advantage over other poultry-producing areas because of its closeness to the huge consumer markets of the Northeast.

Market-related factors are particularly important for retailing firms and service providers. Ron Lubben, president of the Chicago center for the Institute of Store Planning, points out that earlier criteria for selecting retail sites "used to be whether there was decent exposure from the road and if there was a large enough population base."[8] But, as one writer points out:

> Changing demographics and technology have forced retailers to reevaluate their approach to site selection. Automobile transportation has helped open up new residential areas and led to the development of regional and convenience shopping centers . . . Because of the increased number of site choices and a more marketing-oriented approach, retailers are probably more aware than ever of what their primary trade area must look like. Toys "R" Us, the Rochelle, New Jersey–based retailer, requires a market of at least 250,000 people, of which 25 to 28 percent must be children. The market must also be large enough to support four stores, each of which will be located on the path of a major shopping mall.[9]

Tangible cost factors include transportation, utilities, labor, taxes, site costs, and construction costs. Other things being equal, management would prefer cheap, nearby transportation; low utility costs; a ready supply of low-cost but skilled labor; a modest tax structure; and minimal site and construction costs.

Human resource costs account for a major part of the difficulty facing U.S. textile manufacturers in competing with foreign-made products. U.S. apparel workers now average $7 an hour in wages and benefits, compared with $1.74 in Singapore, $1.62 in Hong Kong, and 86 cents in South Korea.[10]

The variations in tangible cost factors require a careful balancing on the part of management. No site meets 100 percent of a firm's ideal standards. Consequently, management is forced to balance favorable and unfavorable factors and choose a site that provides the most favorable blending of all factors.

Intangible factors include local attitude toward industry, zoning and legal regulations, room for growth, climate, schools, churches, hospitals, and recreational opportunities. Some industries have only minimal need to be located near markets, supply sources, or transportation modes; thus, their location decisions are based more on amenity factors such as desirable living conditions for their employees. The population movement to the Sunbelt partially reflects the role of these intangible factors.

PHYSICAL LAYOUT

All phases of production/operations must be carefully considered to design an efficient production facility. A number of alternative layout designs are available. In addition, the necessary inputs at each step of the production/

operations process must be considered and a materials handling system must be designed to blend smoothly with the choice of physical layouts.

BASIC LAYOUTS

There are three basic types of layout: product layouts, process layouts, and fixed position layouts. Each type of layout has a number of advantages and disadvantages, and the production/operations manager must consider a number of factors in choosing the most appropriate type. Major influences in the choice of layout include nature of the product or service, production volume, weight factors, building costs, production mix, and relative fragility of the finished product.

Product Layout. As Figure 18–3 indicates, the *product layout* involves some type of linear flow of the various work activities performed. This design is common in assembly lines and cafeterias. The flow line layout is also used in military induction centers.

The primary advantages of this type of layout are its simplification of production planning and control and the ability to utilize unskilled workers who can quickly learn the tasks involved. In addition, both materials handling and overall processing time are reduced. On the other hand, the product layout is only as strong as its weakest link since each step depends upon all other steps. Products cannot flow through the line faster than the slowest task to be performed. Moreover, this is a relatively expensive type of layout that typically involves substantial investments in special-purpose equipment. Finally, worker monotony often occurs with the product layout approach.

Process Layout. Sometimes the most appropriate physical layout is based on a department grouping or a division on the basis of each process to be

FIGURE 18–3.   Example of a Product Layout for Product on Assembly Line

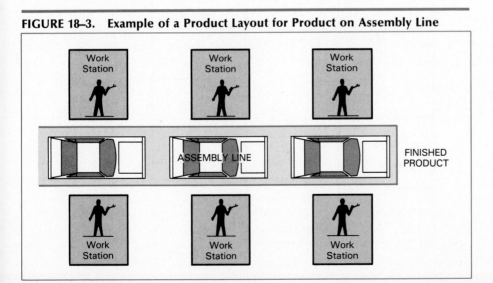

performed. In such instances, all equipment and personnel performing the same activity are separated into departments or groups. Figure 18–4 illustrates the *process layout* by describing the various processes involved in the production of a wooden desk. Insurance claims offices, colleges and universities, banks, and automobile repair shops are other examples of this approach to physical layout.

Since the personnel in each department are likely to perform a larger number of tasks than would employees in a manufacturing facility using a product line layout, the process layout approach has the advantages of flexibility of equipment and personnel and increased worker satisfaction because of the diversity of tasks. In addition, the process layout approach typically requires a smaller investment in equipment because duplication is not necessary unless volume is large. Finally, expertise is developed since the supervisors for each department become highly knowledgeable about their functions.

A major shortcoming of this approach involves costs and reduced efficiency. Backtracking and long movements may occur in materials handling, thereby lowering efficiency in this area. In addition, timing inefficiencies may occur, with work having to wait between tasks. Since workers must have broad skills, higher wages than those paid to assembly line workers may be necessary to attract qualified employees. Because each job is different, there are different setups and operator training requirements. Frequently, the result is lowered productivity.

FIGURE 18–4.   Example of a Process Layout for a Wooden Desk

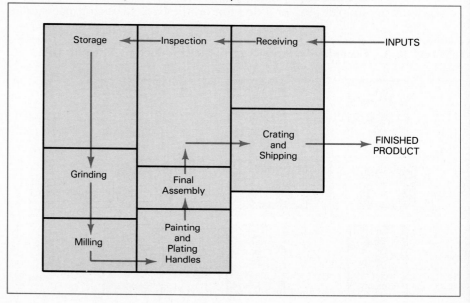

Fixed Position Layout. Shipbuilding, home construction, and the manufacture of products like airplanes and computers follow a *fixed position layout.* This format is typically used for large or fragile products that cannot be readily moved from place to place. Figure 18–5 shows the use of this approach in aircraft production, where workers, machinery, and pre-assembled parts are brought to the stationary product.

Since movement of the work item is minimal, it is less likely to be damaged during the production process. A second advantage of this layout approach is that since the item does not go from one department to another, there is more continuity of the assigned work force. This reduces the problems of replanning and the need to instruct people each time a new type of activity is to begin.

One disadvantage of the fixed position layout is that since the same workers are involved in more operations, skilled and versatile workers are required. The necessary combination of skills may be difficult to find, and high pay levels may be necessary. Secondly, movement of people and equipment to and from the work site may be expensive. Finally, equipment utilization may be low because the equipment may be left at a location where it will be needed again in a few days rather than moved to another location where it would be productive.

Table 18–1 summarizes the advantages and disadvantages of each type of layout.

FIGURE 18–5.   Use of Fixed-Position Layout in Jet Aircraft Production

TABLE 18–1   COMPARING THE THREE MAJOR ALTERNATIVE PLANT LAYOUTS

Layout Classification	Advantages	Disadvantages
Product	1. Reduced materials handling 2. Reduced total processing time 3. Simplified production planning and control systems 4. Simplification of tasks, enabling unskilled workers to learn tasks quickly	1. Facility modification may be required if product changes 2. Product cannot flow through the line faster than the slowest task can be accomplished unless the task is performed at several work stations 3. Large investment for special-purpose equipment 4. Dependence of the whole on each part 5. Worker monotony often occurs
Process	1. Personnel and equipment flexibility 2. Smaller investment in equipment 3. Expertise developed by supervisors, who become highly knowledgeable about their functions 4. Work more satisfying for people who prefer diversity because of wide variety of tasks	1. Lack of materials handling efficiency 2. Lack of efficiency in timing 3. Complication of production planning and control 4. Higher wages for workers with broad skills result in higher costs 5. Different setups and operator learning required for different jobs result in lowered productivity
Fixed Position	1. Reduced damage and costs of moving the product 2. Reduced need for continual replanning and instruction because of continuity of work force	1. Higher wages for workers with broad skills result in higher costs 2. Moving people and equipment to and from work site may be expensive 3. Equipment utilization may be low

ENERGY CONSIDERATIONS

An important ingredient in production decisions concerning the most efficient layout is efficient utilization of energy inputs. Not only is energy an important cost component in production, it can be an effective avenue for further cost savings. Moreover, since energy supplies are limited, minimizing the use of such energy inputs as electricity, oil, and natural gas increases the likelihood of its continued availability.

An excellent example of a state-of-the-art energy management system is located at IBM's Tucson, Arizona facility. The heating and cooling needs of the eleven buildings in the complex are controlled by two IBM computers. Thirteen thermal storage tanks hold hot and cold water for use in heating and cooling. Even the buildings are turned at angles designed to cut cooling costs. The complex has two wells that supply a self-contained water system. All water used at the plant is recycled.[11]

A growing number of firms are producing their own power by taking advantage of previously wasted by-products of their production processes. The world's largest paper mill, a Union Camp facility located in Savannah, Georgia generates sufficient energy to produce seven million pounds of paper and paperboard a day. The plant, shown in Figure 18–6, uses a process called cogeneration in which both steam and electricity for operating the facility are produced in the same power plant.

FIGURE 18–6.   Use of Cogeneration to Reduce Energy Costs in Power-Intensive Industries
Source: Reprinted by permission of Raytheon Company.

Now the world's largest paper mill runs on its own power.

Seven million pounds of paper and paperboard a day, every day. That's the capacity of Union Camp's mill in Savannah, Georgia. Yet, paper production—even in these enormous quantities—is, after all, what a paper mill is all about.

Production of electricity, however, is *not* ordinarily what a paper mill is all about.

But this is not your ordinary paper mill. This one has the capability of being self-sufficient in electricity.

The secret? Cogeneration—the production of both steam and electricity for industrial processes in the same power plant, utilizing energy that might otherwise be lost.

For engineering and design, Union Camp chose United Engineers & Constructors, a Raytheon company. With the new system in place, Union Camp now enjoys the best of two worlds: they maintain their record production while greatly reducing the cost of the fuel and electricity required to do it.

Cogeneration is a concept that's sparking wide interest throughout power-intensive industry, and United has several such assignments in various stages of planning and construction. All these projects are natural extensions of United's long experience in designing and engineering for both utilities and industry, experience that positions them solidly in a market that is expected to total $30 billion between now and the year 2000.

United Engineers & Constructors is an important part of Raytheon, a five and a half billion dollar company in electronics, aviation, appliances, energy, construction, and publishing. For our latest financial reports, write to Raytheon Company, Public Relations, 141 Spring Street, Lexington, MA 02173.

MATERIALS HANDLING

Materials handling is the physical movement of materials and products within a work facility.

Materials handling is the physical movement of materials and products within a work facility. It can range from an overhead crane used in a factory to a robot that delivers and picks up mail in a larger office. In manufacturing operations, the primary pieces of materials handling equipment are conveyors, industrial trucks, and cranes and hoists. Substantial cost and efficiency benefits can stem from effective use of materials handling equipment. Chrysler, for example, was forced to shut its Dodge Main assembly plant in Hamtramck, Michigan, in 1980 because the eight-story factory was outdated. Dodge Main's thirty-two freight elevators were no longer competitive with automated single-floor plants.

JOB DESIGN

Job design is a process of task delineation necessary to meet various personal, work, organizational, and environmental requirements.

Job content consists of work activities assigned to a particular job.

The choices of physical facilities location and the most appropriate process flows are crucial for production/operations management. Of equal importance is the careful design of the jobs necessary to perform the activities involved in converting production inputs into finished products and services. *Job design,* discussed earlier in Chapter 9, refers to the process of task delineation necessary to meet various personal, work, organizational, and environmental requirements. The job that is eventually specified should be technically, economically, and behaviorally feasible. Job design includes both job content and the physical environment in which the job is performed.

Job content refers to the work activities that are assigned to a particular job. The early Gilbreth studies identified seventeen therbligs, or motions, involved in work. The Gilbreth research illustrates job content research at its most micro level. Other basic questions concern the degree of job specialization, relative use of machines (see the section on automation), job enlargement, and job enrichment (see pages 379–380).

THE PHYSICAL ENVIRONMENT

The physical environment has a considerable impact on work effectiveness. In fact, an entirely separate field of study—human engineering or ergonomics—has been created to deal with this aspect of production management. *Human factors engineering* applies relevant information about human characteristics and behavior to the design of things people use, how they are used, and the environment in which people live and work.

Human factors engineering is the application of information about human characteristics and behavior to the design of tools and the work environment.

Human factors engineering is concerned with such subjects as tool design and environmental factors like temperature, noise, and lighting. But safety may be one of its most important topics. Production management always regards an improved safety record as one of its highest priorities.

The Occupational Safety and Health Act of 1970 set up an administrative agency, the Occupational Safety and Health Administration (OSHA), to oversee the protection of workers on the job site. Most private employers are required to comply with the safety and health standards set by OSHA. Some 1,200 OSHA inspectors enforce the agency's requirements, and financial penalties can be assessed for violations.

QUALITY CIRCLES

One of the latest trends in production/operations management is the use of *quality circles,* volunteer groups of employees who meet on a regular basis to identify, discuss, and recommend solutions to problems affecting the firm's output. A typical circle is comprised of five to ten workers who are paid for the time devoted to such meetings. Such programs are designed to provide job satisfaction through participation. In addition, they may result in employees becoming more intimately involved in designing various aspects of their own job activities.

Quality circles are volunteer groups of operative employees who periodically brainstorm on how to increase the firm's output, improve quality, or improve the efficiency of the work place.

Quality circles are used extensively in Japan and are increasingly common in the United States. General Motors, Ford, American Airlines, and Martin Marietta are examples of U.S. firms using this concept. The sponsoring firm typically expects to recoup its investment through improvements suggested by the circle members, and substantial cost savings have indeed been reported. One quality circle at a Westinghouse plant near Baltimore produced a $22,000 cost saving with the simple idea that one employee report to work fifteen minutes early in order to turn on some wire-bonding machines. The result was that other workers were no longer idle during the machine startup time.[12]

PRODUCTION CONTROL ████████████

One would think that Wendy's with its 256 kinds of hamburgers, would face a difficult production control problem. However, the multitude of combinations is a product of the number of burgers used in a Wendy's and the eight condiments and cheese that are offered. Wendy's outlet managers are able to resolve their product control situation by training their cooks to begin grilling a hamburger as soon as someone drives up outside. With only five basic products, Wendy's knows that a vast majority of its customers will buy a hamburger.

Wendy's situation may be somewhat simplistic as compared with that faced in many manufacturing operations, but the concept is basically the same. *Production control* is a system designed to produce maximum output with minimal input contributions, and at the lowest possible cost. Production control can be thought of as a series of sequential steps. The starting point is aggregate output planning. This is followed by resource allocation and activity scheduling.

Production control is a system designed to produce the maximum output with minimal input contributions and at the lowest cost.

A model of the production planning and control system is shown in Figure 18–7. Decisions involving output objectives, allocation of human, material, and energy resources, scheduling of activities, and control are made to produce the desired level of goods and services at predetermined quality levels.

MANAGEMENT FAILURES

The Firestone 500 Automobile Tire

In a recent article, John J. Nevin, chairman, president, and chief executive of the Firestone Tire & Rubber Company, described the problems resulting from the Firestone 500 radial tire.

It was a different story at Firestone when, in 1978, the National Highway Traffic Safety Administration concluded that the Firestone 500 radial tire had caused an exceptional number of accidents, injuries, and deaths, and therefore, should be recalled. In this case, the effort to resolve a safety issue because of the conflicts between a company and an agency of the federal government became one that the parties sought to resolve in the courts, congressional hearing rooms, and the news media rather than a testing laboratory.

Firestone officials were willing to admit that the field adjustment rate on this tire was substantially greater than those of other Firestone tires at that time. However, they insisted that the Firestone 500 was not unsafe. In looking

back at the situation, Firestone chief executive Nevin now feels that the company should have voluntarily withdrawn the tire from the market and made replacement offers to its purchasers rather than wait for the NHTSA to demand a recall.

There was no credible evidence from which to conclude that the 500 was unsafe, but Firestone had good reason to conclude that the 500 would not meet the expectations of its owners. When the problem arose, Firestone had a seventy-five year history of product ex-

AGGREGATE OUTPUT PLANNING

The first step in production control is to forecast the overall output over a specified time period such as a month or year. Aggregate figures such as tons of steel were traditionally used, but computer models now make it possible to forecast specific products rather than some standard measurement of the product mix.

Aggregate output planning has two basic objectives. The first objective is to determine whether the planned output is feasible. This step prevents the company from making impossible commitments to buyers. The operation's capacity limit sets the outside parameters for this assessment since

cellence. A recall of the troublesome 500 tires could and should have been undertaken solely because the tire did not meet the quality and reliability expectations of Firestone's customers.

Nevin has also held senior management positions at Zenith, a firm with a long-standing reputation for quality products. His experiences have led him to two major conclusions about business, its products, and its customers.

The first is that customer satisfaction should be assigned the highest priority in any company. When consumers enter the market to purchase any product, they invariably place more weight on their own past experience than on advertising claims or celebrity endorsements. There is simply no surer way for a manufacturer to give competitors a lift and employees and stockholders a headache than to deliver a product that does not meet the expectations of its buyers.

Nevin's second conclusion is that the currently popular notion that the quality of products produced by U.S. workers is inferior to Japanese output is a myth. Repeating this myth is also an injustice to the men and women who work in American factories.

Zenith's television receivers—consistently rated by consumers as higher in quality than competing Japanese-made sets—were built in plants in Springfield, Missouri, at the edge of the Ozarks, and on Chicago's West Side. More than 70 percent of the work force in the Chicago plants came from Chicago's black or Spanish-speaking minorities. These Americans, who would describe themselves as hillbillies, blacks, or Hispanics, consistently matched or exceeded Japanese quality and performance standards.

Nevin's closing comment summed up his faith in the capabilities of U.S. manufacturing: "The idea that American workers cannot manufacture products of the highest quality is bunk."

Source: Quotations from John J. Nevin, "The Importance of Quality," *Business Week's Guide to Careers,* Spring/ Summer 1985, p. 19.

the building of additional facilities is considered a long-range rather than an intermediate-range project.

The second objective is to optimize the costs and other inputs necessary to meet a planned level of output. A given production level can be reached by a variety of methods. The key is to determine the optimal mix of inputs.

Many of the techniques discussed earlier in the planning section are applicable here. Aggregate output planning is basically a forecasting problem and is subject to solution by trial and error, intuition, linear programming, and a variety of othe techniques—depending on the particular situation.

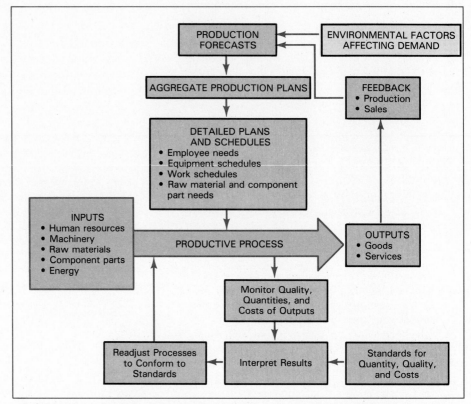

FIGURE 18–7.   Model of the Production Planning and Control System
Source: Adapted from Elwood S. Buffa, *Modern Production/Operations Management* (New York: Wiley, 1980), p. 159. © 1980 by John Wiley & Sons, Inc. Used by permission.

RESOURCE ALLOCATION

The firm's production system results in the transformation of inputs into outputs by the organization. This transformation process requires the careful allocation of inputs—raw materials, employees, financial resources, component parts, and equipment. Resource allocation is an extremely important and complex subject for the decision maker.

One of the basic resource allocation decisions is whether the firm should manufacture or purchase the input. This is often referred to as the *make-or-buy question.* This decision is typically made on the basis of such factors as production costs, transportation costs, availability, quality control needs, and confidentiality requirements.

Value analysis is a common procedure in the resource allocation stage of production control. *Value analysis* is a formal study of purchases to determine the true needs, relative costs, and alternatives in an effort to minimize overall expenditures. Task forces consisting of production, en-

Value analysis is the formal study of purchases to determine needs, relative costs, and alternatives in an effort to minimize total expenditures.

gineering, and purchasing personnel are a common format for implementing value analysis.

ACTIVITY SCHEDULING

Activity scheduling refers to the sequence and timing of work activities so that the transformation process is completed as efficiently as possible. Scheduling typically consists of two activities. First, *loading* refers to the assignment of a job to some designated plant, work center, or department. Second, *dispatching* refers to the actual scheduling of specific activities within a department such as when a certain cut will be made on a given machine.

Activity scheduling is the sequential timing of work activities in an effort to maximize efficiency.

Several analytical techniques are useful in activity scheduling. A Gantt Schedule Chart, such as the one shown in Figure 18–8, can be employed to monitor the current status of a job. In this example, the stand being fabricated is ahead of schedule but the compressor is lagging behind.

The Gantt Chart was developed in 1917, and it was not until 1956–1958 that another major activity scheduling breakthrough occurred. Two new techniques with similar qualities were developed independently of each other during the 1950s. Both used a network format to assist in scheduling.

FIGURE 18–8.   A Gantt Schedule Chart
Source: Reprinted with permission from James B. Dilworth, *Production and Operations Management* 2d ed. (New York: Random House, 1983), p. 282.

Week	1	2	3	4	5	6	7	8	9	10
Obtain Steel	Order			Receive						
Fabricate Stand					Cut	Weld				
Side Panels	Shear	Setup Form	Weld							
Top, Bottom		Shear	Weld							
Compressor	Order				Receive					
Assembly						Assemble Paint				
Wiring								[ ]		
Insulation								[ ]		

[Scheduled Start   ▓▓▓   Actual Progress   Current Date

]   Scheduled Completion   ⊠   Time Reserved for Setup or Maintenance

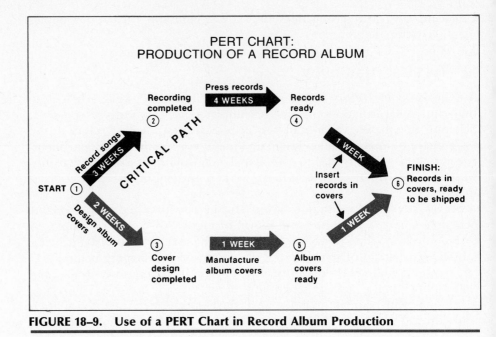

FIGURE 18–9. Use of a PERT Chart in Record Album Production

CPM (Critical Path Method) was created by Du Pont and Remington Rand to improve maintenance and construction scheduling at Du Pont's widespread plants. *PERT (Program Evaluation and Review Technique)* was the product of a joint effort by the Navy, Lockheed, and Booz, Allen & Hamilton. The project was the submarine-launched Polaris missile system. Both CPM and PERT can be used as network scheduling techniques in complex projects involving numerous activities—some sequential and some overlapping.

The illustration shown in Figure 18–9 illustrates the use of these network scheduling techniques. The PERT chart shows the steps in producing a record album, dividing them into separate paths of activities, events, and time periods. Here the critical path is recording the songs and pressing the records. Less time is needed for design and production of the album covers, but the operation will not be complete until the records are ready for shipment.

INVENTORY CONTROL

Inventory control is a method of balancing the need to have sufficient raw materials, work in progress, and finished goods on hand to meet demand with the costs involved in carrying the inventory.

A major component of production/operations control is *inventory control*. Smoothly operating production systems depend upon availability of needed raw materials, component parts, and processed materials and parts. But if excess inventory is kept on hand, the firm will incur unnecessary costs in purchasing and storing materials and parts until they are needed.

Inventory can be defined as any idle resource held for future use. It may take the form of raw materials, partially processed materials, or finished goods that become components of the final product. The typical manufacturer has two years' worth of profits invested in inventory, according to government statistics. In terms of annual sales, inventory accounts for about 13 percent for manufacturers, 12 percent for retailers, and 10 percent for wholesalers.

Manufacturers maintain adequate quantities of inventory on hand for a number of reasons. First, inventory allows production management to fulfill orders immediately, thus cutting or eliminating lead time. In addition, quantity purchases often permit the purchaser to negotiate lower costs, thereby reducing unit costs of the final product. Finally, inventory protects the company from unexpected surges in sales, strikes, and shortages.

TYPES OF INVENTORY CONTROL SYSTEMS

Inventory control systems are typically selected according to the demand situation facing the product being produced. For example, the demand situation may be classified as independent or dependent, based upon whether it is related to the demand for another good.

The most common inventory control systems include fixed quantity systems, fixed interval systems, minimum-maximum systems, budget allocation systems, ABC classification systems, materials requirement planning (MRP), and just-in-time (JIT) inventory systems. Firms using a *fixed quantity system* simply add the same amount to inventory each time it reaches some specified reorder level. The *fixed interval system* is similar to the fixed quantity system. In this case, however, the inventory level is monitored at designated times and then replenished to some predetermined amount. The *minimum-maximum* approach to inventory control involves checking inventory levels at designated times. However, no reorders are placed unless an inventory level is below some specified minimum.

Retail managers are likely to use the *budget allocation* method in inventory control. An overall dollar budget amount is established, and, within these limits, department managers are given flexibility in determining the precise mix of inventories they wish to have available for their customers.

The *ABC classification* format for inventory control groups accounts for inventory items according to their relative importance. The classification is typically based on the annual expenditures for such items. Inventory items labeled as *A items* are considered more critical and, therefore, would require close control. Other categories (B and C items), would receive relatively less attention.

MATERIALS REQUIREMENT PLANNING

Dependent demand situations call for an alternative inventory control system. *Materials requirement planning (MRP)* is such a system. This widely used system is frequently found in production operations involving com-

Materials requirement planning (MRP) is a computer-based method to ensure that needed component parts and materials are available at the right time and place without stockpiling unnecessary inventory.

plex products assembled with parts and materials secured from outside suppliers. The basic function of MRP is to make certain that needed raw materials and component parts are available at the place where they are needed when they are needed without stockpiling unnecessary inventory. The 1987 Fiero is made from over 10,000 components purchased by Pontiac from hundreds of outside suppliers. To perform this function while depending upon hundreds of suppliers to provide thousands of production inputs, the typical MRP system utilizes computer programs to store and retrieve needed data in addition to maintaining a perpetual inventory count and making automatic placement of additional orders when materials and parts are needed.[13]

MRP begins with the master production schedule and the scheduled quantities of materials and parts needed, as well as the dates on which each quantity is needed. After determining what components and materials are needed, the program refers to the time involved between placement of an order and its receipt. These factors are then used to determine what should be ordered, when it should be ordered, the size of the order, and the supplier to be contacted. The result is availability of materials and parts as they are needed.

JUST-IN-TIME INVENTORY CONTROL SYSTEMS

Just-in-time (JIT) inventory control is an inventory control system designed to minimize inventory at production facilities.

A new approach to inventory borrowed from the Japanese is rapidly gaining acceptance in the United States. This approach, known as the *just-in-time (JIT) inventory control system*, involves minimizing inventory on hand at each production facility and eliminating stockpiles. The JIT system, known in Japan as *kanban*, is designed to deliver parts and materials to each production step precisely when they are required for the production process.

Production managers benefit from such a system because of the marked reduction in inventory carrying costs. At Hewlett-Packard, parts inventories are set at a single day's production needs. As each part goes onto the assembly line for installation as part of a finished H-P product, it automatically reorders for the next day's production.

Chrysler board chairman Lee Iacocca points out that JIT inventory control systems were used in the U.S. auto industry sixty years ago:

> As far back as the 1920s, when the ore boats used to arrive at Ford's River Rouge plant, that ore was turned into steel and then to engine blocks within twenty-four hours. But during the boom years between 1945 and 1978, the American car industry fell into some bad habits. One of the many changes we made was to speed up the way our parts and supplies reached the assembly plants. For example, we used to ship transaxles by train from Kokomo, Indiana, to Belvidere, Illinois. By switching to trucks, we got them there the same day, which streamlined the whole operation. After a few months, our just-in-time system became so efficient that when our Detroit engine plant staged a wildcat strike, our assembly plant in Windsor ran out of engines four hours later![14]

One result of the move to JIT systems has been the relocating of supplier firms in close proximity to their industrial customers. When General Motors Corporation decided to emulate the Toyota City approach of their Japanese competitor by modernizing its Buick City complex in Flint, Michigan, the firm's management installed a JIT inventory system. The firm's primary supplier of steel components, Kasle Steel, constructed a $7.5 million facility adjacent to the Buick plant. One result is the ability of Kasle Steel to meet the Buick requirement of delivering needed materials every four hours. As General Motors Corporation chairman Roger Smith stated, "The old ways of dealing with suppliers are as obsolete as a hand crank to start a car."[15]

ECONOMIC ORDER QUANTITY

A number of different costs are associated with inventory. Some rise when inventory levels increase: the costs of capital, storage space, taxes, insurance, deterioration, and obsolescence. Still others decrease with higher inventory levels: the costs of ordering, setup, production control, and missed sales. In addition, larger inventory purchases may permit quantity discounts. Production management is responsible for balancing these various costs (which can be roughly classified as either holding or order costs) and achieving the best order size—the so-called *economic order quantity (EOQ)*.

The graphical determination of EOQ is shown in Figure 18–10. Economic order quantity can also be calculated from the following formula:

Economic order quantity (EOQ) is a method of achieving optimal order size, based on a balancing of the various costs associated with inventory.

FIGURE 18–10.   Graphical Determination of EOQ

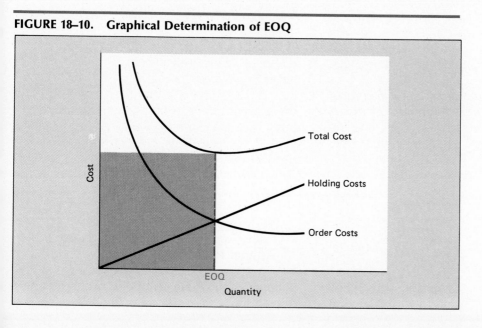

COMPUTERS IN MANAGEMENT

Inventory Control by Laser

Bar codes will soon be appearing on everything from hospital patients to hand grenades.

Grocery shoppers have been growing familiar with the codes since 1973, when the supermarket industry introduced its Universal Product Code. The black and white stripes, when passed over a laser beam, help speed checkouts. In fact the system was developed earlier, in the 1930s and in 1967 the railroad industry adopted it to trace the movement of rail cars.

Today the codes are going almost everywhere. "Bar coding can go on any product, whether it's an automobile or a shipment of caviar," says John Hill, former president of the Materials Handling Institute.

In a bar code, a string of numbers or letters is represented by thin and wide lines on a label. These characters have access to information about the product through a computer memory system. A scanning device shines a ray of light across the bars to record or confirm the bar code. Such information as the product's maker or its country of origin is encoded in the lines.

The coding systems, also popular in Europe, Japan and Britain, are favored for their speed in tracking the movement of goods and accuracy in identifying products, which saves companies money.

In 1967, for example, General Motors installed the system at its Oldsmobile plant in Flint, Mich. The system cost $25,000 to install but it replaced a manual record keeping system that cost $75,000 in salaries, says Edmund Anderson, president of Automatic Identification Manufacturers Inc.

Workers at Ford Motor Co. plants scan bar codes on auto parts to send information about damaged items to repair shops. Workers at Southeast Paper Co., in Dublin, Ga., use the codes to keep track of containers they handle. The hospital industry is poised to put bar codes on patient-identification bracelets to better record their medical histories. And Nicholas Turkey Farms in Santa Rosa, Calif., uses the system to trace its best turkey stock, burying a bar code in each hen's tail so that it can be scanned when the bird produces an egg with a healthy chick inside.

$$EOQ = \sqrt{\frac{2 \times \text{Order Costs} \times \text{Annual Usage}}{\text{Annual Holding Costs}}}$$

Consider the following example of how an economic order quantity would be calculated at a furniture store:

The registration form for runners in last year's New York Marathon used a bar code to record a name, identification number, average scoring time, and predicted finishing time.

Last March, the health industry adopted a standard to track cartons entering and leaving hospitals. At American Medical International Hospital in Beverly Hills, Calif., employees will soon use badges with bar codes on them, enabling scanners to record their check-in and check-out times.

The U.S. Army also adopted the codes two years ago, to identify all government shipping containers, helicopters, furniture, cars and even gasoline pumps. "You drive up to a pump and scan the vehicle, and bill it directly to the correct department," says a Pentagon spokesman. In three years, bar coding will appear on grenades, bombs and guns.

Domestic automakers have one of the most sophisticated bar-coding technologies. Today, the Automotive Industry Action Group, a bar-code trade association, is studying ways to use the system to automatically route parts to shipping docks, delivery trucks and storage areas, as well as shelves for inventory control. Group members plan to create a bar code standard for distinguishing labels used in the auto industry, like the Food and Drug Administration's Universal Product Code. Standardized bar codes will increase and speed organizing among auto vendors.

More than 130 companies comprise the bar coding business, which turns over $250 million of equipment annually. They make such tools as electromagnetic wands, laser scanners and high-speed printers, some creating up to 900 bar codes each minute.

The industry is dominated by small businesses, but such giant companies as Hewlett-Packard Co. and General Electric Co. have bought into the growing market.

Bar coding isn't without its bugs. An electrical engineering trade group developed its own secret codes but discovered none of them could be read, at least by a U.S.-made scanner. And some retail and grocery-store cashiers complain that their scanners too often bleep red, for an inaccurate output, when they should bleep green. Theresa Sugar, a cashier at a Giant Eagle grocery in Pittsburgh, says that sometimes she must run a food item over the scanner three or four times before it registers. Frequently she winds up punching in the price on her register herself.

Industry experts predict more efficient technologies will leave bar coding behind over the next two decades. But for now, studies indicate that they are more accurate than competing identification technologies such as optical character recognition (block-form digits used in retail stores) and the magnetic stripes usually found on bank cards.

Source: Linda M. Watkins, "Bar Codes Are Black-and-White Stripes and Soon They Will Be Read All Over," *Wall Street Journal*, 8 January 1985, p. 39. Reprinted by permission.

Veneer Furniture Company handles several lines of furniture, one of which is the popular Layback Model T chair, which the company purchases from a plant only ten miles from the store. Since the source is so near, Veneer has not bothered to stock a large number of the chairs in its warehouse. Instead, it sends its truck to "pick up a few" when there is none on the showroom floor. Slim Veneer, the owner, has observed that many times when he needs his truck to make a delivery, it is tied up making trips to the Layback plant, and he suspects his ordering practices may not be optimal. He has decided to use the EOQ model to determine the best quantity to obtain in each order.

Mr. Veneer has determined from past invoices that he has sold about 200 chairs during each of the past two years at a fairly uniform rate, and he expects to continue at that rate. He has estimated that preparing an order; paying for the driver, truck, and invoicing; and other variable costs associated with each order are about $10, and that it costs him about 1.5 percent per month, or 18 percent per year, to hold items in stock. His cost for the chair is $87, so it costs him $0.18 \times \$87 = \$15.66$ to hold a chair for one year. (Of course, a chair does not stay in stock that long, but Slim uses annual usage rates, and the holding costs must be based on the same unit of time as the usage rate. He could use a monthly-use rate and the cost to hold a chair for a month. Any other time base could be used, so long as it was used for both the usage rate and the costs to hold an item.) Veneer's calculations show that

$$EOQ = \sqrt{\frac{2 \times \text{Order Costs} \times \text{Annual Usage}}{\text{Annual Holding Costs}}}$$

$$= \sqrt{\frac{2(10)(200)}{15.66}} = \sqrt{255.43} = 15.98 \text{ units}$$

He has, therefore, told the buyer that each time she orders Layback chairs, she should order sixteen of them.[16]

SAFETY STOCKS

The inventory control systems discussed earlier deal with replenishment of what is called *cycle stocks,* the amounts that are expected to be used during the cycle established by the particular system. If usage could be predicted accurately every time, there would be no need for inventory beyond the cycle stock. But such is not the case in most instances. So a *safety stock* must be established to protect against unexpected high usage. It can be defined as the inventory kept on hand in addition to the cycle stock—what is available when replenishment orders arrive. Safety stock is particularly important in situations where *stockouts* (a zero inventory situation) are costly in terms of increased production or labor costs, or lost sales.

Production management assumes the major responsibility in matters of inventory control, including the maintenance of adequate safety stocks. Most production processes are contingent upon having adequate, low-cost inventories of both inputs and finished products.

QUALITY CONTROL

Quality controls are the processes and associated tasks designed to assure that a product or service meets acceptable standards. Quality controls have three components:

1. The product or service must be designed to be at least the minimum appropriate grade for its use.

2. It should conform to the standards of the design.

3. The consumer should receive the necessary training and service support so that his or her use of the product is satisfactory within reasonable expectations.

Consistently high quality standards are a major competitive tool for a firm or an industry—in both domestic and international markets. The high cost of product liability litigation is another reason for establishing an effective quality control program.

Quality plays a major role in the ability of U.S. firms to compete in the world market. In Japan, where the phrase "made in Japan" was converted from a symbol of shoddy, inferior goods to one of quality products in a quarter-century, the top industrial prize is awarded each year to the company and person that makes the greatest contribution to raising quality levels. Many of the quality control techniques used by Japanese firms trace their origins to the United States. In fact, the annual Deming prize for outstanding efforts in quality improvement is named for the American W. Edwards Deming, whose quality-control programs were largely ignored in the 1950s and 1960s by U.S. managers, but found a receptive audience among Japanese companies.

A growing number of American organizations are making major strides in enhancing quality levels of their products. Accomplishing these objectives frequently requires better training for workers, re-engineering products, redesigning the workplace, and reshaping attitudes so that the quality of the product is as important as the quantity of goods being produced. Tennant Co., a Minneapolis manufacturer of maintenance equipment for industrial floors, was able to reduce manufacturing defects by 52 percent as a result of a concentrated quality improvement program. It involved at least 40 hours of classroom training for the firm's 1,200 employees, improved business and production processes, and gradual reshaping of worker and manager attitudes about the importance of improved quality and the firm's commitment to this objective.[17]

Some evidence of success in quality improvements is already evident. In 1980, when Hewlett-Packard tested 300,000 semiconductors from three U.S. and three Japanese suppliers, the Japanese chips had a failure rate of one-sixth that of the American chips. When the test was repeated two years later, the U.S. companies had virtually closed the gap. Similar progress has been achieved in automobiles.

> Ford's Ranger trucks, built in Louisville, Tennessee, offer an especially dramatic example. In just three years, the number of "concerns" registered by the Louisville plant (the automaker's measure of quality deficiencies as recorded at monthly audits) dropped to less than one-third its previous high. Today, the Ranger's quality is nearly equal to that of Toyota's SR5, its chief Japanese rival.[18]

QUALITY CONTROL INSPECTIONS

Quality control inspections should take place at three different points in the production process: receiving, transformation, and final inspection. Inputs are checked in the receiving stage to see that they comply with established standards. Quality control checks are also set up during the actual transformation process to assure that standards are being met before further work is done. In some cases, unacceptable items can be reworked before continuing their journey through the transformation process. A final inspection checks the outputs of the transformation process.

FIGURE 18–11.   Final Quality Control Inspection

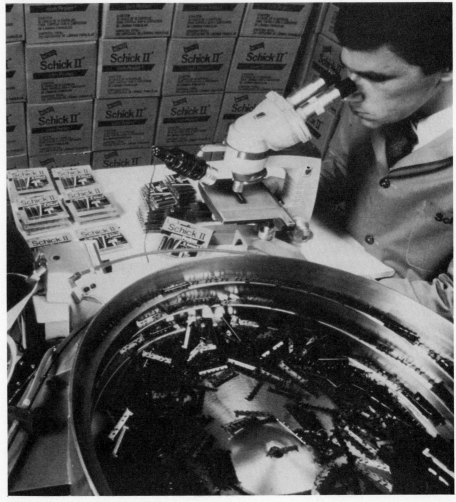

QUALITY CONTROL SYSTEMS

Quality control systems can be classified as 100 percent inspection; sampling by attributes; and sampling by variables. A complete—or 100 percent—quality control plan means that all factors involved in the items are examined to assure that they are 100 percent satisfactory. Inspecting a new aircraft illustrates this type of system since the product must be completely reliable.

Sampling by attributes distinguishes acceptable and unacceptable products or groups of products according to whether the items meet minimum standards. Sampling by variables assesses the variations from standards set for specific product characteristics. Both of these systems may be employed for *acceptance sampling*, which refers to a random sampling plan used to classify a lot as acceptable, as unacceptable, or as one requiring complete screening of each item to eliminate defective items.

Quality control is the final ingredient in the overall production/operations system. It is production management's grading procedure and an important evaluative component of any organization.

Acceptance sampling is a quality control method using random samples to classify a lot as acceptable, unacceptable, or as one requiring complete individual screening.

PRODUCTIVITY

The first census of the United States, conducted in 1790, revealed that over 50 percent of the labor force was engaged in agriculture. Over half of all workers were required to feed the new nation of 3.9 million. In the nearly 200 years since then, vast changes in technology and farm production methods have resulted in crop yields that would have amazed our eighteenth-century ancestors. In 1940, 30 million people worked on farms in the United States. Farm production has increased 600 percent over the past four decades, but the number of farm workers has dwindled to fewer than 3.5 million. Today, 3 percent of the work force feeds a nation of 240 million (and generates surpluses for consumers throughout the world).

Throughout much of its history, growth in other sectors of the U.S. economy roughly paralleled that in agriculture. Technological innovations, a growing work force, and infusions of adequate capital to construct new facilities and equipment for mass production combined to produce productivity increases that sustained economic growth and led to continued improvements in the standards of living for American workers. From the end of World War II through the 1960s, productivity increased at an annual average rate of 3.3 percent. However, during the 1970s, the rate of productivity improvement was only 1.4 percent. Productivity grew at a slightly faster rate of 2.1 percent during 1984, but the annual gain in 1985 amounted to only three-tenths of one percent.[19]

The recent economic ills of the United States and other economies throughout the world have focused increased attention on productivity improvements as the answer to inflation, unemployment, and economic growth. On an aggregate basis, increased production with a given bundle of resources results in a richer nation. More is available for profits, for wages, and for use in achieving social goals. Increases in productivity can offset cost increases in such inputs as energy, materials, and human resources. It is a major factor in determining the competitive position of U.S. firms in the international marketplace. The link between productivity growth and improved living standards makes such improvements major objectives at the national level.

Productivity is also vital to the individual organization, since it reflects the efficiency of a department or a firm. Improved efficiency affects a profit-seeking firm's competitive position, its costs, and its profits. Increased productivity allows a nonprofit organization to provide additional services for the same level of resource inputs.

WHAT IS PRODUCTIVITY?

Productivity is a measure of the output relative to input of goods and services for a nation, an industry, or a firm.

Productivity can be defined as the relationship between the number of units of goods produced and the number of inputs of human and other resources necessary to produce them. It is a ratio of output to input. When a constant amount of inputs generates increased outputs, an increase in productivity has occurred.

Total productivity considers all inputs necessary to produce a given quantity of outputs. Stated in equation form

$$\text{Total Productivity} = \frac{\text{Output (products or services produced)}}{\text{Input (human resources, land, and capital)}}$$

Most productivity ratios focus upon only one of the inputs of the equation: labor productivity or the output per worker per hour. Stated in equation form, partial productivity considers the relationship of output to a single major category of input:

$$\text{Partial Productivity} = \frac{\text{Output (products or services produced)}}{\text{Partial Input (such as worker hours)}}$$

Since productivity—partial or total—is an estimate of outputs for a given amount of inputs, it is a notoriously poor measure, especially for short-term changes. Over longer periods, however, such estimates do indicate real trends. In recent years such trends have been disturbing.

DECLINES IN THE PRODUCTIVITY GROWTH RATE

Although the United States and other nations actually experienced a *decline* in productivity for a period during the severe recession beginning in 1979, productivity rates have continued to increase throughout the twentieth century. The current concerns involve a decline in the *rate* of productivity growth.

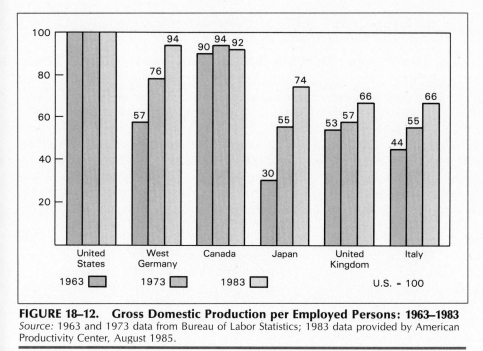

FIGURE 18–12. Gross Domestic Production per Employed Persons: 1963–1983
Source: 1963 and 1973 data from Bureau of Labor Statistics; 1983 data provided by American
Productivity Center, August 1985.

As Figure 18–12 shows, the U.S. output per worker hour is higher than in any other nation. Figure 18–12 compares the gross domestic production per employed worker in Canada, West Germany, the United Kingdom, Italy, and Japan with that of the United States. Although these nations appear to be moving faster than the United States in the drive for productivity, France and West Germany are our closest competitors with 94 percent as much output per worker, while Japan produces only 74 percent of the U.S. output per worker.

Although productivity in the United States is greater than in other nations, the gap is rapidly closing. A number of factors have influenced the decline in the U.S. rate of productivity growth. These include:

- *A decline in the capital-labor ratio.* During the 1970s the growth of capital spending dropped from 3.9 percent a year to 1.4 percent. Capital spending results in the creation of new equipment, factories, machinery, and processes. With more and better tools for the work force, more goods can be produced.

- *Changes in the demographic composition of the labor force.* During the previous decade, some 20 million additional workers joined the U.S. labor force. A great number of them belonged to the baby-boom generation of the 1940s and 1950s and were young and well educated, but unskilled. Not only did the work force expand more rapidly than

MANAGEMENT: THE LIGHTER SIDE

What Happens When Japanese Managers Meet U.S. Production Workers?

Time clocks are banned from the premises. Managers and workers converse on a first-name basis and eat lunch together in the company cafeteria. Employees are briefed once a month by a top executive on sales and production goals and are encouraged to air their complaints. Four times a year, workers attend company-paid parties. Says Betty Price, 54, an assembly-line person: "Working for Sony is like working for your family."

Her expression, echoed by dozens of other American Sony workers in San Diego, is a measure of the success achieved at the sprawling two-story plant, where both the Stars and Stripes and the Rising Sun fly in front of the factory's glistening white exterior. In 1981, the San Diego plant turned out over 700,000 color television sets, one-third of Sony's total world production. More significantly, company officials now proudly say that the plant's productivity approaches that of its Japanese facilities.

Plant Manager Shiro Yamada, 58, insists that there are few differences between workers in the United States and Japan. Says he:

"Americans are as quality conscious as the Japanese. But the question has been how to motivate them." Yamada's way is to bathe his U.S. employees in personal attention. Workers with perfect attendance records are treated to dinner once a year at a posh restaurant downtown. When one employee complained that a refrigerator for storing lunches was too small, it was replaced a few days later with a larger one. Vice-President Masayoshi Morimoto, known as Mike around the plant, has mastered Spanish so he can talk with his many Hispanic workers. The company has installed telephone hot lines on which workers can anonymously register suggestions or complaints.

The firm strives to build strong ties with its employees in the belief that the workers will then show loyalty to the company in return. It carefully promotes from within, and most of the assembly-line supervisors are high school graduates who rose through the ranks because of their hard work and dedication to the company. During the 1973-75 recession, when TV sales dropped and production slowed drastically, no one was fired. Instead, workers were kept busy with plant maintenance and other

the nation's capital formation, but the addition of the younger workers to the labor force reduced its average level of skill and experience.

- *Reduced spending on research and development.* In real terms, spending for research and development (R&D) has declined since 1970. R&D as a percentage of total gross national product declined from 3 percent in 1964 to 2.1 percent in 1977. By 1985, however, it had increased to 2.7 percent.

- *Interindustry shifts.* In recent decades, the U.S. economy has increasingly moved away from basic industries and in the direction of sophisticated electronics, information, and services. Over 50 percent of

chores. In fact, Sony has not laid off a single employee since 1972, when the plant was opened. The Japanese managers were stunned when the first employee actually quit within just one year. Says Richard Crossman, the plant's human relations expert: "They came to me and wanted to know what they had done wrong. I had to explain that quitting is just the way it is sometimes in Southern California."

This personnel policy has clearly been a success. Several attempts to unionize the work force have been defeated by margins as high as 3 to 1. Says Jan Timmerman, 22, a parts dispatcher and former member of the Retail Clerks Union: "Union pay was better, and the benefits were probably better. But basically I'm more satisfied here."

Sony has not forced Japanese customs on American workers. Though the company provides lemon-colored smocks for assembly-line workers, most prefer to wear jeans and running shoes. The firm does not demand that anyone put on the uniforms. A brief attempt to establish a general exercise period for San Diego workers, similar to the kind Sony's Japanese employees perform, was dropped when managers saw that it was not wanted.

Inevitably, there have been minor misunderstandings because of the difference in language and customs. One worker sandblasted the numbers 1 2 6 4 on a series of parts she was testing before she realized that her Japanese supervisor meant that she was to label them "1 to 64." Mark Dempsey, 23, the plant's youngest supervisor, admits that there is a vast cultural gap between the Japanese and the Americans. Says he: "They do not realize that some of us live for the weekend, while lots of them live for the week—just so they can begin to work again." Some workers grumble about the delays caused by the Japanese system of managing by consensus, seeing it instead as an inability to make decisions. Complains one American: "There is a lot of indecision. No manager would ever say do this or do that."

Most American workers, though, like the Japanese management style, and some do not find it all that foreign. Says supervisor Robert Williams: "A long time ago, Americans used to be more people-oriented, the way the Japanese are. It just got lost somewhere along the way."

Source: "Consensus in San Diego," Time, 30 March 1981, p. 58. Reprinted by permission from TIME, The Weekly Newsmagazine, copyright TIME, Inc., 1981. All rights reserved.

the work force is now employed in service industries, which typically are more labor-intensive than manufacturing.

- *Government regulations.* During the past two decades, governmental regulations concerning industrial safety, product specifications, and environmental protection have generated additional costs in equipment and increased paper work. The growth of such regulations may have contributed to reductions in productivity growth rates.

- *Economic orientation to short-term profits.* The continual search for short-term profits may be at the expense of investments designed to create long-term profitability. Critics of well-established, publicly held corporations have argued that short-term measures such as quarterly earnings statements and dividend payments may adversely affect fundamental decisions concerning product innovation and technological development. Although empirical evidence is lacking, critics of short-term thinking frequently point to the Japanese economy and its greater emphasis upon longer-term objectives as a case study in productivity management.

JAPANESE PRODUCTIVITY AND THEORY Z

In attempting to explain the major strides in the Japanese economy in the decades since World War II, a number of writers have analyzed the Japanese workers and their special relationships with their employers. The Japanese approach to management views involved workers as the key to increased productivity. Under this system, employment is a lifetime guarantee. No one is ever dismissed or laid off; each worker participates in decision making; and tasks are rotated to avoid boredom, extreme specialization, and rigidity. The contrasts between organizations in Japan and the typical U.S. organization are shown in Table 18–2.

An estimated 35 percent of Japan's work force is under life-time employment, primarily in large companies and government bureaus. "Lifetime employment means that a major firm or government bureau hires once a year, in the spring, when young people graduate from junior high school, high school, and the university. A major firm that hires only 'rookies' takes on a large inventory of new employees all at once, although it typically does not have work for all of them immediately. Promotions are entirely from within, and a person with one, five, or twenty years at one company will not be hired or even considered by another company. Once hired, the new employee is retained until mandatory retirement at age fifty-five. An employee will not be terminated for anything less than a

TABLE 18–2   COMPARING JAPANESE AND U.S. ORGANIZATIONS

Japanese Organizations	U.S. Organizations
Lifetime Employment	Short-term Employment
Slow Evaluation and Promotion	Rapid Evaluation and Promotion
Nonspecialized Career Paths	Specialized Career Paths
Implicit Control Mechanisms	Explicit Control Mechanisms
Collective Decision Making	Individual Decision Making
Collective Responsibility	Individual Responsibility

Source: William G. Ouchi, *Theory Z* (Reading, Mass.: Addison-Wesley, 1981) p. 58. Copyright © 1981 by Addison-Wesley Publishing Co., Inc. Reprinted by permission.

major criminal offense, and termination is a harsh punishment, since the one who has been fired has no hope of finding employment in a comparable firm and instead must turn either to a minor firm that pays comparatively low wages and offers little security, or else must return to his hometown."[20]

UCLA business professor William G. Ouchi has proposed that U.S. organizations would benefit by adopting many of the characteristics of Japanese organizations, particularly their approach of focusing on employee involvement in every phase of corporate life. This approach, which Ouchi has labeled as *Theory Z,* would provide long-term employment for employees and a sharing of responsibility for making decisions and implementing them. Employees would be provided with varied and nonspecialized experience to broaden their promotion potential and evaluations and promotions would be relatively infrequent.

> **Theory Z** is a management approach emphasizing employee involvement and shared decision making, long-term employment, relatively slow promotions and evaluations, and varied and nonspecialized job assignments.

Ouchi argues that the adoption of Theory Z characteristics by U.S. firms would result in productivity increases and improved worker satisfaction. However, a number of major differences between the two countries exist. Japanese business-government relations are frequently so close that the label "Japan, Inc." has been applied to the entire nation. In addition, the markedly dissimilar cultural backgrounds of the two countries produce great differences in worker attitudes. Although a few attempts have been made to apply Theory Z approaches in such U.S. firms as Hewlett-Packard, Dayton-Hudson, Rockwell International, and Intel, little empirical research has been conducted on its impact in non-Japanese organizations.[21]

A number of writers and practicing managers feel that the Japanese economic miracle is the result of a number of factors. They argue that the Japanese management system alone does not account for the success of Japanese products in world markets. Former ITT chief executive Harold Geneen has made the following observations:

> Japanese labor costs are far below ours; their factories, built there after the devastation of World War II, are newer, more modern, and far more efficient than ours. It costs them $1500–$1800 less to build a car than it costs us. They can afford to invest some of that margin in quality controls that Detroit manufacturers apparently felt were not possible for them up to now. Beyond lower costs, Japanese industry reaps the benefits of all the help their government can give them; because their small island nation is utterly dependent upon its export market, Japan's government and its powerful national banks work hand in hand with Japanese corporations to develop products that will sell abroad and bring wealth into the country. They have a national industry policy. We do not. . . .
>
> Since World War II, when we emerged as the wealthiest and only unscathed industrial power in the world, we have lived off the fat of the land, paying the highest wages in the world while cutting the demands upon the productivity of our labor force; we allowed our factories to age and become obsolete; and, ultimately, we as a people grew slack and flabby. Theory Z touches on none of this.[22]

PRODUCTIVITY IMPROVEMENT

At the federal level, sporadic attempts to deal with the issue of productivity have occurred since 1970 when the National Commission on Productivity was created. In recent years, changes in tax laws and investment credits were designed to stimulate additional investment in private industry.

At the individual firm level, a number of organizations have instituted productivity improvement programs. Among them are General Foods, Corning Glass, Burger King, Hughes Aircraft, and Beatrice Foods.[23] Although the nature of the various programs differs, all of them incorporate three vital ingredients: productivity measurement; organizational commitment; and feedback on results achieved. While such programs demand commitments of both time and effort by managers and operative employees, they have already been proven effective in increasing productivity and improving the firm's competitive position.

SUMMARY

Production/operations consists of the processes and activities necessary to transform various inputs into goods and/or services. Determination of inputs, systems design, and production planning and control are the primary activities of the production/operations function. While production is only one part of the total management system, it plays a key role in any organization.

Two basic types of production systems exist: continuous flow and intermittent flow. The establishment of a production system requires identification of the product or service to be produced, site selection, physical layout, job design, production control procedures, inventory control systems, and quality control requirements. All of these decisions involve a series of component decisions.

Site selection must consider market factors as well as tangible and intangible costs. Physical layout involves decisions concerning materials handling and the basic layout plan (product flow lines, process layout, or fixed position layouts) to be used. Job design must consider job content and the physical environment in which the job is performed. Pro-

duction control involves aggregate output planning, resource allocation, and activity scheduling. Inventory control must be based on decisions as to type of system, economic order quantity, and safety stocks.

The efficiency of a production/operations management system can be expressed in terms of productivity. Productivity is a ratio of outputs to a given quantity of human and other inputs. Although U.S. output per worker hour is the highest in the world, the rate of annual increases in productivity has been declining in recent years. Factors associated with this decline include a decline in the capital-labor ratio, changes in the demographic composition of the labor force, reduced spending on research and development, interindustry shifts, government regulations, and economic orientation to short-term profits. Continuing improvements in productivity are required to maintain and improve organizational profitability, increase worker compensation, achieve social goals, and sustain the United States' competitive strength in the international marketplace.

SOLVING THE STOP ACTION CASE

Jaguar Cars, Ltd.

John Egan initiated numerous changes in Jaguar's production operations in his efforts to produce an improved product at competitive prices. He sped up production lines, installed quality controls modeled on streamlined Japanese precedents, and reduced the number of employees from 10,500 in 1980 to 6,900 in 1982.

Several other basic steps emerged as the means to increased productivity. First, fewer hands doing more jobs translated into greater individual expertise. "Practice really does make perfect, and the fact that the employees are doing more work, more often simply means they're better at it.

Secondly, the company began inspecting output before the production run had finished. "We began inspecting output before the line was done, so we wouldn't find mistakes too late."

On Egan's command, Jaguar also started to play hard ball with its suppliers, stringently inducing them to deliver superior component parts. "We began to lay down much stronger laws for parts," explained Mike Dale, Jaguar's vice-president, marketing for the United States. "If the failure rate rose above 1.5 percent, the supplier then had to not only replace the parts, but pay for the labor to install them."

The combined result of these efforts is an improved automobile and a greatly strengthened image for quality among luxury car buyers. The new image is that the current Jaguar is, as the company advertisement states, "the best Jaguar ever built." The improved reliability image is strengthened by Jaguar's new three-year, 36,000 mile limited warranty.

Today, Jaguar's work force has once again increased to the 10,000-plus mark. But its output has grown even faster. Current annual production is triple the number of Jaguars being produced in 1980. Of equal interest to Jaguar managers, assembly-line personnel, and stockholders is the fact that the elevated production levels are in response to heightened buyer demand for the English motorcar.

Source: Quotations in paragraphs 2, 3, and 4 from Gay Jervey, "Jaguar Pays the Price to Get Back in Hunt," *Advertising Age,* 12 April 1982, p. 4. Updated data supplied by Michael L. Cook, Public Relations Manager, Jaguar Cars, Ltd., August 8, 1985.

"The Best Jaguar Ever Built."

FACT OR FICTION REVEALED

1. Fiction   2. Fact   3. Fiction   4. Fact   5. Fiction   6. Fact   7. Fiction   8. Fiction

MANAGEMENT TERMS

production/operations function
automation
robot
technological displacement
computer-aided design (CAD)
computer-aided manufacturing
   (CAM)
materials handling
job design

job content
human factors engineering
quality circle
production control
value analysis
activity scheduling
inventory control
materials requirement planning
   (MRP)

just-in-time (JIT) inventory
economic order quantity (EOQ)
cycle stock
safety stock
quality control
acceptance sampling
productivity
Theory Z

REVIEW QUESTIONS

1. Differentiate between a continuous flow production system and an intermittent flow production system.

2. Identify the various factors that must be considered in the site selection decision and the stages of the selection decision process.

3. What are the major advantages and disadvantages of each of the basic types of physical layout?

4. Discuss the various aspects of job design.

5. Differentiate among the various inventory control systems.

6. Determine the economic order quantity for a small manufacturer who plans to order 3,500 units of a major product component for the coming year. Each unit costs $50. Estimated costs of placing each order amount to $40, and inventory carrying costs are 20 percent.

7. Identify the components of an effective quality control program.

8. Distinguish between total productivity and partial productivity.

9. Identify the factors influencing recent declines in the rate of productivity growth.

10. What are the major characteristics of a Theory Z organization?

PROBLEMS AND EXPERIENTIAL EXERCISES

1. The typical exploratory oil well in the Anadarko Basin in Texas and Oklahoma costs $5,855,000. Offshore wells are even more expensive. How might this huge expense affect the production process in the petroleum industry?

2. Visit a factory or other production facility. Then prepare a report on what you observed during the visit that relates to one of the following: (a) type of production system, (b) site selection, (c) physical layout, (d) job design, (e) production control, (f) quality control, (g) productivity improvements programs.

3. The number of Americans receiving patents has declined some 25 percent since 1971. But for-eign patent holders have increased 14 percent over the same time span. Comment.

4. Pick a business that interests you. Then develop a study that would identify a new location for this firm. Examples might include a new plant for some locally based company or a new location for a sports franchise.

5. Review the factors influencing the recent declines in the rate of productivity growth. Can any of these factors be eliminated or modified? Should they be changed or modified?

MANAGERIAL INCIDENT: Project Saturn

Nowhere was the impact of the assembly line as profound as in the manufacture of automobiles. For nearly a century, those creeping conveyor belts that Henry Ford borrowed from the meatpacking industry have symbolized Detroit. But that technol-ogy may be reaching the end of the road. Just as Ford Motor Co.'s assembly line became the mainstay of U.S. industry, General Motors Corp.'s new Saturn Corp. subsidiary may pave the way for the elusive "factory of the future."

GM's Saturn subsidiary is a $5 billion bid to do nothing short of revolutionizing automobile manufacturing. The details are still being ironed out, but GM is trying to pull together the most advanced manufacturing technology possible. By replacing the assembly line with a fully computerized production system that extends from the dealer to the factory floor, GM is betting that it can close the estimated $2,000-per-unit gap between its production costs and those of its Japanese competitors.

'PAPERLESS' PLANTS. "It's an exciting approach that transcends just labor costs," says John H. Hammond Jr., director of automotive services at Data Resources Inc. "They can wipe out all of the inertia of the U.S. auto industry with one stroke."

Saturn will change nearly every aspect of auto-making operations. "It really severed all connections to the existing corporate culture," says David E. Cole, a University of Michigan professor who heads the school's automotive transportation program. GM Chairman Roger B. Smith wants his new subsidiary to have its own labor contracts with the United Auto Workers. But most significant, Saturn will tie together GM's collection of advanced technology in robots, machine vision, and computers, which the company has assembled over the past few years. A big part of that integration job will be done by Electronic Data Systems Corp. (EDS), the Texas computer services company that GM acquired for $2.5 billion last year.

Saturn's goal is to drive down costs on all fronts. Direct labor for major power-train components, stamping, and final assembly will be cut to as low as 21 hours per car, down from 55 hours today and nearly 80 hours just five years ago. "Anything in the 25 to 30 hours-per-car range is leading-edge performance in the auto industry today," says Thomas G. Gunn, an Arthur D. Little Inc. vice-president who manages the company's computer-integrated manufacturing section.

GM's EDS has also been directed to make Saturn as nearly "paperless" as possible—minimizing nonproduction staffs and cutting indirect labor costs. The goal is to reduce indirect labor to 30% of the total man-hours needed to build an automobile, considerably less than the 40% average for durable-goods manufacturing.

EDS faces a monumental software engineering task in trying to forge Saturn into what will be the most highly computerized system in basic manufacturing. Computer hardware and software are expected to make up 40% of Saturn's total cost.

GM, which has long been frustrated in trying to get its myriad computer systems to communicate, has already taken a leadership position in developing the procedures that will enable all of its computers to exchange data. EDS is building a network that will hook together computers working in such diverse areas as design, engineering, and purchasing—even hooking up with individual dealers. "We envision all these links

(Continued on next page.)

going out to engineering offices, so if a process isn't working right, you can link right to the engineer who designed it," says W. John Eichler, program director for plant network systems on GM's advanced product and manufacturing engineering staff.

'JUST IN TIME.' Saturn's major departure from traditional auto making will be in bringing component production and assembly together on one site. To cut down on transportation and warehousing costs, the Saturn complex will include at least a half-dozen component manufacturing plants and an assembly plant. This setup will make it possible to create a fully integrated line that could, for example, cast engine blocks, machine them, and assemble the engine.

Such integration will enable Saturn to break new ground in so-called just-in-time parts production, where one day's requirement is delivered directly to the factory floor rather than produced in large quantities for inventory. Observers expect that parts suppliers—some of whom may even set up plants within the Saturn complex—will be linked directly to the central computer to keep closer tabs on production. And to make it possible to make faster design changes, many parts will be produced on machines that can quickly switch from one type of component to another. Parts will also be tested automatically and moved to assembly sites by automatic carts or conveyors as needed.

ROBOT REVOLUTION. Instead of putting together a car piece-by-piece on a traditional moving assembly line, separate teams of workers will put together each of the major Saturn modules. For example, one group will handle the engine and transmission, another will fit together the dashboard with all the gauges and controls, and one will assemble the bumper, grill, radiator, and headlamps into a front-end unit. After testing, these modules will be delivered by computer-controlled vehicles to a final assembly line that combines the modules into finished cars.

Robots will play a far greater role in the process than ever before. Saturn "is going to advance significantly the state of the art in automated assembly," says Jimmy L. Haugen, vice-president for automotive assembly systems at GMFANUC Robotics Corp., the joint venture of GM and Fanuc Ltd., a Japanese robot maker. "It will be the most robotized of any GM plant—and probably any plant in the world."

Robots with limited functions are widely used now in auto assembly plants for such repetitive tasks as welding and painting, but GM plans to take advantage of robots that "see," employing them in a far broader range of tasks on the factory floor. Saturn is expected to use robots to position the sheet metal for car roofs so that other robots can weld them. Robots will also install windshields and possibly rear windows. GMFANUC is working with Saturn on a robot with machine vision that will install car doors. Robots will probably put on the wheels, install the seats, and eventually install the modules in the car.

When the Saturn production lines are up and running in 1988 or 1989, GM expects to be able to manufacture and deliver one of the new compact cars just days after it is ordered. A dealer ordering a car today typically must wait six to eight weeks.

TOP TO BOTTOM. Can GM make it all work? The final proof will not be the technology that Saturn uses but the quality of the car it builds. "If they turn out a dog of a car, it won't matter what they've done with manufacturing systems," says Arthur D. Little's Gunn. However, many observers are convinced that the auto maker has gotten on the right track. "I think GM has really made a very profound decision. What it is doing is top-to-bottom computer-integrated manufacturing," comments Daniel Roos, a professor at Massachusetts Institute of Technology and the co-author of *The Future of the Automobile.*

Even if Saturn doesn't succeed in completely closing the cost gap with the Japanese, the manufacturing technology that it is pioneering seems certain to take U.S. industrial productivity a giant step forward.

Questions and Problems

1. What are the major advantages and drawbacks of a highly automated system such as the GM facility described in this case?

2. Relate the Saturn auto-assembly facility to the following production/operations concepts:
   a. Type of production system
   b. Site selection
   c. Physical layout
   d. Job design
   e. Production control
   f. Quality control
   g. Productivity

Source: "How GM's Saturn Could Run Rings Around Old-Style Carmakers," *Business Week,* 28 January 1985, p. 126. Reprinted by permission. © 1985 by McGraw-Hill, Inc.

CASES FOR PART FIVE

CASE 9   Transpo Electronics, Inc.

Transpo Electronics, Inc., was founded by Frank Oropeza to produce replacement automotive parts such as voltage regulators, armatures, solenoids, and other parts that wear out. Transpo is the third business venture for Mr. Oropeza. Earlier ventures had been less successful due to their faddish nature. Those previous ventures taught Oropeza that he needed a business venture that had a basic product with repeat business.

Oropeza and his wife, Ann, mortgaged their house and developed a voltage regulator that is high quality and dependable. Oropeza left his engineering position with a *Fortune 500* firm and began the manufacture of voltage regulators in his garage. Oropeza was also the salesman. He believed that his engineering ability enabled him to design, develop, and manufacture products of sufficient quality to enable him to give a money-back guarantee to his customers for trying Transpo products.

Transpo's sales in their first year were $257,000 and profits of $87,000; in the second year sales were $895,000 and profits of $225,000. Estimated third year sales are $1.8 million.

MARKETING

After the initial year of operation, Transpo began using WATS lines to call customers on a regular basis to determine their replacement parts needs. Oropeza's intentions are to continue expansion to the entire United States, with possible consideration of international markets. (Exhibit 1 is a portion of the price list of Transpo.)

PRODUCTION

Transpo Electronics, Inc., wants to be known as a quality supplier. To achieve that end Oropeza personally develops the engineering and production rationale for each product. Each of the twenty-two employees is constantly reminded of the strict quality control standards of Oropeza. Less than .01 percent of Transpo products are returned for credit for manufacturing defects.

Transpo's goal is to ship every order complete within twenty-four hours of receiving the order. At times during the third year this goal has been difficult to meet. In general, however, the goal is met.

FINANCE

Oropeza desires no stockholders other than himself and his family. He also wants to avoid debt to the extent possible. Exhibit 2 contains the balance sheet of Transpo Electronics, Inc.

Oropeza recognizes the increased need for professional management techniques but does not want to sacrifice many of the personal goals noted. To this end Mr. Oropeza has requested your assistance to identify possible problem areas and give suggested alternatives.[24]

QUESTIONS

1. Relate this case to Part V of the textbook.

2. What types of control does Oropeza need to establish for his firm?

This case was prepared by Professor Terry Campbell. Adapted and reprinted by permission of the author and the University of Central Florida.

EXHIBIT 1 Transpo Electronics, Inc.—Price List

VOLTAGE REGULATOR PRICE LIST
F.E.T. INCLUDED
PART NUMBERS CAN BE MIXED FOR VOLUME PRICING
NOTE: Delco integrals, trios and remanufactured voltage regulators do not apply.

	QUANTITY				
LEECE NEVILLE REGULATORS	1-9	10-24	25-49	50-99	100
Replacement					
LN79000	$18.04	$16.93	$15.82	$15.41	$15.13
LN79000P	17.94	16.83	15.71	15.31	15.02
LN79000T	15.87	14.94	14.26	13.67	12.97
LN77973	19.17	18.04	16.94	16.57	16.23
LN77973P	19.07	17.94	16.84	16.47	16.13
LN77973T	17.21	16.24	15.37	14.81	14.39
LN97300	19.41	18.27	17.19	16.77	16.43
LN97300P	19.31	18.17	17.09	16.67	16.33
LN97300T	17.39	16.39	15.59	15.11	14.59
LN78855	18.89	17.37	16.39	15.97	15.67
LN78855P	20.41	18.87	17.87	17.21	16.91
LN79350	18.89	17.37	16.39	15.97	15.67
LN79350P	20.41	18.87	17.87	17.21	16.91
Delco Remy Regulators					
Replacement					
1892812	18.27	16.47	15.69	15.27	14.91
1892812T	17.04	15.49	14.81	14.39	13.77
1892813	19.79	18.73	17.51	17.09	16.67
1892817	18.27	16.47	15.69	15.27	14.91
1892817T	17.04	15.49	14.81	14.39	13.77
1892824	19.33	17.81	16.71	16.21	15.69
1892824T	18.19	16.71	15.69	15.21	14.71
1892832	22.77	20.77	19.49	18.81	18.11
9000590 Super	18.57	16.65	15.49	14.89	13.97
9000591 Super	18.91	16.97	16.04	15.41	14.67
9000593 Super	19.83	17.89	16.93	16.49	15.73
Potted Modules					
9000590	9.37	9.17	8.93	8.74	8.47
9000591	9.49	9.26	9.09	8.83	8.61
9000592	9.81	9.61	9.41	9.17	8.97
9000593	12.67	12.37	12.13	11.83	11.63

(Continued on next page.)

	QUANTITY				
LEECE NEVILLE REGULATORS	1-9	10-24	25-49	50-99	100
Prestolite					
Replacement					
VSH 6201(12V)	17.67	16.37	15.11	14.10	13.07
VSH 6201-1(12V)	18.17	16.87	15.66	14.60	13.57
VSH 6401 (24V)	18.27	17.11	15.89	14.73	13.76
Universal Voltage Regulator					
VR 1001	9.03	8.71	8.51	8.24	7.84
VR 1002	9.23	8.91	8.71	8.44	8.04
VR 1003	9.17	8.97	8.79	8.53	8.31
VR 1004	9.42	9.22	9.04	8.78	8.56
VR 1005	9.23	8.91	8.71	8.44	8.04
VR 1006	9.42	9.22	9.04	8.78	8.56
VR 1007	9.03	8.71	8.51	8.24	7.84
VR 1008	9.23	8.91	8.71	8.44	8.04
VR 1009	9.23	8.91	8.71	8.44	8.04
VR 1010	9.37	9.17	8.93	8.74	8.47
VR 1011	9.03	8.71	8.51	8.24	7.84
VR 1013	9.49	9.26	9.09	8.83	8.61
VR 1014	9.17	8.97	8.79	8.53	8.31

ORIGINAL EQUIPMENT REMANUFACTURED REGULATORS TO OEM SPECIFICATIONS
F.E.T. INCLUDED

REGULATOR NO.		QUANTITY			CORE
Delco		1-9	10-24	25 UP	CHARGE
1116374	12V	$14.00	$13.50	$12.50	$3.50
1116377	12V	12.50	12.00	11.50	3.50
1116378	12V	14.00	13.50	12.50	3.50
9000551*	12V	34.50	32.50	—	—
9000551* (panel)	12V	28.50	26.50	—	—
9000590	12V	12.50	12.00	11.50	3.00
9000591	24V	14.50	13.50	13.00	3.50
9000592*	30V	16.50	16.00	—	—
9000593*	32V	16.50	16.00	—	5.00
9000597*	24V	34.50	32.50	—	—
9000597* (panel)	24V	28.50	26.50	—	—
1963875*	24V	18.50	17.50	—	—
1963876*	12V	18.50	17.50	—	—
Leece-Neville					
5013	12V	12.50	12.00	11.50	3.50
5022	12V	13.50	13.00	12.50	3.50

REGULATOR NO.		QUANTITY			CORE
Leece-Neville		1-9	10-24	25 UP	CHARGE
5016	12V	12.50	12.00	11.50	3.50
5062*	32V	17.50	17.00	16.50	4.50
5078*	12V	14.00	13.00	12.50	4.00
B.U.T.E.C R2/1*	12V	14.50	13.50	—	—
Ford					
GR374	12V	13.50	13.00	12.50	4.00
GR504	12V	13.50	13.00	12.50	4.00

WARRANTY: 90 days

* Due to core shortages, core must be supplied to Transpo with orders.

EXHIBIT 2   Transpo Electronics, Inc. and Subsidiary—Consolidated Balance Sheet

TRANSPO ELECTRONICS, INC., AND SUBSIDIARY
CONSOLIDATED BALANCE SHEET
MARCH 31, 198X

ASSETS

Current Assets:		
Cash in Banks	$ 23,494.69	
Accounts Receivable	142,440.32	
Inventories (Note 1)	186,486.72	
Total Current Assets		$352,421.73
Fixed Assets At Cost (Note 1):		
Vehicles	11,203.12	
Furniture & Fixtures	7,607.64	
Equipment	20,744.91	
Total Fixed Assets	39,555.67	
Less: Allowance for Depreciation	(5,831.50)	
Depreciable Value of Fixed Assets		33,724.17
Other Assets:		
Patent Rights	185.00	
Deposits	2,800.00	
Total Other Assets		2,985.00
TOTAL ASSETS		$389,130.90

LIABILITIES & STOCKHOLDERS' EQUITY

Current Liabilities:		
Accounts Payable	$ 58,111.35	
Payroll Taxes Withheld & Accrued	5,215.95	

(Continued on next page.)

LIABILITIES & STOCKHOLDERS' EQUITY

Accrued Interest	1,634.00	
Excise Tax Payable	10,767.40	
Note Payable Bank (Note 2)	60,000.00	
Note Payable Banks—Current Portion	3,445.40	
Federal & State Income Tax Payable (Note 3)	49,786.07	
Total Current Liabilities		$188,960.17
Long-Term Liabilities:		
Security Deposits	2,150.00	
Loan from Stockholders	77,581.75	
Note Payable Banks—Non-Current Portion	4,987.72	
Total Long-Term Liabilities		84,719.47
Stockholders' Equity:		
Common Stock—100 Shares Issued & Outstanding,		
Par Value $1.00 Per Share	100.00	
Retained Earnings	115,351.26	
Total Stockholders' Equity		115,451.26
TOTAL LIABILITIES & STOCKHOLDERS' EQUITY		$389,130.90

CASE 10

The American Machine Co.: A New System Is Needed

The American Machine Co., a division of a major corporation, is a heavy machining industry. The company functions as a job-shop and produces a unique product that has sales of $100,000,000 per year.

To retain this leadership position, Joe Bennington, the general manager, has instructed his section managers to install computer control systems where feasible and to reduce manpower. Joe has reasoned that if some headway were made in these areas, the American Machine Co. could keep its market share despite fierce competition from domestic and foreign sources.

Since cycle time, the time required to complete an order, was critical in the marketplace, American Machine had started to modernize its shop area. It was changing from conventional machinery to numerical control equipment. The stock room was going on line, the Materials Requirement Planning had been put into effect. Management was contemplating switching from piece work to day work.

With the shop modernization almost complete, an alternative system for shop loading had to be implemented. The hourly cost of the equipment was $80 for machine time and

$12 for labor. Because of these costs, it was essential for American Machine to install an effective method for recording shop input and to provide the shop with a timely measurement so that the optimal use of the special purpose machinery could be made.

Don Hiller, manager of the manufacturing systems, had been given the project of changing the dispatch (piece work system) to a system that could, in time, become an on-line system. The dispatch system, which had been an outgrowth of piece work, was a total manual commitment. As paper work was received from configuration and documentation control, the dispatchers would log it in on large cards that were keyed to the drawing numbers. The order in which the paperwork was filed depended on the shop order. The general foreman (later the unit manager) gave the supervisor of dispatch a card that listed the shop orders by priority (Exhibit 1). The dispatchers used this card to position the paper work in the files for each station.

The dispatchers were responsible for passing out work and also stamping off operations as they were complete. Since this involved piece work, they turned in the voucher to payroll so that the operators could get paid (Exhibit 2). When operators came to the dispatch window for work, the dispatcher gave them only enough for the day, plus a little carryover. No more work was given to the operators until they had turned in what they had taken previously. This method kept the amount of actual work at the machines to a minimum. As an operation was completed, the dispatcher would set up the paper work at the next station in accordance with previously mentioned dispatch system filing methods. The dispatcher would also log in the voucher payments on a sheet by operations, pay numbers, and so forth, so that a record was kept of who received what payments.

EXHIBIT 1   The American Machine Co.— Shop Order Priority Card

SHOP ORDER		F/M
153267/319		7851
151138/139		7901
153002/003		7901
152196		7902
153327/328		7902
153174/175		7905
150610		7906
152197		7908
151140/141		7909
122892/893		7910
152198		7910
123795		7911
152199		7911
153270/71/72		7911
153084/085		7916
151158/159		7918
153189/190		7919
122959/960	CGE	7920
122921/922		7921
153273/74/75		7924
151170/71/72		7926

Once a week dispatchers would audit all the stations they were responsible for, and thus they knew what was really active at a station. They used this method to take note of what was overdue as well as to define the status of supply jobs. With this information the dispatchers would then expedite their completion. The dispatchers would, on occasion, have to search the shop for lost material and Quality Reports (QRs) so that they could be expedited.

Jobs that were good paying never became lost or missing, only the jobs that nobody wanted to do ended up in this category.

(Continued on next page.)

These constant search and find missions were the only way the dispatchers could control the amount of lost material and QRs. A meeting was held with the general foreman (unit manager) once a week to outline the process of the main parts. At this time the company utilized an ABC Inventory Classification System. This was a totally manual-clerical operation and, as such, could not really take advantage of techniques developed for computer applications.

Exhibits 3 and 4 show the organizational structure and work flow of this system.

QUESTIONS

1. What changes would you recommend to improve and update this system?

2. Develop a time table for the implementation of the recommendations developed in Question 1.

3. Do you feel that this operation should take advantage of computerized inventory techniques? If so, detail a system that would accomplish the conversion and include a time table for implementation. If not, present arguments against it.

This case was prepared by John W. Moran and James M. McCulloch at the Graduate School of Business—Rivier College. Adapted and reprinted by permission of the authors.

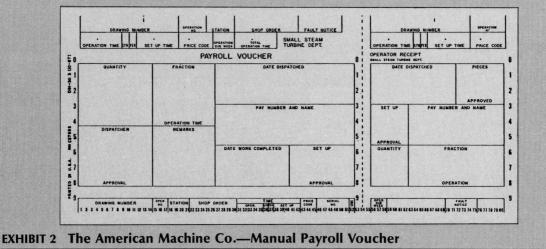

EXHIBIT 2   The American Machine Co.—Manual Payroll Voucher

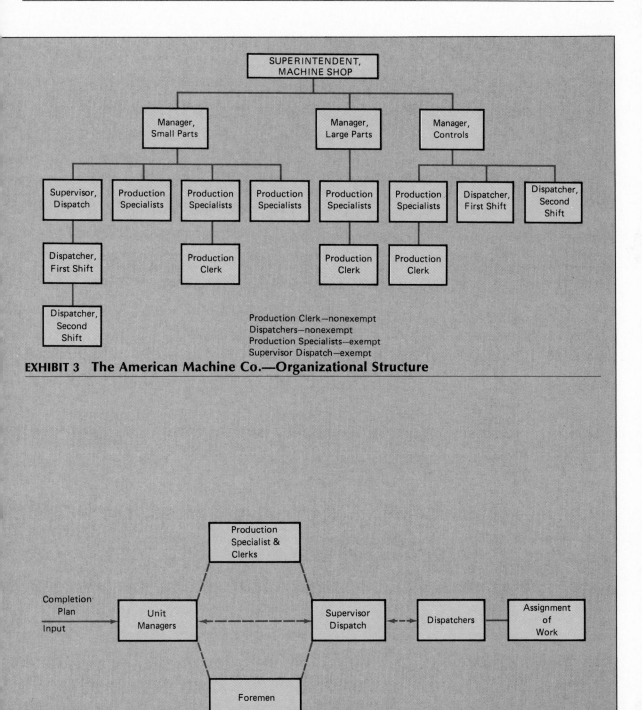

EXHIBIT 3   The American Machine Co.—Organizational Structure

Production Clerk—nonexempt
Dispatchers—nonexempt
Production Specialists—exempt
Supervisor Dispatch—exempt

EXHIBIT 4   The American Machine Co.—Work Flow Diagram

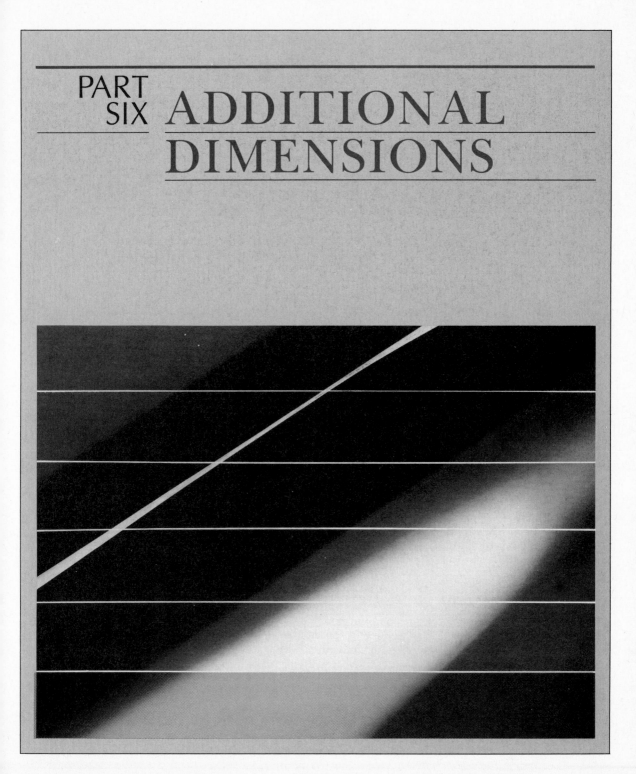

PART
SIX

ADDITIONAL DIMENSIONS

19 INTERNATIONAL AND COMPARATIVE MANAGEMENT

LEARNING OBJECTIVES

After studying this chapter you should be able to

1. Explain the importance of adaptability in international management.

2. Outline the sequence of international business development and its related concepts.

3. Identify the environmental differences affecting international management.

4. Identify the basic functions of management and relate them to an international context.

Materials Resource Corporation

Materials Resource Corporation is an Orangeburg, New York–based ceramics and equipment manufacturer, with a 700-person workforce. The recession of the early 1980s hit the firm hard. Sales dropped from $71 million in 1981 to $60 million in 1982. Net income fell from $2.3 million to $728,000. MRC chairman Sheldon Weinig knew that 100 employees were not needed. Laying them off would save $4 million in payroll costs. Weinig's top executives recommended that the layoff be initiated immediately. But Weinig worried about the limited supply of skilled labor near his plant. Where was he going to recruit a workforce after this recession lifted, if MRC laid people off now?

Weinig wondered if a Japanese-style lifetime employment policy was feasible at Materials Resource Corporation.

Use the materials in this chapter to determine whether Sheldon Weinig should institute a no-layoff policy at MRC.

International managers must have an adaptability that is rarely found in other elements of the organization. Flexibility and a willingness to learn about the merits of other systems are the hallmark of managers who function effectively abroad. Many firms routinely assign rising executives to overseas operations in order to give them a broader perspective than they could obtain otherwise. In the late 1980s business is truly a worldwide venture that extends to the farthest reaches of the globe. And people who want to lead such organizations must have the ability to relate to a mix of cultures, societies, and business systems.

Just as entrepreneurship and the management of domestic enterprises are important dimensions of contemporary management, so are international and comparative management. This exciting topic is explored in the chapter that follows.

THE CONCEPTS OF INTERNATIONAL BUSINESS AND INTERNATIONAL MANAGEMENT

Exporting (the marketing of one's merchandise to another nation) and *importing* (the purchase and shipment of merchandise from another country) are the basic tasks in what is known as *international business*—a term that can be roughly defined as all economic activities that cross national boundaries. Similarly, the term *international management* can be used to refer to the decision making involved in international business activities. It might refer to the activities of the head of a firm's export or import department, or to a privately employed person engaged in such activities. An international manager might also be someone who works abroad in one of his or her firm's subsidiaries or sales offices. International managers have duties similar to those of domestic managers, except that their functions must be performed in a different environment.

The multinational company, often abbreviated *MNC,* is the ultimate level of international business. An MNC is a firm that views itself as essentially global in nature. Its business activities are conducted in numerous national markets and at a variety of different levels ranging from simple export to full-scale foreign companies with comprehensive production and marketing capabilities.

Exporting is the marketing of one's merchandise to other nations.

Importing is the purchase and shipment of merchandise from another nation.

International business refers to all economic activity that crosses national boundaries.

International management refers to the decision making involved in international business activities.

MNC (multinational company) is a firm that views itself as essentially global in nature, and which conducts business in numerous national markets at a variety of levels.

MANAGEMENT FACT OR FICTION

	FACT	FICTION		FACT	FICTION
1. The temporary suspension of the sale of Soviet vodka in 15 states after the KAL 007 tragedy is an example of an economic boycott.	☐	☐	ture at the operational level is known as a matrix organization.	☐	☐
2. The planning function in Saudi Arabia is very detailed, but it is not linked to larger goals or objectives.	☐	☐	4. It only costs about $40,000 annually to send a $50,000 a year manager overseas since living costs are typically lower abroad.	☐	☐
3. A multinational company with a functionally organized corporate headquarters and a geographical struc-			5. Japanese management is usually classified as a systems type of leadership.	☐	☐
			6. International business units tend to be very centralized.	☐	☐

The materials in this chapter will assist you in separating management fact from fiction. Your answers can be checked on page 641.

Licensing is granting the right to an outside firm to produce and/or distribute a firm's products in another country.

The experience of numerous firms suggests that international business activities tend to follow a standardized developmental sequence (see Figure 19–1). First, firms begin to export, usually through an agent who facilitates the transactions with a foreign buyer. An alternative strategy frequently employed by smaller firms is licensing. *Licensing* is granting the right to an outside firm to produce and/or distribute the firm's product in another country. As export sales expand, the company concludes that it can justify its own foreign sales subsidiary and it sets up an overseas marketing arm. The final step is when management decides to begin producing the product abroad.[1]

Effective international management is required in all phases of the developmental process. Foreign sales agents, heads of sales subsidiaries abroad, and a variety of people working in foreign production facilities can be considered international managers. International management per-

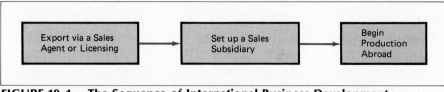

FIGURE 19–1.   The Sequence of International Business Development

meates the entire spectrum of international commerce. Management is the mechanism for getting things done in international business, just as in domestic markets.

ENVIRONMENTAL DIFFERENCES AFFECTING INTERNATIONAL MANAGEMENT

In Chapter 3 we discussed the importance of environmental factors in the framework for management. As important as these circumstances are to domestic management, they are magnified many times over in the international sphere. A multitude of environmental differences affect international management and its related decision-making process. In fact, the variety and extensiveness of such differences often dominate many discussions of international business and management.

These environmental differences may be broadly divided into three categories: political, cultural, and economic. Further subclassification is possible, but it will be avoided here in order to keep the discussion in its proper perspective.

POLITICAL DIFFERENCES

Ben Pon failed when he tried to import Volkswagens in 1949. Too many people remembered that Hitler had ordered Ferdinand Porsche to build a "people's car" that could carry four or five passengers at 60 miles per hour on the new "autobahns" being constructed in Nazi Germany. Hitler further specified that the car average 33 miles per gallon (gasoline was expensive in Nazi Germany) and have an air-cooled engine to avoid frozen radiators. Porsche devised a small car with the engine in the rear, which Hitler called the "Kdf" or "Kraft durch Freude." The name translates as "Strength Through Joy"; the car's name was later changed to Volkswagen "Beetle" in the United States. By 1949, American newspaper advertisements were billing the Beetle as a symbol of totalitarian Nazi rule. Given this background it is little wonder that Ben Pon's importing venture—coming only four years after the end of World War II—failed.[2]

Political differences can have a profound impact on international business. Management must recognize the potential problems and risks associated with business activities that must bridge different political systems

THE MANAGER'S BOOKSHELF

Re-inventing the Corporation, by John Naisbitt

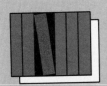

John Naisbitt's *Megatrends* was a months-long best-seller and eventually sold over six million copies. Therefore, it comes as no surprise that Naisbitt put out a sequel, this time a look at how American companies can (and do) adjust to the new "information society." In *Re-inventing the Corporation* (Warner Books, 1985), which Naisbitt co-authored with Patricia Aburdene, the authors contend that business success no longer depends very much on balance sheets and production goals. Now it is all a matter of motivating employees.

Re-inventing the Corporation offers an enormous grab bag of company innovations and exciting worker-oriented ideas that foster creativity and individuality. These examples, culled from such "new-style" companies as W. L. Gore and Associates and People Express, are of macro and micro importance. They run the gamut from buying into new businesses to calling everybody by their first names.

Naisbitt and Aburdene first trace the changes that are restructuring the American economic landscape. These include the omnipresence of computers, increased education, rising health care costs, the large number of women in the labor force, and a forecasted labor shortage in the 18- to 24-year-old age group. These changes, say the authors, will add up to a new orientation toward workers on the part of management. Workers will increasingly be drawn to "re-invented corporations," those companies "that create the most nourishing environments for personal growth."

In these new nourishing environments, managers will no longer pass orders down through the ranks. Now they will serve as coaches, teachers, and mentors. And to hold on to its most talented workers, a company will have to completely rethink its operations. Not only should it consider plunging into new businesses, but it should spend a great deal of its time and effort enriching its employees' working lives. This will mean anything from having executives answer their own phones and calling all workers "partners" to introducing flexible hours, job rotation, day-care facilities, and job analysis programs to reduce wage inequities.

Source: David J. Cherrington, "Re-Inventing the Corporation." Reprinted from the September 1985 issue of *Venture,* For Entrepreneurial Business Owners & Investors, by special permission. © 1985 Venture Magazine, Inc., 521 Fifth Ave., New York, N.Y. 10175.

and philosophies. Many nations—the United States included—have viewed international trade as one element of their overall foreign and domestic political policy.

Some governments use international business in a positive way to improve economic conditions at home. These governments actively subsidize management in achieving their objectives abroad, since these revenues eventually flow back to the source nation to support its standard of living and level of employment. Japan is often cited as such a nation.

Other countries have threatened to halt international business in order

International Business and Management

Managers of international and multinational concerns must have a broad understanding of the political, cultural and economic environment of the country in which they do business. Careful business management is critical in international markets where the possibility for loss or gain is high, and many complex factors can affect the outcome. Management functions, planning, organizing, leading, and controlling, must suit both national and foreign employees.

Despite its complexity, the promise for international and multinational business is great, not only in monetary terms, but also in the accumulation of knowledge, especially in new business ideas and methods.

Foreign managers are often eager to invest in the United States for reasons which include the availability of a wealthy consumer market and a favorable labor market. American labor is viewed as more stable, productive, and cheaper than comparable work forces in, for example, Europe. Here, American employees of New United Motor Manufacturing, Inc. are being trained at Toyota's plants in Japan in preparation for the start of operations in Freemont, CA.

American businesses, like Wendy's, are increasingly successful in foreign markets. One key ingredient has been adaptability, as in the case of this Wendy's restaurant located in Seoul, Korea.

(Left) The Japanese view the company like a family and run their businesses to foster lifetime employment and loyalty. Fringe benefits, like a day of sports, are seen as important motivators, as shown in this example of a companywide field day, held at the Toyota Sport Center for all Toyota employees.

(Below) Political differences can ruin even a product with great potential. For example, associations with Hitler and Nazi Germany made the introduction of the Volkswagen into the American market a disaster in 1949. By the 1960s, Volkswagens were as familiar a shape as the Coke bottle. However, complex factors led to their more recent loss in market share to other imports, including those from Japan.

(Above) Only companies sensitive to the fact that businesses have to be run within the framework of Islamic religious and moral concepts can be successful in Saudi Arabia. Clearly, General Electric had to consider this when they decided to establish an operation in Jeddah, Saudi Arabia.

THE MANAGER'S BOOKSHELF

The M-Form Society, by William Ouchi

The author, well known in management circles for his 1981 best-seller, *Theory Z* (described in Chapter 18), has turned his attention to a macro-view of the problems involving how different organizations relate to one another and to government. His book, *The M-Form Society* (Addison-Wesley, 1984), advocates the infrastructural redesign and institutional reorganization of the entire American economy. Basically, what Ouchi suggests is that American companies give up their single-minded devotion to individual profits and learn how to cooperate with each other and with government to benefit everybody.

An M-Form (short for multidivisional form) organization is a mixture of centralized and decentralized forms that both taps individual competitive efforts and fosters group consensus. An M-Form corporation, for instance, contains independent divisions that seek to maximize profits while simultaneously sharing such corporate resources as R&D, planning, and finance. In the allocation of those limited resources, individual divisions' quest for gratification of self-interest is balanced by central control. Divisions don't necessarily mind giving up something, because they know this will be remembered and repaid in the future.

An M-Form society functions in much the same way. It creates social integration by balancing the need for government regulation with the need for unbridled business activity. Ouchi proposes an "action agenda" for reaching an M-Form society in the United States, although he does not suggest we try to transplant the Japanese model. He points to both the American Electronics Association (a grass-roots organization of computer companies) and the city of Minneapolis as two good American examples of M-Form organizations.

Like many business books, *The M-Form Society* presents a program that seems highly desirable in the abstract. The possibility of actually instituting Ouchi's program, however, seems somewhat remote. And who's to say the same kind of politicking that now pervades the relationship between government and business wouldn't eventually overtake the M-Form organizations as well?

One of Ouchi's central messages, through both this book and his 1981 book, *Theory Z,* has been that it's not the Japanese character and culture that accounts for Japan's competitive advantage, but simply the way they arrange things. Ouchi may not have completely spelled out how to transform the American economy into an M-Form society (though he's tried), and it may not be clear that the American character will ever accept the kind of self-restraint he proposes. Nevertheless, Ouchi has pointed in the right direction with *The M-Form Society.* One can hardly argue with his thesis that if business and government cooperated more effectively, everyone would benefit.

---

to penalize political adversaries. *Economic boycotts* occur when a nation prohibits trade or commerce with another country, typically as an act of political retaliation. The United States has economically boycotted Cuba and other nations in recent years. The 1982 Argentine invasion of the Falkland Islands prompted the United States to restrict some trade with

Economic boycott is a situation where a nation prohibits trade or commerce with another country, typically as an act of political retaliation.

that South American nation. And in 1983, after a Soviet fighter shot down Korean Airlines flight 007, killing all the passengers aboard, 15 states suspended the sale of Soviet vodka. For most of these states, this boycott proved to be short lived; within a year, half of them once again allowed the sale of Stolichnaya—the Russians' leading liquor export—to customers.[3]

Elaborate legal requirements also play an important role in international management decisions. Most of this legislative framework is a derivative of the internal and international political circumstances existing at a particular time. The domination of some U.S. markets by foreign manufacturers has led to public pressure to impose import restrictions on foreign products.

International management must be constantly aware of changing political and legal situations in the nations in which their firms operate. Political differences can affect all the functions performed by international managers, and in some cases these factors can spell the difference between success and failure.

CULTURAL DIFFERENCES

Consider the managerial decision-making process in Israel. In that nation private enterprise controls about 40 percent of the national output, government accounts for 35 percent, and the remaining 25 percent consists of firms owned by the Israeli labor federation, known as Histadrut. As an employer Histadrut ranks second only to the government. The union's involvement in operating business enterprises began in the 1920s, when few investors were willing to buy a stake in the desert that became Israel in 1948.

Israel is a mix of private enterprise and socialism. Much of this pattern is derived from the country's unique cultural and historical background. *Industrial democracy,* a system in which all employees are actively involved in an organization's decision-making process, is widely practiced in Israel. While limited in the private sector, industrial democracy is required by law in the government sector. And management in Histadrut firms are appointed by elected union officials.

The ultimate degree of industrial democracy flourishes in a moshaw or a kibbutz, the rural socialist collectives and enterprises that control most of Israel's agricultural output. All who live and work in these situations are Histadrut members. Management positions and most of the jobs are rotated periodically. Executive officers are elected. A moshaw differs from a kibbutz only in that private family homes and farm plots are permitted. There is no private property in a kibbutz. Everyone eats together in a central hall and shares equally according to a socialist philosophy.[4]

Cultural differences clearly play a big role in the way Israeli managers must operate.[5] Similarly, the well-known Japanese desire to expand exports has been explained by that culture's extreme anxiety over its own

Industrial democracy is a system in which all employees are actively involved in an organization's decision-making processes.

MANAGEMENT: THE LIGHTER SIDE

Cultural Mistakes in International Management

Often, a simple translation error can cause problems in international management. Ford Motor Company experienced major success in the Philippines with its Fiera, so it naturally assumed the vehicle would go over well in Thailand. But it barely sold at all in Thailand and it also succeeded in damaging Ford's reputation. It seems that many Thais routinely overload their vehicles, two or three times beyond normal capacity, and the resulting breakdowns were all blamed on Ford.

Finally, there's the U.S. manufacturer of mixed feed for poultry, which refused to learn from its mistakes. It wanted to start a market in Spain, although local business people advised them that there would be resistance. The U.S. company built a factory, brought in a technical staff, started operations, and sold nothing. Since there was nothing to do with all that feed, the company decided to cover itself by purchasing its own chicken farms. That took care of some of the feed, but no one bought the chickens.

Source: These incidents are reported in David A. Ricks, *Big Business Blunders* (Dow-Jones—Irwin, 1983), pp. 79, 115, 119.

---

economic vulnerability. Over 120 million people inhabit a usable land area only about the size of South Carolina. The Japanese must import a substantial portion of their food supplies and raw materials. The national effort to create exports to pay for such necessities is certainly understandable.

Among the most important cultural differences affecting management are the varied national viewpoints on competition. The prevailing concept of competition can influence the relative aggressiveness of a manager's actions, the type of people hired, leadership styles, motivational practices, and a firm's compensation system. Table 19–1 shows that the American belief in the virtue of competition is not always shared by other cultures. The table illustrates a type of analysis known as *comparative management*, the cross-cultural study of management practices and techniques. The differences shown in Table 19–1 can help explain the difficulties American businesspeople sometimes have in adjusting to international management positions.

Comparative management is the analysis of cross-cultural management practices and techniques.

Stories of American management's inability to adjust to cultural differences are legion. Dozens of failures have resulted from an international manager's insensitivity to local cultural and societal patterns. A common mistake is to assume that our way of doing things is the correct (or even only) way to do them. Consider our penchant for precise legal language with extensive explanations and descriptions of the contemplated act. One

TABLE 19–1   NATIONAL CONCEPTS OF COMPETITION

Nature and Effect of Competition	Typical American Viewpoints	Typical European Viewpoints	Typical Japanese Viewpoints
Nature of Competition	Competition is a strong moral force: it contributes to character building.	Competition is neither good nor bad.	There is conflict inherent in nature. To overcome conflicts man must compete; but man's final goal is harmony with nature and his fellow man.
Business Competition Compared	Business competition is like a big sport game.	Business competition affects the livelihood of people and quickly develops into warfare.	The company is like a family. Competition has no place in a family. Aggressive action against competitors in the marketplace is in order for the survival and growth of the company.
Motivation	One cannot rely on an employee's motivation unless extra monetary inducements for hard work are offered in addition to a base salary or wage.	A key employee is motivated by the fact that he has been hired by the company.	Same as the European viewpoint.
Reward System	Money talks. A person is evaluated on the basis of his image (contribution) to the company. High tipping in best hotels, restaurants, etc., is expected.	An adequate salary, fringe benefits, opportunities for promotion, but no extra incentives—except in sales. Very little tipping (service charge is included in added-value tax).	Same as the European viewpoint.
Excessive Competition	Competition must be tough for the sake of the general welfare of society. No upper limit on the intensity and amount of competition is desirable.	Too much competition is destructive and is in conflict with brotherly love and Christian ethic.	Excessive competition is destructive and can create hatred. Only restrained competition leads to harmony and benefits society.

Nature and Effect of Competition	Typical American Viewpoints	Typical European Viewpoints	Typical Japanese Viewpoints
Hiring Policy	Aggressive individuals who enjoy competition are ideal employees. Individuals who avoid competition are unfit for life and company work.	Diversity of opinion. How competitiveness or aggressive behavior of an individual is viewed varies with national ideology and the type of work. In England it is not a recommendation to describe a job applicant as being "aggressive."	Individuals are hired usually not for specific jobs but on the basis of their personality traits and their ability to become an honorable "company member." Team play and group consensus are stressed.

Source: Hugh E. Kramer, "Concepts of Competition in America, Europe, and Japan," *Business and Society* (Fall 1977): 22-23. Copyright 1977 by Roosevelt University. Published by the Walter E. Heller College of Business Administration of Roosevelt University. Reprinted by permission.

American firm was forced to back out of a plan to manage a government-owned manufacturing operation in an African nation. The traditional "whereases" section of the contract noted that the government had been unsuccessful with the operation. It then went on to note the American firm's extensive international management and technical resources. To the host nation, the implication was that American management know-how would save the incompetent Africans. When a local student newspaper began attacking the "foreign imperialism" of the control language, management had to beat a hasty retreat from a potentially advantageous agreement.[6]

Another story is told about the American executive who was miffed when an Asian businessperson asked to change the American's arrival just ten days before the scheduled date. The American did not realize that his Asian counterpart had asked a religious advisor to suggest a more promising date for an event he considered so important. The Asian's action was a compliment that was missed by the American, who was unsophisticated in such cultural differences.[7]

ECONOMIC DIFFERENCES

Economic differences are quite extensive in international business. They can range from minor technological differences to sizable gaps in personal income and wealth. Economic events affect international management in two primary ways: (1) changing business opportunities; and (2) the response required by a significant economic event.

International management must be quick to recognize shifts in potentially profitable opportunities in worldwide commerce. American business response to the opening of trade with several Communist bloc countries is an example. Perhaps the best illustration has been foreign management's movement into U.S. markets. Americans are good customers for imported products, but they harbor little resistance to foreign-owned firms operating within the United States.

Foreign investment in the United States has soared in recent years. Foreign-owned and managed companies exist in virtually every segment of the United States economy. A report to Congress by the comptroller general of the United States indicated that European investors were attracted by several features of our business environment.[8]

- *Profit motive.* Foreign firms are attracted by our large, wealthy market and the favorable acquisition costs of investing in American companies and property.

- *Favorable labor market.* American labor is viewed as more stable and productive and cheaper than comparative work forces in Europe. Management technology is viewed as more sophisticated than in Europe, where management education has only recently been made available.

- *Stable business environment.* A variety of factors such as a sizable domestic market and a resilient private enterprise system are indications of a stable business environment.

- *State development agencies.* Many states maintain business development offices in Europe and openly attempt to solicit investments in their states.

The comptroller general also reported several obstacles to foreign investment:

- *Foreign investment restrictions.* The United States, like many countries, prohibits foreign investments in what are termed national interest areas.

- *Business regulations.* Two aspects of U.S. business regulations are viewed as distressing. First, the open disclosure requirements (which sometimes apply to the parent European company in addition to the U.S. subsidiary) violate practices common in European firms. Second, U.S. antitrust procedures are viewed as indefinite because the firm does not always know its legal position before the investment is made. This is in marked contrast to European governments, which make their stance clear in advance of such a decision.

- *Market complexity.* The size and complexity of the U.S. market are problems to small European companies. Negative stereotypes are also perceived. The complicated American legal framework is another negative factor for foreign investment.

Significant economic events also have a powerful effect on international management. Consider the slide of the Canadian dollar as compared with the U.S. dollar. The value of the Canadian dollar declined until the *exchange rate* (the ratio of one currency to another) dropped to less than eighty cents in American monies. This made Canadian products and vacations less expensive for Americans. But it made similar U.S. purchases by Canadians more expensive. The management of both U.S. and Canadian firms had to adjust accordingly.

Exchange rate is the ratio of one currency to another.

THE BASIC FUNCTIONS OF INTERNATIONAL MANAGEMENT

In Chapter 1 we noted that managerial functions are usually applicable (as adapted) to all managerial situations, including their international context. Planning, organizing, staffing, leading, and controlling are as important—if not more so—to the international manager as they are to a home-based peer. Only the environmental circumstances differ. Of course, in some cases, these factors can force radical alterations in the way a manager operates.

The importance of environmental constraints is clearly shown in Saudi Arabian planning. The oil-rich but labor-deficient desert kingdom uses loosely structured five-year plans in its economic development process. The Saudis have decided to concentrate on two export industries—petrochemicals and basic metals.

Saudi planning is quite detailed, often relying on numerous feasibility studies. But, unlike Western planning, they do not relate the planning to large goals or objectives. These plans are also loose since Saudi planners do not feel compelled to meet deadlines. Revisions and modifications are an expected part of their planning. All Saudi planning is conducted within the framework of Islamic religious and moral concepts. The Saudis go to considerable effort to preserve the traditional values and social structure of their nation.[9] International managers operating in Saudi Arabia (and there are a lot of them) must pay close attention to their host's cultural heritage and to the values prized by the Saudi people. The characteristics of Saudi planning should also be appreciated by those seeking to do business there.

PLANNING

As the Saudi example illustrates, planning is important, and in many nations the government plays a significant role in the planning done in international settings. Japan, for instance, has its Ministry of International Trade and Industry (MITI), which plans that nation's economic future.

Technocrats are specialists within the bureaucracy who dominate national economic planning.

Technocrats, the staff specialists like engineers, budget analysts, and the like who hold influential positions in the bureaucracy, dominate the planning activities of many foreign countries. International managers must understand the practices and beliefs of these people and interact effectively with them if they are to succeed. National economic planning by technocrats often sets the conditions under which international managers must do their own planning.

Nowhere is the value of planning in international management better shown than in Chrysler's effort—over a decade ago—to develop a "world car," one that incorporates European economy and road-handling features with the American penchant for comfort and luxury. Chrysler actually considered such a subcompact as early as 1969, but decided against the "25-car," which was really a Valiant with a clipped rear end. By 1973 Chrysler engineers were working with their European counterparts at a Chrysler affiliate to develop a world car. The Arab oil boycott and the government mandate on corporate fleet mileages convinced Chrysler management to go ahead. On March 21, 1975, the plan was launched, code named "L-car" in the United States and "C2" in Europe. Planners were originally targeting for the 1979 model year, but top management moved the introduction up to 1978.

66 We have got to decide what free and fair trade is all about, and we've got to level the playing field to be competitive. These are the gut issues. 99

Lee Iacocca

Chrysler originally hoped to use common components in both American and European models. But because of the new capital costs that would have been involved, they opted for separate projects with the maximum amount of common development possible. The two groups of planners and engineers blended their efforts and on November 21, 1977, the first of the successful Omnis and Horizons came off the assembly line.[10] The planning effort of managers on both sides of the Atlantic had come to fruition.

ORGANIZING

Organizations also must be adapted to conditions abroad. What works at home is not always appropriate in another nation. For example, French, Italian, Swiss, and Dutch managers prefer a traditional formal organization structure, while German and Scandinavian executives opt for a less rigid structure.[11]

66 The meek shall inherit the world, but they'll never increase market share. 99

William G. McGowan
Chairman, MCI Communications

Organizational structures for international management are linked to strategies that the firm attempts to implement.[12] American Motors Corp. is a good illustration of such an organizational adaptation. AMC's cars were commanding only 2 percent of the U.S. market, while its Jeep and AM General buses and military vehicles were selling well. The firm did not really have a viable product in the high-mileage market segment of the automobile industry. Rumors of its eventual withdrawal from the passenger car market were rampant. So AMC sought and obtained a link with Renault, the French government-owned automaker. Renault had some problems of its own. While the French firm annually sold about 1.1 million vehicles worldwide, only 13,000 were sold in the United States. Renault,

FIGURE 19–2.   The Top-Selling Renault Encore
Source: Courtesy American Motors Corp.

which now owns 46 percent of AMC, gained access to AMC's U.S. and Canadian dealer network. Similarly, Jeeps were to be sold through Renault dealers in other countries (a plan that has been since developed). And Renaults are now produced at a U.S. plant. In fact, the Renault Alliance and Encore produced by American Motors have been top sellers (see Figure 19–2). Both companies were decisive in adapting their organizations to meet changing corporate strategies.[13]

Multinational companies employ five basic organizational structures.[14] Initially, most companies set up an *international division*. This unit resembles a domestic product division except that it serves a worldwide market. A second structure is the *worldwide product division,* where each product unit is given international responsibilities. The *area or geographical division* is a third possibility. This format has a separate division for specific parts of the firm's marketplace such as Europe, North America, and South America. A popular new structure is the *matrix organization,* where corporate headquarters is organized functionally while a geographical organization exists at operational levels. A fifth alternative is the *focused market unit,* which sets up a market-oriented division to service potential customers regardless of their location. GE's Strategic Business Unit concept is an example.

Matrix organization is one in which the corporate headquarters is organized functionally while a geographical organization exists at operational levels.

None of these structures is correct in every case. Circumstances vary, and so should the structure. Table 19–2 shows the relative suitability of basic MNC organizational structures to specified corporate concerns. For example, area or geographical divisions would be poorly suited to a high-technology company. Similarly, availability of a limited team of experienced

TABLE 19-2   SUITABILITY OF BASIC MNC ORGANIZATIONAL STRUCTURES TO CORPORATE CONCERNS

Area of Corporate Concern	Level of Suitability				
	Inter-National Division	World-Wide Product Division	Area Division	Matrix	Focused Market Units
Rapid growth	M	H	M	H	H
Diversity of products	L	H	L	H	H
High technology	M	H	L	H	H
Few experienced managers	H	M	L	L	L
Close corporate control	M	H	L	H	H
Close government relations	M	L	H	M	M
Resource allocation:					
Product considerations should dominate	L	H	L	M	M
Geographic considerations should dominate	M	L	H	M	M
Functional considerations should dominate	L	M	L	H	M
Relative cost	M	M	L	H	M

H = high   M = medium   L = low

Source: John Hutchinson, "Evolving Organizational Forms," *Columbia Journal of World Business* (Summer 1976): 51. Reprinted with permission from the Summer 1976 issue of the *Columbia Journal of World Business.* Copyright © 1976 by the Trustees of Columbia University in the City of New York.

managers might suggest that the international division is the most appropriate organizational structure.

STAFFING

Few international managers encounter the staffing problems of a Russian manager. The USSR has a chronic labor shortage caused by a low birth rate, an aging population, and the loss of 20 million people in World War II. This situation has steadily worsened since the late 1970s with the decline in the number of working-age Russians and in the number of people who are moving from rural to urban areas. To make staffing problems worse, a critical population decrease is occurring among Russia's European population who live closest to existing industrial plants and who make up Russia's traditional industrial labor force. To meet staffing requirements, Russian planners must move large numbers of workers from the Asian

66 I would not like to be a Russian leader. They never know when they're being taped. 99

Richard Nixon

and Caucasian republics into the European industrial areas. However, the friction that exists between the Europeans and these groups makes such a large scale movement difficult to achieve. The other option—building factories close to the available supply of workers—is equally unattractive since Russian planners are unwilling to invest their industrial resources in areas of the country that do not enthusiastically embrace the Russian regime.[15]

Staffing is a major responsibility of those involved in international management. Traditionally, the chief international manager in an overseas unit and all of his or her key subordinates would be executives posted from corporate headquarters. However, in the past five years, U.S. corporations increasingly have been forced to turn to foreign nationals to fill many key positions. This is due, in part, to the reluctance of host countries to issue work permits to U.S. nationals. This situation sometimes stems from American restrictions on work permits for the host nation's citizens in the United States.[19]

The perquisites, or "perks"—another term for fringe benefits and privileges associated with a position—are often very attractive in overseas assignments. Company-provided housing, automobiles, servants, and vacations back home are common for those given such assignments. U.S. citizens working abroad are also allowed to exclude part of their income for tax purposes. But the cost of living abroad has escalated far faster than it has in North America. As a result, most firms are now required to increase an executive's salary considerably for an overseas assignment just to keep the individual even with the domestic standard of living.

International managers can be divided into those who view their assignment as a career position, much the way a diplomat would view his or her current career assignment, and those who are serving a stint in international management to broaden their background so they can assume increased responsibilities at home. This is a common career pattern for successful executives.

Companies are increasingly relying on the nationals of a host country to fill positions in their international organization. Typically, these people have been utilized in operative and lower-level supervisory positions. As they acquire experience in the particular industry, they are given the chance to compete for major executive positions in the firm's international organization.

Foreign nationals have several advantages in this competition:

- *Training costs may be lower.* Language and cultural sensitivity training can often be eliminated or drastically cut back, thus saving the firm a considerable expenditure.

- *Executive deployment costs may also be lower.* It is now estimated that it costs $120,000 annually—exclusive of social welfare fringes—to deploy a $50,000 a-year U.S. executive abroad.[17] Use of foreign nationals can provide a considerable savings in most instances.

- *Culture shock is avoided.* Culture shock is the disorientation encountered when an individual is forced to deal with a totally unfamiliar cultural setting. It can render a person managerially useless for a period of time. The foreign national has an awareness of the culture in which he or she will be operating and can adapt more easily.

- *There is a political advantage.* Some nations require that foreign firms provide a specified degree of employment for local citizens. Extensive use of nationals of the host nation can be of considerable political advantage.

- *There is a marketing awareness.* Foreign nationals are more likely to be attuned to business opportunities abroad than executives from corporate headquarters. More important, they may help the firm avoid potential marketing errors that might be overlooked by people unfamiliar with the particular marketplace.

LEADING

Effective leadership styles vary according to international settings. A popular international comparison in managerial leadership is between Japanese and American styles.[18] U.S. management is usually classified as a *systems type leadership*. All corporate activities, whether organized functionally or on a decentralized basis, are directed toward the achievement of specified objectives. The various subsystems are linked within a set of constraints such as those set externally or by company policy. Management's role is to design the system and then to make plans and decisions required to achieve the overall corporate objectives. American managers are viewed as professionals who place the highest priority on efficient decision making.

By contrast, Japanese firms employ an *organic type leadership*. The firm is thought of as a collective unit, and company personnel identify with the organization rather than with the specific function to which they are assigned, such as accounting, engineering, or marketing. Members are vertically identified within the firm rather than horizontally with other engineers, accountants, and sales executives. The emphasis is on good human relations.

Table 19–3 compares the characteristics of top management in the United States and Japan. The U.S. manager leads through his or her professional decision-making ability, while the Japanese manager acts as a facilitator and social leader. The Japanese executive relies on *consensus management* where various groups, committees, and task forces are formed to reach an organization-wide agreement on a particular decision. The Japanese emphasis on group strength is in marked contrast to the American system. The U.S. manager counts on the firm's hierarchical command system to arrive at decisions. The Japanese firm may have a similar organizational structure, but the Japanese executive reaches decisions and

Systems type leadership is a style in which all corporate activities are directed toward the achievement of specified objectives.

Organic type leadership is a style in which the firm is thought of as a collective unit; personnel identify with the organization rather than with their particular function.

Consensus management is a style in which chief executives rely on various committees, groups, and task forces to reach organization-wide agreement on a particular decision.

TABLE 19–3   CHARACTERISTICS OF TOP MANAGEMENT: A COMPARISON

Systems Type (U.S.)	Organic Type (Japan)
Decision maker	Facilitator
Professional	Social leader
Individual initiative and creativity	Group strength
Hierarchical command	Free-form command
Emphasis on functional relationships	Emphasis on human relations
Management by objectives	Management by consensus
Decentralization	Centralization
System adapts to changes	Leader adapts to changes

Source: Charles Y. Yang, "Management Styles: American Vis-à-Vis Japanese," *Columbia Journal of World Business* (Fall 1977): 25. Reprinted with permission from the Fall 1977 issue of the *Columbia Journal of World Business*. Copyright © 1977 by the Trustees of Columbia University in the City of New York.

operates through numerous groups of subordinates from throughout the organization. Again, human relations are held in higher regard than decision-making efficiency. For instance, after Matsushita Electric Industrial Co. bought Motorola's television plants and formed Quasar Electronics Co., it took Japanese style consensus management three years to work out a new financial package with its distributors. The independent distributors were involved, along with Quasar financial, sales, marketing, and branch managers.[19]

Which of the two management styles is more effective? Since both have resulted in nearly the same profit performance, it is more meaningful to evaluate the various factors important to profitability. Three such factors can be identified:

1. *Entrepreneurial quality,* defined as "the degree of innovativeness and propensity for "risk-taking."

2. *Level of aspiration,* defined as "the confidence that management instills within the organization (internal relations) as well as outside the organization (external relations)."

3. *Executive quality,* defined as "the decision-making ability of executives in terms of the speed and accuracy of decision-making as well as the flexibility in adjusting and rectifying decision errors."[20]

The relative performance of U.S. systems type and Japanese organic type leadership is shown in Table 19–4. This evaluation is presented in terms of both the traditional environment facing each country and the new common set of situational circumstances. Finally, suggestions for both minor and major modifications in each system are noted. The analysis points out that the American systems approach needs to make a significant

TABLE 19–4   COMPARISON OF THE QUALITY OF MANAGEMENT IN THE UNITED STATES AND JAPAN IN DIFFERENT SITUATIONAL CONFIGURATIONS

	Quality of Entrepreneurship		Level of Aspiration		Effectiveness of Decision Making		
	Innovativeness	Risk-Taking	Internal	External	Speed	Accuracy	Adjustment
Evaluation							
American management (systems type)	fair	fair	poor to fair	poor	good	good	good
Japanese management (organic type)	poor	poor	good	good	poor	good	poor
Management requirements in past situations							
American situational configuration prior to the oil crisis: moderate to high economic growth, moderate external influence and technological leader	required	required	required	not strongly required	strongly required	strongly required	strongly required
Japanese situational configuration prior to the oil crisis: high economic growth, strong external influence and technological follower	not strongly required	not strongly required	strongly required	strongly required	not strongly required	required	required
Management requirements under new situational configuration							
New situational configuration: common to the U.S. and Japan: low economic growth, high external influence and technological leadership	required	required	strongly required	strongly required	strongly required	strongly required	strongly required
Modifications needed to cope with the new situation							
American management	minor	minor	minor	major	strongly required	strongly required	strongly required
Japanese management	minor	minor	minor	major	strongly required	strongly required	minor

Source: Charles Y. Yang, "Management Styles: American Vis-à-Vis Japanese," *Columbia Journal of World Business* (Fall 1977), p. 29. Reprinted with permission from the Fall 1977 issue of the *Columbia Journal of World Business.* Copyright © 1977 by the Trustees of Columbia University in the City of New York.

effort to improve its external level of aspiration, while the Japanese organic approach needs to find new ways to speed up its traditional decision-making process.

EVALUATION AND CONTROL

International managers are also involved in evaluating and controlling operations. Some of this assessment is done locally, some at corporate headquarters. The process is as important to international operations as it is to domestic ones. Business performance is always monitored. And it seems logical to assume that social performance will increasingly be evaluated.

Table 19–5 shows the nature of the supervision and evaluation process among international units. The data suggest that most international units have a broad span in which to operate. Total centralization of decisions occurs in less than 5 percent of the cases cited. On the other hand, complete decentralization prevailed in less than 2 percent of the firms.

The exact location of the monitoring procedure is not as important as its existence and relative effectiveness somewhere within the managerial structure. The evaluative and control procedure should be operational

TABLE 19–5   CONTROL OF MANAGERIAL DECISIONS IN INTERNATIONAL UNITS BY CORPORATE HEADQUARTERS

Nature of Supervision by Corporate Headquarters	Percentage of Respondents
Total decentralization. International units are independent and autonomous. Nominal ties only.	1.6
Complete autonomy in internal operations. Loose financial controls only.	15.6
Broad policies and guidelines with responsibilities and authority delegated to international units. Only important policy decisions such as new investments are made at the corporate headquarters.	35.9
International units are moderately controlled. In addition to all important policy decisions, some internal operating decisions are made at corporate headquarters.	31.3
Operational decisions are highly centralized.	10.9
Total centralization. All operating decisions are made at corporate headquarters.	4.7

Source: Guvenc G. Alpander, "Multinational Corporations: Homebase—Affiliate Relations," *California Management Review* (Spring 1978): 51. Copyright © 1978 by the Regents of the University of California. Reprinted from *California Management Review* XX, no. 3, p. 51, Table 3, by permission of the Regents.

and capable of providing the same degree of feedback that it does at home.

INTERNATIONAL MANAGEMENT—THE AUTHORS' VIEWPOINT

It is readily apparent that American business is becoming increasingly multinational in scope. Most large U.S. firms already receive a substantial portion of their sales and/or profits from abroad. American management cannot afford the complacency of commercial isolation.

Tomorrow's managers must have a working knowledge of overseas business situations. Many will gain this experience through an international assignment; others will acquire it while completing their regular duties. But regardless of how the knowledge is obtained, it surely must be obtained.

The authors suggest that today's business students pay very close attention to the international aspects of all their studies—management, finance, economics, and marketing. You are tomorrow's leaders, and tomorrow's leaders will have to be international leaders.

SUMMARY

Modern international management has adopted a contingency approach to worldwide operations. Adaptability is the key to effective international management.

It is important to distinguish international business concepts from international management concepts. International business is all business activity that crosses international boundaries. International management refers to the decision-making involved with international business activities. The multinational company (MNC) is the ultimate level of international business. An MNC views itself as global in nature. The sequence of international business development from exporting to sales subsidiaries to foreign production is outlined in this chapter.

Various environmental differences affect international management. These include political, cultural, and economic differences. The impact of these inherent variations is highlighted. Terms such as industrial democracy, technocrat, and exchange rate are also explained in this chapter.

The management functions of planning, organizing, staffing, leading, and controlling are as applicable abroad as they are at home. Each of the functional activities is explained in regard to its place in international management. Chapter 19 concludes with the authors' viewpoint on the key role of international management since future worklives will likely involve that dimension.

SOLVING THE STOP ACTION CASE

Materials Resource Corporation

MRC chairman Sheldon Weinig rejected the advice of his executive corps. Instead of laying people off, he made a public pledge to never again lay anyone off.

And what did Weinig get for his $4 million investment in excess wages? Loyalty for one thing. MRC would no longer have any problem recruiting a work force in the tough Rockland County labor market. Employee loyalty has long been considered one of the primary advantages of Japan's lifetime employment concept—a concept that Weinig had endorsed.

MRC also wisely took advantage of its extra employees. It put MRC employees in jobs that had traditionally been hired out: guard jobs and cleaning jobs. And it started its engineers and scientists working on projects they had not found the time for when the company was running at full tilt. There was suddenly time, also, to make customer calls, and this strategy shored up MRC's relations with its clientele.

The lifetime employment policy also seems to have kept unions out, although it was not instituted with that in mind. Weinig says the policy is actually only part of a long-term business plan, which includes heavy research and development spending. The emphasis at MRC is on performance and MRC has begun to perform like a winner. A 25 percent growth ratio is predicted for 1986.

MRC is not the only American company with a no-layoff plan. Such industry giants as Eli Lilly, IBM and Hewlett-Packard are also committed to keeping their workers during economic lulls. This is actually a stronger commitment to employees than Japan's much-touted lifetime employment policy, since Japan only guarantees jobs for men, and since Japanese workers can be forced to retire in their 50s. At MRC, it's all part of Sheldon Weinig's conception of his employee force. "People are very expensive assets," he says. "You should always protect the assets of a company."[24]

Source: Stan Luxenberg, "Lifetime Employment, U.S. Style," *New York Times,* 17 April 1983, p. 12F.

FACT OR FICTION REVEALED

1. Fact   2. Fact   3. Fact   4. Fiction   5. Fiction   6. Fiction

MANAGEMENT TERMS

exporting	**licensing**	**technocrat**
importing	**economic boycott**	**matrix organization**
international business	**industrial democracy**	**systems type leadership**
international management	**comparative management**	**organic type leadership**
MNC	**exchange rate**	**consensus management**

REVIEW QUESTIONS

1. Define the following terms: (a) exporting, (b) importing, (c) international business, (d) inter- national management, (e) MNC, (f) licensing, (g) economic boycott, (h) industrial democracy,

(i) comparative management, (j) exchange rate, (k) technocrat, (l) matrix organization, (m) systems type leadership, (n) organic type leadership, (o) consensus management.

2. Explain why adaptability is so important in international management.

3. Differentiate between international business and international management.

4. Compare and contrast the terms international management and comparative management.

5. Describe the sequence of international business development.

6. Discuss the various environmental differences affecting international management.

7. What features of the U.S. business environment are attractive to foreign investors?

8. What investment obstacles do foreigners perceive to exist in the United States?

9. Describe how the various functions of management operate within an international context.

10. Contrast the Japanese and American styles of management.

PROBLEMS AND EXPERIENTIAL EXERCISES

1. A recent report says that managers must be careful when giving business gifts overseas. They suggest avoiding:
   Clocks in China because clock sounds like funeral in China.
   Red roses in Germany, where they signify romance and would be inappropriate in a business situation.
   Black or purple colored gifts in Latin America since those colors are associated with penitence.[21]
   Relate these warnings to the material found in Chapter 19.

2. By the year 2025, it is estimated that 20.6 percent of Japan's population will be over sixty-five. The comparable figures will be 19.5 percent in the United States and 18.4 percent in Europe.[22] What impact will its aging population have on Japanese management in future decades?

3. The People's Republic of China has increased agricultural output by allowing workers on collective farms to produce and sell on the open market some of the output from their individual plots of land.[23] What can be learned from this experiment in private enterprise?

4. Texas Instruments (TI), the large, Dallas-based consumer electronics firm, has a style similar to the Japanese, TI's leading competitors. Texas Instruments prefers to hire new college graduates and train them, rather than hire away experienced professionals from other firms. "People involvement teams" are featured prominently in the TI organization. Few long-service employees are ever fired. Texas Instruments values employee seniority and loyalty. One vice-president even proclaimed: "The TI culture is a religion."[24] Prepare a report on the relative merits of TI's management style.

5. Do you agree with the trend toward using nationals of the host country to staff overseas positions? Explain.

MANAGERIAL INCIDENT: Toyota Motor Co.

Toyota Motor Co. has eight plants in Toyota City (population 290,000) in central Japan.

The company's presence is everywhere. Some 52,000 people work for Toyota here.

The company provides a fantastic array of benefits to its personnel. Here is a partial list: a free hospital; food and clothing from the company's retail cooperative; subsidized housing including dorms, apartments, and individual homes (in fact, in crowded Japan, Toyota's housing options are considered a major benefit); a low-interest loan fund; seventy-nine sports and cultural clubs; a 150-acre sports center complete with twelve tennis courts and an indoor swimming pool; seven mountain and coastal resorts; a private high school; and, Toyota's company saving plan pays nearly twice the going interest rates.

While many Americans might find the company's paternalistic presence confining, Toyota employees obviously approve. Assembly line turnover is only 3 to 4 percent annually and most higher ranked employees stay until retirement.

Questions

1. Would you like to work in a job environment like Toyota City? Why or why not?

2. Should Toyota use a similar approach in its U.S. plants? Discuss.

Source: Jim Abrams, "Toyota Eases Workers Down Assembly Line of Life," *Seattle Times,* 12 June 1982, p. 1C. Reprinted by permission of the Associated Press.

20 SOCIAL RESPONSIBILITY AND MANAGEMENT ETHICS

LEARNING OBJECTIVES

After studying this chapter you should be able to

1. Explain the concept of social responsibility.

2. Outline the phases of management's social responsibility.

3. Identify the current status of management ethics.

4. Describe the various levels of social responsibility.

5. Discuss the Sethi model of corporate behavior.

6. Explain the measurement of social responsibility.

STOP ACTION CASE

Hershey Chocolate Co.

The typical American eats fifteen pounds of chocolate annually. A lot of it comes from Hershey Chocolate Co. The Pennsylvania firm's product has been a consumer favorite for decades. But on March 28, 1979, the company faced one of the biggest crises in its history.

A few minutes away from the largest chocolate factory in the world, the Three-Mile Island nuclear power plant experienced a widely publicized radiation leak. The nuclear accident had a potentially far-reaching effect on Hershey. Its plant requires fifty tons of milk a day and much of it came from nearby dairy farmers. And experts cited milk—should it contain radiation contamination—as a major cause of thyroid cancer in children.

Hershey's management faced a crisis of major proportions. How could it best react to the Three-Mile Island situation in a socially responsible manner?

Use the materials in this chapter to develop a strategy that will enable Hershey Chocolate Co. to protect consumers from radiation contamination to the greatest extent possible.

Social responsibility has almost as many definitions as there are people willing to define the concept.[1] At its extremes, management's social responsibility can be alternatively described as profit maximization, or as a total corporate immersion in society's problems, as through philanthropy. A reasonable definition of *social responsibility* is those management philosophies, policies, procedures, and actions that have the advancement of society's welfare as one of their primary objectives. This view acknowledges the equivalent importance of traditional profitability objectives and attempts to balance them with socially oriented objectives.

The key to setting contemporary standards of social responsibility is to be able to tie the idea of corporate involvement in social and public issues to traditional standards of profitability. FMC Corp.—a diversified manufacturer with products ranging from industrial chemicals to airfreight equipment—takes this approach in determining how and where it will direct its contributions.[2] FMC has two basic requirements: (1) its contribution will help areas in which FMC facilities are located, or in which its employees live; and (2) the corporation's business environment should be improved by such a donation. Examples of FMC's specific guidelines to supporting educational institutions include:

- Give financial support to colleges and universities that supply our manpower needs or are located in communities where we have facilities (provided that the other guidelines mentioned in this list are also met).

- Make grants to schools that present the case for the competitive enterprise philosophy and those that present a balanced perspective of our economic system.

- Make grants in support of minority programs in fields relevant to the company's business.

In order to understand the modern social responsibility climate, it is useful to look briefly at the evolution of this concept in management. While *Management* concludes with a discussion of social responsibility and

Social responsibility refers to those management philosophies, policies, procedures, and actions that have the advancement of society's welfare as one of their primary objectives.

MANAGEMENT FACT OR FICTION

	FACT	FICTION
1. The trustee management era in social responsibility was based solely on profit maximization.	☐	☐
2. A public opinion survey ranked business executives third in a list of 25 occupations in terms of the perceived adherence to ethical standards.	☐	☐
3. Managers view themselves as less ethical than physicians and college professors.	☐	☐
4. Most executives support ethical codes that prefer specific practice codes rather than general precept codes.	☐	☐
5. Adam Smith is associated with the enlightened self interest view of social responsibility.	☐	☐
6. Community projects, contributions, equal employment opportunity, environmental concerns, energy conservation, voluntarism, and social investments can all be used to measure social responsibility.	☐	☐

The materials in this chapter will assist you in separating management fact from fiction. Your answers can be checked on page 661.

executive behavior, the authors readily acknowledge the many arguments for covering this material much earlier in the course. We believe that this chapter is a concise, self-contained unit that provides a valuable introduction to this important topic.

THREE HISTORICAL PHASES OF MANAGEMENT'S SOCIAL RESPONSIBILITY

Social responsibility in organizations has evolved through three distinct phases or stages. Each required its own unique managerial value system.

The phases are: Phase 1—Profit maximizing management; Phase 2—Trusteeship management; and Phase 3—"Quality of life" management.

Profit maximizing management was based on Adam Smith's concept that people acting in their self-interest would provide or create an invisible hand that would guide the advancement of society. Managers with this orientation believed that their sole goal was to maximize profits. Profit maximization was viewed as a socially responsible action because it created a stronger economy. Applicable business laws were the only requirement to be met by managers of this era—the nineteenth century and early part of the twentieth century.

Trusteeship management, a product of the 1920s and 1930s, acknowledged that other groups such as employees, customers, creditors, and the like had claims on the organization that competed with those of the firm's owners. Trusteeship management was responsible to all these contributor groups. Thus, the concept of social responsibility was broadened beyond its original narrow base of profit maximization.

Phase 3 can be dated from about 1950. Popular concern with the quality of life dictated that management direct some of its efforts and resources to the solution of broader societal issues. Phase 3 goes beyond improving the national standard of living by emphasizing quality, not merely quantity, standards.

The third phase saw an increasing number of managers devoting considerable time and corporate effort to such social responsibilities as developing special programs to improve hiring and promotion opportunities for women and minority employees; developing improved pollution control systems; and making a concerted effort to hire handicapped workers. In many instances these actions were undertaken by managers who recognized that these measures were part of their societal responsibilities. In other instances they resulted from government laws and regulations.

The current view of social responsibility is mixed. Most modern managers are devotees of the Phase 2 viewpoint. An increasing number advocate the characteristics of Phase 3. The general trend is in the direction of Phase 3, partly due to growing acceptance of social obligations and partly due to government requirements.[3]

MANAGEMENT ETHICS

In 1985, the General Dynamics Corporation, the nation's third largest defense contractor, was accused of padding the bills it submits to the federal government with such improper overhead expenses as the cost of boarding an executive's dog and the significantly higher cost of political lobbying. The Navy also pointed to the improper gifts General Dynamics made to the late Adm. Hyman G. Rickover, who until his retirement in 1982 directed the Navy's nuclear submarine program. The year 1985 also saw the giant securities firm E. F. Hutton plead guilty to defrauding more

66 I made my money by supplying a public demand. If I break the law, my customers, who number hundreds of the best people in Chicago, are as guilty as I am. The only difference between us is that I sell and they buy. Everybody calls me a racketeer. I call myself a businessman. When I sell liquor, it's bootlegging. When my patrons serve it on a silver tray on Lake Shore Drive it's hospitality. 99

Al Capone

MANAGEMENT SUCCESSES

Champion of Environmental Protection

 Wearing his battered cowboy hat, Robert Anderson looks the part of a self-made oil-and-ranching baron.

As founder and chairman of the Atlantic Richfield Company, Anderson, 67, travels the world in a private jet.

. . .

Yet ecologists describe the son of a Chicago investment banker as a corporate leader who is uncommonly supportive of environmental protection.

During a bitter two-year congressional battle over amendments to the Clean Air Act in the mid-1970s, Anderson broke ranks with corporate leaders by insisting that motor-vehicle emissions be controlled. "He has the ability to face reality and saw the reality of the need to control air pollution," comments Russell Train, former head of the Environmental Protection Agency.

Anderson became deeply interested in environmental protection 20 years ago when the Egyptian government asked him to serve on a committee deciding the fate of the 3,000-year-old Temple of Dendur, which was about to be flooded by the Aswan Dam project. The stone temple wound up in the Metropolitan Museum of Art in New York, away from the ravages of air pollution.

"It needed air conditioning to protect it from the air that you and I breathe. When a stone building 3,000 years old cannot be moved anywhere except to an air-conditioned atmosphere, it is time to give some thought to what we are doing," he says.

Since then, Anderson has been a catalyst for many environmental causes. He provided seed money for the Friends of the Earth, a major U.S. environmental group, as well as for the London-based International Institute for Environment and Development.

Anderson founded the Aspen Institute for Humanistic Studies in Colorado, where business people discuss social issues with scholars, scientists and artists.

Under Anderson, ARCO granted money to the Nature Conservancy, a nonprofit land-protection organization, to help it buy Santa Cruz Island in California. He also hired Angus Gavin, a leading wildlife-protection expert, for advice on minimizing oil spills after huge reserves were discovered on Alaska's North Slope in 1968. ARCO's techniques for handling emergencies at sea are now so advanced that tugboats can surround a burning tanker and contain a spill within 3 minutes.

Recently, ARCO has begun placing massive concrete pyramid cones over natural oil seeps in the Pacific to capture more crude oil and to get an emission-reduction credit that can be used to balance out pollution elsewhere.

Anderson ranks environment and conservation among his top interests, along with politics and his vast land holdings—more than a million acres in New Mexico and Texas.

Says he: "We are trying to maintain nearly 5 billion people on a planet that has an environmentally optimum capacity of 2 or 3 billion. As the population increases and people want a higher and better standard of living, the pressure on the environment is going to increase."

than 400 banks of millions of dollars through an elaborate scheme that allowed the company to overdraw its accounts. Hutton took advantage of money in transit from one bank to another to obtain interest-free use of bank cards.

These incidents indicate the range and diversity of the ethical problems that face executives.[4] *Management ethics* refers to the moral premises upon which executive decisions are made. Most people view ethical business practices as an inherent part of management's responsibility to society.

Management ethics refers to the moral premises upon which executive decisions are made.

THE PUBLIC'S VIEWPOINT

How does the public evaluate the status of management ethics? The Gallup polling organization found that business executives ranked fifteenth in a list of twenty-five occupations ranked according to their perceived adherence to ethical standards. Clergymen, pharmacists, medical doctors, dentists, college teachers, engineers, policemen, bankers, TV reporters and commentators, journalists, newspaper reporters, lawyers, and stockbrokers were ranked higher. Table 20–1 shows the ranking of all twenty-five occupations.

Another survey focused on the responses by business executives. Managers viewed themselves as less ethical than medical doctors and college professors. However, the executives saw themselves as more ethical than politicians, lawyers, union leaders, and officials of government agencies.[5]

HOW MANAGEMENT ETHICS CHANGE

The *Harvard Business Review* published a 1977 follow-up on a 1961 study about the ethics of U.S. business executives. This comparison produced the following conclusions:

- There is a substantial disagreement among respondents as to whether ethical standards in business today have changed from what they were.

- Respondents are somewhat more cynical about the ethical conduct of their peers than they were.

- Most respondents favor ethical codes, although they strongly prefer general precept codes to specific practice codes.

- The dilemmas respondents experience and the factors they feel have the greatest impact on business ethics suggest that ethical codes alone will not substantially improve business conduct.

- Most respondents have overcome the traditional ideological barriers to the concept of social responsibility and have embraced its practice as a legitimate and achievable goal for business.

TABLE 20–1 THE PUBLIC'S RANKINGS OF HONESTY AND ETHICAL STANDARDS OF SELECTED OCCUPATIONAL GROUPS

	Very High, High	Very High	High	Average	Low	Very Low	No Opinion
Clergymen	64%	24%	40%	27%	3%	1%	5%
Druggists, pharmacists	61	14	47	33	3	1	2
Medical doctors	52	14	38	35	7	4	2
Dentists	51	8	43	41	3	2	3
College teachers	47	10	37	38	4	1	10
Engineers	45	7	38	39	2	1	13
Policemen	41	7	34	45	7	4	3
Bankers	38	5	33	49	7	2	4
TV reporters, commentators	33	5	28	47	11	4	5
Funeral directors	29	5	24	43	12	7	9
Journalists	28	4	24	47	13	4	8
Newspaper reporters	26	3	23	52	12	4	6
Lawyers	24	5	19	43	18	9	6
Stockbrokers	19	2	17	45	8	3	25
Business executives	18	3	15	55	15	5	7
Senators	16	2	14	48	21	9	6
Building contractors	18	3	15	53	18	5	6
Local political officeholders	16	2	14	49	21	8	6
Congressmen	14	3	11	43	26	12	5
Realtors	13	2	11	52	21	7	7
State political officeholders	13	2	11	49	23	8	7
Insurance salesmen	13	1	12	49	22	12	4
Labor union leaders	12	2	10	35	24	20	9
Advertising practitioners	9	2	7	42	26	13	10
Car salesmen	6	1	5	34	32	23	5

Source: The Gallup Report (July 1983), Report No. 214 (Princeton, NJ: The Gallup Poll).

- Most respondents rank their customers well ahead of shareholders and employees as the client group to whom they feel the greatest responsibility.[6]

The study suggests a variety of factors that influence standards. Some act to raise standards, others tend to lower them. Table 20–2 presents a listing of these influencing factors. The three most frequently cited factors causing higher standards were public disclosure, increased public concern, and government regulation. By contrast, the most often mentioned factors leading to *lower* standards were a lowering of society's standards, competition, political ethics and climate, and public awareness of unethical acts.

TABLE 20-2   FACTORS INFLUENCING ETHICAL STANDARDS

Factors Causing Higher Standards	Percentage of Respondents Listing Factor
Public disclosure; publicity; media coverage; better communication	31%
Increased public concern; public awareness, consciousness, and scrutiny; better informed public; societal pressures	20
Government regulation, legislation, and intervention; federal courts	10
Education of business managers; increase in manager professionalism and education	9
New social expectations for the role business is to play in society; young adults' attitudes; consumerism	5
Business's greater sense of social responsibility and greater awareness of the implications of its acts; business responsiveness; corporate policy changes; top management emphasis on ethical action	5
Other	20
Factors Causing Lower Standards	
Society's standards are lower; social decay; more permissive society; materialism and hedonism have grown; loss of church and home influence; less quality, more quantity desires	34%
Competition; pace of life; stress to succeed; current economic conditions; costs of doing business; more businesses compete for less	13
Political corruption; loss of confidence in government; Watergate; politics; political ethics and climate	9
People more aware of unethical acts; constant media coverage; TV; communications create atmosphere for crime	9
Greed; desire for gain; worship the dollar as measure of success; selfishness of the individual; lack of personal integrity and moral fiber	8
Pressure for profit from within the organization from superiors or from stockholders; corporate influences on managers; corporate policies	7
Other	21

Source: Reprinted by permission of the *Harvard Business Review.* Excerpt from "Is the Ethics of Business Changing?" by Stephen N. Brenner and Earl A. Molander (January–February 1977). Copyright © 1977 by the President and Fellows of Harvard College; all rights reserved.

NOTE: Some respondents listed more than one factor, so there were 353 factors in all listed as causing higher standards and 411 in all listed as causing lower ones. Categories may not add up to 100 due to rounding errors.

SELECTED VIEWPOINTS ON MANAGEMENT'S SOCIAL RESPONSIBILITY

A subject as complex as social responsibility is certain to produce a multitude of views among management theorists, writers, practitioners, and others. One useful classification contains three components: (1) the popular viewpoint; (2) the traditional viewpoint; and (3) enlightened self-interest.[7]

THE POPULAR VIEWPOINT

This viewpoint might be termed the Steiner-Davis argument since it is often associated with George Steiner and Keith Davis, two leading management theorists. The Steiner-Davis view is "that the doctrine of corporate social responsibility has evolved from a changing managerial philosophy which explicitly recognizes the obligations of the corporation to society and eschews the narrow goal of simply increasing profits or earnings."[8] In other words the popular view of social responsibility goes beyond a mere profit orientation.

Management professor Joseph W. McGuire is also associated with the popular viewpoint. He puts it this way:

> A socially responsible company is one in which the ownership utility function does not dominate those of other claimants in all situations and at all times. It is a company where the satisfactions of non-owner claimants are taken into account, and where the totality of organizational satisfactions is widely shared. The more equitable the distribution of organizational satisfactions, the greater the social responsibility of the company.[9]

The popular viewpoint, then, is of the businessperson who realizes the full extent of his or her social responsibilities. Those responsibilities are then built into the decision-making process.

THE TRADITIONAL VIEWPOINT

The traditional viewpoint is that expressed by economists relying on Adam Smith's *Wealth of Nations*.[10] The basic premise is that an "invisible hand" of self-interest is the best guide for the business system. Profit maximization is the accepted goal.

Milton Friedman, a recipient of the Nobel Prize for economics, is the best-known advocate of this position. Friedman feels that management's responsibility is to represent the interests of stockholders—not of other groups as a whole. Friedman argues that social issues are best confronted by government, not by private enterprise.[11] Adam Smith's words will ring true for proponents of this viewpoint: "I have never known much good

66 Capitalism is humanitarianism. 99

Margaret Thatcher

done by those who affected to trade for the public good."[12] Similarly, Robert Mercer, Goodyear's CEO, told a student audience:

> The number one corporate responsibility is to make a profit . . . this sounds like you're not even thinking of society, your fellow man or anybody else. It sounds like you're selfish. But profit is like breathing. If you can't do that, you can forget about doing anything else. Once a corporation learns how to breathe, or make a profit, then it can turn to the other corporate responsibilities, like creating jobs and adding to GNP (gross national product).[13]

ENLIGHTENED SELF-INTEREST

Enlightened self-interest is a description of how many modern managers view their responsibilities. This third viewpoint merges the popular and traditional concepts by recognizing that being socially responsible is simply good business.

Henry Ford noted that corporate failure to respond to societal challenges often results in heavy-handed government intervention. Citing an example from his own industry, Ford noted: "Maybe we wouldn't have won any prizes if we had answered auto-safety charges more effectively before the consumerists moved into the area, but we would have saved ourselves—and our customers—some nightmarish regulations."[14]

Du Pont's retired board chairman, Irving S. Shapiro, is a leading proponent of this viewpoint. Shapiro, who spent 30 to 40 percent of his time dealing with public issues, noted:

> I think we're a means to an end, and while producing goods and providing jobs is our primary function, we can't live successfully in a society if the hearts of its cities are decaying and its people can't support their families. We've got to help make the whole system work, and that involves more than just having a safe workplace and providing jobs for the number of people we can hire. It means that just as you want libraries, and you want schools, and you want fire departments and police departments, you also want businesses to help do something about unsolved social problems.[15]

The enlightened self-interest viewpoint is that being socially responsible is also good business practice in that it will lead to greater long-run profits. Management must also make the level of social responsibility compatible with other corporate goals and their own set of business ethics. The different levels of social responsibility are discussed in the section that follows.

> 66 I believe that every right implies a responsibility; every opportunity, an obligation; every possession, a duty. 99
>
> John D. Rockefeller, Jr.

LEVELS OF SOCIAL RESPONSIBILITY

A number of levels exist in management's response to social responsibility issues. One way to look at this problem is to focus on the extremes. The

THE MANAGER'S BOOKSHELF

The 100 Best Companies to Work for in America, by Robert Levering, Milton Moskowitz, and Michael Katz

The authors of this recent best-seller argue that most books on management (and the business press in general) tend to judge companies only by their growth and profit figures, not by "the human condition inside business." In other words, we rarely get to see what American workers think about the place where they spend so many of their waking hours. Rarer still are comparisons of American companies strictly from the standpoint of the employees. Levering, Katz, and Moskowitz set out to provide just such information and their book, *The 100 Best Companies to Work for in America* (Addison-Wesley, 1984), is a compendium of the country's best employers and, implicitly, a look at what produces a harmonious organization.

The authors began by asking friends, relatives, consultants, publishers, and anyone else they could find, which companies they regarded as the best places in America to work. That yielded 350 possibilities, which were whittled down to 135 by reading through whatever literature the authors could talk those companies into sending them. That literature convinced the authors that they needed to visit the companies and see firsthand how they worked. The authors then spent a year visiting 114 companies in 27 states, observing and interviewing people at all company levels.

This admittedly less-than-scientific procedure resulted in the authors' selection of the 100 "best" companies, which they then ranked according to a five-part rating system: pay, benefits, job security, chance to move up, and corporate ambience. The companies who made the cut included the usual IBMs, Procter & Gambles, and General Electrics, but it also offered some surprises: the Los Angeles

most rudimentary position is for management simply to be aware that a social responsibility does exist in a given set of circumstances.[16] At the other extreme is the thorough integration of social responsibility considerations into the organization. Intermediate level responses may be viewed as falling somewhere on a spectrum between these two alternatives—as illustrated in Figure 20–1.

Instead of attempting to place the entire organization at some point along the social responsibility continuum, it may prove more useful to focus on specific social responsibility areas. For instance, fair employment practices may be fully integrated throughout the organization and located at the far right in Figure 20–1. Energy-saving programs might rank in the middle range, while a special program to encourage voluntarism among employees may be just beginning. Such programs would fall to the extreme left in the social responsibility continuum. This focus on levels of social

Dodgers, for instance, and Celestial Seasonings. Generally, the authors found employees like best those companies that sell a high-quality product or service, offer liberal benefits and such perks as stock options, have a nonadversary posture toward their employees, promote from within, and protect their employees from layoffs.

But companies also have special qualities that the authors have categorized under "ambience." These qualities often reveal themselves in interesting ways. *Reader's Digest,* for instance, gives twelve paid holidays a year, at least four weeks vacation for anyone who's been there over a year, and closes down completely every Friday in May because "May is such a pretty month." S. C. Johnson & Sons provides its workers with a 147-acre park containing softball fields, tennis courts, jogging trails, golf driving ranges, picnic areas, and a gym with two basketball courts, volleyball courts, squash, racquetball, archery, and meeting rooms.

The corporate cultures of the 100 best companies are hardly uniform. They range from that of Intel Corporation, where employees push themselves in an intensely competitive environment, to the atmosphere at W. L. Gore & Associates, Inc., where a business school grad, on his first day, was told to "Look around and find something you'd like to do." Wal-Mart Stores, Inc. inspires employees to dedication with numerous personal awards and an intense family feeling, whereas Tandy Corporation motivates its workers with the possibility that they too may make a fortune with the company, like the sixty company employees so far (and not just executives) who have become millionaires.

Though the profiled 100 best companies cannot be neatly squeezed into one picture of the ideal place to work, there does seem to be a general quality that runs through all worker-respected companies: a breaking down of the barriers between workers and management. Smaller companies tend to be better at this than larger ones; consequently, employees tended to rank them as better places to work than the larger ones. And those larger companies that were rated high tended to maintain some small-company traits, often on purpose.

responsibility for a large number of individual social responsibility areas may prove much more insightful than an attempt to categorize the entire organization.

FIGURE 20–1.   Spectrum of Social Responsibility

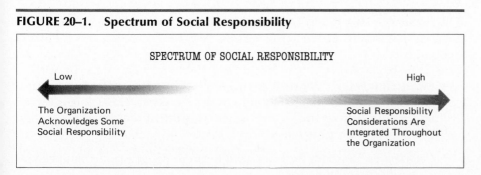

THE SETHI MODEL OF CORPORATE BEHAVIOR

Management tends to respond to a dual set of social forces: market and nonmarket. The firm can adapt its competitive strategy to meet marketplace demands and its success may be evaluated by volume and profitability standards. Nonmarket forces—often called *externalities*—have placed an increased burden on management. Traditionally, such externalities as pollution have been dealt with by the whole society. Today, however, business is being asked to play a greater role in the solution of these problems. How has business responded?

University of Texas business professor S. Prakash Sethi has identified three stages in corporate behavior: (1) social obligation; (2) social responsibility; and (3) social responsiveness.[17]

Social obligation refers to corporate behavior designed to deal only with legal requirements and competitive market factors. The second stage, social responsibility, refers to corporate behavior that complies with contemporary values, norms, and expectations of society. Since many societal standards will later become part of the legal framework for management, stage two may be viewed as prescriptive in nature, rather than descriptive as was the case in stage one. Social responsiveness is the third stage of corporate behavior. Here, management is expected to anticipate various changes and to take appropriate preventive action. As Table 20–3 shows, the Sethi model relates the three stages to various dimensions of corporate behavior.

Externalities are nonmarket social forces.

MEASURING SOCIAL RESPONSIBILITY

There have been numerous proposals and attempts to measure social responsibility. While these efforts are to be applauded, their findings are often mixed. One of the primary problems seems to be indecision as to what should be measured. A closely related issue is how to measure such items.

WHAT SHOULD BE MEASURED?

The insurance industry is often cited as a leader in the measurement of social responsibility. Its social reporting program includes the following categories:

- *Community projects* defined as those in which the company played a significant role or provided substantial support. These include civic and cultural programs, youth activities, student and school activities, and local health programs.

- *Contributions* to federated drives, education programs, urban/civic affairs, and cultural activities.

Social Responsibility

Businesses choose to act in a socially responsible manner for many reasons, including good public relations, the stated corporate mission and values; and even long-term economic gain for the company and also for its surrounding community. Aware of the rewards of socially responsible behavior, many companies have undertaken a variety of actions to meet this objective.

The various cases in this photo essay provide a broad spectrum of examples of the many benefits to business and to our society of specific socially responsible activities.

(Above) The Atlantic Richfield Corporation is involved with community development projects. Their La Plaza de la Raza is an educational center serving the Hispanic community.

(Left) The Clear Lake plant of Celanese Chemical Company is a good neighbor of the Bayou. It maintains a clean lake and a healthy work and living environment.

(Right) Control Data Corporation's HOME-WORK program provides vocational training for people who are disabled. The program produces qualified and competent potential employees—a valuable human resource for Control Data Corporation.

(Below) Young women athletes are provided an opportunity to test themselves in the Colgate Women's Games sponsored by Colgate-Palmolive.

(Below) Burlington Industries assisted drought-stricken farms in North Carolina with "Operation Hayride."

(Left) An Exxon grant provided essential funds to the Houston Zoo.

Below) Shell Oil's SERVE program offers many community services. In Houston, TX, volunteers helped to renovate an elderly woman's home.

(Right) The Toyota Motor Corporation sponsors an annual Traffic Safety Program to teach children how to be safe pedestrians.

(Left) Northrup Corporation expects to train a segment of its future work force with its high school-involvement program. Seniors get credit for work in aerospace and advanced technology.

(Right) The Telephone Pioneers of America sponsor an annual "Doll Drive" to bring joy to children who would otherwise have no dolls with which to play.

Dimensions of Behavior	Stage One: Social Obligation Prescriptive	Stage Two: Social Responsibility Prescriptive	Stage Three: Social Responsiveness Anticipatory and Preventive
Response to social pressures	Maintains low public profile, but, if attacked, uses PR methods to upgrade its public image; denies any deficiencies; blames public dissatisfaction on ignorance or failure to understand corporate functions; discloses information only where legally required.	Accepts responsibility for solving current problems; will admit deficiencies in former practices and attempt to persuade public that its current practices meet social norms; attitude toward critics conciliatory; freer information disclosures than stage one.	Willingly discusses activities with outside groups; makes information freely available to public; accepts formal and informal inputs from outside groups in decision making; is willing to be publicly evaluated for its various activities.
Activities pertaining to governmental actions	Strongly resists any regulation of its activities except when it needs help to protect its market position; avoids contact; resists any demands for information beyond that legally required.	Preserves management discretion in corporate decisions, but cooperates with government in research to improve industrywide standards; participates in political processes and encourages employees to do likewise.	Openly communicates with government; assists in enforcing existing laws and developing evaluations of business practices; objects publicly to governmental activities that it feels are detrimental to the public good.
Legislative and political activities	Seeks to maintain status quo; actively opposes laws that would internalize any previously externalized costs; seeks to keep lobbying activities secret.	Willing to work with outside groups for good environmental laws; concedes need for change in some status quo laws; less secrecy in lobbying than stage one.	Avoids meddling in politics and does not pursue special interest laws; assists legislative bodies in developing better laws where relevant; promotes honesty and openness in government and in its own lobbying activities.
Philanthropy	Contributes only when direct benefit to it clearly shown; otherwise, views contributions as responsibility of individual employees.	Contributes to noncontroversial and established causes; matches employee contributions.	Activities of stage two, plus support and contributions to new, controversial groups whose needs it sees as unfulfilled and increasingly important.

Source: S. Prakash Sethi, "A Conceptual Framework for Environmental Analysis of Social Issues and Evaluation of Business Response Patterns," Academy of Management Review 4, no. 1 (January 1979): 67. Reprinted with permission of the author.

- *Equal employment opportunity* for women and minority group members, including both initial employment and promotions.

- *Environmental concerns and energy conservation* defined as the existence of policies or procedures directed at energy conservation.

- *Voluntarism* measured according to the number and hours contributed by persons loaned to or given release time for public service work; and the percentage of companies having programs to encourage individual involvement.

- *Social investments* that would not have been made under the company's customary lending standards, or those in which social consideration played a substantial part in the investment decision.[18]

After studying the insurance industry's social reporting program, former Commerce Secretary Juanita Kreps once suggested that the federal government establish a "social performance index." Some firms owned by the governments of the United Kingdom and France have "social contracts" that reward the firms for their social contributions. A variety of other proposals have surfaced in recent years.[19] But what are the actual practices of American industry in this critical area?

FIGURE 20–2.   Percentages of Companies Making Social Responsibility Disclosures by Category
Source: Adapted by permission from Dennis R. Beresford and Scott S. Cowen, "Surveying Social Responsibility Disclosure in Annual Reports," *Business* (March–April 1979): 16. Published by Georgia State University.

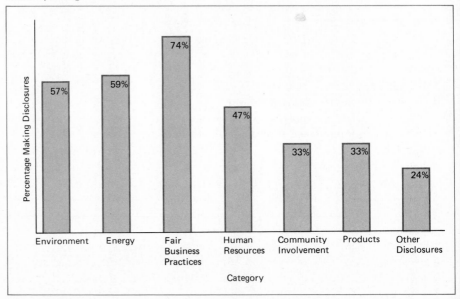

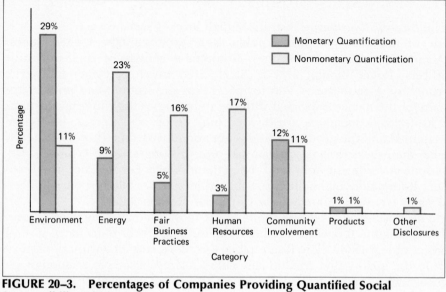

FIGURE 20–3.   Percentages of Companies Providing Quantified Social Responsibility Disclosures

THE ERNST & WHINNEY SURVEY

Ernst & Whinney, a major public accounting firm, has surveyed companies about their involvement in/and disclosure of social responsibility issues.[20] They focused on the nation's 500 largest industrial companies, 50 largest life insurance firms, and 50 biggest banks, as listed in *Fortune* magazine.

Almost 9 of every 10 of *Fortune*'s 500 now make social responsibility disclosures. Some 40 percent of the respondents have a special social responsibility section in their annual reports.

Social responsibility disclosures vary by the categories used in the Ernst & Whinney study. As Figure 20–2 reveals, comments about fair business practice are the most cited disclosure category. Energy rates second.

Some firms supplement their social responsibility disclosures with quantified information—either in monetary or nonmonetary terms. The extent of this supplementary disclosure is shown in Figure 20–3.

The Ernst & Whinney data demonstrate that a socially responsible management philosophy is the norm in American industry. The accounting firm's research provides some benchmarks in this crucial area, even though it is limited to only a select group of major companies and their annual report disclosures. In fact, one analyst suggests that "most U.S. companies participate in more socially responsible activities than are indicated in their annual reports."[21]

THE BUSINESS ROUNDTABLE

Business Roundtable is a group of top managers from different organizations who meet to discuss public issues and report their opinions as business representatives.

The *Business Roundtable* illustrates a high level of social responsibility. It is one of the most prestigious public issue groups in the United States. Organized in 1972, the Business Roundtable consists of chief executive officers. Roger Blough of U.S. Steel, Fred Borch of General Electric, economist Arthur Burns, and former Texas Governor John Connally are some of the names associated with the founding of this important forum.

Roundtable members are divided into various task forces. Issues are examined and the group's positions are announced. The Business Roundtable then seeks to make its views known to Congress, the White House, various government units, and the general public. For instance, the Business Roundtable highlighted the importance of socially responsible decisions by issuing a "Statement of Corporate Responsibility."

The Business Roundtable is one of the most effective groups of its kind in Washington. It is widely credited with influencing the outcome of several pieces of legislation. The Roundtable also represents an abrupt departure from the apathy that traditionally characterized business's relations with government. Today, several states have groups patterned after the national organization.[22]

SUMMARY

Social responsibility refers to management philosophies, policies, procedures, and actions that have the advancement of society's welfare as one of their primary objectives. The social responsibility issue had gone through three distinct stages. In stage one, management viewed profit maximization as its primary obligation. Stage two can be called trustee management, when executives realized that such groups as employees, customers, and vendors also had claims on the organization. Trustee management was responsible to all these contributor groups. In stage three, concern with the quality of life meant that management had to direct some of its efforts and resources to the solution of societal issues.

Ethical business practice is closely tied to management's social responsibility. Management ethics refers to the moral premises upon which executive decisions are made. The current state of management ethics gets mixed reviews. A Gallup Poll reported that, in the public's eyes, executives ranked fifteenth in a list of twenty-five occupations in terms of their honesty and ethical standards. A longitudinal report on management ethics by the *Harvard Business Review* noted that respondents tended to disagree on whether or not business ethics had improved over the years.

Most viewpoints on management's social responsibility can be categorized into one of three groupings: popular, traditional, or enlightened self-interest. The first view is of a management that realized the full extent of its social responsibilities. The traditional viewpoint is that management exists to serve the firm's stockholders and that profit maximization should be the prevailing corporate objective. Enlightened self-interest attempts to merge the first two concepts by realizing that being socially responsible is simply good business.

This chapter also examines the various levels of social responsibility. Table 20–3 shows the Sethi model, which identifies three stages of corporate behavior: social obligation, social responsibility, and social responsiveness. An open discussion of management's views on public affairs is an approach to social responsibility practiced by the Business Roundtable—a public issue group consisting of chief executive officers.

The insurance industry—often cited as one of the leaders in the measurement of social responsibility—uses the following categories to assess its social performance: community projects, contributions, equal employment opportunity, environmental concerns and energy conservation, voluntarism, and social investments.

The chapter also discusses the findings of Ernst & Whinney's survey of industry's involvement in/and disclosure of social responsibility issues. The accounting firm's data show that about nine out of every ten corporations in the *Fortune* 500 list make social responsibility disclosures. Fair business practice is the most often cited disclosure category. Energy places second.

SOLVING THE STOP ACTION CASE

Hershey Chocolate Co.

The Three-Mile Island incident presented Hershey Chocolate Co. with a major crisis since its plant was located nearby. The Hershey management quickly instituted new, more stringent controls to cover all milk and other materials coming into the plant from within a seventy-five mile radius. Although radiation tests indicated no problems, management went a step further by isolating the milk received from a ten-mile radius of the Three-Mile Island site. None proved to be contaminated. Another decision was to convert milk brought from local farmers into powder that could be held until all possible radiation content disappeared. A Hershey spokesperson summed up the firm's actions this way: "While we have no indication of anything wrong with any product, if we are going to err we want to err on the safe side."

Hershey Chocolate's management conducted itself in a highly professional and socially responsible manner. While few executives will ever have to face health threats of this magnitude, Hershey's immediate and comprehensive response to the Three-Mile Island incident suggests the ethical standards maintained by most contemporary managers.

Source: Dennis Montgomery, "Candy Firm Monitoring Atomic Risk," *Detroit News,* 2 April 1979, pp. 3A, 6A.

FACT OR FICTION REVEALED

1. Fiction   2. Fiction   3. Fact   4. Fiction   5. Fiction   6. Fact

MANAGEMENT TERMS

social responsibility   **externalities**   **Business Roundtable**
management ethics

REVIEW QUESTIONS

1. Define the following terms: (a) social responsibility, (b) management ethics, (c) externalities, (d) Business Roundtable.

2. Outline the historical phases of the social responsibility issue.

3. Discuss the current status of management ethics.

4. Contrast the popular, traditional, and enlightened self-interest views of social responsibility.

5. Discuss the varying levels of social responsibility.

6. Describe the Sethi model of corporate behavior.

7. Why might a corporation give money to support cultural activities?

8. How can society measure management's social responsibility?

9. What does the Ernst & Whinney survey reveal about the level of social responsibility in the United States?

10. Does a local version of the Business Roundtable exist in your area? If so, what are the issues with which it is currently dealing?

PROBLEMS AND EXPERIENTIAL EXCERCISES

1. Outline what you think are Union Carbide's social responsibilities with respect to the Bhopal chemical disaster. Outline an action plan that Union Carbide might follow in this situation.

2. *Fortune* surveyed 8,000 managers, financial analysts, and outside directors about the regulation of various large corporations. The highest-ranked in terms of community and environmental responsibility were Eastman Kodak, Johnson & Johnson, IBM, and 3M.[23] Why do you think these firms were so highly regarded?

3. Mutual Benefit Life Company polled chief executive officers about the role of volunteerism in contemporary business. Eighty-six percent said community involvement enhanced the firm's profitability. Over 85 percent said it improved employee morale. Seventy-two percent concluded that volunteers expand their business contacts. And 50 percent of the chief executives said volunteerism increased organizational productivity.[24] Do you agree with the conclusions reached in the Mutual Benefit study? Why or why not?

4. First Federal Savings and Loan Association of Cumberland, Maryland, once fired a teller because she refused to contribute to the local United Way. Prior to this incident, the firm had a record of 100 percent participation for twenty-five years. But the teller refused to donate because of moral objections to some of the organizations supported by United Way. The association later issued an apology and offered to rehire the teller.[25] What can be learned from this incident?

5. Membership on a firm's board of directors has often been treated as an honorary position for people not actually employed by the organization. But both "outside" and "inside" directors (those who are also employees) are increasingly being held responsible for the actions of management and employees. Do you think directors should be the ones who must accept the ultimate social responsibility? If so, under what conditions would your judgment apply?

MANAGERIAL INCIDENT: Alexander Manufacturing Inc.

Nicolas Alexander was a 13-year-old Polish underground fighter when he was captured by the Germans in World War II. When the war ended, the young prisoner of war emigrated to England. He later moved to the United States, and ended up in Portland, Oregon. Today, Alexander's fixture firm supplies various hotels and restaurants in 37 states. Alexander Manufacturing Inc.—located in suburban Portland—has annual sales of $8 million, and employs 100 people.

Alexander is well known for his attention to his customers and employees. He prides himself on the fact that he has never delivered a job late. He also looks out for his employees by providing an extensive array of fringe benefits including legal and tax planning services, financial planning, and even low-interest loans. When employees have to install Alexander's fixtures out of town, he pays for their families to join them, or pays for the employees to come home on weekends.

Employees are also given an hour of overtime each week to donate to charity. Alexander has given substantial sums to charitable projects, and has set up a foundation to award scholarships.

Alexander's feelings about his success and remarkable record of social responsibility are best expressed in his statement that: ". . . the U.S.A. is definitely the best country in the world. The opportunities are almost unlimited if you work hard."

Questions

1. How does Alexander Manufacturing illustrate the saying that "Socially responsible decision-making is good business practice"? Discuss.

2. Relate this case to the material presented in Chapter 20.

Source: Gussie McRobert, "The Horatio Alger of Gresham," *Oregon Business* (June 1985), p. 36.

CASE FOR PART SIX

CASE 11   Honeywell Pace: Cases A and B

CASE A

Until January 1982, Bob Naylor, factory manager of Honeywell's High Technology Unit (HTU) in Newhouse, Scotland, had been concerned with ensuring firm orders for his products so that he could manufacture in the high-volume stable quantities for which his plant was designed. During two years of steady growth, he had succeeded in persuading Honeywell's Process Automation Center Europe (PACE) in Brussels, the only outlet for HTU's products, to place firm orders six months before production, and had permitted only a 20 percent variation on orders placed for the second quarter and no variance for the first quarter.

But when in January 1982 he became the first operations manager of PACE, reporting to its director, John Dickens, Naylor saw the issue from a different perspective. One of his first tasks had been to review PACE's 1982 inventory plan. Controller[1] usage, as shown in Exhibit 1, had grown steadily since 1978, and he knew from an earlier meeting held in October 1981 to plan HTU's production schedule that PACE had expected demand to rise to 2,500 units in 1982. Before becoming operations manager of PACE, he had laid plans to increase controller production at HTU from 35 to 50 units per week.

However, the decline in world commodity prices and demand had suddenly begun to affect investment levels in PACE's customer industries and expected orders had failed to materialize. The January business forecast revised projections downwards to 2,120 controllers, but checks with sales subsidiaries made Naylor suspect that even this figure was optimistic, and he settled for a revised plan of 2,000 units. The February forecast reduced expected usage yet again to 1,700 units. Because at this point Naylor had already accumulated an excess inventory of 380 controllers, more than enough to meet his total needs for three months, he realized that drastic action was called for. He telephoned Jack Fraser, HTU's new factory manager. "Get ready to close and take a vacation," he warned, only half-joking. "I won't be needing any more deliveries for three months." A few hours later he received a telephone call from Peter Williams, president of Honeywell Europe, who insisted that HTU could not close and that Naylor would have to accept deliveries from HTU.

EXHIBIT 1   PACE Controller Usage

YEAR	USAGE
1978	537
1979	1106
1980	1479
1981	1791

Quite apart from the immediate problem, Naylor wondered how he could prevent similar problems from occurring in the future. He determined that one of his first tasks as operations manager at PACE would be to establish a better system for inventory planning and control.

HISTORY OF HONEYWELL

In 1906 Mark C. Honeywell founded the Honeywell Heating Specialties Company in

Wabash, Indiana, to build water-heating equipment. Through a series of mergers and acquisitions, the company developed expertise in manufacturing automatic temperature controls for industrial processes and later for heating regulation in office buildings. Prewar experimental work in electronics led to the development of the first successful electronic autopilot in 1941, which was used on U.S. bombers in World War II.

After the war, Honeywell continued to expand its control system operations, developing domestic, commercial, industrial, and military applications. Much of the expansion was overseas, including the establishment of the Belgian subsidiary in 1946, and the first factory in Newhouse, Scotland, which was opened in 1950. Sales grew rapidly in the postwar period from $13.5 million in 1946 to exceed $100 million for the first time in 1950 and $1 billion by 1957.

At the same time Honeywell developed interests in the new data processing industry, purchasing Raytheon's interests in Datamatic Corporation in 1957 and merging with General Electric's computer division in 1970. In 1971 Honeywell reorganized into two large worldwide operating units: Control Systems and Information Systems. By 1982, Honeywell earned net profits of $273 million on worldwide sales of $5.49 billion and employed 100,000 people.

Over the years, Honeywell Control Systems divided into five groups, each specializing in products for different markets: Commercial Buildings, Residential Components, Industrial Products, Aerospace, and Defense. A sixth group, International Operations, controlled overseas operations for the product groups and was divided into four large geographic segments: Europe, Far East and Australia, Latin America, and Canada (see Exhibit 2).

THE TDC 2000

Within the Industrial Products Group (IPG) were several divisions, including the largest, the Process Control Division (PCD), which manufactured a range of 2,400 instruments to measure and control industrial process variables. (See Exhibit 3.)

In 1975 PCD launched a product that represented a new approach to industrial process control systems, the TDC 2000. A first attempt to offer industrial users a complete package of control instruments organized into a coherent system, it consisted of instruments to measure process variables such as flow, pressure, and temperature that were linked to "controller" units. The systems could contain several controllers, each of which measured up to eight variables, and presented information about them in a digestible form to operators. In most cases the system also regulated automatically the process it measured. Because complete reliability was essential to users for whom even a brief breakdown could mean serious safety hazards and costly production losses, all systems contained backup units to take over if any part of the system failed.

Because the number and combination of variables that users wished to measure differed considerably, until the launch of TDC 2000 the users or their contractors had designed their own systems based on the range of components offered by Honeywell and other competitors.

Design of a highly reliable low-cost system that was flexible enough to meet the very different needs of users in a wide range of industries had required five years of intensive research and development effort. The final product consisted of a hundred or so different modules that could be mass-produced as standard items from which Honeywell sys-

(Continued on next page.)

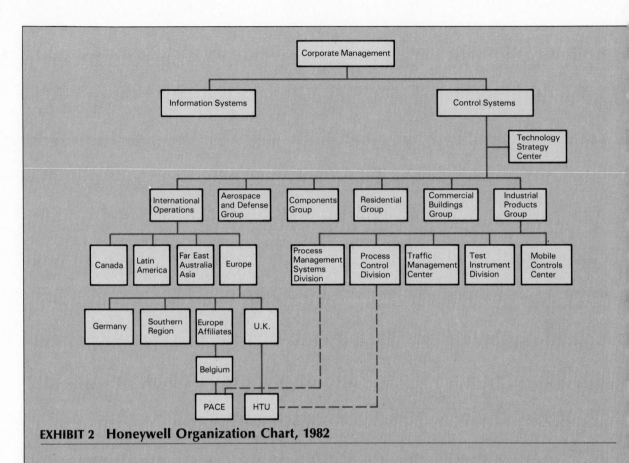

EXHIBIT 2   Honeywell Organization Chart, 1982

tems engineers could select in consultation with customers to design a custom-built system that met the customer's exact requirements.

The PCD recognized that module production and system assembly required very different skills and decided from the outset to keep the two steps of the manufacturing process completely separate. Units to manufacture standard modules were established in existing CD factories at PCD's Fort Washington headquarters and in Phoenix. A few low-volume models were also made at the Kamata/Isehara plant in Japan, but no module was made in more than one location.

Because systems design and assembly of modules required close contact and cooper-

ation with customers, a network of five systems centers was established from the outset near the main user markets. A headquarters center was opened in Phoenix, a second U.S. center was in Fort Washington, and overseas centers were located in Canada, Australia, Japan, and Europe. Each center served its local market only, ordering the modules it required from PCD factories. In 1979 a separate Process Management Systems Division (PMSD) was formed to control the systems centers worldwide (see Exhibit 3 for details of the PCD and PMSD factory networks). While overseas manufacturing and sales were managed by the International Operations Division, PCD and PMSD retained control of key areas such as future product research

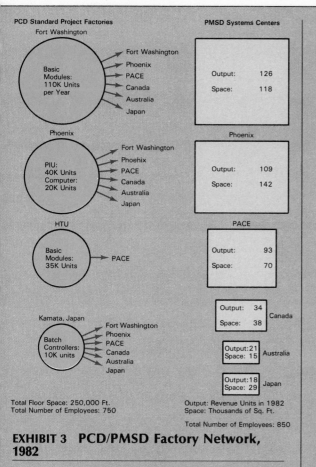

EXHIBIT 3   PCD/PMSD Factory Network, 1982

and development and determined the international transfer prices at which PCD sold standard modules to PMSD.

TDC 2000 found an immediate market among the large petroleum and petrochemical companies in refining and distilling plants throughout the world, which accounted for half of its sales. Other users were producers of major processed commodities such as steel, sugar, cement, wood pulp/paper, and electricity (for a profile of major European purchasers see Exhibit 4).

Half of the sales were for new plants. The system accounted for only a fraction of plant cost—a $500-million plant would require typically a system costing $1 million. Other sales were to replace existing instrumentation, because it was obsolete, or because installation could be justified on the basis of cost reduction through process optimization. In later years, a further important source of sales was existing TDC 2000 users who wished to expand their system.

When Honeywell launched TDC 2000 in 1975, it had defined a new product market, which its ability to demonstrate a track record for reliability and a strong international customer base made it difficult for other companies to enter. When competition did arrive in the early 1980s, it was accompanied by a sudden decline in investment levels in the process industries, and both of these factors contributed to lower order levels during 1982. Nevertheless, TDC 2000 still accounted for about 40 percent of world sales. There were two or three international competitors and a few national competitors in each of the major Organization for Economic Cooperation and Development countries that normally enjoyed an advantage in bidding for their government contracts. A new generation of TDC 2000s development, which involved the introduction of higher-order computer controls for total plant management, was due in 1983–1984, and was expected to strengthen Honeywell's technical leadership of the market.

TDC 2000 IN EUROPE

In 1975, John Dickens, formerly head of Systems Development Engineering at Honeywell's U.K. subsidiary, was given responsibility for establishing the European Systems Center for design and assembly of TDC

(Continued on next page.)

EXHIBIT 4   PACE Multinational Accounts for TDC 2000

	PROJECTS	LOOPS
Company A[a]	9	1,152
Company B	3	800
Company C	7	1,936
Company D	7	618
Company E	5	448
Company F	7	902
Company G	34	3,876
Company H	15	2,430
Company I	64	13,202
Company J	31	3,440
Company K	5	228
Company L	4	608
Company M	6	2,904
Company N	22	1,742
Company O	8	380
Company P	18	3,600
Company Q	65	4,024
Company R	23	3,804
Company S	10	2,030
Company T	28	3,214

[a] These are very large multinational companies such as BASF, Dow, Mobil, BP, Shell, Union Carbide, Exxon, Alcoa, Dupont, and ICI.

2000. The Process Automation Center Europe (PACE) was established in Belgium in vacant office and factory space within Honeywell Europe's headquarters on the outskirts of Brussels.

Company documents defined PACE's basic charter as follows:

It is a prime objective of Honeywell to supply digital control systems of high quality in cost effective configurations and with delivery lead times to meet customer schedules. PACE is a central source for such systems and the activities which relate to them, including: presales support, technical consultation, system design, project management, assembly, test and commissioning/service back-up. It was founded to provide the efficiency of a single high-volume operation, concentrated direct lines of com-

munication with the factory sources and management, and a central pool of product and application knowledge.

Dickens believed that PACE had a twofold role:

For logistic reasons, PACE acts as a coordination center between the sixteen European sales subsidiaries. Since most of our customers are multinational in size and scope, it is important that there is coordination on design standards and pricing.

There are also considerable economic advantages from having a centralized organization. For example, by having only one central Guest Center where the system can be demonstrated to potential customers there is a substantial reduction in investment required in demonstration systems.

Additionally, by centralizing the systems design and engineering function, we can maintain specialized expertise that could neither be developed nor justified economically on a country by country basis.

Between 1975 and 1980, sales of TDC 2000 in Europe grew rapidly from a few thousand dollars to over $100 million (see Exhibit 5). Throughout most of this period of steady growth, PACE successfully achieved both sales and profit targets while meeting customer delivery schedules for more than 95 percent of orders. This required a constant expansion of PACE's manufacturing floor space and personnel. After renting additional space locally, PACE finally moved into its own permanent offices and factory adjacent to the Honeywell Europe headquarters in mid-1982.

Growth of PACE was matched by the other systems centers, and by 1978 the PCD recognized that the level of future expected worldwide sales could not be met by the production of modules from the existing PCD plants.

In considering how to increase production, PCD reviewed its original policy of making each module in only one location, which it felt made TDC 2000 particularly vulnerable to sudden stoppages in one of the plants: shortages of a single module could delay shipment of an entire system. In particular, there was concern that any labor unrest in the United States could affect assembly operations in Europe. The PCD therefore decided to establish a special plant in Europe to provide a duplicate source for PACE of the main modules, thereby reducing its dependence on the U.S. factories. The new factory would supply none of the other assembly centers, because it was feared that this would be seen by the U.S. plant unions as a threat to their continued existence.

Newhouse in Scotland was chosen as the most appropriate site for the factory, called the High Technology Unit (HTU) to distinguish it from other local firms using older electronic technologies. Honeywell's own plant at Newhouse had been established in 1950 to manufacture analog instruments and pen recorders, but the market for them had declined by 1978 as they neared the end of their life cycle. Numbering 7,000 at its peak, the work force had fallen to 1,500 and further reductions were planned. Although HTU was able to use the administrative services (personnel, finance, et cetera) of the main factory, HTU required different manufacturing skills and was therefore able to include only a few existing Honeywell employees in its 100-strong work force.

Bob Naylor, formerly a production manager in Burroughs' U.K. subsidiary, was recruited as factory manager of HTU, reporting to Honeywell's Scottish factories manager based at Newhouse. He established HTU from scratch in an unused 26,000-sq.-ft. building adjacent to the main factory and began by manufacturing TDC 2000 modules that had the highest volume usage, gradually duplicating more of the products previously made only in the United States. When HTU reached capacity it was intended to supply about 80 percent of PACE's long-term needs. In this way HTU would be protected from variations in PACE's demand, which would be met from other PCD plants, so that it could manufacture in high-volume stable quantities. In most cases, HTU used similar or identical production machinery and techniques to those used in the United States, and its performance was judged against cost standards set for the U.S. factories. Because HTU's transfer prices to PACE were the same as those fixed for the U.S. factories, matching

(Continued on next page.)

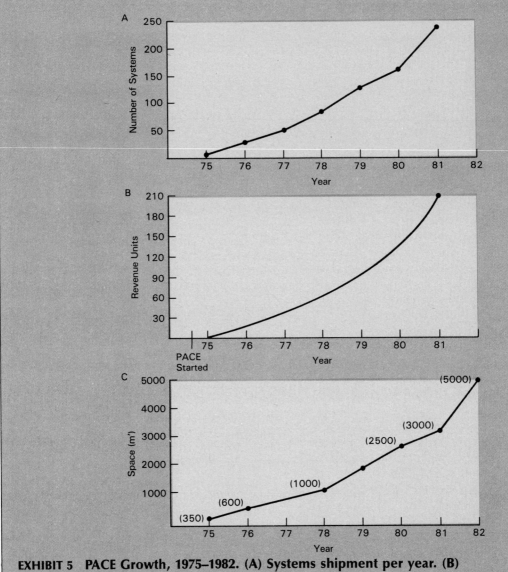

EXHIBIT 5   PACE Growth, 1975–1982. (A) Systems shipment per year. (B) Installed base, cumulative. (C) Production space evolution

U.S. cost standards was essential for profitable operations.

About 60 percent of HTU's total costs were for raw materials, half of which were purchased locally and the rest from other Honeywell divisions or from Honeywell-approved vendors. Lead times varied considerably but could be up to 3 months for circuit boards and 12 months for integrated circuits.

These constraints meant that HTU had to

plan its production schedules a year to 18 months in advance and could not respond quickly to sudden increases or decreases in demand from PACE. Therefore Naylor insisted on firm orders six months in advance from PACE. The HTU held no finished goods inventory, shipping all modules to PACE as soon as they were completed and invoicing PACE for them on the dispatch date.

ORGANIZATION OF HONEYWELL EUROPE

Honeywell Europe was split into four geographic regions—West Germany, United Kingdom, European Affiliates, and Southern Region—each with approximately equal sales (see Exhibit 6). The latter two divisions were further subdivided by country. Each country was a separate profit center, responsible for both local selling activity and manufacturing operations, and its performance was evaluated on the basis of its success in maximizing sales profits and minimizing factory costs.

PACE reported directly to the managing director of the Belgian subsidiary; HTU reported to the manager of Honeywell's Scottish factories, who in turn reported to the chairman of Honeywell U.K. The structure of the 16-country selling organizations varied according to their size, but TDC 2000 sales were normally a responsibility of an Industrial Products Group (IPG) sales manager, to whom several salespersons reported, some of whom would be TDC 2000 specialists.

Honeywell Europe also had vice presidents of finance and administration, of technology and operations, and of marketing, and a director of employee relations, to whom PACE and HTU reported in a matrix structure, drawing on services and specialist expertise they provided. The functional vice presidents provided important links between countries, coordinating aspects of strategy and policy

between them and resolving intercountry disputes. They were the only formal link between PACE and HTU below the president of European operations.

PACE IN 1982

In 1980 sudden sales growth had for the first time led to problems in meeting delivery dates, with inventory shortages causing delays in 25 percent of deliveries. To resolve the problem and to prepare for expected continuing expansion in sales, Dickens decided to recruit an operations manager. Bob Naylor, with his intimate knowledge of HTU's operations, was considered an ideal person to manage the important relationship with HTU, and Dickens recruited him to fulfill the new role. After working closely with PACE during 1981, he finally moved to Brussels in January 1982.

After Naylor's arrival, Dickens restructured PACE as shown in Exhibit 6. Besides an important support staff providing technical, financial, and administrative services, the organization was designed to focus on three key areas: management of individual projects, management of day-to-day operations, and strategic planning of future development.

Project Management Serge Du Pont was responsible for systems engineering. Reporting to him were four project managers, each of whom was in charge of a team of four or five engineers. The project manager was assigned to a project at an early stage, often before the order was confirmed, and he was responsible for all stages in coordination with the appropriate department (see Exhibit 7 for details of a typical project flow through PACE). During early discussions with a potential pur-

(Continued on next page.)

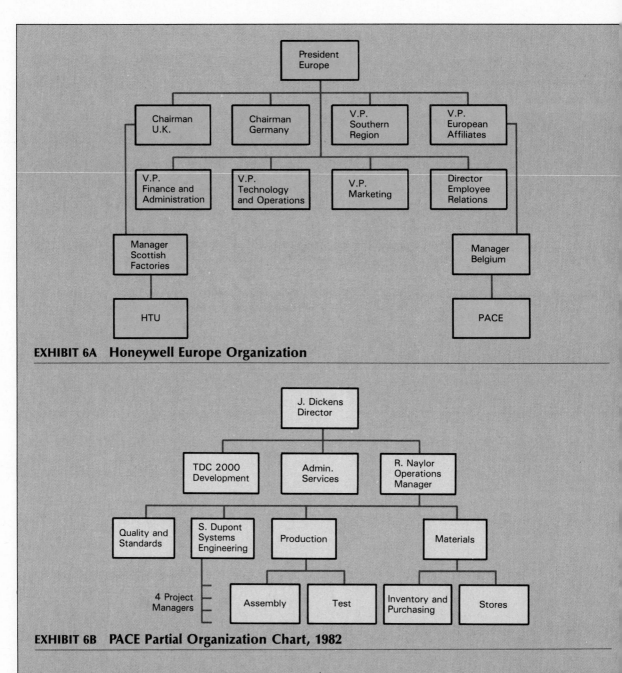

EXHIBIT 6A   Honeywell Europe Organization

EXHIBIT 6B   PACE Partial Organization Chart, 1982

chaser, the project manager and PACE team in general provided technical support and coordination with the sales subsidiary, particularly where projects were for multinational companies, were large (e.g., over $750,000), had new or complex process applications, or had intrinsic safety requirements.

With advice from PACE, the sales subsidi-

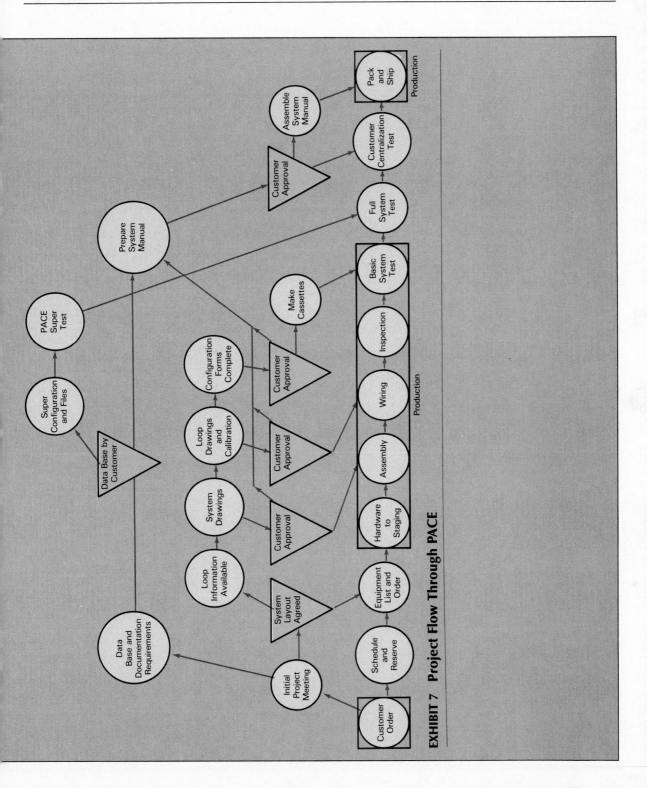

EXHIBIT 7   Project Flow Through PACE

ary then prepared a final job quotation that included a general system specification, a price, and a delivery date. At this point, the project manager reserved the bulk materials required for assembly and a slot in the production schedule. As soon as the order became firm, the project manager issued a project plan and a project milestone schedule (see Exhibit 8) specifying the freeze dates by which customers had to approve progressively more detailed aspects of the system's design. The systems engineers then designed the detailed system layout, confirmed the materials requirements, and prepared detailed drawings for use by the production department during assembly.

In the production, 17 assembly workers with general fitting skills were managed by a foreman who assigned specific orders to small teams that completed all phases of the assembly operations. The system was thoroughly tested at PACE before shipment to the subsidiary and delivery to the customers. Customer acceptance was either at the PACE test station or when installation at the customer's plant was completed. A project took from three to nine months to complete according to size, and the customer was billed progressively via the country sales subsidiary as costs were incurred.

Operations While project managers coordinated the progress of individual projects through production, Naylor oversaw overall operations and worked on development of standards and systems for all stages of the design, assembly, and testing procedures. Commenting on his role, Naylor said:

I'm a great believer in having adequate information, and then analyzing it to extract useful data. This is not only for my sake, but for the benefit of those reporting to me as well. As I often explain to them, they need good data as

much as I do. Without it they cannot justify their actions and the productivity of their departments.

At the same time, computer printouts are no substitute for practical knowledge of the job. For example, I insist that my schedulers know not only part numbers, but the function of the part as well. This means that if one part is out of stock they can make sensible suggestions to the systems engineers about possible substitutes.

He believed that it was important to instill these attitudes in all his subordinates. With these attitudes, he wished to establish formal performance standards to introduce what he described as "the disciplines of a real factory." In 1982 he was considering which were the key parameters he should set out to measure.

Strategic Planning Naylor's arrival allowed Dickens to devote more of his time to the longer-term planning of PACE's development, leaving day-to-day operating concerns to Naylor. In particular, he was able to coordinate future sales strategy with the country subsidiaries and to work on the development of TDC 2000.

Recently Naylor was appointed to represent Europe on the Industrial Products Group Worldwide Manufacturing Council, which meets two or three times a year to consider the future management of PMSD and PCD factories and products throughout the world, and he was also a member of the Worldwide Systems Centers Council, which considered operating issues and future strategy for the PMSD system centers. Because of the complexity of Honeywell's formal reporting structure, these were valuable opportunities to discuss important issues for PACE and to coordinate the activities of system centers worldwide.

Dickens also spent much of his time developing PACE's formal strategic and opera-

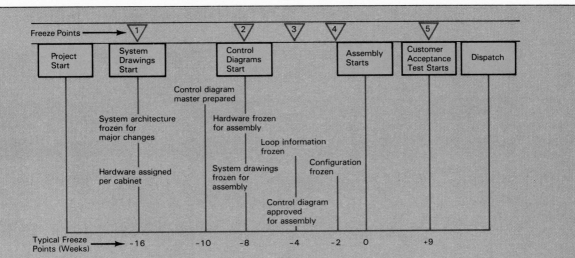

Typical Freeze Points (Weeks) → -16   -10   -8   -4   -2   0   +9

Freeze Point	Information	Situation Before Freeze	Situation After Freeze	Effect of Changes After Freeze on:	
				Delivery	Cost
▽1	System architecture/ content fixed to within ±10%	Equipment ordered in bulk quantities. Modifications to quantities and types permitted.	Bulk equipment is assigned to special cabinet layouts. Changes to equipment content accepted if less than ±10%; similarly minor changes to cabinet layout can be incorporated.	None	None
▽2	System layout/ assignment frozen for assembly purposes	Changes to system drawings can be implemented. Limited changes to hardware content (±10%) and rearrangement can be accepted (stock levels should avoid delivery delays).	Any modifications to system drawings will not necessarily be included in system assembly. Hardware changes will be implemented either after acceptance test or on-site.	Yes	Yes
▽3	Loop data frozen	Modification to loop/process data will be incorporated in drawings and assembly (unless magnitude or impact of changes prevents this).	Modifications will only be accepted for implementation in documentation and system after acceptance test.	Yes	Yes
▽4	Configuration data frozen	Configuration data will be checked and discussed etc. but will not be entered into system.	Configuration data will be entered. Modification and corrections will be inserted during acceptance test.	None	None
▽5	Documentation	Changes accepted for modification to drawings and print-out of configuration made if required.	No changes accepted (transparencies provided to customer print-out of data case if required).	None	None

EXHIBIT 8   Project Milestone Schedule

tional plans, which in 1982 it presented separately from the Belgian subsidiary to the European Board. The two-stage cycle began

in April with a strategic review. Dickens reviewed PACE's past strategy and presented

(Continued on next page.)

his view of PACE's future mission and his proposed methods for achieving goals in specific areas. The plan was discussed, amended, and approved by July. The approved strategy provided the basis for developing an operational plan that defined detailed financial objectives for the following year. The plan was first presented in mid-September and discussed during the next six weeks before final acceptance.

SOLVING THE INVENTORY PROBLEM

Naylor felt that inadequate forecasting was at the root of PACE's inventory problems. "One of the difficulties," he explained, "is that we have long lead times in this business, but we can only see a few months ahead."

The forecasting unit at Honeywell's European headquarters at that time provided predictions of overall dollar sales revenue for the year ahead, divided into quarters. It based its forecasts on overall economic variables such as capital spending levels in PACE's customer industries. Recently these forecasts had failed to foresee the downturn in sales. Naylor decided to supplement this overall business view with his own review of expected sales levels at each of the subsidiaries. To compile these forecasts Dickens recruited Veronique Meister, who had worked for Honeywell Europe for 12 years and knew well the people working in the sales subsidiaries.

Veronique Meister made monthly telephone calls to all 16 sales subsidiaries to review all likely orders for the forthcoming year with sales managers, asking them to assign a booking date, and a probability that the job would be booked. Using her own knowledge and judgment to assess the accuracy of their predictions, she included in her forecast any order she thought had a more than 60 percent probability of being placed. The forecasts provided aggregate data concerning

value of sales at customer prices, which Naylor converted into controller usage because these were a main determinant of system cost. In 1982 Naylor estimated that one controller was used per $22,000 of sales. By analyzing past data, Naylor had developed a simple computer model that gave him an average usage of each module per 1,000 controllers. Thus he could convert sales data into an expected usage of each standard module per months.

In this way, Naylor managed to tap the large amount of hard information available in the sales subsidiaries and use it to adjust his assembly schedule, which he planned by week for the six months ahead. Because the schedule for the first quarter was based substantially on actual orders, it usually required little change, but demand for the rest of the year was less certain and Naylor found the forecasts helpful to develop rough assembly plans that he changed as the booking picture developed. Naylor also used the forecasts to develop his inventory plan, which he discussed monthly with Jack Fraser, HTU's manager, who used PACE's inventory plan to organize his production schedule and materials ordering.

Materials ordering for HTU was a more complex process because each module contained several thousand components, some of which had to be ordered up to a year in advance. These lead times were a major constraint on HTU's flexibility. HTU used a computerized MRP schedule to produce data for component requirements.

Business forecasts indicated that sales would show no improvement until the end of 1983. While PACE was flexible enough to withstand the slump in sales reasonably well, the consequences were more serious for HTU, which was preparing plans to move to a four-day work week in 1983 and was concerned that if short-time working continued it would lose its highly trained work force to new factories that were opening nearby, leaving it unable to meet the upturn in demand predicted for 1984.

By the end of 1982, despite substantially improved forecasting methods, PACE had not been able to resolve its inventory problems. The substantial cost of holding unused modules, running to several years' supply of some low-usage models, had depressed PACE's profits in 1982. Both Dickens and Naylor had become convinced that the problem would not be resolved until HTU shared with PACE responsibility for meeting inventory holding costs. Accordingly, they requested a meeting of senior Honeywell Europe staff so that they could make recommendations for changes in the formal relationship between PACE and HTU. Shortly before Christmas 1982, they met to discuss how they would present their case.

CASE B

In January 1983, John Dickens and Bob Naylor presented their inventory plans for 1983 to a meeting attended by the president of Honeywell Europe and the vice president of manufacturing technology and operations, as well as representatives of the U.K. subsidiary and Jack Fraser, factory manager of HTU.

After lengthy discussion, a consensus gradually emerged. It was agreed that during the first quarter of 1983, PACE would accept a limited stock from HTU, but that deliveries would dwindle to a trickle in the second quarter, allowing PACE to reduce drastically its excess inventories. Any orders to HTU would only be to meet PACE's specific stock needs. During the third and fourth quarters, orders would again reflect PACE's forecast of its actual usage.

This arrangement meant that if HTU decided to continue production above PACE's very limited needs during the first half of the year to balance its annual production schedule, it would have to meet inventory holding costs itself.

QUESTIONS

1. Classify and describe Honeywell's international organizational structure.

2. Discuss the international management problems raised in this case.

3. Do you agree with the eventual decisions about the inventory plans? Why or why not?

Source: Reprinted from the *Journal of Management Case Studies* (Spring 1985). Copyright © Kasra Ferdows and Christopher Spray, 1985.

Certain names and figures in this case are disguised.
[1] Controllers, manufactured at HTU, were a major component of the process control system by PACE, the TDC 2000.

NOTES

Chapter 1

1. Kevin Johnson, "Clinic Franchises Cure-All for Waiting," *USA Today,* 3 July 1985, p. 2B.
2. D. R. Land, Media Relations Specialist, Fluor Corporation, letter, 10 June 1985.
3. Based on "A Friendly Frontier for Female Pioneers," *Fortune,* 25 June 1984, pp. 78-79; and Earl C. Gottshalk, Jr., "More Women Start Up Their Own Business with Major Successes," *Wall Street Journal,* 17 May 1983. A 1985 update was provided by Allison Hairmann of ASK Computer Systems.
4. Toni Mack, "Browning-Ferris Cleaning Up," *Forbes,* 5 July 1981, pp. 101-102. *See also* James Cook, "Par for Course," *Forbes,* 9 September 1985, pp. 70, 72. Update provided by Browning-Ferris Industries, letter, 21 May 1985.
5. A questioning viewpoint is expressed in Myron D. Fottler, "Is Management Really Generic?" *Academy of Management Review* (January 1981): 1-12.
6. Michael Kolbenschlag, "Bechtel's Biggest Job Constructing Its Own Future," *Forbes,* 7 December 1981, pp. 139, 142.
7. "Candid Reflections of a Businessman in Washington," *Fortune,* 29 January 1979, p. 36.
8. Donald Rumsfeld, "A Politi-cian-Turned-Executive Surveys Both Worlds," *Fortune,* 10 September 1979, p. 91.
9. The diversity of the not-for-profit sector is noted in William H. Newman and Harvey W. Wallender III, "Managing Not-For-Profit Enterprises," *Academy of Management Review* (January 1978): 25-26.
10. *Ibid.,* p. 26. Reprinted by permission.
11. The remainder of this section is based on Cecily Cannon Selby, "Better Performance for Nonprofits," *Harvard Business Review* (September–October 1978): 93-95.
12. Heidrick and Struggles, Inc., *Profile of a Chief Executive Officer* © copyright 1984 by Heidrick and Struggles, Inc.
13. Robert L. Katz, "Skills of an Effective Administrator," *Harvard Business Review* (September–October 1974): 90-102.
14. Henry Mintzberg, "The Manager's Job: Folklore and Fact," *Harvard Business Review* (July–August 1975): 49-61; *see also* "Managerial Work: Analysis from Observation," *Management Science* (October 1971): B97-B110.
15. The conclusion that management should be classified as a science is supported by papers such as Ronald F. Gribbins and Shelby D. Hunt, "Is Management a Science?" *Academy of Management Review* (January 1978): 139-144.
16. Roy Rowan, "Those Business Hunches Are More Than Blind Faith," *Fortune,* 23 April 1979, p. 111.
17. The discussion of management and the artistic process is based on Henry O. Boettinger, "Is Management Really an Art?" *Harvard Business Review* (January–February 1975): 54-64. The concluding quote is from p. 64.
18. Miller quoted in Gary F. Schuster, "Decision Number Six," *Detroit News Magazine,* 11 March 1979, p. 46.

Warhol's *Vanity Fair* quote is from "Other Comments," *Forbes,* 25 March 1985, p. 28.

The Frost quote is from Barbara Rowes, *The Book of Quotes* (New York: Ballantine Books, 1978), p. 18.

The Anderson quote is from Fred Moody, "Manager for a Month," *The Weekly* (September 19-September 25, 1984).

Chapter 2

1. Daniel A. Wren and Robert D. Hay, "Management Historians and Business Historians: Differing Perceptions of Pioneer Contributors," *Academy of Management Journal* (September 1977): 470-476.

2. Daniel Wren, *The Evolution of Management Thought* (New York: Ronald Press, 1972), p. 14.

3. Claude S. George, Jr., *The History of Management Thought* (Englewood Cliffs, N.J.: Prentice-Hall, 1968), pp. xiii-xiv, 20-21. Reprinted by permission of Prentice-Hall, Inc.

4. The problems involved in this adjustment are described in Wren, *The Evolution of Management Thought*, pp. 43-52.

5. The discussion of Owen, Babbage, Ure, and Dupin is based on Wren, *The Evolution of Management Thought*, pp. 63-79.

6. Wren's terminology—*administrative theory*—has been adopted to describe the contributions of Fayol and Weber.

7. This section is based on George, *The History of Management Thought,* pp. 105-111; Peter Chambers, "Europe's Greatest Management Pioneer," *International Management* (June 1974): 49-51; "Famous Firsts: Discoveries from Looking Inward," *Business Week,* 6 June 1964, pp. 152ff; *Grande Larousse Encyclopedique* in six volumes, s.v. "Fayol"; Hano Johannsen and G. Terry Page, *International Dictionary of Management: A Practical Guide,* s.v. "Fayol, Henri," and Norman M. Pearson, "Fayolism as the Necessary Complement of Taylorism," *American Political Science Review* (February 1945): 68-80.

8. Henry Fayol, *General and Industrial Management* (London: Pitman, 1949), pp. 19-20. Quoted in George, *The History of Management Thought,* p. 109. Reprinted by permission of Pitman Publishing Limited.

9. Kenneth McNeil, "Understanding of Organizational Powers: Building on the Weberian Legacy," *Administrative Science Quarterly* (March 1978): 65; *see also* Wren, *The Evolution of Management Thought,* p. 229.

10. McNeil, "Understanding of Organizational Powers," pp. 67-68.

11. Victor A. Thompson, *Modern Organization* (New York: Knopf, 1961), p. 11.

12. Earlier neglect of Weber's contributions is suggested in Wren, *The Evolution of Management Thought,* p. 234.

13. Taylor's career is discussed in Daniel Nelson, "Scientific Management, Systematic Management, and Labor, 1880-1915," *Business History Review* (Winter 1974): 482-483; and in George, *The History of Management Thought,* p. 87.

14. Frederick W. Taylor, *Principles of Scientific Management* (New York: Harper, 1911), pp. 36-37. Copyright 1911 by Frederick W. Taylor, renewed 1939 by Louise S. M. Taylor. Reprinted by permission of Harper & Row, Publishers, Inc.

15. These mechanisms are listed in Taylor, *Principles of Scientific Management,* pp. 129-130. Cited in George, *The History of Management Thought,* p. 91.

16. These features are listed in Nelson, "Scientific Management," p. 490.

17. Nelson, "Scientific Management," pp. 479, 486. *See also* W. Jack Duncan, "The History and Philosophy of Administrative Thought," *Business and Society* (Spring 1971): 29.

18. Edwin A. Locke, "The Ideas of Frederick W. Taylor: An Evolution," *Academy of Management Review* (January 1982): 22-23.

19. Frank Gilbreth's early work in motion study is described in George, *The History of Management Thought,* pp. 96-98.

20. Lillian Gilbreth's contributions are described in John E. Burns, "A Biographical Memoir of Lillian Moller Gilbreth," *Industrial Management* (September–October 1978): 28-32.

21. *See* "Dr. Lillian Gilbreth," *Fortune* (September, 1935), p. 82; *Current Biography* (1944), s.v. "Gilbreth, Frank Bunker (Jr.,) and Carey, Ernestine (Moller) Gilbreth," pp. 224-226; and *Current Biography* (1940), s.v. "Gilbreth, Lillian Evelyn," pp. 336-337.

22. George, *The History of Management Thought,* p. 98.

23. This section is based on Wren, *The Evolution of Management Thought,* pp. 148-158; *Dictionary of American Biography* (New York: Charles Scribner & Sons, Inc., 1932), pp. 129-130; Claude S. George, Jr., *The History of Management Thought,* 2nd ed. (Englewood Cliffs, N.J.: Prentice-Hall Inc., 1972); and *National Cyclopedia of American Biography* s.v. "Gantt, Henry Lawrence." For an interesting account of one of Gantt's consulting assignments, see Daniel Nelson and Stuart Campbell, "Taylorism Versus Welfare Work in American Industry: H. L. Gantt and the Bancrofts,"

Business History Review (Spring 1972): 1-16.

24. Nelson, "Scientific Management," pp. 488-500.

25. This interesting account appears in Charles D. Wrege and Anne Marie Stotka, "Cooke Creates a Classic: The Story Behind F. W. Taylor's Principles of Scientific Management," *Academy of Management Review* (October 1978): 736-749.

26. Elliot M. Fox and Lyndall Urwick, eds., *Dynamic Administration: The Collected Papers of Mary Parker Follett* (London: Pitman Publishing, 1973). *See also* L. D. Parker, "Control in Organizational Life: The Contribution of Mary Parker Follett," *Academy of Management Review* (October 1984): 731-745.

27. Stuart Chase, "Calling All Social Scientists," *Nation,* 4 May 1946, pp. 538-540; P. Sargant Florence, "Professor Elton Mayo," (Obituary), *Nature* 15 October 1949, p. 646; "The Fruitful Errors of Elton Mayo," *Fortune* 34, November 1946, pp. 180-183, 238, 241-242, 244, 247-249; and John W. McConnell, "George Elton Mayo: 1880-1949" (Obituary), *Industrial and Labor Relations Review* 3, January 1950, pp. 305-306. *See also* George, *The History of Management Thought,* p. 143; and Lyle Yorks and David A. Whitsett, "Hawthorne, Topkea, and the Issue of Science versus Advocacy in Organizational Behavior," *Academy of Management Journal* (January, 1985): 21-30.

28. Abraham H. Maslow, "A Theory of Human Motiva-

tion," *Psychological Review* (July 1943): 370-396.

29. McGregor's work is outlined in Wren, *The Evolution of Management Thought,* pp. 448-452. His theory is presented in Douglas McGregor, *The Human Side of Enterprise* (New York: McGraw-Hill, 1960).

30. The material on Argyris is from Wren, *The Evolution of Management Thought,* pp. 446-448. Wren cites Argyris's book *Personality and Organization: The Conflict Between the System and the Individual* (New York: Harper & Row 1957) as his source.

31. Donald C. King, "Model I: A Model-T Approach to Effective Professional Behavior," *Contemporary Psychology* 20, no. 9 (1975): 710-711. (A review of *Theory in Practice: Increasing Professional Effectiveness,* by Chris Argyris and Donald A. Schon); review of *Management and Organizational Development,* by Chris Argyris, *Personnel Journal* (November 1972): 848-849; Veronica F. Nieva, "Perspectives on Improving Leadership," review of *Increasing Leadership Effectiveness,* by Chris Argyris, *Contemporary Psychology* 22, no. 12 (1970): 874-876; review of *Theory in Practice: Increasing Professional Effectiveness,* by Chris Argyris and Donald A. Schon, *Journal of Higher Education* XLVII, no. 1 (January–February, 1976): 113-115; and Peter B. Vaill, "Learning to Learn to Learn to . . . ," a review of *Organizational Learning: A Theory of Action Perspective,* by Chris Argyris and Donald A. Schon, *Contemporary Psychol-*

ogy 24, no. 6 (1979): 514-515.

32. Will Durant, *The Story of Civilization* (New York: Simon and Schuster, 1939), 2:632. This is cited by George, *The History of Management Thought,* p. 150.

33. Seymour Tilles, "The Manager's Job: A Systems Approach," *Harvard Business Review* (January–February 1963): 73.

34. Elias M. Awad, *Systems Analysis and Design* (Homewood, Ill.: Irwin, 1979), p. 4. *See also* August W. Smith, *Management Systems: Analysis and Applications* (Hinsdale, Ill.: Dryden, 1982), p. 3.

35. "Dr. Lillian Gilbreth," *Fortune,* September 1935, p. 82. *Current Biography* (1949) s.v. "Gilbreth, Frank Bunker (Jr.), and Carey, Ernestine (Moller) Gilbreth," pp. 224-226. *Current Biography* (1940) s.v. "Gilbreth, Lillian Evelyn," pp. 336-337. Quote from p. 336.

The Henry quotation is from "Historical Perspective," an advertisement of the Association of American Railroads, Department 507, 1920 L Street N.W., Washington, D.C., 20036.

The Coolidge quotation is from Laurence J. Peter, *Peter's Quotations* (New York: Morrow, 1977), p. 84.

The Nixon quotation is from Barbara Rowes, *The Book of Quotes* (New York: Ballantine Books, 1978), p. 140.

Chapter 3

1. P. N. Khandwalla, *The Design of Organization* (New York:

Harcourt Brace Jovanovich, 1977), pp. 333-340. An excellent discussion of Khandwalla's work appears in Robert E. Callahan, C. Patrick Fleenor, and Harry R. Knudson, *Understanding Organizational Behavior* (Columbus, Ohio: Charles E. Merrill Publishing Company, 1986), pp. 314-316. The term "environment modifier" is suggested in their sources.

2. Reprinted from Terrence E. Deal and Allan A. Kennedy, *Corporate Culture* (Reading, Mass.: Addison-Wesley Publishing Co., 1982), pp. 3-4.

3. *Ibid.*, p. 23.

4. Daniel Machalaba, "Newhouse Chain Stays with Founder's Ways, and with His Heirs," *The Wall Street Journal,* 12 February 1982, p. 1.

5. This section is based on Deal and Kennedy, pp. 13-19, 23, 85-87.

6. *Ibid.*, p. 60.

7. This story is from M. Dale Beckman, David L. Kurtz, and Louis E. Boone, *Foundations of Marketing* (Toronto: Holt Rinehart & Winston of Canada, Ltd., 1982), p. 213. The information is from Jan Morin and Michel Ostiguy, "View from the Top," *Marketing,* 1 June 1981, p. 28.

8. "The Uneasy Partnership," *Newsweek,* 14 June 1982, p. 27.

9. Data provided by the American Productivity Center, August 1985.

10. Bill Saporito, "Black and Decker's Gamble on 'Globalization',," *Fortune,* 14 May 1984, p. 142.

11. *Forbes,* 15 September 1978, Portfolio 87.

12. *Ibid.*, Portfolio 88.

13. "The Battle of the Lightweights," *Forbes,* 1 May 1978, p. 24.

14. Kemmons Wilson's story is chronicled in John F. Mariane, "If You Haven't Slept in His Bed, You Must Have Tasted His Tobacco," *Detroit News,* 16 April 1978, pp. 44-48.

15. Ian H. Wilson, "Business Management and the Winds of Change," *Journal of Contemporary Business* (Winter 1978): 46-47.

16. George S. Odiorne, "A Management Style for the Eighties," *University of Michigan Business Review* (March 1978): 3-6. Reprinted by permission of the publisher, the Graduate School of Business Administration, the University of Michigan.

17. George S. Odiorne, "A Management Style for the Eighties," *University of Michigan Business Review* (March 1978): 2.

Van Buren quote is from "Thoughts on the Business of Life," *Forbes,* 5 November 1984, p. 304.

Roderick quote is from William C. Symonds, "U.S. Steel's Roderick: A Chairman Who Doesn't Flinch," *Business Week,* 25 February 1985, p. 55.

Trowbridge quote is from "On the Road," *Time,* 23 April 1984, p. 75.

Chapter 4

1. Ewing W. Reilley, "Planning the Strategy of the Business," *Advanced Management* (December 1955): 8-12.

2. Russell Ackoff, *A Concept of Corporate Planning* (New York: Wiley/Interscience, 1970), pp. 2-4.

3. Stanley S. Thune and Robert J. House, "Where Long-Range Planning Pays Off," *Business Horizons* (August 1970); pp. 81-87.

4. David M. Herald, "Long-Range Planning and Organizational Performance: A Validation Study," *Academy of Management Journal* (March 1972): 91-102.

5. D. Robley Wood, Jr., and R. Lawrence LaForge, "The Impact of Comprehensive Planning on Financial Performance," *Academy of Management Journal* (September 1979): 516-526; Ross Stagner, "Corporate Decision Making," *Journal of Applied Psychology* (February 1979): 1-13; Joseph Eastlack, Jr., and Philip McDonald, "CEO's Role in Corporate Growth," *Harvard Business Review* (May–June 1970): 150-163.

6. Information provided by Pam Olson, Public Relations Department, Rolm Corporation, 20 May 1985.

7. Robert Kreitner, *Management* (Boston: Houghton Mifflin Co., 1983), p. 114. *See also* Robert E. Linneman and Rajan Chandran, "Contingency Planning: A Key to Swift Managerial Action in the Uncertain Tomorrow," *Managerial Planning* (January–February 1981): 23-27; and R. L. Dilenschneider and

Richard C. Hyde, "Crisis Communications: Planning for the Unplanned," *Business Horizons* (January–February 1985): 35-38.

8. Kodak's plans are described in "How Kodak Is Trying to Move Mount Fuji," *Business Week,* 2 December 1985, pp. 62-64.

9. Kathleen Day, "Costly Misses: Success Tales Have Flip Side," *USA Today,* 30 June 1983, p. B1.

10. The commitment principle was first proposed by Harold Koontz and Cyril O'Donnell. See their *Principles of Management* (New York: McGraw-Hill, 1955), p. 442.

11. Some writers confuse the different types of standing plans. For a discussion of this problem, see Milton Leontiades, "The Confusing Words of Business Policy," *Academy of Management Review* (January 1982): 25-34.

12. Alfred D. Chandler, Jr., *Strategy and Structure* (Cambridge, Mass.: MIT Press, 1962), p. 13.

13. Robert M. Randolph, *Planagement—Moving Concept into Reality* (New York: AMACOM, 1975), p. 5.

14. Robert S. Sobek, "A Manager's Primer on Forecasting," *Harvard Business Review* (May–June 1973): 6ff.

15. For a description of the use of simulation in a major firm, see Terry W. Rothermel, "Forecasting Resurrected," *Harvard Business Review* (March–April 1982): 139-147.

16. Don Lebell and O. J. Krasner, "Selecting Environmental Forecasting Techniques for Business Planning Requirements," *Academy of Manage-ment Review* (July 1977): 373-383.

17. Harold W. Henry, "Delphi Forecasting," *Tennessee Survey of Business* (October 1972): 12. *See also* E. Bruce Peters, "Technological Forecasting: An Investment Analysis Aid," *Managerial Planning* (July–August 1978): 5.

18. Myron Magnet, "Who Needs a Trend-Spotter?" *Fortune,* 9 December 1985, p. 52.

19. "The New Breed of Strategic Planner," *Business Week,* 17 September 1984, p. 66.

20. Michael E. Porter, "How Competitive Forces Shape Strategy," *Harvard Business Review* (March–April 1979): 137-145.

21. Shea Smith III and John Walsh, Jr., *Strategies in Business* (New York: Wiley/Interscience, 1978), p. 220. *See also* Frederick W. Gluck, "Taking the Mystique out of Planning," *Across the Board* (July–August 1985): 56-61.

22. "Ways to Stop Wasting Time on the Job," *U.S. News & World Report,* 5 March 1979, p. 60.

23. Ronald N. Askenas and Robert H. Schaffer, "Managers Can Avoid Wasting Time," *Harvard Business Review* (May–June 1982): 99.

24. Michael LeBeouf, "Managing Time Means Managing Yourself," *Business Horizons* (February 1980): 42.

25. Rudyard Kipling, "The Elephant's Child," from *Just So Stories.* Reprinted by permission of the National Trust and Doubleday & Company, Inc.

Napoleon quotation from "Thoughts on the Business of Life," *Forbes,* 30 December 1985, p. 140.

Chapter 5

1. Alfred D. Chandler, Jr., *Strategy and Structure: Chapters in the History of the Industrial Enterprise* (Cambridge, Mass.: MIT Press, 1962), p. 13. *See also* Larry J. Rosenberg and Charles D. Schewe, "Strategic Planning: Fulfilling the Promise," *Business Horizons* (July–August 1985): 54-62.

2. Dan E. Schendel and Charles W. Hofer, eds., *Strategic Management: A New View of Business Policy and Planning* (Boston: Little, Brown, 1979).

3. Peter F. Drucker, *Management: Tasks, Responsibilities, Practices* (New York: Harper & Row, 1974), pp. 123-125.

4. Gerald A. Michaelson, "Sales vs. Marketing," *Sales & Marketing Management,* 3 June 1985, p. 19.

5. Thomas P. Hustad and Ted J. Mitchell, "Creative Market Planning in a Partisan Environment," *Business Horizons* (March–April 1982): 58-65.

6. V. K. Narayanan and Liam Fahey, "The Micro-Politics of Strategy Formulation," *Academy of Management Review* (January 1982): 25-34.

7. John A. Pearce II, "An Executive-Level Perspective on the Strategic Management Process," *California Management Review* (Fall 1981): 40.

8. Quoted in James K. Brown, "Corporate Soul-Searching," *Across the Board* (March 1984): 44. *See also* Craig C. Lundberg, "Zero-In: A Technique for Formulating Better Mis-

sion Statements," *Business Horizons* (September–October 1984): 30-33.

9. Northwestern Mutual Life mission statement supplied by Thomas W. Towers, Manager of Public Relations, the Northwestern Mutual Life Insurance Company.

10. Excerpted from "After the Merger," by Harold Stieglitz, *Across the Board* (December 1984) © 1984 The Conference Board.

11. John Merwin, "The Sad Case of the Dwindling Orange Roofs," *Forbes*, December 1985, 78-79. Reprinted by permission of *Forbes* Magazine, December 30, 1985. © Forbes Inc., 1985.

12. Gary P. Latham and Gary P. Yukl, "A Review of the Application of Goal Setting in Organizations," *Academy of Management Journal* (December 1975): 824-825. *See also* John M. Ivancevich and J. Timothy McMahon, "The Effects of Goal Setting, External Feedback, and Self-Generated Feedback on Outcome Variables: A Field Experiment," *Academy of Management Journal,* (June 1982): 359-372.

13. Edwin A. Locke, "The Ubiquity of the Technique of Goal Setting in Theories and Approaches to Employee Motivation," *Academy of Management Review* (July 1978): 594-601. *See also* Gary P. Latham and Edwin A. Locke, "Goal Setting—A Motivational Technique," *Organizational Dynamics* (Autumn 1979): 68-80.

14. Peter F. Drucker, *The Practice of Management* (New York: Harper & Row, 1954), p. 37.

15. "Intermedics: Out to Be Number One in the Medical Implants Market," *Business Week,* 18 January 1982, pp. 58, 60.

16. Y. K. Shetty, "New Look at Corporate Goals," *California Management Review* (Winter 1979): 71-79.

17. George W. England, "Organizational Goals and Expected Behavior of American Managers," *Academy of Management Journal* (June 1967): 107-117. *See also* Kamal M. Abouzeid and Charles N. Weaver, "Social Responsibility in the Corporate Goal Hierarchy," *Business Horizons* (June 1978): 29-35.

18. See Charles H. Granger, "The Hierarchy of Objectives," *Harvard Business Review* (May–June 1964): 63ff.

19. Drucker, *The Practice of Management,* pp. 128-129.

20. George Odiorne, *Management by Objectives: A System of Managerial Leadership* (New York: Pitman, 1965), p. 55. Three other major contributions to the MBO literature are Stephen J. Carroll, Jr., and Henry L. Tosi, Jr., *Management by Objectives: Applications and Research* (New York: Macmillan, 1973); Douglas M. McGregor, "An Uneasy Look at Performance Evaluation," *Harvard Business Review* (May–June 1957): 89-94; and George S. Odiorne, *MBO II: A System of Managerial Leadership for the 80s* (Belmont, Calif.: Fearon Pitman, 1979).

21. Dale D. McConkey, *MBO for Nonprofit Organizations* (New York: AMACOM, 1975); Mark A. Covaleski and Mark B. Dismith, "MBO and Goal Directedness in a Hospital

Context," *Academy of Management Review* (July 1981): 409-418.

22. Fred E. Schuster and Alva F. Kindall, "Management by Objectives: Where We Stand—A Survey of the Fortune 500," *Human Resources Management* (Spring 1974): 8-11. For a survey of empirical research on MBO effectiveness, *see* Jack N. Kondrasuk, "Studies in MBO Effectiveness," *Academy of Management Review* (July 1981): 419-430.

23. Adapted from W. J. Reddin, *Effective Management by Objectives* (New York: McGraw-Hill, 1970), p. 122.

24. Robert W. Hollman and David A. Tansik, "A Life Cycle Approach to Management by Objectives," *Academy of Management Review* (October 1977): 682. *See also* Charles M. Kelly, "Remedial MBO," *Business Horizons* (September–October 1983): 62-66.

25. Bruce D. Jamieson, "Behavioral Problems with Management by Objectives," *Academy of Management Review* (September 1973): 496-505; Charles H. Ford, "MBO: An Idea Whose Time Has Gone," *Business Horizons* (December 1979): 48-55. Ivancevich has conducted two small-scale studies that suggest that the positive effects of MBO may wear off over time. See John M. Ivancevich, "A Longitudinal Assessment of Management by Objectives," *Administrative Science Quarterly* (March 1972): 126; and John M. Ivancevich, "Different Goal Setting Treatments and Their Effects on Performance and Job Satisfaction,"

Academy of Management Journal (September 1977): 406.

26. Glenn H. Varney, *Management by Objectives* (Chicago: Dartnell Corporation, 1971), pp. 39-40.

27. Daniel Katz and Robert L. Kahn, *The Social Psychology of Organizations* (New York: Wiley, 1966), p. 25.

28. John R. Opel, chief executive officer at IBM, quoted in Nancy J. Perry, "America's Most Admired Corporation," *Fortune,* 9 January 1984, p. 54.

29. James A. F. Stoner, *Management* (Englewood Cliffs, N.J.: Prentice-Hall, 1982), p. 114. The sequence is based upon a discussion in Dan E. Schendel and Charles W. Hofer, eds., *Strategic Management: A New View of Business Policy and Planning* (Boston: Little, Brown, 1978), pp. 244-253.

30. Information provided by Buck Williams, Communications Director, Allstate Insurance Group, 21 August 1985.

31. "A Sampling of Strategic Planning's Track Record," *Business Week,* 17 September 1984, pp. 64-65.

32. Derek F. Abell, "Strategic Windows," *Journal of Marketing* (July 1978): 21-26.

33. This and the following two paragraphs are reprinted from John K. Ryans, Jr., and William L. Shanklin, *Strategic Planning: Concepts and Implementation* (New York: Random House, 1985), p. 11.

34. Margaret Loeb, "R. J. Reynolds Turns to Lines It Knows Best," *Wall Street Journal,* 25 May 1984, p. 31.

35. "Caterpillar is Betting Big on Pint-Size Machines," *Business Week,* 25 November 1985, p. 41.

36. Francine Schwadel, "Burned by Mistakes, Campbell Soup Co. Is in Throes of Change," *Wall Street Journal,* 14 August 1985, p. 1.

37. Philippe Haspeslagh, "Portfolio Planning: Uses and Limits," *Harvard Business Review* (January–February 1982): 58. *See also* Anil K. Gupta and V. Govindarajan, "Business Unit Strategy, Managerial Characteristics, and Business Unit Effectiveness at Strategy Implementation," *Academy of Management Journal* (March 1984): 25-41.

38. William K. Hall, "SBUs: Hot New Topic in the Management of Diversification," *Business Horizons* (February 1979): 21. *See also* Yoram Wind and Vijay Mahajan, "Designing Product and Business Portfolios," *Harvard Business Review* (January–February 1981): 155-165.

39. Walter Kiechel III, "Playing by the Rules of the Corporate Strategy Game," *Fortune,* 24 September 1979, p. 114.

40. Harold Geneen, *Managing* (New York: Doubleday, 1984), p. 27.

41. Walter Kiechel III, "Oh Where, Oh Where Has My Little Dog Gone? Or My Cash Cow? Or My Star?" *Fortune,* 2 November 1982, p. 149.

Wood quotation from Alfred D. Chandler, Jr., *Strategy and Structure* (Cambridge, Mass.: MIT Press, 1962), p. 325. Tsu quotation from Systems & Computer Technology Corporation advertisement appearing in the May 15, 1985 issue of *The Chronicle of Higher Education.*

Chapter 6

1. Talcott Parsons, *Structure and Process in Modern Organizations* (New York: The Free Press, 1960); James D. Thompson, *Organizations in Action* (New York: McGraw-Hill, 1967); and George P. Huber, *Managerial Decision Making* (Glenview, Ill.: Scott, Foresman, 1980).

2. Charles Perrow, "A Framework for the Comparative Analysis of Organizations," *American Sociological Review* (April 1967): 194-208.

3. Peter F. Drucker, "How to Make People Decisions," *Harvard Business Review* (July–August 1985): 22-24.

4. Myron Magnet, "How Top Managers Make a Company's Toughest Decision," *Fortune,* 18 March 1985, pp. 56-57.

5. Herbert A. Simon, *The New Science of Management Decisions* (New York: Harper & Row, 1960), pp. 5-6. One writer describes programed decisions as puzzle solving. *See* Chimezie A. B. Osigweh, Yg., "Puzzles or Problems? Cutting Through the Manager's Dilemma," *Business Horizons* (May–June 1985): 69-73.

6. James G. March and Herbert A. Simon, *Organizations* (New York: Wiley, 1958), p. 170. *See also* Marjorie Caballero and Roger Dickinson, "Beyond Rationality," *Business Horizons* (July–August 1984): 55-58.

7. The systematic approach to decision making has been

treated by a number of writers. *See* John Dewey, *How We Think* (New York: Heath, 1910), pp. 101-105; Peter F. Drucker, *The Practice of Management* (New York: Harper & Row, 1954), pp. 354-365; Charles H. Kepner and Benjamin B. Tregoe, *The Rational Manager* (New York: McGraw-Hill, 1965); and "How to Make a Business Decision: An Analysis of Theory and Practice," *Management Review* (February 1980): 43-47.

8. Alvar Elbing, *Behavioral Decisions in Organizations* (Glenview, Ill.: Scott, Foresman, 1978), p. 110. Copyright © 1978 by Scott, Foresman and Company. Reprinted by permission.

9. The "Five Ms" concept was first suggested by L. T. White. *See* U.S. Small Business Administration, *Strengthening Small Business Management: Collections from the Pages of L. T. White,* ed. Joseph C. Schabacker (Washington, D.C.: U.S. Government Printing Office, 1971), p. 21.

10. W. J. J. Gordon, *Synectics* (New York: Harper & Row, 1961).

11. Frank Barron, *Creative Person and Creative Process* (New York: Holt, Rinehart and Winston, 1968), p. 133. *See also* Timothy A. Matherly and Ronald E. Goldsmith, "The Two Faces of Creativity," *Business Horizons* (September–October 1985): 8-11.

12. F. D. Barrett, "Creativity Techniques: Yesterday, Today, and Tomorrow," *Advanced Management* (Winter 1978): 25-35.

13. Alex Osborn, *Applied Imagi-nation* (New York: Scribners, 1958).

14. S. J. Parnes and H. F. Harding, *A Source Book of Creative Thinking* (New York: Scribners, 1962).

15. Douglas R. Emery and Francis D. Tuggle, "On the Evaluation of Decisions," *MSU Business Topics* (Spring 1976): 42-48.

16. Elbing, *Behavioral Decisions in Organizations.*

17. Lee Iacocca with William Novak, *Iacocca: An Autobiography* (New York: Bantam Books, 1984), p. 52.

18. James H. Davis, *Group Performance* (Reading, Mass.: Addison-Wesley, 1969); L. Richard Hoffman, *The Group Problem Solving Process: Studies of a Valence Model* (New York: Praeger, 1979); and J. Keith Murnighan, "Group Decision Making: What Strategies Should You Use?" *Management Review* (February 1981): 55-62.

19. Irving Lorge, David Fox, Joel Dantz, and Marlin Brenner, "A Survey of Studies Contrasting the Quality of Group Performance and Individual Performance: 1920-1957," *Psychological Bulletin* (November 1958): 337-372.

20. Irving Janis, *Victims of Groupthink* (Boston: Houghton Mifflin, 1972).

21. An excellent summary of the strengths and weaknesses of group decisions is included in Norman R. F. Maier, "Assets and Liabilities in Group Problem Solving," *Psychological Review* (July 1967): 239-249.

22. Victor H. Vroom and Philip W. Yetton, *Leadership and De-cison Making* (Pittsburgh: University of Pittsburgh Press, 1973). *See also* Victor H. Vroom, "A New Look at Managerial Decision Making," *Organizational Dynamics* (Spring 1973): 66-80.

23. Promising results have been obtained in early attempts to test the model's validity. *See* Victor H. Vroom and Arthur G. Jago, "On the Validity of the Vroom-Yetton Model," *Journal of Applied Psychology* (April 1978): 151-162; C. Margerison and R. Glube, "Leadership Decision-Making: An Empirical Test of the Vroom and Yetton Model," *Journal of Management Studies* 16 (1979): 45-55; and Arthur G. Jago and Victor H. Vroom, "An Evaluation of Two Alternatives to the Vroom-Yetton Normative Model," *Academy of Management Journal* (June 1980): 347-355.

Wilson quotation from "Thoughts on the Business of Life," *Forbes,* 16 January 1984, p. 140.

Baruch quotation from "Thoughts on the Business of Life," *Forbes,* 24 October 1983, p. 236.

Williams quote is from "Thoughts on the Business of Life," *Forbes,* 28 July 1986, p. 236.

Hubbard quote is from "Thoughts on the Business of Life," *Forbes,* 14 July 1986, p. 132.

Chapter 7

1. The Wal-Mart success is de-

scribed in "Sam Walton of Wal-Mart: Just Your Basic Homespun Billionaire," *Business Week*, 14 October 1985, pp. 142-147.

2. James B. Dilworth, *Production and Operations Management* (New York: Random House, 1983), p. 26.

3. David R. Anderson, Dennis J. Sweeney, and Thomas A. Williams, *An Introduction to Management Science* (St. Paul, Minn.: West Publishing Co., 1985), p. 2.

4. W. N. Ledbetter and J. F. Cox, "Are OR Techniques Being Used?" *Industrial Engineering* (February 1977): 19-21; and Colin Eden, "Problem Construction and the Influence of OR," *Interfaces* (April 1982): 50-60.

5. William J. Kearney and Desmond D. Martin, "Quantitative Methods in Management Development," *Business Horizons* (August 1974): 52.

6. The need for operations research specialists and line managers to work together in implementing and integrating quantitative techniques in decision making is discussed in John C. Anderson and Thomas R. Hoffman, "A Perspective on the Implementation of Management Science," *Academy of Management Review* (July 1978); 563-571. *See also* Richard Richels, "Building Good Models Is Not Enough," *Interfaces* (August 1981): 48-54; and Richard H. McClure, "Educating the Future Users of O.R.," *Interfaces* (October 1981): 108-112.

7. Thomas M. Cook and Robert A. Russell, *Introduction to Management Science* (Engle-

wood Cliffs, N.J.: Prentice-Hall, 1985), p. 10.

8. Anderson, Sweeney, and Williams, *An Introduction to Management Science*, p. 6.

9. Dilworth, *Production and Operations Management*, p. 36.

10. Gilbert Gordon and Israel Pressman, *Quantitative Decision-Making for Business* (Englewood Cliffs, N.J.: Prentice-Hall, 1978), p. 340.

11. Anderson, Sweeney, and Williams, *An Introduction to Management Science*, p. 10.

12. Arthur C. Laufer, *Operations Management* (Cincinnati: South-Western, 1984), p. 32.

13. Lars Lonnstedt, "Factors Related to the Implementation of Operations Research Solutions," *Interfaces* (February 1975): 24.

14. Stephen P. Shao, *Mathematics and Quantitative Method for Business and Economics* (Cincinnati: South-Western, 1976), p. 148.

15. Frank J. Fabozzi and Joseph Valente, "Mathematical Programming in American Companies: A Sample Survey," *Interfaces* (November 1976): 97.

16. Richard I. Levin, Charles A. Kirkpatrick, and David S. Rubin, *Quantitative Approaches to Management* (New York: McGraw-Hill, 1982), pp. 334-335.

17. Ira Horowitz, *An Introduction to Quantitative Business Analysis* (New York: McGraw-Hill, 1972), p. 7.

18. Two excellent basic linear programing books are R. Stansbury Stockton, *Introduction to Linear Programming* (Homewood, Ill.: Irwin, 1971); and Saul Gass, *Illustrated Guide to Linear Program-*

ming (New York: McGraw-Hill, 1970).

19. This section is reprinted by permission from David J. Rachman and Michael H. Mescon, *Business Today* (New York: Random House, 1985), pp. 504, 506.

20. James B. Boulden and Elwood S. Buffa, "Corporate Models: On-Line, Real-Time Systems," *Harvard Business Review* (July–August 1970): 65.

21. *Business Week*, 28 April 1975.

22. Levin, Kirkpatrick, and Rubin, *Quantitative Approaches to Management*, p. 541.

23. Ledbetter and Cox, "Are OR Techniques Being Used?" p. 19. *See also* Fred C. Weston, "Operations Research Techniques Relevant to Corporate Planning Practices: An Investigative Look," *Operations Research Bulletin* (Spring 1971).

24. Jack Byrd, Jr., "The Value of Queuing Theory," *Interfaces* (May 1978): 22-26.

25. Ledbetter and Cox, "Are OR Techniques Being Used?" p. 19.

26. Barry Shore, *Quantitative Methods for Business Decisions: Text and Cases* (New York: McGraw-Hill, 1978), pp. 118-119.

27. An excellent discussion of decision-tree analysis is contained in Jacob W. Ulvila and Rex V. Brown, "Decision Analysis Comes of Age," *Harvard Business Review* (September–October 1982): 130-141.

Taylor quotation from testimony before the Special House Committee.

Chesterton quotation from Laurence J. Peter, *Peter's Quotations* (New York: Morrow, 1977), p. 408.

Watson quotation from "Thoughts on the Business of Life," *Forbes*, 24 October 1983, p. 236.

Wilmot quotation from "Thoughts on the Business of Life," *Forbes*, 30 June 1986, p. 160.

Chapter 8

1. "Day in Life of UAB Police Office," *Atmore* (Ala.) *Advance*, 30 October 1985, p. 2A.
2. Peter M. Blau and W. Richard Scott, *Formal Organizations* (San Francisco: Chandler, 1962), pp. 5, 14.
3. Howard M. Carlisle, *Management: Concepts and Situations* (Chicago: Science Research Associates, Inc., 1976), p. 333. Fayol quotation from Henri Fayol, *General and Industrial Management* (London: Sir Isaac Pitman and Sons, Ltd., 1949), p. 35.
4. William G. Scott, "Organization Theory: An Overview and Appraisal," *Academy of Management Journal* (April 1961): 7-26.
5. James D. Thompson, *Organizations in Action* (New York: McGraw-Hill, 1967).
6. Charles Perrow, *Complex Organizations: A Critical Essay* (Glenview, Ill.: Scott, Foresman, 1972).
7. Alfred D. Chandler, Jr., *Strategy and Structure: Chapters in the History of the Industrial Enterprise* (Cambridge, Mass.: MIT Press, 1962), p. 13. *See also* Jeffrey D. Ford and W. Harvey Hegarty, "Decision Makers' Beliefs About the Causes and Effects of Structure: An Exploratory Study,"

Academy of Management Journal (June 1984): 271-291.
8. Daniel Katz and Robert L. Kahn, *The Social Psychology of Organizations* (New York: Wiley, 1966), pp. 19-26.
9. W. Lambert Gardiner, *Psychology: A Story of a Search* (Belmont, Calif.: Brooks/Cole, 1970), p. 13.
10. Katz and Kahn, *The Social Psychology of Organizations*, p. 25.
11. George H. Rice, Jr. and Dean W. Bishoprick, *Conceptual Models of Organization* (New York: Appleton-Century-Crofts, 1971), p. 15.
12. James D. Thompson, *Organizations in Action* (New York: McGraw-Hill, 1967), p. 4.
13. Paul R. Lawrence and Jay W. Lorsch, *Organization and Environment* (Boston: Division of Research, Graduate School of Business Administration, Harvard University, 1967), pp. 7-8.
14. Adapted from Edgar F. Huse, *The Modern Manager* (St. Paul, Minn.: West Publishing Co., 1979), p. 347.
15. Theo Haimann, William G. Scott, and Patrick E. Conner, *Managing the Modern Organization* (Boston: Houghton Mifflin, 1978), pp. 252-253.
16. Francis Cornford, *The Republic of Plato* (New York: Oxford University Press, 1959), pp. 165-167.
17. Jay R. Galbraith, *Organization Design* (Reading, Mass.: Addison-Wesley, 1977), pp. 13-14.
18. Sanford L. Jacobs, "Owners See Need to Delegate Authority as Concerns Grow," *Wall Street Journal*, 18 July 1983, p. 21.

19. Quoted in David D. Van Fleet and Arthur G. Bedeian, "A History of the Span of Management," *Academy of Management Review* (July 1977): 358. The term *span of management* was coined by Harold Koontz and Cyril O'Donnell in their book *Principles of Management* (New York: McGraw-Hill, 1964).
20. V. A. Graicunas, "Relationships in Organizations," *Papers on the Science of Administration*, ed. Luther H. Gulick and Lyndall F. Urwick (New York: Institute of Public Administration, Columbia University, 1937), pp. 182-187.
21. James A. F. Stoner, *Management* (Englewood Cliffs, N.J.: Prentice-Hall, 1982), p. 294.
22. James C. Worthy, "Organization Structure and Employee Morale," *American Sociological Review* (April 1950): 169-179.
23. Edwin E. Ghiselli and Jacob Siegel, "Leadership and Managerial Success in Tall and Flat Organization Structures," *Personnel Psychology* (Winter 1972): 617-624; Lyman Porter and Edward Lawler, "The Effects of Flat and Tall Organization Structures on Managerial Job Satisfaction," *Personnel Psychology* 17 (1964): 135-148.
24. Rensis Likert, *New Patterns of Management* (New York: McGraw-Hill, 1961).
25. George F. Wieland and Robert A. Ullrich, *Organizations: Behavior, Design and Change* (Homewood, Ill.: Richard D. Irwin, Inc., 1976), p. 244. *See also* Marc J. Dollinger, "Environmental Boundary Spanning and Information Processing Effects on Organiza-

tional Performance," *Academy of Management Journal* (June 1984): 351-368.

26. Robert Townsend, *Up the Organization* (New York: Alfred A. Knopf, Inc., 1970), p. 93.

Ripley quotation from "Thoughts on the Business of Life," *Forbes*, 5 July 1982, p. 196.

Chapter 9

1. Ricky W. Griffin, *Management* (Boston: Houghton Mifflin, 1984), p. 261.
2. William G. Scott, *Organization Theory: A Behavioral Analysis of Management* (Homewood, Ill.: Richard D. Irwin, 1967).
3. Harold J. Leavitt, *Managerial Psychology* (Chicago: University of Chicago Press, 1978), p. 282.
4. Jay R. Galbraith, *Organization Design* (Reading, Mass.: Addison-Wesley, 1977), p. 36.
5. Tom Burns and Gerald M. Stalker, *The Management of Innovation* (London: Tavistock Publications, 1961).
6. *Ibid.*, p. 5.
7. *Ibid.*
8. Charles Perrow, *Organizational Analysis: A Sociological View* (Belmont, Calif.: Wadsworth, 1970).
9. Joan Woodward, *Industrial Organization: Theory and Practice* (London: Oxford University Press, 1965).
10. Paul R. Lawrence and Jay W. Lorsch, *Organization and Environment* (Cambridge, Mass.: Harvard University Graduate School of Business Administration, 1967).
11. J. Richard Hackman and Greg R. Oldham, "Development of the Job Diagnostic Survey," *Journal of Applied Psychology* 60 (1975): 159-170. *See also* Greg R. Oldham, "Job Characteristics and Internal Motivation: The Moderating Effect of Interpersonal and Individual Variables," *Human Relations* 29 (1976): 559-569.
12. Robert J. Kuhne and Courtney O. Blair, "Flexitime," *Business Horizons* (April 1978): 42-44. *See also* Paul Blyton, *Changes in Working Time: An International Review* (New York: St. Martin's Press, 1986); and Randall B. Dunham and Jon L. Pierce, "Attitudes Toward Work Schedules: Construct Definition, Instrument Development, and Validation," *Academy of Management Journal* (March 1986): 170-182.
13. Mark Memmott, "4-Day Workweek Still Rare," *USA Today*, 11 August 1986, p. 4B.
14. Harvey F. Kolodny, "Evolution to a Matrix Organization," *Academy of Management Review* (October 1979): 543-544. *See also* H. R. Smith, "A Socio-Biological Look at Matrix," *Academy of Management Review* (October 1978): 922-926.
15. Stanley M. Davis and Paul R. Lawrence, "Problems of Matrix Organizations," *Harvard Business Review* (May–June 1978): 134.
16. Stephen P. Robbins, *Managing Organizational Conflict* (Englewood Cliffs, N.J.: Prentice-Hall, 1974), p. 23.
17. Daniel Katz and Robert L. Kahn, *The Social Psychology of Organizations* (New York: Wiley, 1966), p. 184.
18. David R. Hampton, Charles E. Summer, and Ross A. Weber, *Organization Behavior and the Practice of Management* (Glenwood, Ill.: Scott, Foresman, 1978), p. 676.
19. Richard E. Walter, *Interpersonal Peacemaking: Confrontations, and Third Party Consultation* (Reading, Mass.: Addison-Wesley, 1969).

Howe quotation from "Thoughts on the Business of Life," *Forbes*, 19 May 1986, p. 234.

Chapter 10

1. Maureen Pratsher, "Exclusive Job Survey Reveals Upbeat Mood," *Restaurants & Institutions*, 29 May 1985, p. 100.
2. "EEOC, Burlington Northern Settlement to Provide $10 Million in Back Pay and $40 Million in Affirmative Relief," *EEOC News*, 8 November 1983.
3. "Human Resources Managers Aren't Corporate Nobodies Anymore," *Business Week*, 2 December 1985, p. 59.
4. *Ibid.*, pp. 58, 59.
5. *ASPA-BNA Survey No. 48: Personnel Activities, Budgets, and Staffs: 1984–1985* (Washington, D.C.: U.S. Government Printing Office, Bureau of National Affairs, May 23, 1985).
6. *Affirmative Action & Equal Employment: A Guide Book for Employers* (Washington, D.C.: U.S. Equal Employment Opportunity Commission, 1974). *See also* Alice G. Sargent, *Beyond Sex Roles* (St. Paul, Minn.: West Publishing Co., 1977).
7. "EEOC, General Motors, and Union Sign Record-Setting Equal Opportunity Accord," *EEOC News*, 18 October 1983.

8. J. W. Miller, "Up on the Wall: Posting Salaried Openings," *Business Horizons* (May–June 1984): 69-74.

9. Sanford L. Jacobs, "Changes in Employment Laws Can Trap Unwary Companies," *Wall Street Journal*, 4 February 1985, p. 25.

10. *Personnel Management: Policies and Practices, Report #22* (Englewood Cliffs, N.J.: Prentice-Hall, 1975).

11. Theodore T. Pettus, *One on One: Win the Interview, Win the Job* (New York: Random House, 1981).

12. Winifred Yu, "Firms Tighten Resume Checks of Applicants," *Wall Street Journal*, 20 August 1985, p. 31.

13. Jeremy Main, "New Ways to Teach Workers What's New," *Fortune*, 1 October 1984, pp. 85-94.

14. Gerard R. Roche, "Much Ado About Mentors," *Harvard Business Review* (January–February 1979): 24.

15. Desmond D. Martin and William J. Kearney, "The Behavioral Sciences in Management Development Programs," *Journal of Business* (May 1978): 28.

16. "How Much Does Career Success Depend Upon A Helping Hand From Above?" *International Management* (April 1982): 17. *See also* M. K. Badawy, "Finding and Using a Mentor," *Machine Design*, 9 August 1984, pp. 57-60; and David M. Hunt and Carol Michael, "Mentorship: A Career Training and Development Tool," *Academy of Management Review* (July 1983): 475-485.

17. Douglas Cederblom, "The Performance Appraisal Interview: A Review, Implica-tions, and Suggestions," *Academy of Management Review* (April 1982): 219-227.

18. Mark R. Edwards and J. Ruth Sproull, "Safeguarding Your Employee Rating System," *Business* (April–June 1985): 17-27.

19. Elliott Jaques, "Taking Time Seriously in Evaluating Jobs," *Harvard Business Review* (September–October 1979): 39-42.

20. "Coaches' Corner," *The Sporting News*, 30 September 1985, p. 33.

21. J. H. Foegen, "The Creative Flowering of Employee Benefits," *Business Horizons* (May–June 1982): 9-13.

22. "Rank Has Its ... Space," *Wall Street Journal*, 10 September 1985, p. 1.

Disney quotation from "Thoughts on the Business of Life," *Forbes*, 5 July 1982, p. 196.

Chapter 11

1. Richard Pascale, "Fitting New Employees into the Corporate Culture," *Fortune*, 28 May 1984, pp. 30, 34.

2. Randall S. Schuler, "Organizational and Individual Change," *Bulletin of Business Research* (November 1977): 6-7.

3. The bank wiring room research is described in F. J. Roethlisberger and William J. Dickson (with Harold A. Wright), *Management and the Worker* (New York: Wiley, 1964), pp. 379-548. Another perspective on the Hawthorne studies is contained in H. McIlvaine Parsons, "What Caused the Hawthorne Ef-fect? A Scientific Detective Story," *Administration and Society* (November 1978): 259-283.

4. Lester Coch and John R. P. French, Jr., "Overcoming Resistance to Change," *Human Relations* (August 1948): 512-532.

5. An excellent discussion of participative management appears in William E. Hallal and Bob S. Brown, "Participative Management: Myth and Reality," *California Management Review* (Summer 1981): 20-32.

6. An interesting article is Gregory H. Gaertner, Karen N. Gaertner, and David M. Akinnusi, "Environment, Strategy, and the Implementation of Administrative Change: The Case of Civil Service Reform," *Academy of Management Journal* (September 1984): 525-543.

7. Change agents are discussed in Richard N. Ottoway and Gary L. Cooper, "Moving Toward a Taxonomy of Change Agents," *International Studies of Management and Organization* (Spring–Summer 1978): 7-21.

8. Ted Kade, "Ford Firm Still 'Runs' at Age 75," *Detroit News*, 14 July 1978, pp. 1A, 4A.

9. Kurt Lewin, "Frontiers in Group Dynamics: Concept, Method, and Reality in Social Science," *Human Relations* (June 1947): 34-35.

10. This section is based on Larry E. Greiner, "Patterns of Organization Change," *Harvard Business Review* (May–June 1967): 119-122, 125-130.

11. This section is based on and

quotes are from Richard Beckhard, *Organizational Development: Strategies and Models* (Reading, Mass.: Addison-Wesley, 1969), pp. 9-14.

12. These sources are suggested in Wendell French and Cecil Bell, "A Brief History of Organization Development," *Journal of Contemporary Business* (Summer 1972): 1-4. This paper is based on French and Bell's book, *Organization Development: Behavioral Science Interventions for Organization Improvements* (Englewood Cliffs, N.J.: Prentice-Hall, 1973), pp. 21-26. A similar discussion appears in Wendell French and Cecil Bell, *Organization Development: Behavioral Science Interventions for Organizaton Improvements,* 2d ed. (Englewood Cliffs, N.J.: 1978), pp. 20-24.

13. *Ibid.*

14. An interesting discussion of T-groups and sensitivity training appears in Robert A. Luke, Jr., "Matching the Individual and the Organization," *Harvard Business Review* (May–June 1975): 17-18, 20, 24, 28, 30, 32, 34, 165.

15. *See* note 12.

16. *Ibid.*

17. This section is based on and quotes are from French and Bell, "A Brief History of Organization Development," pp. 2-3. *See also* French and Bell, *Organization Development: Behavioral Science Interventions* (1973), pp. 22-25. A similar discussion appears in French and Bell, *Organization Development: Behavioral Science Interventions,* 2d ed., pp. 20-24.

18. Robert R. Blake, Jane S. Mouton, Louis B. Barnes, and Larry E. Greiner, "Breakthrough in Organization Development," *Harvard Business Review* (November–December 1964): 133-155.

19. Robert R. Blake and Jane S. Mouton, *The Managerial Grid* (Houston: Gulf Publishing Company, 1964).

20. This section is based on and quotes are from Michael E. McGill, *Organization Development for Operating Managers* (New York: AMACOM, 1977), pp. 77-79. *See also* Thomas H. Patten, Jr., "Team Building Part I—Designing the Intervention," *Personnel* (January–February 1979): 11-21.

Kettering quotation from "Thought for the Month," *Sales Memo* (June 1983).

Sevareid quotation from Barbara Rowes, *The Book of Quotes* (New York: Ballantine Books, 1979), p. 242.

Drucker quotation from Laurence J. Peter, *Peter's Quotations* (New York: Morrow, 1977), p. 85.

The Chinese Symbol for Crisis. Copyright 1981 by the Foundation for the School of Business at Indiana University. Reprinted by permission.

Chapter 12

1. The importance of power is discussed in John P. Kotter, "Power, Dependence, and Effective Management," *Harvard Business Review* (July–August 1977): 125-136. Another interesting article is Richard S. Blackburn, "Lower Participant Power: Toward A Conceptual Integration," *Academy of Management Review* (January 1981): 127-131.

2. John R. P. French, Jr. and Bertram Raven, "The Bases of Social Power," in *Group Dynamics: Research and Theory,* 2d ed., ed. Dorwin Cartwright and Alvin Zander (Evanston, Ill.: Row, Peterson, 1960), pp. 607-623.

3. Both positive and punitive rewards are discussed in Robert T. Keller and Andrew D. Szilagyi, "Employer Reactions to Leader Reward Behavior," *Academy of Management Journal* (December 1976): 619-627.

4. Amitai Etzioni, *Modern Organizations* (Englewood Cliffs, N.J.: Prentice-Hall, 1964), pp. 59-61.

5. Douglas McGregor, *The Human Side of Enterprise* (New York: McGraw-Hill, 1960), pp. 33-34.

6. Likert's concepts are outlined in *New Patterns of Management* (1961) and *The Human Organization* (1967), both published by McGraw-Hill.

7. This section is based on Robert Tannenbaum and Warren Schmidt's original article, "How to Choose a Leadership Pattern," *Harvard Business Review* (March–April 1958): 95-101; and the "Retrospective Commentary," that appeared fifteen years later. *See Harvard Business Review* (May–June 1973): 166-168.

8. Jeffrey C. Barrow, "The Variables of Leadership: A Review and Conceptual Framework," *Academy of Management Review* (April 1977): 232.

9. Hoyt Gimlin (Editorial Research Reports), "Niche of Silent Cal Undisturbed," *Jour-*

nal-American, 9 January 1983, p. 5D.

10. This discussion of Ghiselli's work is based on James F. Gavin, "A Test of Ghiselli's Theory of Managerial Traits," *Journal of Business Research* (February 1976): 45-52. *See also* E. E. Ghiselli, *Explorations in Managerial Talent* (Pacific Palisades, Calif.: Goodyear, 1971).

11. Quoted in Steven H. Appelbaum, "Management by Co-operation: The Views of Seven Chief Executive Officers," *University of Michigan Business Review* (November 1977): 20.

12. A recent article of interest is Jonathan E. Smith, Kenneth P. Carson, and Ralph Alexander, "Leadership: It Can Make A Difference," *Academy of Management Journal* (December 1984): 765-776.

13. Ralph M. Stogdill, Ellis L. Scott, and William E. Jaynes, *Leadership and Role Expectations* (Columbus: Bureau of Business Research, Ohio State University, 1956), p. 132.

14. William Foote Whyte and Lawrence K. Williams, "Supervisory Leadership: An International Comparison," in *Proceedings, CIOS XIII Internatonal Management Congress* (New York: Council for International Progress in Management, 1963), p. 485.

15. Robert Kahn and Daniel Katz, "Leadership Practices in Relation to Productivity and Morale," in *Group Dynamics: Research and Theory,* 2d ed., ed. Dorwin Cartwright and Alvin Zander (Evanston, Ill.: Row, Peterson, 1960), pp. 554-570; Frederick Herz-

berg, Bernard Mausner, and Barbara Block Snyderman, *The Motivation to Work* (New York: Wiley, 1959).

16. *1985 General Motors Public Interest Report,* p. 20.

17. A. Paul Hare, *Handbook of Small Group Research* (New York: Free Press, 1962), p. 231.

18. M. E. Shaw, "Some Effects of Problem Complexity Upon Problem Solution Efficiency in Different Communication Nets," *Journal of Experimental Psychology* (January 1954): 211-217.

19. Paul R. Lawrence and Jay W. Lorsch, *Organization and Environment* (Boston: Graduate School of Business Administration, Harvard University, 1967), pp. 31-36.

20. Information provided by Robert J. O'Gara of Koppers, June 20, 1985; and S. B. Stoffle of Phillips Petroleum Co., June 4, 1985.

21. Donald C. Pelz, "Influence: A Key to Effective Leadership in the First-Line Supervisor," *Personnel* (December 1952): 209-217.

22. Personal needs and characteristics are examined in articles such as Douglas E. Durand and Walter R. Nord, "Perceived Leader Behavior as a Function of Personality Characteristics of Superiors and Subordinates," *Academy of Management Journal* (September 1976): 427-438; and Donald L. Helmich and Paul F. Erzen, "Leadership Style and Leader Needs," *Academy of Management Journal* (June 1975): 397-402.

23. Peter M. Blau and W. Richard Scott, *Formal Organizations: A Comparative Approach* (San

Francisco: Chandler, 1962), p. 159.

24. Hare, *Handbook of Small Group Research,* p. 292.

25. This section is based on Chester A. Schriesheim, James M. Tolliver, and Orlando C. Behling, "Leadership Theory: Some Implications for Managers," *MSU Business Topics* (Summer 1978): 35-36; and Barrow, "The Variables of Leadership," pp. 232-233.

26. This section is based on Barrow, "The Variables of Leadership," pp. 235-236.

27. Robert R. Blake and Jane S. Mouton, *The Managerial Grid* (Houston: Gulf Publishing Co., 1964); Robert R. Blake, Jane S. Mouton, Louis B. Barnes, and Larry Greiner, "Breaking Through in Organization Development," *Harvard Business Review* (November–December 1964): 133-155.

28. William J. Reddin, "The 3-D Management Style Theory," *Training and Development Journal* (April 1967): 8-17; William J. Reddin, *Managerial Effectiveness* (New York: McGraw-Hill, 1970).

29. Fiedler's model is summarized in Barrow, "The Variables of Leadership," p. 234. Some of this discussion follows that summary.

30. Fred E. Fiedler and Martin M. Chemers, *Leadership and Effective Management* (Glenview, Ill.: Scott, Foresman, 1974), p. 87.

31. This section is based on, and quotes and adaptations are from, Robert J. House and Terence R. Mitchell, "Path-Goal Theory of Leadership," *Journal of Contemporary Business* (Autumn 1974): 81-97.

Used by permission of *Journal of Contemporary Business* (University of Washington). *See also* Robert J. House, "Retrospective Comment," in *The Great Writings in Management and Organization Behavior,* ed. Louis E. Boone and Donald D. Bowen (New York: Random House, 1987).

32. James J. Polyczynski, Robert Graham, Stanford Orma, and LeRoy Cougle, "Increasing Productivity Through Front-Line Supervision and Expectancy Theory," *Pittsburgh Business Review* (June 1978): 9-14. Another interesting article on expectancy theory is Laurence R. Walker and Kenneth W. Thomas, "Beyond Expectancy Theory: An Integrative Motivational Model from Health Care," *Academy of Management Review* (April 1982); 187-194. *See also* Richard W. School, "Differentiating Organizational Commitment From Expectancy As a Motivating Force," *Academy of Management Review* (October 1981): 589-599.

33. *The Detroit News,* 24 September 1978, p. 11A. Reprinted with permission.

34. "Answers to Ailing Industry: Overhaul at the Very Top," *U.S. News & World Report,* 17 January 1983, p. 39.

35. Abraham Zoleznik, "Managers and Leaders: Are They Different?" *Harvard Business Review* (May–June 1977): 67-78.

Regan quotation from "The Chief of Staff," *Newsweek,* 21 January 1985, p. 19.

Emery quotation from "Maneu-vering in a Dogfight," *Across The Board* (March 1985): p. 22.

Johnson quotation from "Thoughts on the Business of Life," *Forbes,* 4 July 1983, p. 196.

Chapter 13

1. An excellent article on motivation is Terence R. Mitchell, "Motivation: New Directions for Theory, Research, and Practice," *Academy of Management Review* (January 1982): 80-88.

2. Kurt Lewin, *Field Theory in Social Science* (New York: Harper & Row, 1951), p. 62.

3. A. H. Maslow, "A Theory of Human Motivation," *Psychological Review* (July 1943): 370-396.

4. *Ibid.,* p. 383.

5. *Ibid.,* p. 396.

6. Saul W. Gellerman, *Motivation and Productivity* (New York: American Management Associations, 1963), pp. 185-199.

7. Except for the citation in note 10, this section is based on David C. McClelland and David H. Burnham, "Power is the Great Motivator," *Harvard Business Review* (March–April 1976): 100-110. The McClelland-Burnham article notes that the three needs are from David C. McClelland's *The Achieving Society* (Princeton, N.J.: Van Nostrand, 1961), and *Power: The Inner Experience* (New York: Irvington, 1975).

8. Herbert G. Hicks and C. Ray Gullett, *Organizations: Theory and Behavior* (New York: McGraw-Hill, 1975), p. 282.

9. Frederick Herzberg, Bernard Mausner, and Barbara Block Snyderman, *The Motivation to Work* (New York: Wiley, 1959), pp. 113-119.

10. Frederick Herzberg, "One More Time: How Do You Motivate Employees?" *Harvard Business Review* (January–February 1968), pp. 57-58.

11. Information provided by Renald M. Romain of Eaton Corporation, July 8, 1985.

12. Michael R. Malinovsky and John R. Barry, "Determinants of Work Attitudes," *Journal of Applied Psychology* (December 1965): 446-451; Richard Centers and Daphne E. Burgental, "Intrinsic and Extrinsic Job Motivations Among Different Segments of the Working Population," *Journal of Applied Psychology* (June 1966): 193-197; and Donald C. Ott, "The Generality of Herzberg's Two-Factor Theory of Motivation (Ph.D. dissertation, Ohio University, Athens, Ohio) in *Dissertation Abstracts* vol. 26, no. 3 (1965): 1767-1768.

13. B. F. Skinner, *About Behaviorism* (New York: Knopf, 1974), p. 40.

14. *Ibid.,* p. 46.

15. This section is based on Gary Dessler, *Human Behavior: Improving Performance at Work* (Reston: Reston Publishing, 1980), pp. 87-89; and Bernard L. Rosenbaum, *How to Motivate Today's Workers* (New York: McGraw-Hill, 1982), pp. 23-24.

16. Victor H. Vroom, *Work and Motivation* (New York: Wiley, 1964), p. 17.

17. *Ibid.,* pp. 15-19.

18. The remainder of this section follows Edward E. Lawler, III and Lyman W. Porter, "The

Effect of Performance on Job Satisfaction," *Industrial Relations* (October 1967): 20-28.

19. Another interesting article on expectancy theory is Hugh J. Arnold, "A Test of the Validity of the Multiplicative Hypothesis of Expectancy-Valence Theories of Work Motivation," *Academy of Management Journal* (March 1981): 128-141.

20. Michael Korda, *Power* (New York: Ballantine Books, 1975).

21. This section is based on an unpublished paper by William B. Gavin and C. Patrick Fleenor, "The Relationship of the Locus of Control Construct in an Industrial Environment to the Expectancy-Valence Model of Behavior." Other interesting discussions appear in Dan R. Dalton and William D. Tudor, "Union Steward Locus of Control, Job, Union Involvement, and Grievance Behavior," *Journal of Business Research* (March 1982): 85-101; and Danny Miller, Manfred F. R. Kets D. Vries, and Jean-Marie Toulous, "Top Executive Locus of Control and Its Relationship to Strategy-Making, Structure, and Environment," *Academy of Management Journal* (June 1982): 237-253.

22. *See* Julian B. Rotter, *Social Learning and Clinical Psychology* (Englewood Cliffs, N.J.: Prentice-Hall, 1954); and "Generalized Expectancies for Internal Versus External Control of Reinforcement: Psychological Monographs," *General and Applied* 80, no. 1 (1966): 1-28. *See also* Rotter and R. C. Muhry, "Internal Versus External Control of

Reinforcement and Decision Time," *Journal of Personality and Social Psychology* 2, no. 4 (1965): 598-604.

23. "Pay for the Performance—Good News or Bad?" *U.S. News & World Report,* 11 March 1985, p. 74.

24. "Pay for the Performance—Good News or Bad?" *U.S. News & World Report,* 11 March 1985, p. 74.

25. Reported in "Low Morale," *Wall Street Journal,* 9 September 1985, p. 23. Data from Equitable Life Insurance Society.

26. Truman quotation is from "Thoughts on the Business of Life," *Forbes,* 5 February 1979, p. 118. Nixon quotation is from "Well, Hello Richard," *Newsweek,* 18 December 1978, p. 38.

27. Updated information provided by Pam Olson, Public Relations staff, ROLM Corporation, May 20, 1985.

28. Quoted in B. C. Forbes, *Men Who Made America Great,* p. 68. This is a reprint from a 1917 work originally entitled *Men Who Are Making America Great.* Reprinted by Hamilton Press, Box 583, Brookfield, Wisc. 53005.

Morgan quotation from "Thoughts on the Business of Life," *Forbes,* 11 February 1985, p. 210.

Lombardi quotation from Angelo M. Vecchio's "Letter to the Editor," *U.S. News & World Report,* 20 May 1985, p. 7.

Holmes quotation from "Now Hear This," *Fortune,* 10 December 1984, p. 11.

Chapter 14

1. S. E. Asch, "Effects of Group Pressure Upon the Modification and Distortion of Judgments," in *Group Dynamics: Research and Theory,* 2d ed., ed. Dorwin Cartwright and Alvin Zander (Evanston, Ill.: Row, Peterson, 1960), pp. 193-194.

2. B. Tuckman, "Developmental Sequence in Small Groups," *Psychological Bulletin* 63 (1965): 384-399. Tuckman's work is described in John P. Wanous, Arnon E. Walters, and S. D. Malik, "Organizational Socialization and Group Development: Toward An Integrated Perspective," *Academy of Management Review* (October 1984): 673.

3. This is described in "Why the Kremlin Can't Make Ivan Work," *U.S. News & World Report,* 9 September 1985, p. 50.

4. Thomas F. O'Boyle and Carol Hymowitz, "More Corporate Chiefs Seek Direct Contact with Staff, Customers," *Wall Street Journal,* 27 February 1985, pp. 1, 25.

5. Quoted in Barbara Rowes, *The Book of Quotes* (New York: Ballantine Books, 1979), p. 25.

6. Marvin Stone, "Happy Birthday, Mr. Coolidge," *U.S. News & World Report,* 9 July 1984, p. 78.

7. F. J. Roethlisberger and William J. Dickson (with Harold A. Wright), *Management and the Worker* (New York: Wiley, 1964). A new perspective on the Hawthorne studies is contained in H. McIlvaine Parsons, "What Caused the Hawthorne Effect? A Scientific Detective Story," *Administra-*

tion and Society (November 1978): 259-283.

8. This section is based on Raymond E. Miles, "Human Relations or Human Resources?" Harvard Business Review (July–August 1965): 148, 163.

9. William Foote Whyte, Money and Motivation (New York: Harper & Row, 1955).

10. Stanley F. Seashore, Group Cohesiveness and the Industrial Work Group (Ann Arbor: Survey Research Center, University of Michigan, 1954).

11. Equity theory is discussed in Michael R. Carrell and John E. Dittrich, "Equity Theory: The Recent Literature, Methodological Considerations, and New Directions," Academy of Management Review (April 1978): 202-210; and Sam Gould, "An Equity-Exchange Model of Organizational Involvement," Academy of Management Review (January 1979): 53-62.

12. Thomas F. O'Boyle, "Loyalty Ebbs At Many Companies As Employers Grow Disillusioned," Wall Street Journal, 11 July 1985, p. 29.

13. Martin Patchen, "A Conceptual Framework and Some Empirical Data Regarding Comparison of Social Rewards," in Readings in Reference Group Theory and Research, ed. Herbert H. Hyman and Eleanor Singer (New York: Free Press, 1960), pp. 169-184.

14. L. B. Barnes, Organizational Systems and Engineering Groups: A Comparative Study of Two Technical Groups in Industry (Boston: Division of Research, Harvard Business School, Harvard Uni-

versity, 1960); Alvin W. Gouldner, "Cosmopolitans and Locals: Toward An Analysis of Latent Social Roles-I," Administrative Science Quarterly (March 1958): 444-480; and Peter M. Blau and W. Richard Scott, Formal Organizations: A Comparative Approach (San Francisco: Chandler, 1962), pp. 73-74.

15. Talcott Parsons, Robert F. Bales, and Edward A. Shils, Working Papers in the Theory of Action (New York: Free Press, 1953).

16. Robert L. Kahn, "Productivity and Job Satisfaction," Personnel Psychology (Autumn 1960): 275-287.

17. Victor H. Vroom, Work and Motivation (New York: Wiley, 1964), pp. 181-186.

18. Rensis Likert, New Patterns of Management (New York: McGraw-Hill, 1961); and Likert, The Human Organization (New York: McGraw-Hill, 1967). A recent article of interest is Rabi S. Bhagat, "Conditions Under Which Stronger Job Performance–Job Satisfaction Relationships May Be Observed: A Closer Look at Two Situational Contingencies," Academy of Management Journal (December 1978): 772-789.

19. Interesting discussions of work values appear in M. R. Cooper, B. S. Morgan, P. M. Foley, and L. B. Kaplan, "Changing Employee Values: Deepening Discontent?" Harvard Business Review (January–February 1979): 117-125; and David Glenn Bowers and Jerome L. Franklin, "American Work Values and Preferences," University of Michigan Business Review (March 1977): 14-22.

20. See earlier references to these studies.

21. Steve Lohr, "Overhauling America's Business Management," New York Times Magazine, 4 January 1981, pp. 44-45.

22. Alan Fram, "A Worker-Owned Experiment That Is Succeeding," Journal-American, 20 June 1982, p. B2. Updated by General Motors, May 27, 1985. William Sersin, "Experiments in Employee Ownership Facing Test," New York Times, 4 December 1984.

Gehrig quotation from "Thoughts on the Business of Life," Forbes, 8 April 1985, p. 196.

Schweitzer quotation from "Thoughts on the Business of Life," Forbes, 14 January 1985, p. 308.

John Paul II's quotation reported in "The Pope Gets to Work," Newsweek, 28 September 1981, p. 59.

Chapter 15

1. The importance of information to decision making is discussed in Charles A. O'Reilly, III, "Variations in Decision Makers' Use of Information Sources: The Impact of Quality and Accessibility of Information," Academy of Management Journal (December 1984): 756-771.

2. Reported in Clifford Houston and Gloria Wilson, "Body Talk—The Unspoken Language," Management World (July 1978): 16.

3. Another list of barriers appears in Leonard R. Sayles and George Strauss, Human Behavior in Organizations (Englewood Cliffs, N.J.: Pren-

tice-Hall, 1966), pp. 238-246. Similar lists appear in a variety of other sources. *See also* Mary Polfer, "Communications: The Secret of Success in the World of Business," *Pittsburgh State University Business and Economic Review* (February 1979): 3-6.

4. Roger Bellows, Thomas Q. Gilson, and George S. Odione, *Executive Skills* (Englewood Cliffs, N.J.: Prentice-Hall, 1962), pp. 60-61.

5. A classic discussion of this roadblock appears in Carl R. Rogers and F. J. Roethlisberger, "Barriers and Gateways to Communication," *Harvard Business Review* (July–August 1952): 46-52.

6. "The Right Way, The Wrong Way, and the Army Way," *Forbes,* 20 May 1985, p. 232.

7. William V. Haney, "A Comparative Study of Unilateral and Bilateral Communication," *Academy of Management Journal* (June 1964): 128-136; and Harold J. Leavitt and Ronald A. H. Mueller, "Some Effects of Feedback on Communications," *Human Relations* (November 1951): 401-410.

8. Management's problems in obtaining accurate feedback about situations are discussed in Chris Argyris, "Double-loop Learning in Organizations," *Harvard Business Review* (September–October 1977): 115-125.

9. Stuart Chase, *Power of Words* (New York: Harcourt, Brace, 1954), p. 165.

10. S. I. Hayakawa, *Language in Thought and Action,* 3rd ed. (New York: Harcourt Brace Jovanovich, 1974), p. 258.

11. Rogers and Roethlisberger, "Barriers and Gateways," p. 48.

12. George C. Homans, *The Human Group* (New York: Harcourt, Brace, 1950), p. 111.

13. This is discussed at length by James G. March and Herbert A. Simon, *Organizations* (New York: Wiley, 1958), p. 66.

14. This was illustrated in research by Elton Mayo and George F. Lombard, *Teamwork and Labor Turnover in the Aircraft Industry of Southern California,* Business Research Report No. 32 (Boston: Graduate School of Business Administration, Harvard University, 1944), p. 8.

15. Studies showing this can be found in Alexander Paul Hare, *Handbook of Small Group Research* (New York: Free Press, 1976), pp. 229-230.

16. This pattern is described in *ibid.,* pp. 51-52.

17. Harold J. Leavitt, "Some Effects of Certain Communication Patterns on Group Performance," *Journal of Abnormal and Social Psychology* (January 1951): 38-50; M. E. Shaw, "Some Effects of Problem Complexity upon Problem Solution Efficiency in Different Communication Nets," *Journal of Experimental Psychology* 47 (1954): 211-217; and Harold J. Leavitt, *Managerial Psychology,* 2d ed. (Chicago: University of Chicago Press, 1964).

18. Alan Filley, "Committee Management: Guidelines from Social Science Research," *California Management Review* (Fall 1970): 13.

19. Discussed in Peter M. Blau and

W. Richard Scott, *Formal Organizations: A Comparative Approach* (San Francisco: Chandler, 1962), pp. 118-119.

20. A study showing this can be found in Kurt Lewin, "Forces Behind Food Habits and Methods of Change," *Bulletin of National Resources Council* (1943): 35-65.

21. Blau and Scott, *Formal Organizations,* pp. 121-124.

22. Henry Mintzberg, "The Manager's Job: Folklore and Fact," *Harvard Business Review* (July–August 1975): 49-61. Part of this article is condensed from *The Nature of Managerial Work* (New York: Harper & Row, 1973).

23. "A Productive Way to Vent Employee Gripes," *Business Week,* 16 October 1978, pp. 170-171.

24. Bruce Harriman, "Up and Down the Communications Ladder," *Harvard Business Review* (September–October 1974): 143-151. Updated by New England Telephone in 1985.

25. A good discussion of suggestion systems is contained in Vincent G. Reuter, "Suggestion Systems: Utilization, Evaluation, and Implementation," *California Management Review* (Spring 1977): 78-79.

26. Reactions to overload are explored in James G. Miller, "Information Input, Overload, and Psychopathology," *American Journal of Psychiatry* (February 1960): 695-704.

27. Mary Bralove, "Some Chief Executives Bypass, and Irk, Staffs in Getting Information," *Wall Street Journal,* 12 January 1983, pp. 1, 20.

28. Keith Davis, "Management

Communication and the Grapevine," *Harvard Business Review* (September–October 1953): 43-49.

29. Dorwin Cartwright, et al., "A Study of a Rumor: Its Origin and Spread," *Human Relations* (August 1948): 483-485. An excellent discussion of rumor also appears in Keith Davis, *Human Behavior at Work*, 5th ed. (New York: McGraw-Hill, 1976), pp. 268-270.

30. This is discussed in John W. Thibaut and Harold H. Kelley, *The Social Psychology of Groups* (New York: Wiley, 1959), p. 39.

31. *See* note 17.

32. Survey data is from a table labeled, "Weak Writers," *Wall Street Journal,* 14 June 1985, p. 27. The data source is Hodge-Cronin & Associations, Inc.

33. Reported in "Reading Uses 824 Key Words," *Detroit News,* 25 January 1978, p. 6F (UPI story).

34. Donald L. Kirkpatrick, "Communications: Everybody Talks About It, But . . .," *Personnel Administrator* (January 1978): 46.

Hemingway quotation from "Thoughts on the Business of Life," *Forbes,* 10 May 1982, p. 332.

Stevenson quotation from Laurence J. Peter, *Peter's Quotations* (New York: Morrow, 1977), p. 503.

Regan quotation from "Now Hear This," *Fortune,* 29 April 1985, p. 11.

Chapter 16

1. E. F. Schumacher, *A Guide for the Perplexed* (New York: Harper & Row, 1977), p. 127.

2. Reported in Lindley H. Clark, Jr., "The Great Depression Had Its Big Winners Along with the Losers," *Wall Street Journal,* 26 October 1979, p. 34.

3. Arthur G. Bedeian and William F. Glueck, *Management,* (Hinsdale, Ill.: Dryden Press, 1983), p. 7.

4. Standards provided by Joe Stroop, Manager of Corporate Communications, American Airlines, June 7, 1985.

5. Edgar F. Huse, *The Modern Manager* (St. Paul, Minn.: West, 1979), p. 185.

6. These characteristics are discussed in Harold Koontz and Cyril O'Donnell, *Essentials of Management* (New York: McGraw-Hill, 1974), pp. 362-365; and Robert L. Trewatha and M. Gene Newport, *Management: Functions and Behavior* (Dallas: Business Publications, 1979), pp. 260-264.

7. Louis A. Allen, *Making Managerial Planning More Effective* (New York: McGraw-Hill, 1982), p. 8.

8. Selvin W. Becker and David Green, Jr., "Budgeting and Employee Behavior," *Journal of Business* (October 1962): 392-402. *See also* Neil C. Churchill, "Budget Choice: Planning vs. Control," *Harvard Business Review* (July–August 1984): 150-164.

9. Robert Anthony and Regina Herzlinger, *Management Control in Nonprofit Organizations* (Homewood, Ill.: Irwin, 1975), p. 129.

10. Peter A. Phyrr, *Zero-Base Budgeting: A Practical Management Tool for Evaluating Expenses* (New York: Wiley, 1973). *See also* Barry J. Ewell, "To Budget, Start From Zero," *Sales & Marketing Management,* 22 April 1985, pp. 46-48.

11. Derek F. du Toit, "Confessions of a So-So Controller," *Harvard Business Review* (July–August 1985): 50-56.

12. Stephen C. Harper, "A Developmental Approach to Performance Appraisal," *Business Horizons* (September–October 1983): 68-74.

13. Mark R. Edwards, Walter C. Borman, and J. Ruth Sproull, "Solving the Double Bind in Performance Appraisal: A Saga of Wolves, Sloths, and Eagles," *Business Horizons* (May–June 1985): 59-68; Cynthia Lee, "Increasing Performance Appraisal Effectiveness: Matching Task Types, Appraisal Process, and Rater Training," *Academy of Management Review* (April 1985): 322-331.

14. Peter F. Drucker, "A New Scorecard for Management," *Wall Street Journal,* 24 September 1976, p. 16.

15. Edward E. Lawler III and John Grand Rhode, *Information and Control in Organizations* (Pacific Palisades, Calif.: Goodyear Publishing Co., 1976), pp. 83-94.

16. Cortlandt Cammann and David A. Nadler, "Fit Control Systems to Your Managerial Style, *Harvard Business Review* (January–February 1976) 65.

de Gaulle quotation from David Schoenbrun, "The Battle of Gettysburg," *Parade,* 2 February 1986, p. 9.

Thoreau quote from Louis A. Allen, *Making Managerial Planning More Effective* (New York: McGraw-Hill, 1982), p. 251.

Shah quote from Pravin P. Shah, *Cost Control and Information Systems* (New York: McGraw-Hill, 1981), p. 127.

Drucker quote from Peter F. Drucker, *An Introductory View of Management* (New York: Harper & Row, 1977), p. 431.

Bailey quote from *Publisher's Weekly* (January 13, 1975). Reprinted by permission of Herbert S. Baily, Jr.

Chapter 17

1. Quoted in C. Richard Roberts and Louis E. Boone, "MIS Development in American Industry: The Apex," *The Journal of Business Strategy* (Winter 1983).
2. Marie Spadoni, "Harley-Davidson Revs Up to Improve Image," *Advertising Age,* 5 August 1985, p. 30.
3. Samuel V. Smith, Richard H. Brien, and James E. Stafford, *Readings in Marketing Information Systems* (Boston: Houghton Mifflin, 1968), p. 7.
4. Louis E. Boone, "Proposed Cure for the Information Explosion," *Business Horizons* (December 1972). *See also* Michael E. Porter and Victor E. Millar, "How Information Gives You Competitive Advantage," *Harvard Business Review* (July–August 1985): 149-160.
5. Keith K. Cox and Ben M. Enis, *The Marketing Research Process* (Santa Monica, Calif.: Goodyear Publishing Co., 1972), p. 19.
6. This widely accepted taxonomy was developed by Robert N. Anthony. *See his Planning and Control Systems: A Framework for Analysis* (Boston: Division of Research, Harvard Business School, 1965), pp. 16-18.
7. This section is based on David B. Montgomery and Glen L. Urban, "Marketing Decision-Information Systems: An Emerging View," *Journal of Marketing Research* (May 1970): 226-234.
8. David B. Montgomery and Charles B. Weinberg, "Toward Strategic Intelligence Systems," *Journal of Marketing* (Fall 1979): 46.
9. "Data Bases Rediscovered," *Personal Computing,* December 1985, pp. 95-101.
10. John G. Burch, Felix R. Strater, and Gary Grudnitski, *Information Systems: Theory and Practice* (New York: Wiley, 1979), pp. 149-150.
11. Roberts and Boone, "MIS Development in American Industry," p. 13.
12. James B. Bouden and Elwood S. Buffa, "Corporate Models: On-Line, Real-Time Systems," *Harvard Business Review* (July–August 1970).
13. "Managing Information: Two Insurance Giants Forge Divergent Paths," *Business Week,* 8 October 1984, p. 120.
14. Benny Gilad and Tamar Gilad, "A Systems Approach to Business Intelligence," *Business Horizons* (September–October 1985): 65-70; Jugoslav S. Milutinovich, "Business Facts for Decision Makers: Where to Find Them, *Business Horizons* (March–April 1985): 63-80.
15. Arnold E. Amstutz, "The Marketing Executive and Management Information Systems" in *Science, Technology, and Marketing,* ed. Raymond M. Haas (Chicago: American Marketing Association, 1967), pp. 69-86.
16. Allen S. King, "Computer Decision Support Systems Must Be Credible, Consistent, and Provide Timely Data," *Marketing News,* 12 December 1980, p. 11; *See also* Bernard C. Reimann, "Decision Support Systems: Strategic Management Tools for the Eighties," *Business Horizons* (September–October 1985): 71-77.
17. H. C. Lucas, Jr., *Why Information Systems Fail* (New York: Columbia University Press, 1975). *See also* Daniel Robey, "User Attitudes and Management Information System Use," *Academy of Management Journal* (September 1979): 527; Kate Kaiser and Ananth Srinivasan, "User-Analyst Differences: An Empirical Investigation of Attitudes Related to Systems Development," *Academy of Management Journal* (September 1982): 630-646.
18. These characteristics are suggested by Amstutz in "The Marketing Executive and Management Information Systems." The discussion of each characteristic is based upon his work.
19. F. Warren McFarlan, "Information Technology Changes the Way You Compete," *Harvard Business Review* (May–June 1984): 98-102.
20. Phillip Ein-Dor and Eli Segev, "Information-System Responsibility," *MSU Business*

Topics (Autumn 1977): 33-40. *See also* F. Warren McFarlan, "Portfolio Approach to Information Systems," *Harvard Business Review* (September–October 1981): 142-150.

21. Adapted from Russell L. Ackoff, "Management Misinformation Systems," *Management Science* (December 1967): 147-156. Used with permission.

Chapter 18

1. Steven C. Wheelwright and Robert H. Hayes, "Competing Through Manufacturing," *Harvard Business Review* (January–February 1985): 99-108.

2. Much of the material in this chapter is adapted from James B. Dilworth, *Production and Operations Management: Manufacturing and Nonmanufacturing*, 2d ed. (New York: Random House, 1983). This includes the following: production systems (pp. 10-11); location factors (pp. 457, 458-461); stages of site location (pp. 463, 466); materials handling (pp. 484-494, 503-505); job design (pp. 521-523); job content, methods improvement, physical environment, and sociotechnical factors (pp. 520-552); production control (pp. 106-171, 172-199, 270-359); inventory control (pp. 183-186, 188-195, 203-214, 218-230, 239-252); and quality control (pp. 381-419).

3. Theodore Levitt's viewpoints are outlined in "The 'Big Mac' Theory of Economic Progress," *Forbes*, 15 April 1977, pp. 187-188.

4. Data supplied by John T. Wheeler, Public Affairs Department, Du Pont, July 15, 1985.

5. Hirotaka Takeuchi and Ikujiro Nonaka, "The New Product Development Game," *Harvard Business Review* (January–February 1986): 137-146.

6. Data supplied by Jeff Burnstein, Robot Industries Association, July 30, 1985.

7. Edward M. Knod, Jr., Jerry L. Wall, John P. Daniels, Hugh M. Shane, and Theodore A. Wernimont, "Robotics: Challenges for the Human Resources Manager," *Business Horizons* (March–April 1984): 38-46; Fred K. Foulkes and Jeffrey L. Hirsch, "People Make Robots Work," *Harvard Business Review* (January–February 1984): 94-102; "'Overblown, Oversold, Over-Everythinged,'" *Forbes*, 25 March 1985, pp. 191, 194; and Charles J. Hollon and George N. Rogol, "How Robotization Affects People," *Business Horizons* (May–June 1985): 74-80.

8. Janet Neiman, "Retailers Should Know Their Place," *Advertising Age*, 1 November 1982, p. M22.

9. Neiman, "Retailers Should Know Their Place."

10. Donald L. Battle, "'Buy American' Crusade Struggles On," *U.S. News & World Report*, 27 January 1986, p. 52.

11. Information provided by Rick Bause, IBM Corporation, July 17, 1985.

12. Merle O'Donnell and Robert J. O'Donnell, "Quality Circles—The Latest Fad or a Real Winner?" *Business Horizons* (May–June 1984): 48-52; John D. Blair and Carlton J. Whitehead, "Can Quality Circles Survive in the United States?" *Business Horizons* (September–October 1984): 17-22; Edward E. Lawler III and Susan A. Mohrman, "Quality Circles After the Fed," *Harvard Business Review* (January–February 1985): 65-71; and Larry R. Smeltzer and Ben L. Kedia, "Knowing the Ropes: Organizational Requirements for Quality Circles," *Business Horizons* (July–August 1985): 30-34.

13. Sumer C. Aggarwal, "MRP, JIT, OPT, FMS?" *Harvard Business Review* (September–October 1985): 8-16; John C. Anderson and Roger G. Schroeder, "Getting Results from Your MRP System," *Business Horizons* (May–June 1984): 57-64.

14. Lee Iacocca, *Iacocca: An Autobiography* (New York: Bantam Books, 1984), pp. 186-187.

15. Amal Nag, "Auto Companies Push Parts Makers to Raise Efficiency, Cut Costs," *Wall Street Journal*, 31 July 1984, p. 1.

16. James B. Dilworth, *Production and Operations Management: Manufacturing and Nonmanufacturing* (New York: Random House, 1983), pp. 210-211.

17. Ed Bean, "Cause of Quality-Control Problems Might Be Managers—Not Workers," *Wall Street Journal*, 10 April 1985, p. 31.

18. David A. Garvin, "Quality on the Line," *Harvard Business Review* (September–October 1983): 73.
19. Matt Yancey, "Productivity Nosedives," *Mobile Register,* 30 January 1986, p. 10A.
20. William G. Ouchi, *Theory Z* (Addison-Wesley, 1981), p. 17.
21. Jeremiah J. Sullivan, "A Critique of Theory Z," *Academy of Management Review* (January 1983): 132-142. *See also* Andrew Weiss, "Simple Truths of Japanese Manufacturing," (July–August 1984), pp. 119-125.
22. Harold Geneen, *Managing* (New York: Doubleday, 1984), pp. 23, 24.
23. Y. K. Shetty, "Key Elements of Productivity Improvement Programs," *Business Horizons* (March–April 1982): 15-22.

Chapter 19

1. The sequence and Figure 19-1 are suggested in Jan Johanson and Jan-Erils Vahlore, "The Internationalization Process of the Firm—A Model of Knowledge Development and Increasing Foreign Market Commitments," *Journal of International Business Studies* (Spring–Summer 1977): 24.
2. Michael Grant, "VW Satisfied Basic Needs," *Ypsilanti* (Mich.) *Press,* 18 June 1978, p. 68 (Copley News Service).
3. Eugene Carlson, "Boycotting of Russian Vodka Ended or Eased by Most States," *Wall Street Journal,* 18 September 1984, p. 33.
4. Harry Bernstein, "Socialism Marches to a Different Drummer in Israel," *Detroit News,* 3 July 1978, pp. 1C, 2C. Another interesting discussion of Israeli management appears in Yoav Vardi, Arie Shirom, and Dan Jacobson, "A Study of Leadership Beliefs of Israeli Managers," *Academy of Management Journal* (June 1980): 367-374.
5. An interesting discussion of Israeli management appears in Dale Zand, "Management in Israel," *Business Horizons* (August 1978): 36-46.
6. Louis T. Wells, Jr., "Negotiating with Third World Governments," *Harvard Business Review* (January–February, 1977): 76.
7. This illustration is attributed to Professor Ashok Kapoor of New York University. *See* David Richlefs, "For the Businessman Headed Abroad, Some Basic Training," *Wall Street Journal,* 16 January 1978, p. 14.
8. These lists of advantages and disadvantages are found in *Controlling Foreign Investment in National Interest Sectors of the U.S. Economy,* Report to the Congress by the Comptroller General of the United States, October 7, 1977 (Washington, D.C.: General Accounting Office), pp. 27-31.
9. Robert D. Crane, "Planning, Islamic Style," *Fortune,* 25 September 1978, pp. 114-116.
10. Clark Hallas, "The L-Car," *Detroit News Magazine,* 2 April 1978, pp. 14, 41.
11. "Europe's New Managers," *Business Week,* 24 May 1982, p. 117.
12. John Hutchinson, "Evolving Organizational Forms," *Columbia Journal of World Business* (Summer 1976): 48. *See also* W. H. Davidson and Philippe Haspeslaugh, "Shaping A Global Product Organization," *Harvard Business Review* (July–August 1982): 125-132.
13. Ted Kade, "Renault Says 'Oui' to AMC," *Detroit News,* 1 April 1978, pp. 1A, 5A. Updated by Ed G. Snyder, Manager of News and Financial Information, American Motors, May 17, 1985.
14. This discussion is based on Hutchinson, "Evolving Organizational Forms," pp. 48-50. Another excellent article on this general subject is Stanley M. Davis, "Trends in the Organization of Multinational Corporations," *Columbia Journal of World Business* (Summer 1976): 59-71. *See also* Gerard H. Garnier, "Context and Decision Making Autonomy in the Foreign Affiliates of U.S. Multinational Corporations," *Academy of Management Journal* (December 1982): 893-903.
15. Daniel Seligman, "Gridlock for the Soviet Economy," *Fortune,* 15 April 1985, pp. 142-143.
16. Homer Garren, Runzheimer International, telephone conversation, May 12, 1985.
17. Estimated by executive recruiter George P. Craighead. *See* Phillip Greer and Myron Kandel, "Go Abroad to Climb Corporate Ladder," *Detroit News,* 9 October 1978, p. 5D. Another interesting article is Michael G. Harvey, "The Multinational Corporation's

Expatriate Problem: An Application of Murphy's Law," *Business Horizons* (January–February 1983): 71-78.

18. This comparison is based on and quotes are from Charles Y. Yang, "Management Styles: American Vis-à-Vis Japanese," *Columbia Journal of World Business* (Fall 1977): 23-31.

19. David P. Garino, "Takeover by Japanese Hasn't Hurt After All, Quasar Workers Find," *Wall Street Journal,* 10 October 1978, p. 16.

20. Quotes are from Yang, "Management Styles," p. 24.

21. "Business Gifts Abroad," *United Airlines Magazine,* May 1982, p. 20; "It's a Gift," *Journal-American,* 23 November 1981, p. 7B (AP story).

22. U.S. data from the Bureau of the Census. European and Japanese data from United Nations, "World Population Prospects, Estimates, and Projections As Assessed in 1982" (published in 1985).

23. Revolution Down on the Farm" *Time,* 23 November 1981, p. 51.

24. "Under Its Ten-Gallon Hat, A Japanese-Style Culture," *Business Week,* 18 September 1978, pp. 68-69.

Iacocca quotation from "We're A Colony Again, This Time of Japan," *U.S. News & World Report,* 16 April 1984, p. 63.

McGowan quotation from "Now Hear This," *Fortune,* 23 August 1982, p. 8.

Nixon quotation from Barbara Rowes, *The Book of Quotes* (New York: Ballantine Books, 1978), p. 147.

Chapter 20

1. Definitions of social responsibility are discussed in Thomas J. Zenisek, "Corporate Social Responsibility: A Conceptualization Based on Organizational Literature," *Academy of Management Review* (July 1979): 359-362. An excellent discussion appears in Dan R. Dalton and Richard A. Cosier, "The Four Faces of Social Responsibility," *Business Horizons* (May–June 1982): 19-27; and Kenneth E. Goodpaster and John B. Matthews, Jr., "Can A Corporation Have a Conscience?" *Harvard Business Review* (January–February 1982): 132-141.

2. The discussion about FMC's program is based on and quotes are from Robert H. Malott, "Corporate Support of Education: Some Strings Attached," *Harvard Business Review* (July–August 1978): 137-138. Updated in 1982 by FMC Foundation.

3. This section is based on Robert Hay and Ed Gray, "Social Responsibilities of Business Managers," *Academy of Management Journal* (March 1974): 135-143. Another excellent discussion of the various eras of social responsibility is contained in Patrick E. Murphy, "An Evolution: Corporate Social Responsiveness," *University of Michigan Business Review* (November 1978): 19-24.

4. Management ethics are discussed in Kristine Hanson and Robert Solomon, "The Real Business Ethics," *Business and Society* (Spring 1982): 58-59; George K. Sand, "Business Ethics: Where Are We Going?" *Academy of Management Review* (April 1981): 269-276; Darrell J. Fasching, "A Case for Corporate and Management Ethics," *California Management Review* (Summer 1982): 62-76; and Harold L. Johnson, "Ethics and the Executive," *Business Horizons* (May–June 1981): 53-59.

5. Steven Brenner and Earl A. Molander, "Is the Ethics of Business Changing," *Harvard Business Review* (January–February 1977): 59.

6. *Ibid.* Reprinted by permission.

7. Management author Gerald Keim has suggested the popular-traditional dichotomy. The third category, enlightened self-interest, has evolved partially from the views of leading business executives. *See* Gerald Keim, "Managerial Behavior and the Social Responsibility Debate: Goals Versus Constraints," *Academy of Management Journal* (March 1978): 57-69.

8. *Ibid.,* p. 58.

9. Joseph W. McGuire, "The Changing Nature of Business Responsibilities" (Paper delivered at Oklahoma State University's College of Business Administration Honors Lecture, March 9, 1978, p. 10.

10. Keim, "Managerial Behavior," p. 57-58.

11. Milton Friedman, "The Social Responsibility of Business Is to Increase Its Profits," *New York Times Magazine,* 13 September 1970, pp. 122-126. Friedman's views are discussed in Robert Hay and Ed Gray, "Social Responsibilities

of Business Managers," *Academy of Management Review* (March 1974): 141.

12. Adam Smith quotation from Milton Friedman, "Social Responsibilities: A Subversive Doctrine," *National Review,* 24 August 1965, p. 723.

13. Mercer quotation from "Goodyear President Visits," *Focus EMU,* 3 April 1979, p. 5.

14. Ford quotation from Ted Kade, "Henry Ford II Admits Errors: Questions Capitalist Virtues," *Detroit News,* 27 April 1979, p. 13A.

15. Shapiro quotation from "Today's Executive: Private Steward and Public Servant," *Harvard Business Review* (March–April 1978): 101.

16. This is suggested in Kenneth Rowe and John Schlacter, "Integrating Social Responsibility Into Corporate Structure," *Public Relations Quarterly* (Fall 1978): 7-12.

17. This section is based on S. Prakash Sethi, "A Conceptual Framework for Environmental Analysis of Social Issues and Evaluation of Business Response Patterns," *Academy of Management Review* (January 1979): 63-74. Another interesting article is David W. Fischer, "Strategies Toward Political Pressures: A Typology of Firm Responses,"

Academy of Management Review (January 1983): 71-78.

18. Adapted from *1978 Special Report of the Life and Health Insurance Business* (Washington, D.C.: Clearinghouse on Corporate Social Responsibility, 1978).

19. Stanley G. Karson, "A Social Index for Business," *Response* (November 1977): 2; Walter F. Abbott and R. Joseph Monsen, "On the Measurement of Corporate Social Responsibility: Self-Reported Disclosures as a Method of Measuring Corporate Social Involvement," *Academy of Management Journal* (September 1979): 501.

20. The remainder of this section is based on Dennis R. Beresford and Scott S. Cowen, "Surveying Social Responsibility Disclosure in Annual Reports," *Business* (March–April 1979): 15-20. The Ernst & Whinney research is also discussed in Abbott and Monsen, "On the Measurement of Corporate Social Responsibility," pp. 501-515.

21. Beresford and Cowen, "Surveying Social Responsibility Disclosure," p. 19.

22. Walter Guzzardi, Jr., "Business Is Learning How to Win in Washington," *Fortune,* 27 March 1978, p. 53. Material based on the original article

and reprinted by special permission; © 1978 TIME, Inc. Update from Kenneth Mason, "The Future of Private Enterprise Initiatives in the 1980s," (Presentation given in Washington, D.C., May 13, 1982).

23. Patricia Sellers, "America's Most Admired Corporations," *Fortune,* 7 January 1985, pp. 18-30.

24. Rebecca Case, "Get Involved in Your Community, Chairman of Seafirst Corp. Urges," *Journal-American,* 21 September 1984, p. D1.

25. "Apology: Bank Offers to Rehire Worker Who Spurned United Way." *Seattle Times,* 1 December 1981, p. 16A.

Capone quotation attributed to Daniel Boorstin, *The Americans.* Quoted in John Barbour, "Prohibition," *Journal-American,* 4 December 1983, p. B4.

Thatcher quotation from Malcolm S. Forbes, "Fact and Comment," *Forbes,* 15 October 1979, p. 31.

Rockefeller quotation from "Ten Principles: Address in Behalf of United Service Organizations," New York, July 9, 1941. Quoted in John Bartlett, *Familiar Quotations,* 14th ed. (Boston: Little, Brown, 1968), p. 932.

Glossary

Acceptance sampling is a type of quality control method using random samples to classify a lot as acceptable, unacceptable or as one requiring complete individual screening. (597)*

Accountability is the act of holding subordinates liable for performing those activities for which they have been delegated the necessary authority and responsibility. (266)

Activity scheduling is the sequential timing of work activities in an effort to maximize efficiency. (587)

Affirmative action programs are government programs designed to increase opportunities for females, minorities, and other protected categories of workers through recruitment, training, and promotion so that they are fairly represented in the work force. (341)

Analog model is a physical representation of a real object or situation that does not have the same appearance of that which it represents. (199)

Analytical methods bank is an MIS component that processes and analyzes data inputs. (545)

Analytical sophistication refers to the complexity of the model and analytical methods banks of the MIS. (552)

Apprenticeship training is a combination of on-the-job training and off-the-job instruction. (349)

Authority is the legitimate power a manager possesses to act and make decisions in carrying out responsibilities. (266)

Automation is a process of performing a mechanical operation by means of automatically controlled equipment with little or no human involvement. (572)

Behavioral school is an approach to management thought that emphasizes effective employee motivation as a primary determinant of organizational and managerial effectiveness. (39)

Body language is the form of nonverbal communication that employs eye contact, gestures, and posture. (459)

Bottom line reflects company profitability on the income statement. (14)

Boundary spanner can be defined as someone who links the organization to its external environment or other organizations.

Bounded rationality is a term for boundaries or limits that exist in any problem situation that necessarily restrict the manager's picture of the world and so his or her ability to make decisions. (159)

Brainstorming is a technique used to bring forth many alternative solutions; it involves a group of people brought together with the purpose of exchanging ideas. (170)

Breakeven analysis is a technique used to determine the number of products or services that must be produced and sold at a specified price to generate sufficient volume to cover total costs. (211)

Buckpassing is a phenomenon present in some committees in which individual members blame one another for a poorly made compromise decision or the lack of a decision. (180)

Budget is a financial plan listing the resources or funds assigned to a particular program, project, product, or division. (93)

Bureaucracy refers to a management approach based on a formal organizational structure with set rules and regulations. (33)

Business incubator is a facility that is rented at below market rates to several start-up firms that share accounting, computer, and secretarial services.

Business Roundtable is a group of top managers from different organizations who meet to discuss public issues and report their opinions as business representatives. (660)

Career development refers to the methods for effectively employing and shifting personnel within the organization

Career management is the firm's attempt to match

*The numbers in parentheses refer to the pages on which each term is defined.

G-1

employee goals with organizational opportunities.

Career planning is the personal determination of one's career path.

Career plateau is a stage in one's career from which further advancement is not expected.

Cash cows are products or businesses with high market share but low growth prospects. (144)

Causes are the underlying factors that combine to create a problem and allow it to exist. (167)

Centralization is an organizational philosophy in which managers retain considerable authority, relying on subordinates to implement assignments. (312)

Certainty refers to a decision situation in which sufficient information exists to predict the results of each alternative prior to its implementation. (153)

Change agent is the person who initiates a change within an organization.

Climate surveys examine work attitudes and situations within individual work units or departments with the idea of improving communication. (472)

Closed system is a set of interacting elements operating without any exchange with the environment in which they exist. (251)

Coaching is a management development technique in which junior executives work closely with a senior manager called a *mentor* or *sponsor*. (350)

Cognitive dissonance refers to the discrepancy between existing beliefs and attitudes and new perceptions. (463)

Commitment principle states that managers should plan for a period of time in the future sufficient to fulfill commitments resulting from current decisions. (91)

Committees are groups of people who render decisions or offer advice to management. (469)

Communication is the transfer of information via an understandable message from a sender to others. (459)

Comparative management is the analysis of cross-cultural management practices and techniques. (627)

Competitive environment refers to the firm's relative situation in the marketplace. (57)

Compressed work week is a work scheduling system in which employees spend fewer than five days a week on the job, but work approximately the same number of hours as under the traditional 40-hour, five-day week system. (311)

Computer-aided design (CAD) involves the use of special computer programs and graphics to design products. (573)

Computer-aided manufacturing (CAM) involves the use of computers to control machinery used in the production process. (573)

Conflict comprises the disagreements that occur within and among people in a work group. (439)

Conflict is opposition or antagonistic interaction resulting from scarcity of power, resources, or social position, and different value structures on the part of individuals or groups. (315)

Conflict avoidance is a simplistic, ineffective method of dealing with conflict in which the individual ignores it, withdraws from it, or pretends it does not exist. (319)

Confronting is a method of dealing with conflict in which parties in the conflict are required to meet, discuss the conflict, and seek solutions acceptable to everyone. (323)

Consensus management is a style in which chief executives rely on various committees, groups, and task forces to reach organization-wide agreement on a particular decision. (636)

Contingency plan is an alternative plan to be put into effect if certain events occur.

Contingency plans provide alternative scenarios for use in case of deviations from expected trends. (66)

Contingency theory, often called *situational management,* is an approach to management that emphasizes adjusting managerial actions and styles to the specific circumstances of the situation confronting the organization. (45)

Controlling is the continual analysis and measurement of actual operations against the established standards developed during the planning process. (88)

Corporate culture refers to generally accepted behavior patterns within an organization that are adopted by each new generation of employees. (54)

Cross-functional team is a boundary-spanning mechanism involving the creation of relatively permanent groups to deal with continually recurring interdepartmental problems. (275)

Cycle of events refers to the process by which an open system receives inputs from its environment, transforms them, and generates output. (253)

Cycle stock is the amount of inventory expected to be used during a particular cycle. (594)

Data are facts, statistics, opinions, or predictions categorized on some basis for storage and retrieval. (539)

Data bank is an MIS component consisting of raw

data as assembled, recorded, stored, and retrieved. (541)

Data base is a centralized, manageable repository
of the organization's data resources—procedures, computer programs, and specialized personnel. (543)

Decentralization is an organizational philosophy
in which managers disperse considerable authority to subordinates. (312)

Decision making involves choosing among two or
more alternatives by following the steps of problem recognition, developing and analyzing alternative courses of action, selecting and implementing a course of action, and obtaining
feedback to determine the effectiveness of the
decision. (84)

Decision tree is a branched model that is helpful
in identifying and evaluating alternative courses
of action. (219)

Delegation is the assignment of authority and responsibility to subordinates.

Delphi forecasting is a method of forecasting in
which a group of experts in a given field work
individually until a consensus about the future is
reached. (99)

Departmentalization is the subdividing of activities
and responsibility areas into units within the organization.

Differentiation is a structural force in organizations whereby the system develops specialized
functions among its various components as it
grows and becomes more complex. (256)

Dismissal is involuntary separation from one's job.

Dogs are products or businesses with both low
market share and poor growth prospects. (144)

Dynamic homeostasis is the process by which the
open system maintains equilibrium over a period of time. (255)

Economic boycott is a situation where a nation
prohibits trade or commerce with another country, typically as an act of political retaliation.

Economic order quantity (EOQ) is a method of
achieving optimal order size, based on a balancing of the various costs associated with inventory. (591)

Effectiveness is a measure of the extent to which
a decision alternative meets the stated objective
regardless of the costs involved. (173)

Efficiency is a comparison of the costs involved in
implementing a course of action with the expected returns; the ratio of outputs to inputs.
(173)

Empathy is identification with another person's
perspective. (465)

Entrepreneur is a person who takes financial and
other risks to start a business entity.

Equal employment opportunity is the right of all
persons to work and to advance on the basis of
merit, ability, and potential without any form of
discrimination because of race, color, religion,
sex, or national origin. (338)

Equifinality is the principle that organizational objectives can be achieved through more than one
course of action. (138)

Equity theory has been offered to explain the human tendency to balance work efforts or inputs
with the rewards received. (445)

Exception principle is an organizational concept
stating that managers should permit their subordinates to make routine, recurring decisions
and that only unusual or highly important problems should be referred to higher levels in the
organization. (265)

Exchange rate is the ratio of one currency to another. (631)

Expectancy theory holds that a person's perception of achieving a prized reward or goal via effective job performance will motivate the individual. Expectancy theory forms the basis of
path-goal leadership. (412)

Exporting is the marketing of one's merchandise
to other nations. (621)

External environment refers to factors outside the
organization. (51)

Externalities are nonmarket social forces.

External objectives are organizational aims focusing upon service to customers and to society as a
whole. (128)

Feedback is information transmitted by a receiver
back to the original sender of a message. (464)

Feedback mechanism is an open systems component that informs the organization of deviations
from objectives and may lead to adjustment in
activities. (254)

Financial analysis is the use of specific techniques
used to analyze the firm's financial statements in
controlling the liquidity, profitability, and overall
financial health of the organization. (521)

Flexitime is a work scheduling system permitting
employees to set their own working hours
within constraints specified by the organization.
(311)

Forcing is the application of power to resolve conflicts. (320)

Forecasts are estimates or predictions of future
events or outcomes for a specified time period.
(98)

Formal communication channel is the pattern of

communication approved and recognized by management. (471)

Fringe benefits are indirect compensation such as insurance, retirement plans, paid vacations, holidays, and the like. (358)

Functional authority is the power to direct or require certain procedures, policies, or specific practices in other departments not under the direct supervision of the person or department possessing this authority. (278)

Future-oriented managers are those who think ahead and take appropriate steps to stay ahead. (66)

Game theory is a technique for determining the strategy that is likely to produce maximum profits in a competitive situation.

Global strategy is one that adopts standardized manufacturing and marketing approaches to serve markets worldwide. (62)

Goal displacement is a phenomenon in which employees view the performance measures used in the control system as more important than the organizational objective upon which they are based. (528)

Grapevine is a term sometimes used by managers to refer to the informal communication channel. (474)

Great Man Theory states that only an exceptional person is capable of playing a prominent leadership role. (402)

Groupthink is a phenomenon present in some committee decisions which the desire for group consensus and cohesiveness is stronger than the desire for the most appropriate decision. (180)

Hawthorne effect refers to the positive impact on employee motivation of factors other than money and job security, as revealed by the Hawthorne studies. (442)

Hawthorne studies were a series of investigations that revealed that money and job security are not the only sources of employee motivation. They led to the development of the human relations approach to employee motivation. (442)

Headhunter is a term used to describe an executive search firm.

Homan's interaction hypothesis states that people who interact will grow to like each other, assuming they have compatible goals and needs, and this will lead to more interaction (or communication), thus establishing a cycle of cohesiveness. (468)

Human factors engineering is the application of information about human characteristics and

behavior to the design of tools and the work environment. (582)

Human relations approach refers to management attempts to improve and increase employees' production by boosting their morale. (443)

Human resources management involves planning for human resource needs, recruitment, selection, development, compensation, and evaluation. (333)

Human resources model suggests that management should be responsible for establishing an environment that best utilizes all the human resources for improved decision making and performance. (444)

Iconic model is a physical replica or scale representation that looks like the object it represents. (198)

Importing is the purchase and shipment of merchandise from another nation. (621)

Industrial democracy is a system in which all employees are actively involved in an organization's decision-making processes. (626)

Industrial revolution was the mid-eighteenth century movement of English manufacturing to a factory system (where products are produced in a centralized location) from a cottage system (where production was contracted to family living/work units). (27)

Informal communication channels are communication patterns that exist outside of or in addition to management-approved channels. (474)

Informal group leader is a leader in a group who functions as a social-emotional task leader. (448)

Information is data relevant to the manager in making decisions.

Information aggregation is the amount of detail with which information is maintained in the data bank. (551)

Information recency is the time lapse between the occurrence of an event and the inclusion of data recording that event in the MIS. (549)

Inputs are human and other resources that are necessary to operate and maintain the system or subsystem.

Institutional decisions involve long-term planning and policy formulation with the aim of assuring the organization's survival as a productive part of the economy and society.

Integrating role is a boundary-spanning mechanism whereby an organizational member with little or no formal authority coordinates decisions and work activities involving several different departments by influencing those individuals in control of the functional units involved. (276)

Integration refers to the structural force in organizations involving the degree to which members of various departments within the organization work together in a coordinated, unified way. (259)

Intergroup conflict is conflict occurring between departments or work groups as a result of such issues as authority, jurisdiction, control of work flow, and/or access to scarce resources. (319)

Internal environment refers to factors within the firm itself. (51)

Internal objectives are organizational aims designed to satisfy groups within the organization. (128)

International business refers to all economic activity that crosses national boundaries. (621)

International management refers to the decision making involved in international business activities. (621)

Interpersonal conflict is conflict occurring between two or more organizational members as a result of such factors as differences in managerial philosophies, values, and problem-solving styles or competition for power or promotion. (318)

Intervention refers to the changes that are introduced to either individuals or the organization. (372)

Interview is a personal meeting in which the employer evaluates a prospective employee and the applicant assesses opportunities offered by the firm.

Intrapersonal conflict is conflict occurring within a single member of the organization as a result of role conflict and/or job stress. (315)

Intrapreneurship is the adoption of entrepreneurial concepts—and even separate organizations—within the established structures of large firms.

Inventory control is a method of balancing the need to have sufficient raw materials, work in progress, and finished goods on hand to meet demand with the costs involved in carrying the inventory. (588)

Job analysis is the systematic study of jobs, consisting of identifying the requirements of the person assigned to the job and the elements and characteristics of the job. (336)

Job application is a form designed to obtain information that will allow the employer to determine if the job seeker meets basic qualifications and is suitable for further screening.

Job content refers to work activities assigned to a particular job. (582)

Job description is a written statement describing the objectives of a job, the work to be performed, the skills needed, the responsibilities in-

volved, the relationship of the job to other jobs, and its working conditions. (338)

Job design is the process of task delineation necessary to meet various personal, work, organizational, and environmental parameters. (582)

Job enlargement is the rearrangement of jobs to increase their complexity. (380)

Job enrichment is a rearrangement of jobs in order to get employee involvement in job-oriented decisions.

Job evaluation is a comparison of different jobs on such factors as responsibilities and education, skill, and physical requirements to determine the relative worth of a job. (357)

Job rotation is a management development technique in which managers are assigned to different departments to familiarize them with various operations of the organization. (350)

Job sharing is a work scheduling system in which a single job assignment is divided among two or more persons. (312)

Job specification is a written description of the special qualifications required of a person who fills a particular job, including skills, education, and previous experience. (338)

Just-in-time (JIT) inventory control is a system designed to minimize inventory at production facilities. (590)

Laboratory training refers to the use of unstructured small group discussions to induce interactions that will produce behavior change in the participants. (376)

Leadership is the act of motivating people to perform certain tasks intended to achieve specified objectives. (395)

Leadership style is the way a person uses available power in order to lead others. (397)

Leading is the act of motivating or causing people to perform certain tasks intended to achieve specific objectives. It is the act of making things happen.

Legal environment consists of federal, state, and local regulations, as well as those of foreign nations in which the business may operate. (59)

Liaison role is a boundary-spanning mechanism whereby one or more members of a department serve as a linkage between two highly interdependent departments. (275)

Licensing is granting the right to produce and/or to distribute a firm's products in another country to an outside firm. (622)

Line authority refers to the relationship existing between a superior and a subordinate in an organization. (276)

Linear programming is a mathematical technique

used to find the best solution to a given problem from a set of feasible solutions when resources are scarce. (207)

Linking pin theory is an organizational concept viewing managers as links between the groups they manage and the higher group to which they report, permitting them to integrate the efforts of the two groups. (273)

Locus of control refers to a person's perception of the controlling factors in his or her own destiny. (431)

Long-range objectives are organizational aims to be achieved within a time period longer than one year. (128)

Management is the use of people and other resources to accomplish objectives. (3)

Management access time is the time lapse between the manager's request for certain information and its receipt. (551)

Management audit is a professional review and evaluation of an organization's total activities from the perspective of management. (527)

Management by objectives (MBO) is a process whereby the superior and subordinate managers of an organization identify objectives common to each, define areas of responsibility, and use these measures as guides for operating the unit and assessing the contribution of each member of the organization. (131)

Management ethics refers to the moral premises upon which executive decisions are made. (649)

Management information system (MIS) is a structured, interacting complex of persons, machines, and procedures designed to generate an orderly flow of information. (538)

Managerial decisions are those related to the coordination and support of the core activities of the organization. (155)

Materials handling is the physical movement of materials and products within a work facility. (582)

Materials requirement planning (MRP) is a computer-based method to ensure that needed component parts and materials are available at the right time and place without stockpiling unnecessary inventory. (589)

Mathematical model (*See* Symbolic model.)

Matrix organization is one in which the corporate headquarters is organized functionally while a geographical organization exists at operational levels. (633)

Matrix approach is an organization arrangement in which specialists from different areas of the organization are brought together to work on specific projects; typically used simultaneously with a line-and-staff organization structure. (313)

Mechanistic structure is an organizational design frequently used in stable, relatively simple environments characterized by low uncertainty, high task specialization, and managers who rely more on formal authority structures, directives and rules, and high centralization. (295)

Mission is a general, enduring statement of company intent. (119)

MNC (multinational company) is a firm that views itself as essentially global in nature, and that conducts business in numerous national markets at a variety of levels. (621)

Model is a representation, or abstraction, of a real object, situation, or system. (197)

Model bank is an MIS component that integrates various models for use in describing, predicting, and possibly controlling organizational behavior. (545)

Motion study refers to the determination of the best sequence and number of motions to accomplish a specified task. (36)

Motivation refers to the forces leading to behavior directed toward the satisfaction of some need. (419)

Multinational strategy is one by which products are designed and marketed for specific overseas markets. (62)

Multiplexing is the supplementing of formal communication channels with other channels. (472)

Negative entropy is the ability of a system to repair itself, survive, and grow by importing resources from its environment and transforming them into outputs. (253)

Noise refers to any situation that interferes with or distorts the message being communicated. (461)

Nonprogrammed decisions are those that deal with unusual or novel problems. (158)

Objectives are guideposts in defining standards of what the organization should accomplish and in providing direction and motivation. (122)

"Old boy" network is an array of friends and associates that functions as a support system for executives.

On-the-job training consists of learning the specifics of a job in the actual work environment. (349)

Open system is a set of interacting elements that interact with the environment and whose structure will evolve over time as a result of this interaction. (253)

Operant behavior is voluntary behavior. (428)

Operations research is the application of mathematical techniques to managerial planning, decision making, and problem solving. (192)

Organic structure is an organizational design frequently used in complex, dynamic environments characterized by high uncertainty, low specialization, and managers who rely more on low levels of formalization, authority based on knowledge rather than formal authority positions, and decentralization. (296)

Organic type leadership is a style in which the firm is thought of as a collective unit; personnel identify with the organization rather than with their particular function. (636)

Organization chart is a blueprint of the organization, indicating lines of authority within it. (268)

Organization design is the specific blending of organizational structural components—people, tasks, structure, information, and environment—that makes each organization unique. (289)

Organization development (OD) is an effort by management to increase organization effectiveness by planned intervention in the organization's processes. (376)

Organization structure refers to the common elements of people, tasks, structure, information and environment that characterize all organizations. (289)

Organizing is the process of arranging people and physical resources to carry out plans and accomplish organizational objectives. (7)

Outplacement firms consist of consultants who help a fired employee adjust to unemployment and then help him or her find a new position.

Path-goal theory indicates that effective leadership is dependent on clearly defining the paths of goal achievement and the degree to which the leader is able to influence subordinates' attaining such goals. (412)

People-group conflict is conflict resulting from individual opposition to group norms or rules of behavior. (318)

Performance gap refers to the difference between the predicted or expected level of performance and the actual level. (162)

Phased retirement means that a person is gradually provided additional leisure time as he or she approaches the planned retirement age.

Planning is a process by which managers set objectives, assess the future, and develop courses of action to accomplish these objectives. (83)

Plans are detailed expressions of actions necessary to accomplish stated organizational objectives. (83)

Policies are general guidelines for decision making. (94)

Postcontrols are techniques applied following the completion of an activity that serve as the basis for developing precontrols and steering controls for subsequent activities. (513)

Power is the ability of one person to influence the behavior of another. (396)

Precontrols are preventive measures developed to eliminate the causes of any deviations that might occur in the execution of organizational plans. (512)

Probability is the likelihood of the occurrence of some uncertain event or condition. (206)

Problems are barriers to the achievement of organizational goals. (162)

Procedures are guides to action that specify in detail the manner in which activities are to be performed. (95)

Production control is a system designed to produce the maximum output with minimal input contributions and at the lowest cost. (583)

Production/operations function refers to the processes and activities necessary to transform various inputs into goods and/or services. (564)

Productivity is a measure of the output relative to input of goods and services for a nation, an industry, or a firm. (598)

Professional manager refers to persons who are hired for their training and skills in managerial techniques but who were not involved in establishing the enterprise.

Program is a large-scale, single-use plan involving numerous interrelated activities. (93)

Programmed decisions are those involving simple, common, frequently occurring problems that have well-established and understood solutions. (158)

Program planning budgeting system (PPBS) is a five-step system of budgeting that has been adopted by a number of nonprofit organizations. (520)

Project is a single-use plan that is a component part of a program or is on a smaller scale than a program. (93)

Promotion is movement to a position with additional compensation, responsibility, and added status. (360)

Qualitative forecasts are subjective estimates or predictions of future events or outcomes based upon customer surveys, sales force estimates, key executives, and other industry experts. (99)

Quality circles are volunteer groups of operative employees who periodically brainstorm on how to increase the firm's output, improve quality, or improve the efficiency of the work place. (583)

Quality control deals with establishing and maintaining specified quality levels for a firm's goods or services. (594)

Quantitative forecasts are estimates or predictions of future events or outcomes based upon statistical techniques. (98)

Question marks are products or businesses with low market share in a high-growth market. (144)

Queuing model is a technique for solving problems caused by waiting lines by determining the appropriate balance between the cost of providing extra service and the cost of having people, machines, or materials wait.

Ratio analysis is a performance evaluation technique measuring the liquidity, profitability, extent of debt financing, and effectiveness of the firm's use of its resources and permitting comparison with other firms and with past performance. (522)

Rationalizing is the distortion of a message to bring it into line with one's own beliefs. (464)

Reference groups are those sets or categories of people with which a person identifies. (447)

Reflex behavior is involuntary behavior. (428)

Reinforcement is the process by which behavior is modified by either positive or negative factors (428)

Resume is a summary of one's qualifications for employment.

Retirement shock refers to the personal adjustment problems caused by going from full-time work to full-time leisure.

Risk is a decision situation in which sufficient information exists to estimate the likelihood of the outcome of each alternative. (154)

Robot is a programmable machine used in performing repetitive tasks involving programmed manipulation of tools and materials. (572)

Rules are statements of actions that must be taken or not taken in a given situation. (95)

Safety stock is inventory kept in addition to the cycle stock to ensure availability in case of unexpectedly high usage. (594)

Salary refers to compensation for white-collar workers based on a unit of time. (357)

Satisficing is the term used by Herbert Simon to describe the way modern managers must, necessarily, make decisions with incomplete information, by choosing from among a few likely alternatives. (159)

Scalar principle is an organizational concept stating that authority and responsibility should flow in a clear, unbroken line from top management to supervisory levels; also called *chain of command*. (266)

Scientific management is a school of management popularized during the early 1900s that is based upon the application of the scientific method to the workplace and other management activities. (34)

Scientific method is a systematic and logical approach to the identification and solution of problems facing the decision maker. (193)

Self-concept is the image a person has of who he or she is; it is shaped over a long period of time by many outside forces. (423)

Sensitivity training is a process of group dynamics that influences a T-group participant's behavior. (376)

Separation refers to resignation, layoff, dismissal, or retirement. (360)

Short-range objectives are organizational aims to be accomplished within a period of one year or less. (128)

Simulation is a process for replicating the major aspects of an existing system or process by using probability distributions to describe elements, then combining them in various ways to study their effect on the model. (217)

Single-use plans are predetermined courses of action developed for nonrepetitive situations. (92)

Situational management (*See* Contingency theory.)

Smoothing is an ineffective method of dealing with conflict in which the individual delays decisions and appeals to reason as methods of suppressing overt signs of conflict. (320)

Social objectives are organizational aims designed with the larger interests of society in mind. (128)

Social responsibility refers to those management philosophies, policies, procedures, and actions that have the advancement of society's welfare as one of their primary objectives. (645)

Span of management is an organizational concept referring to the optimum number of subordinates a person can effectively manage; also called *span of control*. (266)

Spreadsheet is a decision-oriented computer program designed to answer "What if?" questions by analyzing different groups of data provided by the manager. (215)

Staff authority is the power to conduct investigations and advise line managers, but not to implement these recommendations. (276)

Staff planning groups are specialists who assist managers by developing a planning system, gathering and evaluating information, and aiding the development of corporate and divisional plans. (104)

Standard is the level of activity established by management as a model for evaluating performance. (506)

Standing plans are predetermined courses of action developed for repetitive situations. (93)

Stars are products or businesses that are high-growth market leaders. (144)

Steering controls are techniques used to detect deviations and allow corrective actions to be taken while the activity is being performed. (513)

Strategic business units (SBUs) are divisions composed of key businesses within multiproduct companies with specific managers, resources, objectives, and competitors. SBUs may encompass a division, a product line, or a single product. (143)

Strategic planning is the process of determining the major objectives of an organization and then adopting the courses of action and allocating the resources necessary to achieve those objectives. (96, 116)

Strategic window is a limited time period during which the "fit" between the key requirements of a market and the particular competencies of a firm is at an optimum. (140)

Survey research and feedback refers to action research involving attitude surveys and the resulting feedback to employees. (377)

Symbolic model is a model using equations or groups of equations to express the relationship among factors in a given process or system being modeled; also called *mathematical model.* (199)

Symptom is a visible indicator resulting in awareness that a problem exists. (167)

Synectics is a technique widely used to generate alternative solutions by examining analogous methods and perceptions of other fields to gain insight into management problems. (170)

System is an organized group of parts, components, or subsystems linked together according to a plan in order to achieve specific objectives (45)

System authority refers to the amount of authority delegated to the MIS. (553)

Systems type leadership is a style in which all corporate activities are directed toward the achievement of specified objectives. (636)

Tactical planning focuses on short-term implementation of current activities and the allocation of resources for those activities. (97, 118)

Task force is a boundary-spanning mechanism involving the creation of temporary groups to solve problems affecting several departments. (275)

Tasks consist of activities performed by the organization in accomplishing its objectives; the transformation of inputs from the environment into outputs. (297)

Team building is a process designed to improve the effectiveness of a work group with emphasis on work procedures and interpersonal relationships. (381)

Technical decisions are those involving the process whereby inputs are changed into outputs. (155)

Technocrats are specialists within the bureaucracy who dominate national economic planning. (632)

Technological displacement refers to the loss of employment due to technological changes. (573)

Technology is the science of applying information and knowledge to problem-solving situations. (61)

Theory X proposes that subordinates dislike work and require an autocratic style of leadership. (399)

Theory Y advocates a democratic style of leadership in which employees are encouraged to participate in the decision-making process. (399)

Theory Z is a management approach emphasizing employee involvement and shared decision making, long-term employment, relatively slow promotions and evaluations, and varied and non-specialized job assignments. (603)

Therbligs is the term coined by the Gilbreths to refer to the seventeen basic hand motions they identified in the course of their studies of motion. (37)

Trait theory concerns the identification and measurement of traits or attitudes that are associated with a leader's behavior. (402)

Transfer is lateral movement to another position which usually does not include a pay increase or added responsibilities. (360)

Uncertainty is a decision situation in which insufficient information exists to estimate the likelihood of the outcome of various alternatives. (154)

Unity of command is an organizational concept stating that each organizational member should report to only one supervisor for any single function. (265)

Value analysis is a formal study of purchases to determine needs, relative costs, and alternatives in an effort to minimize total expenditures. (586)

Vestibule training allows the individual to perform the work in a training area under the supervision of a trainer before being assigned to the actual work area. (349)

Wage is employee compensation based on the number of hours worked or the number of units produced. (357)

Work ethic is a belief in the inherent value of work in a society.

Yes-no controls are techniques used at one or more screening points where specific approval is needed to permit the activity to continue. (513)

Zero-base budgeting is the forced periodic justification of any expenditure program, rather than incremental changes in such a program. (521)

Photo Credits

TEXT PHOTOS

3: Courtesy of Microsoft Corporation. **6:** Courtesy of the New York National League Baseball Club. **21:** Courtesy of Microsoft Cororation. **28:** Hirmer Fotoarchiv, Munich. **36:** Figure 2–1, Courtesy of Frank B. Gilbreth. **58:** Courtesy of Olivetti Corporation. **60:** Don MacLeod/MacLeod Studio. **86:** Courtesy of RCA. **108:** Courtesy of Stouffer Foods Corporation. **111:** Courtesy of Piedmont Aviation. **127:** Courtesy of Carlson Companies, Inc. **147:** Courtesy of BMW. **161:** Courtesy of TV Guide—Triangle Publications, Inc. **185:** Courtesy of Gerber Products Company. **190:** Courtesy of Burger King. **212:** Courtesy of Pan American World Airways, Inc. **324:** Courtesy of Chobat. **331:** Courtesy of Delta Business Systems, Inc. **358:** Harry Wilks/courtesy of IBM. **367:** Courtesy of 3M Corpora-

tion. **373:** Courtesy of Johnson and Johnson, Inc. **434:** Courtesy of Lincoln Electric Company. **455:** Courtesy of Romac Industries, Inc. **501:** Figure 16–1; Peter Southwick/Stock Boston. **526:** Courtesy of Savin Corporation. **535:** Courtesy of Fisher Camuto Group. **538:** Figure 17–1, Photo By Stephen Wilkes, courtesy of Honeywell/Harley-Davidson. **544:** Courtesy of Ideal Basic Industries. **556:** Courtesy of Shaklee Corporation. **564:** Courtesy of Jaguar Cars, Inc. **568:** Courtesy of Emergency One, Inc. subsidiary of Federal Signal Corporation. **579:** Figure 18–5, Courtesy of Douglas Aircraft Company. **584:** Courtesy of Firestone. **592:** Courtesy of Uniform Product Code Council, Inc. **596:** Dick Luria/Science Source-Photo Researchers. **607:** Courtesy of General Motors Corporation.

COLOR PHOTO ESSAYS

Photo Essay 1: Entrepreneurship and Intrapreneurship
Page 1: Both, courtesy of Noble Roman's, Inc. Page 2: Top left, courtesy of AT&T; top right, courtesy of Mary Kay Cosmetics, Inc.; bottom left, Doug Wilson/Black Star; bottom right, courtesy of General Mills.

Photo Essay 2: Milestones in the Development of Management Thought 336-323 B.C.: Staatliche Museen Zu Berlin. 1822: Courtesy of IBM. 1898: Courtesy of Joan C. Tonn and the Urwick Management Center, Slough, England. 1911: The Smithsonian Institution. 1916: International Management Magazine. 1917: Courtesy of Stephens Institute of Technology. 1927: Courtesy of Western Electric. 1957: Courtesy of Harvard University Graduate School of Education. 1960: Courtesy of Antioch College. 1981: Courtesy of William G. Ouchi.

Photo Essay 3: Micro-Computers in Management
Page 1: Right, courtesy of Ashton Tate; left, courtesy of Hewlett-Packard Company. Page 2: Top, courtesy of Holiday Inns, Inc.; center, courtesy of Innovative Software; bottom, courtesy of Evans and Sutherland, Salt Lake City, Utah and Rediffusion Simulation.

Photo Essay 4: Technology and Production
Page 1: Left, courtesy of Chrysler Corporation; right, courtesy of Chrysler Corporation. Page 2: Top, courtesy of Parker Hannifin Corporation; bottom left, courtesy of General Motors Corporation; bottom right, courtesy of Owens-Illinois.

Photo Essay 5: Leadership and Corporate Culture
Page 1: Left, courtesy of Parker Hannifin Corporation; right, photo by Bachrach, courtesy of ITT and Harold S. Geneen. Page 2: Top, courtesy of The Pillsbury Company; bottom left, courtesy of Fogelman Properties; bottom right, courtesy of Physio-Control Corporation.

Photo Essay 6: International Business and Management
Page 1: Top, courtesy of Toyota Motor Corporation; bottom, courtesy of Wendy's International, Inc. Page 2: Top, courtesy of Toyota Motor Corporation; bottom left, William Strode/Woodfin Camp & Associates; bottom right, courtesy of Volkswagen of America, Inc.

Photo Essay 7: Social Responsibility
Page 1: Left, courtesy of Celanese Chemical Company; right, courtesy of Atlantic Richfield Company. Page 2: Top, courtesy of Control Data

Corporation; bottom left, courtesy of Colgate-Palmolive; bottom right, courtesy of Burlington Industries. Page 3: Top, courtesy of Exxon Corporation; bottom, courtesy of Shell Oil Corporation.

Page 4: Top, courtesy of Toyota Motor Corporation; center, courtesy of Northrup Corporation; bottom, courtesy of Telephone Pioneers of America.

Name Index

Subject Index